The *GRE*® General Test

The *new path*

to success

You're making your way in the world, passionately pursuing your own definition of success. So choose the only business school admissions test that gives you more freedom to do things your way — skip questions, change answers and control which scores schools will see. Show the world's top business schools your best.

Accepted at the world's top-ranked business schools.

Learn more at TakeTheGRE.com

Measuring the Power of Learning.®

2019 EDITION

Best Business Schools

HOW TO ORDER: Additional copies of U.S. News & World Report's **Best Business Schools 2019** guidebook are available for purchase at usnews.com/businessbook or by calling (800) 836-6397. To order custom reprints, please call (877) 652-5295 or email usnews@wrightsmedia.com. For permission to republish articles, data or other content from this book, email permissions@usnews.com.

Northwestern's Kellogg School of Management
ALYSSA SCHUKAR FOR USN&WR

MBA | MFIN | MSBA | MPAc | Ph.D. | ExecEd

WE ARE INNOVATORS. ENTREPRENEURS. #RADYMADE

Attend the top graduate business school in the center of San Diego's innovation economy. Experience the entrepreneurial mindset infused in all curriculum and activities at the Rady School of Management.

ARE YOU RADY?

rady.ucsd.edu

Rady | School of Management
UNIVERSITY OF CALIFORNIA SAN DIEGO

CONTENTS

42

74

CHAPTER 4

The U.S. News Rankings

GEORGIA. MBA

TOP RANKED PROGRAM
ON AND OFF THE FIELD

BEST GRAD SCHOOLS
U.S.News & WORLD REPORT
BUSINESS 2019

A Top 20 Public MBA Program
According to U.S. News & World Report

@USNEWS.COM/EDUCATION

Prospective business students researching their options will find the U.S. News website (home of the Best Graduate Schools and Best Colleges rankings) full of tips on everything from choosing a school to landing the most generous scholarships. Here's a sampling:

MBA Admissions Blog
usnews.com/mbaadmissions

Get admissions advice from blogger Stacy Blackman, a business school specialist with degrees from Wharton and Kellogg and co-author of "The MBA Application Roadmap: The Essential Guide to Getting into a Top Business School." Learn how to master application essays, prepare for interviews and find the money for business school.

Applying to Business School
usnews.com/businessapp

Planning for graduate school involves deciding what to study, finding the right school and applying to competitive programs. Find out how to plan for the application process, what the ROI of business school can be and what insider tips you should know.

Paying for Business School
usnews.com/payformba

Higher education is expensive, but students who choose to pursue a business program face especially steep costs. Paying for school involves exploring scholarships, employer reimbursement and student loans, as well as smart financial planning. Learn more about how to navigate your way through paying for an MBA.

Online Education
usnews.com/online

Want to get that MBA without spending time in the classroom? See our rankings of the best online degree programs in business (as well as in education, engineering, computer information technology, criminal justice and nursing). And read time-management and funding tips from students who have completed online degree programs.

Morse Code Blog
usnews.com/morsecode

Get an insider's view of the rankings from Chief Data Strategist Bob Morse, the mastermind behind them. Morse explains the methods we use to rank undergraduate and graduate programs and keeps you up to date on all the commentary and controversy.

Best Graduate Schools
usnews.com/grad

Check out our latest graduate school rankings in business, education, engineering, law, medicine and nursing, as well as the humanities and sciences.

U.S. News Graduate School Compass
usnews.com/gradcompass

Gain access to the U.S. News Graduate School Compass (subscribe at usnews.com/compassdiscount to get a 25 percent discount) and view our profiles of more than 1,900 graduate programs in an array of disciplines. Tap into a wealth of searchable data with tools and an expanded directory of programs. Are you curious about how much you could make coming out of business school? Find out – and get admissions, student body and career data that will help you find your perfect B-school match.

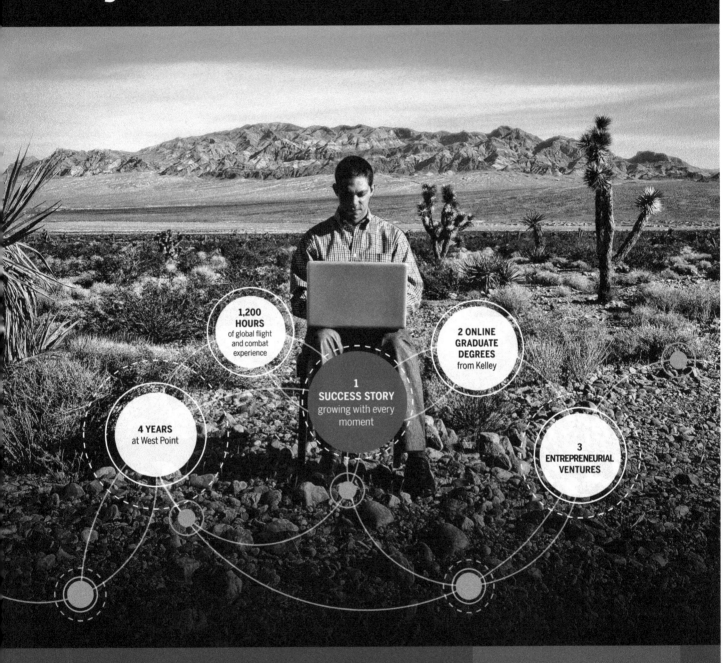

Find the Best B-

In the library at the
Stanford Graduate School
of Business

Business schools are reinventing graduate education

 ORE CHOICES, more flexibility, more emphasis on experiential learning and internationally flavored curricula – these are the hallmarks of a new breed of graduate business programs, spawned by student demand for offerings that better meet their professional and personal needs. U.S. News' Best Business Schools guidebook will take you inside top MBA programs that have been reimagined to include niche concentrations, incubators for entrepreneurs, and robust opportunities to gain hands-on experience at major companies or to study abroad. Not quite sure an MBA is the answer? We also survey the expanding array of professional master's programs and look at the explosion of mini-MBAs and certificates available to early and midcareer professionals who want to buff up certain skills – or their leadership cred.

And, as always, we feature the U.S. News rankings of Best Business programs, while providing smart advice on getting in, getting hired and financing your education. Read on for all this and much more. ●

School for You

CHAPTER 1 PICKING A

PROGRAM

7
Ways the
MBA
Is
Changing

BY KATHERINE HOBSON

Ross MBA students Aaron
Schmit (left) and Victor
Casana Angulo readying for a
presentation at luxury goods
startup Shinola in Detroit

DWIGHT CENDROWSKI

The traditional two-year MBA degree has been getting a makeover lately as B-schools work harder to see that the investment pays off

LORA EKPE-IDANG knew exactly what she wanted from business school. She was working in multicultural digital advertising in Los Angeles, but had long hoped to build a company making dolls representing different ethnicities – and knew that a grounding in finance and supply chain management would be essential. She chose Babson College for its focus on entrepreneurship and its WIN Lab (for Women Innovating Now), which nurtures female founders of early-stage companies with peer support and coaching by entrepreneurs.

"It pushed me," says Ekpe-Idang, 29, who "used to be uncomfortable" telling people about her idea. All the strategizing, analyzing and pitching involved in the Babson program solved that problem. And she does more than talk these days: While working in marketing at Target since graduation last year, she's also been building Corage Dolls.

Ekpe-Idang was typical of today's prospective MBA student: She was ambitious, in need of specific skills, and motivated by a purpose beyond making money. And she found a program that met her needs. That's more possible than ever in today's B-school climate, where demand for the traditional two-year program, a daunting investment of time and money for many, has been softening lately. While the appeal of traditional programs – which equip students with a broad range of business knowledge, from accounting to marketing – remains strong at top institutions, many schools are working harder to make that investment pay off. They're giving students a chance to gain more industry-specific expertise, for example, and are building in work experience. In some cases, they're shortening the time to a degree (story, Page 20) and punching up a global perspective (Page 30.)

Here are seven common ways MBA programs are evolving to better satisfy grads:

THEY'RE GETTING MORE SPECIALIZED. If you know which industry you'd like to land in, whether it's clean tech, data analytics, health care or sports business, you can probably find a program

tailored to your intended path. Specialization – more electives, more areas of concentration, even distinct degrees – is hot. At the University of California–Berkeley's Haas School of Business, for example, MBA students can pick from one of 11 specializations, including energy and clean technology, real estate, and health management. In addition, there are plenty of classes on cutting-edge topics. Gregory La Blanc, a lecturer at Haas, has launched three in the last four years, in data science, the future of the workplace, and blockchain (the secure, decentralized ledger of online transactions that is behind bitcoin and that many experts say will transform a host of industries). "The outside world is moving very, very quickly," he says. "If students feel like the stuff they're learning isn't relevant or is outdated, they'll be frustrated."

That ability to keep pace with the rapid changes in tech and finance has been valuable to Blakey Larsen, 31, who graduates from Haas this spring. She got interested in business while she was teaching computer science and consulting in the Peace Corps in Samoa, when she saw the potential for technology to increase access to financial services. At Haas, she served as co-president of the FinTech Club, which focuses on the intersection of finance and technology, and now hopes to work for either a startup or a traditional business with a mission to help everyone access financial services, no matter where they live.

Where industry demand for specific knowledge is strong, some schools are creating entirely separate degrees. New York University's Leonard N. Stern School of Business will welcome students this spring to two new one-year MBA programs, one for those interested in fashion and luxury goods and one in technology for those who want to add business skills to their tech expertise. The goal, says Raghu Sundaram, vice dean for MBA programs at Stern, is to combine the breadth of an MBA with the depth you'd get in coursework for a master's in data science, say.

THEY'RE FOCUSING ON DOING GOOD. A big part of Haas' appeal for Larsen was its emphasis on meaningful work. That desire is common among today's students, says Meeta Kothare, managing director of the Social Innovation Initiative at the University of Texas–Austin's McCombs School of Business. "They expect that their jobs and careers and the products they buy and companies in which they invest will reflect their values," she says. Job opportunities aren't limited to nonprofits or socially conscious startups, either; even Fortune 500 companies are paying attention to environmental and social impacts on their bottom lines and hiring accordingly.

At McCombs, the Social Innovation Institute provides suggested course sequences to guide students to expertise in four areas: how organizations can take into account environmental and social considerations in their decision-making; how investors can take account of such concerns in choosing where to put their money; social entrepreneurship, or starting new ventures with a social or environmental purpose in addition to making a profit; and how the public and social sectors can innovate to tackle problems. And there are plenty of extracurricular options too; for example, Haas, McCombs and other schools have programs that allow MBA students to take temporary nonvoting seats on nonprofit boards.

The appeal of social entrepreneurship is such that when the University of Vermont relaunched its traditional MBA program in 2014, it went all-in on sustainable innovation. The 12-month program, which preps students to work in nonprofits, the public sector or the private sector, partners with corporations so students get experience solving problems – for example, how coffee and coffeemaker company Keurig Green Mountain might develop a sustainable supply chain.

THEY'RE MAKING WORK REAL. That sort of real-world experience is an increasingly important part of the MBA curriculum, given the velocity of change in business wrought by tech and globalization. "We have to put students in situations that very closely mirror the world we're preparing them for," says Scott DeRue, dean of the University of Michigan's Ross School of Business. At NYU, for example, MBA students participate in Stern Solutions, which partners with companies and nonprofits including the San Antonio Spurs, HBO and the World Wildlife Fund on projects that serve as "live case studies," says Sundaram.

In addition to consulting gigs, Ross now offers MBA students a chance to embed with a company with the objective of taking responsibility for a business segment. Aaron Schmit, who will graduate in 2018, was intrigued by the chance to work with Shinola, the Detroit-based luxury goods startup. Schmit, 29, whose pre-MBA experience was in investment management, saw it as a chance to get experience in corporate finance as an employee (albeit an unpaid one) rather than as a student working on a project. He and fellow students were part of the team working on Shinola's recently launched high-end headphones, from scaling up manufacturing to marketing to pricing.

THEY'RE STARTING IT UP. "We see so many applicants who have been working for Fortune 500 companies and who see business school as a way to transition to something more entrepreneurial or to a fast-growth tech firm," says Matt Symonds, co-founder and director of business school admissions consultancy Fortuna Admissions. So schools are catering to would-be founders, adding entrepreneurship coursework and concentrations and accelerators like Babson's WIN Lab. In an eight-month program, lab participants get training, coaching

SPOTLIGHT ON

Krannert School of Management

PURDUE UNIVERSITY
WEST LAFAYETTE, INDIANA

U.S. NEWS RANK
#53

Purdue University's engineering program has long been a top draw, and in fact, more than half of the MBA students at the Krannert School of Management have a STEM background. The campus in West Lafayette is "a sandbox" for people who want to work at the intersection of tech and business, says Dean David Hummels. Students can specialize in manufacturing/technology management, for instance, or technology innovation and entrepreneurship.

Second-year MBA student Steve Sanders, 28, volunteers at the Purdue Foundry, an entrepreneurship hub, where he assists tech startups in developing their business plans. He is also part of a group that helps the university decide which startups are worth investing in. "They rely on the MBA students to help them maximize profit," he says. Also strong in data analytics, Krannert hosts 24-hour "data dives," during which chief data strategists from companies such as Walmart and Cisco allow groups of students to examine their raw data files to solve business problems for the companies. *–Lindsay Cates*

▶ **More @ usnews.com/purdue**

SPOTLIGHT ON

W. P. Carey
School of Business

ARIZONA STATE UNIVERSITY, TEMPE

U.S. NEWS RANK #29 In 2016, the W. P. Carey School of Business rolled out its revamped Forward Focus curriculum, which includes career coaching; mentoring from industry executives; courses on leadership, data analytics and entrepreneurship; and cross-disciplinary learning labs where B-school students partner with peers across other ASU schools on real community challenges. In one collaboration with the School of Sustainability, students helped create a renewable energy program for the city of Tempe, which they presented to the city council, says John Wisneski, director of the full-time MBA program.

Along with the new curriculum, ASU offered all full-time MBA students accepted for fall 2016 a scholarship that covers the full cost of tuition and fees for the two-year program (about $94,000 for out-of-staters). ASU plans to continue providing funds for each incoming class of roughly 120 MBAs for the foreseeable future, Wisneski says. In return, students serve as graduate assistants for 10 hours a week. *–Mariya Greeley*

▶ **More @ usnews.com/asu**

and feedback as they develop a growth strategy and funding plan for their business. "We want them to build confidence and get the skills they need so that when they graduate, they are ready" to actually run it, says Heatherjean MacNeil, WIN Lab's co-founder and global director.

Rady School of Management at the University of California–San Diego launched in 2003 with entrepreneurship as its focus. Every MBA student takes a three-course lab-to-market sequence covering idea generation, market testing, coming up with a viable product, and working in teams to develop a growth path. Alums have launched 150 ongoing businesses, says Robert Sullivan, Rady's dean. He notes that the same skills that make entrepreneurs successful are also essential for "intrapreneurs" who want to manage change within an established company.

THEY'RE STRESSING SOFT SKILLS. In today's job market, students who stand out know how "to thrive in highly ambiguous situations" where change is constant, says DeRue. When the National Association of Colleges and Employers asked members what skills were in demand, top vote-getters were the ability to work in a team, a knack for problem-solving, written and verbal communication skills, and a strong work ethic.

Communication skills are especially in demand, says Jeff McNish, assistant dean of the career development center at the University of Virginia's Darden School of Business. "Employers want students to be able to articulate an idea in a compelling, convincing and concise way," he says. That means an increased emphasis on these skills in the core classes, faculty teaching business students skills like persuasion and strategic writing, and writing centers where students can get individual help.

At American University's Kogod School of Business, students can reduce their anxiety by practicing their public speaking skills in front of a friendly audience – dogs. "Their heart rate goes down, they have a smile on their face, and they start to associate public speaking with something they can enjoy," says Caron Martinez, director of Kogod's Center for Business Communications. And Kogod students learn that they need to write with an eye to the audience and the context, says Martinez, whether it's a one-page memo or a strategic five-year plan.

THEY'RE EMPHASIZING LEADERSHIP. Academic interest in perhaps the ultimate soft skill – leadership – isn't new. "But over the last 10 years or so there's been an increased focus on the need for MBA students not just to be great functional managers, but also great managers of people," says Sridhar Balasubramanian, senior associate dean of MBA programs at the University of North Carolina's Kenan-Flagler Business School. At Kenan-Flagler, students complete a 360-degree evaluation before they start, getting feedback from co-workers and bosses at their previous job. Then they home in on strengths they can build on and weaknesses they can improve. And a six-

HATCHING THE NEXT BIG IDEA

If you've ever stood in a drugstore wondering whether to choose a name-brand product over a generic, Meg Greenhalgh, a second-year MBA student at the University of Virginia's Darden School of Business, can help. She developed Brandefy in Darden's i.Lab Incubator – a startup that pays trained volunteers with gift cards to compare products and inform shoppers via its blog or just-launched app when they can save money by buying quality generics. The nearly 10,000-square-foot i.Lab, a cooperative effort of all 11 schools in the UVA system, provides budding entrepreneurs – at no charge – with workspace, mentors, $5,000 in funding for their new ventures, and workshops on everything from trademarks to project management. UVA law students, working with practicing attorneys, help entrepreneurs with documents like incorporation papers.

During the summer, some 25 startup teams (28 percent of those that applied in

Inside the i.Lab at UVA's Darden School of Business

2017) take part in an intensive 10-week accelerator program designed to advance their ventures. Greenhalgh and her partner worked on creating Brandefy's blog and monitoring site traffic to confirm their potential market. After getting about

2,500 visitors in a month, they felt ready to build a web prototype of their app.

Venture teams can be comprised of students from across the UVA system as well as faculty and community members. The interdisciplinary mix of participants can be a major asset. For example, Greenhalgh was able to consult with a Ph.D. candidate in chemical engineering working on his own venture about testing products. "That kind of interaction is really what makes the i.Lab so special," she says.

Once the school year begins, student teams often continue working on their businesses in the i.Lab. These committed entrepreneurs are "the group that you end up staying there until midnight or 1 a.m. with," Greenhalgh says.

Charlottesville has become a major startup hub, and the i.Lab holds regular events so entrepreneurs can mingle with local businesspeople, including one with the Virginia biotech industry. "The angel [investor] community here is unbelievably supportive," says Jason Brewster, the incubator director, and many members have invested time and money in i.Lab companies. –*Mariya Greeley*

---

credit course dealing entirely with leadership skills includes challenges of all types – for example, a surprise assignment to manage the school's cafeteria for a day – to help students learn to think and act on their feet.

At the UCLA Anderson School of Management, a new leadership development program has participants methodically work on four skills per quarter such as collaboration and managing conflict. These capabilities will pay off even if graduates aren't immediately in a top management role, says Gary Fraser, assistant dean of student affairs for the full-time MBA program; students also need to learn how to influence people when they don't have direct authority over them.

THEY'RE COACHING FOR CAREER SUCCESS. Career coaching and one-on-one advising have come to business school. "We really work with individual students to understand who they are, what their value proposition is, and how they fit into the marketplace," says John Rooney, director of graduate business career services at Mendoza College of Business at the University of Notre Dame. "What are your

MORE @ USNEWS.COM

CHECK OUT THE U.S. NEWS ONLINE GUIDE TO BUSINESS SCHOOLS
You'll find a wealth of detail on the country's MBA programs as well as comprehensive advice on getting in and finding the money. Plus: Where are the jobs? ▶ *usnews.com/bschool*

strengths? What are your preferences? Your values?"

At Indiana University's Kelley School of Business, students work to nail down their personal brand and story in the two weeks before school starts, through the Me Inc. program. "We want to give each student an opportunity to better understand their personal values and transferrable skills," says Eric Johnson, Kelley's executive director of graduate career services. Scott Price, 29, says the program really made him think about what was important to him in a future job and why. He started his MBA with an eye toward going into brand management and marketing, but soon realized he was more of a generalist. "It's not just preparing for job interviews," he says. Though he did well on those, too: After graduating this year, he'll head to Louisville, Kentucky, to join the leadership development program at GE Appliances. ●

A Faster Track

Demand is rising for the accelerated MBA

BY BARBARA SADICK

AFTER GRADUATING from the U.S. Military Academy in 2006, Ian Folau served as a military intelligence officer for nine years in Germany and Afghanistan. But besides managing teams of people gathering data on enemy actions, he also built side businesses allowing homeowners near an Arizona army base to rent out rooms to government employees on temporary assignment and started an online rugby supply company. After discharge, he wanted to develop a full-time business helping companies make open-source technologies safe to use. An MBA degree would prepare him to launch a startup, he thought, but he didn't want to leave the workforce for the typical two-year stretch. When he found the one-year Johnson Cornell Tech MBA program, he knew it was the right fit.

The Cornell Tech program, which is offered on a new Roosevelt Island campus in New York City, admits students with technical experience in the workforce who want to add business knowledge to their portfolio. They begin by spending 10 intensive summer weeks on Cornell's Ithaca campus taking accelerated core courses such as finance and marketing. In New York City, the curriculum melds business and tech content and emphasizes teamwork with other master's students in engineering, computer science, and connective media and design. The program's "studio" curriculum has interdisciplinary teams of students developing new product and business ideas to pitch to investors. A fall term project gives students a chance to work as management consultants for Israeli startup companies and culminates with a short stay in Israel.

"I've come away from this MBA program understanding how businesses are built from the ground up," says Folau, 35, who finished the program in May 2016 and has since started his company.

Desire for speed. The demand for a quicker route to an MBA seems to be gaining strength, and business schools have responded with accelerated tracks that can take as little as a year. Beyond the top-ranked B-schools, interest in two-year MBA programs has been waning, says Andrew Ward, associate dean for graduate programs at Lehigh University's College of Business and Economics, which introduced a one-year option last year and has no full-time two-year program. Many people who have already been earning a paycheck are not inclined these days to take so much time without one, he says. "The cost of an extra year is high."

Indeed, tuition for a two-year MBA at a top school can run $140,000, and then there is the extra year of lost salary, which is estimated at an additional $63,000 or so, according to Ward. Total tuition for the new one-year MBA at Lehigh is $64,750. Moreover, he adds, the one-year program is the dominant model in Europe, and foreign students, too, are now looking for such programs in the U.S.

Accelerated MBA programs are designed for students who show up with more experience in traditional business roles than two-year students, notes Kristin McAndrew, director of admissions for graduate business programs at the University of Notre Dame's Mendoza College of Business. The one-year option adds knowledge, a network and a credential that may hasten their career progression.

The typical one-year path begins with a summer session during which the core subjects two-year students complete in their first year are covered in an intensive fashion. Then the single-year cohort essentially gets the equivalent of the second year, typically merging with a two-year class if there is one. "When you enter an accelerated one-year program, a lot of information will come at you in a very short time and you have to be very focused," says Johary Rivera, 29, an MBA student with a health care consulting concentration at the Samuel Curtis Johnson Graduate School of Management on Cornell's Ithaca campus. (The New York City Cornell Tech campus offers a one-year MBA only.)

What do one-year students give up? A shortened schedule allows for less time to explore business fields by packing in electives. Because there's no summer internship, MBA candidates also don't have as much

The view from the Cornell Tech New York campus – and students in class

opportunity to gain experience working with companies that might hire them once they graduate, says Brian Mitchell, associate dean for full-time MBA programs at Emory University's Goizueta Business School. Emory, a pioneer in the one-year MBA, launched its program in 1983. By contrast, two-year programs typically involve summer internships that frequently lead to jobs. In certain fields such as investment banking, employers tend to hire newly minted MBAs only from internship pools, says Mitchell.

"Employers like the opportunity to interact with candidates during the internship experience, reducing the risk in hiring decisions," says Bill Valenta, assistant dean of MBA and executive programs at the University of Pittsburgh's Joseph M. Katz Graduate School of Business. On the other hand, bosses who want to add to their employees' credentials find appeal in the accelerated programs: One-year students at Katz and other schools often have been sent to class by their companies with the understanding that they will return.

Some accelerated programs carve out especially defined niches. Brandeis' Heller School for Social Policy and Management, for example, offers an MBA program in nonprofit management for those interested in working for an organization with a social justice mission. Students spend 16 months gaining the business acumen needed to take a leadership position and help the organization succeed.

In place of an internship, Heller students complete a capstone project for which they work in teams to find solutions to management problems brought to the school by all sorts of mission-driven entities. "Our group's task was to deliver a roadmap for how the city of Haverhill, Massachusetts, could transition from incremental budgeting to performance-based budgeting" so as to better finance its priorities, says Elaine Theriault, 25, who worked for a couple of years with community organizations through AmeriCorps after college before deciding she wanted to effect social change on a larger level. She says most of her core classes have been taught from two points of view – that of a for-profit and that of a nonprofit organization.

A wide angle. Georgette Phillips, dean of Lehigh's College of Business and Economics, says the goal of Lehigh's new MBA program is to produce business leaders who are trained to look at and solve modern business problems by taking various perspectives rather than any single disciplinary approach. The skills employers are looking for – analytical skills, business acumen, problem-solving abilities, project management and teamwork – are not exclusive to the traditional longer program, she argues.

"As more universities offer solid one-year MBA programs," predicts Phillips, it will become clearer and clearer that graduates "are as skilled and talented as those who have taken a more leisurely route to the same end." ●

BY MARGARET LOFTUS

The growing "go-to" option for business students who have a specialized goal and want an expedited time frame

The New Niche

ATTHEW MOTTOLA was wrapping up his undergraduate degree in accounting and finance at the University of Massachusetts–Lowell and was set to pursue an MBA when he began to second-guess his plan. Funding for a financial tech startup he'd co-founded had just fallen through, and he was disappointed at the lack of support for his venture among his peers and mentors. He knew an MBA would net him a decent job, but would it sufficiently nurture his entrepreneurial spirit?

Worried that it wouldn't, Mottola, 25, set his sights 30 miles south on an ultrafocused one-year master of science degree in entrepreneurial leadership at Babson College's F.W. Olin Graduate School of Business. The specialized program is geared toward students who want to start their own companies. "There's a mindset there that anything is possible," he says. "Instead of telling you what to do, they give you the resources, and you figure it out on your own."

Traditionally the go-to degree for those seeking a leg up in the job market, the MBA now has plenty of company. In the last decade,

U.S. business schools have been rolling out one-year niche degrees at a furious pace, in subjects ranging from accounting to finance to business analytics to health care management. Budding entrepreneurs "don't want to spend two years doing MBA-learning about all the roles in a corporation," notes Helena Yli-Renko, who co-chairs the entrepreneurship programs at the University of Southern California's Marshall School of Business. Applications to Marshall's one-year Master of Science in Entrepreneurship and Innovation program, launched four years ago, have tripled since it was introduced. With five required and four elective courses, the yearlong (or part-time over two years) curriculum is highly experiential, focusing on developing and launching the students' ventures.

By carving out deeper niches, schools say

Degrees

they're responding to the demands of the marketplace. "What we're finding is that students need more skills going into their first jobs than they're able to attain in their undergrad as the world becomes more connected," says Michael Faulkender, associate dean for master's programs at the University of Maryland–College Park's Robert H. Smith School of Business, which introduced two specialty master's last year and now offers eight in subjects from quantitative finance to marketing analytics to supply chain management.

In the last five years, the number of MBA degrees earned in the U.S. has declined by 5.7 percent while specialized business master's have increased nearly 45 percent, according to a member survey by AACSB International–The Association to Advance Collegiate Schools of Business. "The MBA has evolved to be more of a post-experience degree," says Dan LeClair, AACSB's executive vice president and chief strategy and innovation officer.

About three-quarters of applicants to these niche degree programs have three or fewer years of experience, according to a recent survey by the Graduate Management Admission Council. While the level in each class varies, the most recent group to enter Babson's entrepreneurial program had an average of 10 months under their belts. "This is for folks who haven't been corporatized yet," says Richard Goulding, faculty director of the Babson program. "They are the raw form of entrepreneur energy." LeClair suggests that, increasingly, there may be room for both degrees at different stages of a career: a specialized degree following college and an MBA after five to eight years in the work world.

The Babson and Marshall programs are two of a number of niche entrepreneurship degrees that have popped up in the last five years. Marshall's Lloyd Greif Center for Entrepreneurial Studies also offers a master's in social entrepreneurship for those who want to start a business with a social impact. Babson's program is broken down into two 14-week semesters separated by a global experience. Faculty initially focus on introducing participants to major forces in the business world. For example, last year, the class explored how autonomous and electric vehicles will impact entrepreneurial activity in insurance, urban infrastructure and the fuel sector.

The second half of the program covers business development, from pitch to funding to launch. At one point, each student pitches his or her business idea to the class, which then votes on the best ones and divides into teams to flesh them out. Five of the projects launched by the Class of 2016 have become viable commercial enterprises.

The entrepreneurial mindset is prized by corporations, too, and degrees focused on innovation are being designed to meet that need. "A lot of companies are looking for 'intrapreneurs,' someone who can come into an established company and create new things," says Gregg Schoenfeld, director of management education research for GMAC. Northeastern University's D'Amore-McKim School of Business, for example, offers a program geared toward working professionals who want to become innovation leaders within their organizations. It's offered online or on campus; the in-person classes meet on Saturdays for a year. Students in the program work on real-world experiential assignments, and also on individual innovation projects for their employers.

The Northeastern degree has allowed Pam Abel – who already had an MBA and was working in project management for an aerospace company – to make a career change to new product development in the consumer packaged goods industry. "When you're dealing with innovation, there's no history or benchmark to work from," notes Abel, 36, who is now a commercialization manager at Ocean Spray in Lakeville, Massachusetts. "So how do you become successful with a brand new idea that's not out there?" The program, she says, helped her to ask the right questions when shepherding a new product to market.

Also on the hot list: business analytics. Applications for UMD Smith's analytics program have exceeded expectations the last two years. Why? "Companies are seeing exponential growth in the amount of information that's available," Faulkender says. They're looking for hires with a set of analytic skills to harness it to better serve their customers. Analytics programs like Smith's immerse students in technical coursework such as data mining, quantitative modeling, and optimization, equipping them for careers in everything from business intelligence to logistics.

At Duke University's Fuqua School of Business, a new master's in quantitative management, or MQM, is aimed at students with a strong STEM background who want to apply their analytical skills in one of four areas: finance, marketing, forensics or strategy. Someone who chooses forensics, say, might work as an internal auditor, analyzing data to determine any inefficiencies in an organization. And a grad with a focus on strategy could go on to work as a strategic analyst, helping company leadership identify and quantify growth opportunities, for instance.

The MQM touts a big helping of soft skills, which some say is often missing in analytics programs. It's one thing to know how to make sense of data that's available, says Bill Boulding, dean of Fuqua. But how do you communicate it to others? "You have to be able to translate into digestible information for people who aren't as quantitatively sophisticated," he says. The school also just introduced an online-only program focused solely on health analytics. Graduates will be prepared to analyze patterns in data that could help improve medical outcomes, for example.

The soft skills component sold Rutu Shah, 27, a CPA who enrolled in Fuqua's MQM program to transition from forensic accounting at PwC in Mumbai, India, where she worked in fraud investigations, into financial services. "What happens with analytics programs is they have the tendency to get very technical," she says. "If you want to work with everybody you need to know how to tell your story."

Meanwhile, Mottola is telling his story to potential clients in a sales role for Gigster, a San Francisco startup that builds custom software. He says his job would not have been possible had the failure of his startup in college not sent him to Babson. "At Babson, you fall in love with problems and learn how to solve them with minimal resources and in environments of extreme uncertainty," he says. "Rather than providing answers, they pointed us toward frameworks for asking the right questions." •

SPOTLIGHT ON

McCombs School of Business
UNIVERSITY OF TEXAS–AUSTIN

U.S. NEWS RANK #17

Thanks to Austin's position as an emerging hub for technology and innovation, the region's sizable energy market, and a lively arts and music scene, students at the McCombs School of Business have plenty of opportunities to tap into in the Lone Star State capital. After a semester of core classes, the school's roughly 530 full-time MBA students have the flexibility to design their own program. They choose one of 23 optional concentrations (examples include energy finance and real estate), have the ability to study abroad in one of 25 countries, and apply to fellows programs where they dive into a particular interest – marketing or operations, say – with a focused curriculum and real-world consulting projects.

Through Venture Fellows, for instance, Alana Williams, 32, worked with Austin-based Whole Foods Market on its global growth and business development team analyzing market data on the food and beverage industry. She also got to attend weekly seminars from successful investors in the private equity and venture capital space. –*Lindsay Cates*

▶ **More @ usnews.com/utaustin**

The Job Market

Here are some of the fastest growing, best-paying career options for business grads

BY MARIYA GREELEY

MARKETING MANAGER

These pros use market research, branding, pricing strategies and creative multimedia campaigns to increase interest in products and generate sales. Critical to companies that want to maintain healthy bottom lines, positions for marketing managers are expected to grow at a solid 10 percent clip between 2016 and 2026. The median salary in 2016 was just over $131,000, according to the Bureau of Labor Statistics.

HEALTH CARE ADMINISTRATOR

Behind the scenes at hospitals, home health care agencies, and other facilities, these administrators work to improve how care is delivered and managed. They may cut unnecessary spending, say, or help implement technology that improves the security of patient records. Careers in health care administration are poised to see high growth as the need for services increases with people living and staying active longer. Between 2016 and 2026, jobs for these administrators are expected to increase by 20 percent. The median salary in 2016 was about $96,000.

VENTURE CAPITAL ASSOCIATE

These specialists at VC firms evaluate pitches from entrepreneurs who hope to get the funding they need to launch or grow their businesses. VC associates analyze every angle

SPOTLIGHT ON:
PRODUCT MANAGEMENT

CHRISTOPHER KAO

University of Southern California
Marshall School of Business, 2017

Christopher Kao, 37, grew up loving video games. Now Kao is a Southern California-based product manager for Zynga Games, a social gaming company with global hits like "Words with Friends" and "FarmVille." At Zynga, Kao pulls insights from "an ocean of data" and helps formulate strategic decisions like when to put a game on sale. As product manager, he interacts with developers, marketers and executives. For example, "I have to be able to explain why these numbers are important, why this new feature should be made, and what the priorities are," Kao says.

He started his career as a quality assurance tester and moved through the developer ranks, but eventually became more interested in high-level business strategy, a change he describes as moving from being a "carpenter" to being "like the architect." While earning his MBA at USC Marshall, a school with strong entertainment industry ties, Kao took marketing and analytics classes and interned in Warner Brothers' mobile games department, working on games like "Lego Star Wars." He cemented his career transition with a Zynga-run product management training course at Marshall.

of a startup's business plan, market demand and the entrepreneurs themselves to determine the venture's viability and whether the firm should make an investment. The median base salary is about $94,000, according to PayScale, and additional compensation, especially for finding companies that succeed and add to the firm's investment fund, is common.

COMMERCIAL REAL ESTATE DEVELOPMENT MANAGER

With their deep market knowledge and finance and management skills, these executives help create and oversee the budget, design and timely execution of commercial construction and renovation projects. Clients look to development managers for their expertise in subjects like zoning, permits and property assessment. Median salary is about $95,000. With bonuses and profit sharing factored in, total compensation can vary from about $50,000 to $160,000.

FINANCIAL ANALYST

These analysts' responsibilities range from helping company leaders decide whether an expansion is financially feasible to helping individuals and institutions make stock, bond and other investment decisions. The employment outlook is expected to remain strong in the immediate future, with job growth projected to be 11 percent over the decade ending in 2026. Median salary is around $81,000, according to the BLS.

DATA SCIENTIST

Once called "the sexiest job of the 21st century" by Harvard Business Review and named the best job in America in 2018, 2017 and 2016 by Glassdoor, data science clearly is hot. These analytic whizzes find patterns in data and come up with actionable insights in nearly every business function and industry. Median base pay for data scientists is $110,000 according to Glassdoor, and IBM predicts that by 2020 there will be over 60,000 openings for data scientists and similar experts.

OPERATIONS RESEARCH ANALYST

Applying statistics and strategic thinking, these specialized analysts help systematically improve company performance. They might provide a report with suggestions on how to optimize crew and plane schedules for an airline, for example. As technology advances over the next decade, companies will look to operations research analysts to cut costs and maximize efficiency, causing their employment opportunities to jump by 27 percent, according to the BLS. Median salary is about $79,000.

INVESTMENT BANKING ASSOCIATE

These financial pros advise their clients – including corporations, governments and hedge funds – on investing and complicated financial moves such as a merger, financing a big project, or becoming a publicly traded company. Median salary is about $77,000 according to PayScale, but top earners can bring in about $125,000 and base salaries are (often heavily) supplemented by bonuses, a measure of compensation for the often long hours.

FINANCIAL MANAGER

At companies of every type and size, financial managers work with their teams to produce financial reports, set long-term earning goals, direct investments, and propose strategies for improvement and growth to top executives. Openings for financial managers are expected to grow by 19 percent between 2016 and 2026, much faster than most occupations, because their risk and money

SPOTLIGHT ON:
MANAGEMENT CONSULTING

CAROLYN SCHNEIDER

Massachusetts Institute of Technology
Sloan School of Management, 2013

After four years helping determine the value of companies and business assets, Carolyn Schneider, 32, decided she wanted to make more of a positive impact by moving into the health care space to help clients improve outcomes and care for patients. She earned her MBA from MIT Sloan in 2013 and joined the Frankel Group, now part of Huron Consulting Group, a boutique, Boston-based firm where she started as an associate and is now a director in the life sciences strategy practice. She works with pharmaceutical and biotech companies on everything from development planning to acquisitions to launching new drugs.

In B-school she joined management consulting and health care clubs, took courses with experiential consulting components, and attended networking events to learn the differences between management consulting firms. Huron's specialized focus on health care and the consultants' passion about their mission and work made the company the perfect fit for Schneider. "The industry is always changing and problems are complex," she says. "One could never get bored in this line of work."

Consulting can be "sort of an extension of an MBA program in some ways," Schneider notes. "You're continuing to build strategy skills. You're learning constantly." It provides great opportunities to grow, she says, whether you plan on staying in consulting or returning to industry down the road.

MORE @ USNEWS.COM

BEST JOBS FOR MBAS
Learn more about the best careers for MBA graduates and, as a bonus, learn how Fortune 500 CEOs got to where they are, starting with their business school education. ▶usnews.com/mbajobs

management skills will be in high demand, according to the BLS. The median salary is just over $121,000.

PERSONAL FINANCIAL ADVISOR

Helping individuals manage their finances can be both fulfilling and lucrative work. These advisors help clients with everything from investing to saving for college and estate planning. They possess both the technical skills to create strong risk management and investing strategies and the interpersonal skills to build relationships with their clients. Their median salary is about $90,000 a year and demand is projected to grow by 15 percent between 2016 and 2026 as the population ages and more people look for long-term investment help.

TRAINING-AND-DEVELOPMENT MANAGER

These managers ensure employees get the skills they need to stay at the top of their game. They plan and oversee everything from new-employee training and team-building events to skill-development workshops and performance review programs. There is a constant need for workforce training and development, especially in fields like manufacturing and cybersecurity where executives struggle to fill open positions with skilled workers. Job openings in training-and-development management are expected to grow faster than average, according to the BLS – about 10 percent in the decade ending in 2026. Median yearly income is almost $106,000.

SUPPLY CHAIN MANAGER

If you want to get products from point A (the supplier) to point Z (the retailer or customer) in the most efficient way possible, then you need an expert in supply chain management. Amazon customers can thank these pros for the company's trademark speedy deliveries, for example. These coordination experts design and supervise logistics policies and practices, including negotiating contracts with suppliers, maintaining the right amount of inventory for fluctuating demand and traveling to check in on production, warehouse or retail locations along the supply chain. Median annual salary is about $81,500, according to PayScale. ●

GOING

GLOBAL

The University of
Oxford in England

ROB STOTHARD FOR USN&WR

SPOTLIGHT ON THE B-SCHOOL AT:
University of California–Berkeley 34

Business
Without
Borders

B-schools are preparing MBAs to thrive in an interconnected world

BY COURTNEY RUBIN

AST FALL, WHEN Grace McLarty, a 23-year-old management consultant in Chicago, was assigned a project with a colleague in South America, she knew she should not necessarily expect immediate responses to out-of-business-hours emails and made sure to discuss with her partner their respective work styles. "I already knew what questions to ask, and that her work-life balance would be different than mine," McLarty notes. It sounds like such a small thing, she says, but it helped the project run smoothly and on time.

McLarty credits her ease working with people from different countries and cultures to a new 10-month program she completed in 2017 that simultaneously earned her two business degrees and a certificate from schools on three continents. A partnership between the University of Virginia's McIntire School of Commerce,

Lingnan (University) College at Sun Yat-sen University in Guangzhou, China, and ESADE Business School in Barcelona, Spain, the program sends students to live and study as a cohort at all three institutions for stints ranging from nine to 15 weeks. Participants take courses focused on global business strategy and practices to help them understand the unique aspects of doing business in the U.S., China and the European Union. Graduates earn a master's in global commerce from UVA, a master's in global strategic management from ESADE, and a certificate in international management from Lingnan. The program debuted in 2016, and the Class of 2018 includes 60 students from 15 countries.

UVA's program reflects a growing trend among U.S. B-schools to beef up their international offerings for students who want to prepare themselves

ASIA SCHOOL OF BUSINESS. MBA students at the brand-new institution prep for a factory tour in Malaysia.

for a more interconnected global economy. Though elite U.S. B-schools are still a big draw to students from other countries, in recent years they have lagged behind their foreign counterparts in global academic offerings. According to a 2016 ranking of the "most international" MBA programs by business education website Poets&Quants, the Massachusetts Institute of Technology Sloan School of Management was the top U.S. finisher – in 39th place.

But that trend is starting to turn around as U.S. business schools aggressively reimagine their standard MBA curricula. Many schools have introduced globally focused courses such as "Chinese Economy and Financial Markets" (at the University of Chicago Booth School of Business) or "The Political Economy of China" (at Stanford). And since 2016, all full-time MBA students at the Yale School of Management have been required to take a course called "Global Virtual Teams," where they work with students from other network schools abroad tackling, for example, a 24-hour factory simulation. In such an experience, students oversee a hypothetical production line and serve in mock business roles, making key operations management decisions while getting a feel for working across cultures and time zones. Now, other institutions are taking things even further with deep immersion programs, academic alliances with global partners, and even a brand-new global business school – all designed to attract more international students and

and "more cultural, more big picture, more on the pure fun end" excursions on the side, says Barbara Bennett Ostdiek, senior associate dean of degree programs. In 2018, full-time students will travel to Brazil, and Ostdiek expects a continued emphasis on emerging markets in the years ahead. Many other schools, such as B-schools at the College of William and Mary, the University of Florida and the University of Michigan, offer global immersion opportunities but don't require them.

The Leonard N. Stern School of Business at New York University still makes international academic experiences optional for MBA students, but the number who have embraced global offerings has grown substantially in recent years, says Jamie

turn domestic ones into culturally sensitive – and effective – multinational business leaders.

Emphasizing immersive experience. Though study-abroad options have been standard fare for years, business schools at Pennsylvania State University, Dartmouth, Harvard, and Rice University have made them core requirements, often in the form of short immersion trips. Though Rice has required so-called global immersion programs for its executive MBA students for a few years, the full-time MBA class entering in the fall of 2018 will now also have to complete a mandatory field experience before graduation. An immersion lasts roughly 10 days, with about half of that time devoted to intense coursework (including meetings with local academics and business leaders)

RICE. A street-art walking tour in Bogota, Colombia, site of one of Rice's global experiences

Tobias, assistant dean of student engagement. Some 130 MBA students took part in programs with a study-abroad component in 2004-2005 compared to nearly 500 in 2016-2017. In 2016, MBAs in the traditional two-year program could opt for a one- or two-week "Doing Business in ..." elective course held in one of about a dozen countries – including Australia, Israel and Hungary – where they talk to academics, make company visits and, as at Rice, also have cultural experiences. Many students also partner with faculty and go abroad through Stern Solutions to help solve a real-world business problem. A recent group collaborated with the World Wildlife Fund and the United Arab Emirates' Fujairah municipality to launch the country's first

A Strong Cultural Mix

U.S. NEWS has compiled a list of the full-time and part-time MBA programs (from among ranked programs) that, for 2017, had the highest percentage of international students enrolled. U.S. News collected this data directly from each MBA program in the fall of 2017 and early 2018. Advantages of choosing a program with a high proportion of international students are that participants can more frequently engage with peers from different cultures and the curriculum is apt to be more globally oriented. The first data column below indicates the percentage of the full- or part-time 2017 enrollment that was international; the second gives the total full- or part-time enrollment of the program.

MBA programs with the most international students

Full Time

School	% International students	'17 enrollment
Stevens Institute of Technology (NJ)	94.2%	914
Hult International Business School–Boston (MA)	90.2%	245
Syracuse University (Whitman) (NY)	73.1%	52
Babson College (Olin) (MA)	72.3%	328
University of California–Riverside (Anderson)	69.7%	119
University of Connecticut	64.5%	107
Rochester Institute of Technology (Saunders) (NY)	56.8%	146
Pace University (Lubin) (NY)	52.1%	192
University of Tampa (Sykes) (FL)	51.7%	344
University of San Diego (CA)	50.6%	81
University of Delaware (Lerner)	50.5%	111
University of California–Irvine (Merage)	47.9%	167
University of Rochester (Simon) (NY)	46.9%	211
San Diego State University (Fowler) (CA)	46.5%	230
University of San Francisco (CA)	46.3%	82
Purdue University–West Lafayette (Krannert) (IN)	44.5%	119
Clark University (MA)	43.7%	87
Chapman University (Argyros) (CA)	43.3%	67
George Washington University (DC)	43.2%	169
Case Western Reserve U. (Weatherhead) (OH)	41.7%	108

Part Time

School	% International students	'17 enrollment
University of Northern Iowa	67.8%	149
Saginaw Valley State University (MI)	49.2%	61
University of California–Riverside (Anderson)	48.2%	114
Adelphi University (NY)	45.8%	402
Hofstra University (Zarb) (NY)	44.7%	751
University of Texas–Dallas	41.4%	759
University of Texas–Arlington	41.0%	442
University of North Carolina–Charlotte (Belk)	39.7%	368
St. Joseph's University (Haub) (PA)	36.1%	421
Indiana University (Kelley)	32.7%	294
Loyola University Chicago (Quinlan) (IL)	32.1%	557
University of Nebraska–Lincoln	31.7%	41
University of Massachusetts–Boston	31.1%	296
Seton Hall University (Stillman) (NJ)	31.0%	216
California State University–San Bernardino	30.6%	222
California State University–Fullerton (Mihaylo)	30.5%	285
Bradley University (Foster) (IL)	30.4%	46
Chapman University (Argyros) (CA)	30.0%	140
St. John's University (Tobin) (NY)	25.7%	319
Worcester Polytechnic Institute (MA)	25.7%	214

Full- and part-time MBA enrollment data are as of March 1, 2018. Only ranked schools are eligible to be included on this list.

national park. Students spent two weeks in the UAE before the start of the semester, then they worked to come up with a strategy before presenting it by videoconference.

Forging dual-degree partnerships. Much of the new B-school emphasis on global studies is coming in master's degree programs, which are fast-growing as an alternative to the MBA. Reflecting this trend, the Yale SOM announced in September a new master's initiative called M2M along with four other schools – the University of British Columbia's Sauder School of Business, HKUST Business School in Hong Kong, HEC Paris, and Brazil's FGV Escola de Administração de Empresas de São Paulo – that will allow students to simultaneously earn master's degrees at two of the participating schools in a two-year program. (And they'll have access to both schools' alumni networks.) The first cohort of students will begin in August. En-

rollees will pay the tuition costs of whichever institutions they attend. Yale's annual tuition and fees for 2018-2019 will run about $71,600, while those at HEC Paris are roughly $30,200 in U.S. currency. Travel and living expenses are not included.

Giving students the skills to work in a global marketplace is "what recruiters tell us they're looking for," says David Bach, Yale SOM's deputy dean. In 2012, Yale helped bring together a group of schools from around the world to form the Global Network for Advanced Management, which provides a range of both curricular and extracurricular travel and other activities for students at the 32 schools that now participate.

As at Yale, UVA's McIntire program places a lot of emphasis on tapping the expertise of each school and location involved in the partnership. Business students start at McIntire, where they take advantage of working with a foreign company doing

SPOTLIGHT ON

Haas
School of Business

UC – BERKELEY

U.S. NEWS RANK

#7

When she was choosing a business school, Carolyn Chuong, 29, was struck by the "incredibly talented, yet very down-to-earth" students at Berkeley's Haas School of Business. The school's reputation in both the tech sector and in making a difference for society was also appealing to her. Interested in education technology, Chuong led a team to Makerere University in Uganda to help launch a center to improve youth employment rates during her first year and spent a summer interning at Amazon Education in Seattle.

About 80 percent of "Haasies" participate in at least one program through the school's Center for Social Sector Leadership, such as serving on the board of a local nonprofit or tackling an investing project focused on helping others. Most of the school's roughly 540 full-time MBA students choose to concentrate on at least one of the school's 11 "areas of emphasis," which include subjects like corporate social responsibility and energy and clean tech. *–Mariya Greeley*

More @ usnews.com/berkeley

business in the U.S. to study global strategic management, global market research and cross-cultural decision-making. The program is taught in English in all three countries. After 15 weeks, they move on to China, where they focus on global finance and operations and take advantage of visiting high-tech companies in Hong Kong and Southern China. Finally, at ESADE in Spain, they focus on entrepreneurship, corporate social responsibility, and innovation and global alliances. Graduation is in Barcelona. Students pay approximately $36,000 in tuition, plus roughly $10,000 in housing expenses for the 10 months. Travel expenses are not included.

Members of the 2017-2018 class of five dozen students live together during their time on all three continents in cross-cultural apartments. "Students are teaching each other all the time" in both formal and less formal ways, says Lynn Hamilton, the academic director for McIntire. The cohort has organized an international cooking night, and students are known to share their own language lessons.

Hamilton says she can see the program eventually expanding to include even more country choices for students. But she sees the biggest value in students working through the experience together, as opposed to having individualized study-abroad experiences. "We really want to stick with this cohort aspect because we see it as so critical," she says.

Although no American graduate from the partnership's first cohorts has yet landed a job in China or Spain, students have found a range of postgrad positions across the world, says Denise Egan, McIntire's assistant dean for career services. Egan notes that one 2017 U.S. grad who landed an opportunity in Singapore with Tinkle, an international marketing agency, credits it partly to his knowledge of Asian and European business practices and his experience collaborating on projects through the McIntire program. Other graduates of the inaugural class have landed jobs at Amazon, Google, Marriott International, Rolls-Royce, Tencent, Volvo, GSK and Vodafone.

A global school. A growing interest in international degrees has even led to the creation of a new global MBA school – so new it doesn't even have its own campus yet. The Asia School of Business is a partnership between MIT Sloan and Bank Negara Malaysia, the central bank of Malaysia. The 82 first- and second-year students currently enrolled represent 21 different countries. The program is heavily experiential. "We are teaching [students] how to go into a country they've never been in before and build a business, build networks," says Charles Fine, dean of the Asia School of Business and a professor of management at MIT.

The program is based in Kuala Lumpur, where classes currently take place in the central bank's training center while campus is being built. Over the course of four to five weeks out of each 14-week semester, student teams travel to different countries in Southeast Asia to work with companies on place-specific projects. Some recently went to Myanmar, for example, to help Procter & Gamble figure out how to market hair care and skin care products there. Students also spend six weeks in the U.S. They first visit Silicon Valley, Washington D.C., and New York City; then, they spend about a month in residence at MIT, where they take specially focused classes taught by MIT faculty.

The courses in Malaysia cover typical MBA topics like finance and marketing, but students have to be nimble, as scheduling often depends on when MIT professors are able to travel abroad. A course on finance, for instance, might be broken up into several weeklong modules taught in the fall, winter and spring. (MIT faculty split teaching duties with a group of 10 local faculty members, who come from nine different countries.) For now, classes are "almost all aligned with MIT Sloan content and are not particularly Asia-specific," Fine says, though they will likely become more specialized as the school recruits and develops more professors locally. The language of instruction is English, and no foreign languages are offered yet, though Fine says this may also change as the school grows.

The program lasts 20 months and costs roughly $100,000, including campus housing, travel and lodging costs incurred for the trip to the U.S. Graduates receive an MBA from the ASB and a certificate from MIT Sloan. The traditional two-year MBA at MIT runs about $71,300 a year for tuition and fees alone.

When she learned about the MIT program, Alexandra Hill Snedeker, 27, thought "it was an intriguing opportunity to see a new part of the world," she says, as well as to become well rounded in management topics and to expand her skills. She has a bachelor's degree in environmental science from the University of North Carolina–Chapel Hill and was a Venture For America fellow at a series of environmental startups in New Orleans before enrolling. Snedeker says she is going to use the

UNIVERSITY OF VIRGINIA. UVA students do some team-building at ESADE in Barcelona, a partner school along with another in Guangzhou, China.

experience to help determine the next steps she wants to take in her career.

While students may miss some of the traditional career opportunities (like large and long-established job fairs) that standard MBA programs might offer, 2018 graduate Katherine Robinson, 25, notes that she has gotten more travel and project-based experiences than many students in traditional MBA programs. "We spend so much time doing hands-on work – being there and going and doing as opposed to being in a classroom," she says.

What do potential employers make of students who can bring international experience with their degree? "The short answer is, they love it," says Troy Steece, a project manager at Korn Ferry, an executive search and recruiting firm. But the particulars of the experience matter. A weeklong study tour will rarely "separate you from the pack" compared to, say, spending a semester abroad and doing an internship, Steece says. Bonus points if your experience is somewhere your potential employer is growing or has plans to expand. In general, demonstrating substantive experience can really help your résumé rise to the top of the pile. ●

MORE @ USNEWS.COM

INDEX OF BEST BUSINESS SCHOOLS
Check here for our index of the top business schools, which will give you instant online access to the rank of and a wealth of data on every school in our rankings. ▶ usnews.com/topbschools

Getting Your MBA Abroad

Four popular overseas programs for Americans

BY ARLENE WEINTRAUB

F INTERNATIONAL experience is increasingly valuable, why not simply get your MBA abroad? You certainly wouldn't be alone. Last year, 65 percent of MBA programs in the United Kingdom and 67 percent of schools in other European countries reported increasing numbers of applicants from elsewhere, and many of them from the U.S., according to the Graduate Management Admission Council's 2017 Applications Trends Survey.

European programs attract the most U.S. students (though programs in other regions are gaining traction, such as China Europe International Business School in Shanghai and Melbourne Business School in Australia). That's because many are based in appealing business hubs like London, and several compress the two-year MBA curriculum into 18 months or a year. That, coupled with the dollar's strength compared to European currencies, can greatly reduce the cost of getting an MBA.

Tuition costs range roughly from $73,000 to $95,000 for one-year programs in Europe to just over $100,000 for two-year programs, not counting room and board. In contrast, tuition and fees for a number of top-20 U.S. MBA programs in 2017 ranged from roughly $120,000 to $160,000.

European degrees can also appeal to hiring managers. "The top U.S. companies are international themselves and need people who have the ability to work across borders," says Caroline Diarte Edwards, an MBA admissions consultant based in Palo Alto, California. She's an alumna and former director of INSEAD in France, one of the world's leading business programs. "Going to a top international school will give you that insight into working with different cultures and teach you how things work in different parts of the world."

Americans looking to study in Europe will find a range of options. HEC Paris attracts students interested in technology and entrepreneurship, for exam-

Oxford. A tour group takes in the beauty and history of the university, which is home to the Saïd Business School.

ple, while Switzerland's IMD – the Institute for Management Development – fosters tomorrow's CEOs with its focus on leadership development.

Applying to these schools is similar to the process in the U.S. You'll need to complete essays and submit your undergraduate transcript, plus GMAT or GRE scores. But the specifics and timing may differ depending on the school, so be sure to leave plenty of time to research your options. Here are the distinctive features of four of the most popular choices for Americans who want to earn their MBAs in Europe.

University of Oxford Saïd Business School

When Californian Katie-Coral Sicora, 31, decided to go to Saïd for her MBA, her goal wasn't just to study in London, one of the world's premier financial centers. Sicora, who got her undergrad degree in political communications and advocacy from Emerson College in Boston, is passionate about climate change, so she wanted to go to a school that would allow her to explore that topic as well as accounting and finance.

Sicora is enrolled in Oxford's 1 + 1 MBA, a two-year program that awards an additional master's degree from one of 14 other departments, including medicine, history and music. Sicora spent her first year earning a master's from Oxford's School of Geography and the Environment – training that got her hired as an intern at Whirlpool, where she'll work with executives in several parts of the business to hone her interest in developing en-

vironmentally friendly products. "I'm intrigued by the challenge of rethinking how we make products so they meet the needs of consumers better and make a social impact," she says.

The 1 + 1 program is one of several options that make Oxford a top choice for Americans, who account for 20 percent of the Class of 2018. Saïd also offers a one-year MBA program. All students are offered a range of experiences, from consulting projects for large multinational companies like L'Oréal to advising financial-technology startups in Africa. Tuition for 2018-2019 is about $76,000 at early 2018 exchange rates and the school estimates that room and board would range from about $17,000 to $26,000.

Entrepreneurship is one of three broad themes that shape the MBA curriculum at Saïd, which admits about 320 MBA students a year. Everyone participates in an entrepreneurship module, teaming up to develop ideas for startups. "We teach students to think broadly about entrepreneurship and how they can apply what they learn broadly across all organizations," says MBA program director Ian Rogan. All students are required to complete two additional modules as well: "Global Rules of the Game," which focuses on laws and norms that govern business transactions, such as anticorruption agreements and trade laws; and "Responsible Business," where students focus on ethical decision-making.

Another common experience is Global Opportunities and Threats Oxford, a project that brings together faculty and students from across the university to address a different international issue each year. The 2017-2018 class focused on health care, working in groups to identify business opportunities related to the global aging of the population. "We do believe students should be prepared to be leaders in a world where the private sector has a huge influence on society above and beyond what people buy, and that we as a business school have a responsibility to address these larger issues," Rogan says.

London Business School. Americans accounted for 16 percent of the student body last year.

INSEAD

INSEAD calls itself "the business school for the world" – and not just because students can move between its flagship location in Fontainebleau, France, and its Singapore campus. (Some participants also do a rotation at the school's Abu Dhabi campus). INSEAD is the only top European MBA program with a language requirement. All classes are taught in English, but students must have a basic working knowledge of two other languages by the time they graduate from the 10-month program.

Of the roughly 1,000 students who enter the program in one of two intakes per year, about 8 percent come from the U.S. University of Georgia grad Andrew Ward, who finishes this summer, had already mastered German while working for German companies. He took Spanish classes at INSEAD. It has been daunting, he says. But "the languages are opening up regions of the world to me for work opportunities."

The INSEAD curriculum is split into five two-month periods, accommodating core business classes, electives and a capstone project. The tuition cost for 2017-2018 was nearly $100,000, plus fees and living expenses.

INSEAD's international campuses offer the opportunity to gain deep experience working with companies that are either based in those countries or that are trying to establish themselves in a region. Google, for example, called upon INSEAD

students in Abu Dhabi to create an open online platform for news organizations in Africa. Participants generally pick their location of study based on their career goals, says Urs Peyer, associate professor of finance and dean of INSEAD's master's programs. "People who want to work in Asia will need to network there and look for job opportunities, so we recommend that during part of their program they are in Singapore."

The INSEAD experience is highly customizable. Students who choose to enter the program in January have the option of completing eight-week summer internships with organizations ranging from the World Bank in Washington, D.C., to private equity firms in Dubai. Ward, 32, decided to take four

model that has long been popular in the U.S., with core courses like accounting and marketing taught in the first year, followed by electives. That being said, the school recognizes that taking time out of the workforce for two years isn't feasible for every student, so programs can be tailored to be completed in 15, 18 or 21 months. All students now have three possible options for their summer term: They can line up at least one paid internship, be one of a handful of top students to get hands-on experience in consulting or take advantage of the Entrepreneurship Summer School to work on a new business idea. Students who participate in the international exchange program also now have the option to shorten the length of their time overseas so they can fit that into a condensed curriculum.

Another distinctive element of the LBS MBA is that students are expected to participate in some of the 75 themed clubs on campus designed to help them prepare for their chosen careers. The choices include finance; retail and luxury goods; and technology and media. Sardesai, 28, joined the entrepreneurship and health care clubs, both of which are preparing him to transition into a career in health care venture capital.

University of Navarra IESE Business School

Once a year in Barcelona, MBA students at IESE Business School band together to stage an international conference called Doing Good Doing Well. The theme of the conference – responsible business practices – mirrors the MBA curriculum at IESE, which is designed to train students to make managerial decisions that positively impact the world. The student-run showcase provides the opportunity "to share different models that are being used around the world for social-impact investing, alternative energy and many other ethical issues," notes Julia Prats, associate dean of MBA programs.

"There's a strong emphasis on social responsibility and service that I find really attractive," says Thomas Atwell, 29, who will graduate from the program in May. Atwell, who got his undergrad degree at the University of Wisconsin–Madison, says he also likes the fact that the curriculum is mainly taught through case studies that build in a discussion of the ethical implications of strategies and "what the impact of a particular decision might be on workers or the environment."

About 12 percent of IESE's 710 students come from North America. They spend most of their 19 months in the program studying in Barcelona. IESE offers 133 electives, giving students multiple options to drill deeply into topics from wealth management and real estate finance to mergers and acquisitions. Students who want to start their own businesses can spend the entire summer term in an entrepreneurship boot camp, developing a business plan for their startup. IESE also offers an exchange program; Atwell, for example, spent his second-to-last term taking business courses at Yale.

IESE charges roughly $108,000 in tuition and fees for the program. The school advises students to budget about $2,468 per month for room and board off campus. ●

months of classes at the Singapore campus. That experience, he notes, "is allowing me to see how work gets done in various regions."

London Business School

During his second year at the London Business School, Californian Nolan Sardesai came back to New York to spend one term studying at Columbia University's B-school. LBS has exchange agreements with around 30 universities in a dozen countries, including China, Australia, Mexico and the U.S. "I picked Columbia because I wanted to build my network in a part of the U.S. I hadn't worked in before," says Sardesai, who graduated with a degree in biomedical engineering from the University of Southern California in 2011 and went on to earn a master's in the field there.

LBS admits more students from the U.S. than any other country, and in 2017, Americans comprised 16 percent of the total student body of 431. Students who start the two-year program in August 2018 will pay about $108,000 in total tuition.

The exchange program is part of a larger mission at LBS to get students thinking about business challenges in a global context, says Gareth Howells, executive director of the MBA program. During the second half of their studies, every student takes part in an immersive Global Business Experience in one of a number of other countries, including South Africa, Israel, China, Peru and Myanmar. The weeklong program includes faculty briefings, panels, workshops, company visits and project work. In the fall of 2017, for example, 80 MBA students worked with small-business owners in South Africa to implement improvements that would boost their profits.

LBS's program is somewhat similar to the typical two-year

3

MIDCAREER

MOVES

The Foster School of
Business, University
of Washington

LINDSEY WASSON FOR USN&WR

The Executive MBA Edge

Ready to lead? An EMBA program can prepare you

BY KATHERINE HOBSON

IFFANY WILLIS saw the writing on the wall. She had plenty of corporate experience in accounting, auditing and consulting, but knew she would need more if she hoped to lead a team: Job listings for positions she wanted said "MBA preferred." And she admired how colleagues who had the degree approached problems. "I was missing out," she says. So she enrolled in a program at Emory University's Goizueta Business School that put her in class every other weekend. When Willis graduated in 2015, she had multiple job offers and landed at financial services technology company Fiserv as vice president for operational audit and advisory services.

Willis, now in her early 40s, is a prime example of the kind of person likely to benefit from an executive MBA program, which offers the same credential as a traditional full-time program but is formatted for professionals who want to keep their day jobs. She was at a career crossroads, highly motivated and clear on what she wanted to get out of her investment of time and money.

And demand is growing for EMBA programs. In 2017, 54 percent of those surveyed by the Graduate Management Admission Council reported an increase in applications. The structure var-

ies, but EMBA programs are typically about 20 months long and designed so classes take place in a concentrated fashion. Students spend all day Friday on campus one week and all day Saturday the next, for example, or a few days at a stretch once a month. The common ground: "No one is quitting their job and going to live on campus," says Michael Desiderio, executive director of the EMBA Council, which represents the industry.

Indeed, targeted students tend to be like Willis – in the middle of their careers; the average age of participants is about 38. The goal is to equip peo-

Terry College of Business. At the University of California–Berkeley's Haas School of Business, for example, students can take electives in entrepreneurship, leadership and strategy on top of the nuts and bolts. George Mason University in Virginia offers an EMBA focused on national security; in 2017 the University of Pittsburgh Katz Graduate School of Business launched a 19-month program for health care professionals in which each class is customized to cover health care topics, from pharmaceutical development to insurance. At St. Mary's College of California, the Global Executive MBA focuses on corporate social responsibility, ethics and sustainability.

As with a traditional MBA, face time with professors and teamwork with fellow students – and the networking opportunities both create – are considered crucial. And many programs include blocks of travel time to give students international experience as a group. But mindful of the difficulties of balancing a full-time job and family life with academics, a number of schools now broadcast some classes online so participants can occasionally skip the commute.

At St. Mary's, for example, EMBA programs involve 50 percent in-person classes and 50 percent live videoconferencing. "We try to use technology to replicate the traditional face-to-face experience," explains Zhan Li, dean of the school of economics and business administration.

ple with knowledge that they can parlay into greater responsibility and a bigger paycheck.

That paycheck may be more key than ever. Employers used to be willing to cover all or most of the tuition. No longer. An EMBAC survey found that just 20 percent of students were fully funded by their employer in 2017, with another 35 percent getting some help.

More choice, please. As students have picked up more of the check, they've demanded an experience more finely tailored to their goals and interests. "Nowadays, the demand for choice is much greater," says Richard Daniels, director of executive and professional MBA programs at the University of Georgia's

When employers were footing the bill – and, in return, expecting their newly minted MBAs to stay on for some period – career services for EMBA students weren't essential. That, too, has changed. Many people intend a job switch or career change. So prospective students should ask about services such as executive coaching, help with résumés and positioning, and access to the alumni and student networks. And it's best to be clear about what career outcomes you're expecting, advises Joan Coonrod, senior director of the MBA career management center for working professionals at Goizueta. Willis credits Coonrod and her colleagues – her "career board of directors"

– for pushing her to consider what skills she would need to rise to the C-suite as well as to hold out for a job that would make use of her new degree.

Anyone contemplating an EMBA should realize that it's not a magic bullet, advises Hallie Crawford, an Atlanta-based certified career coach. It's important to take stock of what you hope to gain. Does the job band above you require an MBA? Are you looking to fill gaps in your experience so you can make a lateral move in your company, such as from technology to the business side?

Once enrolled in a program, you can improve the odds of achieving your goal by staying tightly focused on it, says Crawford. Take classes that address gaps in your experience. Some kind of independent or team project will be required, such as consulting work for a local business; pick projects relevant to

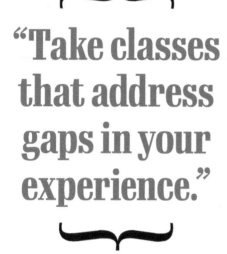

> ## "Take classes that address gaps in your experience."

your job plans. And if you are aiming for a pivot into a new industry, prepare to be patient and possibly make multiple job moves to get there.

Tony Stobbe, 46, credits the EMBA he earned from Haas in 2014 for helping him understand how the leadership skills he developed over two decades in the Coast Guard could translate to the corporate world. Trained as an engineer, he saw the program as a way to pick up skills in finance, accounting and marketing – and to develop a network of fellow students that he could tap in the future. Now at Tesla, where he manages the company's external warehouses in the Bay Area, he says he would recommend an EMBA to those who have true intellectual curiosity about business and aren't simply looking "to put an 'MBA' after their name." Given the highly demanding schedule, an EMBA requires a full commitment. ●

SPOTLIGHT ON

McDonough School of Business

GEORGETOWN UNIVERSITY
WASHINGTON, D.C.

U.S. NEWS RANK #25

Located at the intersection of government, international diplomacy and industry, the McDonough School of Business gives students plenty of opportunities to "have a seat at the table" when decisions are made in Washington, says Dean Paul Almeida. The capital, along with the university's Jesuit-inspired mission of advancing social justice, attracted Kelly Bies, 26, a 2018 MBA candidate and a former Teach for America teacher who snagged an internship in federal consulting (and a postgrad job offer) at Deloitte. Bies joined the pro bono consulting club, and in one project helped develop a science curriculum for local students focused on solving challenges energy companies face, such as incorporating environmentally friendly practices into their business initiatives.

To help them think globally, each of the school's roughly 560 full-time MBA students must complete an international consulting project. For example, this year some students are going to Hong Kong to help a hotel chain develop its social media strategy. Others will work on projects in South Africa, Brazil, India, Kenya and elsewhere. –*Lindsay Cates*

▶ **More @ usnews.com/georgetown**

ACADEMIC INSIGHTS
YOUR SCHOOL BY THE NUMBERS

Designed for schools, U.S. News Academic Insights provides instant access to a rich historical archive of undergraduate and graduate school rankings data.

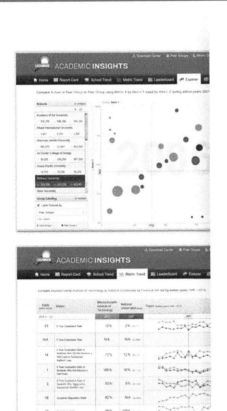

Advanced Visualizations
Take complex data and turn it into six easily understandable and exportable views.

Download Center
Export large data sets from the new Download Center to create custom reports.

Dedicated Account Management
Have access to full analyst support for training, troubleshooting and advanced reporting.

Peer-Group Analysis
Flexibility to create your own peer groups to compare your institution on more than 5 M + data points.

Historical Trending
Find out how institutions have performed over time based on more than 350 metrics.

To request a demo visit **AI.USNEWS.COM**   or call **202.955.2121**

A Part-Time Path

There's growing interest in studying while working

BY MARIYA GREELEY

OPE BOVENZI, a systems engineer at Texas Instruments' Silicon Valley office, knew she wanted to pursue her MBA part time. It wasn't "financially feasible" for her to quit her job for a full-time program, and she didn't want to lose the momentum she'd built in her career, she says. Bovenzi, 28, needed a flexible class schedule, though, because she travels at least once a month for work. She found a fit at UCLA's Anderson School of Management in its Fully Employed MBA Flex option. She takes classes online and then every third weekend flies about 400 miles to UCLA for a packed weekend of classes and events with her peers. Some of her fellow students fly in from places like Rhode Island, Chicago and Utah for the program, which costs about $122,000 in total tuition. "You're learning how to work remotely, but you're also taking that time to work in person," says Bovenzi, which mirrors how she interacts with her TI colleagues around the world.

While enrollment for full-time MBAs decreased significantly in the U.S. between 2005 and 2016, enrollment at part-time programs has risen nearly 20 percent, according to a survey of about 350 accredited B-schools from AACSB International – The Association to Advance Collegiate Schools of Business. Dan LeClair, executive vice president and chief strategy and innovation officer at AACSB, notes that the part-time numbers signal "some really important changes that are happening in higher education." Increasingly, students seem to value the greater convenience of these programs as well as the ability to keep their jobs and salaries.

Clarisa Bonilla, 29, a business project manager in Chicago working for Baker McKenzie, a global law firm, is a part-time MBA student at the Kellogg School of Management at Northwestern University working toward a career in impact investing. Bonilla attends evening classes at Kellogg's downtown Chicago facility and, when available, she also takes courses alongside full-time MBA students at the school's main campus in nearby Evanston. Bonilla credits Kellogg with giving her "a holistic perspective" of business and enabling her to combine her passion for helping others with her interest in finance. "I know I am now a better business leader because of it," she says. The Booth School of Business at the University of Chicago, the Leonard N. Stern School of Business at

New York University, and the Fox School of Business at Temple University also offer flexible part-time models.

As popular as these self-paced programs are, demand for lockstep programs – where students take classes according to a set schedule and graduate within a specified time period – has started to outpace them, according to the Graduate Management

Admission Council. With flexible models, "it's easy to take off here or there and the next thing you know you're not completing the program in a reasonable time frame, or even completing it at all," says Gordon McCray, vice dean of academic programs at the Wake Forest University School of Business. The momentum of the lockstep program at Wake Forest has resulted in "fairly impressive on-time graduation rates," says McCray, running between 90 and 98 percent for the last several years.

Many students also value the in-class networking opportunities that come with having the same classmates throughout the program. At Wake Forest, part-time MBA students are required to take classes year-round, at least one per semester with their cohort (each has 55 people on average), and graduate in two years. Tuition is about $39,000 per year. Students can choose to attend Saturday or evening classes on specified weekdays at a state-of-the-art learning complex in Charlotte or at the school's Winston-Salem campus. Wake Forest is beginning to offer some class

A leadership class at Northwestern Kellogg's part-time MBA program in Chicago

content online as well, says McCray, to help students juggling families and other obligations.

Abrianna Barca, an IT supervisor at the University of Wisconsin–Madison, takes classes in the university's lockstep program two evenings a week. When she graduates in spring 2018, she will have spent three years with her 55-person cohort, including a two-week intensive course in Hong Kong, China and Vietnam. That closeness helped encourage more meaningful discussions, such as students sharing stories of their salary and benefit negotiations in a class on negotiations. "We're all really comfortable with each other," says Barca, 29. The University of Texas–Austin McCombs School of Business, Villanova University School of Business, and the University of Georgia's Terry College of Business all offer similar lockstep programs.

In general, even the most competitive part-time programs tend to be easier to get accepted to than their

full-time counterparts. For example, at NYU Stern, 20 percent of full-time students are accepted versus nearly 66 percent of part-time applicants. (Students can hedge their bets by applying to both programs at once.) However, a significant number of the most competitive schools, including all of the Ivy League, Stanford's Graduate School of Business and the Sloan School of Management at Massachusetts Institute of Technology, don't offer regular part-time MBA programs.

Determining the ideal program requires taking a hard look at one's goals, professional development needs, and constraints, advises LeClair. For those planning to stay in their current industry – an engineer eying a move into management, say

– experts give the part-time track a thumbs-up. Those aiming for a bigger career switch, however – engineers who want to transition into business strategy or finance – may be well served by a full-time program that will give them the time and opportunity to immerse themselves in their desired field through classes and experiential learning, including a summer internship. That's not a hard and fast rule, however. In a survey of 2017 graduates of the University of California–Berkeley's Haas School of Business, 47 percent reported making a career change to a new industry or function while in the part-time program, for example.

Though part-time study makes a summer internship impractical, schools are finding other ways to beef up experiential learning. At the College of Business and Economics at Lehigh University, part-time students this spring will participate in a class researching and devising strategies to help the United Nations engage the private sector in different countries to address sustainable development goals like clean water and sanitation. Kellogg gives part-timers hands-on opportunities to explore whether certain industries or functions are a good fit. Students interested in marketing, say, can help develop advertising strategies for companies like Bank of America and General

SPOTLIGHT ON

Owen Graduate School of Management

*VANDERBILT UNIVERSITY
NASHVILLE, TENNESSEE*

U.S. NEWS RANK #26

For the roughly 170 full-time MBA students who enter each year, Owen focuses on creating "personal scale experiences," says Dean Eric Johnson. The average class size is 28, and every student is paired with an executive coach from industry through the leadership development program. Second-year student Matt Sternberg, 28, chose Owen because of its connections to Nashville's health care industry. He is pursuing an MBA concentration in the field and worked on an organizational performance project for Vanderbilt LifeFlight, an emergency medical operation.

The academic year is split into four eight-week "mods," which allows students to take a wide range of classes (at least 16 per year) and pursue electives early. One-week immersion courses are offered in between mods that put MBA candidates on the front lines of industries that interest them. Real estate students, for example, partner with the University of Tennessee's school of architecture in Knoxville to propose a development project to housing professionals. *–Lindsay Cates*

▶ **More @ usnews.com/vanderbilt**

Electric. In one of her experiential learning labs, Bonilla helped create funding strategies for microfranchise grocery stores in Nicaragua. Part-time students at the D'Amore-McKim School of Business at Northeastern University can apply to the university's venture accelerator or spend a week in Washington, D.C., learning about the intersection of government and business.

Experts agree that full-time students do enjoy more chances to network. But as Barca has discovered at Wisconsin, part-time students still can develop strong relationships. Kelly Blair, 28, a recent grad of the part-time program at Indiana University's Kelley School of Business, says she's "built lifelong connections" with some of the 60 classmates with whom she took core courses. A class connection even helped her land an interview for her current job as a human resources strategy and transformation consultant at Eli Lilly.

And part-time programs are expanding career services. The Stephen M. Ross School of Business at the University of Michigan–Ann Arbor, for example, brings recruiters to campus to mingle with part-time students and offers part-timers and full-timers the same coaching for job searches, interviewing and negotiating job offers. The extra help seems to be paying off:

> **{ "Part-time programs are expanding career services." }**

Nearly 65 percent of 2017 evening MBA grads reported switching organizations within six months of graduation. Still, some schools continue to have separate career offices for part- and full-time students and part-timers often may not have access to all of the same recruiting events as those in full-time programs.

Many part-time MBAs run on a cost-per-credit basis, so tuition isn't inflated by the program's timeline. Part-time and full-time students often end up facing similar overall tuition costs, though the difference varies from program to program, and have the same financing options (story, Page 96). But part-timers often choose their path with an eye toward minimizing debt. While B-schools usually reserve most of their scholarship funds for full-timers who face the loss of a salary while studying, many part-timers can get some help from their employers in addition to their salary. Texas Instruments pays for about a third of Bovenzi's tuition; the rest she covers with savings and her salary. Many companies who reimburse MBA tuition require employees to remain at the organization for a certain period after they get their degree, according to the AACSB; usually that period runs two to five years. Some organizations' support is also contingent on employees completing the program or getting certain grades in their classes.

There are part-time programs "to meet the needs of just about anybody out there," notes LeClair. It's just a matter of finding the best fit. ●

The Online Option

A top degree can now be earned on your laptop

BY COURTNEY RUBIN

WHEN THE UNIVERSITY of Florida debuted its online MBA in 1999 – this is pre-YouTube, pre-Facebook, practically prehistory – the start had already been delayed a year because of then-primitive technology. And when students came to campus for a brief residency, they were sent home with boxes of VHS tapes of lectures for the semester.

Online education has come a long way since, and not just technologically. Whereas once distance coursework was often of dubious quality and typically associated with for-profit universities, now close to 75 percent of U.S. News' top-100 national universities – among them Johns Hopkins, Columbia, Harvard and Georgetown – offer at least one online degree program, according to analysis by the Center for Online Education. An MBA is one of the most popular, observers say; Joshua Casto, director of marketing and communications for the Ohio University College of Business, dates the recent explosion of interest in the online MBA – both among schools and applicants – to 2011 and 2012, in the wake of the last recession. "The online MBA market is countercyclical to the economy," he says. Ohio is one of the many schools that have added an online MBA (ranking, Page 74); others include the University of North Carolina–Chapel Hill and Carnegie Mellon University.

With so much choice, how to find the right fit (and know whether an online degree is a fit at all)? Here are five questions to ask:

What do I want in – and from – a program?

The term "online MBA" doesn't mean the same thing to everybody offering one. There's a wide variety of formats, from "synchronous" learning that requires you to virtually attend class at the same time each week (as at UNC's Kenan-Flagler Business School), to study that is 100 percent doable at whatever hour of the day or night you choose (at Washington State University, for example, and Northeastern University's D'Amore-McKim School of Business). Some programs (like the University of Arizona's) don't expect to physically see you; others have significant residency requirements. The University of Florida has a new fully online option, for example, but its hybrid degree requires seven residential weekends over the two-year period. ("That residency in December can be really nice for folks who've been dealing with snow for a month already," says John Gresley, assistant dean and director of UF's Warrington College of Business MBA program.) More on residencies below.

If minimizing student debt is your top priority, keep in mind that online degrees are not necessarily discounted. Carnegie Mellon's Tepper School of Business charges the same price for its online and residential full-time MBAs, while tuition for Kenan-Flagler's online program falls between the rates for its in-state and out-of-state full-time MBA. Both schools require attendance each week in small classes, with everyone's face visible on screen in tiles à la "The Brady Bunch." There are still bargains to be had, though: The University of Arizona, for example, charges online students in-state tuition, regardless of where they live.

"Know what you're spending and whether what you believe you will gain is worth that cost," advises Stacy Blackman, president of her own MBA admissions consulting firm and author of "The MBA Application Roadmap: The Essential Guide to Getting Into a Top Business School." Are you likely, based on the school's graduation rate and placement performance, to actually finish and land a job that gives you a healthy return on your investment? Will you gain what you need to become better at your current job and potentially advance? If a career change is your target, does this program offer what you will need to reach it?

And keep in mind, says Troy Steece, a college recruiting expert at Korn Ferry, that besides your record and how well you interview, the major thing Fortune 100 companies look at is the reputation of the school you attended – not whether you went to class online or on campus.

How well does a program do online education?

A decade ago, when very few prestigious B-schools had yet entered the online arena, one of the chief concerns of prospective students was whether the school had been accredited. Now, with so many familiar university names in the marketplace, that's less of a worry. But you would do well to investigate which programs are firmly established, advises Sean Galla-

Kristin Minetti, who earned her MBA online from Washington State University (which does offer 24/7 technical support) while working for Target in California: "Screen-shot any assignment submissions so in case there's an issue you have proof you submitted on time."

Are my family, friends, co-workers and supervisor willing to cooperate?

"These programs are nearly impossible to do alone," notes Florida's Gresley. Although the flexibility of an online degree is one of its most touted benefits, many programs do require you to show up at a specific time (which could be 9:00 p.m. or 9:00 a.m. or all points in between, depending on where you live). And yes, attendance is noted.

gher, executive director of the Center for the Future of Higher Education and Talent Strategy at Northeastern University and author of "The Future of University Credentials." Since many institutions "are newer to the market or dabbling in it," he says, they may not have the same extent and quality of services and technology. It's important to find out what kind of access you will have to academic advisers and live technical support. The University of Delaware, for example, gives online MBA students access to a personal career coach for help with their résumé and job search strategy; Villanova University holds online office hours.

At some schools, help desks may only be available during weekday hours – in the time zone of the school. One tip from

For this reason, Scott Grady, 40, who earned his degree online from Temple University in 2017, was inspired to start while his kids were just 4 and 5 years old and their schedules were easier, after watching a co-worker struggle to balance schoolwork and family priorities. "He had to choose: Am I going to go study or go to a swim meet? Whereas most of my kids' activities at that age were on Saturday mornings, and I could take class when they'd be in bed." Online MBA students are often advised to get a calendar and block out when, exactly, they're going to study. Grady, the chief strategy officer of sheet music retailer J.W. Pepper & Son near Philadelphia, suggests also figuring out when and how you're going to make time for family and friends. "We'd sit down and watch a movie on

Friday night, and I'd be thinking about accounting and stats," he says. "You really need to be there at those times emotionally and spiritually – and also because you need a break."

Does the school foster networking and interaction with fellow classmates?

If your sole goal is to advance at your current company, you may not care about having a peer or alumni network (though you may want friendly peers when, say, you're struggling to get online and the help desk isn't available). But otherwise, a network can be an invaluable source of support now and later on. Plus, it's nearly impossible to master soft skills (presentation ability, working well in teams) just sitting alone at your computer.

This is where a residency comes in. It can range from a few days' quick orientation or other interactive event to regular periods on campus. Villanova, for example, brings students together for three days for a "leadership challenge" that includes self-assessment and group exercises focused on influencing others and developing high-performance teams. At the other end of the spectrum is Carnegie Mellon with 16 residential weekends required over 32 months. Each weekend, students attend the first three sessions of the two classes they will then finish virtually over the six-week quarter. Pennsylvania State University requires a five-day residency at the start of the program. Students meet instructors and classmates, attend workshops on networking and online technology, and start earning credit for a team performance class that includes a group project.

Other schools encourage interaction through projects; on average, online MBA students spend nearly 30 percent of their time involved in team projects, according to the 2015 Global Management Education Graduate Survey. Students at the University of Maryland, for example, form virtual teams, identify real-world business problems, attempt to solve them, and present their recommendations over a 14-week period.

Minetti says you reap what you sow when it comes to the effort to "meet" peers. She took full advantage of required group projects, class discussions and the Washington State online MBA Facebook group. She also spent time in Google Hangouts interacting with classmates. "I have friends to this day from the program," she says, "that I have never met in person."

Who is teaching the classes?

Are the profs teaching online classes the same ones who teach on campus? And are they easily accessible for one-on-one help outside of class? "The answer to both of these questions should be 'yes,'" says Terrill Cosgray, executive director of Indiana University's Kelley Direct Online MBA, which launched with 15 students in 1999 at the request of corporate partners including Rolls Royce and Federal Express and now boasts 962. Online students can attend classes "live" or opt to watch the lectures afterward.

Likewise, at the College of William & Mary's Raymond A. Mason School of Business, online MBA students can interact directly with professors; 2017 grad Carrie Harris recalls that they typically responded "immediately – that is, within a few minutes – and occasionally within a few hours" to email queries. They "seemed to really connect with us," she says. "Although it was an online program, somehow it didn't feel that way." ●

SPOTLIGHT ON

Stephen M. Ross School of Business

UNIVERSITY OF MICHIGAN–ANN ARBOR

U.S. NEWS RANK #7 To close out their first year, full-time MBA students at Michigan's Stephen M. Ross School of Business complete one of the school's signature multidisciplinary action projects or "MAP." For seven weeks, teams of students focus on a single consulting challenge, such as working with Hotels.com to create an easy-to-access portal to share consumer research across regions. Tapping into Michigan's 18 other schools and colleges for insight is encouraged, and about half of the projects have an international component; students worked in about 25 countries in 2017. Ching-Yin Chen, 29, who is pursuing both an MBA and a J.D. at Michigan, worked with an Israeli biotech startup trying to break into Japan's health care market.

Michigan Ross has always emphasized action-based learning in its curriculum, and "in recent years, we have taken that to the next level," says Liz Muller, managing director of global initiatives. In a new course called Living Business Leadership Experience, for example, students (with faculty guidance) help run a piece of a real business at companies like Shinola and Ford. *–Mariya Greeley*

▶ **More @ usnews.com/michigan**

MBA Not Needed

Certificate programs provide valuable skills quickly

BY LINDSAY CATES

JOE KOPACZ, a mechanical engineer in Lockheed Martin's engineering leadership development program, realized he didn't have the grasp of finance jargon he needed to feel comfortable interacting with business leaders he was working with. "I couldn't just open up financial documents or quarterly reports and have a good understanding of what was going on there," says Kopacz, 29. To brush up his skills, he enrolled in UNC Kenan-Flagler Business School's UNC Business Essentials, a self-paced online certificate program consisting of six subject modules that students have up to four months to complete. Now, he says, he has a much better understanding of the elements that come together to make a business work.

Over the past five years, as U.S. enrollment in specialized business master's programs has jumped 45 percent (story, Page 22), there's been a similar boom in certificate programs for professionals looking to buff up their management and leadership creds in an even shorter time frame. These certificate programs (sometimes known as mini-MBAs) boil down the key elements of an MBA curriculum to a series of need-to-know topics that can take as little as a few weeks to complete. The programs can prove useful in helping professionals advance in their current company, prepare for a career change, get up to speed after a promotion, or figure out if they want to pursue a full MBA, says Tom Robinson, president and chief executive officer of AACSB International–The Association to Advance Collegiate Schools of Business.

UNC's certificate program costs $2,500 and covers financial accounting, economics, finance, marketing, business operations and business communications. Kopacz says he now has a better understanding of how his own work on a day-to-day basis affects the company's bottom line, and is better at public speaking and effective email writing.

An array of options. At B-schools across the country, on-campus and online certificate programs are popping up not only in business fundamentals but also in niche topics like leadership, data analytics, social media and digital marketing to meet evolving student demand. "Going forward, schools will have to offer a spectrum of programs" beyond the traditional MBA, says Paul Krause, associate vice provost for online learning at Cornell University and CEO of eCornell. The

coursework can be challenging, students say, but the more flexible schedule makes it manageable for someone who wants to keep working full time.

Online options are particularly popular. Students can usually pick a start date and then work through a mix of video lectures, narrated powerpoint presentations, quizzes, case studies and exams at their own pace. After serving 10 years of active duty as a Marine Corps officer, Craig Platt, 33, a product sales leader at GE Aviation, had leadership experience but felt he needed "to fill some gaps" to expand his potential career path at the company. He enrolled in a six-month online certificate program in business administration offered by the University of Notre Dame's Mendoza College of Business that he felt gave him the flexibility he needed as a student with two young kids. Once a week he logged in to a live, instructor-led session and the rest of the week completed coursework and downloaded the 20-minute lectures onto his phone so he could "just jump in" as he had time.

Harvard Business School's HBX CORe certificate offers an online "primer on business fundamentals" that students complete with weekly deadlines for eight to 17 weeks, depending on the program. The $1,950 certificate includes

Student teams take part in a Stanford Ignite design-thinking class to tackle real-world problems.

courses in business analytics, economics for managers and financial accounting, along with a final exam. UT Dallas Naveen Jindal School of Management offers a self-paced $3,995 certificate of management comprised of 16 modules. Students usually take six to 10 months to complete coursework.

The networking edge. Although online formats are convenient, on-campus programs allow middle managers to come together to network and focus on leadership skills. "The network is the factor that separates the in-person versus the online programs," says Peter Methot, executive director of executive education at Rutgers Business School. Mini-MBA students in Rutgers' weeklong programs get to know their classmates well with group work during the day and networking events in

the evening. Rutgers was one of the first to offer a mini-MBA in Business Essentials 15 years ago, and today offers a sizable portfolio of on-campus and online certificates covering dozens of topics. New ones launched in 2017-2018 include Customer-Centric Management and Intergenerational Leadership. About 30 students attend the programs, where they complete two modules a day.

Pepperdine's Graziadio School of Business and Management offers a $5,999 on-campus certificate that meets every other weekend from early February through early April. The program includes sessions on strategy, finance, decision sciences and law, and if a student wants to move to a degree program, the fees can be applied to the tuition. The University of Minnesota's Carlson School of Management offers a five-day certificate for $5,000; while Loyola University Chicago's Quinlan School of Business holds the $3,500 mini-MBA program one evening per week for 10 weeks.

Targeting nonbusiness graduate students and working professionals, Stanford Ignite teaches business essentials and provides training in product design and commercialization for budding innovators. The $14,500 program is offered at Stanford in a four-week full-time or nine-week part-time format, or can be taken abroad in London, Beijing or São Paulo.

Many certificate programs also target experienced professionals who already have an MBA but want to develop a more specific skill set. Pepperdine's portfolio includes a hybrid certificate in cyber risk, and on-campus certificates in applied analytics, healthcare management and leadership, and corporate social responsibility. Cornell offers more than 40 online certificates in topics ranging from commercial real estate to financial success for nonprofits. In 2017 Kenan-Flagler announced a partnership with Fortune to offer certificates for business professionals in topics like Leading with Purpose and Most Powerful Women inspired by Fortune's lists and conferences. Courses are taught by UNC professors, but include Fortune's video content and interviews with Fortune 500 executives.

Certificates can also appeal to veterans with Post-9/11 GI Bill benefits looking to build their business skills. Stanford Ignite hosts a session for post-9/11 veterans, and Rutgers offers a mini-MBA titled Business Management for Military and Veterans.

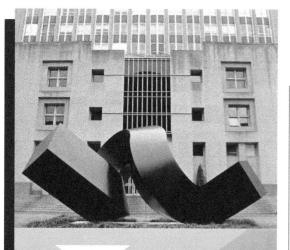

Columbia Business School

COLUMBIA U., NEW YORK CITY

U.S. NEWS RANK #9 To help the 1,300 or so full-time MBA students build a sense of community, Columbia's first-year classes are broken into clusters of 65 to 70 students who take core courses in strategy, economics and other topics together.

Most students cherish the school's deep connections to a wide range of industries in New York, says Michael Malone, associate dean of the MBA program. A steady stream of executives from retail, media, health care and finance firms based in the Big Apple visit to speak, co-teach classes and recruit. Electives include immersion seminars on topics like luxury brands and shareholder activism, where teaching happens both in the classroom and during site visits around the city.

For example, entrepreneurship seminar students spend time in New York's so-called Silicon Alley to see startups in action. Former classroom teacher Ingram Carpenter, 29, planned to get her MBA and work as a school administrator before Columbia opened her eyes to other paths, such as working in tech. "I found that I'm more forward thinking than I ever thought," she says. –*Lindsay Cates*

▶ **More @ usnews.com/columbia**

Intrigued by the possibilities? Here are a few key factors to consider as you look for a program that works best for you:

For-credit or noncredit? Some certificates will enable you to earn university credits, and you can often get financial aid if needed. Many companies will also pitch in for for-credit programs, so make sure you know what your firm's requirements are to qualify. One additional advantage of the for-credit option: Some schools, such as Rutgers, Pepperdine, Florida Tech and University of Colorado–Denver, will allow you to apply those credits later to a full-degree program.

How you learn best. Some students thrive in an online format that allows more time to process information, says Methot. For example, you can replay lectures if you happen to miss something the first time. Other students learn better in a more traditional in-class model and may want to capitalize on the opportunity to network with their peers. Consider which is the best match for your situation and personality.

The record of success. Researching the schools to determine their track record in delivering on their promises to students is critical. Program graduates can be a good resource, says Krause. Amy Glaser, senior vice president at Adecco Staffing, also recommends asking the program director for statistics and real examples of grads who used their certificate successfully to advance in their careers. Confirming accreditation is important,

> { **"Confirming accreditation is important."** }

but just as critical may be discussing with a hiring manager how the program will increase your value to the company, Glaser says. Check out LinkedIn discussion groups to get a sense of what's involved. Some online programs out there "are not much more than a series of YouTube videos," says Krause.

The time commitment. While 87 percent of enrollees for the UNC Business Essentials certificate complete it, administrators note, 13 percent either don't finish it or never start it at all. Evaluate your schedule to ensure you can set aside the time you will need on a regular basis. Most students will spend three to 10 hours per week on online coursework.

For Sara DuCuennois, senior director of alumni relations and annual giving at Florida International University, the confidence boost gained from earning Cornell's online Women in Leadership certificate has proved a valuable advantage. "I had been asking for things – when I did have the nerve to ask for things – in the wrong way," she says. Not only has the coursework helped her personally, she says, but it also provided the tools she needed to more effectively coach women on how to advocate for themselves and their beliefs. As she found, picking the right certificate program from among the thousands being offered can give your career just that lift you're looking for. ●

Inside Goizueta
Business School at
Emory University

JIM LO SCALZO FOR USN&WR

CHAPTER
4

THE
U.S. NEWS
RANKINGS

How We Judge Schools

Objective measures are important, as are the opinions of experts

BY ROBERT J. MORSE

EACH YEAR, U.S. NEWS ranks programs in business: MBA programs, both full- and part-time; executive MBA programs; online MBA and other master's degree programs; and undergraduate programs in business. Most of the rankings are based on two types of data: expert opinions about program excellence and statistical indicators that measure the quality of a school's faculty, research and students. In the case of the executive and undergraduate rankings, results are based on expert opinion alone. Experts were also asked to weigh in on which institutions do the best job of educating students in specialty areas such as accounting, finance and marketing for both MBA and undergraduate business programs.

As you research course offerings and weigh schools' intangible attributes, the data in these pages can help you compare concrete factors such as faculty-student ratio and placement success upon graduation. It's important that you use the rankings to supplement, not substitute for, careful thought and your own research. Statistical indicators fall into two categories: inputs, or measures of the qualities that students and

▶ A strategy class at the University of Washington's Foster School of Business

faculty bring to the educational experience, and outputs, measures of graduates' achievements linked to their degrees. As inputs, for example, we use admission test scores. Output measures for the MBA programs include starting salaries and grads' ability to find jobs. A description of how we ranked full-time and part-time MBA programs follows here; information on the EMBA, online degree and undergraduate rankings appears with each table.

Full-time MBA programs. The universe that U.S. News considers when ranking MBA programs consists of the 480 programs accredited by AACSB International – The Association to Advance Collegiate Schools of Business. We start by surveying all of the schools to collect data on key measures that we consider important indicators of quality, described below. In the most recent fall 2017 and early 2018 data survey, 387 schools responded, with 127 providing the information needed to calculate rankings. In addition, we conduct two peer assessment surveys asking for expert opinion on the quality of education students can expect. The key factors and their weighting in the ranking formula:

Quality assessment: Two peer assessment surveys were conducted in the fall of 2017. Business school deans and directors of accredited MBA programs were asked to rate the overall academic quality of the MBA programs at each school on a scale from marginal (1) to outstanding (5); 43 percent responded. The average score is weighted by .25 in the ranking model. Corporate recruiters and company contacts who hired MBA grads, whose names were supplied by previously ranked MBA programs, also were asked to rate the programs. The last three years' recruiter responses were averaged and are weighted by .15 in the model. This year, programs that had fewer than 10 recruiter and company responses total were assigned the lowest score for this indicator achieved by any ranked MBA program for the purposes of calculating the rankings. These programs have an N/A instead of a recruiter assessment score published in the tables.

Placement success (.35 of the ranking formula): Success is based on average starting salary and bonus (40 percent of this measure) and employment rates for full-time 2017 graduates at graduation (20 percent) and at three months later (40 percent). Calculations for MBA placement rates exclude those not seeking jobs and those for whom the school has no information. To be included in the full-time MBA rankings, a program needed 20 or more of its 2017 full-time graduates – and at least 50 percent of the graduating class – to be seeking employment. Salary is based on the number of graduates reporting data. Signing bonus is weighted by the proportion of graduates reporting salaries who received a bonus, since not everyone received a signing bonus.

Student selectivity (.25): The strength of full-time students who entered in the fall of 2017 was measured by the average GMAT and GRE scores (65 percent of this measure), average undergraduate grade-point average (30 percent), and the proportion of applicants accepted (5 percent). For the first time, when fewer than half of full-time students submitted test scores, we adjusted their weighted percentile distributions downward by the percentage of the student body that submitted test scores. A similar adjustment was made when under half of entering MBA students submitted undergraduate grade-point averages.

Overall rank: We examined the data for individual indicators and standardized the value of each one about its mean. The weight applied to each reflects our judgment about its relative importance, as determined in consultation with experts in the field. Final scores were rescaled so the highest-scoring institution was assigned 100; the others' scores were recalculated as a percentage of that top score. Scores were then rounded to the nearest whole number. Schools with a score of

100 accumulated the highest composite score. An institution's rank reflects the number of schools that sit above it; if three are tied at No. 1, for example, the next will be ranked No. 4. Tied schools are listed alphabetically.

Specialty rankings: These rankings are based solely on the opinions of educators at peer schools. B-school deans and MBA program heads were asked to nominate up to 10 programs for excellence. Those receiving the most nominations are listed.

Part-time MBA programs. The U.S. News part-time MBA rankings are based on five factors: average peer assessment score (50 percent of the overall score), average GMAT score and GRE scores of part-time MBA students entering in the fall of 2017 (15 percent), average undergraduate GPA (12.5 percent), average number of years of work experience (10 percent), and the percentage of the fall 2017 total MBA program enrollment that is in the part-time program (12.5 percent). As with the full-time programs, adjustments were made when fewer than half of new entrants submitted test scores and GPAs. In addition, the ranking factors were weighted somewhat differently than in the past; more detailed information can be found at usnews.com/bschool.

The average peer assessment score is calculated from a fall 2017 survey that asked business school deans and MBA program directors at each of the nation's 301 part-time MBA programs to rate other programs from marginal (1) to outstanding (5); 46 percent responded. To be eligible, a program had to be accredited by the AACSB, have at least 20 students enrolled part time in the fall of 2017, and be ranked in the previous year; 279 programs met those criteria. More information about programs can be found both at usnews.com and in the directories at the back of this book. ●

WISCONSIN MBA GRADUATES ARE

FIERCE
ADVOCATES
COLLABORATIVE
PARTNERS
INNOVATIVE
LEADERS
INSPIRING
ENTREPRENEURS
DISTINCTLY
UW–MADISON.

WISCONSIN
SCHOOL OF BUSINESS
UNIVERSITY OF WISCONSIN–MADISON

TOGETHER
FORWARD®

Wisconsin MBA: Build a

A DISTINGUISHED 170-YEAR HISTORY

The University of Wisconsin–Madison has been a catalyst for the extraordinary since 1848. Today it is ranked the #12 public university in the U.S. and one of the top 10 colleges to produce Fortune 500 CEOs.

At the top-ranked Wisconsin School of Business, you can be part of a proud legacy that continues to produce tomorrow's business leaders and innovators.

Jia Jiang
Author and
TED speaker

DIVERSE PERSPECTIVES

The Wisconsin School of Business is committed to bringing people of diverse backgrounds together. In 1966, we became a founding member of The Consortium for Graduate Study in Management to increase diversity in business. This mission remains at our core as we prepare you to thrive in an ever-changing business environment.

WISCONSIN
SCHOOL OF BUSINESS
UNIVERSITY OF WISCONSIN-MADISON

TOGETHER FORWARD®

·ture. Be part of a legacy.

FAR-REACHING IMPACT

The Wisconsin Idea, conceived in 1905, signifies the university's commitment to public service, applying what is taught in the classroom across the globe to make a real-world impact. Be part of Wisconsin's commitment to improving people's lives worldwide.

Melissa Abney
MBA '19

BUILDING LEADERS FOR THE FUTURE

Today, the Wisconsin MBA Program gives you a competitive career advantage through in-depth learning, real-world experience, and comprehensive leadership preparation. Build your career on the UW–Madison legacy with an MBA education that consistently ranks at the top nationally for exceptional ROI.

IN THE LIBRARY AT HARVARD,
TIED AT NO. 1

Best MBA Programs

Rank	School	Overall score	Peer assessment score (5.0=highest)	Recruiter assessment score (5.0=highest)	'17 full-time average undergrad GPA	'17 full-time average GMAT score	'17 full-time acceptance rate	'17 average starting salary and bonus	'17 graduates employed at graduation	'17 Employed 3 months after graduation	'17 out-of-state tuition and fees	'17 total full-time enrollment
1	Harvard University (MA)	100	4.8	4.5	3.71	731	9.9%	$158,049	78.9%	89.3%	$78,772	1,857
1	University of Chicago (Booth) (IL)	100	4.7	4.5	3.61	730	23.5%	$151,085	88.0%	95.3%	$70,364	1,176
3	University of Pennsylvania (Wharton)	99	4.7	4.4	3.60	730	19.2%	$159,815	82.3%	92.6%	$76,580	1,737
4	Stanford University (CA)	98	4.8	4.4	3.74	737	5.7%	$159,440	63.9%	87.6%	$68,868	853
5	Massachusetts Institute of Technology (Sloan)	97	4.6	4.4	3.57	722	11.6%	$148,451	84.2%	93.9%	$71,312	813
6	Northwestern University (Kellogg) (IL)	95	4.5	4.3	3.60	732	20.2%	$146,259	81.6%	92.6%	$70,435	1,296
7	University of California–Berkeley (Haas)	93	4.5	4.3	3.71	725	12.9%	$146,752	66.3%	89.9%	$59,811	543
7	University of Michigan–Ann Arbor (Ross)	93	4.3	4.2	3.46	716	25.3%	$150,052	89.7%	94.4%	$67,628	824
9	Columbia University (NY)	92	4.4	4.2	3.60	727	14.0%	$151,849	69.9%	89.3%	$74,476	1,297
10	Dartmouth College (Tuck) (NH)	91	4.2	4.3	3.52	722	23.0%	$152,805	80.2%	91.8%	$72,330	582
11	Duke University (Fuqua) (NC)	90	4.3	4.1	3.50	702	22.4%	$147,857	87.0%	92.6%	$68,322	882
11	Yale University (CT)	90	4.3	4.2	3.67	727	17.4%	$137,155	75.2%	90.5%	$68,690	716
13	New York University (Stern)	88	4.2	4.0	3.48	714	20.9%	$146,024	79.1%	91.3%	$71,658	779
13	University of Virginia (Darden)	88	4.0	4.1	3.50	713	24.5%	$153,576	83.4%	90.1%	$65,800	671
15	Cornell University (Johnson) (NY)	87	4.1	4.1	3.36	700	29.9%	$152,207	80.3%	90.9%	$66,894	573
16	University of California–Los Angeles (Anderson)	85	4.0	4.0	3.52	715	22.3%	$141,197	74.4%	88.0%	$62,776	725
17	Carnegie Mellon University (Tepper) (PA)	83	4.0	3.9	3.30	691	29.9%	$145,463	81.1%	88.6%	$64,834	446
17	University of Texas–Austin (McCombs)	83	3.9	4.0	3.48	703	27.8%	$139,406	81.5%	89.9%	$52,654	527
19	U. of North Carolina–Chapel Hill (Kenan-Flagler)	80	3.8	3.9	3.38	701	37.2%	$131,469	79.1%	90.8%	$61,596	581
20	Emory University (Goizueta) (GA)	79	3.6	3.8	3.30	682	34.6%	$143,410	84.6%	92.7%	$59,616	352
20	University of Southern California (Marshall)	79	3.7	3.6	3.48	703	29.1%	$135,812	74.9%	93.6%	$68,194	454
22	University of Washington (Foster)	78	3.5	3.2	3.39	693	22.4%	$143,674	85.2%	98.1%	$48,606	221
23	Rice University (Jones) (TX)	77	3.4	3.7	3.34	711	27.2%	$131,821	83.0%	94.0%	$58,794	228
23	Washington University in St. Louis (Olin) (MO)	77	3.6	3.8	3.50	694	39.7%	$125,420	72.0%	97.2%	$58,710	272
25	Georgetown University (McDonough) (DC)	76	3.6	4.0	3.37	692	47.8%	$130,588	68.3%	91.8%	$56,901	562
26	Vanderbilt University (Owen) (TN)	75	3.5	3.8	3.31	688	43.2%	$134,066	75.8%	91.3%	$54,547	347
27	Indiana University (Kelley)	74	3.7	3.6	3.38	677	34.9%	$120,649	76.8%	86.9%	$49,268	392
28	Georgia Institute of Technology (Scheller)	72	3.3	3.5	3.40	680	31.1%	$124,895	71.9%	93.0%	$42,190	158
29	Arizona State University (Carey)	71	3.4	3.4	3.51	682	24.0%	$111,484	74.3%	95.9%	$46,874	227
29	University of Minnesota–Twin Cities (Carlson)	71	3.4	2.8	3.35	676	36.8%	$122,791	82.9%	95.7%	$53,670	200
31	Ohio State University (Fisher)	70	3.4	3.4	3.47	670	37.2%	$107,806	80.0%	94.4%	$52,611	183
31	Pennsylvania State U.–University Park (Smeal)	70	3.2	3.5	3.47	661	17.1%	$124,858	78.0%	91.5%	$42,094	115
31	University of Notre Dame (Mendoza) (IN)	70	3.5	3.6	3.27	674	41.9%	$123,549	73.1%	86.1%	$52,838	294
34	University of Florida (Warrington)	69	3.3	3.0	3.43	682	14.9%	$115,510	79.6%	89.8%	$31,130	94
35	Brigham Young University (Marriott) (UT)	68	3.0	3.5	3.49	680	46.7%	$119,434	76.8%	89.4%	$12,680	302
36	Texas A&M University–College Station (Mays)	66	3.3	3.5	3.27	638	33.8%	$116,972	72.0%	90.0%	$52,471	122
37	Michigan State University (Broad)	65	3.3	3.2	3.30	674	32.5%	$116,637	75.0%	85.3%	$48,538	143
37	University of California–Davis	65	3.1	3.2	3.36	669	37.2%	$97,325	82.9%	91.4%	$53,199	96
37	University of Wisconsin–Madison	65	3.3	3.4	3.35	678	30.4%	$108,754	57.8%	85.6%	$36,576	203
40	University of Georgia (Terry)	63	3.2	2.8	3.46	647	37.0%	$100,200	75.0%	92.5%	$34,378	103

*Tuition is reported on a per-credit-hour basis. †Total program costs, which may or may not include required fees. Schools receiving less than than 10 ratings from corporate recruiters have N/A displayed instead of corporate recruiter score. Sources: U.S. News and the schools. Assessment data collected by Ipsos Public Affairs.

Rank	School	Overall score	Peer assessment score (5.0=highest)	Recruiter assessment score (5.0=highest)	'17 full-time average undergrad GPA	'17 full-time average GMAT score	'17 full-time acceptance rate	'17 average starting salary and bonus	'17 graduates employed at graduation	Employed 3 months after graduation	'17 out-of-state tuition and fees	'17 total full-time enrollment
40	University of Texas–Dallas	63	3.0	4.2	3.50	678	23.8%	$91,270	41.9%	90.3%	$32,246	100
42	Boston University (Questrom) (MA)	62	3.1	3.0	3.33	680	40.0%	$104,636	59.8%	90.6%	$52,066	320
42	University of California–Irvine (Merage)	62	3.2	3.2	3.46	654	25.0%	$104,413	50.9%	87.3%	$51,480	167
44	Rutgers, The State U. of N.J.–Newark & New Brunswick	61	2.9	3.1	3.21	673	36.6%	$108,939	73.6%	88.7%	$48,415	118
44	University of Rochester (Simon) (NY)	61	3.1	2.8	3.40	666	30.0%	$116,294	71.3%	93.8%	$47,125	211
44	University of Tennessee–Knoxville (Haslam)	61	2.9	3.8	3.48	656	50.5%	$96,995	69.6%	87.5%	$47,592	120
44	University of Utah (Eccles)	61	2.9	3.3	3.49	637	44.0%	$93,869	75.4%	91.2%	$60,000†	133
48	Boston College (Carroll) (MA)	60	3.2	3.3	3.28	637	39.7%	$108,865	64.2%	85.1%	$49,340	175
48	Southern Methodist University (Cox) (TX)	60	3.1	3.1	3.33	660	45.5%	$105,644	64.8%	86.7%	$52,880	222
48	University of Illinois–Urbana-Champaign	60	3.3	3.2	3.29	647	31.3%	$103,435	71.2%	80.3%	$39,296	109
48	University of Maryland–College Park (Smith)	60	3.3	3.3	3.26	629	36.2%	$112,991	65.4%	79.5%	$56,388	200
52	University of Pittsburgh (Katz) (PA)	59	3.1	3.5	3.41	608	33.2%	$95,722	65.8%	89.5%	$68,716†	135
53	Purdue University–West Lafayette (Krannert) (IN)	58	3.4	3.1	3.19	632	37.3%	$101,344	58.8%	88.2%	$42,184	119
55	Case Western Reserve U. (Weatherhead) (OH)	55	3.1	3.2	3.10	612	69.9%	$86,589	69.4%	89.8%	$39,590	108
55	College of William and Mary (Mason) (VA)	55	2.9	4.0	3.33	617	59.7%	$89,390	54.0%	85.7%	$44,778	204
55	CUNY Bernard M. Baruch College (Zicklin) (NY)	55	2.8	3.6	3.31	619	38.4%	$83,173	65.5%	89.7%	$30,709	101
55	University of Massachusetts–Amherst (Isenberg)	55	2.9	3.2	3.44	659	33.1%	$81,467	71.4%	76.2%	$33,047	51
59	Baylor University (Hankamer) (TX)	54	2.8	3.0	3.35	628	51.2%	$77,082	70.0%	93.3%	$44,190	96
59	George Washington University (DC)	54	2.9	3.5	3.30	645	54.2%	$95,990	41.5%	83.1%	$102,000†	169
59	Northeastern University (MA)	54	2.8	3.3	3.34	633	35.3%	$89,243	42.2%	91.1%	$1,560*	166
59	University of Missouri (Trulaske)	54	2.5	3.6	3.58	654	41.3%	$70,653	61.5%	92.3%	$986*	109
63	Fordham University (Gabelli) (NY)	53	3.0	3.9	3.14	643	38.8%	$91,428	55.8%	74.4%	$51,575	83
63	University of Alabama (Manderson)	53	2.7	3.2	3.60	662	82.6%	$68,733	69.2%	87.2%	$30,930	289
65	University of Arkansas–Fayetteville (Walton)	51	2.8	2.4	3.54	655	58.4%	$66,306	71.8%	84.6%	$1,499*	90
65	University of Colorado–Boulder (Leeds)	51	3.0	2.9	3.36	630	68.8%	$79,061	46.9%	84.4%	$1,200*	185
65	University of Miami (FL)	51	2.8	2.9	3.35	645	52.9%	$89,238	15.9%	95.5%	$1,960*	126
65	University of South Carolina (Moore)	51	3.0	3.0	3.50	670	74.1%	$93,530	34.4%	78.1%	$71,580†	53
69	University of Arizona (Eller)	50	3.1	2.8	3.26	642	73.9%	$88,979	40.7%	77.8%	$48,762	86
70	Syracuse University (Whitman) (NY)	49	2.8	3.3	3.43	642	60.0%	$67,589	55.6%	77.8%	$46,202	52
70	University at Buffalo–SUNY (NY)	49	2.6	4.2	3.38	613	64.0%	$61,521	56.5%	84.7%	$29,440	204
72	Pepperdine University (Graziadio) (CA)	48	2.9	3.1	3.20	627	52.8%	$82,533	59.6%	72.3%	$49,580	128
73	Auburn University (Harbert) (AL)	46	2.8	2.8	3.41	584	39.2%	$65,200	66.7%	85.2%	$42,039†	78
73	Rochester Institute of Technology (Saunders) (NY)	46	2.7	3.1	3.37	551	44.7%	$57,795	70.7%	91.5%	$43,840	146
73	University of Kansas	46	2.7	2.6	3.36	618	61.1%	$61,792	50.0%	90.0%	$950*	52
76	Binghamton University–SUNY (NY)	45	2.5	3.3	3.53	612	68.5%	$61,740	72.1%	81.4%	$26,716	107
76	University of Oklahoma (Price)	45	2.6	2.8	3.60	639	59.2%	$76,339	44.4%	74.1%	$54,000†	80
78	Howard University (DC)	44	2.4	2.8	3.14	508	41.2%	$115,122	73.1%	84.6%	$35,571	51
79	American University (Kogod) (DC)	43	2.6	3.5	3.18	580	68.3%	$86,563	69.6%	73.9%	$1,642*	57
79	Chapman University (Argyros) (CA)	43	2.2	3.6	3.35	648	53.0%	$63,570	50.0%	79.2%	$1,590*	67
79	Iowa State University	43	2.6	N/A	3.54	610	61.6%	$71,077	81.3%	84.4%	$25,698	81
79	University of San Diego (CA)	43	2.5	3.3	3.30	611	55.3%	$86,667	53.6%	71.4%	$1,420*	81
83	Babson College (Olin) (MA)	42	3.1	3.2	3.23	620	89.4%	$80,445	53.5%	81.6%	$108,794†	328
83	Louisiana State University–Baton Rouge (Ourso)	42	2.7	2.2	3.30	610	54.8%	$61,926	69.6%	80.4%	$69,208†	94
85	Drexel University (LeBow) (PA)	41	2.6	3.1	3.20	570	44.9%	$65,625	52.2%	82.6%	$64,000†	42
85	University of Connecticut	41	2.7	3.0	3.45	639	38.0%	$102,868	36.1%	55.6%	$36,638	107
85	University of Houston (Bauer) (TX)	41	2.8	2.8	3.23	612	55.1%	$78,938	40.6%	65.6%	$40,042	85
85	University of Louisville (KY)	41	2.4	N/A	3.42	622	51.7%	$66,290	80.6%	83.9%	$32,000†	53
89	University of California–Riverside (Anderson)	39	2.5	2.8	3.26	594	60.4%	$74,805	20.0%	85.7%	$52,110	119
89	University of Cincinnati (Lindner) (OH)	39	2.6	N/A	3.45	670	51.6%	$68,620	62.7%	86.7%	$40,677†	83
89	University of Kentucky (Gatton)	39	2.7	N/A	3.49	597	85.8%	$55,356	54.7%	81.1%	$36,948†	71
92	Clemson University (SC)	36	2.8	N/A	3.21	559	79.6%	$73,666	44.4%	91.7%	$31,172	139
92	North Carolina State University (Poole)	36	2.7	N/A	3.40	626	41.2%	$84,352	62.9%	88.6%	$41,112	93
92	University of Denver (Daniels) (CO)	36	2.7	N/A	3.24	605	60.8%	$76,589	37.8%	78.4%	$87,000†	79

Note: The university that was ranked No.54 among MBA programs has been changed to unranked because of a data reporting error by the school.

Rank	School	Overall score	Peer assessment score (5.0=highest)	Recruiter assessment score (5.0=highest)	'17 full-time average undergrad GPA	'17 full-time average GMAT score	'17 full-time acceptance rate	'17 average starting salary and bonus	'17 graduates employed at graduation	Employed 3 months after graduation	'17 out-of-state tuition and fees	'17 total full-time enrollment
95	College of Charleston (SC)	35	2.1	N/A	3.35	555	64.9%	$65,691	50.0%	100.0%	$16,498†	41
95	Northern Arizona University (Franke)	35	2.1	N/A	3.48	544	97.6%	$54,300	80.0%	100.0%	$24,101†	26
95	Oklahoma State University (Spears)	35	2.7	N/A	3.43	552	62.7%	$60,160	48.0%	88.0%	$849*	79
95	University of Delaware (Lerner)	35	2.6	N/A	3.40	627	46.6%	$97,000	37.5%	62.5%	$1,000*	111
95	University of Mississippi	35	2.4	N/A	3.38	568	32.2%	$59,529	56.4%	87.2%	$53,443†	53

School	Peer assessment score (5.0=highest)	Recruiter assessment score (5.0=highest)	'17 full-time average undergrad GPA	'17 full-time average GMAT score	'17 full-time acceptance rate	'17 average starting salary and bonus	'17 graduates employed at graduation	Employed 3 months after graduation	'17 out-of-state tuition and fees	'17 total full-time enrollment
SCHOOLS RANKED 100 THROUGH 127 ARE LISTED HERE ALPHABETICALLY										
Belmont University (Massey) (TN)	2.1	N/A	3.45	525	82.4%	$49,300	20.8%	79.2%	$56,650†	32
Clark University (MA)	2.1	N/A	3.27	518	71.3%	$56,254	17.0%	63.8%	$67,502†	87
Clarkson University (NY)	2.1	N/A	3.45	601	85.7%	$64,173	34.5%	89.7%	$51,110†	67
Colorado State University	2.6	2.7	3.38	535	81.8%	$50,169	50.0%	50.0%	$1,557*	94
Florida International University	2.2	N/A	3.49	581	39.0%	$60,000	2.8%	2.8%	$47,000†	44
Hult International Business School–Boston (MA)	2.2	N/A	2.95	615	38.1%	$96,729	48.4%	90.2%	$73,000†	245
Jacksonville University (FL)	1.8	N/A	3.42	443	89.4%	$36,250	34.8%	69.6%	$770*	80
La Salle University (PA)	2.1	N/A	3.20	456	94.4%	$55,174	33.3%	95.8%	$24,280	63
Louisiana Tech University	2.0	N/A	3.60	524	57.4%	$51,667	54.0%	77.8%	$12,420	52
Mississippi State University	2.5	N/A	3.60	590	52.9%	$50,844	53.8%	76.9%	$31,185†	23
Oregon State University	2.5	N/A	3.40	559	35.7%	$81,416	32.7%	59.2%	$35,040	150
Pace University (Lubin) (NY)	2.4	3.0	3.59	543	42.3%	$63,578	28.0%	70.0%	$1,230*	192
Portland State University (OR)	2.3	N/A	3.26	572	52.1%	$65,296	32.0%	68.0%	$765*	28
Quinnipiac University (CT)	2.2	N/A	3.33	595	83.6%	$66,818	51.1%	82.0%	$1,010*	183
Rollins College (Crummer) (FL)	2.5	N/A	3.47	546	72.4%	$63,146	57.7%	84.5%	$74,200†	128
Saint Louis University (Chaifetz) (MO)	2.9	3.9	3.19	561	59.0%	$58,965	37.5%	66.7%	$58,456	21
San Diego State University (Fowler) (CA)	2.6	2.5	3.36	603	38.8%	$60,470	39.2%	57.6%	$23,696	230
Stevens Institute of Technology (NJ)	2.2	N/A	3.00	628	62.2%	$74,601	21.1%	93.3%	$35,716	914
University at Albany–SUNY (NY)	2.4	N/A	3.60	560	52.0%	$64,000	52.8%	83.3%	$22,210†	103
University of New Hampshire (Paul)	2.3	N/A	3.15	504	86.0%	$63,660	32.3%	93.5%	$48,033	34
University of North Carolina–Greensboro (Bryan)	2.2	N/A	3.40	527	76.9%	$57,529	59.1%	68.2%	$27,099	43
University of Oregon (Lundquist)	2.8	3.2	3.39	588	50.6%	$73,750	23.3%	51.2%	$42,849	126
University of San Francisco (CA)	2.6	N/A	3.18	579	52.8%	$81,924	38.9%	58.3%	$1,425*	82
University of South Florida	2.2	N/A	3.53	508	39.0%	$42,294	68.0%	84.0%	$913*	55
University of Tampa (Sykes) (FL)	2.2	N/A	3.50	530	40.0%	$54,602	24.2%	62.1%	$603*	344
University of Tulsa (Collins) (OK)	2.3	N/A	3.50	590	66.7%	$71,137	42.9%	66.7%	$900*	36
West Texas A&M University	1.8	N/A	3.48	540	73.6%	$79,000	55.6%	88.9%	$14,000†	370
Willamette University (Atkinson) (OR)	2.1	N/A	3.13	552	59.6%	$56,872	32.8%	65.6%	$40,650	131

Tops in the Specialties

MBA programs ranked best by B-school deans and MBA program directors

ACCOUNTING

1. University of Texas–Austin (McCombs)
2. University of Pennsylvania (Wharton)
3. University of Illinois–Urbana-Champaign
4. Brigham Young University (Marriott) (UT)
4. University of Michigan–Ann Arbor (Ross)
6. Stanford University (CA)
7. University of Chicago (Booth) (IL)
7. University of Southern California (Marshall)
9. New York University (Stern)
10. Indiana University (Kelley)
11. U. of North Carolina–Chapel Hill (Kenan-Flagler)
12. University of Notre Dame (Mendoza) (IN)
13. Gonzaga University (WA)
13. Ohio State University (Fisher)
15. Seattle University (Albers) (WA)
16. Columbia University (NY)
16. Loyola Marymount University (CA)
18. Northwestern University (Kellogg) (IL)
19. Marquette University (WI)
19. University of California–Berkeley (Haas)

ENTREPRENEURSHIP

1. Babson College (Olin) (MA)
2. Stanford University (CA)
3. Massachusetts Institute of Technology (Sloan)
4. Harvard University (MA)
5. University of California–Berkeley (Haas)
6. University of Pennsylvania (Wharton)
7. University of Michigan–Ann Arbor (Ross)
8. University of Southern California (Marshall)
9. Indiana University (Kelley)
9. University of Texas–Austin (McCombs)
11. Loyola Marymount University (CA)
12. Saint Louis University (Chaifetz) (MO)
13. Rice University (Jones) (TX)
14. University of San Francisco (CA)

FINANCE

1. University of Pennsylvania (Wharton)
2. University of Chicago (Booth) (IL)
3. New York University (Stern)
4. Columbia University (NY)
5. Stanford University (CA)
6. Massachusetts Institute of Technology (Sloan)
7. Harvard University (MA)
8. University of California–Berkeley (Haas)
9. University of California–Los Angeles (Anderson)
10. University of Michigan–Ann Arbor (Ross)
11. Northwestern University (Kellogg) (IL)
12. Fairfield University (Dolan) (CT)

13. Duke University (Fuqua) (NC)
13. University of Texas–Austin (McCombs)
15. Carnegie Mellon University (Tepper) (PA)
15. Creighton University (NE)
15. St. Joseph's University (Haub) (PA)
15. Xavier University (Williams) (OH)

INFORMATION SYSTEMS

1. Massachusetts Institute of Technology (Sloan)
2. Carnegie Mellon University (Tepper) (PA)
3. University of Minnesota–Twin Cities (Carlson)
4. University of Texas–Austin (McCombs)
5. University of Arizona (Eller)
6. University of Pennsylvania (Wharton)
7. New York University (Stern)
7. Stanford University (CA)
9. University of Maryland–College Park (Smith)
10. Indiana University (Kelley)
10. Santa Clara University (Leavey) (CA)

INTERNATIONAL

1. University of South Carolina (Moore)
2. Harvard University (MA)
3. University of Pennsylvania (Wharton)
4. University of California–Berkeley (Haas)
5. University of Michigan–Ann Arbor (Ross)
6. New York University (Stern)
7. Columbia University (NY)
7. Thunderbird School of Global Management (AZ)
9. Stanford University (CA)
10. University of Southern California (Marshall)
11. Georgetown University (McDonough) (DC)

MANAGEMENT

1. Harvard University (MA)
2. Stanford University (CA)
3. University of Michigan–Ann Arbor (Ross)
4. Northwestern University (Kellogg) (IL)
5. University of Pennsylvania (Wharton)
6. University of Virginia (Darden)
7. University of California–Berkeley (Haas)
8. Dartmouth College (Tuck) (NH)
9. Duke University (Fuqua) (NC)
10. Columbia University (NY)
11. Yale University (CT)
12. Rockhurst University (Helzberg) (MO)
13. New York University (Stern)

MARKETING

1. Northwestern University (Kellogg) (IL)
2. University of Pennsylvania (Wharton)

3. Duke University (Fuqua) (NC)
4. Harvard University (MA)
4. University of Michigan–Ann Arbor (Ross)
6. Stanford University (CA)
7. Columbia University (NY)
8. University of Chicago (Booth) (IL)
9. University of California–Berkeley (Haas)
10. New York University (Stern)
11. Indiana University (Kelley)
12. Loyola Marymount University (CA)
13. St. Joseph's University (Haub) (PA)

NONPROFIT

1. Yale University (CT)
2. Harvard University (MA)
2. Stanford University (CA)
4. University of California–Berkeley (Haas)
5. University of Michigan–Ann Arbor (Ross)

PRODUCTION / OPERATIONS

1. Massachusetts Institute of Technology (Sloan)
2. Carnegie Mellon University (Tepper) (PA)
3. University of Michigan–Ann Arbor (Ross)
4. University of Pennsylvania (Wharton)
5. Stanford University (CA)
6. Purdue University–West Lafayette (Krannert) (IN)
7. Georgia Institute of Technology (Scheller)
8. Northwestern University (Kellogg) (IL)
9. Harvard University (MA)
10. Michigan State University (Broad)
10. Ohio State University (Fisher)

SUPPLY CHAIN / LOGISTICS

1. Michigan State University (Broad)
2. Massachusetts Institute of Technology (Sloan)
3. Arizona State University (Carey)
4. Ohio State University (Fisher)
5. Pennsylvania State University–University Park (Smeal)
6. Rutgers, The State U. of New Jersey–Newark and New Brunswick
6. University of Michigan–Ann Arbor (Ross)
8. Stanford University (CA)
9. Carnegie Mellon University (Tepper) (PA)
10. University of Tennessee–Knoxville (Haslam)
11. Purdue University–West Lafayette (Krannert) (IN)
12. Loyola University Chicago (Quinlan) (IL)
12. Northwestern University (Kellogg) (IL)
12. University of Pennsylvania (Wharton)

Best Part-Time MBA Programs

ART-TIME BUSINESS programs play a vital role for people who can't go to school full time because of family or financial reasons or who simply prefer to keep working. The U.S. News part-time MBA ranking is based on five factors: the opinions of business school deans and MBA directors about program excellence; average GMAT and GRE scores of part-time MBA students entering in the fall of 2017; average undergraduate GPA; average number of years of work experi-

ence; and the percentage of the fall 2017 total MBA program enrollment that is in the part-time MBA program. The results were weighted – for more detail on how, see Page 56. Finally, the contenders were ranked in descending order by their overall score. To be eligible, a program had to be accredited by AACSB International – The Association to Advance Collegiate Schools of Business, have at least 20 students enrolled part time in the fall of 2017, and have been included in last year's part-time MBA ranking. More @ usnews.com/parttime.

Rank	School	Overall score	Peer assessment score (5.0=highest)	'17 part-time average GMAT score	'17 part-time acceptance rate	'17 total part-time enrollment
1	University of California–Berkeley (Haas)	100	4.5	699	N/A	846
2	University of Chicago (Booth) (IL)	97	4.6	684	N/A	1,377
3	Northwestern University (Kellogg) (IL)	95	4.6	675	65.6%	747
4	New York University (Stern)	91	4.3	667	65.8%	1,300
5	University of California–Los Angeles (Anderson)	90	4.2	675	67.0%	983
6	University of Michigan–Ann Arbor (Ross)	85	4.3	656	74.3%	402
7	Carnegie Mellon University (Tepper) (PA)	79	4.1	651	58.8%	119
7	University of Texas–Austin (McCombs)	79	4.0	632	73.7%	453
9	Ohio State University (Fisher)	75	3.7	643	74.7%	365
9	University of Minnesota–Twin Cities (Carlson)	75	3.6	605	85.4%	919
11	Georgetown University (McDonough) (DC)	74	3.8	635	76.1%	434
11	University of Southern California (Marshall)	74	3.8	629	65.0%	480
13	Indiana University (Kelley)	73	3.7	634	60.2%	294
13	University of Washington (Foster)	73	3.5	635	75.7%	382
15	Emory University (Goizueta) (GA)	72	3.7	647	72.6%	250
15	University of Maryland–College Park (Smith)	72	3.5	588	79.2%	542
17	Rice University (Jones) (TX)	71	3.5	636	76.6%	331
17	Virginia Tech (Pamplin)	71	3.0	620	93.4%	182
17	Wake Forest University (NC)	71	3.2	598	88.8%	311
20	University of Nebraska–Lincoln	69	3.0	593	62.5%	41
20	University of Texas–Dallas	69	3.2	638	69.0%	759
22	University of Iowa (Tippie)	68	3.1	586	95.3%	873
22	University of South Carolina (Moore)	68	3.1	605	93.9%	435

Note: The data listed for acceptance rate and enrollment are for informational purposes only and are not used in the computation of the part-time MBA program rankings.
N/A=Data were not provided by the school. Sources: U.S. News and the schools. Assessment data collected by Ipsos Public Affairs.

Rank	School	Overall score	Peer assessment score (5.0=highest)	'17 part-time average GMAT score	'17 part-time acceptance rate	'17 total part-time enrollment
22	Washington University in St. Louis (Olin) (MO)	68	3.7	594	85.9%	258
25	Arizona State University (Carey)	66	3.5	590	75.1%	232
25	Boston College (Carroll) (MA)	66	3.4	591	92.1%	424
25	Georgia Institute of Technology (Scheller)	66	3.3	606	67.9%	374
25	Lehigh University (PA)	66	2.8	620	61.1%	167
25	University of Massachusetts–Amherst (Isenberg)	66	3.0	576	85.4%	213
30	Case Western Reserve University (Weatherhead) (OH)	65	3.3	598	93.2%	170
30	University of Florida (Warrington)	65	3.3	566	57.4%	344
32	Boston University (Questrom) (MA)	64	3.2	618	88.1%	646
32	Georgia State University (Robinson)	64	3.0	606	42.7%	275
32	Loyola University Chicago (Quinlan) (IL)	64	3.1	554	56.4%	557
32	University of California–Davis	64	3.2	579	75.2%	323
32	University of California–Irvine (Merage)	64	3.3	590	84.4%	330
32	University of Wisconsin–Madison	64	3.4	629	78.9%	157
32	Villanova University (PA)	64	3.0	580	88.4%	128
39	Rutgers, The State U. of New Jersey–Newark and New Brunswick	63	2.9	583	82.0%	1,040
39	Santa Clara University (Leavey) (CA)	63	3.1	619	88.3%	374
39	Texas A&M University–College Station (Mays)	63	3.4	597	83.6%	89
42	Seattle University (Albers) (WA)	62	2.9	545	46.2%	345
42	University of Richmond (Robins) (VA)	62	2.7	618	85.5%	79
44	Florida State University	61	2.9	561	47.6%	108
44	Rutgers, The State University of New Jersey–Camden	61	2.9	560	78.9%	127
44	University of Georgia (Terry)	61	3.2	553	93.5%	308
47	George Mason University (VA)	60	2.8	561	78.6%	252
47	Purdue University–West Lafayette (Krannert) (IN)	60	3.4	581	84.1%	101
47	University of Illinois–Chicago (Liautaud)	60	2.8	568	57.4%	236
47	University of North Carolina–Charlotte (Belk)	60	2.8	579	76.9%	368
51	Fordham University (Gabelli) (NY)	59	3.1	592	53.5%	163
51	Loyola Marymount University (CA)	59	2.9	578	39.6%	89
51	Miami University (Farmer) (OH)	59	2.8	551	66.7%	126
51	Pepperdine University (Graziadio) (CA)	59	3.0	571	81.1%	654
51	University of Colorado–Boulder (Leeds)	59	3.1	586	90.4%	149
56	CUNY Bernard M. Baruch College (Zicklin) (NY)	58	2.8	586	65.4%	460
56	DePaul University (Kellstadt) (IL)	58	2.9	595	86.9%	886
56	University of California–San Diego (Rady)	58	3.1	585	72.5%	122
56	University of Pittsburgh (Katz) (PA)	58	3.2	538	81.0%	294
60	University of Arizona (Eller)	57	3.2	527	87.3%	211
60	University of Oklahoma (Price)	57	2.8	595	85.9%	127
60	University of Utah (Eccles)	57	3.0	567	85.2%	288
60	Xavier University (Williams) (OH)	57	2.9	550	90.9%	546
64	George Washington University (DC)	56	3.1	591	82.4%	209
64	Southern Methodist University (Cox) (TX)	56	3.0	617	69.7%	233
66	Babson College (Olin) (MA)	55	3.2	622	91.0%	246
66	Northeastern University (MA)	55	2.9	589	88.7%	309
66	St. Joseph's University (Haub) (PA)	55	2.8	502	67.2%	421
66	University of Houston (Bauer) (TX)	55	2.8	602	66.2%	327
70	James Madison University (VA)	54	2.7	556	94.4%	42
70	Kennesaw State University (Coles) (GA)	54	2.5	576	52.9%	188
70	Marquette University (WI)	54	2.9	539	85.1%	195
70	University of Wisconsin–Milwaukee (Lubar)	54	2.7	542	63.1%	433
74	Loyola University Maryland (Sellinger)	53	2.7	508	91.1%	306
74	North Carolina State University (Poole)	53	2.7	618	74.3%	281
74	University of Connecticut	53	2.9	523	88.5%	913
74	University of Scranton (PA)	53	2.5	519	69.0%	123
78	Creighton University (NE)	52	2.8	493	50.9%	112

Rank	School	Overall score	Peer assessment score (5.0=highest)	'17 part-time average GMAT score	'17 part-time acceptance rate	'17 total part-time enrollment
78	University of Colorado–Denver	52	2.6	578	64.2%	462
78	University of Kansas	52	2.9	564	90.5%	100
78	University of Rochester (Simon) (NY)	52	3.3	603	85.4%	159
82	Bradley University (Foster) (IL)	51	2.4	557	73.7%	46
82	Butler University (IN)	51	2.5	582	80.6%	171
82	Gonzaga University (WA)	51	2.9	537	74.0%	154
82	Texas Christian University (Neeley)	51	2.9	532	94.4%	147
82	University of Colorado–Colorado Springs	51	2.4	548	76.5%	332
87	Bentley University (MA)	50	2.8	594	91.7%	224
87	College of William and Mary (Mason) (VA)	50	3.0	565	98.0%	196
87	Drexel University (LeBow) (PA)	50	2.7	481	94.6%	143
87	Old Dominion University (VA)	50	2.5	554	56.4%	85
87	University of Denver (Daniels) (CO)	50	2.8	592	80.0%	109
92	Elon University (Love) (NC)	49	2.4	565	76.5%	131
92	Illinois State University	49	2.3	542	89.0%	106
92	Rockhurst University (Helzberg) (MO)	49	2.6	527	99.4%	359
92	University of New Hampshire (Paul)	49	2.4	557	95.5%	139
92	University of North Carolina–Greensboro (Bryan)	49	2.5	544	90.4%	111
97	Seton Hall University (Stillman) (NJ)	48	2.5	463	75.9%	216
97	University of Cincinnati (Lindner) (OH)	48	2.8	632	72.7%	130
97	University of Nebraska–Omaha	48	2.4	559	79.2%	246
97	University of Nevada–Las Vegas	48	2.4	571	49.2%	156
101	Fairfield University (Dolan) (CT)	47	2.7	489	75.0%	65
101	Ohio University	47	2.5	N/A	73.2%	102
101	Oklahoma State University (Spears)	47	2.8	551	81.3%	86
101	Oregon State University	47	2.4	572	50.0%	44
101	St. John's University (Tobin) (NY)	47	2.4	566	80.9%	319
101	University of Louisville (KY)	47	2.5	546	79.0%	169
101	University of Michigan–Flint	47	2.1	529	58.7%	190
101	University of Texas–Arlington	47	2.6	517	71.3%	442
101	University of Washington–Tacoma Milgard	47	2.2	517	87.2%	50
101	Valparaiso University (IN)	47	2.2	580	100.0%	41
111	Clemson University (SC)	46	2.7	594	91.9%	367
111	Colorado State University	46	2.8	520	100.0%	50
111	John Carroll University (Boler) (OH)	46	2.7	613	91.7%	137
111	University of Alabama–Birmingham	46	2.6	521	86.3%	412
111	University of Michigan–Dearborn	46	2.3	579	49.5%	124
111	University of South Florida	46	2.3	575	57.3%	294
111	University of Tennessee–Chattanooga	46	2.4	533	85.3%	150
118	Iowa State University	45	2.7	500	90.5%	55
118	Providence College (RI)	45	2.2	535	92.5%	169
118	San Diego State University (Fowler) (CA)	45	2.6	581	38.6%	228
118	University of Akron (OH)	45	2.1	570	66.3%	310
118	University of Massachusetts–Lowell	45	2.3	550	90.4%	229
118	University of Portland (Pamplin) (OR)	45	2.4	578	90.0%	108
118	Virginia Commonwealth University	45	2.4	545	62.5%	175
125	Duquesne University (Palumbo-Donahue) (PA)	44	2.4	564	81.6%	199
125	Hofstra University (Zarb) (NY)	44	2.4	548	78.6%	751
125	Minnesota State University–Mankato	44	2.0	535	75.0%	52
125	Northern Illinois University	44	2.3	541	98.1%	420
125	University at Buffalo–SUNY (NY)	44	2.7	558	98.8%	201
125	University of Kentucky (Gatton)	44	2.7	620	83.7%	181
125	University of San Diego (CA)	44	2.5	574	86.0%	98
125	University of San Francisco (CA)	44	2.7	553	95.2%	87
133	California State University–Northridge (Nazarian)	43	2.2	600	19.1%	125

Rank	School	Overall score	Peer assessment score (5.0=highest)	'17 part-time average GMAT score	'17 part-time acceptance rate	'17 total part-time enrollment
133	California State University–San Bernardino	43	2.0	519	55.7%	222
133	Florida International University	43	2.3	N/A	51.0%	525
133	Portland State University (OR)	43	2.4	586	68.9%	43
133	University of Alabama–Huntsville	43	2.4	552	79.6%	95
133	University of Central Florida	43	2.3	N/A	58.7%	407
133	University of St. Thomas (MN)	43	2.5	519	100.0%	518
133	Wichita State University (Barton) (KS)	43	2.4	526	66.3%	180
141	Belmont University (Massey) (TN)	42	2.1	507	88.5%	129
141	Rochester Institute of Technology (Saunders) (NY)	42	2.9	538	65.4%	76
141	Rollins College (Crummer) (FL)	42	2.6	N/A	78.4%	177
141	University of Wisconsin–Oshkosh	42	1.9	560	89.8%	397
141	Willamette University (Atkinson) (OR)	42	2.3	538	100.0%	119
146	Berry College (Campbell) (GA)	41	1.8	523	89.5%	29
146	Canisius College (Wehle) (NY)	41	2.3	473	86.9%	234
146	Mercer University–Atlanta (Stetson) (GA)	41	2.1	540	59.4%	317
146	Monmouth University (NJ)	41	1.9	466	87.9%	184
146	Pennsylvania State University–Erie, The Behrend College (Black)	41	2.3	544	82.6%	122
146	Texas State University (McCoy)	41	2.1	556	46.3%	226
152	California State University–Fullerton (Mihaylo)	40	2.3	528	63.2%	285
152	Florida Atlantic University	40	2.1	510	71.3%	176
152	Loyola University New Orleans (Butt) (LA)	40	2.6	490	92.6%	57
152	Southern Illinois University–Edwardsville	40	2.0	515	83.3%	112
152	University of Arkansas–Little Rock	40	2.5	N/A	24.5%	152
152	University of California–Riverside (Anderson)	40	2.8	492	89.0%	114
152	University of Delaware (Lerner)	40	2.5	550	89.1%	163
152	University of Hawaii–Manoa (Shidler)	40	2.7	515	86.4%	49
152	University of Wisconsin–Whitewater	40	2.1	504	68.3%	454
152	West Chester University of Pennsylvania	40	2.0	505	77.5%	427
152	Western Michigan University (Haworth)	40	2.3	518	70.7%	312
163	Bowling Green State University (OH)	39	2.3	N/A	68.1%	90
163	New Mexico State University	39	2.2	497	73.6%	85
163	Saint Louis University (Chaifetz) (MO)	39	3.1	554	77.8%	149
163	San Francisco State University (CA)	39	2.4	501	73.6%	73
163	University of Memphis (Fogelman) (TN)	39	2.4	605	68.0%	141
168	Boise State University (ID)	38	2.3	573	100.0%	79
168	Louisiana State University–Baton Rouge (Ourso)	38	2.7	560	81.4%	57
168	Radford University (VA)	38	1.9	510	80.0%	32
168	University of North Texas	38	2.2	534	65.1%	312
172	American University (Kogod) (DC)	37	2.8	N/A	N/A	42
172	Iona College (Hagan) (NY)	37	2.1	N/A	95.7%	242
172	Pennsylvania State University–Harrisburg	37	2.0	539	69.0%	160
172	Samford University (Brock) (AL)	37	2.0	557	84.4%	98
172	University of Louisiana–Lafayette (Moody)	37	2.1	N/A	64.4%	176
172	University of North Florida (Coggin)	37	2.0	512	63.4%	440
172	University of South Dakota	37	2.1	515	97.6%	210
179	Appalachian State University (Walker) (NC)	36	2.2	N/A	100.0%	45
179	Auburn University–Montgomery (AL)	36	2.6	N/A	N/A	55
179	Eastern Michigan University	36	1.9	540	52.4%	200
179	Oakland University (MI)	36	2.0	504	93.3%	287
179	Sonoma State University (CA)	36	1.9	550	78.3%	59
179	University at Albany–SUNY (NY)	36	2.4	552	82.8%	189
179	University of Dayton (OH)	36	2.3	521	47.1%	83
179	University of Tulsa (Collins) (OK)	36	2.2	551	88.9%	48
187	Sacred Heart University (Welch) (CT)	35	2.0	458	85.7%	145
187	St. Mary's College of California	35	2.2	518	82.5%	123

Rank	School	Overall score	Peer assessment score (5.0=highest)	'17 part-time average GMAT score	'17 part-time acceptance rate	'17 total part-time enrollment
187	University of Nevada–Reno	35	2.0	524	96.8%	208
187	University of North Carolina–Wilmington (Cameron)	35	2.2	N/A	81.1%	78
187	Wayne State University (MI)	35	2.2	N/A	48.6%	1,214
187	Weber State University (Goddard) (UT)	35	1.9	565	85.9%	236
193	Chapman University (Argyros) (CA)	34	2.3	543	95.9%	140
193	Fayetteville State University (NC)	34	1.6	518	91.5%	322
193	Georgia College & State University (Bunting)	34	1.9	520	75.0%	24
193	Stevens Institute of Technology (NJ)	34	2.4	622	74.6%	464
193	University of Illinois–Springfield	34	2.2	484	84.8%	87
193	University of Missouri–Kansas City (Bloch)	34	2.5	572	53.2%	149
193	University of Northern Iowa	34	2.2	520	79.2%	149
193	University of Texas–San Antonio	34	2.1	554	72.2%	174
201	Clarion University of Pennsylvania	33	2.0	520	91.9%	104
201	East Carolina University (NC)	33	2.1	495	65.1%	585
201	La Salle University (PA)	33	2.2	420	98.1%	182
204	University of Massachusetts–Boston	32	2.5	547	54.0%	296
204	University of Minnesota–Duluth (Labovitz)	32	2.5	565	100.0%	37
206	Bloomsburg University of Pennsylvania	31	1.9	490	85.7%	36
206	North Dakota State University	31	2.0	530	85.7%	70
206	Ramapo College of New Jersey	31	1.8	N/A	54.6%	63
206	Rider University (NJ)	31	1.9	510	79.3%	172
206	Robert Morris University (PA)	31	1.9	557	89.3%	164
206	Rowan University (Rohrer) (NJ)	31	2.1	500	33.3%	74
206	Texas A&M International University	31	2.1	N/A	100.0%	113
206	University of Detroit Mercy (MI)	31	2.3	412	100.0%	55

School	Peer assessment score (5.0=highest)	'17 part-time average GMAT score	'17 part-time acceptance rate	'17 total part-time enrollment
SCHOOLS RANKED 214 THROUGH 279 ARE LISTED HERE ALPHABETICALLY				
Adelphi University (NY)	1.7	476	58.3%	402
Alfred University (NY)	1.7	N/A	N/A	20
Bellarmine University (Rubel) (KY)	2.0	516	100.0%	35
Bryant University (RI)	2.2	417	67.0%	70
California State University–East Bay	2.0	522	41.4%	283
Clark University (MA)	2.2	N/A	100.0%	45
Cleveland State University (Ahuja) (OH)	2.2	N/A	N/A	341
Coastal Carolina University (SC)	1.7	N/A	100.0%	34
Columbus State University (Turner) (GA)	1.6	545	78.4%	60
Dominican University (Brennan) (IL)	1.8	415	60.3%	147
Eastern Illinois University (Lumpkin)	1.8	514	52.8%	61
Fairleigh Dickinson University (Silberman) (NJ)	2.0	N/A	72.5%	238
Florida Gulf Coast University (Lutgert)	1.9	547	54.1%	78
Georgia Southern University	2.0	451	87.3%	86
Grand Valley State University (Seidman) (MI)	1.9	557	63.9%	270
Howard University (DC)	2.4	N/A	N/A	23
Indiana University Northwest	1.8	N/A	92.3%	66
Indiana University–Southeast	1.8	520	83.6%	177
Jacksonville University (FL)	1.9	480	93.3%	138
LIU Post (NY)	1.6	400	82.6%	26
Le Moyne College (NY)	2.1	N/A	84.6%	73
Marshall University (Lewis) (WV)	2.2	N/A	82.0%	64
Meredith College (NC)	1.7	N/A	100.0%	29
Montclair State University Feliciano (NJ)	2.0	N/A	82.9%	562
New Jersey Institute of Technology	2.1	533	73.6%	151

BEST MBA PROGRAMS

School	Peer assessment score (5.0=highest)	'17 part-time average GMAT score	'17 part-time acceptance rate	'17 total part-time enrollment
SCHOOLS RANKED 214 THROUGH 279 ARE LISTED HERE ALPHABETICALLY CONTINUED				
Niagara University (NY)	1.9	N/A	N/A	79
Oklahoma City University	1.8	N/A	73.4%	101
Pace University (Lubin) (NY)	2.4	537	31.3%	103
Pittsburg State University (Kelce) (KS)	2.1	550	68.1%	22
Prairie View A&M University (TX)	1.5	N/A	N/A	143
Quinnipiac University (CT)	2.3	660	77.8%	31
SUNY–Oswego (NY)	1.8	543	79.1%	152
Saginaw Valley State University (MI)	1.7	N/A	57.1%	61
Savannah State University (GA)	1.8	501	63.3%	70
Shenandoah University (Byrd) (VA)	1.7	N/A	92.9%	46
Shippensburg University of Pennsylvania (Grove)	1.9	630	80.0%	176
Southeast Missouri State University (Harrison)	1.6	473	44.4%	67
Southeastern Louisiana University	1.7	N/A	N/A	22
St. Bonaventure University (NY)	2.0	N/A	85.7%	27
St. John Fisher College (NY)	2.0	465	82.8%	75
Stetson University (FL)	2.0	N/A	N/A	23
Suffolk University (Sawyer) (MA)	2.2	454	79.3%	247
Tennessee Technological University	1.8	N/A	89.2%	191
The Citadel (SC)	2.4	481	N/A	154
University of Alaska–Fairbanks	2.0	N/A	N/A	68
University of Central Arkansas	1.7	N/A	83.3%	63
University of Houston–Clear Lake (TX)	1.8	470	73.5%	314
University of Houston–Downtown (TX)	2.0	407	88.7%	1,069
University of Massachusetts–Dartmouth	2.3	N/A	91.7%	30
University of Montevallo (AL)	1.7	N/A	53.3%	38
University of New Mexico (Anderson)	2.4	N/A	53.0%	126
University of North Georgia	1.7	443	76.7%	80
University of South Florida–Sarasota-Manatee	1.8	N/A	34.7%	80
University of Southern Indiana	1.8	N/A	N/A	121
University of Southern Maine	1.8	N/A	73.0%	80
University of Southern Mississippi	1.9	496	91.7%	37
University of Tampa (Sykes) (FL)	2.3	550	53.3%	142
University of Texas–Rio Grande Valley	1.8	N/A	N/A	159
University of West Georgia (Richards)	1.7	450	89.1%	103
University of Wisconsin–Parkside	1.9	380	93.8%	55
University of Wisconsin–River Falls	1.9	440	100.0%	65
West Texas A&M University	1.8	540	69.2%	930
Western Carolina University (NC)	1.9	474	92.3%	77
Western Illinois University	1.8	470	70.0%	38
Western New England University (MA)	1.7	480	65.8%	97
Worcester Polytechnic Institute (MA)	2.4	N/A	92.5%	214

Best Executive MBA Programs

THE BEST MOVE for successful professionals who would rather not give up their job (and their paycheck) may be to pursue an executive MBA degree. These intensive programs target people who have made strides in their careers already but may need that credential to continue to advance. Classes take place in a concentrated manner, so that students come together on campus one day a week, say, or for a few days per month.

U.S. News ranks EMBA programs based solely on a fall 2017 survey of B-school deans and MBA program directors, who are asked to nominate up to 10 schools for the excellence of their EMBA programs. Those receiving the most votes in the latest survey are listed here, along with key information (from schools that provided it) about the student body – and the cost.

Rank	School	'17 acceptance rate	'17 average age of new entrants	% women enrolled ('17)	% minority students ('17)	% international students ('17)	'17 total EMBA enrollment	'17 total EMBA program cost
1	University of Chicago (Booth) (IL)	N/A	38	21.5%	42.0%	11.0%	181	$184,000
2	University of Pennsylvania (Wharton)	58.3%	34	28.4%	40.5%	2.3%	444	$198,600
3	Northwestern University (Kellogg) (IL)	N/A	N/A	26.8%	0%	N/A	477	$100,560**
4	Columbia University (NY)	N/A	32	N/A	N/A	N/A	N/A	$3,270*
5	Duke University (Fuqua) (NC)	89.5%	38	27.1%	37.5%	31.3%	48	$158,000
6	University of Michigan–Ann Arbor (Ross)	67.9%	39	24.5%	30.0%	8.0%	200	$64,928**
7	New York University (Stern)	71.0%	37	35.0%	37.1%	6.3%	240	$189,200
8	University of California–Los Angeles (Anderson)	81.0%	38	33.5%	44.5%	8.7%	218	$77,947**
9	University of California–Berkeley (Haas)	N/A	N/A	31.9%	0%	N/A	138	$185,000
10	Massachusetts Institute of Technology (Sloan)	N/A	N/A	N/A	N/A	N/A	N/A	N/A
11	Seattle University (Albers) (WA)	54.3%	46	41.7%	9.7%	0%	72	$96,000
12	Cornell University (Johnson) (NY)	76.1%	35	24.2%	24.2%	7.8%	128	$176,104
13	Marquette University (WI)	100%	38	33.3%	12.8%	0%	39	$72,000
14	Loyola Marymount University (CA)	74.3%	36	45.7%	47.8%	8.7%	46	$97,000
14	University of Southern California (Marshall)	79.4%	38	25.5%	48.6%	1.4%	220	$112,482
16	University of North Carolina–Chapel Hill (Kenan-Flagler)	N/A	36	21.7%	30.4%	0%	46	$110,313
17	St. Joseph's University (Haub) (PA)	75.0%	40	47.7%	33.3%	1.5%	195	$69,300
18	Southern Methodist University (Cox) (TX)	94.7%	37	25.9%	29.5%	11.5%	139	$116,150
18	University of Virginia (Darden)	N/A	N/A	27.0%	0%	N/A	244	$130,000
20	University of Notre Dame (Mendoza) (IN)	91.6%	36	20.6%	24.8%	0%	141	$129,000
20	Xavier University (Williams) (OH)	90.9%	38	39.1%	21.7%	0%	23	$1,225*
22	University of Texas-Austin (McCombs)	64.5%	35	25.4%	31.5%	8.5%	130	N/A
23	Emory University (Goizueta) (GA)	72.6%	36	34.0%	52.4%	6.8%	103	$110,000
23	University of Washington (Foster)	86.6%	37	39.3%	33.3%	11.1%	135	$51,500**
23	Yale University (CT)	N/A	N/A	27.1%	35.7%	8.6%	140	$172,000

*Tuition is reported on a per-credit-hour basis. **Annual tuition and fees. Sources: U.S. News and the schools. Assessment data collected by Ipsos Public Affairs.

Best Online Programs

UR RANKINGS OF online business degree programs have been split into two groups: those that deliver the MBA – still the most popular online graduate degree – and non-MBA master's-level business programs. These include degrees in accounting, finance, insurance, marketing and management.

To start, U.S. News surveyed nearly 450 master's-level business programs at regionally accredited institutions that deliver required classes predominantly online. In both the MBA and non-MBA groups, programs were ranked based on their success at promoting student engagement, the training and credentials of their faculty, the selectivity of their admissions processes, the services and technologies available to remote learners, and the opinions of deans and other academics in the disciplines at peer distance-education programs.

Specific indicators include graduation and retention rates, student indebtedness at graduation, the average undergraduate GPAs and standardized test scores of new entrants, proportion of faculty members with terminal degrees, proportion of full-time faculty who are tenured or tenure-track, whether there is program-level accreditation, and whether students can remotely access support services like mentoring and academic advising. In summary, the rankings measure the extent to which online degree programs have achieved academic quality commensurate with that found at strong brick-and-mortar schools. All the ranked programs are listed below; to see more detail on the methodologies, visit usnews.com/onlinedegrees.

Best Online MBA Programs

Rank	School	Overall score	Average peer assessment score (5.0=highest)	'17 total enrollment	'17-'18 total program cost[1]	Entrance test required	'17 average undergrad GPA	'17 acceptance rate	'17 full-time faculty with terminal degree	'17 tenured or tenure-track faculty[2]	'17 retention rate	'17 three-year graduation rate
2	Carnegie Mellon University (Tepper) (PA)	97	4.1	146	$128,000	GMAT or GRE	3.4	54%	90%	87%	100%	100%
2	Indiana University–Bloomington (Kelley)	97	4.2	703	$67,830	GMAT or GRE	3.4	75%	82%	60%	99%	86%
4	U. of North Carolina–Chapel Hill (Kenan-Flagler)	96	4.1	1,862	$114,048	N/A	3.2	55%	80%	59%	96%	92%
5	Arizona State University (Carey)	89	3.8	402	N/A	GMAT or GRE	3.2	57%	83%	50%	97%	97%
6	University of Florida (Hough)	87	3.7	456	$58,000	GMAT or GRE	3.2	46%	96%	62%	97%	93%
6	University of Texas–Dallas	87	3.2	310	$83,428	GMAT or GRE	3.4	34%	72%	40%	85%	57%
8	University of Southern California (Marshall)	86	3.7	88	$95,618	GMAT or GRE	3.1	56%	93%	50%	100%	N/A
9	University of Maryland–College Park (Smith)	84	3.4	369	$83,970	GMAT or GRE	3.2	74%	100%	59%	94%	100%
10	Pennsylvania State University–World Campus	83	3.3	259	$56,880	GMAT or GRE	3.3	83%	100%	95%	98%	87%
11	Auburn University (Harbert) (AL)	81	3.3	353	$34,425	GMAT or GRE	3.2	78%	100%	100%	96%	77%
12	Arkansas State University–Jonesboro	79	2.1	190	$20,130	GMAT or GRE	3.6	83%	100%	100%	95%	93%
12	Washington State University	79	3.2	852	$34,000	GMAT	3.5	66%	85%	69%	93%	66%
14	North Carolina State University (Poole)	78	3.0	311	$74,555	N/A	3.3	58%	92%	88%	92%	93%
14	University of Wisconsin MBA Consortium	78	2.6	316	$20,250	GMAT or GRE	3.4	82%	91%	91%	96%	88%
16	Ball State University (Miller) (IN)	77	2.8	293	$18,090	GMAT or GRE	3.4	92%	100%	96%	91%	61%
16	Florida State University	77	3.0	213	$31,599	GMAT or GRE	3.4	57%	83%	70%	78%	66%
16	U. of Massachusetts–Amherst (Isenberg)	77	3.2	1,344	$35,100	GMAT or GRE	3.4	85%	95%	63%	91%	55%

Note: The university that was ranked No.1 among online MBA programs has been changed to unranked because of a data reporting error by the school.

N/A=Data were not provided by the school; programs that received insufficient numbers of ratings do not have their peer-assessment scores published.

[1]Tuition is reported for part-time, out-of-state students. [2]Percentage reported of full-time faculty. More detail can be found in the directory of online programs at the back of the book.

Rank	School	Overall score	Average peer assessment score (5.0=highest)	'17 total enrollment	'17-'18 total program cost[1]	Entrance test required	'17 average undergrad GPA	'17 acceptance rate	'17 full-time faculty with terminal degree	'17 tenured or tenure-track faculty[2]	'17 retention rate	'17 three-year graduation rate
19	Kennesaw State University (Coles) (GA)	76	2.7	213	$22,170	GMAT or GRE	3.3	67%	100%	100%	96%	91%
19	Lehigh University (PA)	76	2.8	200	$39,075	GMAT or GRE	3.3	77%	69%	62%	91%	75%
19	Pepperdine University (Graziadio) (CA)	76	3.3	361	$89,180	GMAT or GRE	3.2	72%	85%	40%	94%	73%
22	James Madison University (VA)	75	2.9	45	$37,800	GMAT or GRE	3.2	92%	100%	100%	89%	95%
22	Mississippi State University	75	2.9	245	$13,680	GMAT or GRE	3.3	63%	100%	92%	91%	62%
22	University of Delaware (Lerner)	75	2.8	240	$35,750	GMAT or GRE	3.3	63%	100%	92%	81%	80%
25	University of Mississippi	74	2.8	131	$29,700	GMAT or GRE	3.2	45%	92%	75%	84%	49%
25	University of Utah (Eccles)	74	3.0	119	$58,800	GMAT or GRE	3.4	71%	100%	53%	94%	N/A
25	Worcester Polytechnic Institute (MA)	74	N/A	169	$69,936	GMAT or GRE	3.2	92%	90%	90%	95%	95%
28	University of North Texas	73	2.6	205	$32,952	GMAT or GRE	3.4	61%	100%	88%	82%	69%
28	University of Wisconsin–Whitewater	73	2.5	329	$22,968	GMAT or GRE	3.3	71%	100%	100%	94%	79%
30	Oklahoma State University (Spears)	72	3.0	285	$12,946	GMAT or GRE	3.2	82%	96%	100%	82%	56%
30	U. of South Florida–St. Petersburg (Tiedemann)	72	2.4	296	$32,664	GMAT or GRE	3.3	48%	100%	78%	89%	77%
30	University of Tennessee–Martin	72	2.4	89	N/A	GMAT or GRE	3.1	92%	100%	100%	89%	62%
33	SUNY–Oswego	71	2.4	198	$36,585	GMAT	3.4	78%	88%	88%	89%	71%
33	University of Arizona (Eller)	71	3.3	273	$18,000	GMAT	3.4	85%	75%	55%	74%	92%
33	University of Nevada–Reno	71	2.4	66	$30,000	GMAT or GRE	3.0	100%	82%	91%	82%	96%
36	Clarkson University (NY)	70	2.3	230	$54,624	GMAT or GRE	3.4	45%	86%	61%	88%	79%
36	Hofstra University (Zarb) (NY)	70	2.6	47	N/A	N/A	3.1	75%	100%	100%	81%	91%
36	Kansas State University	70	2.9	81	$32,500	GMAT	3.4	97%	100%	100%	88%	N/A
36	Rochester Institute of Technology (NY)	70	3.0	39	N/A	None	3.2	74%	83%	75%	100%	N/A
36	University of North Dakota	70	2.4	98	$19,152	GMAT or GRE	3.3	79%	100%	86%	100%	64%
36	West Texas A&M University	70	2.0	1,005	$16,035	None	3.6	63%	98%	88%	90%	87%
42	Colorado State University	69	3.2	838	N/A	None	3.1	86%	83%	90%	88%	64%
42	Florida Atlantic University	69	2.4	224	$32,000	None	3.3	68%	100%	30%	88%	N/A
42	Georgia College & State University (Bunting)	69	2.4	59	$22,170	GMAT or GRE	3.1	91%	100%	100%	93%	88%
42	Syracuse University (Whitman) (NY)	69	3.3	1,102	$81,000	N/A	3.1	77%	89%	37%	92%	68%
42	University of Nebraska–Lincoln	69	3.1	389	$30,240	GMAT or GRE	3.4	86%	90%	76%	84%	44%
47	Georgia Southern University	68	2.4	140	$13,302	GMAT or GRE	2.8	92%	100%	100%	92%	N/A
47	Stevens Institute of Technology (NJ)	68	2.3	88	$68,988	GMAT or GRE	3.1	74%	95%	50%	89%	N/A
47	University of Massachusetts–Lowell	68	2.6	564	$19,200	GMAT or GRE	3.5	92%	83%	76%	94%	55%
47	West Virginia University	68	2.6	86	$47,904	GMAT or GRE	3.1	93%	83%	70%	98%	87%
51	Boise State University (ID)	67	2.4	209	$36,750	GMAT or GRE	3.4	76%	90%	90%	97%	83%
51	Louisiana State U.–Baton Rouge (Ourso)	67	2.8	137	$42,462	None	3.3	55%	N/A	N/A	N/A	94%
51	Missouri University of Science & Technology	67	2.0	83	$43,200	GMAT or GRE	3.0	91%	94%	81%	79%	100%
54	Central Michigan University	66	2.4	241	N/A	GMAT	3.3	34%	94%	75%	84%	72%
54	Columbus State University (Turner) (GA)	66	2.1	23	$22,170	GMAT or GRE	3.0	84%	100%	100%	89%	92%
54	Creighton University (NE)	66	2.7	71	$36,300	GMAT or GRE	3.3	56%	89%	84%	100%	N/A
54	Florida International University	66	2.5	650	$42,000	None	3.3	62%	97%	48%	88%	81%
54	George Washington University (DC)	66	3.2	403	N/A	GMAT or GRE	3.1	63%	100%	80%	91%	68%
54	Southern Illinois University–Carbondale	66	2.6	122	$35,868	GMAT or GRE	3.1	80%	100%	90%	87%	86%
54	University of Colorado–Colorado Springs	66	2.7	108	N/A	N/A	3.3	78%	100%	100%	72%	N/A
61	Drexel University (LeBow) (PA)	65	2.7	190	$64,005	GMAT or GRE	3.2	92%	96%	61%	95%	89%
61	Mercer University–Atlanta (Stetson) (GA)	65	2.2	78	$26,640	GMAT or GRE	3.2	57%	100%	90%	95%	N/A
61	Quinnipiac University (CT)	65	N/A	323	$42,550	GMAT or GRE	3.2	63%	100%	91%	71%	63%
61	Rutgers University–Camden (NJ)	65	2.9	208	$52,752	GMAT or GRE	3.2	66%	89%	33%	80%	N/A
61	University of Cincinnati (OH)	65	2.9	218	$31,198	GMAT or GRE	3.3	76%	93%	71%	95%	42%
61	University of Kansas	65	3.0	234	$35,700	GMAT or GRE	3.2	73%	91%	64%	70%	N/A
61	Villanova University (PA)	65	N/A	243	$64,800	GMAT or GRE	3.2	75%	100%	100%	91%	N/A
68	Old Dominion University (VA)	64	2.6	61	$21,520	GMAT or GRE	3.4	63%	88%	92%	62%	N/A
68	Samford University (Brock) (AL)	64	2.2	123	$39,000	GMAT or GRE	3.3	55%	100%	100%	97%	69%
68	Tennessee Technological University	64	2.1	282	$36,420	GMAT or GRE	3.3	54%	100%	83%	88%	83%
68	University of Michigan–Dearborn	64	2.7	117	N/A	GMAT or GRE	3.3	44%	100%	74%	87%	33%
72	Cleveland State University (Ahuja) (OH)	63	2.2	26	$35,000	GMAT or GRE	2.9	79%	92%	83%	86%	68%

Rank	School	Overall score	Average peer assessment score (5.0=highest)	'17 total enrollment	'17-'18 total program cost[1]	Entrance test required	'17 average undergrad GPA	'17 acceptance rate	'17 full-time faculty with terminal degree	'17 tenured or tenure-track faculty[2]	'17 retention rate	'17 three-year graduation rate
72	Longwood University (VA)	63	1.7	27	$42,588	GMAT or GRE	3.4	88%	100%	91%	100%	N/A
72	Robert Morris University (PA)	63	1.8	87	N/A	GMAT	3.3	100%	100%	93%	87%	82%
72	Western Kentucky University (Ford)	63	2.3	92	$21,210	GMAT	3.2	96%	100%	90%	61%	79%
76	Baylor University (Hankamer) (TX)	62	3.1	148	$24,648	None	3.0	69%	86%	86%	82%	77%
76	Marist College (NY)	62	2.2	228	$28,800	GMAT or GRE	3.4	42%	93%	87%	88%	47%
76	Northeastern University (MA)	62	3.1	709	$78,000	None	3.2	88%	91%	77%	74%	50%
76	Portland State University (OR)	62	2.6	119	$41,904	N/A	3.2	75%	75%	75%	N/A	81%
76	Queens University of Charlotte (McColl) (NC)	62	1.9	95	$39,780	None	3.0	85%	93%	100%	60%	N/A
76	University of Miami (FL)	62	3.1	45	$82,320	GMAT	3.1	55%	100%	100%	N/A	N/A
76	University of West Georgia	62	2.2	115	N/A	GMAT or GRE	3.0	90%	100%	100%	95%	91%
83	Ferris State University (MI)	61	1.7	116	$27,072	GMAT or GRE	3.6	34%	93%	100%	87%	70%
83	Southern Utah University	61	1.8	66	$15,505	GMAT or GRE	3.3	83%	89%	89%	73%	95%
85	Southeast Missouri State U. (Harrison)	60	1.9	74	N/A	GMAT or GRE	3.0	100%	95%	91%	79%	62%
85	University of New Hampshire	60	2.4	80	$42,240	GMAT	3.2	94%	88%	82%	96%	42%
85	University of Tennessee–Chattanooga	60	2.6	193	$28,944	GMAT or GRE	3.4	80%	100%	100%	70%	N/A
85	West Chester University of Pennsylvania	60	1.6	399	$15,300	GMAT or GRE	3.3	91%	100%	68%	99%	83%
89	Ohio University	59	2.7	815	$35,805	None	3.1	81%	84%	84%	96%	77%
89	University of Memphis (Fogelman) (TN)	59	2.7	110	$27,753	GMAT or GRE	3.3	95%	92%	92%	N/A	62%
91	East Carolina University (NC)	58	2.3	840	$33,078	GMAT or GRE	3.2	77%	100%	100%	73%	49%
91	St. Joseph's University (Haub) (PA)	58	2.6	374	N/A	GMAT or GRE	3.3	82%	86%	83%	84%	48%
93	New Jersey Institute of Technology	57	2.4	102	N/A	None	3.1	70%	91%	91%	63%	43%
93	U. of Massachusetts–Dartmouth (Charlton)	57	2.8	68	N/A	GMAT	2.8	81%	100%	100%	82%	N/A
93	University of South Dakota	57	2.2	267	$14,660	GMAT	3.3	95%	100%	53%	78%	38%
96	California State University–San Bernardino	56	2.2	135	$36,000	None	3.1	90%	94%	94%	86%	67%
96	DeSales University (PA)	56	1.4	625	N/A	None	3.4	87%	100%	100%	93%	60%
96	Texas A&M International University	56	N/A	99	$14,760	N/A	3.1	100%	100%	83%	92%	83%
96	University of Baltimore (MD)	56	2.2	512	$39,552	GMAT or GRE	3.3	89%	91%	83%	90%	57%
100	American University (Kogod) (DC)	55	2.7	365	$78,816	None	2.9	83%	76%	53%	76%	N/A
100	Babson College (MA)	55	N/A	449	$87,025	None	3.0	90%	90%	62%	98%	93%
100	California Baptist University	55	1.8	91	$23,832	None	3.2	92%	100%	100%	75%	71%
100	Clarion University of Pennsylvania	55	1.7	140	$16,200	GMAT or GRE	3.3	92%	100%	100%	77%	49%
100	Sam Houston State University (TX)	55	2.0	291	$10,800	GMAT	3.3	82%	100%	79%	75%	42%
100	University of Louisiana–Monroe	55	1.9	67	$17,500	GMAT or GRE	3.2	70%	91%	91%	65%	24%
106	Baldwin Wallace University (OH)	54	1.5	52	N/A	GMAT	3.2	65%	90%	80%	100%	79%
106	Fayetteville State University (NC)	54	1.8	248	$16,478	N/A	3.4	72%	100%	93%	80%	40%
108	Embry-Riddle Aeronautical U.–Worldwide (FL)	52	2.1	974	N/A	None	3.2	95%	100%	56%	84%	35%
108	Florida Institute of Technology	52	1.9	968	N/A	None	3.2	42%	100%	0%	82%	50%
108	Fort Hays State University (KS)	52	1.9	120	$12,527	GMAT or GRE	3.2	55%	87%	53%	84%	57%
108	Frostburg State University (MD)	52	2.0	258	$19,116	N/A	3.4	76%	100%	100%	10%	38%
108	Texas A & M University-Central Texas	52	N/A	210	$23,400	None	3.3	97%	100%	40%	19%	100%
108	Texas A&M University–Kingsville	52	2.1	90	$17,831	GMAT or GRE	3.1	87%	100%	100%	74%	71%
108	University of Scranton (PA)	52	2.1	453	$34,740	None	3.1	95%	93%	93%	89%	50%
108	University of Texas–Tyler	52	1.8	1,504	$31,740	GMAT or GRE	3.2	84%	100%	100%	87%	N/A
116	Campbellsville University (KY)	51	1.3	83	$18,900	GMAT or GRE	3.2	49%	100%	100%	88%	58%
116	Shippensburg U. of Pennsylvania (Grove)	51	1.9	172	$18,840	None	3.2	88%	100%	100%	93%	59%
116	St. Mary's College of California	51	1.9	83	$67,000	None	3.0	88%	91%	91%	26%	N/A
116	University of Bridgeport (CT)	51	1.9	145	N/A	None	3.2	60%	100%	100%	81%	N/A
116	University of North Alabama	51	2.0	819	$14,450	N/A	3.1	88%	94%	89%	80%	68%
116	University of St. Francis (IL)	51	1.6	150	N/A	None	3.3	43%	75%	75%	77%	63%
122	Northwood University (MI)	50	N/A	150	$37,080	None	3.1	72%	100%	0%	87%	N/A
122	Regent University (VA)	50	1.6	512	$27,300	None	3.2	32%	100%	100%	77%	50%
122	University of Houston–Clear Lake (TX)	50	2.3	69	$34,728	GMAT	N/A	41%	100%	100%	65%	42%
125	Monroe College (NY)	49	1.3	152	$29,376	None	3.2	57%	86%	0%	88%	65%
125	SUNY Polytechnic Institute	49	2.3	112	$48,768	GMAT or GRE	N/A	95%	89%	89%	74%	89%

AT UNC–CHAPEL HILL, WHOSE ONLINE
MBA PROGRAM RANKS NO. 4.

Rank	School	Overall score	Average peer assessment score (5.0=highest)	'17 total enrollment	'17-'18 total program cost[1]	Entrance test required	'17 average undergrad GPA	'17 acceptance rate	'17 full-time faculty with terminal degree	'17 tenured or tenure-track faculty[2]	'17 retention rate	'17 three-year graduation rate
125	Utica College (NY)	49	1.9	251	N/A	None	3.5	88%	100%	100%	81%	68%
128	Fitchburg State University (MA)	48	1.6	173	$11,310	None	3.2	100%	80%	100%	93%	88%
128	New England Col. of Business and Finance (MA)	48	1.4	166	$36,420	None	3.3	92%	83%	0%	86%	68%
128	Wright State University (Soin) (OH)	48	2.3	667	$50,732	None	3.2	84%	83%	83%	89%	N/A
131	Ashland University (OH)	47	1.3	270	$24,450	None	3.1	87%	75%	88%	93%	100%
131	Emporia State University (KS)	47	1.9	40	$16,920	GMAT or GRE	3.5	93%	100%	100%	N/A	N/A
131	Louisiana Tech University (LA)	47	2.2	39	N/A	GMAT or GRE	3.2	55%	100%	100%	86%	N/A
131	Missouri State University (MO)	47	2.2	143	N/A	GMAT or GRE	3.3	85%	92%	92%	N/A	N/A
131	University of Maine	47	2.3	38	$16,080	GMAT or GRE	N/A	72%	100%	78%	18%	N/A
136	Lindenwood University (MO)	46	1.3	160	$19,500	None	3.3	67%	91%	0%	78%	43%
136	North Park University (IL)	46	1.4	95	$41,410	None	3.2	93%	80%	80%	70%	63%
136	University of Southern Mississippi	46	N/A	52	$18,579	GMAT or GRE	3.3	96%	100%	91%	88%	N/A
139	Liberty University (VA)	45	1.5	4,078	N/A	None	3.2	31%	100%	0%	72%	41%
139	Post University (CT)	45	1.3	412	$26,280	None	3.1	50%	100%	0%	82%	34%
139	Texas A&M University–Commerce	45	2.1	1,252	$18,510	None	2.7	61%	90%	78%	80%	51%
139	Wichita State University (Barton) (KS)	45	N/A	223	N/A	GMAT or GRE	3.4	72%	94%	81%	N/A	N/A
143	Concordia University–St. Paul (MN)	44	1.8	423	$27,500	None	N/A	69%	50%	67%	90%	87%
143	McKendree University (IL)	44	1.3	151	$17,820	None	N/A	60%	75%	75%	98%	89%
143	Valdosta State University (Langdale) (GA)	44	2.3	15	$22,170	GMAT or GRE	N/A	100%	N/A	N/A	76%	N/A
146	Brenau University (GA)	43	1.5	486	$30,825	None	3.1	56%	89%	0%	79%	60%
146	Franklin Pierce University (NH)	43	N/A	224	$25,935	None	3.2	100%	89%	0%	77%	51%
146	University of La Verne (CA)	43	1.5	187	N/A	None	3.3	51%	87%	60%	92%	58%
146	University of the Cumberlands (KY)	43	1.5	227	N/A	None	3.6	77%	100%	43%	90%	88%
150	California State University–Dominguez Hills	42	1.8	47	$13,800	GMAT or GRE	3.1	60%	93%	86%	N/A	67%
150	Cornerstone University (MI)	42	1.2	72	$19,000	None	3.2	51%	50%	50%	82%	62%
150	Eastern Illinois University (IL)	42	2.0	24	$19,800	None	3.2	100%	100%	100%	N/A	N/A
150	Herzing University (WI)	42	1.3	214	$26,130	None	3.2	89%	100%	0%	94%	59%
150	University of Alabama–Birmingham	42	N/A	27	$39,168	N/A	3.4	75%	83%	72%	N/A	N/A
150	University of Texas of the Permian Basin	42	1.8	63	$10,739	GMAT	N/A	53%	100%	100%	58%	6%
156	Dakota State University (SD)	41	1.8	N/A	N/A	GMAT or GRE	3.3	100%	83%	83%	100%	N/A
156	Dakota Wesleyan University (SD)	41	1.5	43	N/A	None	3.2	68%	67%	67%	72%	85%
156	Maryville University of St. Louis (MO)	41	1.5	209	N/A	None	N/A	94%	75%	75%	75%	N/A
156	Minnesota State University– Moorhead	41	N/A	34	$28,786	GMAT	N/A	100%	92%	100%	93%	N/A
156	National University (CA)	41	1.4	728	N/A	None	3.0	100%	90%	0%	79%	60%
156	Park University (MO)	41	1.5	721	$20,592	None	3.3	93%	79%	100%	95%	N/A
156	Schreiner University (TX)	41	N/A	34	N/A	N/A	3.0	100%	100%	100%	N/A	N/A
156	William Woods University (MO)	41	1.2	104	N/A	None	3.4	100%	100%	100%	90%	N/A
164	Brandman University (CA)	40	1.5	186	$30,720	None	3.5	99%	78%	0%	82%	64%
164	California State University–Stanislaus	40	1.8	24	N/A	GMAT or GRE	N/A	71%	100%	100%	N/A	N/A
164	Cameron University (OK)	40	1.5	128	$13,530	GMAT or GRE	3.6	66%	100%	100%	65%	18%
164	Cedarville University (OH)	40	1.2	32	$21,456	None	3.3	79%	80%	70%	94%	58%
164	Rowan University (Rohrer) (NJ)	40	2.0	52	N/A	GMAT or GRE	3.2	52%	100%	0%	92%	N/A
164	Stetson University (FL)	40	2.2	25	$24,150	None	3.5	100%	100%	100%	100%	53%
164	Suffolk University (Sawyer) (MA)	40	N/A	38	N/A	N/A	3.2	85%	100%	67%	100%	29%
164	University of Central Missouri (Harmon)	40	N/A	17	$11,228	GMAT or GRE	3.3	64%	91%	91%	N/A	N/A
172	City University of Seattle (WA)	39	1.4	1,169	$33,024	None	N/A	75%	42%	0%	86%	N/A
172	Colorado Technical University	39	1.7	2,300	$28,080	None	N/A	100%	100%	0%	93%	65%
172	King University (TN)	39	N/A	159	$21,780	None	N/A	52%	100%	0%	84%	78%
172	Lawrence Technological University (MI)	39	1.6	166	N/A	None	2.9	60%	100%	55%	76%	40%
172	Ohio Dominican University	39	1.4	230	$21,600	None	3.1	93%	78%	44%	N/A	73%
172	Troy University (AL)	39	1.9	124	$17,784	GMAT or GRE	3.1	60%	71%	50%	N/A	N/A
172	Walsh University (OH)	39	1.5	200	N/A	GMAT	3.3	78%	90%	80%	49%	N/A
179	California University of Pennsylvania	38	1.6	110	$27,000	None	N/A	65%	53%	100%	71%	N/A
179	DeVry University (IL)	38	1.3	2,283	$36,768	None	3.3	90%	78%	0%	87%	33%

Rank	School	Overall score	Average peer assessment score (5.0=highest)	'17 total enrollment	'17-'18 total program cost[1]	Entrance test required	'17 average undergrad GPA	'17 acceptance rate	'17 full-time faculty with terminal degree	'17 tenured or tenure-track faculty[2]	'17 retention rate	'17 three-year graduation rate
179	Texas Southern University (Jones)	38	2.0	55	N/A	None	2.9	75%	100%	70%	N/A	N/A
182	Columbia College (MO)	37	1.4	806	N/A	None	3.3	93%	67%	100%	80%	58%
182	Webster University (MO)	37	1.6	603	N/A	None	3.0	92%	100%	100%	66%	41%
184	Concordia University Wisconsin	36	1.8	175	$27,261	None	N/A	51%	100%	0%	N/A	N/A
184	Johnson and Wales University (RI)	36	1.7	453	N/A	None	N/A	66%	69%	0%	70%	63%
184	Lynchburg College (VA)	36	1.5	33	N/A	GMAT or GRE	3.2	65%	N/A	N/A	5%	N/A
184	New England College (NH)	36	1.4	170	$23,800	None	3.2	99%	N/A	N/A	98%	82%
184	University of Alaska–Fairbanks	36	2.2	N/A	$18,300	N/A	N/A	N/A	67%	50%	N/A	N/A
189	Andrews University (MI)	35	1.4	35	$17,721	GMAT	3.0	86%	100%	100%	83%	N/A
189	Concordia University Chicago (IL)	35	1.8	218	$25,560	None	N/A	98%	60%	43%	85%	24%
189	Delaware Valley College (PA)	35	N/A	115	N/A	None	3.3	98%	N/A	N/A	87%	72%
189	Lynn University (FL)	35	1.5	604	$26,640	None	N/A	85%	65%	0%	89%	83%
189	University of the Incarnate Word (TX)	35	1.4	319	$27,490	None	N/A	96%	100%	0%	74%	62%
189	Upper Iowa University	35	1.5	471	$19,260	None	N/A	56%	60%	80%	91%	60%
189	Warner University (FL)	35	N/A	N/A	$20,016	N/A	N/A	N/A	100%	0%	84%	76%
196	Lamar University (TX)	34	1.7	107	$19,584	GMAT	3.2	87%	88%	88%	N/A	N/A
196	Southwestern College (KS)	34	1.3	49	N/A	None	N/A	68%	N/A	N/A	85%	53%
196	University of Hartford (Barney) (CT)	34	N/A	349	$35,445	N/A	3.3	67%	89%	0%	N/A	N/A
199	Abilene Christian University (TX)	33	1.7	123	$25,200	None	3.7	96%	100%	50%	10%	N/A
199	Angelo State University (TX)	33	1.4	136	$18,810	GMAT or GRE	3.1	95%	100%	90%	85%	N/A
199	Dallas Baptist University (TX)	33	1.8	580	$32,616	GMAT	N/A	49%	100%	0%	N/A	N/A
199	Jacksonville State University (AL)	33	1.8	79	$11,460	GMAT	3.3	50%	100%	100%	83%	45%
199	Marymount University (VA)	33	N/A	132	N/A	GMAT or GRE	3.1	93%	86%	93%	N/A	N/A
199	Westminster College (UT)	33	1.5	52	$54,600	None	N/A	N/A	100%	0%	N/A	75%

School	Average peer assessment score (5.0=highest)	'17 total enrollment	'17-'18 total program cost[1]	Entrance test required	'17 average undergrad GPA	'17 acceptance rate	'17 full-time faculty with terminal degree	'17 tenured or tenure-track faculty[2]	'17 retention rate	'17 three-year graduation rate
MBA PROGRAMS RANKED 205 THROUGH 267 ARE LISTED HERE ALPHABETICALLY										
Albertus Magnus College (CT)	1.3	201	N/A	None	N/A	N/A	100%	9%	N/A	N/A
Alliant International University (CA)	1.1	22	N/A	None	N/A	N/A	N/A	N/A	N/A	N/A
American InterContinental University (IL)	1.1	2,043	$27,936	None	N/A	100%	100%	0%	94%	54%
Baker University (KS)	1.4	222	$26,620	None	N/A	N/A	100%	100%	N/A	N/A
Bay Path University (MA)	N/A	N/A	N/A	N/A	N/A	N/A	N/A	N/A	N/A	N/A
Belhaven University (MS)	1.5	326	$20,340	None	N/A	50%	100%	38%	85%	43%
Bethel University (TN)	1.6	877	$21,420	None	N/A	80%	100%	0%	N/A	73%
Bryan College (TN)	1.3	92	$19,620	None	N/A	N/A	100%	0%	N/A	N/A
Cardinal Stritch University (WI)	N/A	N/A	$23,400	None	N/A	N/A	N/A	N/A	N/A	N/A
Charleston Southern University (SC)	1.5	50	$20,625	None	N/A	76%	N/A	N/A	N/A	N/A
Chatham University (PA)	N/A	18	N/A	None	3.1	100%	100%	0%	N/A	N/A
Colorado Christian University	N/A	139	$21,645	None	N/A	N/A	N/A	N/A	N/A	N/A
Edgewood College (WI)	1.4	N/A	N/A	GMAT or GRE	N/A	N/A	100%	100%	N/A	N/A
Florida A&M University	2.2	15	N/A	None	N/A	N/A	N/A	N/A	N/A	N/A
Fontbonne University (MO)	1.3	N/A	$26,856	None	N/A	N/A	75%	75%	N/A	N/A
Friends University (KS)	1.3	153	$20,430	None	N/A	78%	50%	100%	74%	N/A
Governors State University (IL)	N/A	12	N/A	N/A	N/A	47%	86%	93%	N/A	N/A
Greenville University (IL)	1.3	59	N/A	None	N/A	N/A	100%	100%	N/A	N/A
Husson University (ME)	1.2	82	$16,704	None	N/A	79%	67%	0%	100%	N/A
Indiana Institute of Technology	1.7	389	N/A	None	N/A	99%	N/A	N/A	N/A	N/A
Jackson State University (MS)	1.9	N/A	N/A	GMAT or GRE	N/A	N/A	100%	100%	N/A	N/A
Keiser University (FL)	N/A	406	N/A	N/A	N/A	N/A	100%	0%	N/A	75%
Kettering University (MI)	1.7	N/A	$42,720	None	N/A	N/A	0%	50%	45%	N/A
Lasell College (MA)	1.2	25	$21,600	None	N/A	95%	67%	0%	64%	N/A

School	Average peer assessment score (5.0=highest)	'17 total enrollment	'17-'18 total program cost[1]	Entrance test required	'17 average undergrad GPA	'17 acceptance rate	'17 full-time faculty with terminal degree	'17 tenured or tenure-track faculty[2]	'17 retention rate	'17 three-year graduation rate
MBA PROGRAMS RANKED 205 THROUGH 267 ARE LISTED HERE ALPHABETICALLY CONTINUED										
Louisiana State University–Shreveport	2.1	1,175	$12,474	N/A	N/A	90%	N/A	N/A	N/A	N/A
Madonna University (MI)	1.1	30	N/A	None	N/A	100%	80%	0%	N/A	65%
Maharishi University of Management (IA)	N/A	N/A	N/A	None	N/A	N/A	100%	100%	N/A	N/A
McNeese State University (Burton) (LA)	1.8	12	N/A	GMAT or GRE	N/A	N/A	82%	0%	N/A	N/A
Mercy College (NY)	1.5	39	N/A	None	N/A	27%	N/A	N/A	N/A	N/A
Mississippi College	N/A	N/A	$17,640	GMAT	N/A	N/A	N/A	N/A	N/A	N/A
Montclair State University (NJ)	2.0	161	$10,383	N/A	N/A	65%	N/A	N/A	N/A	N/A
New Mexico State University	N/A	63	$30,618	N/A	N/A	100%	90%	85%	N/A	N/A
North Greenville University (SC)	1.4	N/A	$18,900	None	N/A	N/A	N/A	N/A	N/A	N/A
Northcentral University (CA)	1.6	N/A	$28,230	None	N/A	N/A	100%	0%	N/A	N/A
Northwest Christian University (OR)	N/A	116	$23,400	N/A	N/A	N/A	N/A	N/A	N/A	N/A
Northwest Missouri State University	1.8	158	$13,530	GMAT or GRE	N/A	N/A	100%	0%	N/A	N/A
Northwest University (WA)	1.7	26	$29,406	None	N/A	79%	50%	100%	75%	N/A
Nova Southeastern University (FL)	N/A	1,493	$37,785	GMAT or GRE	N/A	91%	100%	0%	N/A	N/A
Olivet Nazarene University (IL)	N/A	121	N/A	None	N/A	N/A	N/A	N/A	N/A	N/A
Point Loma Nazarene University (CA)	1.6	11	$34,650	GMAT or GRE	N/A	100%	100%	100%	N/A	N/A
Point Park University (PA)	1.2	78	N/A	None	N/A	88%	0%	0%	N/A	N/A
Regis University (CO)	1.6	932	N/A	None	N/A	91%	25%	0%	91%	58%
Salisbury University (MD)	1.8	20	N/A	GMAT or GRE	N/A	N/A	100%	90%	69%	N/A
Southeastern University (FL)	N/A	N/A	N/A	None	N/A	N/A	N/A	N/A	N/A	N/A
Southern Arkansas University	1.6	N/A	N/A	GMAT or GRE	N/A	N/A	100%	100%	N/A	N/A
St. Bonaventure University (NY)	1.9	56	$30,786	GMAT or GRE	N/A	88%	67%	100%	N/A	N/A
St. Joseph's College New York	1.9	63	$12,854	N/A	N/A	100%	50%	13%	80%	N/A
Tabor College (KS)	1.2	28	$20,476	None	N/A	81%	N/A	N/A	N/A	N/A
Tarleton State University (TX)	1.5	112	N/A	GMAT or GRE	N/A	56%	0%	100%	N/A	N/A
The Citadel (SC)	2.2	N/A	N/A	GMAT or GRE	N/A	N/A	N/A	N/A	N/A	N/A
University of Central Arkansas	1.8	138	N/A	GMAT or GRE	N/A	59%	100%	100%	N/A	N/A
University of Dallas (TX)	N/A	N/A	$37,500	N/A	3.1	N/A	N/A	N/A	N/A	N/A
University of Findlay (OH)	N/A	373	$21,780	None	3.3	88%	100%	91%	N/A	N/A
University of North Carolina–Pembroke	1.9	70	N/A	N/A	N/A	100%	100%	100%	N/A	N/A
University of Sioux Falls (SD)	1.6	21	$13,680	None	3.2	100%	67%	83%	N/A	N/A
University of Southern Indiana	1.8	293	$12,900	GMAT or GRE	3.2	86%	100%	100%	N/A	N/A
University of St. Mary (KS)	1.5	317	$22,140	None	N/A	97%	40%	0%	82%	65%
University of Texas–Rio Grande Valley	N/A	206	N/A	GMAT or GRE	N/A	N/A	N/A	N/A	N/A	N/A
Waynesburg University (PA)	N/A	220	$23,760	N/A	3.1	60%	N/A	N/A	N/A	N/A
Western Illinois University	2.1	N/A	N/A	GMAT or GRE	N/A	N/A	100%	0%	N/A	N/A
Western New England University (MA)	1.7	85	$29,644	GMAT or GRE	N/A	66%	76%	76%	N/A	N/A
Widener University (PA)	1.7	53	N/A	N/A	N/A	87%	N/A	N/A	N/A	N/A
Wilmington University (DE)	N/A	724	N/A	N/A	N/A	100%	0%	0%	N/A	N/A

Best Online Master's Programs

Rank	School	Overall score	Average peer assessment score (5.0=highest)	'17 total enrollment	'17-'18 total program cost[1]	Entrance test required	'17 average undergrad GPA	'17 acceptance rate	'17 full-time faculty with terminal degree	'17 tenured or tenure-track faculty[2]	'17 retention rate	'17 three-year graduation rate
1	Villanova University (PA)	100	3.2	311	$43,200	None	3.3	82%	100%	90%	91%	100%
2	Arizona State University (Carey)	98	3.9	206	N/A	GMAT or GRE	3.3	72%	100%	63%	97%	94%
2	Indiana University–Bloomington (Kelley)	98	4.2	216	$39,900	GMAT or GRE	3.2	69%	81%	64%	99%	70%
4	University of Texas–Dallas	97	3.3	506	$56,538	GMAT or GRE	3.4	44%	72%	40%	84%	64%
5	Pennsylvania State University–World Campus	94	3.2	637	$31,650	GMAT or GRE	3.4	78%	93%	60%	95%	81%

Rank	School	Overall score	Average peer assessment score (5.0=highest)	'17 total enrollment	'17-'18 total program cost[1]	Entrance test required	'17 average undergrad GPA	'17 acceptance rate	'17 full-time faculty with terminal degree	'17 tenured or tenure-track faculty[2]	'17 retention rate	'17 three-year graduation rate
6	Auburn University (Harbert) (AL)	90	3.0	150	$26,550	GMAT or GRE	3.4	67%	100%	100%	89%	93%
6	Florida State University	90	3.1	126	$26,737	GMAT or GRE	3.3	84%	88%	71%	87%	81%
6	University of Connecticut	90	3.3	238	$24,750	GRE	3.5	90%	44%	44%	95%	88%
9	Boston University (MA)	89	3.4	758	$34,400	None	3.3	89%	100%	0%	86%	63%
9	California State U.–Fullerton (Mihaylo)	89	2.5	50	$22,920	GMAT or GRE	3.2	66%	100%	100%	100%	84%
9	Georgetown University (McDonough) (DC)	89	3.5	86	$73,312	GMAT or GRE	3.3	31%	100%	73%	N/A	82%
12	Temple University (Fox) (PA)	88	3.3	112	$33,420	GMAT or GRE	3.2	58%	71%	64%	100%	N/A
13	Georgia College & State U. (Bunting) (GA)	87	2.3	102	$14,010	GMAT or GRE	3.2	89%	100%	88%	87%	N/A
13	University of Alabama (Manderson)	87	2.3	174	N/A	GMAT or GRE	3.4	82%	96%	92%	100%	94%
13	University of Southern California (Marshall)	87	3.6	132	N/A	None	3.3	70%	79%	100%	97%	83%
16	Missouri University of Science & Technology	84	2.1	67	$36,000	GMAT or GRE	3.0	64%	94%	81%	93%	88%
16	University of San Diego (CA)	84	2.9	68	$51,120	None	3.0	79%	100%	100%	90%	83%
18	West Texas A&M University	83	1.9	200	$17,885	None	3.6	64%	100%	100%	86%	84%
19	George Washington University (DC)	82	3.3	56	$59,580	None	3.1	74%	100%	50%	86%	64%
19	Wright State University (Soin) (OH)	82	2.1	33	N/A	None	2.8	72%	100%	100%	100%	97%
21	Florida International University	81	2.5	134	$35,000	None	3.2	40%	77%	58%	91%	85%
21	Michigan State University (Broad)	81	3.4	534	$32,700	None	3.2	94%	100%	56%	93%	89%
21	Rutgers U.–New Brunswick and Newark	81	2.8	295	$36,000	None	3.2	75%	91%	73%	90%	51%
21	University of Georgia (Terry)	81	3.3	26	$26,400	GMAT or GRE	3.0	80%	100%	18%	90%	N/A
25	Creighton University (NE)	80	2.6	121	$36,000	GMAT or GRE	3.2	70%	88%	88%	91%	69%
26	Ferris State University (MI)	79	N/A	72	$27,918	GMAT or GRE	3.4	32%	71%	86%	73%	96%
26	St. Mary's College of California	79	1.9	90	$35,000	GMAT or GRE	3.1	92%	95%	90%	80%	89%
28	Bentley University (MA)	78	2.8	237	$44,450	GMAT or GRE	3.4	84%	78%	51%	97%	82%
28	Stevens Institute of Technology (NJ)	78	2.5	184	$51,741	GMAT or GRE	3.3	66%	97%	45%	93%	37%
30	Oklahoma City University	77	1.8	199	$17,700	None	3.0	91%	100%	100%	96%	N/A
30	Portland State University (OR)	77	2.5	34	$39,936	None	3.2	67%	63%	63%	N/A	74%
30	University of Alabama–Birmingham	77	2.5	100	$32,640	GMAT or GRE	3.1	92%	67%	67%	83%	N/A
30	University of Illinois–Springfield	77	2.6	170	N/A	GMAT or GRE	3.2	85%	100%	100%	86%	45%
30	University of Massachusetts–Lowell	77	2.4	87	$19,200	GMAT or GRE	3.3	90%	92%	83%	93%	N/A
35	Quinnipiac University (CT)	76	2.5	455	$30,525	None	3.2	88%	100%	100%	86%	78%
36	American University (Kogod) (DC)	75	2.9	132	$54,186	None	3.0	79%	79%	50%	86%	N/A
36	St. Joseph's University (Haub) (PA)	75	2.4	311	N/A	GMAT or GRE	3.1	76%	85%	81%	78%	77%
36	U. of Massachusetts–Amherst (Isenberg)	75	2.9	169	$24,000	GMAT or GRE	3.5	80%	50%	0%	95%	N/A
36	University of North Dakota	75	2.3	51	$14,112	GMAT or GRE	3.1	58%	100%	100%	68%	45%
40	Colorado State University (CO)	74	2.9	171	N/A	GMAT or GRE	3.2	86%	100%	83%	88%	41%
40	University of Miami (FL)	74	2.9	130	$62,720	GMAT or GRE	3.1	61%	85%	65%	N/A	N/A
42	Oklahoma State University (Spears)	73	2.9	85	$10,172	GMAT or GRE	3.1	94%	93%	71%	76%	39%
43	Florida Atlantic University	72	2.1	584	$12,800	None	3.4	68%	100%	47%	90%	56%
43	University of Denver (Daniels) (CO)	72	2.8	58	$63,360	None	3.0	100%	100%	86%	92%	59%
45	Marymount University (VA)	71	1.7	93	N/A	None	3.3	98%	100%	100%	72%	85%
45	St. Johns University (Tobin) (NY)	71	2.4	40	N/A	GMAT or GRE	3.3	92%	100%	100%	92%	56%
45	University of South Dakota	71	2.2	103	$13,327	GRE	3.4	69%	83%	83%	78%	36%
48	Georgia Southern University	70	2.2	96	N/A	GMAT or GRE	3.2	73%	100%	100%	82%	67%
48	University of Cincinnati (OH)	70	2.6	44	$24,630	GMAT or GRE	3.4	88%	50%	0%	84%	65%
50	Southern Utah University	69	1.6	90	$14,350	GMAT or GRE	3.5	98%	57%	57%	58%	98%
51	Marist College (NY)	68	1.8	299	$33,600	GMAT	3.2	42%	100%	78%	87%	68%
51	New England Col. of Business and Finance (MA)	68	1.8	170	$30,350	None	3.2	85%	83%	0%	85%	85%
51	Northeastern University (MA)	68	2.9	174	$46,800	None	3.3	90%	93%	60%	64%	42%
51	Stetson University (FL)	68	1.9	23	$25,820	GMAT or GRE	3.4	62%	100%	100%	100%	78%
55	Rider University (NJ)	67	1.7	31	N/A	N/A	3.3	65%	100%	100%	60%	89%
56	George Mason University (VA)	66	2.7	31	N/A	N/A	3.4	89%	71%	57%	87%	N/A
56	Syracuse University (Whitman) (NY)	66	3.2	124	$51,000	N/A	3.2	75%	94%	33%	91%	N/A
56	University of St. Francis (IL)	66	1.4	84	N/A	None	3.3	41%	67%	67%	86%	62%
59	Baylor University (Hankamer) (TX)	65	N/A	148	$24,648	None	3.0	69%	86%	86%	82%	77%

Rank	School	Overall score	Average peer assessment score (5.0=highest)	'17 total enrollment	'17-'18 total program cost[1]	Entrance test required	'17 average undergrad GPA	'17 acceptance rate	'17 full-time faculty with terminal degree	'17 tenured or tenure-track faculty[2]	'17 retention rate	'17 three-year graduation rate
59	California State University–Sacramento	65	2.2	50	$22,200	GRE	3.2	77%	100%	78%	N/A	93%
59	Eastern Michigan University	65	1.9	68	$26,028	None	3.1	61%	89%	78%	N/A	69%
59	Western Carolina University (NC)	65	1.9	189	N/A	GMAT or GRE	3.1	96%	100%	100%	70%	56%
63	Frostburg State University (MD)	64	N/A	258	$19,116	N/A	3.4	76%	100%	100%	15%	38%
63	Northern Arizona University	64	N/A	306	$19,800	None	3.2	99%	92%	40%	90%	71%
63	Ohio University	64	N/A	815	$35,805	None	3.1	81%	84%	84%	96%	77%
63	West Virginia University	64	2.1	47	$23,952	GMAT or GRE	3.3	78%	93%	93%	10%	N/A
67	Clarkson University (NY)	63	1.5	23	$40,968	GMAT or GRE	N/A	52%	100%	100%	100%	N/A
67	Embry-Riddle Aeronautical U.–Worldwide (FL)	63	1.8	2,570	N/A	None	3.1	95%	97%	56%	82%	31%
67	Southeast Missouri State U. (Harrison)	63	1.9	37	N/A	GMAT or GRE	3.5	83%	95%	91%	92%	N/A
70	California University of Pennsylvania	62	N/A	118	$27,000	None	3.2	71%	53%	100%	91%	N/A
70	Regent University (VA)	62	1.4	323	$21,450	None	3.1	38%	100%	100%	84%	56%
70	University of Massachusetts–Boston	62	2.9	80	$20,700	None	3.0	88%	75%	50%	82%	45%
73	Saint Vincent College (PA)	61	N/A	34	$23,832	None	3.2	79%	80%	60%	40%	N/A
73	Stony Brook University–SUNY	61	2.7	162	N/A	None	3.3	96%	N/A	N/A	93%	59%
75	Colorado State University–Global Campus	60	2.2	4,687	$18,000	None	3.1	99%	100%	0%	78%	49%
75	Minot State University (ND)	60	1.4	111	N/A	GMAT or GRE	3.3	96%	80%	90%	N/A	75%
75	Robert Morris University (PA)	60	1.8	21	N/A	N/A	3.3	100%	100%	80%	72%	N/A
75	University of Michigan–Dearborn	60	2.6	36	N/A	GMAT or GRE	3.5	39%	100%	74%	93%	27%
79	North Park University (IL)	59	1.2	60	$41,410	None	3.2	96%	60%	60%	75%	71%
79	SUNY Polytechnic Institute	59	2.4	61	N/A	GMAT or GRE	N/A	97%	57%	57%	58%	44%
79	Sam Houston State University (TX)	59	1.9	16	$10,800	GRE	3.1	86%	100%	57%	100%	N/A
79	Texas A&M University–Commerce	59	2.2	1,416	$18,510	None	2.7	60%	88%	78%	83%	60%
83	Post University (CT)	58	1.3	60	$18,750	None	3.4	83%	100%	0%	100%	N/A
83	University of Houston–Clear Lake	58	2.2	46	$34,728	None	N/A	38%	100%	100%	100%	48%
83	University of Scranton (PA)	58	2.3	145	$26,850	None	N/A	100%	100%	100%	89%	N/A
83	University of Tulsa (Collins) (OK)	58	2.3	115	$30,600	GMAT or GRE	3.4	92%	100%	0%	78%	N/A
87	California Baptist University	57	1.6	38	$19,860	None	3.2	88%	67%	100%	88%	N/A
87	Granite State College (NH)	57	1.4	156	$16,800	None	3.5	98%	50%	0%	74%	64%
87	Mississippi State University	57	2.5	18	$13,680	GMAT or GRE	3.5	44%	100%	100%	100%	N/A
90	Florida Institute of Technology	56	1.8	650	N/A	None	3.1	47%	100%	0%	81%	48%
90	New Jersey Institute of Technology	56	2.1	13	N/A	None	3.3	63%	91%	91%	42%	N/A
92	Clarion University of Pennsylvania	54	1.5	19	$16,200	None	3.4	100%	100%	100%	80%	N/A
92	Emporia State University (KS)	54	1.5	47	$16,920	GMAT or GRE	3.3	100%	100%	100%	N/A	N/A
92	Park University (MO)	54	N/A	281	$19,764	None	3.1	100%	100%	50%	85%	N/A
95	Brandman University (CA)	53	1.3	244	$23,040	None	3.5	100%	78%	0%	80%	74%
95	Duquesne U. (Palumbo-Donahue) (PA)	53	1.9	37	$28,020	GMAT or GRE	3.2	91%	100%	63%	N/A	N/A
95	National University (CA)	53	1.3	666	N/A	None	3.0	100%	95%	0%	80%	52%
95	Texas A & M University-Central Texas	53	N/A	51	$23,400	None	3.3	100%	100%	100%	56%	100%
99	Lindenwood University (MO)	52	1.3	18	$18,500	None	3.0	46%	100%	0%	60%	50%
99	Maine Maritime Academy	52	1.8	19	$28,800	GMAT or GRE	3.3	82%	100%	0%	40%	N/A
101	Austin Peay State University (TN)	51	1.5	71	N/A	N/A	3.5	55%	100%	88%	86%	65%
101	Briar Cliff University (IA)	51	N/A	65	N/A	None	N/A	77%	100%	100%	95%	100%
101	Campbellsville University (KY)	51	1.1	37	$15,750	GMAT or GRE	3.1	71%	100%	100%	70%	61%
101	Friends University (KS)	51	1.0	55	$20,430	None	N/A	80%	60%	100%	91%	N/A
105	Missouri State University	50	N/A	29	N/A	GMAT or GRE	3.2	77%	100%	100%	N/A	N/A
106	DeVry University (IL)	49	1.2	2,519	$34,470	None	3.3	89%	81%	0%	88%	37%
106	University of the Incarnate Word (TX)	49	1.5	717	$27,490	None	N/A	98%	100%	0%	83%	72%
108	Colorado Technical University	48	1.6	1,408	$28,080	None	N/A	100%	91%	0%	93%	54%
108	Lasell College (MA)	48	1.4	168	$21,600	None	N/A	90%	80%	0%	76%	64%
108	Liberty University (VA)	48	1.3	4,534	N/A	None	3.1	74%	100%	0%	67%	26%
108	Webster University (MO)	48	1.5	1,226	N/A	None	3.0	96%	100%	100%	66%	51%
112	City University of Seattle (WA)	47	1.6	163	$30,960	None	N/A	71%	42%	0%	64%	N/A
112	Concordia University–St. Paul (MN)	47	1.6	182	$15,300	None	N/A	79%	67%	67%	73%	64%

Rank	School	Overall score	Average peer assessment score (5.0=highest)	'17 total enrollment	'17-'18 total program cost[1]	Entrance test required	'17 average undergrad GPA	'17 acceptance rate	'17 full-time faculty with terminal degree	'17 tenured or tenure-track faculty[2]	'17 retention rate	'17 three-year graduation rate
114	Northwood University (MI)	46	N/A	92	$23,610	None	2.6	100%	100%	0%	81%	52%
114	Southwestern College (KS)	46	1.0	105	N/A	None	N/A	82%	100%	100%	80%	52%
114	University of Wisconsin–Platteville	46	2.1	850	$19,500	None	N/A	98%	71%	81%	78%	29%
117	Troy University (AL)	45	1.9	807	$17,784	GMAT or GRE	3.0	98%	100%	72%	64%	33%
118	New England College (NH)	44	1.5	251	$27,200	None	3.0	100%	N/A	N/A	93%	66%
119	Concordia University Wisconsin	43	1.5	44	$22,368	None	N/A	67%	100%	0%	N/A	N/A

School	Average peer assessment score (5.0=highest)	'17 total enrollment	'17-'18 total program cost[1]	Entrance test required	'17 average undergrad GPA	'17 acceptance rate	'17 full-time faculty with terminal degree	'17 tenured or tenure-track faculty[2]	'17 retention rate	'17 three-year graduation rate
MASTER'S PROGRAMS RANKED 120 THROUGH 158 ARE LISTED HERE ALPHABETICALLY										
Abilene Christian University (TX)	N/A	35	N/A	None	N/A	87%	N/A	N/A	10%	N/A
Albertus Magnus College (CT)	1.2	147	N/A	None	N/A	N/A	100%	9%	78%	N/A
Azusa Pacific University (CA)	N/A	160	N/A	None	N/A	94%	N/A	N/A	N/A	N/A
Baker University (KS)	1.4	84	$22,135	None	N/A	N/A	100%	0%	N/A	N/A
Bay Path University (MA)	N/A	N/A	N/A	N/A	N/A	N/A	N/A	N/A	N/A	N/A
Belhaven University (MS)	1.3	743	$18,900	None	N/A	71%	100%	56%	84%	48%
Bellevue University (NE)	1.4	886	$20,340	None	N/A	81%	60%	0%	81%	N/A
Charleston Southern University (SC)	1.6	19	$20,625	None	N/A	83%	N/A	N/A	N/A	N/A
Cornerstone University (MI)	1.3	17	$16,560	None	N/A	50%	N/A	N/A	71%	N/A
Dallas Baptist University (TX)	1.3	77	$32,616	GRE	N/A	52%	100%	0%	N/A	N/A
Edgewood College (WI)	1.3	N/A	N/A	GMAT or GRE	N/A	N/A	100%	100%	N/A	N/A
Fontbonne University (MO)	1.2	N/A	$22,380	None	N/A	N/A	N/A	N/A	N/A	N/A
Greenville University (IL)	1.1	20	$14,322	None	N/A	N/A	100%	100%	N/A	N/A
Indiana Institute of Technology	1.6	162	N/A	None	N/A	99%	N/A	N/A	N/A	N/A
Johnson and Wales University (RI)	1.7	111	N/A	None	N/A	65%	69%	0%	80%	N/A
Keiser University (FL)	N/A	88	N/A	N/A	N/A	N/A	100%	0%	N/A	81%
Kettering University (MI)	1.6	N/A	$34,800	None	N/A	N/A	0%	100%	N/A	N/A
Keuka College (NY)	N/A	21	N/A	None	3.4	100%	0%	75%	N/A	N/A
Louisiana State University–Shreveport	N/A	438	$12,474	N/A	N/A	96%	N/A	N/A	N/A	N/A
Maharishi University of Management (IA)	N/A	N/A	$27,000	N/A	N/A	N/A	100%	0%	N/A	N/A
Maryville University of St. Louis (MO)	1.6	187	N/A	None	3.0	97%	56%	72%	N/A	N/A
Mercy College (NY)	1.2	62	N/A	None	N/A	N/A	N/A	N/A	N/A	N/A
North Greenville University (SC)	N/A	139	$16,680	N/A	3.1	97%	100%	0%	N/A	N/A
Northcentral University (CA)	1.1	N/A	$25,770	None	N/A	N/A	100%	0%	N/A	N/A
Nova Southeastern University (FL)	1.7	289	$34,905	GMAT or GRE	N/A	90%	100%	0%	N/A	N/A
Olivet Nazarene University (IL)	N/A	43	N/A	None	N/A	N/A	N/A	N/A	N/A	N/A
Point Park University (PA)	N/A	56	N/A	None	N/A	84%	0%	0%	N/A	N/A
Regis University (CO)	1.8	656	N/A	None	N/A	94%	N/A	N/A	93%	55%
Rochester Institute of Technology (NY)	N/A	56	N/A	None	3.3	86%	0%	0%	N/A	N/A
St. Francis University (PA)	N/A	N/A	$26,250	N/A	N/A	N/A	N/A	N/A	N/A	N/A
St. Joseph's College New York (NY)	1.9	28	N/A	N/A	N/A	100%	50%	13%	70%	N/A
Tarleton State University (TX)	1.4	114	N/A	GMAT or GRE	N/A	68%	0%	100%	N/A	N/A
University of Charleston (WV)	N/A	N/A	N/A	N/A	N/A	N/A	N/A	N/A	N/A	N/A
University of Dallas (TX)	2.4	302	N/A	None	N/A	N/A	93%	0%	N/A	N/A
University of Hartford (Barney) (CT)	N/A	98	N/A	N/A	N/A	68%	N/A	N/A	N/A	N/A
University of Nevada–Reno	N/A	N/A	N/A	N/A	N/A	N/A	N/A	N/A	N/A	N/A
Warner University (FL)	N/A	N/A	$20,016	N/A	N/A	N/A	100%	0%	100%	64%
Western New England University (MA)	N/A	49	$24,720	GMAT or GRE	N/A	91%	76%	76%	N/A	N/A
Wilmington University (DE)	N/A	379	N/A	N/A	N/A	100%	0%	0%	N/A	N/A

Best Undergraduate Programs

ACH YEAR, U.S. NEWS ranks undergraduate business programs accredited by AACSB International – The Association to Advance Collegiate Schools of Business; the results are based solely on surveys of B-school deans and senior faculty. Participants – two at each AACSB-accredited business program – were asked to rate the quality of business programs with which they're familiar on a scale of 1 (marginal) to 5 (distinguished); 38.4 percent of those canvassed responded to the most recent survey conducted in the spring of 2017. Two years of data were used to calculate the average peer assessment score. The ranking sorts, in descending order, the undergraduate business programs by their average peer assessment score. In total, 494 schools were ranked.

Deans and faculty members also were asked to nominate the 10 best programs in a number of specialty areas like accounting, marketing and finance; the 10 schools receiving the most mentions in the 2017 survey appear on page 87. A school or program had to receive seven or more nominations in a specific specialty area to be ranked. The best undergraduate business programs in a specialty area are based solely on the peer assessment survey conducted in spring 2017. More @ usnews.com/undergrad.

Rank	School (State)	Peer assessment score (5.0=highest)
1	University of Pennsylvania (Wharton)	4.8
2	Massachusetts Inst. of Technology (Sloan)	4.6
3	University of California–Berkeley (Haas)	4.5
3	University of Michigan–Ann Arbor (Ross)	4.5
5	New York University (Stern)	4.3
5	University of Texas–Austin (McCombs)	4.3
7	Carnegie Mellon University (Tepper) (PA)	4.2
7	Cornell University (Dyson) (NY)	4.2
7	U. of N. Carolina–Chapel Hill (Kenan-Flagler)	4.2
7	University of Virginia (McIntire)	4.2
11	Indiana University–Bloomington (Kelley)	4.1
11	University of Notre Dame (Mendoza) (IN)	4.1
11	Univ. of Southern California (Marshall)	4.1
14	Washington University in St. Louis (Olin)	4.0
15	Emory University (Goizueta) (GA)	3.8
15	Georgetown University (McDonough) (DC)	3.8
15	Ohio State University–Columbus (Fisher)	3.8
15	U. of Illinois–Urbana-Champaign	3.8
15	Univ. of Minnesota–Twin Cities (Carlson)	3.8
15	Univ. of Wisconsin–Madison	3.8

Rank	School (State)	Peer assessment score (5.0=highest)
21	Pennsylvania State U.–Univ. Park (Smeal)	3.7
21	University of Arizona (Eller)	3.7
21	Univ. of Maryland–College Park	3.7
24	Arizona State University–Tempe (Carey)	3.6
24	Boston College (Carroll)	3.6
24	Michigan State University (Broad)	3.6
24	Purdue U.–West Lafayette (Krannert) (IN)	3.6
24	University of Florida (Warrington)	3.6
24	University of Georgia (Terry)	3.6
24	University of Washington (Foster)	3.6
31	Babson College (MA)	3.5
31	Brigham Young Univ.–Provo (Marriott) (UT)	3.5
31	Case Western Reserve U. (Weatherhead) (OH)	3.5
31	Georgia Institute of Technology (Scheller)	3.5
31	Texas A&M Univ.–College Station (Mays)	3.5
31	University of California–Irvine (Merage)	3.5
31	University of Colorado–Boulder (Leeds)	3.5
31	University of Iowa (Tippie)	3.5
31	University of Pittsburgh	3.5
40	Boston University	3.4

Rank	School (State)	Peer assessment score (5.0=highest)
40	Wake Forest University (NC)	3.4
42	College of William & Mary (Mason) (VA)	3.3
42	George Washington University (DC)	3.3
42	Syracuse University (Whitman) (NY)	3.3
45	Florida State University	3.2
45	Miami University–Oxford (Farmer) (OH)	3.2
45	Pepperdine University (CA)	3.2
45	Southern Methodist University (Cox) (TX)	3.2
45	Temple University (Fox) (PA)	3.2
45	Tulane University (Freeman) (LA)	3.2
45	United States Air Force Acad. (CO)	3.2
45	University of Alabama (Culverhouse)	3.2
45	University of Arkansas (Walton)	3.2
45	Univ. of California–San Diego (Rady)	3.2
45	University of Connecticut	3.2
45	University of Kansas	3.2
45	U. of Massachusetts–Amherst (Isenberg)	3.2
45	Univ. of Nebraska–Lincoln	3.2
45	Univ. of South Carolina (Moore)	3.2
45	University of Tennessee (Haslam)	3.2

Note: Peer assessment survey conducted by Ipsos Public Affairs. To be ranked in a specialty, an undergraduate business school may have either a program or course offerings in that subject area. Extended undergraduate business rankings can be found at usnews.com/undergrad.

THE WHARTON SCHOOL,
NO. 1

Rank	School (State)	Peer assessment score (5.0=highest)
45	University of Utah (Eccles)	3.2
45	Villanova University (PA)	3.2
45	Virginia Tech (Pamplin)	3.2
64	Auburn University (Harbert) (AL)	3.1
64	Baylor University (Hankamer) (TX)	3.1
64	Bentley University (MA)	3.1
64	CUNY–Baruch College (Zicklin)	3.1
64	Fordham University (Gabelli) (NY)	3.1
64	Georgia State University (Robinson)	3.1
64	Northeastern U. (D'Amore-McKim) (MA)	3.1
64	Rensselaer Polytechnic Inst. (Lally) (NY)	3.1
64	Rochester Inst. of Technology (Saunders) (NY)	3.1
64	Santa Clara University (Leavey) (CA)	3.1
64	University of Miami (FL)	3.1
64	University of Oklahoma (Price)	3.1
64	University of Oregon (Lundquist)	3.1
64	University of Texas–Dallas (Jindal)	3.1
78	Clemson University (SC)	3.0
78	DePaul University (Driehaus) (IL)	3.0
78	George Mason University (VA)	3.0
78	Iowa State University	3.0
78	Loyola University Chicago (Quinlan)	3.0
78	Rutgers University–New Brunswick (NJ)	3.0
78	Texas Christian University (Neeley)	3.0
78	University at Buffalo–SUNY	3.0
78	Univ. of California–Riverside	3.0
78	University of Delaware (Lerner)	3.0
78	University of Illinois–Chicago	3.0
78	University of Kentucky (Gatton)	3.0
78	Univ. of Missouri (Trulaske)	3.0
91	American University (Kogod) (DC)	2.9
91	Brandeis University (MA)	2.9
91	Colorado State University	2.9
91	Creighton University (NE)	2.9
91	Lehigh University (PA)	2.9
91	Loyola Marymount University (CA)	2.9
91	Marquette University (WI)	2.9
91	North Carolina State U.–Raleigh (Poole)	2.9
91	Oklahoma State University (Spears)	2.9
91	Rutgers University–Newark (NJ)	2.9
91	Saint Louis University (Cook)	2.9
91	San Diego State University	2.9
91	U.S. Coast Guard Acad. (CT)	2.9
91	University of Cincinnati (Lindner)	2.9
91	University of Colorado–Denver	2.9
91	University of Denver (Daniels)	2.9
91	University of Houston (Bauer)	2.9
91	University of Richmond (Robins) (VA)	2.9
109	Drexel University (LeBow) (PA)	2.8
109	Gonzaga University (WA)	2.8
109	James Madison University (VA)	2.8
109	Kansas State University	2.8
109	Louisiana State Univ.–Baton Rouge (Ourso)	2.8
109	Loyola University Maryland (Sellinger)	2.8
109	Seton Hall University (Stillman) (NJ)	2.8
109	St. Joseph's University (Haub) (PA)	2.8
109	Texas Tech University (Rawls)	2.8
109	University at Albany–SUNY	2.8
109	University of Alabama–Birmingham (Collat)	2.8
109	University of Hawaii–Manoa (Shidler)	2.8
109	University of Louisville (KY)	2.8
109	University of Mississippi	2.8
109	U. of North Carolina–Charlotte (Belk)	2.8
109	University of San Diego	2.8
109	University of San Francisco	2.8
109	Univ. of Wisconsin–Milwaukee (Lubar)	2.8
109	Washington State University (Carson)	2.8
128	Binghamton University–SUNY	2.7
128	Bucknell University (PA)	2.7
128	Butler University (IN)	2.7
128	Cal. Poly. State U.–San Luis Obispo (Orfalea)	2.7
128	California State U.–Los Angeles	2.7
128	Elon University (Love) (NC)	2.7
128	Hofstra University (Zarb) (NY)	2.7
128	Howard University (DC)	2.7
128	Kennesaw State University (Coles) (GA)	2.7
128	Ohio University	2.7
128	Oregon State University	2.7
128	Rollins College (FL)	2.7
128	Rutgers University–Camden (NJ)	2.7
128	Seattle University (Albers)	2.7
128	University of Central Florida	2.7
128	Univ. of Colo.–Colorado Springs	2.7
128	University of Memphis (Fogelman)	2.7
128	University of New Mexico (Anderson)	2.7
128	University of St. Thomas (Opus) (MN)	2.7
128	University of Texas–Arlington	2.7
128	Virginia Commonwealth University	2.7
128	Washington and Lee U. (Williams) (VA)	2.7
128	Xavier University (Williams) (OH)	2.7
151	Ball State University (Miller) (IN)	2.6
151	Calif. State Poly. Univ.–Pomona	2.6
151	California State U.–Fullerton (Mihaylo)	2.6
151	Chapman University (Argyros) (CA)	2.6
151	The Citadel (SC)	2.6
151	Duquesne University (Palumbo) (PA)	2.6
151	Fairfield University (Dolan) (CT)	2.6
151	Florida International University	2.6
151	Kent State University (OH)	2.6
151	Mississippi State University	2.6
151	Northern Illinois University	2.6
151	Pace University (Lubin) (NY)	2.6
151	Providence College (RI)	2.6
151	Purdue University–Northwest (IN)	2.6
151	Quinnipiac University (CT)	2.6
151	San Jose State University (Lucas) (CA)	2.6
151	University of Idaho	2.6
151	Univ. of Massachusetts–Boston	2.6
151	U. of Massachusetts–Dartmouth (Charlton)	2.6
151	University of Minnesota–Duluth (Labovitz)	2.6
151	Univ. of Missouri–Kansas City (Bloch)	2.6
151	Univ. of Missouri–St. Louis	2.6
151	University of Montana	2.6
151	University of Nebraska–Omaha	2.6
151	University of New Hampshire (Paul)	2.6
151	U. of North Carolina–Greensboro (Bryan)	2.6
151	University of Portland (Pamplin) (OR)	2.6
151	University of Rhode Island	2.6
151	Univ. of Tennessee–Chattanooga	2.6
151	University of Vermont	2.6
151	West Virginia University	2.6
151	Worcester Polytechnic Inst. (MA)	2.6
183	Boise State University (ID)	2.5
183	Bowling Green State University (OH)	2.5
183	Bradley University (Foster) (IL)	2.5
183	Bryant University (RI)	2.5
183	Clarkson University (NY)	2.5
183	Clark University (MA)	2.5
183	Drake University (IA)	2.5
183	Georgia College & State Univ. (Bunting)	2.5
183	John Carroll University (Boler) (OH)	2.5
183	Loyola University New Orleans	2.5
183	Northern Arizona University (Franke)	2.5
183	Old Dominion University (Strome) (VA)	2.5
183	Portland State University (OR)	2.5
183	San Francisco State University	2.5
183	Southern Illinois U.–Carbondale	2.5
183	Stevens Institute of Technology (NJ)	2.5
183	St. John's University (Tobin) (NY)	2.5
183	University of Alabama–Huntsville	2.5
183	Univ. of Arkansas–Little Rock	2.5
183	University of Baltimore (Merrick)	2.5
183	University of Dayton (OH)	2.5
183	University of Evansville (Schroeder) (IN)	2.5
183	University of Michigan–Dearborn	2.5
183	University of Nevada–Las Vegas (Lee)	2.5
183	U. of North Carolina–Asheville	2.5
183	U. of North Carolina–Wilmington (Cameron)	2.5
183	University of Scranton (Kania) (PA)	2.5
183	University of South Florida (Muma)	2.5
183	University of Tulsa (Collins) (OK)	2.5
183	University of Wyoming	2.5
183	Utah State University (Huntsman)	2.5
183	Valparaiso University (IN)	2.5
183	Western Michigan University (Haworth)	2.5

Tops in the Specialties

Undergraduate programs ranked best by B-school deans and program directors

ACCOUNTING
1. University of Texas–Austin (McCombs)
2. University of Illinois–Urbana-Champaign
3. Brigham Young Univ.–Provo (Marriott) (UT)
4. University of Pennsylvania (Wharton)
5. University of Michigan–Ann Arbor (Ross)
6. University of Notre Dame (Mendoza) (IN)
7. University of Southern California (Marshall)
8. Indiana University–Bloomington (Kelley)
9. New York University (Stern)
10. Ohio State University–Columbus (Fisher)

ENTREPRENEURSHIP
1. Babson College (MA)
2. Massachusetts Inst. of Technology (Sloan)
3. Indiana University–Bloomington (Kelley)
3. University of California–Berkeley (Haas)
5. University of Pennsylvania (Wharton)
6. University of Southern California (Marshall)
7. University of Texas–Austin (McCombs)
8. U. of North Carolina–Chapel Hill (Kenan-Flagler)
9. Saint Louis University (Cook)
10. University of Arizona (Eller)

FINANCE
1. University of Pennsylvania (Wharton)
2. New York University (Stern)
3. Massachusetts Inst. of Technology (Sloan)
4. University of Michigan–Ann Arbor (Ross)
5. University of Texas–Austin (McCombs)
6. University of California–Berkeley (Haas)
7. U. of North Carolina–Chapel Hill (Kenan-Flagler)
8. Indiana University–Bloomington (Kelley)
9. University of Virginia (McIntire)
10. Carnegie Mellon University (Tepper) (PA)

INSURANCE/RISK MANAGEMENT
1. University of Pennsylvania (Wharton)
2. University of Georgia (Terry)
3. University of Wisconsin–Madison
4. St. Joseph's University (Haub) (PA)
5. Georgia State University (Robinson)
6. Florida State University
6. University of Texas–Austin (McCombs)
8. Temple University (Fox) (PA)
9. New York University (Stern)
10. Pennsylvania State U.–Univ. Park (Smeal)

INTERNATIONAL BUSINESS
1. University of South Carolina (Moore)
2. University of Pennsylvania (Wharton)
3. New York University (Stern)
4. Georgetown University (McDonough) (DC)
5. University of California–Berkeley (Haas)
6. University of Southern California (Marshall)
7. Florida International University
8. Fordham University (Gabelli) (NY)
9. George Washington University (DC)
9. Northeastern University (D'Amore-McKim) (MA)

MANAGEMENT
1. University of Michigan–Ann Arbor (Ross)
2. University of Pennsylvania (Wharton)
3. University of California–Berkeley (Haas)
4. U. of North Carolina–Chapel Hill (Kenan-Flagler)
5. University of Virginia (McIntire)
6. New York University (Stern)
7. University of Texas–Austin (McCombs)
8. Massachusetts Inst. of Technology (Sloan)
9. Indiana University–Bloomington (Kelley)
10. University of Southern California (Marshall)

MANAGEMENT INFORMATION SYSTEMS
1. Massachusetts Inst. of Technology (Sloan)
2. Carnegie Mellon University (Tepper) (PA)
3. University of Arizona (Eller)
4. University of Minnesota–Twin Cities (Carlson)
5. University of Texas–Austin (McCombs)
6. Georgia Institute of Technology (Scheller)
6. Indiana University–Bloomington (Kelley)
8. University of Maryland–College Park
9. University of Pennsylvania (Wharton)
10. Georgia State University (Robinson)

MARKETING
1. University of Pennsylvania (Wharton)
2. University of Michigan–Ann Arbor (Ross)
3. New York University (Stern)
4. University of Texas–Austin (McCombs)
5. University of California–Berkeley (Haas)
6. Indiana University–Bloomington (Kelley)
7. U. of North Carolina–Chapel Hill (Kenan-Flagler)
8. University of Virginia (McIntire)
9. St. Joseph's University (Haub) (PA)
10. University of Wisconsin–Madison

PRODUCTION/OPERATIONS MANAGEMENT
1. Massachusetts Inst. of Technology (Sloan)
2. University of Pennsylvania (Wharton)
3. Carnegie Mellon University (Tepper) (PA)
4. University of Michigan–Ann Arbor (Ross)
5. Purdue Univ.–West Lafayette (Krannert) (IN)
6. University of California–Berkeley (Haas)
6. U. of North Carolina–Chapel Hill (Kenan-Flagler)
8. Michigan State University (Broad)
9. University of Texas–Austin (McCombs)
10. Ohio State University–Columbus (Fisher)

QUANTITATIVE ANALYSIS/METHODS
1. Massachusetts Inst. of Technology (Sloan)
2. Carnegie Mellon University (Tepper) (PA)
3. University of Pennsylvania (Wharton)
4. University of California–Berkeley (Haas)
5. New York University (Stern)
6. Georgia Institute of Technology (Scheller)
6. Purdue University–West Lafayette (Krannert) (IN)
6. University of Michigan–Ann Arbor (Ross)
9. Rockhurst University (Helzberg) (MO)
9. University of Texas–Austin (McCombs)

REAL ESTATE
1. University of Pennsylvania (Wharton)
2. University of California–Berkeley (Haas)
3. University of Wisconsin–Madison
4. New York University (Stern)
5. University of Georgia (Terry)
6. University of Texas–Austin (McCombs)
7. University of Southern California (Marshall)
8. University of Florida (Warrington)
9. Marquette University (WI)
10. Cornell University (Dyson) (NY)

SUPPLY CHAIN MANAGEMENT/LOGISTICS
1. Michigan State University (Broad)
2. Massachusetts Inst. of Technology (Sloan)
3. University of Tennessee (Haslam)
4. Arizona State University–Tempe (Carey)
4. Pennsylvania State U.–Univ. Park (Smeal)
6. Ohio State University–Columbus (Fisher)
7. University of Michigan–Ann Arbor (Ross)
8. Carnegie Mellon University (Tepper) (PA)
9. University of Texas–Austin (McCombs)
10. Purdue University–West Lafayette (Krannert) (IN)

CHAPTER

5

TIPS

&TACTICS

Duke University's Fuqua
School of Business

PHYLLIS B. DOONEY FOR USN&WR

The Keys to Making the Cut

What impresses admissions pros? Several told U.S. News what gives applicants an edge

BY STACEY COLINO

 HEN GUSTAVO MAYEN, 36, first considered applying to business school, he thought his chances were "slim at best." Mayen, who was born in Guatemala and came to the U.S. when he was 10, grew up in a financially strapped household and was the first in his family to complete college. But because he didn't have a high GPA and hadn't taken the GRE, he doubted his candidacy. What Mayen did have: Five years as a Marine, during which he earned an undergraduate and a law degree. "I used what I initially thought were disadvantages as ways of standing out and showing how the adversity and risks I have faced made me a good candidate," says Mayen, who applied to Babson College's MBA program in 2015 after realizing that he could boost the success of his private law practice by sharpening his business skills.

With the MBA continuing to be among the most sought-after credentials, it's important to make your application shine. As Mayen discovered, though, that doesn't necessarily require what you might expect. Sure, your past academic performance matters. But these days, so does your work experience and evidence of your emotional intelligence.

During Mayen's interview, he was asked to describe a time when he'd had to think outside the box. He recounted an incident from one of his two tours in Iraq when a tank broke down in a dangerous area and no spare parts were available. As the mechanic on duty, Mayen discovered the problem was a burned-out cable linking the starter to the engine. He went from vehicle to vehicle, scavenging items to jury-rig a fix, enabling the mission to be completed. Mayen believes his resilience and resourcefulness helped sway the admissions committee, which waived the GRE requirement and instead considered his law degree – and admitted him.

Indeed, many schools increasingly value personal qualities. "We're looking for candidates who will be successful – and good citizens – while working in a collaborative environment with classmates and professors," says Jim Holmen, director of admissions and financial aid for the Kelley School of Business MBA program at Indiana University. Admissions teams also gravitate toward candidates they feel will represent the school well after graduation, he adds. Rely on the following strategies to wow admissions officers.

Know yourself. Before you fill out the application, think about what you hope to gain from earning an MBA. What are your postgraduate goals? How can you contribute to the program? How do you view your strengths and weaknesses? "There is no such thing as a perfect candidate," says Bruce Del-Monico, assistant dean for admissions at the Yale School of Management. Instead of trying to hide your weaknesses, a better strategy is to "address them on your own terms rather than letting us draw our own conclusions about them," he says. "We're trying to infer how you approach issues and how you think about yourself. If you present as someone who is self-aware and has a growth

mindset, that is much more compelling than someone who tries to ignore issues and gloss over imperfections."

John Stacey, director of student community at an educational technology company, used this tactic. "One of the things that helped me was to let myself be vulnerable, transparent and open throughout the process," says Stacey, 31, who applied to the MBA programs at the University of California–Berkeley and Columbia University. To show how hardships had changed him, he chose to reveal in his essays that he had lost his brother a few years earlier and that someone close to him had struggled with depression. "These experiences made me more empathetic and compassionate, and I connected those stories to where I want to go in business school and beyond," he explains. "It's important for leaders to pay attention to mental health." After being admitted to both schools, Stacey joined the evening program at Berkeley.

Pick the test that suits you best. Many business schools don't have a preference for the GRE or GMAT. "We are test-agnostic," says Isser Gallogly, associate dean of MBA admissions and program innovation at the NYU Stern School of Business. "Both are pretty reliable tools." Students who majored in the humanities or social sciences tend to prefer the GRE, while those with a more quantitative or business background often favor the GMAT, says Courtney Elmes, director of the full-time MBA program at the University of California–Irvine Paul Merage School of Business. Some applicants take both tests and send both scores to business schools. "There's no downside to that because we make a decision based on the highest score," Gallogly says. Whichever exam you choose, it's smart to take it more than once; only the highest score will count. Scores range considerably from one school to another but generally the 600-800 range is considered competitive on the GMAT, while 157 and higher (on the verbal section) and 160 and higher (quantitative) are for the GRE.

Make a unique (but genuine) impression. Essays have always given applicants a chance to express who they are in a distinctive fashion, but some business schools have made that easier than ever. NYU's Stern has begun asking MBA applicants to submit a "Pick Six" essay – six images (pictures, charts, artwork or infographics) with captions – to reveal themselves. At the Cornell S.C. Johnson Graduate School of Management, applicants are asked to imagine they are the author of their life story and to write a table of contents for the book. Other schools allow students to answer essay prompts in video format.

As for what ground to cover, it helps to use optional essays "to talk about things that wouldn't otherwise be clear from your application, to guide us in how to interpret your life story," says Shari Hubert, associate dean for admissions at Duke University's Fuqua School of Business. "If there are gaps in your work experience or aspects of your academic experience that were particularly challenging, don't [assume] that we can read into your application." Above all, "present an authentic voice – don't write about what you think the business school admissions committee wants to hear," Holmen cautions. If you haven't had much work experience to highlight, keep in mind that "when evaluating an applicant's work experience, we are simply looking to

Two Essays That Worked

There is no formula for writing a compelling application essay. Bruce DelMonico, assistant dean for admissions at the Yale School of Management, says he looks for evidence of resilience, introspection and initiative. William Rieth, director of graduate enrollment management at Temple University's Fox School of Business, says essays "should reflect your personality and sound like you." Here are two essays by students (identities withheld) who were accepted into the MBA programs at Fox and Yale, annotated with comments by the admissions officials on why they stood out.

> Conveying your personality is an important component of a successful personal statement, Rieth says. This personal statement felt authentic. The voice of the essay sounded like the voice of a real person, and the essay was consistent with the demeanor of the applicant when she was interviewed. "I felt like I was really hearing from the applicant," Rieth says. "This wasn't some template she had downloaded."

> Rieth says he appreciated that the applicant acknowledged that she was an unusual MBA candidate because of her college major. He says her distinctive academic background was an asset, not a deficit. "We don't necessarily want a well-rounded student," he says. "We want a well-rounded class."

> Rieth's favorite sentence in this essay was this one: "I was petrified of selling." He appreciated how upfront the applicant was about her emotions. "That was a really honest moment," he notes.

> Describing a personal transformation can be strong fodder for a personal statement, Rieth says, but only if the transformation seems genuine. "Your personality should come through in the essay, and this really matched with her very well."

> Explaining how a particular school would help you achieve career goals can be an effective strategy. "We want the student to be interested in us, and we want to be interested in them," Rieth says. "We're looking for a real partnership, and she did a good job articulating how we could help her."

> Rieth says it is unusual for students to be specific about why they want to attend a particular school, but that this kind of detail helps establish genuine interest and make the case for admission.

Fox School of Business at Temple University

What past experience prepared or motivated you to pursue this degree? Describe how you would expect to change over the course of the program. What personal and professional values and skills do you hope to acquire beyond the academic content? How will obtaining the degree help you achieve your career goals? (500 word max suggested.)

In May 2010 I graduated from _____ with a degree in English and Creative Writing. I had always wanted to be a writer. I was good at it. I liked it. I thought that was all I needed to know to choose a career path. In September 2010, I began working for _____ Publishing Company, thus starting a four year arc managing the production of the monthly _____ magazine. During my third year at _____ my boss introduced me to the idea of "salesatorial," where editors sell magazine content. I was petrified of selling. I was hired to sit behind a desk and churn out as much content as possible, not smooth talk clients. Then I landed my first sale and discovered a hidden talent.

In August 2014, I moved to an entirely client-facing role when I was promoted to the executive editor of new media and custom publishing. I work for outside clients to come up with creative solutions to their marketing needs, such as video production and print catalogs. I no longer write for my job–and I love it.

Now, when I think of what I want to be in 15 years, it is not a writer. It is the president of media conglomerate Condé Nast. In order to achieve this goal, I plan to work as a consultant at Boston Consulting Group on projects such as one BCG did for an Asian media company, helping them convert their publications from print to online. My experience working for a publishing company combined with the strategic management skills I will gain from my Fox MBA will aid me in creating solutions for BCG's clients.

Because of my interest in consulting, the Enterprise Management Consulting project attracted me to Fox. Discussing the project with Associate Professor TL Hill at Fox Decision Day furthered my interest in the program. He explained that the EMC faculty members create diverse teams of students to fill every need of the project and that students work for a variety of industries.

While the strategic management concentration at Fox interests me for a career in consulting, instead I'd like to sample various electives to get a broad understanding of management. The two samples classes I have attended at Fox—Human Resources Management with Professor McClendon and Finance with Professor Anderson—had a large impact on this decision. Both are courses I never thought would appeal to me, but had me riveted. The expertise of both professors was evident and the energy of the classrooms infectious.

That same energy was carried over through Fox Decision Day, which fully convinced me that Fox is the right program for me. The students, faculty and staff I met spoke of the interesting opportunities at Fox, such as the partnership with a university in Adelaide, Australia and the annual immersion trips. It made me excited to spend two years working with and getting to know the Fox community—and experiencing the programs first hand.

understand their accomplishments and transferable skills," Holmen adds. Mentioning extracurricular activities that involved leadership can also help set you apart.

"I think being authentic by highlighting the uniqueness and diversity of my experience really helped me," says Ashley Ice, 29, who showcased her two years in the Peace Corps in West Africa as well as her three years at a strategic communications firm in the District of Columbia. "Being a woman and working across language barriers was very challenging," says Ice, who started the evening MBA program at Georgetown University in the fall of 2016. "It helped me learn to communicate effectively with a wide variety of people."

Do sweat the details. "You may be tempted to cut corners by squeezing your answers for one school into another school's

Yale School of Management

The Yale School of Management educates individuals who will have deep and lasting impact on the organizations they lead. Describe how you have positively influenced an organization, as an employee, a member, or an outside constituent.

When Janet* visited a hospital for a common ailment, she was refused treatment under the claim that the hospital lacked knowledge on transgender healthcare. When Dan and Tom applied to an apartment, the leasing office said there were no vacancies once it was apparent that Dan and Tom were a couple. Such challenges faced by LGBT individuals in Columbus, Indiana, which had no protections against discrimination, spurred me to start the LGBT SAFE Initiative, a social venture to enable organizations to self-identify as LGBT friendly.

To create the initiative, I formed a cross-sector team of public, private, and nonprofit volunteers. We worked together to identify important stakeholders, conducted fifty interviews, and captured the challenges faced by the local LGBT community. With this groundwork, we won an $18,000 grant from The Cummins Foundation.

Leading a diverse team – individuals with varied professional backgrounds and communication styles – was challenging. Many team members not only had competing priorities and varying levels of commitment, but also had more experience and authority than me. To overcome this challenge, I worked with the team to gain agreement on the overall vision and common goals, enabling us to effectively resolve differences and diversions. I learnt that building consensus based on shared common goals and multiple perspectives is critical for buy-in and shared success.

In early 2015, Indiana passed the controversial RFRA law that sparked national outrage. In Columbus, the LGBT community felt the adverse impact and wanted to respond with an immediate launch of SAFE.

While an immediate launch could harness the passion induced by RFRA, I was concerned about the risks and requested we gauge the pulse of the wider community. The community input highlighted a major risk – launching without a critical number of partner organizations willing to publicly identify with us would jeopardize our long term success. Using this data, I established consensus amongst the stakeholders to launch only after we overcame this hurdle.

I led our team to present evidence collected on the discrimination faced by the LGBT community. We addressed questions, allayed concerns, and highlighted the benefits of our initiative; thereby, convincing 34 major organizations to partner with us to self-identify as LGBT friendly. Our focus on long term success was rewarded.

In June 2015, we launched SAFE along with our 34 community partners. The state media recognized this significant achievement and praised us as an effective antidote to RFRA. The momentum from SAFE along with the grassroots lobbying efforts, which I co-led as an elected board member of Pride Alliance, played a major part in the City Council and Mayor voting to amend city law to include LGBT as a protected class.

Today, Janet can go to the SAFE website to determine which healthcare facility will treat her equally. Dan and Tom can now find a house together secure in the knowledge that they will not be denied housing just because they are a couple. This is the kind of deep and impactful change that I am proud to be a part of.

*Real names have been replaced with fictitious names to protect confidentiality.

Although eloquence is not the primary thing admissions officers look for in personal statements, it never hurts to have a powerful introduction. DelMonico says he was impressed by the way this applicant touched on the reason he began his project right from the start. The ability to explain a vision and frame an issue is a desirable trait in a business school applicant, DelMonico says.

Business school admissions officers like to see evidence that applicants have the grit necessary to succeed. DelMonico says this essay impressed him because it provided details about how the applicant accomplished his goal, including figures such as the amount of money raised and the number of people interviewed for the applicant's project. "The applicant was very concrete about the impact he had," he notes.

DelMonico says he was impressed with the statement for nonpolitical reasons. The applicant demonstrated his ability to translate a viewpoint into an ambitious long-term plan. "We're not looking to admit people who only hold certain political or ideological views," he says. "We're looking at the foundational qualities of how they relate to people." He says he looks for evidence of perseverance and empathy and an ability to think strategically.

This paragraph demonstrated the applicant's ability to evaluate risk, which is an important skill in business.

The ability to think about long-term consequences is a trait that distinguishes good businesspeople from great businesspeople, DelMonico says. This portion of the essay demonstrated the applicant's long-term thinking skills.

This paragraph provides specific details about what happened, which an admissions officer can easily fact-check. "That adds credibility and value to the essay," DelMonico says.

The conclusion focuses on the human impact of the applicant's actions. "It wasn't claiming to have changed the world, and the applicant wasn't just focused on himself," DelMonico says. He says the applicant's humility was attractive, as was his ability to explain the difference he made in concrete terms.

TIPS & TACTICS

application," DelMonico says. "Please resist that temptation. We can tell when you are not answering our specific questions but are trying to 'repurpose' answers from another school's application." Before submitting an application, read (and reread) your essay and other responses closely, perhaps aloud. "Spell-check doesn't compensate for careful proofreading," Holmen says. It's a good idea to explain why a particular school appeals to you, but if you mention the school by name, make sure to use the right name; believe it or not, this is a common mistake.

Choose your cheerleaders wisely. Most schools require at least one recommendation letter, usually from a supervisor who can address your management and leadership potential. "It doesn't need to be someone with a lofty title," Hubert says. "It's more important to focus on the content and substance of what the person can say on your behalf regarding your character and performance." So think carefully about who is in the best position to articulate your strengths and give specific, powerful examples of how you've used them. Importantly, give the person lead time to craft a thoughtful, thorough, personal letter. The goal is to avoid a formulaic recommendation that could apply to any candidate. Keep in mind that schools and employers are placing more of a premium on emotional intelligence. Some MBA programs (such as Stern's) may even require a testimonial from a colleague or advocate who can detail how you've demonstrated your people skills at work.

Show clear interest, within reason. Making the effort to visit the campus, attend a business school event near you, or connect with alumni or students can speak volumes about your interest in the school. "Any touch point a candidate can use to connect with us in a positive way makes the person memorable to us," Elmes says. But don't go overboard. "There may be a point of diminishing returns," says Rodrigo Malta, director of MBA admissions at the McCombs School of Business at the University of Texas–Austin. "If we see the same person over and over again, he or she can be perceived as high maintenance or an attention-seeker."

Dazzle during the interview. Many business schools require an interview with a member of the admissions committee, a student or an alum. If you're selected for an interview, take it seriously and prepare for it. "Think about your story and how you want to present yourself," Gallogly advises. "The interviewer has read your entire application so you can go a lot deeper and have a substantive discussion."

When preparing for the interview, "take inventory of examples of teamwork and leadership you've shown that you can use to demonstrate core competencies," Malta suggests. Compile a list of insightful questions to ask your interviewer with an especially strong one to pose at the end of your discussion. That step, Malta says, can carry you across the finish line. ●

MORE @ USNEWS.COM

ADDITIONAL TIPS FOR GETTING IN
Learn what to do if you're wait-listed, how to up the odds of getting great recommendations, which schools are the most competitive to get into, and more. ▶*usnews.com/businessapp*

SPOTLIGHT ON

Booth School of Business
UNIVERSITY OF CHICAGO

U.S. NEWS RANK #1

Kallie Parchman, 26, takes classes at the University of Chicago's Booth School of Business three days a week and interns at a venture capital firm in the city the other two. Parchman, who is planning for a career investing in or operating startups, credits the B-school's flexible curriculum for allowing her and her peers to tailor the program "to what you're looking for," she says, even as a first-year MBA student. Indeed, the goal is "owning one's own experience," says Stacey Kole, deputy dean for the full-time MBA program, which enrolls about 1,175 students. The MBA can be completed in up to five years, Kole says, and a total of six of the 21 mandatory courses needed for the degree can be completed in other UChicago academic divisions.

Foundation courses in accounting, microeconomics and statistics are required, as are six courses from a set of options covering business functions and management. All students also take Leadership Effectiveness and Development to sharpen their management, communication and interpersonal skills by working closely alongside a small "squad" of seven or eight peers from a class of 60. –*Mariya Greeley*

▶ **More @ usnews.com/chicago**

Graduate students have more options to pay for their education and limit debt than many expect

Finding the

Money

HEN GENEVIEVE KELLY was accepted to Johns Hopkins University to pursue a joint MBA and master's degree in public health, she was looking at a whopping $105,000 in total tuition expenses alone for her accelerated two-year program. So Kelly, who had spent six years working for nonprofits prior to applying to graduate school, got to work pursuing every opportunity she could find to help finance her degree, starting with the college itself.

Kelly, 28, filled out the Free Application for Federal Student Aid and played up her health-related work experience in her applications. She ended up nabbing $40,000 in total scholarship money from Hopkins' Carey Business School and Bloomberg School of Public Health, plus $37,000 in federal loans for the first year. She also got a 10-hour-per-week work-study job with a professor who specializes in sanitation – a position that brings in about $4,000 per year. And when she's not too busy studying for exams, Kelly has a side business walking and boarding dogs for clients she recruits on Rover.com. That brings in an additional $200-$300 a month on average – not to mention ongoing experience running a business. "Plus spending time with dogs gives me a sanity break," Kelly says.

Earning an MBA is far from an inexpensive pursuit. The total median cost of completing an MBA degree, including tuition, room and board, and other expenses, at a top university was $185,747 in 2017, up from $171,000 the year before, according to Poets&Quants, a business school news and information provider. And total cost for a number of schools including Harvard Business School, the University of Chicago Booth School of Business, and Stanford Graduate School of Business tops $200,000.

Students whose parents set aside a 529 college savings plan to pay for their undergrad degree should check to see if those funds are exhausted. If not, then the remainder can be put toward their MBA. But if you are not so fortunate, there are still numerous options for bringing your degree costs way down.

Start with your chosen university. Graduate aid from the government requires that FAFSA form but is calculated based solely on your assets – not your parents'. That means you may get a richer reward than you did for your bachelor's. As for merit aid, there's plenty to go around, experts say. "The sticker prices can be shocking," says John Byrne, founder and editor in chief of Poets&Quants, "but with the amount of scholarship aid out there, the discount can be really significant – as much as 70 percent." In fact, 45 percent of students in full-time MBA programs received financial assistance in 2017, according to the Graduate Management Admission Council.

Apply for aid as early as possible, Byrne advises, since more scholarship money is available at the beginning of the application cycle. Once you have an offer or two in hand, he adds, "you can shop around" and perhaps negotiate for more aid from your No. 1 choice if the initial offer wasn't sufficiently generous. Be sure to check with the schools on the proper protocol for negotiating merit aid. When appealing an offer, say, some schools will require requests to be in writing and for you to answer specific questions to help admissions officers make the decision.

Check for unique aid offerings. Some schools are now offering full-tuition fellowships to all of the MBA students they admit, including Arizona State University and the University of Massachusetts–Amherst, both of which introduced the funding as a way to attract high-quality students. The fellowships can be quite competitive – ASU's W.P. Carey School of Business received 634 applications for 120 spots in 2017, for example – and the savings are significant. Carey's program would normally cost about $58,000 for in-state residents and $94,000 for nonresidents, while the Isenberg School of Management at UMass–Amherst covers tuition and most fees and offers a work stipend that brings in roughly another $10,000.

Paige Hill of Portland, Oregon, applied to a few MBA programs, but the fellowship offer from Isenberg made the decision a no-brainer, she says. Besides having her tuition completely covered, she gets free health care benefits and a job with the business school's director of diversity and inclusion – a position that perfectly matches her desire for a future in social services. "I don't want to have student loan debt be the driving factor in where I decide to work," says Hill, 28, who will graduate in 2019.

Some MBA programs are offering financial support to students based on what they want to do after graduation. Stanford, for example, offers a loan forgiveness program for graduates who enter the nonprofit or government sectors and awards fellowships to citizens of India and of African countries who want to work in those regions. The school also offers a fellowship providing full tuition to students who commit to working in regions of the country that have traditionally been underrepresented at the university. In the 2017-2018 academic year, three students who plan to head back to the Midwest are receiving aid. This fellowship was a perfect fit for Wisconsin native Adam Verhasselt, 25, who spent three years working as a financial analyst for Wells Fargo in Green Bay before arriving at Stanford. The opportunity "will allow me to bring back a lot of ideas and technologies that we're seeing here in the heart of

MORE @ USNEWS.COM

PAYING FOR BUSINESS SCHOOL
Get additional tips on how to up your chance for a full ride, deduct your MBA tuition from your taxes, navigate your loan options, and much more. ▶usnews.com/mbapay

SPOTLIGHT ON

F.W. Olin Graduate School of Business

BABSON COLLEGE
BABSON PARK, MASSACHUSETTS

U.S. NEWS RANK #83 Babson College's Olin Graduate School of Business, located near Boston, champions innovation and entrepreneurial thinking. All 330 or so full-time MBA students are immersed in the school's Entrepreneurial Thought and Action curriculum. They learn skills like recognizing and creating business opportunities by applying empathy and self-reflection and practicing how to deliver results with limited resources, such as executing a mini-venture using only $5. "What you end up doing are these incredibly creative, bootstrap projects," says Alexander Barza, 30, a 2018 MBA candidate.

After mastering the basics of ET&A, students spend their second semester working in teams and applying that entrepreneurial mindset to assist area companies in solving real challenges, such as helping to develop market strategies for new technologies. Whether one chooses to stay focused on entrepreneurship or pursue one of Babson's other concentrations, the expectation of students is "that you will go out and pound pavement and make things happen," says Barza. *–Mariya Greeley*

▶ **More @ usnews.com/babson**

FIND THE BEST ONLINE PROGRAM FOR YOU

Search more than 1,200 online education programs to find one that best fits your needs.

Bachelor's
MBA
Graduate Business
Graduate Criminal Justice
Graduate Education
Graduate Engineering
Graduate Information Technology
Graduate Nursing

U.S.News & WORLD REPORT

Start your search today: **usnews.com/education/online-education**

Silicon Valley," says Verhasselt, who will graduate in 2019.

Embrace work opportunities. MBA degrees that can be earned without leaving the workforce are on the rise, largely due to demand from students who are no longer willing to take years off from their careers – and to suffer the financial consequences of doing so. "The two-year full-time MBA is on a decline," says Norean Sharpe, dean of the Peter J. Tobin College of Business at St. John's University in Queens, N.Y., which offers an evening MBA program. The 36-credit program can be completed in as little as three semesters. More and more universities are taking this route, serving students by introducing flexible part-time programs (story, Page 46) and online MBAs (Page 49), so that they can continue pulling in their full-time salaries and benefits. Among the schools that have launched online MBA programs in the last few years are the University of Southern California, Carnegie Mellon and the University of North Carolina–Chapel Hill. Part-time programs are being offered by various schools like the University of California–Berkeley Haas School of Business and the Kellogg School of Management at Northwestern University.

Staying in your job may offer another benefit, as well: tuition assistance from your employer. More than half of students enrolling in a part-time self-paced MBA program in 2017 expected to receive financial assistance from their employers, as did 38 percent of online MBA students, according to GMAC. It's worth checking your company's policy, even if you're planning to take time off to complete a full-time MBA. Just be aware that only 8 percent of full-time two-year MBA students expected to receive employer support in 2017.

John Stacey III, a part-time MBA student at Berkeley Haas, decided to keep his full-time job as the director of student community at Course Hero, a company that provides supplemental educational resources contributed by students and educators. Course Hero is giving Stacey $5,000 a year toward tuition. And he got a $15,000 merit scholarship from Berkeley Haas that is renewable each year, contingent on his ability to demonstrate leadership skills – something his job allows him to do. All of that, plus his salary, will go a long way toward covering the $135,000 total cost of the program, he predicts. "Maintaining my full-time job is a great way to finance the degree. I expect to come out debt-free," says Stacey, 31, who plans to finish in the spring of 2020.

Go off the beaten path. MBA prospects can find plenty of oppor-

tunities to supplement the scholarships and loans that are provided by their schools with scholarships funded by private organizations, many of which seek to foster graduate education among certain demographic groups. They include the Forté Foundation, which has partnered with more than 50 U.S. and international schools to offer fellowships of $10,000 to $20,000 per year to female MBA students. Forté-awarded fellowships went to 1,085 MBA students graduating in 2018 from institutions like Harvard Business School, HEC Paris and the University of Virginia Darden School of Business. Websites such as GoGrad.org will help you search for scholarships.

There are an array of scholarship opportunities for minorities through groups like the National Black MBA Association and the Association of Latino Professionals for America. And students aiming for certain fields might find scholarships that fit those interests, such as the Government Finance Officers Association Goldberg-Miller Public Finance Scholarship – a $15,000 award for students committed to working in government finance. Derek Brainard, a 32-year-old Navy veteran, attends his online MBA program at Syracuse University's Whitman School of Management free of charge, because the school participates in the Yellow Ribbon program. Under the GI Bill, Yellow Ribbon pays full tuition and fees plus a cost-of-living stipend.

Brainard previously worked for Syracuse University as a financial literacy coordinator, helping other students figure out how to finance their degrees. He typically advised MBA students to do a cost-benefit analysis, weighing the potential bump in their income as a result of having the degree against what it will cost to get it. "Generally speaking, using a variety of ways to generate enough cash flow to finance your MBA yourself, rather than taking out loans, can be really beneficial," especially if you are forgoing all or part of your salary to get the degree, Brainard says.

Get an accelerated degree. One increasingly popular tactic for bringing down the cost of earning an MBA is to fast-track the degree (story, Page 20). Many schools are now offering one-year MBAs, including Notre Dame, Emory and Northwestern. St. John's offers a fast-track option enabling undergrads to start their MBA as seniors and graduate with a BS/MBA in five or six years. "With today's millennial generation, their No. 1 concern is cost, and their second concern is time," says Sharpe. "We're motivated to do anything we can to help those students accomplish their goals."

And if you're willing to go overseas (story, Page 36), you might save even more by attending a one-year

The Payback Picture

U. S. NEWS HAS compiled a list of the schools whose 2017 MBA graduates finished up with the heaviest and lightest debt loads. The average amount borrowed reflects what was incurred to pay grad school expenses – for tuition, fees, room, board, books and miscellaneous costs – and omits any undergraduate debt. The figures include all loans taken out by students from private financial institutions and federal, state and local governments. The first column of data indicates what percentage of full- or part-time 2017 graduates completed their programs owing money (and, by extrapolation, what percentage graduated debt free). "Average amount of debt" refers to the cumulative amount borrowed by those who incurred debt; it's not an average for all students.

Least Debt

Full Time

School	% of grads with debt	Average amount of debt
University of Texas–Dallas	22%	$7,345
University of Kentucky (Gatton)	32%	$8,430
University of Missouri (Trulaske)	13%	$15,509
Mississippi State University	22%	$16,124
Louisiana Tech University	67%	$16,204
Louisiana State U.–Baton Rouge (Ourso)	26%	$17,300
Binghamton University–SUNY (NY)	37%	$18,706
West Texas A&M University	52%	$19,000
College of Charleston (SC)	50%	$19,810
La Salle University (PA)	48%	$20,201

Part Time

School	% of grads with debt	Average amount of debt
Seattle University (Albers) (WA)	29%	$1,075
Providence College (RI)	17%	$3,800
University of Nebraska–Omaha	19%	$4,563
Lehigh University (PA)	7%	$5,410
University of Wisconsin–Whitewater	48%	$5,500
Le Moyne College (NY)	22%	$6,121
West Texas A&M University	28%	$6,600
Texas State University (McCoy)	51%	$6,932
University of Nevada–Reno	10%	$8,500
University of Kentucky (Gatton)	17%	$8,967

Most Debt

Full Time

School	% of grads with debt	Average amount of debt
New York University (Stern)	42%	$120,984
Duke University (Fuqua) (NC)	67%	$114,679
Massachusetts Inst. of Technology (Sloan)	59%	$109,891
University of Michigan–Ann Arbor (Ross)	47%	$107,129
Yale University (CT)	50%	$104,799
University of Virginia (Darden)	61%	$104,686
U. of N. Carolina–Chapel Hill (Kenan-Flagler)	67%	$96,096
University of San Francisco (CA)	40%	$93,937
University of California–Berkeley (Haas)	41%	$90,642
Pepperdine University (Graziadio) (CA)	34%	$90,256

Part Time

School	% of grads with debt	Average amount of debt
U. of California–Los Angeles (Anderson)	49%	$102,279
University of California–Berkeley (Haas)	36%	$93,265
New York University (Stern)	45%	$87,195
U. of California–Riverside (Anderson)	29%	$86,556
Georgia Institute of Technology (Scheller)	24%	$85,902
University of Texas–Austin (McCombs)	55%	$85,243
Meredith College (NC)	100%	$80,805
Pepperdine University (Graziadio) (CA)	60%	$80,273
Rice University (Jones) (TX)	50%	$78,084
University of California–Davis	49%	$77,897

Student debt data are as of March 1, 2018. Only ranked schools are eligible to be included on this list.

program there because of the strength of the U.S. dollar against foreign currencies. The one-year MBA program at Oxford's renowned Saïd Business School costs about $76,000 at exchange rates in early 2018 – a bargain compared to the one-year program at Northwestern's Kellogg School of Management, say, which costs about $95,000.

Borrow – as a last resort. Federal loans are an option for MBA students, though it's important to understand the shortcomings of these funding sources before grabbing them. Unlike undergraduate loans, federal loans for graduate students are never subsidized, meaning your interest will start accruing as soon as you take out the loan, rather than being deferred until you finish the program. Stafford loans are capped at $20,500 per year to a maximum of $138,500 total for both your undergraduate and graduate degrees. Some schools offer Federal Perkins Loans for low-income students, but they max out at $8,000 per year. Higher rate federal Grad PLUS loans are also available to help fill in the gaps. The maximum PLUS loan amount is the cost of attendance minus other financial aid you receive. And be aware that borrowing will cost you more as a grad student: Graduate unsubsidized loans carried interest rates of 6 percent for the 2017-2018 school year, while PLUS loans ran up interest of 7 percent. The interest rates on undergraduate loans, by contrast, were just 4.45 percent. •

8 Experts on How to Get

YOU EXCELLED IN COLLEGE and now you've made it into a leading MBA program. The future looks rosy for a great job with a big multinational or a hot startup, right? Well, maybe. The truth is employers want more than a slick résumé and a top class ranking. They are looking for highly engaged applicants who have done their homework and know how to communicate. During your job search, "treat every interaction with thought and importance," says Jessica Wessely, who led MBA recruiting for JPMorgan Chase last year. Recruiters "have a limited amount of time to get to know people, so students need to make sure that every interaction is productive for their recruiting success." U.S. News reached out to corporate recruiters as well as career specialists at major MBA programs to get their inside tips for getting an inside track. –*Compiled by Elizabeth Whitehead*

NAOMI SANCHEZ
University of Washington Foster School of Business
Assistant Dean, MBA Career Management

Build your interviewing chops. One thing we emphasize is not getting derailed by a difficult interview. I've had students who've been told their answers are not good. Don't lose your composure. Continue trying to respond in a positive manner. Engage with the interviewer. You can ask back, "Did I answer your question?" Try to build that emotional connection even if they don't want to be connected. Finish strong. You need positivity, resilience and grit to ultimately get the job you want.

BONUS TIP It's easy to get attached to a location where you live or have family. But we encourage people to take advantage of international opportunities, like one former student who is now starting his career working in Amazon Japan. Some students love Seattle – it's a happening place – so they may start here and then go abroad. But students should keep in mind that living abroad is very much a part of leadership development now for most multinational companies. If you're going to go to the C-suite, you will need that experience.

KRISTINA LIPHARDT
EY
Americas Campus Recruiting Leader for MBA Recruiting

Show you can "team." One component of our interview day is having candidates sit in a room, and we give them an actual business scenario to solve while they're observed. We've had instances where someone will have interviewed really well till that point, then they get to this exercise, and they will either rise or fall based on how they do. Maybe someone will sit back and be very quiet, and you will see others say to that person, "Hey, do you have any ideas you want to contribute?" Another candidate might suggest a way to solve the case, and a team member might say, "Oh no, that's a bad idea." In consulting you have to team well, so you need to demonstrate these skills to get hired.

BONUS TIP The people who do well are authentic and not afraid to share their experiences honestly. We had an applicant turn us down for an internship and then come back a year later wanting to interview for a full-time position. We asked, "What's different now?" The candidate explained about not having been sure consulting was the right fit and having taken another internship, only later realizing that had been a mistake. The candidate just seemed very sincere and had done so much research on EY, the opportunity and who they were interviewing with that we made an offer.

JASON OLIVER
AT&T
Vice President – Talent Acquisition

Show how you will add value. It's critical to show how you will add value as an employee. Recently, one of our college recruiters interviewed an MBA student who didn't seem to have a solid sense of AT&T's position in the marketplace – overall strategy, recent M&A activity and so forth. Instead, the student seemed more focused on "How much will I make?" or "What is the promotion timeline for new hires?" We seek candidates who are passionate about AT&T and can identify where he or she can add value in the future – like a young woman who registered for one of our "meet and greets" recently. In an initial conversation, she discussed AT&T's mobility product suite, asking, "Have you ever thought about making a differentiated marketing offer?" She proceeded to walk through a one-page document that laid out her proposal in detail. The impressive component wasn't the proposal per se – it was the fact that she came prepared, felt comfortable pitching her idea, and was passionate about driving our business forward.

BONUS TIP Increasingly, we partner with social platforms to target graduate business students. Through these connections, students can talk to members of the recruiting team and various leaders from across the business to learn more about our careers. Be on the lookout and leap at these interactive opportunities – we're hiring a lot of people through this channel.

JESSICA WESSELY
JPMorgan Chase
Technology Investment Banking Business Manager

Start your job search early. We typically begin preidentifying job candidates in April and May – before students enter business school in the fall. We partner with organizations like Toigo, MLT – Management Leadership for Tomorrow – and Forté to host early industry insight conferences. A number target specific ethnicities or women and help students meet with different companies and think about what kind of job or career they want. They're great vehicles for students to get their foot in the door with JPMorgan Chase. We also put on events and competitions throughout the year at different schools. For example, at NYU Stern we

Hired

have an annual investment banking case competition. We take a group of about 100 students, break them into groups and send them off to work on a case study, like a merger or acquisition. The next day each team presents the findings to a group of managing directors from JPMorgan Chase. Students who have banking or financial clubs at their schools should sign up for those because they're a great way of finding out what the financial companies are going to be doing.

5 KAREN HEISE
Washington University
Olin Business School
Interim Director – Weston Career Center

Stick around after company events.
One mistake I see is that students go to an employer-sponsored event but leave without talking to anyone. Most recruiters or company reps stay after the presentation – sometimes for a half hour so people can walk up to them and get to know them personally. Then the student has a business card and connection he or she can use later: "I met so-and-so at your event on campus last month … ." These relationships can be so important later when applying for a job.

6 MICHELLE HOPPING
University of Pennsylvania
The Wharton School
Director, Wharton MBA Career Management

Cultivate your champions.
Developing a conversation over time with company recruiters or reps can pay off. Look for reasons to contact them again that can reflect the skills and value you bring to the table. It could be updates that you see in the news about their company, their team or their individual contribu-

tions. It could be topical suggestions or even recommending a stellar person from your network for a noncompeting role at the company. The idea is you create a relationship. You want to develop advocates who will pound the table for you in a group when people are looked at for a potential internship or for a full-time job.

7 ALLISON FETHER
IBM
Vice President, Human Resources

Dress for success. Culture plays a big role in recruiting. We want to see if applicants fit into the "new IBM." If we tell you to wear business casual, don't show up in a three-piece suit. Folks have even shown up in suits with the tags still on, while the interviewer is wearing jeans and a T-shirt. We always say, "If you're uncertain about something, ask your recruiter.

BONUS TIP Sitting in an airport, I once heard a candidate talking on a cellphone about an IBM interview experience and saying how great it went. But then that person also made critical comments about an interviewer's hairdo, things of that nature. The applicant had no idea that I was nearby and employed by IBM. You never know who might hear you, so save your interview reflections for when you have a private space.

8 SJOERD GEHRING
Johnson & Johnson
VP, Talent Acquisition & Employee Experience

Sell yourself in a 360-degree perspective. We're starting to see more MBA students designing portfolios, not just a résumé but a much more creative and holistic portfolio around who they are as a leader, their academic background, skills and experiences. Recently I interviewed a student with a digital marketing background. She came into the interview with a beautiful portfolio of everything that she had done to date. She ran me through two digital marketing and digital ad campaigns she had supported for clients. She explained her role on the team, the creative campaigns they came up with, the media outlets that they had targeted and their results. She was able to bring her experience to life. Portfolios aren't just for designers; they can be effective for many candidates.
BONUS TIP Do not apply to 50 positions. If you are really interested in a role at J&J, then surely you will take the time to make sure your passions and skills align well to us and the position. By playing the quantity game you're not conveying that "This is the company I really want to work for." ●

DIRECTORY OF

Business

Schools

Directory of On-Campus MBA Programs PAGE D-2

Directory of Online MBA and Business Programs PAGE D-46

Index of On-Campus Programs PAGE D-91

Index of Online Programs PAGE D-94

Schools are listed alphabetically by state
within each category; data are accurate as of
late February 2018. A key to the terminology
used in the directories can be found at the
beginning of each one.

Georgetown's
McDonough School
of Business

On-Campus MBA Programs

THE BUSINESS directory lists all 480 U.S. schools offering master's programs in business accredited by AACSB International – The Association to Advance Collegiate Schools of Business as of summer 2017. Most offer the MBA degree; a few offer the master of business. Three hundred and eighty-seven schools responded to the U.S. News survey conducted in the fall of 2017 and early 2018. Schools that did not respond to the survey have abbreviated entries.

KEY TO THE TERMINOLOGY

1. A school whose name is footnoted with the numeral 1 did not return the U.S. News statistical survey; limited data appear in its entry.
N/A. Not available from the school or not applicable.
Email. The address of the admissions office. If instead of an email address a website is given in this field, the website will automatically present an email screen programmed to reach the admissions office.
Application deadline. For fall 2018 enrollment. "Rolling" means there is no application deadline; the school acts on applications as they are received. "Varies" means deadlines vary according to department or whether applicants are U.S. citizens or foreign nationals.
Tuition. For the 2017-2018 academic year or for the cost of the total graduate business degree program, if specified. Includes required annual student fees.
Credit hour. The cost per credit hour for the 2017-2018 academic year.
Room/board/expenses. For the 2017-2018 academic year.
College-funded aid and international student aid. "Yes" means the school provides its own financial aid to students.
Average indebtedness. Computed for 2017 graduates who incurred business school debt.

Enrollment. Full-time and part-time program totals are for fall 2017.
Minorities. For fall 2017, percentage of students who are black or African-American, Asian, American Indian or Alaska Native, Native Hawaiian or other Pacific Islander, Hispanic/Latino, or two or more races. The minority numbers were reported by each school.
Acceptance rate. Percentage of applicants to the full-time program who were accepted for fall 2017.
Average Graduate Management Admission Test (GMAT) score. Calculated for full-time students who entered in fall 2017.
Average Graduate Record Examinations (GRE) scores. Verbal, quantitative and writing scores calculated for full-time students who entered in fall 2017.
Average undergraduate grade point average (1.0 to 4.0). For full-time program applicants who entered in fall 2017.
Average age of entrants. Calculated for full-time students who entered in fall 2017.
Average months of work experience. Calculated only for full-time program students who entered in fall 2017. Refers to post-baccalaureate work experience only.
TOEFL requirement. "Yes" means that students from non-English-speaking countries must submit

scores for the Test of English as a Foreign Language.
Minimum TOEFL score. The lowest score on the paper TOEFL accepted for admission. (The computer-administered TOEFL is graded on a different scale.)
Most popular departments. Based on highest student demand in the 2017-2018 academic year.
Mean starting base salary for 2017 graduates. Calculated only for graduates who were full-time students, had accepted full-time job offers, and reported salary data. Excludes employer-sponsored students, signing bonuses of any kind and other forms of guaranteed compensation, such as stock options.
Employment locations. For the 2017 graduating class. Calculated only for full-time students who had accepted job offers. Abbreviations: Intl., international; N.E., Northeast (Conn., Maine, Mass., N.H., N.J., N.Y., R.I., Vt.); M.A., Middle Atlantic (Del., D.C., Md., Pa., Va., W.Va.); S., South (Ala., Ark., Fla., Ga., Ky., La., Miss., N.C., S.C., Tenn.); M.W., Midwest (Ill., Ind., Iowa, Kan., Mich., Minn., Mo., Neb., N.D., Ohio, S.D., Wis.); S.W., Southwest (Ariz., Colo., N.M., Okla., Texas); W., West (Alaska, Calif., Hawaii, Idaho, Mont., Nev., Ore., Utah, Wash., Wyo.).

ALABAMA

Auburn University (Harbert)
415 W. Magnolia, Suite 503
Auburn, AL 36849-5240
www.business.auburn.edu/mba
Public
Admissions: (334) 844-4060
Email: mbadmis@auburn.edu
Financial aid: (334) 844-4367
Application deadline: 02/01
In-state tuition: total program: $24,856 (full time); part time: N/A
Out-of-state tuition: total program: $52,882 (full time)
Room/board/expenses: $20,314
College-funded aid: Yes
International student aid: Yes
Average student indebtedness at graduation: $36,956
Full-time enrollment: 78
men: 56%; women: 44%; minorities: 17%; international: 12%
Part-time enrollment: N/A
Acceptance rate (full time): 39%
Average GMAT (full time): 584
Average GRE (full time): 155 verbal; 151 quantitative; 4.0 writing
Average GPA (full time): 3.41
Average age of entrants to full-time program: 24
Average months of prior work experience (full time): 32
TOEFL requirement: Yes
Minimum TOEFL score: 550
Most popular departments: finance, human resources management, management information systems, supply chain management/logistics, quantitative analysis/statistics and operations research
Mean starting base salary for 2017 full-time graduates: $61,675
Employment location for 2017 class: Intl. 0%; N.E. 5%; M.A. 0%; S. 80%; M.W. 5%; S.W. 0%; W. 10%

Auburn University–Montgomery
7300 East Drive
Montgomery, AL 36117
www.aum.edu
Public
Admissions: (334) 244-3623
Email: awarren3@aum.edu
Financial aid: (334) 244-3571
Application deadline: 08/01
In-state tuition: full time: $385/credit hour; part time: $385/credit hour
Out-of-state tuition: full time: $866/credit hour
Room/board/expenses: N/A
College-funded aid: Yes
International student aid: Yes
Average student indebtedness at graduation: $28,053
Full-time enrollment: 38
men: 58%; women: 42%; minorities: 13%; international: 53%
Part-time enrollment: 55
men: 44%; women: 56%; minorities: 33%; international: 13%
Acceptance rate (full time): 73%
Average GMAT (full time): 484

More @ usnews.com/bschool

Average GRE (full time): 144 verbal; 144 quantitative; N/A writing
Average GPA (full time): 3.18
Average age of entrants to full-time program: 28
TOEFL requirement: Yes
Minimum TOEFL score: 500

Jacksonville State University[1]
700 Pelham Road N
Jacksonville, AL 36265
www.jsu.edu/ccba/
Public
Admissions: (256) 782-5268
Email: info@jsu.edu
Financial aid: N/A
Tuition: N/A
Room/board/expenses: N/A
Enrollment: N/A

Samford University (Brock)
800 Lakeshore Drive
Birmingham, AL 35229
www.samford.edu/business
Private
Admissions: (205) 726-2040
Email: gradbusi@samford.edu
Financial aid: (205) 726-2905
Application deadline: 08/01
Tuition: full time: N/A; part time: $813/credit hour
Room/board/expenses: N/A
College-funded aid: Yes
International student aid: Yes
Full-time enrollment: N/A
Part-time enrollment: 98
men: 55%; women: 45%; minorities: 14%; international: 6%
Average GRE (full time): N/A verbal; N/A quantitative; N/A writing
TOEFL requirement: Yes
Minimum TOEFL score: N/A

University of Alabama–Birmingham
1720 2nd Avenue South
Birmingham, AL 35294-4460
www.uab.edu/business/
Public
Admissions: (205) 934-8817
Email: cmanning@uab.edu
Financial aid: (205) 934-8223
Application deadline: 08/01
In-state tuition: full time: $7,866; part time: $437/credit hour
Out-of-state tuition: full time: $17,910
Room/board/expenses: N/A
College-funded aid: Yes
International student aid: Yes
Full-time enrollment: N/A
Part-time enrollment: 412
men: 57%; women: 43%; minorities: 24%; international: 13%
Average GRE (full time): N/A verbal; N/A quantitative; N/A writing
TOEFL requirement: Yes
Minimum TOEFL score: 550
Most popular departments: accounting, finance, health care administration, marketing, management information systems

University of Alabama–Huntsville
BAB 202
Huntsville, AL 35899
www.uah.edu/business
Public
Admissions: (256) 824-6681
Email: gradbiz@uah.edu
Financial aid: (256) 824-2754
Application deadline: 06/01
In-state tuition: full time: $10,224; part time: $730/credit hour
Out-of-state tuition: full time: $22,696
Room/board/expenses: $15,353
College-funded aid: Yes
International student aid: Yes
Average student indebtedness at graduation: $23,647
Full-time enrollment: 39
men: 64%; women: 36%; minorities: 10%; international: 13%
Part-time enrollment: 95
men: 45%; women: 55%; minorities: 18%; international: 5%
Acceptance rate (full time): 83%
Average GMAT (full time): 505
Average GRE (full time): 152 verbal; 153 quantitative; 4.1 writing
Average GPA (full time): 3.20
Average age of entrants to full-time program: 27
Average months of prior work experience (full time): 36
TOEFL requirement: Yes
Minimum TOEFL score: 550
Most popular departments: accounting, general management, manufacturing and technology management, supply chain management/logistics, technology

University of Alabama (Manderson)
Box 870223
Tuscaloosa, AL 35487
www.cba.ua.edu/~mba
Public
Admissions: (888) 863-2622
Email: mba@cba.ua.edu
Financial aid: (205) 348-6517
Application deadline: 04/15
In-state tuition: full time: $13,610; part time: N/A
Out-of-state tuition: full time: $30,930
Room/board/expenses: N/A
College-funded aid: Yes
International student aid: Yes
Full-time enrollment: 289
men: 68%; women: 32%; minorities: 12%; international: 1%
Part-time enrollment: N/A
Acceptance rate (full time): 83%
Average GMAT (full time): 662
Average GRE (full time): 153 verbal; 152 quantitative; N/A writing
Average GPA (full time): 3.60
Average age of entrants to full-time program: 22
Average months of prior work experience (full time): 48
TOEFL requirement: Yes
Minimum TOEFL score: 550

ALASKA

University of Alaska–Anchorage[1]
3211 Providence Drive
Anchorage, AK 99508
www.uaa.alaska.edu/cbpp/
Public
Admissions: (907) 786-1480
Email: admissions@uaa.alaska.edu

Most popular departments: consulting, management information systems, production/operations management, supply chain management/logistics, quantitative analysis/statistics and operations research
Mean starting base salary for 2017 full-time graduates: $66,856
Employment location for 2017 class: Intl. N/A; N.E. 1%; M.A. 15%; S. 63%; M.W. 6%; S.W. 12%; W. 3%

University of Montevallo
Morgan Hall 201, Station 6540
Montevallo, AL 35115
www.montevallo.edu/mba/
Public
Admissions: (205) 665-6544
Email: mba@montevallo.edu
Financial aid: (205) 665-6050
Application deadline: rolling
In-state tuition: full time: N/A; part time: $412/credit hour
Out-of-state tuition: full time: N/A
Room/board/expenses: N/A
College-funded aid: Yes
Full-time enrollment: N/A
Part-time enrollment: 38
men: 58%; women: 42%; minorities: 18%; international: 0%
Average GRE (full time): N/A verbal; N/A quantitative; N/A writing
TOEFL requirement: Yes
Minimum TOEFL score: 525
Most popular departments: general management

University of North Alabama[1]
UNA Box 5077
Florence, AL 35632
www.una.edu/mba/
Public
Admissions: (256) 765-4103
Email: mbainfo@una.edu
Financial aid: N/A
Tuition: N/A
Room/board/expenses: N/A
Enrollment: N/A

University of South Alabama (Mitchell)[1]
307 N. University Boulevard
Mobile, AL 36688
mcob.usouthal.edu
Public
Admissions: (251) 460-6418
Financial aid: N/A
Tuition: N/A
Room/board/expenses: N/A
Enrollment: N/A

Financial aid: N/A
Tuition: N/A
Room/board/expenses: N/A
Enrollment: N/A

University of Alaska–Fairbanks
PO Box 756080
Fairbanks, AK 99775-6080
www.uaf.edu/index.html
Public
Admissions: (800) 478-1823
Email: admissions@uaf.edu
Financial aid: (888) 474-7256
Application deadline: 08/01
In-state tuition: full time: $559/credit hour; part time: $559/credit hour
Out-of-state tuition: full time: $1,175/credit hour
Room/board/expenses: $13,540
College-funded aid: Yes
International student aid: Yes
Full-time enrollment: 25
men: 36%; women: 64%; minorities: 24%; international: 0%
Part-time enrollment: 68
men: 43%; women: 57%; minorities: 25%; international: 1%
Average GRE (full time): N/A verbal; N/A quantitative; N/A writing
Average age of entrants to full-time program: 24
TOEFL requirement: Yes
Minimum TOEFL score: N/A
Most popular departments: finance, general management

ARIZONA

Arizona State University (Carey)
PO Box 874906
Tempe, AZ 85287-4906
wpcarey.asu.edu/mba-programs
Public
Admissions: (480) 965-3332
Email: wpcareymasters@asu.edu
Financial aid: (480) 965-6890
Application deadline: 04/03
In-state tuition: full time: $28,938; part time: $28,188
Out-of-state tuition: full time: $46,874
Room/board/expenses: $19,275
College-funded aid: Yes
International student aid: Yes
Average student indebtedness at graduation: $41,460
Full-time enrollment: 227
men: 59%; women: 41%; minorities: 18%; international: 32%
Part-time enrollment: 232
men: 63%; women: 37%; minorities: 29%; international: 9%
Acceptance rate (full time): 24%
Average GMAT (full time): 682
Average GRE (full time): 156 verbal; 155 quantitative; 3.9 writing
Average GPA (full time): 3.51
Average age of entrants to full-time program: 29
Average months of prior work experience (full time): 67

TOEFL requirement: Yes
Minimum TOEFL score: 550
Most popular departments: entrepreneurship, finance, marketing, supply chain management/logistics, other
Mean starting base salary for 2017 full-time graduates: $98,633
Employment location for 2017 class: Intl. N/A; N.E. 4%; M.A. 3%; S. 8%; M.W. 7%; S.W. 52%; W. 25%

Northern Arizona University (Franke)
PO Box 15066
Flagstaff, AZ 86011-5066
www.franke.nau.edu/graduateprograms
Public
Admissions: (928) 523-7342
Email: fcb-gradprog@nau.edu
Financial aid: (928) 523-4951
Application deadline: rolling
In-state tuition: total program: $18,753 (full time); part time: N/A
Out-of-state tuition: total program: $31,101 (full time)
Room/board/expenses: N/A
College-funded aid: Yes
International student aid: Yes
Full-time enrollment: 26
men: 50%; women: 50%; minorities: 12%; international: 8%
Part-time enrollment: N/A
Acceptance rate (full time): 98%
Average GMAT (full time): 544
Average GRE (full time): 153 verbal; 150 quantitative; 4.3 writing
Average GPA (full time): 3.48
Average age of entrants to full-time program: 23
Average months of prior work experience (full time): 35
TOEFL requirement: Yes
Minimum TOEFL score: 550
Mean starting base salary for 2017 full-time graduates: $54,300

Thunderbird School of Global Management[1]
1 Global Place
Glendale, AZ 85306-6000
www.thunderbird.edu
Public
Admissions: (602) 978-7100
Email: admissions@thunderbird.edu
Financial aid: (602) 978-7130
Tuition: N/A
Room/board/expenses: N/A
Enrollment: N/A

University of Arizona (Eller)
1130 East helen Street
McClelland Hall, Room 417
Tucson, AZ 85721-0108
ellermba.arizona.edu
Public
Admissions: (520) 621-6227
Email: mba_admissions@eller.arizona.edu
Financial aid: (520) 621-5200
Application deadline: 05/01
In-state tuition: full time: $24,312; part time: $25,500

Out-of-state tuition:
full time: $44,262
Room/board/expenses: $15,700
College-funded aid: Yes
International student aid: Yes
Average student indebtedness
at graduation: $35,495
Full-time enrollment: 86
men: 73%; women:
27%; minorities: 20%;
international: 41%
Part-time enrollment: 211
men: 60%; women:
40%; minorities: 30%;
international: 3%
Acceptance rate (full time): 74%
Average GMAT (full time): 642
Average GRE (full
time): N/A verbal; N/A
quantitative; N/A writing
Average GPA (full time): 3.26
Average age of entrants to
full-time program: 28
Average months of prior work
experience (full time): 50
TOEFL requirement: Yes
Minimum TOEFL score: 600
Most popular departments:
entrepreneurship, finance,
health care administration,
marketing, management
information systems
Mean starting base salary for 2017
full-time graduates: $82,315
Employment location for
2017 class: Intl. 0%; N.E.
5%; M.A. 5%; S. 14%; M.W.
19%; S.W. 43%; W. 14%

ARKANSAS

Arkansas State University–Jonesboro
PO Box 970
State University, AR 72467
www2.astate.edu/business/
Public
Admissions: (870) 972-3029
Email: gradsch@astate.edu
Financial aid: (870) 972-2310
Application deadline: 06/01
In-state tuition: full time: $392/
credit hour; part time: N/A
Out-of-state tuition: full
time: $659/credit hour
Room/board/expenses: $15,865
College-funded aid: Yes
International student aid: Yes
Average student indebtedness
at graduation: $39,000
Full-time enrollment: 194
men: 55%; women:
45%; minorities: 10%;
international: 30%
Part-time enrollment: N/A
Acceptance rate (full time): 89%
Average GMAT (full time): 560
Average GRE (full
time): 155 verbal; 154
quantitative; 4.4 writing
Average GPA (full time): 3.50
Average age of entrants to
full-time program: 28
Average months of prior work
experience (full time): 28
TOEFL requirement: Yes
Minimum TOEFL score: 550
Most popular departments:
finance, health care
administration, international
business, management
information systems, supply
chain management/logistics

Mean starting base salary for 2017
full-time graduates: $55,750
Employment location for 2017
class: Intl. 20%; N.E. 10%;
M.A. 20%; S. 30%; M.W.
N/A; S.W. 20%; W. N/A

Arkansas Tech University
1605 North Coliseum Drive
Russellville, AR 72801
www.atu.edu/business/
Public
Admissions: (479) 968-0398
Email: gradcollege@atu.edu
Financial aid: N/A
Application deadline: rolling
In-state tuition: full time:
$284/credit hour; part
time: $284/credit hour
Out-of-state tuition: full
time: $568/credit hour
Room/board/expenses: $11,285
College-funded aid: Yes
International student aid: Yes
Full-time enrollment: 2
men: 100%; women:
0%; minorities: N/A;
international: N/A
Part-time enrollment: 44
men: 32%; women:
68%; minorities: N/A;
international: N/A
Average GRE (full
time): N/A verbal; N/A
quantitative; N/A writing
TOEFL requirement: Yes
Minimum TOEFL score: N/A

Henderson State University[1]
1100 Henderson Street
Box 7801
Arkadelphia, AR 71999-0001
www.hsu.edu/Academics/
GraduateSchool/index.html
Public
Admissions: (870) 230-5126
Email: grad@hsu.edu
Financial aid: (870) 230-5148
Tuition: N/A
Room/board/expenses: N/A
Enrollment: N/A

Southern Arkansas University
100 E. University
Magnolia, AR 71753
web.saumag.edu/graduate/
programs/mba/
Public
Admissions: (870) 235-4150
Email: gradstudies@saumag.edu
Financial aid: (870) 235-4023
Application deadline: 07/01
In-state tuition: full time:
$285/credit hour; part
time: $285/credit hour
Out-of-state tuition: full
time: $425/credit hour
Room/board/expenses: N/A
College-funded aid: Yes
International student aid: Yes
Full-time enrollment: 20
men: 40%; women:
60%; minorities: N/A;
international: N/A

Part-time enrollment: 67
men: 49%; women:
51%; minorities: N/A;
international: N/A
Acceptance rate (full time): 83%
Average GMAT (full time): 416
Average GRE (full
time): N/A verbal; N/A
quantitative; N/A writing
Average GPA (full time): 3.60
Average age of entrants to
full-time program: 23
TOEFL requirement: Yes
Minimum TOEFL score: 550
Most popular departments:
entrepreneurship, general
management, supply chain
management/logistics, other

University of Arkansas–Fayetteville (Walton)
310 Williard J. Walker Hall
Fayetteville, AR 72701
gsb.uark.edu
Public
Admissions: (479) 575-2851
Email: gsb@walton.uark.edu
Financial aid: (479) 575-2711
Application deadline: 04/15
In-state tuition: full time: $573/
credit hour; part time: N/A
Out-of-state tuition: full
time: $1,499/credit hour
Room/board/expenses: $33,536
College-funded aid: Yes
International student aid: Yes
Full-time enrollment: 90
men: 60%; women:
40%; minorities: 8%;
international: 18%
Part-time enrollment: N/A
Acceptance rate (full time): 58%
Average GMAT (full time): 655
Average GRE (full
time): 155 verbal; 157
quantitative; 3.7 writing
Average GPA (full time): 3.54
Average age of entrants to
full-time program: 25
Average months of prior work
experience (full time): 41
TOEFL requirement: Yes
Minimum TOEFL score: 550
Most popular departments:
entrepreneurship, finance,
marketing, management
information systems, supply
chain management/logistics
Mean starting base salary for 2017
full-time graduates: $64,016
Employment location for
2017 class: Intl. 0%; N.E.
3%; M.A. 3%; S. 61%; M.W.
18%; S.W. 12%; W. 3%

University of Arkansas–Little Rock
2801 S. University Avenue
Little Rock, AR 72204
ualr.edu/cob
Public
Admissions: (501) 569-3356
Email: mbaadvising@ualr.edu
Financial aid: (501) 569-3035
Application deadline: 07/15
In-state tuition: full time: N/A;
part time: $345/credit hour
Out-of-state tuition: full time: N/A
Room/board/expenses: N/A
College-funded aid: Yes

International student aid: Yes
Average student indebtedness
at graduation: $39,738
Full-time enrollment: N/A
Part-time enrollment: 152
men: 41%; women:
59%; minorities: 15%;
international: 23%
Average GRE (full
time): N/A verbal; N/A
quantitative; N/A writing
TOEFL requirement: Yes
Minimum TOEFL score: 550
Most popular departments:
human resources
management, other

University of Central Arkansas
201 Donaghey
Conway, AR 72035
www.uca.edu/mba
Public
Admissions: (501) 450-5308
Email: markmc@uca.edu
Financial aid: (501) 450-3140
Application deadline: 07/15
In-state tuition: full time:
$267/credit hour; part
time: $267/credit hour
Out-of-state tuition: full
time: $534/credit hour
Room/board/expenses: $18,753
College-funded aid: Yes
International student aid: No
Average student indebtedness
at graduation: $18,437
Full-time enrollment: 45
men: 58%; women:
42%; minorities: 18%;
international: 33%
Part-time enrollment: 63
men: 49%; women:
51%; minorities: 25%;
international: 11%
Acceptance rate (full time): 88%
Average GRE (full
time): N/A verbal; N/A
quantitative; N/A writing
Average age of entrants to
full-time program: 24
Average months of prior work
experience (full time): 36
TOEFL requirement: Yes
Minimum TOEFL score: 550
Most popular departments:
e-commerce, finance,
health care administration,
international business,
quantitative analysis/statistics
and operations research
Mean starting base salary for 2017
full-time graduates: $65,000

CALIFORNIA

California Polytechnic State University–San Luis Obispo (Orfalea)
1 Grand Avenue
San Luis Obispo, CA 93407
www.cob.calpoly.edu/
gradbusiness/
Public
Admissions: (805) 756-2311
Email: admissions@calpoly.edu
Financial aid: (805) 756-2927
Application deadline: 04/01

In-state tuition: full time:
$25,626; part time: N/A
Out-of-state tuition:
full time: $38,298
Room/board/expenses: $17,721
College-funded aid: Yes
Full-time enrollment: 38
men: 53%; women:
47%; minorities: N/A;
international: N/A
Part-time enrollment: N/A
Acceptance rate (full time): 60%
Average GMAT (full time): 593
Average GRE (full
time): N/A verbal; N/A
quantitative; N/A writing
Average GPA (full time): 3.30
TOEFL requirement: Yes
Minimum TOEFL score: 550
Most popular departments:
accounting, economics, general
management, tax, other

California State Polytechnic University–Pomona
3801 W. Temple Avenue
Pomona, CA 91768
www.cpp.edu/cba/grad
Public
Admissions: (909) 869-3210
Email: admissions@cpp.edu
Financial aid: (909) 869-3700
Application deadline: 05/31
In-state tuition: total
program: $26,000 (full
time); part time: N/A
Out-of-state tuition: total
program: $38,000 (full time)
Room/board/expenses: $18,718
College-funded aid: Yes
International student aid: Yes
Full-time enrollment: 78
men: 53%; women:
47%; minorities: N/A;
international: N/A
Part-time enrollment: N/A
Acceptance rate (full time): 38%
Average GMAT (full time): 503
Average GRE (full
time): N/A verbal; N/A
quantitative; N/A writing
Average GPA (full time): 3.21
TOEFL requirement: Yes
Minimum TOEFL score: 550

California State University–Bakersfield[1]
9001 Stockdale Highway
Bakersfield, CA 93311-1099
www.csub.edu/BPA
Public
Admissions: (661) 664-3036
Email: admissions@csub.edu
Financial aid: N/A
Tuition: N/A
Room/board/expenses: N/A
Enrollment: N/A

California State University–Chico
Tehama Hall 301
Chico, CA 95929-0001
www.csuchico.edu/MBA
Public
Admissions: (530) 898-6880
Email: graduatestudies@
csuchico.edu

Financial aid: (530) 898-6451
Application deadline: 03/21
In-state tuition: full time:
$8,786; part time: N/A
Out-of-state tuition:
full time: $14,726
Room/board/expenses: $12,000
College-funded aid: Yes
International student aid: Yes
Full-time enrollment: 74
men: 58%; women:
42%; minorities: N/A;
international: N/A
Part-time enrollment: N/A
Acceptance rate (full time): 58%
Average GMAT (full time): 605
Average GRE (full
time): 148 verbal; 153
quantitative; N/A writing
Average GPA (full time): 3.20
Average age of entrants to
full-time program: 28
Average months of prior work
experience (full time): 31
TOEFL requirement: Yes
Minimum TOEFL score: 550

California State University–East Bay

25800 Carlos Bee Boulevard
Hayward, CA 94542
www.csueastbay.edu
Public
Admissions: (510) 885-3973
Email: admissions@
csueastbay.edu
Financial aid: (510) 885-2784
Application deadline: 05/15
In-state tuition: total
program: $29,800 (full
time); $31,336 (part time)
Out-of-state tuition: total
program: $29,800 (full time)
Room/board/expenses: N/A
College-funded aid: Yes
International student aid: No
Full-time enrollment: 23
men: 35%; women:
65%; minorities: 74%;
international: 9%
Part-time enrollment: 283
men: 51%; women:
49%; minorities: 48%;
international: 22%
Acceptance rate (full time): 67%
Average GRE (full
time): N/A verbal; N/A
quantitative; N/A writing
Average GPA (full time): 3.06
Average months of prior work
experience (full time): 5
TOEFL requirement: Yes
Minimum TOEFL score: 550
Most popular departments:
finance, general management,
human resources management,
marketing, supply chain
management/logistics

California State University– Fresno (Craig)[1]

5245 N. Backer Avenue
Fresno, CA 93740-8001
www.craig.csufresno.edu/mba
Public
Admissions: (559) 278-2107
Email: mbainfo@csufresno.edu
Financial aid: N/A
Tuition: N/A

Room/board/expenses: N/A
Enrollment: N/A

California State University–Fullerton (Mihaylo)

PO Box 6848
Fullerton, CA 92834-6848
business.fullerton.edu/
Public
Admissions: (657) 278-4035
Email: mihaylogradprograms@
fullerton.edu
Financial aid: (657) 278-3125
Application deadline: 04/01
In-state tuition: full time:
N/A; part time: $6,896
Out-of-state tuition: full time: N/A
Room/board/expenses: N/A
College-funded aid: Yes
International student aid: Yes
Full-time enrollment: N/A
Part-time enrollment: 285
men: 59%; women:
41%; minorities: 32%;
international: 31%
Average GRE (full
time): N/A verbal; N/A
quantitative; N/A writing
TOEFL requirement: Yes
Minimum TOEFL score: 583
Most popular departments:
accounting, economics, general
management, management
information systems

California State University– Long Beach

1250 Bellflower Boulevard
Long Beach, CA 90840-8501
www.csulb.edu/
cba-graduate-programs
Public
Admissions: (562) 985-4767
Email: mba@csulb.edu
Financial aid: (562) 985-4141
Application deadline: 06/01
In-state tuition: total program:
$45,600 (full time); part
time: $870/credit hour
Out-of-state tuition: total
program: $45,600 (full time)
Room/board/expenses: N/A
College-funded aid: Yes
International student aid: Yes
Full-time enrollment: 29
men: 55%; women:
45%; minorities: 0%;
international: 48%
Part-time enrollment: 80
men: 56%; women: 44%;
minorities: 0%; international: 8%
Acceptance rate (full time): 36%
Average GMAT (full time): 507
Average GRE (full
time): 149 verbal; 150
quantitative; 3.0 writing
Average GPA (full time): 3.17
Average age of entrants to
full-time program: 24
Average months of prior work
experience (full time): 26
TOEFL requirement: Yes
Minimum TOEFL score: N/A
Most popular departments:
human resources management

California State University– Los Angeles

5151 State University Drive
Los Angeles, CA 90032-8120
www.calstatela.edu/business/
gradprog
Public
Admissions: (323) 343-2810
Email: jratan@calstatela.edu
Financial aid: (323) 343-6260
Application deadline: 05/15
In-state tuition: full time:
N/A; part time: N/A
Out-of-state tuition: full time: N/A
Room/board/expenses: N/A
College-funded aid: Yes
International student aid: Yes
Full-time enrollment: 323
men: 55%; women:
45%; minorities: N/A;
international: N/A
Part-time enrollment: N/A
Acceptance rate (full time): 55%
Average GRE (full
time): N/A verbal; N/A
quantitative; N/A writing
TOEFL requirement: Yes
Minimum TOEFL score: 550

California State University–Northridge (Nazarian)

18111 Nordhoff Street
Northridge, CA 91330-8380
www.csun.edu/mba/
Public
Admissions: (818) 677-2467
Email: mba@csun.edu
Financial aid: (818) 677-4085
Application deadline: 05/01
In-state tuition: full time:
$13,164; part time: $10,152
Out-of-state tuition:
full time: $20,292
Room/board/expenses: N/A
College-funded aid: Yes
International student aid: Yes
Full-time enrollment: N/A
Part-time enrollment: 125
men: 49%; women:
51%; minorities: 52%;
international: 6%
Average GRE (full
time): N/A verbal; N/A
quantitative; N/A writing
TOEFL requirement: Yes
Minimum TOEFL score: 550
Most popular departments:
accounting, finance,
general management,
marketing, management
information systems

California State University– Sacramento[1]

6000 J Street
Sacramento, CA 95819-6088
www.csus.edu/cba/graduate/
index.html
Public
Admissions: (916) 278-6772
Email: CBA-MBAAdmissions@
csus.edu
Financial aid: (916) 278-6980
Tuition: N/A
Room/board/expenses: N/A
Enrollment: N/A

California State University– San Bernardino

5500 University Parkway
San Bernardino, CA 92407
jhbc.csusb.edu/mba
Public
Admissions: (909) 537-5703
Email: mba@csusb.edu
Financial aid: (909) 537-5227
Application deadline: 06/11
In-state tuition: full time:
$8,319; part time: $5,307
Out-of-state tuition:
full time: $17,823
Room/board/expenses: N/A
College-funded aid: Yes
International student aid: Yes
Full-time enrollment: N/A
Part-time enrollment: 222
men: 65%; women:
35%; minorities: 42%;
international: 31%
Average GRE (full
time): N/A verbal; N/A
quantitative; N/A writing
TOEFL requirement: Yes
Minimum TOEFL score: 550
Most popular departments:
accounting, entrepreneurship,
finance, general
management, other

California State University–Stanislaus

1 University Circle
Turlock, CA 95382
www.csustan.edu/grad
Public
Admissions: (209) 667-3129
Email: graduate_school@
csustan.edu
Financial aid: (209) 667-3336
Application deadline: 06/30
In-state tuition: full time:
N/A; total program:
$23,000 (part time)
Out-of-state tuition: full time: N/A
Room/board/expenses: N/A
College-funded aid: Yes
International student aid: No
Full-time enrollment: N/A
Part-time enrollment: 60
men: 45%; women:
55%; minorities: N/A;
international: N/A
Average GRE (full
time): N/A verbal; N/A
quantitative; N/A writing
TOEFL requirement: Yes
Minimum TOEFL score: 550

Chapman University (Argyros)

1 University Drive
Orange, CA 92866
www.chapman.edu/argyros
Private
Admissions: (714) 997-6596
Email: mba@chapman.edu
Financial aid: (714) 628-2510
Application deadline: 06/01
Tuition: full time: $1,590/
credit hour; part time:
$1,590/credit hour
Room/board/expenses: $24,626
College-funded aid: Yes
International student aid: Yes
Average student indebtedness
at graduation: $62,693

Full-time enrollment: 67
men: 60%; women:
40%; minorities: 22%;
international: 43%
Part-time enrollment: 140
men: 52%; women:
48%; minorities: 33%;
international: 30%
Acceptance rate (full time): 53%
Average GMAT (full time): 648
Average GRE (full
time): 153 verbal; 156
quantitative; 3.7 writing
Average GPA (full time): 3.35
Average age of entrants to
full-time program: 27
Average months of prior work
experience (full time): 52
TOEFL requirement: Yes
Minimum TOEFL score: N/A
Most popular departments:
entrepreneurship, finance,
general management,
international business,
marketing
Mean starting base salary for 2017
full-time graduates: $63,570
Employment location for
2017 class: Intl. N/A; N.E.
N/A; M.A. 6%; S. N/A; M.W.
N/A; S.W. N/A; W. 94%

Claremont Graduate University (Drucker)

150 E. 10th Street
Claremont, CA 91711
www.cgu.edu/school/
drucker-school-of-
management/
Private
Admissions: (909) 607-7811
Email: admissions@cgu.edu
Financial aid: (909) 621-8337
Application deadline: 08/15
Tuition: full time: N/A;
part time: N/A
Room/board/expenses: N/A
College-funded aid: Yes
International student aid: Yes
Full-time enrollment: 84
men: 60%; women:
40%; minorities: 32%;
international: 50%
Part-time enrollment: 20
men: 55%; women:
45%; minorities: 55%;
international: 0%
Average GRE (full
time): N/A verbal; N/A
quantitative; N/A writing
TOEFL requirement: Yes
Minimum TOEFL score: N/A
Most popular departments: arts
adiminstration, finance, general
management, marketing, supply
chain management/logistics

Loyola Marymount University

1 LMU Drive, MS 8387
Los Angeles, CA 90045-2659
mba.lmu.edu
Private
Admissions: (310) 338-2848
Email: Mba.office@lmu.edu
Financial aid: (310) 338-2753
Application deadline: 06/01
Tuition: full time: N/A; total
program: $88,500 (part time)
Room/board/expenses: N/A
College-funded aid: Yes

International student aid: Yes
Full-time enrollment: N/A
Part-time enrollment: 89
men: 66%; women:
34%; minorities: 37%;
international: 21%
Average GRE (full
time): N/A verbal; N/A
quantitative; N/A writing
TOEFL requirement: Yes
Minimum TOEFL score: 600
Most popular departments:
entrepreneurship, finance,
general management,
international business,
marketing

Naval Postgraduate School[1]

555 Dyer Road
Monterey, CA 93943
www.nps.edu/academics/
schools/GSBPP/
Public
Admissions: N/A
Financial aid: N/A
Tuition: N/A
Room/board/expenses: N/A
Enrollment: N/A

Pepperdine University (Graziadio)

24255 Pacific Coast Highway
Malibu, CA 90263-4100
bschool.pepperdine.edu
Private
Admissions: (310) 568-5530
Email: gsbmadm@
pepperdine.edu
Financial aid: (310) 568-5530
Application deadline: 05/01
Tuition: full time: $49,580;
part time: $1,715/credit hour
Room/board/expenses: $9,800
College-funded aid: Yes
International student aid: Yes
Average student indebtedness
at graduation: $90,256
Full-time enrollment: 128
men: 54%; women:
46%; minorities: 16%;
international: 35%
Part-time enrollment: 654
men: 53%; women:
47%; minorities: 30%;
international: 3%
Acceptance rate (full time): 53%
Average GMAT (full time): 627
Average GRE (full
time): 155 verbal; 153
quantitative; 4.0 writing
Average GPA (full time): 3.20
Average age of entrants to
full-time program: 29
Average months of prior work
experience (full time): 60
TOEFL requirement: Yes
Minimum TOEFL score: 500
Most popular departments:
finance, general
management, leadership,
marketing, management
information systems
Mean starting base salary for 2017
full-time graduates: $78,294
Employment location for
2017 class: Intl. 12%; N.E.
6%; M.A. N/A; S. 9%; M.W.
N/A; S.W. 9%; W. 65%

San Diego State University (Fowler)

5500 Campanile Drive
San Diego, CA 92182-8228
business.sdsu.edu
Public
Admissions: (619) 594-6336
Email: admissions@sdsu.edu
Financial aid: (619) 594-6323
Application deadline: 03/01
In-state tuition: full time:
$14,588; part time: $10,742
Out-of-state tuition:
full time: $23,696
Room/board/expenses: $17,015
College-funded aid: Yes
International student aid: Yes
Average student indebtedness
at graduation: $41,732
Full-time enrollment: 230
men: 57%; women:
43%; minorities: 20%;
international: 47%
Part-time enrollment: 228
men: 55%; women:
45%; minorities: 33%;
international: 10%
Acceptance rate (full time): 39%
Average GMAT (full time): 603
Average GRE (full
time): 151 verbal; 154
quantitative; 3.6 writing
Average GPA (full time): 3.36
Average age of entrants to
full-time program: 27
Average months of prior work
experience (full time): 52
TOEFL requirement: Yes
Minimum TOEFL score: N/A
Most popular departments:
accounting, entrepreneurship,
finance, marketing, management
information systems
Mean starting base salary for 2017
full-time graduates: $60,274

San Francisco State University

835 Market Street, Suite 600
San Francisco, CA 94103
mba.sfsu.edu
Public
Admissions: (415) 817-4300
Email: mba@sfsu.edu
Financial aid: (415) 338-1581
Application deadline: 05/31
In-state tuition: full time:
$17,572; part time: $11,320
Out-of-state tuition:
full time: $27,076
Room/board/expenses: $32,000
College-funded aid: Yes
International student aid: Yes
Full-time enrollment: 79
men: 43%; women:
57%; minorities: 24%;
international: 53%
Part-time enrollment: 73
men: 52%; women:
48%; minorities: 55%;
international: 12%
Acceptance rate (full time): 74%
Average GMAT (full time): 545
Average GRE (full
time): 150 verbal; 152
quantitative; 3.8 writing
Average GPA (full time): 3.52
Average age of entrants to
full-time program: 27
Average months of prior work
experience (full time): 46
TOEFL requirement: Yes

Minimum TOEFL score: 590
Most popular departments:
accounting, finance, marketing,
management information
systems, quantitative
analysis/statistics and
operations research

San Jose State University (Lucas)

1 Washington Square
San Jose, CA 95192-0162
www.sjsu.edu/lucasgsb
Public
Admissions: (408) 924-1000
Email: admissions@sjsu.edu
Financial aid: (408) 283-7500
Application deadline: 05/01
In-state tuition: total
program: $32,721 (full
time); N/A (part time)
Out-of-state tuition: total
program: $49,350 (full time)
Room/board/expenses: N/A
College-funded aid: Yes
International student aid: No
Full-time enrollment: 152
men: 55%; women:
45%; minorities: 47%;
international: 30%
Part-time enrollment: N/A
Acceptance rate (full time): 43%
Average GRE (full
time): N/A verbal; N/A
quantitative; N/A writing
Average age of entrants to
full-time program: 26
TOEFL requirement: Yes
Minimum TOEFL score: N/A
Most popular departments:
accounting, general
management

Santa Clara University (Leavey)

Lucas Hall 116
Santa Clara, CA 95053
www.scu.edu/business
Private
Admissions: (408) 554-2752
Email: gradbusiness@scu.edu
Financial aid: (408) 554-4505
Application deadline: rolling
Tuition: full time: N/A; part
time: $1,068/credit hour
Room/board/expenses: N/A
College-funded aid: Yes
International student aid: Yes
Average student indebtedness
at graduation: $59,240
Full-time enrollment: N/A
Part-time enrollment: 374
men: 59%; women:
41%; minorities: 47%;
international: 24%
Average GRE (full
time): N/A verbal; N/A
quantitative; N/A writing
TOEFL requirement: Yes
Minimum TOEFL score: N/A
Most popular departments:
entrepreneurship, finance,
leadership, marketing, other

Sonoma State University

1801 E. Cotati Avenue
Rohnert Park, CA 94928
www.sonoma.edu/admissions
Public
Admissions: (707) 664-2252
Email: rosanna.kelley@
sonoma.edu
Financial aid: (707) 664-2389
Application deadline: 04/30
In-state tuition: total
program: $22,520 (full
time); $22,103 (part time)
Out-of-state tuition: total
program: $30,455 (full time)
Room/board/expenses: N/A
College-funded aid: Yes
International student aid: Yes
Full-time enrollment: N/A
Part-time enrollment: 59
men: 49%; women: 51%;
minorities: 8%; international: 8%
Average GRE (full
time): N/A verbal; N/A
quantitative; N/A writing
TOEFL requirement: Yes
Minimum TOEFL score: 550
Most popular departments:
general management,
leadership, other

Stanford University

655 Knight Way
Stanford, CA 94305-7298
www.gsb.stanford.edu/mba
Private
Admissions: (650) 723-2766
Email: mba.admissions@
gsb.stanford.edu
Financial aid: (650) 723-3282
Application deadline: 04/04
Tuition: full time: $68,868;
part time: N/A
Room/board/expenses: $43,929
College-funded aid: Yes
International student aid: Yes
Average student indebtedness
at graduation: $86,929
Full-time enrollment: 853
men: 60%; women:
40%; minorities: N/A;
international: N/A
Part-time enrollment: N/A
Acceptance rate (full time): 6%
Average GMAT (full time): 737
Average GRE (full
time): 165 verbal; 164
quantitative; 4.9 writing
Average GPA (full time): 3.74
Average months of prior work
experience (full time): 52
TOEFL requirement: Yes
Minimum TOEFL score: 600
Most popular departments:
entrepreneurship,
finance, general
management, leadership,
organizational behavior
Mean starting base salary for 2017
full-time graduates: $144,455
Employment location for
2017 class: Intl. 11%; N.E.
16%; M.A. 2%; S. 2%; M.W.
2%; S.W. 5%; W. 63%

St. Mary's College of California

1928 Saint Marys Road
Moraga, CA 94575
www.smcmba.com
Private
Admissions: (925) 631-4503
Email: smcmba@stmarys-ca.edu
Financial aid: (925) 631-4370
Application deadline: 12/15
Tuition: total program: $29,700
(full time); $59,400 (part time)
Room/board/expenses: N/A
College-funded aid: Yes
International student aid: Yes
Full-time enrollment: 15
men: 47%; women:
53%; minorities: 33%;
international: 7%
Part-time enrollment: 123
men: 63%; women:
37%; minorities: 60%;
international: 3%
Average GRE (full
time): N/A verbal; N/A
quantitative; N/A writing
TOEFL requirement: Yes
Minimum TOEFL score: N/A
Most popular departments:
entrepreneurship, finance,
international business,
marketing, quantitative
analysis/statistics and
operations research
Mean starting base salary for 2017
full-time graduates: $50,000
Employment location for
2017 class: Intl. N/A; N.E.
N/A; M.A. N/A; S. N/A; M.W.
N/A; S.W. N/A; W. 100%

University of California– Berkeley (Haas)

545 Student Services Building
Berkeley, CA 94720-1900
mba.haas.berkeley.edu
Public
Admissions: (510) 642-1405
Email: mbaadm@
haas.berkeley.edu
Financial aid: (510) 643-0183
Application deadline: 04/05
In-state tuition: full time:
$58,794; part time:
$3,265/credit hour
Out-of-state tuition:
full time: $59,811
Room/board/expenses: $27,470
College-funded aid: Yes
International student aid: Yes
Average student indebtedness
at graduation: $90,642
Full-time enrollment: 543
men: 60%; women:
40%; minorities: 20%;
international: 34%
Part-time enrollment: 846
men: 71%; women:
29%; minorities: N/A;
international: N/A
Acceptance rate (full time): 13%
Average GMAT (full time): 725
Average GRE (full
time): 164 verbal; 161
quantitative; 5.0 writing
Average GPA (full time): 3.71
Average age of entrants to
full-time program: 28

Average months of prior work experience (full time): 63
TOEFL requirement: Yes
Minimum TOEFL score: 570
Most popular departments: entrepreneurship, finance, leadership, marketing, technology
Mean starting base salary for 2017 full-time graduates: $125,572
Employment location for 2017 class: Intl. 11%; N.E. 5%; M.A. 1%; S. 1%; M.W. 1%; S.W. 2%; W. 79%

University of California–Davis

1 Shields Avenue
Davis, CA 95616-8609
gsm.ucdavis.edu
Public
Admissions: (530) 752-7658
Email: admissions@gsm.ucdavis.edu
Financial aid: (530) 752-7363
Application deadline: 04/18
In-state tuition: full time: $40,954; total program: $93,960 (part time)
Out-of-state tuition: full time: $53,199
Room/board/expenses: $23,988
College-funded aid: Yes
International student aid: Yes
Average student indebtedness at graduation: $68,861
Full-time enrollment: 96
men: 56%; women: 44%; minorities: 32%; international: 38%
Part-time enrollment: 323
men: 59%; women: 41%; minorities: 46%; international: 11%
Acceptance rate (full time): 37%
Average GMAT (full time): 669
Average GRE (full time): 159 verbal; 162 quantitative; 3.8 writing
Average GPA (full time): 3.36
Average age of entrants to full-time program: 29
Average months of prior work experience (full time): 67
TOEFL requirement: Yes
Minimum TOEFL score: 600
Most popular departments: entrepreneurship, finance, marketing, organizational behavior, technology
Mean starting base salary for 2017 full-time graduates: $95,603
Employment location for 2017 class: Intl. 9%; N.E. N/A; M.A. N/A; S. 6%; M.W. N/A; S.W. 3%; W. 81%

University of California–Irvine (Merage)

5300 SB1, 4293 Pereira Drive
Irvine, CA 92697-3125
merage.uci.edu/
Public
Admissions: (949) 824-4622
Email: mba@merage.uci.edu
Financial aid: (949) 824-7967
Application deadline: 04/01
In-state tuition: full time: $43,831; total program: $95,697 (part time)

Out-of-state tuition: full time: $51,480
Room/board/expenses: $32,488
College-funded aid: Yes
International student aid: Yes
Average student indebtedness at graduation: $75,714
Full-time enrollment: 167
men: 72%; women: 28%; minorities: 21%; international: 48%
Part-time enrollment: 330
men: 64%; women: 36%; minorities: 62%; international: 3%
Acceptance rate (full time): 25%
Average GMAT (full time): 654
Average GRE (full time): 157 verbal; 158 quantitative; 4.3 writing
Average GPA (full time): 3.46
Average age of entrants to full-time program: 29
Average months of prior work experience (full time): 72
TOEFL requirement: Yes
Minimum TOEFL score: 600
Most popular departments: finance, marketing, organizational behavior, quantitative analysis/statistics and operations research, other
Mean starting base salary for 2017 full-time graduates: $97,808
Employment location for 2017 class: Intl. 4%; N.E. 0%; M.A. 2%; S. 0%; M.W. 0%; S.W. 0%; W. 94%

University of California–Los Angeles (Anderson)

110 Westwood Plaza
Box 951481
Los Angeles, CA 90095-1481
www.anderson.ucla.edu
Public
Admissions: (310) 825-6944
Email: mba.admissions@anderson.ucla.edu
Financial aid: (310) 825-2746
Application deadline: 04/16
In-state tuition: full time: $61,245; part time: $44,554
Out-of-state tuition: full time: $62,776
Room/board/expenses: $34,203
College-funded aid: Yes
International student aid: Yes
Average student indebtedness at graduation: $84,802
Full-time enrollment: 725
men: 66%; women: 34%; minorities: 26%; international: 32%
Part-time enrollment: 983
men: 68%; women: 32%; minorities: 45%; international: 9%
Acceptance rate (full time): 22%
Average GMAT (full time): 715
Average GRE (full time): 164 verbal; 164 quantitative; 4.5 writing
Average GPA (full time): 3.52
Average age of entrants to full-time program: 28
Average months of prior work experience (full time): 63
TOEFL requirement: Yes

Minimum TOEFL score: 560
Most popular departments: accounting, consulting, finance, marketing, technology
Mean starting base salary for 2017 full-time graduates: $119,964
Employment location for 2017 class: Intl. 8%; N.E. 6%; M.A. 0%; S. 1%; M.W. 1%; S.W. 3%; W. 81%

University of California–Riverside (Anderson)

900 University Avenue
Riverside, CA 92521-0203
agsm.ucr.edu
Public
Admissions: (951) 827-6200
Email: ucr_agsm@ucr.edu
Financial aid: (951) 827-7249
Application deadline: 09/01
In-state tuition: full time: $39,864; part time: $1,379/credit hour
Out-of-state tuition: full time: $52,110
Room/board/expenses: $15,045
College-funded aid: Yes
International student aid: Yes
Average student indebtedness at graduation: $52,257
Full-time enrollment: 119
men: 55%; women: 45%; minorities: 22%; international: 70%
Part-time enrollment: 114
men: 58%; women: 42%; minorities: 38%; international: 48%
Acceptance rate (full time): 60%
Average GMAT (full time): 594
Average GRE (full time): 150 verbal; 159 quantitative; 3.4 writing
Average GPA (full time): 3.26
Average age of entrants to full-time program: 26
Average months of prior work experience (full time): 43
TOEFL requirement: Yes
Minimum TOEFL score: 550
Most popular departments: accounting, finance, general management, marketing, supply chain management/logistics
Mean starting base salary for 2017 full-time graduates: $70,305
Employment location for 2017 class: Intl. 37%; N.E. 0%; M.A. 0%; S. 0%; M.W. 0%; S.W. 3%; W. 60%

University of California–San Diego (Rady)

9500 Gilman Drive #0553
San Diego, CA 92093-0553
www.rady.ucsd.edu/
Public
Admissions: (858) 534-0864
Email: RadyGradAdmissions@ucsd.edu
Financial aid: (858) 534-4480
Application deadline: 06/01
In-state tuition: full time: $48,961; part time: $1,152/credit hour
Out-of-state tuition: full time: $55,546

Room/board/expenses: $15,000
College-funded aid: Yes
International student aid: Yes
Full-time enrollment: 117
men: 67%; women: 33%; minorities: N/A; international: N/A
Part-time enrollment: 122
men: 35%; women: 65%; minorities: N/A; international: N/A
Acceptance rate (full time): 48%
Average GMAT (full time): 668
Average GRE (full time): 157 verbal; 157 quantitative; 3.7 writing
Average GPA (full time): 3.26
Average age of entrants to full-time program: 29
Average months of prior work experience (full time): 62
TOEFL requirement: Yes
Minimum TOEFL score: 550
Most popular departments: entrepreneurship, finance, general management, marketing, technology
Mean starting base salary for 2017 full-time graduates: $84,858
Employment location for 2017 class: Intl. 17%; N.E. N/A; M.A. N/A; S. 6%; M.W. 6%; S.W. N/A; W. 72%

University of San Diego

5998 Alcala Park
San Diego, CA 92110-2492
www.sandiego.edu/mba
Private
Admissions: (619) 260-4860
Email: gradbus@sandiego.edu
Financial aid: (619) 260-4514
Application deadline: 05/01
Tuition: full time: $1,420/credit hour; part time: $1,420/credit hour
Room/board/expenses: $18,918
College-funded aid: Yes
International student aid: Yes
Average student indebtedness at graduation: $83,677
Full-time enrollment: 81
men: 64%; women: 36%; minorities: 15%; international: 51%
Part-time enrollment: 98
men: 63%; women: 37%; minorities: 28%; international: 7%
Acceptance rate (full time): 55%
Average GMAT (full time): 611
Average GRE (full time): 154 verbal; 155 quantitative; 4.0 writing
Average GPA (full time): 3.30
Average age of entrants to full-time program: 28
Average months of prior work experience (full time): 52
TOEFL requirement: Yes
Minimum TOEFL score: 580
Most popular departments: entrepreneurship, finance, general management, marketing, supply chain management/logistics
Mean starting base salary for 2017 full-time graduates: $81,278

University of San Francisco

101 Howard Street, Suite 500
San Francisco, CA 94105-1080
www.usfca.edu/management/graduate/
Private
Admissions: (415) 422-2221
Email: management@usfca.edu
Financial aid: (415) 422-2020
Application deadline: 06/15
Tuition: full time: $1,425/credit hour; part time: $1,425/credit hour
Room/board/expenses: N/A
College-funded aid: Yes
International student aid: Yes
Average student indebtedness at graduation: $93,937
Full-time enrollment: 82
men: 57%; women: 43%; minorities: 27%; international: 46%
Part-time enrollment: 87
men: 53%; women: 47%; minorities: 52%; international: 2%
Acceptance rate (full time): 53%
Average GMAT (full time): 579
Average GRE (full time): 152 verbal; 151 quantitative; 3.9 writing
Average GPA (full time): 3.18
Average age of entrants to full-time program: 28
Average months of prior work experience (full time): 57
TOEFL requirement: Yes
Minimum TOEFL score: 580
Most popular departments: entrepreneurship, finance, marketing, organizational behavior, quantitative analysis/statistics and operations research
Mean starting base salary for 2017 full-time graduates: $80,071
Employment location for 2017 class: Intl. 14%; N.E. N/A; M.A. N/A; S. N/A; M.W. N/A; S.W. N/A; W. 86%

University of Southern California (Marshall)

University Park
Los Angeles, CA 90089-1421
www.marshall.usc.edu
Private
Admissions: (213) 740-7846
Email: marshallmba@marshall.usc.edu
Financial aid: (213) 740-1111
Application deadline: 04/15
Tuition: full time: $68,194; part time: $1,847/credit hour
Room/board/expenses: $23,555
College-funded aid: Yes
International student aid: Yes
Full-time enrollment: 454
men: 68%; women: 32%; minorities: 26%; international: 31%
Part-time enrollment: 480
men: 69%; women: 31%; minorities: 51%; international: 2%
Acceptance rate (full time): 29%
Average GMAT (full time): 703

Average GRE (full time): 160 verbal; 159 quantitative; 4.4 writing
Average GPA (full time): 3.48
Average age of entrants to full-time program: 28
Average months of prior work experience (full time): 60
TOEFL requirement: Yes
Minimum TOEFL score: 600
Mean starting base salary for 2017 full-time graduates: $118,110
Employment location for 2017 class: Intl. 6%; N.E. 6%; M.A. N/A; S. 1%; M.W. 2%; S.W. 2%; W. 83%

University of the Pacific (Eberhardt)
3601 Pacific Avenue
Stockton, CA 95211
www.pacific.edu/mba
Private
Admissions: (209) 946-2629
Email: mba@pacific.edu
Financial aid: (209) 946-2421
Application deadline: 03/01
Tuition: total program: $70,296 (full time); part time: N/A
Room/board/expenses: $30,420
College-funded aid: Yes
International student aid: Yes
Full-time enrollment: 22
men: 45%; women: 55%; minorities: 64%; international: 9%
Part-time enrollment: N/A
Acceptance rate (full time): 63%
Average GMAT (full time): 567
Average GRE (full time): 152 verbal; 150 quantitative; 4.0 writing
Average GPA (full time): 3.28
Average age of entrants to full-time program: 23
Average months of prior work experience (full time): 17
TOEFL requirement: Yes
Minimum TOEFL score: 550
Most popular departments: general management, health care administration

Woodbury University[1]
7500 N. Glenoaks Boulevard
Burbank, CA 91504
woodbury.edu/
Private
Admissions: (818) 252-5221
Email: admissions@woodbury.edu
Financial aid: (818) 252-5273
Tuition: N/A
Room/board/expenses: N/A
Enrollment: N/A

Colorado State University
1270 Campus Delivery
Fort Collins, CO 80523-1270
biz.colostate.edu/Academics/Graduate-Programs/Master-of-Business-Administration
Public
Admissions: (970) 491-1129
Email: gradadmissions@business.colostate.edu

Financial aid: (970) 491-6321
Application deadline: 06/01
In-state tuition: full time: $757/credit hour; part time: $757/credit hour
Out-of-state tuition: full time: $1,557/credit hour
Room/board/expenses: $12,000
College-funded aid: Yes
International student aid: Yes
Average student indebtedness at graduation: $42,014
Full-time enrollment: 94
men: 51%; women: 49%; minorities: 11%; international: 37%
Part-time enrollment: 50
men: 62%; women: 38%; minorities: 22%; international: 4%
Acceptance rate (full time): 82%
Average GMAT (full time): 535
Average GRE (full time): 152 verbal; 151 quantitative; 3.4 writing
Average GPA (full time): 3.38
Average age of entrants to full-time program: 26
Average months of prior work experience (full time): 56
TOEFL requirement: Yes
Minimum TOEFL score: N/A
Most popular departments: finance, general management, leadership, marketing, management information systems
Mean starting base salary for 2017 full-time graduates: $49,942

Colorado State University–Pueblo[1]
2200 Bonforte Boulevard
Pueblo, CO 81001
hsb.colostate-pueblo.edu
Public
Admissions: (719) 549-2461
Email: info@colostate-pueblo.edu
Financial aid: N/A
Tuition: N/A
Room/board/expenses: N/A
Enrollment: N/A

University of Colorado–Boulder (Leeds)
995 Regent Drive 419 UCB
Boulder, CO 80309
www.colorado.edu/business
Public
Admissions: (303) 492-2061
Email: leedsmba@Colorado.edu
Financial aid: (303) 492-8223
Application deadline: 04/01
In-state tuition: full time: $900/credit hour; total program: $49,800 (part time)
Out-of-state tuition: full time: $1,200/credit hour
Room/board/expenses: $20,500
College-funded aid: Yes
International student aid: Yes
Full-time enrollment: 185
men: 66%; women: 34%; minorities: 15%; international: 17%
Part-time enrollment: 149
men: 62%; women: 38%; minorities: 9%; international: 6%

Acceptance rate (full time): 69%
Average GMAT (full time): 630
Average GRE (full time): 156 verbal; 154 quantitative; 4.0 writing
Average GPA (full time): 3.36
Average age of entrants to full-time program: 29
Average months of prior work experience (full time): 64
TOEFL requirement: Yes
Minimum TOEFL score: N/A
Most popular departments: entrepreneurship, finance, general management, real estate, other
Mean starting base salary for 2017 full-time graduates: $75,774
Employment location for 2017 class: Intl. 7%; N.E. 2%; M.A. 2%; S. 2%; M.W. 6%; S.W. 72%; W. 9%

University of Colorado–Colorado Springs
1420 Austin Bluffs Parkway
Colorado Springs, CO 80918
www.uccs.edu/mba
Public
Admissions: (719) 255-3122
Email: cobgrad@uccs.edu
Financial aid: (719) 255-3460
Application deadline: 06/01
In-state tuition: full time: N/A; part time: $726/credit hour
Out-of-state tuition: full time: N/A
Room/board/expenses: N/A
College-funded aid: Yes
International student aid: Yes
Full-time enrollment: N/A
Part-time enrollment: 332
men: 57%; women: 43%; minorities: 22%; international: 3%
Average GRE (full time): N/A verbal; N/A quantitative; N/A writing
TOEFL requirement: Yes
Minimum TOEFL score: 550
Most popular departments: accounting, finance, general management, marketing, other

University of Colorado–Denver
Campus Box 165
PO Box 173364
Denver, CO 80217-3364
www.ucdenver.edu/business/
Public
Admissions: (303) 315-8200
Email: bschool.admissions@ucdenver.edu
Financial aid: (303) 315-1850
Application deadline: 04/16
In-state tuition: full time: $45,200; part time: $621/credit hour
Out-of-state tuition: full time: $45,200
Room/board/expenses: N/A
College-funded aid: Yes
International student aid: Yes
Full-time enrollment: 22
men: 64%; women: 36%; minorities: 5%; international: 0%

Part-time enrollment: 462
men: 62%; women: 38%; minorities: 16%; international: 4%
Acceptance rate (full time): 91%
Average GMAT (full time): 578
Average GRE (full time): N/A verbal; N/A quantitative; N/A writing
Average GPA (full time): 3.31
Average age of entrants to full-time program: 30
TOEFL requirement: Yes
Minimum TOEFL score: 560

University of Denver (Daniels)
2101 S. University Boulevard
Denver, CO 80208
www.daniels.du.edu/
Private
Admissions: (303) 871-3416
Email: daniels@du.edu
Financial aid: (303) 871-7860
Application deadline: 05/01
Tuition: total program: $87,000 (full time); $75,000 (part time)
Room/board/expenses: $18,642
College-funded aid: Yes
International student aid: Yes
Full-time enrollment: 79
men: 59%; women: 41%; minorities: 18%; international: 11%
Part-time enrollment: 109
men: 60%; women: 40%; minorities: 17%; international: 4%
Acceptance rate (full time): 61%
Average GMAT (full time): 605
Average GRE (full time): 156 verbal; 154 quantitative; 4.1 writing
Average GPA (full time): 3.24
Average age of entrants to full-time program: 28
Average months of prior work experience (full time): 54
TOEFL requirement: Yes
Minimum TOEFL score: 587
Most popular departments: ethics, finance, international business, marketing, quantitative analysis/statistics and operations research
Mean starting base salary for 2017 full-time graduates: $74,885
Employment location for 2017 class: Intl. 7%; N.E. 3%; M.A. 0%; S. 3%; M.W. 7%; S.W. 76%; W. 3%

University of Northern Colorado (Monfort)
800 17th Street
Greeley, CO 80639
mcb.unco.edu/
Public
Admissions: (970) 351-2831
Email: Graduate.School@unco.edu
Financial aid: (970) 351-2502
Application deadline: rolling
In-state tuition: full time: $598/credit hour; part time: $592/credit hour
Out-of-state tuition: full time: $1,131/credit hour
Room/board/expenses: $16,628

College-funded aid: Yes
International student aid: Yes
Average student indebtedness at graduation: $15,583
Full-time enrollment: 13
men: 77%; women: 23%; minorities: 15%; international: 8%
Part-time enrollment: 17
men: 41%; women: 59%; minorities: 18%; international: 12%
Acceptance rate (full time): 90%
Average GMAT (full time): 535
Average GRE (full time): N/A verbal; N/A quantitative; N/A writing
Average GPA (full time): 3.44
Average age of entrants to full-time program: 25
TOEFL requirement: Yes
Minimum TOEFL score: N/A

Central Connecticut State University
1615 Stanley Street
New Britain, CT 06050
www.ccsu.edu/mba
Public
Admissions: (860) 832-2350
Financial aid: (860) 832-2200
Application deadline: 06/10
In-state tuition: full time: N/A; part time: $629/credit hour
Out-of-state tuition: full time: N/A
Room/board/expenses: N/A
College-funded aid: Yes
Full-time enrollment: N/A
Part-time enrollment: 199
men: 56%; women: 44%; minorities: 33%; international: 1%
Average GRE (full time): N/A verbal; N/A quantitative; N/A writing
TOEFL requirement: Yes
Minimum TOEFL score: N/A
Most popular departments: accounting, finance, other

Fairfield University (Dolan)
1073 N. Benson Road
Fairfield, CT 06824
www.fairfield.edu/dsb/graduateprograms/mba/
Private
Admissions: (203) 254-4000
Email: dsbgrad@fairfield.edu
Financial aid: (203) 254-4000
Application deadline: 08/01
Tuition: full time: N/A; part time: $925/credit hour
Room/board/expenses: N/A
College-funded aid: Yes
International student aid: No
Full-time enrollment: N/A
Part-time enrollment: 65
men: 62%; women: 38%; minorities: 14%; international: 11%
Average GRE (full time): N/A verbal; N/A quantitative; N/A writing
TOEFL requirement: Yes
Minimum TOEFL score: 550

Most popular departments: accounting, finance, general management, marketing, other

Quinnipiac University

275 Mount Carmel Avenue
Hamden, CT 06518
www.quinnipiac.edu/
Private
Admissions: (800) 462-1944
Email: graduate@quinnipiac.edu
Financial aid: (203) 582-8384
Application deadline: 08/10
Tuition: full time: $1,010/credit hour; part time: $1,010/credit hour
Room/board/expenses: $22,448
College-funded aid: Yes
International student aid: Yes
Average student indebtedness at graduation: $27,074
Full-time enrollment: 183
men: 52%; women: 48%; minorities: 16%; international: 10%
Part-time enrollment: 31
men: 58%; women: 42%; minorities: 6%; international: 6%
Acceptance rate (full time): 84%
Average GMAT (full time): 595
Average GRE (full time): 146 verbal; 146 quantitative; N/A writing
Average GPA (full time): 3.33
Average age of entrants to full-time program: 23
Average months of prior work experience (full time): 5
TOEFL requirement: Yes
Minimum TOEFL score: 577
Most popular departments: finance, general management, health care administration, marketing, supply chain management/logistics
Mean starting base salary for 2017 full-time graduates: $57,218
Employment location for 2017 class: Intl. 1%; N.E. 97%; M.A. 0%; S. 1%; M.W. 1%; S.W. 0%; W. 0%

Sacred Heart University (Welch)

5151 Park Avenue
Fairfield, CT 06825
www.sacredheart.edu/johnfwelchcob.cfm
Private
Admissions: (203) 365-4716
Email: gradstudies@sacredheart.edu
Financial aid: (203) 371-7980
Application deadline: rolling
Tuition: full time: N/A; part time: $905/credit hour
Room/board/expenses: N/A
College-funded aid: No
International student aid: No
Full-time enrollment: N/A
Part-time enrollment: 145
men: 57%; women: 43%; minorities: 16%; international: 24%
Average GRE (full time): N/A verbal; N/A quantitative; N/A writing
TOEFL requirement: Yes
Minimum TOEFL score: 570

Most popular departments: accounting, finance, human resources management, marketing, other

University of Connecticut

2100 Hillside Road, Unit 1041
Storrs, CT 06269-1041
www.business.uconn.edu
Public
Admissions: (860) 728-2440
Email: mba@uconn.edu
Financial aid: (860) 486-2819
Application deadline: 06/01
In-state tuition: full time: $15,328; part time: $825/credit hour
Out-of-state tuition: full time: $36,638
Room/board/expenses: $27,000
College-funded aid: Yes
International student aid: Yes
Average student indebtedness at graduation: $41,000
Full-time enrollment: 107
men: 65%; women: 35%; minorities: 7%; international: 64%
Part-time enrollment: 913
men: 66%; women: 34%; minorities: 34%; international: 0%
Acceptance rate (full time): 38%
Average GMAT (full time): 639
Average GRE (full time): 149 verbal; 153 quantitative; 3.8 writing
Average GPA (full time): 3.45
Average age of entrants to full-time program: 29
Average months of prior work experience (full time): 77
TOEFL requirement: Yes
Minimum TOEFL score: 575
Most popular departments: finance, general management, marketing, portfolio management, other
Mean starting base salary for 2017 full-time graduates: $94,947
Employment location for 2017 class: Intl. N/A; N.E. 79%; M.A. N/A; S. 11%; M.W. N/A; S.W. N/A; W. 11%

University of Hartford (Barney)[1]

200 Bloomfield Avenue
West Hartford, CT 06117
www.hartford.edu/barney/
Private
Admissions: (860) 768-5003
Email: knight@hartford.edu
Financial aid: (860) 768-4296
Tuition: N/A
Room/board/expenses: N/A
Enrollment: N/A

University of New Haven

300 Boston Post Rd
West Haven, CT 06516
www.newhaven.edu
Private
Admissions: (203) 932-7440
Email: gradinfo@newhaven.edu
Financial aid: (203) 932-7315
Application deadline: rolling

Tuition: full time: $890/credit hour; part time: $890/credit hour
Room/board/expenses: N/A
College-funded aid: Yes
International student aid: Yes
Full-time enrollment: 127
men: 53%; women: 47%; minorities: 28%; international: 35%
Part-time enrollment: 68
men: 57%; women: 43%; minorities: 32%; international: 9%
Acceptance rate (full time): 87%
Average GMAT (full time): 418
Average GRE (full time): 143 verbal; 148 quantitative; 2.8 writing
Average GPA (full time): 3.29
Average age of entrants to full-time program: 25
TOEFL requirement: Yes
Minimum TOEFL score: N/A
Most popular departments: accounting, finance, human resources management, marketing, sports business

Yale University

165 Whitney Avenue
New Haven, CT 06511-3729
som.yale.edu
Private
Admissions: (203) 432-5635
Email: mba.admissions@yale.edu
Financial aid: (203) 432-5875
Application deadline: 04/18
Tuition: full time: $68,690; part time: N/A
Room/board/expenses: $24,210
College-funded aid: Yes
International student aid: Yes
Average student indebtedness at graduation: $104,799
Full-time enrollment: 716
men: 57%; women: 43%; minorities: 27%; international: 37%
Part-time enrollment: N/A
Acceptance rate (full time): 17%
Average GMAT (full time): 727
Average GRE (full time): 165 verbal; 164 quantitative; 4.7 writing
Average GPA (full time): 3.67
Average age of entrants to full-time program: 28
Average months of prior work experience (full time): 65
TOEFL requirement: No
Minimum TOEFL score: N/A
Most popular departments: economics, entrepreneurship, finance, general management, marketing
Mean starting base salary for 2017 full-time graduates: $119,371
Employment location for 2017 class: Intl. 19%; N.E. 44%; M.A. 6%; S. 3%; M.W. 2%; S.W. 4%; W. 21%

Delaware State University[1]

1200 DuPont Highway
Dover, DE 19901
www.desu.edu/business-administration-mba-program
Public
Admissions: (302) 857-6978
Email: dkim@desu.edu
Financial aid: (302) 857-6250
Tuition: N/A
Room/board/expenses: N/A
Enrollment: N/A

University of Delaware (Lerner)

One South Main Street,
Graduate and MBA Programs,
Second Floor
Newark, DE 19716
lerner.udel.edu/
Public
Admissions: (302) 831-2221
Email: mbaprogram@udel.edu
Financial aid: (302) 831-8761
Application deadline: 07/01
In-state tuition: full time: $780/credit hour; part time: $780/credit hour
Out-of-state tuition: full time: $1,000/credit hour
Room/board/expenses: $9,000
College-funded aid: Yes
International student aid: Yes
Average student indebtedness at graduation: $33,812
Full-time enrollment: 111
men: 58%; women: 42%; minorities: 15%; international: 50%
Part-time enrollment: 163
men: 58%; women: 42%; minorities: 28%; international: 6%
Acceptance rate (full time): 47%
Average GMAT (full time): 627
Average GRE (full time): 149 verbal; 157 quantitative; 3.9 writing
Average GPA (full time): 3.40
Average age of entrants to full-time program: 26
Average months of prior work experience (full time): 38
TOEFL requirement: Yes
Minimum TOEFL score: 600
Most popular departments: finance, health care administration, international business, leadership, quantitative analysis/statistics and operations research
Mean starting base salary for 2017 full-time graduates: $92,000
Employment location for 2017 class: Intl. 5%; N.E. 5%; M.A. 75%; S. N/A; M.W. 5%; S.W. N/A; W. 10%

American University (Kogod)

4400 Massachusetts Avenue NW
Washington, DC 20016
kogod.american.edu
Private
Admissions: (202) 885-1913
Email: kogodgrad@american.edu
Financial aid: (202) 885-1907

Application deadline: 05/01
Tuition: full time: $1,642/credit hour; part time: $1,642/credit hour
Room/board/expenses: $22,252
College-funded aid: Yes
International student aid: Yes
Full-time enrollment: 57
men: 63%; women: 37%; minorities: 18%; international: 37%
Part-time enrollment: 42
men: 50%; women: 50%; minorities: 21%; international: 10%
Acceptance rate (full time): 68%
Average GMAT (full time): 580
Average GRE (full time): 152 verbal; 152 quantitative; 3.6 writing
Average GPA (full time): 3.18
Average age of entrants to full-time program: 28
Average months of prior work experience (full time): 47
TOEFL requirement: Yes
Minimum TOEFL score: N/A
Most popular departments: consulting, finance, international business, marketing, management information systems
Mean starting base salary for 2017 full-time graduates: $81,518
Employment location for 2017 class: Intl. 7%; N.E. N/A; M.A. 87%; S. 7%; M.W. N/A; S.W. N/A; W. N/A

Georgetown University (McDonough)

Rafik B. Hariri Building
37th and O Streets NW
Washington, DC 20057
msb.georgetown.edu
Private
Admissions: (202) 687-4200
Email: georgetownmba@georgetown.edu
Financial aid: (202) 687-4547
Application deadline: 10/10
Tuition: full time: $56,901; part time: $1,860/credit hour
Room/board/expenses: $25,969
College-funded aid: Yes
International student aid: Yes
Full-time enrollment: 562
men: 69%; women: 31%; minorities: 21%; international: 33%
Part-time enrollment: 434
men: 61%; women: 39%; minorities: 22%; international: 5%
Acceptance rate (full time): 48%
Average GMAT (full time): 692
Average GRE (full time): 157 verbal; 157 quantitative; 4.3 writing
Average GPA (full time): 3.37
Average age of entrants to full-time program: 28
Average months of prior work experience (full time): 64
TOEFL requirement: Yes
Minimum TOEFL score: 600
Most popular departments: consulting, finance, general management, marketing, technology

Mean starting base salary for 2017 full-time graduates: $112,501

George Washington University

2201 G Street NW
Washington, DC 20052
business.gwu.edu/programs/
masters-of-business-
administration/global-mba/
Private
Admissions: (202) 994-1212
Email: gwmba@gwu.edu
Financial aid: (202) 994-7850
Application deadline: 05/01
Tuition: total program:
$105,115 (full time); part
time: $1,765/credit hour
Room/board/expenses: $25,000
College-funded aid: Yes
International student aid: Yes
**Average student indebtedness
at graduation:** $87,402
Full-time enrollment: 169
men: 57%; women:
43%; minorities: 21%;
international: 43%
Part-time enrollment: 209
men: 58%; women:
42%; minorities: 40%;
international: 5%
Acceptance rate (full time): 54%
Average GMAT (full time): 645
**Average GRE (full
time):** 155 verbal; 153
quantitative; 4.1 writing
Average GPA (full time): 3.30
**Average age of entrants to
full-time program:** 28
**Average months of prior work
experience (full time):** 54
TOEFL requirement: Yes
Minimum TOEFL score: 600
Most popular departments:
consulting, finance, international
business, marketing, other
**Mean starting base salary for 2017
full-time graduates:** $87,548
**Employment location for 2017
class:** Intl. 4%; N.E. 19%;
M.A. 48%; S. 4%; M.W.
13%; S.W. 4%; W. 9%

Howard University

2600 Sixth Street NW, Suite 236
Washington, DC 20059
www.bschool.howard.edu
Private
Admissions: (202) 806-1725
Email:
MBA_bschool@howard.edu
Financial aid: (202) 806-2820
Application deadline: 04/01
Tuition: full time: $35,571; part
time: $1,840/credit hour
Room/board/expenses: $26,518
College-funded aid: Yes
International student aid: Yes
**Average student indebtedness
at graduation:** $64,267
Full-time enrollment: 51
men: 55%; women:
45%; minorities: 88%;
international: 12%
Part-time enrollment: 23
men: 48%; women:
52%; minorities: 96%;
international: 4%
Acceptance rate (full time): 41%
Average GMAT (full time): 508

**Average GRE (full
time):** 153 verbal; 148
quantitative; N/A writing
Average GPA (full time): 3.14
**Average age of entrants to
full-time program:** 25
**Average months of prior work
experience (full time):** 46
TOEFL requirement: Yes
Minimum TOEFL score: 550
Most popular departments:
finance, general management,
international business,
marketing, supply chain
management/logistics
**Mean starting base salary for 2017
full-time graduates:** $107,026
**Employment location for 2017
class:** Intl. N/A; N.E. 18%;
M.A. 36%; S. 9%; M.W.
14%; S.W. 9%; W. 14%

FLORIDA

Barry University[1]

11300 N.E. Second Avenue
Miami Shores, FL 33161-6695
www.barry.edu/mba
Private
Admissions: (305) 899-3146
Email: dfletcher@mail.barry.edu
Financial aid: (305) 899-3673
Tuition: N/A
Room/board/expenses: N/A
Enrollment: N/A

Florida Atlantic University

777 Glades Road
Boca Raton, FL 33431
www.business.fau.edu
Public
Admissions: (561) 297-3624
Email: graduatecollege@fau.edu
Financial aid: (561) 297-3530
Application deadline: 07/01
In-state tuition: full time: N/A;
part time: $304/credit hour
Out-of-state tuition: full time: N/A
Room/board/expenses: N/A
College-funded aid: Yes
International student aid: Yes
Full-time enrollment: N/A
Part-time enrollment: 176
men: 51%; women:
49%; minorities: N/A;
international: N/A
**Average GRE (full
time):** N/A verbal; N/A
quantitative; N/A writing
TOEFL requirement: Yes
Minimum TOEFL score: 600
Most popular departments:
accounting, general
management, health
care administration,
international business, tax

Florida Gulf Coast University (Lutgert)

10501 FGCU Boulevard S
Fort Myers, FL 33965-6565
lutgert.fgcu.edu
Public
Admissions: (239) 590-7988
Email: graduate@fgcu.edu
Financial aid: (239) 590-7920
Application deadline: 06/01
In-state tuition: full time:
$373/credit hour; part
time: $372/credit hour

Out-of-state tuition: full
time: $1,301/credit hour
Room/board/expenses: $17,562
College-funded aid: Yes
International student aid: Yes
**Average student indebtedness
at graduation:** $20,878
Full-time enrollment: 32
men: 53%; women:
47%; minorities: 19%;
international: 19%
Part-time enrollment: 78
men: 53%; women:
47%; minorities: 26%;
international: 0%
Acceptance rate (full time): 83%
Average GMAT (full time): 503
**Average GRE (full
time):** 154 verbal; 153
quantitative; N/A writing
Average GPA (full time): 3.16
**Average age of entrants to
full-time program:** 26
TOEFL requirement: Yes
Minimum TOEFL score: 550
Most popular departments:
accounting, finance,
general management,
marketing, management
information systems

Florida International University

1050 S.W. 112 Avenue, CBC 300
Miami, FL 33199-0001
business.fiu.edu
Public
Admissions: (305) 348-7398
Email: chapman@fiu.edu
Financial aid: (305) 348-7272
Application deadline: 07/01
In-state tuition: total
program: $37,000 (full
time); $48,000 (part time)
Out-of-state tuition: total
program: $47,000 (full time)
Room/board/expenses: $18,000
College-funded aid: Yes
International student aid: Yes
Full-time enrollment: 44
men: 52%; women:
48%; minorities: 16%;
international: 32%
Part-time enrollment: 525
men: 41%; women:
59%; minorities: 84%;
international: 4%
Acceptance rate (full time): 39%
Average GMAT (full time): 581
**Average GRE (full
time):** 149 verbal; 150
quantitative; 3.4 writing
Average GPA (full time): 3.49
**Average age of entrants to
full-time program:** 26
**Average months of prior work
experience (full time):** 55
TOEFL requirement: Yes
Minimum TOEFL score: 550
Most popular departments:
finance, general
management, health care
administration, international
business, marketing
**Mean starting base salary for 2017
full-time graduates:** $55,000
**Employment location for 2017
class:** Intl. 0%; N.E. 0%;
M.A. 0%; S. 100%; M.W.
0%; S.W. 0%; W. 0%

Florida Southern College

111 Lake Hollingsworth Drive
Lakeland, FL 33801
www.flsouthern.edu/
Private
Admissions: (863) 680-4205
Financial aid: (863) 680-4140
Application deadline: 07/01
Tuition: total program: $34,500
(full time); part time: N/A
Room/board/expenses: N/A
College-funded aid: Yes
International student aid: Yes
Full-time enrollment: 77
men: 45%; women:
55%; minorities: 16%;
international: 9%
Part-time enrollment: N/A
Acceptance rate (full time): 52%
Average GMAT (full time): 396
**Average GRE (full
time):** 148 verbal; 146
quantitative; 3.0 writing
Minimum TOEFL score: N/A
Most popular departments:
accounting, general
management, health care
administration, supply chain
management/logistics
**Mean starting base salary for 2017
full-time graduates:** $48,700
**Employment location for 2017
class:** Intl. N/A; N.E. N/A;
M.A. N/A; S. 100%; M.W.
N/A; S.W. N/A; W. N/A

Florida State University

Graduate Programs
233 Rovetta Building
Tallahassee, FL 32306-1110
business.fsu.edu/academics/
graduate-programs/
masters-degrees
Public
Admissions: (850) 644-6455
Email: gradprograms@
business.fsu.edu
Financial aid: (850) 644-5716
Application deadline: 06/01
In-state tuition: full time:
$480/credit hour; part
time: $480/credit hour
Out-of-state tuition: full
time: $1,110/credit hour
Room/board/expenses: $18,693
College-funded aid: Yes
International student aid: Yes
**Average student indebtedness
at graduation:** $19,458
Full-time enrollment: 52
men: 65%; women:
35%; minorities: 25%;
international: 6%
Part-time enrollment: 108
men: 65%; women:
35%; minorities: 19%;
international: 10%
Acceptance rate (full time): 83%
Average GMAT (full time): 562
**Average GRE (full
time):** 152 verbal; 153
quantitative; N/A writing
Average GPA (full time): 3.38
**Average age of entrants to
full-time program:** 24
**Average months of prior work
experience (full time):** 28
TOEFL requirement: Yes

Minimum TOEFL score: 600
Most popular departments:
accounting, finance,
general management,
insurance, marketing
**Mean starting base salary for 2017
full-time graduates:** $50,250
**Employment location for
2017 class:** Intl. N/A; N.E.
N/A; M.A. N/A; S. 75%; M.W.
13%; S.W. N/A; W. 13%

Jacksonville University

2800 University Boulevard N
Jacksonville, FL 32211
www.ju.edu
Private
Admissions: (904) 256-7000
Email: admiss@ju.edu
Financial aid: (904) 256-7062
Application deadline: 08/01
Tuition: full time: $770/credit
hour; part time: $770/credit hour
Room/board/expenses: $14,298
College-funded aid: Yes
International student aid: Yes
Full-time enrollment: 80
men: 68%; women:
33%; minorities: 25%;
international: 24%
Part-time enrollment: 138
men: 51%; women:
49%; minorities: 30%;
international: 1%
Acceptance rate (full time): 89%
Average GMAT (full time): 443
**Average GRE (full
time):** 140 verbal; 141
quantitative; 3.2 writing
Average GPA (full time): 3.42
**Average age of entrants to
full-time program:** 24
**Average months of prior work
experience (full time):** 62
TOEFL requirement: Yes
Minimum TOEFL score: 500
Most popular departments:
accounting, finance,
general management,
leadership, marketing
**Mean starting base salary for 2017
full-time graduates:** $36,250
**Employment location for 2017
class:** Intl. N/A; N.E. N/A;
M.A. 11%; S. 89%; M.W.
N/A; S.W. N/A; W. N/A

Rollins College (Crummer)

1000 Holt Avenue
Winter Park, FL 32789-4499
www.rollins.edu/business/
Private
Admissions: (407) 628-2405
Email: MBAADMISSIONS@
rollins.edu
Financial aid: (407) 646-2395
Application deadline: 07/01
Tuition: total program: $74,440
(full time); $58,240 (part time)
Room/board/expenses: $25,927
College-funded aid: Yes
International student aid: Yes
**Average student indebtedness
at graduation:** $58,343
Full-time enrollment: 128
men: 59%; women:
41%; minorities: 23%;
international: 5%

Part-time enrollment: 177
men: 53%; women:
47%; minorities: 34%;
international: 0%
Acceptance rate (full time): 72%
Average GMAT (full time): 546
Average GRE (full
time): N/A verbal; N/A
quantitative; N/A writing
Average GPA (full time): 3.47
Average age of entrants to
full-time program: 23
Average months of prior work
experience (full time): 12
TOEFL requirement: Yes
Minimum TOEFL score: N/A
Most popular departments:
entrepreneurship, finance,
general management,
international business,
marketing
Mean starting base salary for 2017
full-time graduates: $61,292
Employment location for
2017 class: Intl. 2%; N.E.
5%; M.A. 5%; S. 82%; M.W.
2%; S.W. 2%; W. 3%

Stetson University

421 N. Woodland Boulevard
DeLand, FL 32723
www.stetson.edu/graduate
Private
Admissions: (386) 822-7100
Email: gradadmissions@
stetson.edu
Financial aid: (800) 688-7120
Application deadline: 08/01
Tuition: full time: $1,009/
credit hour; part time:
$1,009/credit hour
Room/board/expenses: $15,326
College-funded aid: Yes
International student aid: Yes
Average student indebtedness
at graduation: $26,028
Full-time enrollment: 69
men: 55%; women:
45%; minorities: 26%;
international: 13%
Part-time enrollment: 23
men: 30%; women:
70%; minorities: 35%;
international: 0%
Acceptance rate (full time): 68%
Average GMAT (full time): 517
Average GRE (full
time): N/A verbal; N/A
quantitative; N/A writing
Average GPA (full time): 3.33
Average age of entrants to
full-time program: 27
TOEFL requirement: Yes
Minimum TOEFL score: N/A
Mean starting base salary for 2017
full-time graduates: $48,778

University of Central Florida

PO Box 161400
Orlando, FL 32816-1400
www.ucf.edu
Public
Admissions: (407) 235-3917
Email: cbagrad@ucf.edu
Financial aid: (407) 823-2827
Application deadline: 07/01
In-state tuition: total
program: $39,000 (full
time); part time: $5,550
Out-of-state tuition: total
program: $39,000 (full time)

Room/board/expenses: $15,886
College-funded aid: Yes
International student aid: Yes
Average student indebtedness
at graduation: $33,288
Full-time enrollment: 26
men: 58%; women:
42%; minorities: 46%;
international: 8%
Part-time enrollment: 407
men: 51%; women:
49%; minorities: 40%;
international: 2%
Acceptance rate (full time): 36%
Average GRE (full
time): N/A verbal; N/A
quantitative; N/A writing
Average GPA (full time): 3.20
Average age of entrants to
full-time program: 26
Average months of prior work
experience (full time): 31
TOEFL requirement: Yes
Minimum TOEFL score: 577
Most popular departments:
accounting, entrepreneurship,
general management, human
resources management,
sports business

University of Florida (Warrington)

Hough Hall 310
Gainesville, FL 32611-7152
www.floridamba.ufl.edu
Public
Admissions: (352) 392-7992
Email:
floridamba@warrington.ufl.edu
Financial aid: (352) 392-1275
Application deadline: 03/15
In-state tuition: full time:
$12,737; part time: $26,622
Out-of-state tuition:
full time: $30,130
Room/board/expenses: $17,700
College-funded aid: Yes
International student aid: Yes
Average student indebtedness
at graduation: $32,510
Full-time enrollment: 94
men: 70%; women:
30%; minorities: 16%;
international: 15%
Part-time enrollment: 344
men: 68%; women:
32%; minorities: 32%;
international: 11%
Acceptance rate (full time): 15%
Average GMAT (full time): 682
Average GRE (full
time): N/A verbal; N/A
quantitative; N/A writing
Average GPA (full time): 3.43
Average age of entrants to
full-time program: 27
Average months of prior work
experience (full time): 61
TOEFL requirement: Yes
Minimum TOEFL score: 550
Most popular departments:
consulting, finance, human
resources management,
marketing, supply chain
management/logistics
Mean starting base salary for 2017
full-time graduates: $100,863
Employment location for
2017 class: Intl. 0%; N.E.
9%; M.A. 5%; S. 61%; M.W.
11%; S.W. 5%; W. 9%

University of Miami

PO Box 248027
Coral Gables, FL 33124-6520
www.bus.miami.edu/grad
Private
Admissions: (305) 284-2510
Email: mba@miami.edu
Financial aid: (305) 284-2270
Application deadline: 05/15
Tuition: full time: $1,960/
credit hour; part time: N/A
Room/board/expenses: $25,190
College-funded aid: Yes
International student aid: Yes
Full-time enrollment: 126
men: 67%; women:
33%; minorities: 29%;
international: 32%
Part-time enrollment: N/A
Acceptance rate (full time): 53%
Average GMAT (full time): 645
Average GRE (full
time): 156 verbal; 154
quantitative; 4.0 writing
Average GPA (full time): 3.35
Average age of entrants to
full-time program: 28
Average months of prior work
experience (full time): 63
TOEFL requirement: Yes
Minimum TOEFL score: N/A
Most popular departments:
finance, international business,
marketing, real estate,
quantitative analysis/statistics
and operations research
Mean starting base salary for 2017
full-time graduates: $84,000
Employment location for
2017 class: Intl. 0%; N.E.
10%; M.A. 7%; S. 71%; M.W.
5%; S.W. 5%; W. 2%

University of North Florida (Coggin)

1 UNF Drive
Jacksonville, FL 32224-2645
www.unf.edu/coggin
Public
Admissions: (904) 620-1360
Email: graduateschool@unf.edu
Financial aid: (904) 620-5555
Application deadline: 08/01
In-state tuition: full time: N/A;
part time: $494/credit hour
Out-of-state tuition: full time: N/A
Room/board/expenses: N/A
College-funded aid: Yes
International student aid: Yes
Full-time enrollment: N/A
Part-time enrollment: 440
men: 50%; women:
50%; minorities: 29%;
international: 10%
Average GRE (full
time): N/A verbal; N/A
quantitative; N/A writing
TOEFL requirement: Yes
Minimum TOEFL score: 550
Most popular departments:
accounting, e-commerce,
finance, general
management, supply chain
management/logistics

University of South Florida

4202 Fowler Avenue
BSN 3403
Tampa, FL 33620
www.mba.usf.edu
Public
Admissions: (813) 974-3335
Email: bsn-mba@usf.edu
Financial aid: (813) 974-4700
Application deadline: 07/01
In-state tuition: full time:
$467/credit hour; part
time: $467/credit hour
Out-of-state tuition: full
time: $913/credit hour
Room/board/expenses: $28,000
College-funded aid: Yes
International student aid: Yes
Average student indebtedness
at graduation: $56,415
Full-time enrollment: 55
men: 56%; women:
44%; minorities: 25%;
international: 15%
Part-time enrollment: 294
men: 63%; women:
37%; minorities: 27%;
international: 20%
Acceptance rate (full time): 39%
Average GMAT (full time): 508
Average GRE (full
time): 150 verbal; 150
quantitative; N/A writing
Average GPA (full time): 3.53
Average age of entrants to
full-time program: 24
Average months of prior work
experience (full time): 10
TOEFL requirement: Yes
Minimum TOEFL score: 550
Most popular departments:
entrepreneurship, finance,
leadership, marketing,
sports business
Mean starting base salary for
2017 full-time graduates: $41,812
Employment location for 2017
class: Intl. N/A; N.E. 10%;
M.A. 5%; S. 67%; M.W.
10%; S.W. 10%; W. 0%

University of South Florida–Sarasota-Manatee

8350 N. Tamiami Trail
Sarasota, FL 34243
usfsm.edu/college-of-business
Public
Admissions: (941) 359-4331
Email: admissions@sar.usf.edu
Financial aid: (941) 359-4200
Application deadline: 07/01
In-state tuition: full time:
$381/credit hour; part
time: $381/credit hour
Out-of-state tuition: full
time: $805/credit hour
Room/board/expenses: N/A
College-funded aid: Yes
International student aid: Yes
Full-time enrollment: N/A
Part-time enrollment: 80
men: 56%; women:
44%; minorities: 38%;
international: 0%
Average GRE (full
time): N/A verbal; N/A
quantitative; N/A writing

TOEFL requirement: Yes
Minimum TOEFL score: 550

University of South Florida–St. Petersburg[1]

140 7th Ave S, BAY III
St. Petersburg, FL 33701
www.usfsp.edu/ktcob
Public
Admissions: (727) 873-4567
Email: applygrad@usfsp.edu
Financial aid: (727) 873-4128
Tuition: N/A
Room/board/expenses: N/A
Enrollment: N/A

University of Tampa (Sykes)

401 W. Kennedy Boulevard
Tampa, FL 33606-1490
grad.ut.edu
Private
Admissions: (813) 257-3642
Email: utgrad@ut.edu
Financial aid: (813) 253-6219
Application deadline: rolling
Tuition: full time: $603/
credit hour; part time:
$603/credit hour
Room/board/expenses: $12,424
College-funded aid: Yes
International student aid: Yes
Average student indebtedness
at graduation: $49,332
Full-time enrollment: 344
men: 57%; women:
43%; minorities: 12%;
international: 52%
Part-time enrollment: 142
men: 54%; women:
46%; minorities: 32%;
international: 1%
Acceptance rate (full time): 40%
Average GMAT (full time): 530
Average GRE (full
time): 151 verbal; 154
quantitative; 4.0 writing
Average GPA (full time): 3.50
Average age of entrants to
full-time program: 26
TOEFL requirement: Yes
Minimum TOEFL score: 577
Most popular departments:
accounting, entrepreneurship,
finance, marketing, technology
Mean starting base salary for 2017
full-time graduates: $54,167
Employment location for
2017 class: Intl. 4%; N.E.
5%; M.A. 6%; S. 79%; M.W.
4%; S.W. 0%; W. 1%

University of West Florida[1]

11000 University Parkway
Pensacola, FL 32514
uwf.edu
Public
Admissions: (850) 474-2230
Email: mba@uwf.edu
Financial aid: N/A
Tuition: N/A
Room/board/expenses: N/A
Enrollment: N/A

GEORGIA

Augusta University[1]
1120 15th Street
Augusta, GA 30912
www.gru.edu/hull/grad/mba.php
Public
Admissions: (706) 737-1418
Email: hull@gru.edu
Financial aid: N/A
Tuition: N/A
Room/board/expenses: N/A
Enrollment: N/A

Berry College (Campbell)
PO Box 495024
Mount Berry, GA 30149-5024
www.berry.edu/academics/campbell/
Private
Admissions: (706) 236-2215
Email: admissions@berry.edu
Financial aid: (706) 236-1714
Application deadline: 07/20
Tuition: full time: $635/credit hour; part time: $635/credit hour
Room/board/expenses: N/A
College-funded aid: Yes
International student aid: Yes
Full-time enrollment: 1
men: 100%; women: 0%; minorities: N/A; international: N/A
Part-time enrollment: 29
men: 66%; women: 34%; minorities: N/A; international: N/A
Average GRE (full time): N/A verbal; N/A quantitative; N/A writing
TOEFL requirement: Yes
Minimum TOEFL score: 550
Most popular departments: general management

Clark Atlanta University
223 James P. Brawley Drive SW
Atlanta, GA 30314
www.cau.edu
Private
Admissions: (404) 880-8443
Email: mbaadmissions@cau.edu
Financial aid: (404) 880-6265
Application deadline: 04/01
Tuition: full time: $28,026; part time: N/A
Room/board/expenses: $16,290
College-funded aid: Yes
International student aid: No
Full-time enrollment: 41
men: 39%; women: 61%; minorities: 71%; international: 15%
Part-time enrollment: 8
men: 50%; women: 50%; minorities: 50%; international: 50%
Acceptance rate (full time): 59%
Average GRE (full time): 141 verbal; 141 quantitative; 2.9 writing
Average GPA (full time): 3.20
Average age of entrants to full-time program: 26
TOEFL requirement: Yes
Minimum TOEFL score: 500

Clayton State University[1]
2000 Clayton State Boulevard
Morrow, GA 30260-0285
www.clayton.edu/mba
Public
Admissions: (678) 466-4113
Email: graduate@clayton.edu
Financial aid: (678) 466-4185
Tuition: N/A
Room/board/expenses: N/A
Enrollment: N/A

Columbus State University (Turner)
4225 University Avenue
Columbus, GA 31907
cobcs.columbusstate.edu
Public
Admissions: (706) 507-8800
Email: alexander_viola@columbusstate.edu
Financial aid: (706) 507-8807
Application deadline: 06/30
In-state tuition: full time: $255/credit hour; part time: $255/credit hour
Out-of-state tuition: full time: $1,000/credit hour
Room/board/expenses: N/A
College-funded aid: Yes
International student aid: Yes
Average student indebtedness at graduation: $15,600
Full-time enrollment: 40
men: 68%; women: 33%; minorities: 40%; international: 8%
Part-time enrollment: 60
men: 67%; women: 33%; minorities: 20%; international: 7%
Acceptance rate (full time): 70%
Average GMAT (full time): 512
Average GRE (full time): 152 verbal; 149 quantitative; N/A writing
Average GPA (full time): 3.27
Average age of entrants to full-time program: 30
Average months of prior work experience (full time): 44
TOEFL requirement: Yes
Minimum TOEFL score: 550

Emory University (Goizueta)
1300 Clifton Road NE
Atlanta, GA 30322
www.goizueta.emory.edu
Private
Admissions: (404) 727-6311
Email: mbaadmissions@emory.edu
Financial aid: (404) 727-6039
Application deadline: 03/09
Tuition: full time: $59,616; total program: $73,600 (part time)
Room/board/expenses: $23,764
College-funded aid: Yes
International student aid: Yes
Average student indebtedness at graduation: $74,199
Full-time enrollment: 352
men: 73%; women: 27%; minorities: 22%; international: 30%

Part-time enrollment: 250
men: 66%; women: 34%; minorities: 28%; international: 10%
Acceptance rate (full time): 35%
Average GMAT (full time): 682
Average GRE (full time): N/A verbal; N/A quantitative; N/A writing
Average GPA (full time): 3.30
Average age of entrants to full-time program: 28
Average months of prior work experience (full time): 68
TOEFL requirement: Yes
Minimum TOEFL score: N/A
Most popular departments: consulting, finance, general management, marketing, production/operations management
Mean starting base salary for 2017 full-time graduates: $119,665
Employment location for 2017 class: Intl. 2%; N.E. 15%; M.A. 2%; S. 56%; M.W. 11%; S.W. 4%; W. 10%

Georgia College & State University (Bunting)
Campus Box 019
Milledgeville, GA 31061
mba.gcsu.edu
Public
Admissions: (478) 445-6283
Email: grad-admit@gcsu.edu
Financial aid: (478) 445-5149
Application deadline: 07/01
In-state tuition: full time: N/A; part time: $288/credit hour
Out-of-state tuition: full time: N/A
Room/board/expenses: N/A
College-funded aid: Yes
International student aid: Yes
Full-time enrollment: N/A
Part-time enrollment: 24
men: 46%; women: 54%; minorities: 38%; international: 0%
Average GRE (full time): N/A verbal; N/A quantitative; N/A writing
TOEFL requirement: Yes
Minimum TOEFL score: 550
Most popular departments: management information systems

Georgia Institute of Technology (Scheller)
800 W. Peachtree Street NW
Atlanta, GA 30332-0520
scheller.gatech.edu
Public
Admissions: (404) 894-8722
Email: mba@scheller.gatech.edu
Financial aid: (404) 894-4160
Application deadline: 06/01
In-state tuition: full time: $31,242; part time: $1,218/credit hour
Out-of-state tuition: full time: $42,190
Room/board/expenses: $17,840
College-funded aid: Yes
International student aid: Yes
Average student indebtedness at graduation: $63,723

Full-time enrollment: 158
men: 77%; women: 23%; minorities: 15%; international: 25%
Part-time enrollment: 374
men: 70%; women: 30%; minorities: 28%; international: 4%
Acceptance rate (full time): 31%
Average GMAT (full time): 680
Average GRE (full time): 158 verbal; 162 quantitative; 4.4 writing
Average GPA (full time): 3.40
Average age of entrants to full-time program: 28
Average months of prior work experience (full time): 54
TOEFL requirement: Yes
Minimum TOEFL score: N/A
Most popular departments: consulting, entrepreneurship, production/operations management, supply chain management/logistics, technology
Mean starting base salary for 2017 full-time graduates: $106,115
Employment location for 2017 class: Intl. 4%; N.E. 2%; M.A. 2%; S. 74%; M.W. 0%; S.W. 2%; W. 17%

Georgia Southern University
PO Box 8002
Statesboro, GA 30460-8050
coba.georgiasouthern.edu/mba
Public
Admissions: (912) 478-2357
Email: mba@georgiasouthern.edu
Financial aid: (912) 478-5413
Application deadline: 07/31
In-state tuition: full time: N/A; part time: N/A
Out-of-state tuition: full time: N/A
Room/board/expenses: N/A
College-funded aid: Yes
International student aid: Yes
Full-time enrollment: N/A
Part-time enrollment: 86
men: 62%; women: 38%; minorities: 24%; international: 6%
Average GRE (full time): N/A verbal; N/A quantitative; N/A writing
TOEFL requirement: Yes
Minimum TOEFL score: 550

Georgia Southwestern State University[1]
800 Georgia Southwestern State University Drive
Americus, GA 31709
gsw.edu/
Public
Admissions: N/A
Financial aid: N/A
Tuition: N/A
Room/board/expenses: N/A
Enrollment: N/A

Georgia State University (Robinson)
35 Broad Street
Atlanta, GA 30302-3989
robinson.gsu.edu/
Public
Admissions: (404) 413-7305
Email: rcbgradadmissions@gsu.edu
Financial aid: (404) 413-2600
Application deadline: 06/01
In-state tuition: full time: N/A; part time: $491/credit hour
Out-of-state tuition: full time: N/A
Room/board/expenses: N/A
College-funded aid: Yes
International student aid: Yes
Full-time enrollment: N/A
Part-time enrollment: 275
men: 56%; women: 44%; minorities: 39%; international: 9%
Average GRE (full time): N/A verbal; N/A quantitative; N/A writing
TOEFL requirement: Yes
Minimum TOEFL score: 610
Most popular departments: finance, general management, health care administration, management information systems, quantitative analysis/statistics and operations research

Kennesaw State University (Coles)
560 Parliament Garden Way
MD 0401
Kennesaw, GA 30144
www.kennesaw.edu/graduate/admissions
Public
Admissions: (470) 578-4377
Email: ksugrad@kennesaw.edu
Financial aid: (470) 578-2044
Application deadline: 07/01
In-state tuition: full time: N/A; part time: $346/credit hour
Out-of-state tuition: full time: N/A
Room/board/expenses: N/A
College-funded aid: Yes
International student aid: Yes
Full-time enrollment: N/A
Part-time enrollment: 188
men: 56%; women: 44%; minorities: 37%; international: 0%
Average GRE (full time): N/A verbal; N/A quantitative; N/A writing
TOEFL requirement: Yes
Minimum TOEFL score: N/A
Most popular departments: accounting, economics, general management, international business, marketing

Mercer University– Atlanta (Stetson)
3001 Mercer University Drive
Atlanta, GA 30341-4155
business.mercer.edu
Private
Admissions: (678) 547-6300
Email: business.admissions@mercer.edu
Financial aid: (678) 547-6444
Application deadline: 06/15

Tuition: full time: $818/credit hour; part time: $740/credit hour
Room/board/expenses: N/A
College-funded aid: No
International student aid: No
Average student indebtedness at graduation: $17,343
Full-time enrollment: 54
men: 46%; women: 54%; minorities: N/A; international: N/A
Part-time enrollment: 317
men: 54%; women: 46%; minorities: N/A; international: N/A
Acceptance rate (full time): 60%
Average GMAT (full time): 517
Average GRE (full time): 150 verbal; 153 quantitative; N/A writing
Average GPA (full time): 3.25
Average age of entrants to full-time program: 27
Average months of prior work experience (full time): 36
TOEFL requirement: Yes
Minimum TOEFL score: 550
Most popular departments: accounting, economics, finance, health care administration, marketing
Mean starting base salary for 2017 full-time graduates: $59,573

Savannah State University

PO Box 20359
Savannah, GA 31404
www.savannahstate.edu/coba/programs-mba.shtml
Public
Admissions: (912) 358-3393
Email: mba@savannahstate.edu
Financial aid: (912) 358-4162
Application deadline: rolling
In-state tuition: total program: N/A (full time); $10,500 (part time)
Out-of-state tuition: total program: N/A (full time)
Room/board/expenses: N/A
College-funded aid: Yes
Full-time enrollment: N/A
Part-time enrollment: 70
men: 24%; women: 76%; minorities: 81%; international: 9%
Average GRE (full time): N/A verbal; N/A quantitative; N/A writing
TOEFL requirement: Yes
Minimum TOEFL score: N/A

University of Georgia (Terry)

600 South Lumpkin Street
Athens, GA 30602
terry.uga.edu/mba
Public
Admissions: (706) 542-5671
Email: ugamba@uga.edu
Financial aid: (706) 542-6147
Application deadline: 03/15
In-state tuition: full time: $15,670; total program: $56,400 (part time)
Out-of-state tuition: full time: $34,378
Room/board/expenses: $23,950
College-funded aid: Yes
International student aid: Yes

Average student indebtedness at graduation: $33,625
Full-time enrollment: 103
men: 66%; women: 34%; minorities: 14%; international: 23%
Part-time enrollment: 308
men: 62%; women: 38%; minorities: 35%; international: 5%
Acceptance rate (full time): 37%
Average GMAT (full time): 647
Average GRE (full time): 157 verbal; 156 quantitative; 4.3 writing
Average GPA (full time): 3.46
Average age of entrants to full-time program: 27
Average months of prior work experience (full time): 41
TOEFL requirement: Yes
Minimum TOEFL score: N/A
Most popular departments: finance, human resources management, marketing, management information systems, production/operations management
Mean starting base salary for 2017 full-time graduates: $90,250
Employment location for 2017 class: Intl. 3%; N.E. 3%; M.A. 0%; S. 62%; M.W. 5%; S.W. 11%; W. 16%

University of North Georgia

82 College Circle
Dahlonega, GA 30597
ung.edu/mike-cottrell-college-of-business/academic-programs/the-cottrell-mba.php
Public
Admissions: (706) 864-1543
Email: grads@ung.edu
Financial aid: (706) 864-1412
Application deadline: 04/01
In-state tuition: full time: N/A; part time: $520/credit hour
Out-of-state tuition: full time: N/A
Room/board/expenses: N/A
College-funded aid: Yes
International student aid: Yes
Full-time enrollment: N/A
Part-time enrollment: 80
men: 50%; women: 50%; minorities: 21%; international: 0%
Average GRE (full time): N/A verbal; N/A quantitative; N/A writing
TOEFL requirement: Yes
Minimum TOEFL score: 550
Most popular departments: technology

University of West Georgia (Richards)

1601 Maple Street
Carrollton, GA 30118-3000
www.westga.edu/academics/business/index.php
Public
Admissions: (678) 839-5355
Email: hudombon@westga.edu
Financial aid: (678) 839-6421
Application deadline: 07/15
In-state tuition: full time: N/A; part time: $227/credit hour

Out-of-state tuition: full time: N/A
Room/board/expenses: N/A
College-funded aid: Yes
International student aid: Yes
Full-time enrollment: N/A
Part-time enrollment: 103
men: 48%; women: 52%; minorities: 37%; international: 6%
Average GRE (full time): N/A verbal; N/A quantitative; N/A writing
TOEFL requirement: Yes
Minimum TOEFL score: 550
Most popular departments: accounting, economics, finance, general management

Valdosta State University (Langdale)[1]

1500 N. Patterson Street
Valdosta, GA 31698
www.valdosta.edu/lcoba/grad/
Public
Admissions: (229) 245-3822
Email: mschnake@valdosta.edu
Financial aid: (229) 333-5935
Tuition: N/A
Room/board/expenses: N/A
Enrollment: N/A

University of Hawaii–Manoa (Shidler)

2404 Maile Way
Business Administration C-204
Honolulu, HI 96822
www.shidler.hawaii.edu
Public
Admissions: (808) 956-8266
Email: mba@hawaii.edu
Financial aid: (808) 956-7251
Application deadline: N/A
In-state tuition: full time: $21,288; part time: $887/credit hour
Out-of-state tuition: full time: $38,352
Room/board/expenses: $20,500
College-funded aid: Yes
International student aid: Yes
Full-time enrollment: 47
men: 55%; women: 45%; minorities: 70%; international: 11%
Part-time enrollment: 49
men: 59%; women: 41%; minorities: 80%; international: 0%
Acceptance rate (full time): 66%
Average GMAT (full time): 563
Average GRE (full time): N/A verbal; N/A quantitative; N/A writing
Average GPA (full time): 3.37
Average age of entrants to full-time program: 28
Average months of prior work experience (full time): 66
TOEFL requirement: Yes
Minimum TOEFL score: N/A
Most popular departments: accounting, entrepreneurship, finance, health care administration, international business
Employment location for 2017 class: Intl. N/A; N.E. N/A; M.A. N/A; S. N/A; M.W. N/A; S.W. 100%; W. N/A

Boise State University

1910 University Drive
MBEB4101
Boise, ID 83725-1600
cobe.boisestate.edu/graduate
Public
Admissions: (208) 426-3116
Email: graduatebusiness@boisestate.edu
Financial aid: (208) 426-1664
Application deadline: rolling
In-state tuition: full time: $8,754; part time: $382/credit hour
Out-of-state tuition: full time: $24,070
Room/board/expenses: $14,204
College-funded aid: Yes
International student aid: Yes
Average student indebtedness at graduation: $34,250
Full-time enrollment: 66
men: 47%; women: 53%; minorities: 15%; international: 21%
Part-time enrollment: 79
men: 62%; women: 38%; minorities: 10%; international: 4%
Acceptance rate (full time): 74%
Average GMAT (full time): 603
Average GRE (full time): 150 verbal; 149 quantitative; 3.9 writing
Average GPA (full time): 3.52
Average age of entrants to full-time program: 26
TOEFL requirement: Yes
Minimum TOEFL score: 587
Mean starting base salary for 2017 full-time graduates: $54,110

Idaho State University[1]

921 S. 8th Avenue, Stop 8020
Pocatello, ID 83209
www.isu.edu/cob/mba.shtml
Public
Admissions: (208) 282-2966
Email: mba@isu.edu
Financial aid: N/A
Tuition: N/A
Room/board/expenses: N/A
Enrollment: N/A

University of Idaho[1]

PO Box 443161
Moscow, ID 83844-3161
www.uidaho.edu
Public
Admissions: (800) 885-4001
Email: graduateadmissions@uidaho.edu
Financial aid: N/A
Tuition: N/A
Room/board/expenses: N/A
Enrollment: N/A

Bradley University (Foster)

1501 W. Bradley Avenue
Peoria, IL 61625
www.bradley.edu/academic/colleges/fcba/programs/grad/mba/
Private
Admissions: (309) 677-3714
Email: mba@bradley.edu

Financial aid: (309) 677-3085
Application deadline: 08/01
Tuition: full time: N/A; part time: $870/credit hour
Room/board/expenses: N/A
College-funded aid: No
International student aid: Yes
Full-time enrollment: N/A
Part-time enrollment: 46
men: 63%; women: 37%; minorities: 11%; international: 30%
Average GRE (full time): N/A verbal; N/A quantitative; N/A writing
TOEFL requirement: Yes
Minimum TOEFL score: N/A
Most popular departments: finance, general management

DePaul University (Kellstadt)

1 E. Jackson Boulevard
Chicago, IL 60604-2287
www.kellstadt.depaul.edu/
Private
Admissions: (312) 362-8810
Email: kgsb@depaul.edu
Financial aid: (312) 362-8091
Application deadline: 08/01
Tuition: full time: $1,040/credit hour; part time: $1,040/credit hour
Room/board/expenses: $15,000
College-funded aid: Yes
International student aid: Yes
Average student indebtedness at graduation: $65,274
Full-time enrollment: 50
men: 60%; women: 40%; minorities: 6%; international: 18%
Part-time enrollment: 886
men: 56%; women: 44%; minorities: 30%; international: 2%
Acceptance rate (full time): 30%
Average GMAT (full time): 596
Average GRE (full time): 154 verbal; 152 quantitative; 3.8 writing
Average GPA (full time): 3.34
Average age of entrants to full-time program: 27
Average months of prior work experience (full time): 43
TOEFL requirement: Yes
Minimum TOEFL score: 550
Mean starting base salary for 2017 full-time graduates: $74,750
Employment location for 2017 class: Intl. N/A; N.E. 7%; M.A. N/A; S. N/A; M.W. 93%; S.W. N/A; W. N/A

Dominican University (Brennan)

7900 West Division Street
River Forest, IL 60305
www.dom.edu/business
Private
Admissions: (708) 524-6796
Email: bmueller@dom.edu
Financial aid: (708) 524-6950
Application deadline: rolling
Tuition: full time: N/A; part time: $980/credit hour
Room/board/expenses: N/A
College-funded aid: Yes
International student aid: Yes

Full-time enrollment: N/A
Part-time enrollment: 147
men: 32%; women: 68%; minorities: 23%; international: 17%
Average GRE (full time): N/A verbal; N/A quantitative; N/A writing
TOEFL requirement: Yes
Minimum TOEFL score: N/A
Most popular departments: finance, health care administration, international business, marketing, quantitative analysis/statistics and operations research

Eastern Illinois University (Lumpkin)
600 Lincoln Avenue
Charleston, IL 61920-3099
www.eiu.edu/mba/
Public
Admissions: (217) 581-3028
Email: mba@eiu.edu
Financial aid: (217) 581-6405
Application deadline: 08/01
In-state tuition: full time: $292/credit hour; part time: $292/credit hour
Out-of-state tuition: full time: $701/credit hour
Room/board/expenses: $12,423
College-funded aid: Yes
International student aid: Yes
Full-time enrollment: 43
men: 40%; women: 60%; minorities: 12%; international: 30%
Part-time enrollment: 61
men: 44%; women: 56%; minorities: 13%; international: 0%
Acceptance rate (full time): 52%
Average GMAT (full time): 458
Average GRE (full time): N/A verbal; N/A quantitative; N/A writing
Average age of entrants to full-time program: 24
TOEFL requirement: Yes
Minimum TOEFL score: 550
Most popular departments: accounting, general management, other

Governors State University
1 University Parkway
University Park, IL 60484
www.govst.edu
Private
Admissions: (708) 534-4490
Email: admissions@govst.edu
Financial aid: (708) 534-4480
Application deadline: 06/15
Tuition: full time: N/A; part time: $406/credit hour
Room/board/expenses: N/A
College-funded aid: Yes
International student aid: No
Full-time enrollment: N/A
Part-time enrollment: 123
men: 42%; women: 58%; minorities: 54%; international: 11%
Average GRE (full time): N/A verbal; N/A quantitative; N/A writing
TOEFL requirement: Yes

Minimum TOEFL score: 550
Most popular departments: accounting, finance, leadership, management information systems, supply chain management/logistics

Illinois Institute of Technology (Stuart)[1]
10 W. 35th Street
Chicago, IL 60616
www.stuart.iit.edu
Private
Admissions: (312) 567-3020
Email: admission@stuart.iit.edu
Financial aid: (312) 567-7219
Tuition: N/A
Room/board/expenses: N/A
Enrollment: N/A

Illinois State University
MBA Program
Campus Box 5570
Normal, IL 61790-5570
business.illinoisstate.edu/mba/
Public
Admissions: (309) 438-2181
Email: admissions@ilstu.edu
Financial aid: (309) 438-2231
Application deadline: 07/01
In-state tuition: full time: N/A; part time: $389/credit hour
Out-of-state tuition: full time: N/A
Room/board/expenses: N/A
College-funded aid: Yes
International student aid: Yes
Full-time enrollment: N/A
Part-time enrollment: 106
men: 60%; women: 40%; minorities: 7%; international: 24%
Average GRE (full time): N/A verbal; N/A quantitative; N/A writing
TOEFL requirement: Yes
Minimum TOEFL score: 550
Most popular departments: finance, human resources management, insurance, leadership, marketing

Loyola University Chicago (Quinlan)
820 N. Michigan Avenue
Chicago, IL 60611
www.luc.edu/quinlan/
Private
Admissions: (312) 915-8908
Email: quinlangrad@luc.edu
Financial aid: (773) 508-7704
Application deadline: 07/15
Tuition: full time: N/A; part time: $1,496/credit hour
Room/board/expenses: N/A
College-funded aid: Yes
International student aid: Yes
Full-time enrollment: N/A
Part-time enrollment: 557
men: 45%; women: 55%; minorities: 21%; international: 32%
Average GRE (full time): N/A verbal; N/A quantitative; N/A writing
TOEFL requirement: Yes
Minimum TOEFL score: 550

Most popular departments: accounting, finance, health care administration, human resources management, supply chain management/logistics

Northeastern Illinois University
5500 North St. Louis Avenue
Chicago, IL 60625-4699
www.neiu.edu/academics/college-of-business-and-management/graduate-programs-business/master-business-administration
Public
Admissions: (773) 442-6114
Email: cobm-grad@neiu.edu
Financial aid: N/A
Application deadline: rolling
In-state tuition: full time: N/A; part time: N/A
Out-of-state tuition: full time: N/A
Room/board/expenses: N/A
Full-time enrollment: 23
men: 57%; women: 43%; minorities: 30%; international: 30%
Part-time enrollment: 50
men: 54%; women: 46%; minorities: 32%; international: 8%
Average GRE (full time): N/A verbal; N/A quantitative; N/A writing
TOEFL requirement: Yes
Minimum TOEFL score: 550

Northern Illinois University
Office of MBA Programs
Barsema Hall 203
De Kalb, IL 60115-2897
cob.niu.edu/departments/mba-programs/index.shtml
Public
Admissions: (866) 648-6221
Email: mba@niu.edu
Financial aid: (815) 753-1300
Application deadline: 07/15
In-state tuition: total program: $49,250 (full time); part time: $896/credit hour
Out-of-state tuition: total program: $61,750 (full time)
Room/board/expenses: $15,000
College-funded aid: Yes
International student aid: Yes
Full-time enrollment: 14
men: 64%; women: 36%; minorities: 29%; international: 7%
Part-time enrollment: 420
men: 69%; women: 31%; minorities: 33%; international: 6%
Acceptance rate (full time): 75%
Average GMAT (full time): 475
Average GRE (full time): N/A verbal; N/A quantitative; N/A writing
Average GPA (full time): 3.22
Average age of entrants to full-time program: 23
Average months of prior work experience (full time): 6
TOEFL requirement: Yes
Minimum TOEFL score: N/A

Most popular departments: accounting, finance, health care administration, human resources management, supply chain management/logistics
Employment location for 2017 class: Intl. 6%; N.E. N/A; M.A. N/A; S. N/A; M.W. 94%; S.W. N/A; W. N/A

Northwestern University (Kellogg)
2211 Campus Drive
Evanston, IL 60208-2001
www.kellogg.northwestern.edu
Private
Admissions: (847) 491-3308
Email: mbaadmissions@kellogg.northwestern.edu
Financial aid: (847) 491-3308
Application deadline: 04/11
Tuition: full time: $70,435; part time: $6,683/credit hour
Room/board/expenses: $22,497
College-funded aid: Yes
International student aid: Yes
Full-time enrollment: 1,296
men: 60%; women: 40%; minorities: N/A; international: N/A
Part-time enrollment: 747
men: 72%; women: 28%; minorities: N/A; international: N/A
Acceptance rate (full time): 20%
Average GMAT (full time): 732
Average GRE (full time): N/A verbal; N/A quantitative; N/A writing
Average GPA (full time): 3.60
Average age of entrants to full-time program: 27
Average months of prior work experience (full time): 61
TOEFL requirement: Yes
Minimum TOEFL score: N/A
Most popular departments: economics, finance, general management, marketing, organizational behavior
Mean starting base salary for 2017 full-time graduates: $128,192
Employment location for 2017 class: Intl. 10%; N.E. 19%; M.A. 2%; S. 2%; M.W. 29%; S.W. 4%; W. 33%

Southern Illinois University–Carbondale
133 Rehn Hall
Carbondale, IL 62901-4625
business.siu.edu/academics/mba/
Public
Admissions: (618) 453-3030
Email: gradprograms@business.siu.edu
Financial aid: (618) 453-4334
Application deadline: 07/31
In-state tuition: full time: $530/credit hour; part time: N/A
Out-of-state tuition: full time: $1,220/credit hour
Room/board/expenses: N/A
College-funded aid: Yes
International student aid: Yes
Average student indebtedness at graduation: $46,196

Full-time enrollment: 55
men: 56%; women: 44%; minorities: 40%; international: 0%
Part-time enrollment: N/A
Acceptance rate (full time): 71%
Average GRE (full time): N/A verbal; N/A quantitative; N/A writing
Average GPA (full time): 3.60
Average age of entrants to full-time program: 27
Average months of prior work experience (full time): 88
TOEFL requirement: Yes
Minimum TOEFL score: 550
Most popular departments: finance, general management, marketing, other

Southern Illinois University–Edwardsville
Box 1051
Edwardsville, IL 62026-1051
www.siue.edu/business
Public
Admissions: (618) 650-3840
Email: mba@siue.edu
Financial aid: (618) 650-3880
Application deadline: rolling
In-state tuition: full time: N/A; part time: $317/credit hour
Out-of-state tuition: full time: N/A
Room/board/expenses: N/A
College-funded aid: Yes
International student aid: Yes
Full-time enrollment: N/A
Part-time enrollment: 112
men: 55%; women: 45%; minorities: 13%; international: 3%
Average GRE (full time): N/A verbal; N/A quantitative; N/A writing
TOEFL requirement: Yes
Minimum TOEFL score: 550
Most popular departments: accounting, finance, general management, management information systems

St. Xavier University[1]
3700 West 103rd Street
Chicago, IL 60655
www.sxu.edu/academics/colleges_schools/gsm/
Private
Admissions: (773) 298-3053
Email: graduateadmission@sxu.edu
Financial aid: (773) 398-3070
Tuition: N/A
Room/board/expenses: N/A
Enrollment: N/A

University of Chicago (Booth)
5807 S. Woodlawn Avenue
Chicago, IL 60637
ChicagoBooth.edu
Private
Admissions: (773) 702-7369
Email: admissions@ChicagoBooth.edu
Financial aid: (773) 702-7369
Application deadline: 04/03
Tuition: full time: $70,364; part time: $6,854/credit hour

Room/board/expenses: $25,870
College-funded aid: Yes
International student aid: Yes
Full-time enrollment: 1,176
men: 59%; women:
41%; minorities: 27%;
international: 35%
Part-time enrollment: 1,377
men: 74%; women:
26%; minorities: 26%;
international: 18%
Acceptance rate (full time): 24%
Average GMAT (full time): 730
Average GRE (full
time): N/A verbal; N/A
quantitative; N/A writing
Average GPA (full time): 3.61
Average age of entrants to
full-time program: 28
Average months of prior work
experience (full time): 51
TOEFL requirement: Yes
Minimum TOEFL score: 600
Most popular departments:
economics, entrepreneurship,
finance, organizational
behavior, other
Mean starting base salary for 2017
full-time graduates: $129,442
Employment location for
2017 class: Intl. 11%; N.E.
23%; M.A. 2%; S. 2%; M.W.
36%; S.W. 4%; W. 22%

University of Illinois–Chicago (Liautaud)

601 South Morgan Street
University Hall, 11th Floor
Chicago, IL 60607
business.uic.edu/liautaud
Public
Admissions: (312) 996-4573
Email: lgsb@uic.edu
Financial aid: (312) 996-3126
Application deadline: 07/15
In-state tuition: full time:
$24,952; part time: $18,060
Out-of-state tuition:
full time: $37,192
Room/board/expenses: N/A
College-funded aid: Yes
International student aid: Yes
Full-time enrollment: N/A
Part-time enrollment: 236
men: 66%; women:
34%; minorities: 33%;
international: 12%
Average GRE (full
time): N/A verbal; N/A
quantitative; N/A writing
TOEFL requirement: Yes
Minimum TOEFL score: 550
Most popular departments:
accounting, entrepreneurship,
finance, general
management, marketing

University of Illinois–Springfield

1 University Plaza
MS UHB 4000
Springfield, IL 62703
www.uis.edu/admissions
Public
Admissions: (888) 977-4847
Email: admissions@uis.edu
Financial aid: (217) 206-6724
Application deadline: N/A
In-state tuition: full time:
$329/credit hour; part
time: $329/credit hour

Out-of-state tuition: full
time: $675/credit hour
Room/board/expenses: N/A
College-funded aid: Yes
International student aid: Yes
Full-time enrollment: N/A
Part-time enrollment: 87
men: 49%; women:
51%; minorities: 13%;
international: 11%
Average GRE (full
time): N/A verbal; N/A
quantitative; N/A writing
TOEFL requirement: Yes
Minimum TOEFL score: N/A

University of Illinois–Urbana-Champaign

515 E. Gregory Drive
3019 BIF, MC 520
Champaign, IL 61820
www.mba.illinois.edu
Public
Admissions: (217) 333-8221
Email: mba@illinois.edu
Financial aid: (217) 333-0100
Application deadline: 03/04
In-state tuition: full time:
$27,284; part time: $26,177
Out-of-state tuition:
full time: $39,296
Room/board/expenses: $18,560
College-funded aid: Yes
International student aid: Yes
Average student indebtedness
at graduation: $56,871
Full-time enrollment: 109
men: 66%; women:
34%; minorities: 18%;
international: 32%
Part-time enrollment: 97
men: 62%; women:
38%; minorities: N/A;
international: N/A
Acceptance rate (full time): 31%
Average GMAT (full time): 647
Average GRE (full
time): 154 verbal; 153
quantitative; N/A writing
Average GPA (full time): 3.29
Average age of entrants to
full-time program: 27
Average months of prior work
experience (full time): 52
TOEFL requirement: Yes
Minimum TOEFL score: 610
Most popular departments:
consulting, finance,
general management,
marketing, technology
Mean starting base salary for 2017
full-time graduates: $95,295
Employment location for
2017 class: Intl. 4%; N.E.
8%; M.A. 6%; S. 0%; M.W.
55%; S.W. 11%; W. 17%

Western Illinois University

1 University Circle
Macomb, IL 61455
www.wiu.edu/cbt
Public
Admissions: (309) 298-2442
Email: wj-polley@wiu.edu
Financial aid: (309) 298-2446
Application deadline: rolling
In-state tuition: full time:
$324/credit hour; part
time: $324/credit hour
Out-of-state tuition: full
time: $485/credit hour

Room/board/expenses: N/A
College-funded aid: Yes
International student aid: Yes
Full-time enrollment: 27
men: 56%; women:
44%; minorities: N/A;
international: N/A
Part-time enrollment: 38
men: 63%; women:
37%; minorities: N/A;
international: N/A
Acceptance rate (full time): 65%
Average GMAT (full time): 488
Average GRE (full
time): N/A verbal; N/A
quantitative; N/A writing
Average GPA (full time): 3.35
TOEFL requirement: Yes
Minimum TOEFL score: 550
Most popular departments:
accounting, economics, finance,
general management, supply
chain management/logistics

Ball State University (Miller)[1]

Whitinger Building,147
Muncie, IN 47306
www.bsu.edu/mba/
Public
Admissions: (765) 285-1931
Email: mba@bsu.edu
Financial aid: (765) 285-5600
Tuition: N/A
Room/board/expenses: N/A
Enrollment: N/A

Butler University

4600 Sunset Avenue
Indianapolis, IN 46208-3485
www.butlermba.com
Private
Admissions: (317) 940-9842
Email: mba@butler.edu
Financial aid: (317) 940-8200
Application deadline: 07/15
Tuition: full time: N/A; part
time: $820/credit hour
Room/board/expenses: N/A
College-funded aid: No
International student aid: No
Full-time enrollment: N/A
Part-time enrollment: 171
men: 65%; women:
35%; minorities: 13%;
international: 3%
Average GRE (full
time): N/A verbal; N/A
quantitative; N/A writing
TOEFL requirement: Yes
Minimum TOEFL score: 550
Most popular departments:
entrepreneurship, finance,
international business,
leadership, marketing

Indiana State University

MBA Program
30 N 7th Street
Federal Hall, Room 114
Terre Haute, IN 47809
www.indstate.edu/mba/
Public
Admissions: (812) 237-2002
Email: ISU-MBA@
mail.indstate.edu
Financial aid: (800) 841-4744
Application deadline: rolling

In-state tuition: full time:
$404/credit hour; part
time: $404/credit hour
Out-of-state tuition: full
time: $793/credit hour
Room/board/expenses: $13,454
College-funded aid: Yes
International student aid: Yes
Average student indebtedness
at graduation: $19,890
Full-time enrollment: 50
men: 58%; women:
42%; minorities: 12%;
international: 40%
Part-time enrollment: 64
men: 67%; women:
33%; minorities: 13%;
international: 0%
Acceptance rate (full time): 54%
Average GMAT (full time): 534
Average GRE (full
time): N/A verbal; N/A
quantitative; 0.0 writing
Average GPA (full time): 3.36
Average age of entrants to
full-time program: 28
Average months of prior work
experience (full time): 60
TOEFL requirement: Yes
Minimum TOEFL score: 550
Most popular departments:
accounting, finance, marketing,
production/operations
management, supply chain
management/logistics
Mean starting base salary for 2017
full-time graduates: $28,000
Employment location for
2017 class: Intl. 0%; N.E.
0%; M.A. 0%; S. 25%; M.W.
75%; S.W. 0%; W. 0%

Indiana University (Kelley)

1275 E. 10th Street
Suite CG 2010
Bloomington, IN 47405-1703
kelley.iu.edu/programs/
full-time-mba
Public
Admissions: (812) 855-8006
Email: iumba@indiana.edu
Financial aid: (812) 855-1618
Application deadline: 04/15
In-state tuition: full time:
$28,405; part time:
$796/credit hour
Out-of-state tuition:
full time: $49,268
Room/board/expenses: $18,736
College-funded aid: Yes
International student aid: Yes
Average student indebtedness
at graduation: $60,155
Full-time enrollment: 392
men: 71%; women:
29%; minorities: 19%;
international: 33%
Part-time enrollment: 294
men: 84%; women:
16%; minorities: 16%;
international: 33%
Acceptance rate (full time): 35%
Average GMAT (full time): 677
Average GRE (full
time): 160 verbal; 157
quantitative; 4.3 writing
Average GPA (full time): 3.38

Average age of entrants to
full-time program: 28
Average months of prior work
experience (full time): 63
TOEFL requirement: Yes
Minimum TOEFL score: 600
Most popular departments:
finance, general management,
marketing, supply chain
management/logistics, other
Mean starting base salary for 2017
full-time graduates: $100,874
Employment location for
2017 class: Intl. 4%; N.E.
10%; M.A. 2%; S. 10%; M.W.
46%; S.W. 8%; W. 20%

Indiana University–Kokomo[1]

2300 S. Washington Street
Kokomo, IN 46904-9003
www.iuk.edu/index.php
Public
Admissions: (765) 455-9275
Financial aid: N/A
Tuition: N/A
Room/board/expenses: N/A
Enrollment: N/A

Indiana University Northwest

3400 Broadway
Gary, IN 46408-1197
www.iun.edu/business/
index.htm
Public
Admissions: (219) 980-6635
Email: iunbiz@iun.edu
Financial aid: (219) 980-6778
Application deadline: 08/01
In-state tuition: full time: N/A;
part time: $340/credit hour
Out-of-state tuition: full time: N/A
Room/board/expenses: N/A
College-funded aid: Yes
International student aid: No
Full-time enrollment: N/A
Part-time enrollment: 66
men: 61%; women:
39%; minorities: N/A;
international: N/A
Average GRE (full
time): N/A verbal; N/A
quantitative; N/A writing
TOEFL requirement: Yes
Minimum TOEFL score: 550

Indiana University-Purdue University–Fort Wayne (Doermer)[1]

2101 E. Coliseum Boulevard
Fort Wayne, IN 46805-1499
www.ipfw.edu/mba
Public
Admissions: (260) 481-6498
Email: mba@ipfw.edu
Financial aid: (260) 481-6820
Tuition: N/A
Room/board/expenses: N/A
Enrollment: N/A

Indiana University–South Bend

1700 Mishawaka Avenue
PO Box 7111
South Bend, IN 46634-7111
business.iusb.edu
Public
Admissions: (574) 520-4839
Email: graduate@iusb.edu
Financial aid: (574) 520-4357
Application deadline: 07/15
In-state tuition: full time: N/A; part time: $340/credit hour
Out-of-state tuition: full time: N/A
Room/board/expenses: N/A
College-funded aid: Yes
International student aid: Yes
Full-time enrollment: N/A
Part-time enrollment: 90
men: 59%; women: 41%; minorities: 17%; international: 8%
Average GRE (full time): N/A verbal; N/A quantitative; N/A writing
TOEFL requirement: Yes
Minimum TOEFL score: N/A
Most popular departments: finance

Indiana University–Southeast

4201 Grant Line Road
New Albany, IN 47150
www.ius.edu/graduatebusiness
Public
Admissions: (812) 941-2364
Email: iusmba@ius.edu
Financial aid: (812) 941-2246
Application deadline: 07/20
In-state tuition: full time: N/A; part time: $414/credit hour
Out-of-state tuition: full time: N/A
Room/board/expenses: N/A
College-funded aid: Yes
International student aid: Yes
Full-time enrollment: N/A
Part-time enrollment: 177
men: 72%; women: 28%; minorities: 13%; international: 0%
Average GRE (full time): N/A verbal; N/A quantitative; N/A writing
TOEFL requirement: Yes
Minimum TOEFL score: 550

Purdue University–Northwest

2200 169th Street
Hammond, IN 46323
academics.pnw.edu/business/mba/
Public
Admissions: (219) 989-3150
Email: Kimberly.Nikolovski@pnw.edu
Financial aid: (219) 989-2301
Application deadline: 07/16
In-state tuition: full time: N/A; part time: $288/credit hour
Out-of-state tuition: full time: N/A
Room/board/expenses: N/A
College-funded aid: Yes
Full-time enrollment: N/A

Part-time enrollment: 121
men: 57%; women: 43%; minorities: 25%; international: 21%
Average GRE (full time): N/A verbal; N/A quantitative; N/A writing
TOEFL requirement: Yes
Minimum TOEFL score: N/A
Most popular departments: accounting, management information systems

Purdue University–West Lafayette (Krannert)

100 S. Grant Street
Rawls Hall, Room 2020
West Lafayette, IN 47907-2076
www.krannert.purdue.edu/masters/home.php
Public
Admissions: (765) 494-0773
Email: krannertmasters@purdue.edu
Financial aid: (765) 494-0998
Application deadline: 05/01
In-state tuition: full time: $22,408; part time: $24,870
Out-of-state tuition: full time: $42,184
Room/board/expenses: $13,030
College-funded aid: Yes
International student aid: Yes
Average student indebtedness at graduation: $41,806
Full-time enrollment: 119
men: 68%; women: 32%; minorities: 16%; international: 45%
Part-time enrollment: 101
men: 70%; women: 30%; minorities: 21%; international: 8%
Acceptance rate (full time): 37%
Average GMAT (full time): 632
Average GRE (full time): 153 verbal; 161 quantitative; 4.0 writing
Average GPA (full time): 3.19
Average age of entrants to full-time program: 29
Average months of prior work experience (full time): 66
TOEFL requirement: Yes
Minimum TOEFL score: 600
Most popular departments: finance, human resources management, marketing, production/operations management, supply chain management/logistics
Mean starting base salary for 2017 full-time graduates: $91,491
Employment location for 2017 class: Intl. 5%; N.E. 3%; M.A. 8%; S. 10%; M.W. 49%; S.W. 21%; W. 5%

University of Notre Dame (Mendoza)

204 Mendoza College of Business
Notre Dame, IN 46556
mendoza.nd.edu/programs/mba-programs/
Private
Admissions: (574) 631-8488
Email: mba.business@nd.edu
Financial aid: (574) 631-6436

Application deadline: 03/17
Tuition: full time: $52,838; part time: N/A
Room/board/expenses: $20,450
College-funded aid: Yes
International student aid: Yes
Full-time enrollment: 294
men: 76%; women: 24%; minorities: 16%; international: 25%
Part-time enrollment: N/A
Acceptance rate (full time): 42%
Average GMAT (full time): 674
Average GRE (full time): 158 verbal; 157 quantitative; 4.4 writing
Average GPA (full time): 3.27
Average age of entrants to full-time program: 27
Average months of prior work experience (full time): 63
TOEFL requirement: Yes
Minimum TOEFL score: N/A
Most popular departments: consulting, finance, leadership, marketing, other
Mean starting base salary for 2017 full-time graduates: $107,230
Employment location for 2017 class: Intl. 4%; N.E. 15%; M.A. 3%; S. 9%; M.W. 38%; S.W. 15%; W. 16%

University of Southern Indiana

8600 University Boulevard
Evansville, IN 47712
www.usi.edu/business/
Public
Admissions: (812) 465-7015
Email: graduate.studies@usi.edu
Financial aid: (812) 464-1767
Application deadline: rolling
In-state tuition: full time: $368/credit hour; part time: $368/credit hour
Out-of-state tuition: full time: $723/credit hour
Room/board/expenses: $11,198
College-funded aid: Yes
International student aid: Yes
Full-time enrollment: 234
men: 47%; women: 53%; minorities: 13%; international: 3%
Part-time enrollment: 121
men: 62%; women: 38%; minorities: 13%; international: 1%
Average GRE (full time): N/A verbal; N/A quantitative; N/A writing
TOEFL requirement: Yes
Minimum TOEFL score: 550
Most popular departments: general management, health care administration, human resources management, quantitative analysis/statistics and operations research, other

Valparaiso University

Urschel Hall, 1909 Chapel Drive
Valparaiso, IN 46383
www.valpo.edu/mba/
Private
Admissions: (219) 465-7952
Email: mba@valpo.edu
Financial aid: (219) 464-5015
Application deadline: 06/30

Tuition: full time: $833/credit hour; part time: $833/credit hour
Room/board/expenses: $22,090
College-funded aid: No
International student aid: No
Average student indebtedness at graduation: $44,016
Full-time enrollment: 9
men: 56%; women: 44%; minorities: 11%; international: 33%
Part-time enrollment: 41
men: 68%; women: 32%; minorities: 20%; international: 5%
Acceptance rate (full time): 79%
Average GMAT (full time): 620
Average GRE (full time): 140 verbal; 165 quantitative; 3.0 writing
Average GPA (full time): 3.06
Average age of entrants to full-time program: 25
Average months of prior work experience (full time): 49
TOEFL requirement: Yes
Minimum TOEFL score: 575
Most popular departments: finance, general management, manufacturing and technology management, technology
Mean starting base salary for 2017 full-time graduates: $75,000
Employment location for 2017 class: Intl. N/A; N.E. N/A; M.A. N/A; S. N/A; M.W. 100%; S.W. N/A; W. N/A

IOWA

Drake University

2847 University Avenue
Des Moines, IA 50311
www.drake.edu/mba
Private
Admissions: (515) 271-2188
Email: cbpa.gradprograms@drake.edu
Financial aid: (515) 271-2905
Application deadline: 08/01
Tuition: full time: N/A; part time: $640/credit hour
Room/board/expenses: N/A
College-funded aid: No
International student aid: Yes
Full-time enrollment: N/A
Part-time enrollment: 94
men: 54%; women: 46%; minorities: 7%; international: 4%
Average GRE (full time): N/A verbal; N/A quantitative; N/A writing
TOEFL requirement: Yes
Minimum TOEFL score: 550
Most popular departments: finance, general management, health care administration, leadership, other

Iowa State University

1360 Gerdin Business Building
Ames, IA 50011-2027
www.business.iastate.edu
Public
Admissions: (515) 294-8118
Email: busgrad@iastate.edu
Financial aid: N/A
Application deadline: 06/01
In-state tuition: full time: $11,986; part time: N/A/credit hour
Out-of-state tuition: full time: $25,698

Room/board/expenses: N/A
College-funded aid: Yes
International student aid: Yes
Full-time enrollment: 81
men: 62%; women: 38%; minorities: 4%; international: 37%
Part-time enrollment: 55
men: 64%; women: 36%; minorities: 18%; international: 0%
Acceptance rate (full time): 62%
Average GMAT (full time): 610
Average GRE (full time): 154 verbal; 156 quantitative; 3.0 writing
Average GPA (full time): 3.54
Average age of entrants to full-time program: 25
Average months of prior work experience (full time): 34
TOEFL requirement: Yes
Minimum TOEFL score: 600
Most popular departments: finance, marketing, management information systems, supply chain management/logistics, other
Mean starting base salary for 2017 full-time graduates: $68,750
Employment location for 2017 class: Intl. N/A; N.E. 11%; M.A. N/A; S. 4%; M.W. 81%; S.W. N/A; W. 4%

University of Iowa (Tippie)

108 John Pappajohn Business Building, Suite W160
Iowa City, IA 52242-1000
tippie.uiowa.edu/future-graduate-students/mba-programs
Public
Admissions: (319) 335-0864
Email: iowamba@uiowa.edu
Financial aid: N/A
Application deadline: 07/30
In-state tuition: full time: N/A; part time: $665/credit hour
Out-of-state tuition: full time: N/A
Room/board/expenses: N/A
Full-time enrollment: N/A
Part-time enrollment: 873
men: 63%; women: 37%; minorities: 12%; international: 5%
Average GRE (full time): N/A verbal; N/A quantitative; N/A writing
TOEFL requirement: Yes
Minimum TOEFL score: 600
Most popular departments: finance, general management, leadership, marketing, quantitative analysis/statistics and operations research

University of Northern Iowa

Curris Business Building 316
Cedar Falls, IA 50614-0123
www.cba.uni.edu/mba/
Public
Admissions: (319) 273-6243
Email: mba@uni.edu
Financial aid: (319) 273-2700
Application deadline: 05/30
In-state tuition: full time: $11,887; part time: $592/credit hour

Out-of-state tuition:
full time: $22,361
Room/board/expenses: N/A
College-funded aid: Yes
International student aid: No
Full-time enrollment: N/A
Part-time enrollment: 149
men: 52%; women:
48%; minorities: 3%;
international: 68%
**Average GRE (full
time):** N/A verbal; N/A
quantitative; N/A writing
TOEFL requirement: Yes
Minimum TOEFL score: 550
Most popular departments:
general management

KANSAS

Emporia State University[1]
1 Kellogg Circle
ESU Box 4039
Emporia, KS 66801-5087
emporia.edu/business/
programs/mba
Public
Admissions: (800) 950-4723
Email: gradinfo@emporia.edu
Financial aid: (620) 341-5457
Tuition: N/A
Room/board/expenses: N/A
Enrollment: N/A

Kansas State University
2004 Business Building
1301 Lovers Lane
Manhattan, KS 66506-0501
www.cba.ksu.edu/cba/
Public
Admissions: (785) 532-7190
Email: gradbusiness@ksu.edu
Financial aid: (785) 532-6420
Application deadline: 02/01
In-state tuition: full time:
$415/credit hour; part
time: $415/credit hour
Out-of-state tuition: full
time: $936/credit hour
Room/board/expenses: $22,000
College-funded aid: Yes
International student aid: Yes
Full-time enrollment: 50
men: N/A; women:
N/A; minorities: 26%;
international: 20%
Part-time enrollment: 21
men: 48%; women:
52%; minorities: 19%;
international: 5%
Acceptance rate (full time): 89%
Average GMAT (full time): 540
**Average GRE (full
time):** N/A verbal; N/A
quantitative; N/A writing
Average GPA (full time): 3.40
**Average age of entrants to
full-time program:** 27
**Average months of prior work
experience (full time):** 32
TOEFL requirement: Yes
Minimum TOEFL score: 550
Most popular departments:
finance, general management,
management information
systems, supply chain
management/logistics

Pittsburg State University (Kelce)
1701 S. Broadway
Pittsburg, KS 66762
www.pittstate.edu/business/
departments-programs/mba
Public
Admissions: (620) 235-4180
Email: jsmiller@pittstate.edu
Financial aid: (620) 235-4240
Application deadline: 07/15
In-state tuition: full time: $9,288;
part time: $333/credit hour
Out-of-state tuition:
full time: $19,654
Room/board/expenses: $8,700
College-funded aid: Yes
International student aid: Yes
Full-time enrollment: 87
men: 61%; women:
39%; minorities: N/A;
international: N/A
Part-time enrollment: 22
men: 59%; women:
41%; minorities: N/A;
international: N/A
Acceptance rate (full time): 97%
Average GMAT (full time): 483
**Average GRE (full
time):** N/A verbal; N/A
quantitative; N/A writing
Average GPA (full time): 3.42
TOEFL requirement: Yes
Minimum TOEFL score: 550

University of Kansas
1654 Naismith Drive
Lawrence, KS 66045-7585
www.mba.ku.edu
Public
Admissions: (785) 864-6738
Email: bschoolmba@ku.edu
Financial aid: (785) 864-4700
Application deadline: 06/01
In-state tuition: full time:
$408/credit hour; part
time: $458/credit hour
Out-of-state tuition: full
time: $950/credit hour
Room/board/expenses: $14,000
College-funded aid: Yes
International student aid: Yes
**Average student indebtedness
at graduation:** $32,756
Full-time enrollment: 52
men: 69%; women:
31%; minorities: 19%;
international: 4%
Part-time enrollment: 100
men: 75%; women:
25%; minorities: 13%;
international: 9%
Acceptance rate (full time): 61%
Average GMAT (full time): 618
**Average GRE (full
time):** 149 verbal; 155
quantitative; 2.8 writing
Average GPA (full time): 3.36
**Average age of entrants to
full-time program:** 27
**Average months of prior work
experience (full time):** 30
TOEFL requirement: Yes
Minimum TOEFL score: N/A
Most popular departments:
finance, general management,
marketing, supply chain
management/logistics
**Mean starting base salary for 2017
full-time graduates:** $59,375

**Employment location for
2017 class:** Intl. 11%; N.E.
N/A; M.A. N/A; S. N/A; M.W.
78%; S.W. 11%; W. N/A

Washburn University[1]
1700 S.W. College Avenue
Topeka, KS 66621
www.washburn.edu/business
Public
Admissions: N/A
Financial aid: N/A
Tuition: N/A
Room/board/expenses: N/A
Enrollment: N/A

Wichita State University (Barton)
1845 N. Fairmount, Box 48
Wichita, KS 67260-0048
www.wichita.edu/mba
Public
Admissions: (316) 978-3230
Email: grad.business@
wichita.edu
Financial aid: (316) 978-3430
Application deadline: 07/01
In-state tuition: full time: N/A;
part time: $295/credit hour
Out-of-state tuition: full time: N/A
Room/board/expenses: N/A
College-funded aid: Yes
International student aid: Yes
Full-time enrollment: N/A
Part-time enrollment: 180
men: 62%; women:
38%; minorities: 27%;
international: 9%
**Average GRE (full
time):** N/A verbal; N/A
quantitative; N/A writing
TOEFL requirement: Yes
Minimum TOEFL score: 570
Most popular departments:
economics, finance, health care
administration, management
information systems, other

KENTUCKY

Bellarmine University (Rubel)
2001 Newburg Road
Louisville, KY 40205-0671
www.bellarmine.edu/mba/
Private
Admissions: (502) 272-7200
Email: gradadmissions@
bellarmine.edu
Financial aid: (502) 452-8124
Application deadline: rolling
Tuition: total program: $30,992
(full time); $30,992 (part time)
Room/board/expenses: $0
College-funded aid: Yes
International student aid: Yes
Full-time enrollment: 33
men: 61%; women:
39%; minorities: 21%;
international: 0%
Part-time enrollment: 35
men: 66%; women: 34%;
minorities: 9%; international: 6%
Acceptance rate (full time): 97%
Average GMAT (full time): 434
**Average GRE (full
time):** 151 verbal; 149
quantitative; 3.6 writing
Average GPA (full time): 3.22

**Average age of entrants to
full-time program:** 26
TOEFL requirement: Yes
Minimum TOEFL score: 550
Most popular departments:
consulting, finance, health care
administration, marketing, tax

Eastern Kentucky University[1]
521 Lancaster Avenue
Richmond, KY 40475
cbt.eku.edu/
Public
Admissions: (859) 622-1742
Email: graduateschool@eku.edu
Financial aid: N/A
Tuition: N/A
Room/board/expenses: N/A
Enrollment: N/A

Morehead State University[1]
Combs Building 214
Morehead, KY 40351
www.moreheadstate.edu/mba
Public
Admissions: (606) 783-2000
Email: admissions@
moreheadstate.edu
Financial aid: N/A
Tuition: N/A
Room/board/expenses: N/A
Enrollment: N/A

Murray State University (Bauernfeind)[1]
109 Business Building
Murray, KY 42071
murraystate.edu/business.aspx
Public
Admissions: (270) 809-3779
Email:
Msu.graduateadmissions@
murraystate.edu
Financial aid: (270) 809-2546
Tuition: N/A
Room/board/expenses: N/A
Enrollment: N/A

Northern Kentucky University[1]
Suite 401, BEP Center
Highland Heights, KY 41099
cob.nku.edu/
graduatedegrees.html
Public
Admissions: (859) 572-6336
Email: mbusiness@nku.edu
Financial aid: N/A
Tuition: N/A
Room/board/expenses: N/A
Enrollment: N/A

University of Kentucky (Gatton)
359 Gatton College of
Business and Economics
Lexington, KY 40506-0034
gatton.uky.edu
Public
Admissions: (859) 257-1306
Email: ukmba@uky.edu
Financial aid: (859) 257-3172
Application deadline: 05/11

In-state tuition: total program:
$33,486 (full time); part
time: $886/credit hour
Out-of-state tuition: total
program: $38,486 (full time)
Room/board/expenses: $14,000
College-funded aid: Yes
International student aid: Yes
**Average student indebtedness
at graduation:** $8,430
Full-time enrollment: 71
men: 66%; women:
34%; minorities: 6%;
international: 10%
Part-time enrollment: 181
men: 60%; women:
40%; minorities: 10%;
international: 7%
Acceptance rate (full time): 86%
Average GMAT (full time): 597
**Average GRE (full
time):** 155 verbal; 163
quantitative; 3.9 writing
Average GPA (full time): 3.49
**Average age of entrants to
full-time program:** 25
**Average months of prior work
experience (full time):** 4
TOEFL requirement: Yes
Minimum TOEFL score: 550
Most popular departments:
entrepreneurship, finance,
general management,
marketing, supply chain
management/logistics
**Mean starting base salary for 2017
full-time graduates:** $54,971
**Employment location for
2017 class:** Intl. 0%; N.E.
0%; M.A. 7%; S. 63%; M.W.
28%; S.W. 2%; W. 0%

University of Louisville
Belknap Campus
Louisville, KY 40292
business.louisville.edu/uoflmba
Public
Admissions: (502) 852-7257
Email: mba@louisville.edu
Financial aid: (502) 852-5517
Application deadline: 07/01
In-state tuition: total
program: $32,202 (full
time); $32,202 (part time)
Out-of-state tuition: total
program: $32,202 (full time)
Room/board/expenses: $13,000
College-funded aid: Yes
International student aid: Yes
**Average student indebtedness
at graduation:** $33,023
Full-time enrollment: 53
men: 64%; women:
36%; minorities: 15%;
international: 0%
Part-time enrollment: 169
men: 60%; women:
40%; minorities: 18%;
international: 7%
Acceptance rate (full time): 52%
Average GMAT (full time): 622
**Average GRE (full
time):** 160 verbal; 159
quantitative; 5.0 writing
Average GPA (full time): 3.42
**Average age of entrants to
full-time program:** 26
**Average months of prior work
experience (full time):** 36
TOEFL requirement: Yes

Minimum TOEFL score: 550
Most popular departments: entrepreneurship, finance, health care administration, marketing, quantitative analysis/statistics and operations research
Mean starting base salary for 2017 full-time graduates: $64,614
Employment location for 2017 class: Intl. N/A; N.E. N/A; M.A. N/A; S. 96%; M.W. N/A; S.W. N/A; W. 4%

Western Kentucky University (Ford)

434 A. Grise Hall
Bowling Green, KY 42101-1056
www.wku.edu/mba/
Public
Admissions: (270) 745-2446
Email: mba@wku.edu
Financial aid: (270) 745-2755
Application deadline: 03/15
In-state tuition: full time: $589/credit hour; part time: N/A
Out-of-state tuition: full time: $873/credit hour
Room/board/expenses: N/A
College-funded aid: Yes
International student aid: No
Average student indebtedness at graduation: $19,030
Full-time enrollment: 17
men: 59%; women: 41%; minorities: 6%; international: 18%
Part-time enrollment: 2
men: 100%; women: 0%; minorities: 100%; international: 0%
Acceptance rate (full time): 67%
Average GMAT (full time): 483
Average GRE (full time): N/A verbal; N/A quantitative; N/A writing
Average GPA (full time): 3.50
Average age of entrants to full-time program: 24
TOEFL requirement: Yes
Minimum TOEFL score: 550
Most popular departments: accounting, economics, general management

LOUISIANA

Louisiana State University–Baton Rouge (Ourso)

4000 Business Education Complex
Baton Rouge, LA 70803
mba.lsu.edu
Public
Admissions: (225) 578-8867
Email: busmba@lsu.edu
Financial aid: (225) 578-3103
Application deadline: 05/15
In-state tuition: total program: $42,240 (full time); $55,088 (part time)
Out-of-state tuition: total program: $75,848 (full time)
Room/board/expenses: $20,000
College-funded aid: Yes
International student aid: Yes
Average student indebtedness at graduation: $17,300

Full-time enrollment: 94
men: 63%; women: 37%; minorities: 12%; international: 11%
Part-time enrollment: 57
men: 68%; women: 32%; minorities: 21%; international: 0%
Acceptance rate (full time): 55%
Average GMAT (full time): 610
Average GRE (full time): 151 verbal; 153 quantitative; 3.9 writing
Average GPA (full time): 3.30
Average age of entrants to full-time program: 24
Average months of prior work experience (full time): 26
TOEFL requirement: Yes
Minimum TOEFL score: 550
Most popular departments: consulting, human resources management, management information systems, supply chain management/logistics, quantitative analysis/statistics and operations research
Mean starting base salary for 2017 full-time graduates: $59,296
Employment location for 2017 class: Intl. 3%; N.E. 3%; M.A. 9%; S. 49%; M.W. N/A; S.W. 29%; W. 9%

Louisiana Tech University

PO Box 10318
Ruston, LA 71272
www.latech.edu/graduate_school
Public
Admissions: (318) 257-2924
Email: gschool@latech.edu
Financial aid: (318) 257-2641
Application deadline: 08/01
In-state tuition: full time: $7,689; part time: $3,705
Out-of-state tuition: full time: $12,420
Room/board/expenses: $12,163
College-funded aid: Yes
International student aid: Yes
Average student indebtedness at graduation: $16,204
Full-time enrollment: 52
men: 63%; women: 37%; minorities: 17%; international: 23%
Part-time enrollment: 16
men: 81%; women: 19%; minorities: 0%; international: 19%
Acceptance rate (full time): 57%
Average GMAT (full time): 524
Average GRE (full time): 150 verbal; 146 quantitative; 4.5 writing
Average GPA (full time): 3.60
Average age of entrants to full-time program: 23
Average months of prior work experience (full time): 36
TOEFL requirement: Yes
Minimum TOEFL score: 550
Most popular departments: accounting, finance, marketing, management information systems
Mean starting base salary for 2017 full-time graduates: $51,667

Loyola University New Orleans (Butt)

6363 St. Charles Avenue
Campus Box 15
New Orleans, LA 70118
www.business.loyno.edu
Private
Admissions: (504) 864-7953
Email: mba@loyno.edu
Financial aid: (504) 865-3231
Application deadline: 06/30
Tuition: full time: $1,005/credit hour; part time: $1,005/credit hour
Room/board/expenses: N/A
College-funded aid: Yes
International student aid: Yes
Average student indebtedness at graduation: $51,306
Full-time enrollment: 23
men: 52%; women: 48%; minorities: 26%; international: 17%
Part-time enrollment: 57
men: 42%; women: 58%; minorities: 30%; international: 7%
Acceptance rate (full time): 100%
Average GMAT (full time): 497
Average GRE (full time): N/A verbal; N/A quantitative; N/A writing
Average age of entrants to full-time program: 30
TOEFL requirement: Yes
Minimum TOEFL score: 580
Most popular departments: entrepreneurship, finance, marketing, production/operations management, quantitative analysis/statistics and operations research

McNeese State University[1]

PO Box 91660
Lake Charles, LA 70609
www.mcneese.edu/colleges/bus
Public
Admissions: (337) 475-5576
Email: mba@mcneese.edu
Financial aid: (337) 475-5065
Tuition: N/A
Room/board/expenses: N/A
Enrollment: N/A

Nicholls State University[1]

PO Box 2015
Thibodaux, LA 70310
www.nicholls.edu/business/
Public
Admissions: (985) 448-4507
Email: becky.leblanc-durocher@nicholls.edu
Financial aid: (985) 448-4048
Tuition: N/A
Room/board/expenses: N/A
Enrollment: N/A

Southeastern Louisiana University

SLU 10735
Hammond, LA 70402
www.selu.edu/acad_research/programs/grad_bus
Public
Admissions: (985) 549-5637

Email: admissions@selu.edu
Financial aid: (985) 549-2244
Application deadline: 07/15
In-state tuition: full time: $8,772; part time: $487/credit hour
Out-of-state tuition: full time: $21,250
Room/board/expenses: $13,200
College-funded aid: Yes
International student aid: Yes
Full-time enrollment: 65
men: 52%; women: 48%; minorities: 14%; international: 8%
Part-time enrollment: 22
men: 32%; women: 68%; minorities: 18%; international: 14%
Acceptance rate (full time): 98%
Average GMAT (full time): 485
Average GRE (full time): 144 verbal; 152 quantitative; N/A writing
Average age of entrants to full-time program: 24
TOEFL requirement: Yes
Minimum TOEFL score: 500
Most popular departments: general management

Southern University and A&M College[1]

PO Box 9723
Baton Rouge, LA 70813
www.subr.edu/index.cfm/page/121
Public
Admissions: (225) 771-5390
Email: gradschool@subr.edu
Financial aid: N/A
Tuition: N/A
Room/board/expenses: N/A
Enrollment: N/A

Tulane University (Freeman)

7 McAlister Drive
New Orleans, LA 70118-5669
freeman.tulane.edu
Private
Admissions: (504) 865-5410
Email: freeman.admissions@tulane.edu
Financial aid: (504) 865-5410
Application deadline: 05/01
Tuition: full time: $55,878; part time: $1,723/credit hour
Room/board/expenses: $19,598
College-funded aid: Yes
International student aid: Yes
Full-time enrollment: 87
men: 64%; women: 36%; minorities: 20%; international: 14%
Part-time enrollment: 131
men: 54%; women: 46%; minorities: 31%; international: 5%
Acceptance rate (full time): 61%
Average GMAT (full time): 648
Average GRE (full time): 154 verbal; 152 quantitative; N/A writing
Average GPA (full time): 3.12
Average age of entrants to full-time program: 28
Average months of prior work experience (full time): 66
TOEFL requirement: Yes
Minimum TOEFL score: N/A

Most popular departments: entrepreneurship, finance, general management, international business, other
Mean starting base salary for 2017 full-time graduates: $91,269
Employment location for 2017 class: Intl. N/A; N.E. 21%; M.A. N/A; S. 53%; M.W. N/A; S.W. 16%; W. 11%

University of Louisiana–Lafayette (Moody)

USL Box 43545
Lafayette, LA 70504-3545
gradschool.louisiana.edu/
Public
Admissions: (337) 482-6965
Email: gradschool@louisiana.edu
Financial aid: (337) 482-6506
Application deadline: 06/30
In-state tuition: full time: $9,450; part time: $523/credit hour
Out-of-state tuition: full time: $23,178
Room/board/expenses: N/A
College-funded aid: Yes
International student aid: Yes
Full-time enrollment: N/A
Part-time enrollment: 176
men: 48%; women: 52%; minorities: 15%; international: 10%
Average GRE (full time): N/A verbal; N/A quantitative; N/A writing
TOEFL requirement: Yes
Minimum TOEFL score: 550
Most popular departments: accounting, finance, health care administration, international business, production/operations management

University of Louisiana–Monroe

700 University Avenue
Monroe, LA 71209
www.ulm.edu/cbss/
Public
Admissions: N/A
Financial aid: N/A
Application deadline: rolling
In-state tuition: full time: N/A; part time: N/A
Out-of-state tuition: full time: N/A
Room/board/expenses: N/A
College-funded aid: Yes
International student aid: Yes
Full-time enrollment: 34
men: 65%; women: 35%; minorities: N/A; international: N/A
Part-time enrollment: N/A
Average GRE (full time): N/A verbal; N/A quantitative; N/A writing
TOEFL requirement: Yes
Minimum TOEFL score: N/A
Most popular departments: general management, health care administration, public administration, other

University of New Orleans

2000 Lakeshore Drive
New Orleans, LA 70148
www.uno.edu/admissions/
contact.aspx
Public
Admissions: (504) 280-6595
Email: pec@uno.edu
Financial aid: (504) 280-6603
Application deadline: N/A
In-state tuition: full time:
N/A; part time: N/A
Out-of-state tuition: full time: N/A
Room/board/expenses: N/A
College-funded aid: Yes
International student aid: Yes
Full-time enrollment: 79
men: 42%; women:
58%; minorities: N/A;
international: N/A
Part-time enrollment: 79
men: 42%; women:
58%; minorities: 24%;
international: 9%
Average GRE (full
time): N/A verbal; N/A
quantitative; N/A writing
TOEFL requirement: Yes
Minimum TOEFL score: N/A

University of Maine[1]

Donald P. Corbett Business
Building
Orono, ME 04469-5723
www.umaine.edu/business/mba
Public
Admissions: (207) 581-1971
Email: mba@maine.edu
Financial aid: (207) 581-1324
Tuition: N/A
Room/board/expenses: N/A
Enrollment: N/A

University of Southern Maine

PO Box 9300
Portland, ME 04104
www.usm.maine.edu/sb
Public
Admissions: (207) 780-4184
Email: mba@usm.maine.edu
Financial aid: (207) 780-5250
Application deadline: N/A
In-state tuition: full time:
$393/credit hour; part
time: $393/credit hour
Out-of-state tuition: full
time: $1,063/credit hour
Room/board/expenses: N/A
College-funded aid: Yes
International student aid: Yes
Full-time enrollment: N/A
Part-time enrollment: 80
men: 61%; women: 39%;
minorities: 4%; international: 3%
Average GRE (full
time): N/A verbal; N/A
quantitative; N/A writing
TOEFL requirement: Yes
Minimum TOEFL score: 550

Frostburg State University

101 Braddock Road
Frostburg, MD 21532-2303
www.frostburg.edu/colleges/
cob/mba/
Public
Admissions: (301) 687-7053
Email: gradservices@
frostburg.edu
Financial aid: (301) 687-4301
Application deadline: N/A
In-state tuition: full time:
$413/credit hour; part
time: $413/credit hour
Out-of-state tuition: full
time: $531/credit hour
Room/board/expenses: N/A
College-funded aid: Yes
International student aid: Yes
Full-time enrollment: 33
men: 58%; women:
42%; minorities: 15%;
international: 0%
Part-time enrollment: 143
men: 46%; women:
54%; minorities: 23%;
international: 2%
Average GRE (full
time): N/A verbal; N/A
quantitative; N/A writing
TOEFL requirement: Yes
Minimum TOEFL score: N/A

Johns Hopkins University (Carey)[1]

3400 N Charles Street
Baltimore, MD 21218
carey.jhu.edu/
Private
Admissions: N/A
Financial aid: N/A
Tuition: N/A
Room/board/expenses: N/A
Enrollment: N/A

Loyola University Maryland (Sellinger)

4501 N. Charles Street
Baltimore, MD 21210-2699
www.loyola.edu/sellinger/
Private
Admissions: (410) 617-5020
Email: graduate@loyola.edu
Financial aid: (410) 617-2576
Application deadline: 08/20
Tuition: total program:
$59,450 (full time); part
time: $950/credit hour
Room/board/expenses: N/A
College-funded aid: Yes
International student aid: Yes
Full-time enrollment: 27
men: 59%; women:
41%; minorities: 41%;
international: 4%
Part-time enrollment: 306
men: 58%; women:
42%; minorities: 18%;
international: 1%
Acceptance rate (full time): 90%
Average GMAT (full time): 530
Average GRE (full
time): N/A verbal; N/A
quantitative; N/A writing
Average GPA (full time): 3.40
Average age of entrants to
full-time program: 23

Average months of prior work
experience (full time): 9
TOEFL requirement: Yes
Minimum TOEFL score: 550

Morgan State University (Graves)

1700 E. Cold Spring Lane
Baltimore, MD 21251
www.morgan.edu/sbm
Public
Admissions: (443) 885-3396
Email:
gravesschool@morgan.edu
Financial aid: (443) 885-3170
Application deadline: 03/15
In-state tuition: full time:
$412/credit hour; part
time: $412/credit hour
Out-of-state tuition: full
time: $810/credit hour
Room/board/expenses: N/A
College-funded aid: Yes
International student aid: Yes
Average student indebtedness
at graduation: $2,500
Full-time enrollment: 64
men: 56%; women:
44%; minorities: 58%;
international: 41%
Part-time enrollment: 10
men: 70%; women:
30%; minorities: 80%;
international: 20%
Acceptance rate (full time): 79%
Average GMAT (full time): 400
Average GRE (full
time): 144 verbal; 287
quantitative; 3.5 writing
Average GPA (full time): 3.30
Average age of entrants to
full-time program: 26
Average months of prior work
experience (full time): 49
TOEFL requirement: Yes
Minimum TOEFL score: N/A
Most popular departments:
accounting, finance,
management information
systems
Mean starting base salary for 2017
full-time graduates: $65,000
Employment location for 2017
class: Intl. 20%; N.E. N/A;
M.A. 60%; S. N/A; M.W.
20%; S.W. N/A; W. N/A

Salisbury University

1101 Camden Avenue
Salisbury, MD 21801-6860
www.salisbury.edu/Schools/
perdue/welcome.html
Public
Admissions: (410) 543-6161
Email: admissions@
salisbury.edu
Financial aid: (410) 543-6165
Application deadline: 03/01
In-state tuition: full time:
$392/credit hour; part
time: $392/credit hour
Out-of-state tuition: full
time: $703/credit hour
Room/board/expenses: N/A
College-funded aid: Yes
International student aid: Yes
Full-time enrollment: 34
men: 50%; women:
50%; minorities: 26%;
international: 6%

Part-time enrollment: 25
men: 52%; women:
48%; minorities: 20%;
international: 8%
Acceptance rate (full time): 58%
Average GRE (full
time): N/A verbal; N/A
quantitative; N/A writing
Average age of entrants to
full-time program: 26
TOEFL requirement: Yes
Minimum TOEFL score: 550

University of Baltimore[1]

11 W. Mt. Royal Avenue
Baltimore, MD 21201
www.ubalt.edu/mba
Public
Admissions: (410) 837-6565
Email: gradadmission@ubalt.edu
Financial aid: (410) 837-4763
Tuition: N/A
Room/board/expenses: N/A
Enrollment: N/A

University of Maryland–College Park (Smith)

2308 Van Munching Hall
College Park, MD 20742
www.rhsmith.umd.edu
Public
Admissions: (301) 405-0202
Email: mba_info@
rhsmith.umd.edu
Financial aid: (301) 405-2301
Application deadline: 03/01
In-state tuition: full time:
$47,208; part time: $15,322
Out-of-state tuition:
full time: $56,388
Room/board/expenses: N/A
College-funded aid: Yes
International student aid: Yes
Full-time enrollment: 200
men: 66%; women:
35%; minorities: 24%;
international: 35%
Part-time enrollment: 542
men: 61%; women:
39%; minorities: 29%;
international: 9%
Acceptance rate (full time): 36%
Average GMAT (full time): 629
Average GRE (full
time): 156 verbal; 153
quantitative; 4.3 writing
Average GPA (full time): 3.26
Average age of entrants to
full-time program: 29
Average months of prior work
experience (full time): 69
TOEFL requirement: Yes
Minimum TOEFL score: 600
Most popular departments:
consulting, entrepreneurship,
finance, general
management, marketing
Mean starting base salary for 2017
full-time graduates: $100,934
Employment location for 2017
class: Intl. 0%; N.E. 15%;
M.A. 67%; S. 2%; M.W.
2%; S.W. 3%; W. 11%

Babson College (Olin)

231 Forest Street
Babson Park, MA 02457-0310
www.babson.edu/graduate
Private
Admissions: (781) 239-4317
Email: gradadmissions@
babson.edu
Financial aid: (781) 239-4219
Application deadline: rolling
Tuition: total program:
$108,794 (full time); part
time: $1,718/credit hour
Room/board/expenses: $54,556
College-funded aid: Yes
International student aid: Yes
Average student indebtedness
at graduation: $74,838
Full-time enrollment: 328
men: 69%; women:
31%; minorities: 8%;
international: 72%
Part-time enrollment: 246
men: 62%; women:
38%; minorities: 13%;
international: 8%
Acceptance rate (full time): 89%
Average GMAT (full time): 620
Average GRE (full
time): 151 verbal; 152
quantitative; 3.5 writing
Average GPA (full time): 3.23
Average age of entrants to
full-time program: 28
Average months of prior work
experience (full time): 61
TOEFL requirement: Yes
Minimum TOEFL score: N/A
Most popular departments:
entrepreneurship, finance,
marketing, technology, other
Mean starting base salary for 2017
full-time graduates: $78,123
Employment location for
2017 class: Intl. 24%; N.E.
56%; M.A. 4%; S. 8%; M.W.
4%; S.W. 1%; W. 3%

Bentley University

175 Forest Street
Waltham, MA 02452-4705
admissions.bentley.edu/
graduate
Private
Admissions: (781) 891-2108
Email: applygrad@bentley.edu
Financial aid: (781) 891-3441
Application deadline: rolling
Tuition: full time: $41,510;
part time: $1,992
Room/board/expenses: $21,170
College-funded aid: Yes
International student aid: Yes
Average student indebtedness
at graduation: $34,664
Full-time enrollment: 122
men: 49%; women:
51%; minorities: 12%;
international: 61%
Part-time enrollment: 224
men: 54%; women:
46%; minorities: 20%;
international: 4%
Acceptance rate (full time): 82%
Average GRE (full
time): N/A verbal; N/A
quantitative; N/A writing
Average age of entrants to
full-time program: 27

Average months of prior work experience (full time): 48
TOEFL requirement: Yes
Minimum TOEFL score: 600
Most popular departments: accounting, finance, marketing, management information systems, quantitative analysis/statistics and operations research

Boston College (Carroll)

140 Commonwealth Avenue
Fulton Hall 320
Chestnut Hill, MA 02467
www.bc.edu/mba
Private
Admissions: (617) 552-3920
Email: bcmba@bc.edu
Financial aid: (800) 294-0294
Application deadline: 04/17
Tuition: full time: $49,340; part time: $1,676/credit hour
Room/board/expenses: $22,648
College-funded aid: Yes
International student aid: Yes
Average student indebtedness at graduation: $63,081
Full-time enrollment: 175
men: 69%; women: 31%; minorities: 16%; international: 26%
Part-time enrollment: 424
men: 65%; women: 35%; minorities: 18%; international: 9%
Acceptance rate (full time): 40%
Average GMAT (full time): 637
Average GRE (full time): 153 verbal; 153 quantitative; 4.0 writing
Average GPA (full time): 3.28
Average age of entrants to full-time program: 28
Average months of prior work experience (full time): 54
TOEFL requirement: Yes
Minimum TOEFL score: 600
Most popular departments: accounting, finance, general management, marketing, quantitative analysis/statistics and operations research
Mean starting base salary for 2017 full-time graduates: $100,698
Employment location for 2017 class: Intl. 4%; N.E. 79%; M.A. 4%; S. 5%; M.W. N/A; S.W. 2%; W. 7%

Boston University (Questrom)

595 Commonwealth Avenue
Boston, MA 02215-1704
www.bu.edu/questrom
Private
Admissions: (617) 353-2670
Email: mba@bu.edu
Financial aid: (617) 353-2670
Application deadline: 03/19
Tuition: full time: $52,066; part time: $1,622/credit hour
Room/board/expenses: $19,119
College-funded aid: Yes
International student aid: Yes
Full-time enrollment: 320
men: 57%; women: 43%; minorities: 19%; international: 30%

Part-time enrollment: 646
men: 56%; women: 44%; minorities: 24%; international: 6%
Acceptance rate (full time): 40%
Average GMAT (full time): 680
Average GRE (full time): 157 verbal; 158 quantitative; N/A writing
Average GPA (full time): 3.33
Average age of entrants to full-time program: 27
Average months of prior work experience (full time): 57
TOEFL requirement: Yes
Minimum TOEFL score: 600
Most popular departments: health care administration, leadership, marketing, not-for-profit management, other
Mean starting base salary for 2017 full-time graduates: $95,471
Employment location for 2017 class: Intl. 12%; N.E. 69%; M.A. 0%; S. 6%; M.W. 1%; S.W. 0%; W. 12%

Brandeis University[1]

415 South Street
Waltham, MA 02454-9110
www.brandeis.edu/global
Private
Admissions: (781) 736-4829
Email: admissions@lembergbrandeis.edu
Financial aid: N/A
Tuition: N/A
Room/board/expenses: N/A
Enrollment: N/A

Clark University

950 Main Street
Worcester, MA 01610
www.clarku.edu/gsom
Private
Admissions: (508) 793-7559
Email: jczub@clarku.edu
Financial aid: (508) 793-7559
Application deadline: 02/01
Tuition: total program: $69,582 (full time); $69,582 (part time)
Room/board/expenses: $12,000
College-funded aid: Yes
International student aid: Yes
Full-time enrollment: 87
men: 53%; women: 47%; minorities: 6%; international: 44%
Part-time enrollment: 45
men: 38%; women: 62%; minorities: 24%; international: 4%
Acceptance rate (full time): 71%
Average GMAT (full time): 518
Average GRE (full time): 148 verbal; 149 quantitative; 3.0 writing
Average GPA (full time): 3.27
Average age of entrants to full-time program: 26
Average months of prior work experience (full time): 35
TOEFL requirement: Yes
Minimum TOEFL score: N/A
Most popular departments: general management, marketing
Mean starting base salary for 2017 full-time graduates: $55,209

Harvard University

Soldiers Field
Boston, MA 02163
www.hbs.edu
Private
Admissions: (617) 495-6128
Email: admissions@hbs.edu
Financial aid: (617) 495-6640
Application deadline: 04/02
Tuition: full time: $78,772; part time: N/A
Room/board/expenses: $28,028
College-funded aid: Yes
International student aid: Yes
Average student indebtedness at graduation: $87,300
Full-time enrollment: 1,857
men: 58%; women: 42%; minorities: N/A; international: N/A
Part-time enrollment: N/A
Acceptance rate (full time): 10%
Average GMAT (full time): 731
Average GRE (full time): N/A verbal; N/A quantitative; N/A writing
Average GPA (full time): 3.71
Average age of entrants to full-time program: 27
Average months of prior work experience (full time): 54
TOEFL requirement: Yes
Minimum TOEFL score: N/A
Mean starting base salary for 2017 full-time graduates: $137,293
Employment location for 2017 class: Intl. 13%; N.E. 44%; M.A. 5%; S. 4%; M.W. 6%; S.W. 3%; W. 25%

Hult International Business School–Boston

1 Education Street
Cambridge, MA 02141
www.hult.edu
Private
Admissions: (161) 774-6199
Email: admissions@hult.edu
Financial aid: N/A
Application deadline: 06/06
Tuition: total program: $73,000 (full time); part time: N/A
Room/board/expenses: $26,000
College-funded aid: Yes
International student aid: Yes
Full-time enrollment: 245
men: 62%; women: 38%; minorities: 0%; international: 90%
Part-time enrollment: N/A
Acceptance rate (full time): 38%
Average GMAT (full time): 615
Average GRE (full time): 152 verbal; 154 quantitative; N/A writing
Average GPA (full time): 2.95
Average age of entrants to full-time program: 31
Average months of prior work experience (full time): 89
TOEFL requirement: Yes
Minimum TOEFL score: N/A
Mean starting base salary for 2017 full-time graduates: $94,822

Massachusetts Institute of Technology (Sloan)

100 Main Street, Building E62
Cambridge, MA 02142
mitsloan.mit.edu/mba
Private
Admissions: (617) 258-5434
Email: mbaadmissions@sloan.mit.edu
Financial aid: (617) 253-4971
Application deadline: 04/19
Tuition: full time: $71,312; part time: N/A
Room/board/expenses: $34,858
College-funded aid: Yes
International student aid: Yes
Average student indebtedness at graduation: $109,891
Full-time enrollment: 813
men: 59%; women: 41%; minorities: 23%; international: 36%
Part-time enrollment: N/A
Acceptance rate (full time): 12%
Average GMAT (full time): 722
Average GRE (full time): N/A verbal; N/A quantitative; N/A writing
Average GPA (full time): 3.57
Average age of entrants to full-time program: 28
Average months of prior work experience (full time): 58
TOEFL requirement: No
Minimum TOEFL score: N/A
Most popular departments: entrepreneurship, finance, international business, manufacturing and technology management, production/operations management
Mean starting base salary for 2017 full-time graduates: $128,301
Employment location for 2017 class: Intl. 13%; N.E. 38%; M.A. 3%; S. 3%; M.W. 4%; S.W. 4%; W. 34%

Northeastern University

360 Huntington Avenue
350 Dodge Hall
Boston, MA 02115
www.damore-mckim.northeastern.edu/academic-programs/graduate-programs
Private
Admissions: (617) 373-5992
Email: gradbusiness@northeastern.edu
Financial aid: (617) 373-5899
Application deadline: 04/15
Tuition: full time: $1,560/credit hour; part time: $1,560/credit hour
Room/board/expenses: $25,350
College-funded aid: Yes
International student aid: Yes
Full-time enrollment: 166
men: 57%; women: 43%; minorities: 14%; international: 38%
Part-time enrollment: 309
men: 59%; women: 41%; minorities: 21%; international: 5%
Acceptance rate (full time): 35%
Average GMAT (full time): 633

Average GRE (full time): 156 verbal; 158 quantitative; 3.7 writing
Average GPA (full time): 3.34
Average age of entrants to full-time program: 27
Average months of prior work experience (full time): 46
TOEFL requirement: Yes
Minimum TOEFL score: 600
Most popular departments: entrepreneurship, finance, international business, marketing, supply chain management/logistics
Mean starting base salary for 2017 full-time graduates: $87,773
Employment location for 2017 class: Intl. 2%; N.E. 90%; M.A. 0%; S. 5%; M.W. 0%; S.W. 2%; W. 0%

Simmons College[1]

300 The Fenway
Boston, MA 02115
www.simmons.edu/som
Private
Admissions: N/A
Financial aid: N/A
Tuition: N/A
Room/board/expenses: N/A
Enrollment: N/A

Suffolk University (Sawyer)

8 Ashburton Place
Boston, MA 02108
www.suffolk.edu/business
Private
Admissions: (617) 573-8302
Email: grad.admission@suffolk.edu
Financial aid: (617) 573-8470
Application deadline: 03/15
Tuition: full time: $42,772; part time: $1,424/credit hour
Room/board/expenses: $20,400
College-funded aid: Yes
International student aid: Yes
Average student indebtedness at graduation: $54,014
Full-time enrollment: 96
men: 46%; women: 54%; minorities: 19%; international: 41%
Part-time enrollment: 247
men: 43%; women: 57%; minorities: 23%; international: 1%
Acceptance rate (full time): 63%
Average GMAT (full time): 509
Average GRE (full time): 146 verbal; 151 quantitative; 3.2 writing
Average GPA (full time): 3.39
Average age of entrants to full-time program: 27
Average months of prior work experience (full time): 28
TOEFL requirement: Yes
Minimum TOEFL score: 550
Most popular departments: accounting, finance, marketing, tax
Mean starting base salary for 2017 full-time graduates: $62,273
Employment location for 2017 class: Intl. 8%; N.E. 83%; M.A. 0%; S. 0%; M.W. 0%; S.W. 0%; W. 8%

University of Massachusetts–Amherst (Isenberg)

121 Presidents Drive
Amherst, MA 01003
www.isenberg.umass.edu/
programs/masters/mba
Public
Admissions: (413) 545-5608
Email:
mba@isenberg.umass.edu
Financial aid: (413) 545-0801
Application deadline: 04/01
In-state tuition: full time: $13,930;
part time: $900/credit hour
Out-of-state tuition:
full time: $30,533
Room/board/expenses: $13,904
College-funded aid: Yes
International student aid: Yes
Average student indebtedness
at graduation: $26,998
Full-time enrollment: 51
men: 43%; women:
57%; minorities: 18%;
international: 20%
Part-time enrollment: 213
men: 69%; women:
31%; minorities: 26%;
international: 11%
Acceptance rate (full time): 33%
Average GMAT (full time): 659
Average GRE (full
time): 159 verbal; 157
quantitative; 4.2 writing
Average GPA (full time): 3.44
Average age of entrants to
full-time program: 29
Average months of prior work
experience (full time): 77
TOEFL requirement: Yes
Minimum TOEFL score: 600
Most popular departments:
entrepreneurship, finance,
general management, hotel
administration, sports business
Mean starting base salary for 2017
full-time graduates: $78,300

University of Massachusetts–Boston

100 Morrissey Boulevard
Boston, MA 02125-3393
www.umb.edu/cmgrad
Public
Admissions: (617) 287-7720
Email: gradcm@umb.edu
Financial aid: (617) 287-6300
Application deadline: 06/01
In-state tuition: full time: N/A;
part time: $739/credit hour
Out-of-state tuition: full time: N/A
Room/board/expenses: N/A
College-funded aid: No
International student aid: Yes
Full-time enrollment: N/A
Part-time enrollment: 296
men: 52%; women:
48%; minorities: 15%;
international: 31%
Average GRE (full
time): N/A verbal; N/A
quantitative; N/A writing
TOEFL requirement: Yes
Minimum TOEFL score: 600
Most popular departments:
accounting, finance,
general management,
marketing, management
information systems

University of Massachusetts–Dartmouth

285 Old Westport Road
North Dartmouth, MA 02747
www.umassd.edu/charlton/
programs/graduate
Public
Admissions: (508) 999-8604
Email: graduate@umassd.edu
Financial aid: (508) 999-8643
Application deadline: 07/01
In-state tuition: full time: $16,259;
part time: $549/credit hour
Out-of-state tuition:
full time: $28,690
Room/board/expenses: $15,651
College-funded aid: Yes
International student aid: No
Average student indebtedness
at graduation: $17,813
Full-time enrollment: 151
men: 53%; women:
47%; minorities: 11%;
international: 64%
Part-time enrollment: 30
men: 43%; women:
57%; minorities: 13%;
international: 0%
Acceptance rate (full time): 79%
Average GMAT (full time): 422
Average GRE (full
time): 139 verbal; 148
quantitative; 2.8 writing
Average GPA (full time): 3.12
Average age of entrants to
full-time program: 26
TOEFL requirement: Yes
Minimum TOEFL score: 550
Most popular departments:
general management,
health care administration,
leadership, technology, other
Mean starting base salary for 2017
full-time graduates: $58,657
Employment location for
2017 class: Intl. 25%; N.E.
75%; M.A. N/A; S. N/A; M.W.
N/A; S.W. N/A; W. N/A

University of Massachusetts–Lowell

1 University Avenue
Lowell, MA 01854
www.uml.edu/grad
Public
Admissions: (978) 934-2390
Email: graduate_admissions@
uml.edu
Financial aid: (978) 934-4220
Application deadline: rolling
In-state tuition: full time:
$835/credit hour; part
time: $835/credit hour
Out-of-state tuition: full
time: $1,489/credit hour
Room/board/expenses: $18,782
College-funded aid: Yes
International student aid: Yes
Average student indebtedness
at graduation: $25,317
Full-time enrollment: 63
men: 57%; women:
43%; minorities: 32%;
international: 30%
Part-time enrollment: 229
men: 62%; women:
38%; minorities: 31%;
international: 10%
Acceptance rate (full time): 90%
Average GMAT (full time): 507

Average GRE (full
time): N/A verbal; N/A
quantitative; N/A writing
Average GPA (full time): 3.30
Average age of entrants to
full-time program: 27
Average months of prior work
experience (full time): 49
TOEFL requirement: Yes
Minimum TOEFL score: 600
Most popular departments:
accounting, finance,
general management,
marketing, management
information systems

Western New England University

1215 Wilbraham Road
Springfield, MA 01119-2684
www1.wne.edu/academics/
graduate/index.cfm#?
category=2
Private
Admissions: (800) 325-1122
Email: study@wne.edu
Financial aid: (413) 796-2080
Application deadline: rolling
Tuition: full time: N/A; part
time: $824/credit hour
Room/board/expenses: N/A
College-funded aid: No
International student aid: No
Full-time enrollment: N/A
Part-time enrollment: 97
men: 54%; women: 46%;
minorities: 8%; international: 1%
Average GRE (full
time): N/A verbal; N/A
quantitative; N/A writing
TOEFL requirement: Yes
Minimum TOEFL score: N/A
Most popular departments:
accounting, general
management, leadership, other

Worcester Polytechnic Institute

100 Institute Road
Worcester, MA 01609
business.wpi.edu
Private
Admissions: (508) 831-6345
Email: business@wpi.edu
Financial aid: (508) 831-5469
Application deadline: 07/15
Tuition: full time: $1,457/
credit hour; part time:
$1,457/credit hour
Room/board/expenses: $24,233
College-funded aid: Yes
International student aid: Yes
Average student indebtedness
at graduation: $33,741
Full-time enrollment: 190
men: 41%; women:
59%; minorities: 4%;
international: 92%
Part-time enrollment: 214
men: 57%; women:
43%; minorities: 13%;
international: 26%
Acceptance rate (full time): 34%
Average GRE (full
time): 148 verbal; 161
quantitative; 3.2 writing
Average age of entrants to
full-time program: 24

TOEFL requirement: Yes
Minimum TOEFL score: 577
Most popular departments:
manufacturing and technology
management, marketing,
management information
systems, production/operations
management, technology

Central Michigan University[1]

252 ABSC - Grawn Hall
Mount Pleasant, MI 48859
www.cmich.edu/colleges/cba/
Pages/default.aspx
Public
Admissions: (989) 774-4723
Email: grad@cmich.edu
Financial aid: N/A
Tuition: N/A
Room/board/expenses: N/A
Enrollment: N/A

Eastern Michigan University

Gary M. Owen Building
300 W Michigan Avenue
Ypsilanti, MI 48197
www.cob.emich.edu
Public
Admissions: (734) 487-4444
Email: cob.graduate@emich.edu
Financial aid: (734) 487-0455
Application deadline: 05/15
In-state tuition: full time: N/A;
part time: $722/credit hour
Out-of-state tuition: full time: N/A
Room/board/expenses: N/A
College-funded aid: Yes
International student aid: Yes
Full-time enrollment: N/A
Part-time enrollment: 200
men: 46%; women:
54%; minorities: 25%;
international: 7%
Average GRE (full
time): N/A verbal; N/A
quantitative; N/A writing
TOEFL requirement: Yes
Minimum TOEFL score: 550
Most popular departments:
finance, general management,
human resources management,
marketing, supply chain
management/logistics

Grand Valley State University (Seidman)

50 Front Avenue SW
Grand Rapids, MI 49504-6424
www.gvsu.edu/Seidman
Public
Admissions: (616) 331-7400
Email: go2gvmba@gvsu.edu
Financial aid: (616) 331-3234
Application deadline: rolling
In-state tuition: full time:
$686/credit hour; part
time: $686/credit hour
Out-of-state tuition: full
time: $686/credit hour
Room/board/expenses: N/A
College-funded aid: Yes
International student aid: Yes
Full-time enrollment: N/A

Part-time enrollment: 270
men: 59%; women:
41%; minorities: 10%;
international: 5%
Average GRE (full
time): N/A verbal; N/A
quantitative; N/A writing
TOEFL requirement: Yes
Minimum TOEFL score: N/A
Most popular departments:
accounting, finance, health care
administration, international
business, manufacturing and
technology management

Michigan State University (Broad)

Eppley Center
645 N. Shaw Lane, Room 211
East Lansing, MI 48824-1121
www.mba.msu.edu
Public
Admissions: (517) 355-7604
Email: mba@msu.edu
Financial aid: (517) 355-7604
Application deadline: 04/01
In-state tuition: full time:
$30,638; part time: N/A
Out-of-state tuition:
full time: $48,538
Room/board/expenses: $21,016
College-funded aid: Yes
International student aid: Yes
Average student indebtedness
at graduation: $54,196
Full-time enrollment: 143
men: 71%; women:
29%; minorities: 11%;
international: 41%
Part-time enrollment: N/A
Acceptance rate (full time): 32%
Average GMAT (full time): 674
Average GRE (full
time): 155 verbal; 152
quantitative; 3.7 writing
Average GPA (full time): 3.30
Average age of entrants to
full-time program: 28
Average months of prior work
experience (full time): 52
TOEFL requirement: Yes
Minimum TOEFL score: N/A
Most popular departments:
consulting, finance, general
management, marketing, supply
chain management/logistics
Mean starting base salary for 2017
full-time graduates: $101,836
Employment location for
2017 class: Intl. 5%; N.E.
10%; M.A. 2%; S. 17%; M.W.
38%; S.W. 10%; W. 17%

Michigan Technological University

1400 Townsend Drive
Houghton, MI 49931-1295
www.mtu.edu/business/
graduate/techmba
Public
Admissions: (906) 487-3055
Email: techmba@mtu.edu
Financial aid: (906) 487-3055
Application deadline: 07/01
In-state tuition: full time: $950/
credit hour; part time: N/A
Out-of-state tuition: full
time: $950/credit hour
Room/board/expenses: $14,627

College-funded aid: Yes
International student aid: Yes
Full-time enrollment: 30
men: 47%; women:
53%; minorities: 3%;
international: 27%
Part-time enrollment: N/A
Acceptance rate (full time): 19%
Average GMAT (full time): 490
Average GRE (full
time): N/A verbal; N/A
quantitative; N/A writing
Average GPA (full time): 3.31
Average age of entrants to
full-time program: 25
Average months of prior work
experience (full time): 56
TOEFL requirement: Yes
Minimum TOEFL score: 590
Most popular departments:
entrepreneurship,
manufacturing and technology
management, technology
Mean starting base salary for 2017
full-time graduates: $53,917

Northern Michigan University

1401 Presque Isle Avenue
Marquette, MI 49855
www.nmu.edu/graduatestudies
Public
Admissions: (906) 227-2300
Email: graduate@nmu.edu
Financial aid: (906) 227-2327
Application deadline: rolling
In-state tuition: full time:
$623/credit hour; part
time: $623/credit hour
Out-of-state tuition: full
time: $623/credit hour
Room/board/expenses: $23,728
College-funded aid: Yes
International student aid: Yes
Full-time enrollment: 16
men: 63%; women:
38%; minorities: 13%;
international: 13%
Part-time enrollment: 5
men: 40%; women:
60%; minorities: 0%;
international: 20%
Acceptance rate (full time): 100%
Average GMAT (full time): 503
Average GRE (full
time): N/A verbal; N/A
quantitative; N/A writing
Average GPA (full time): 3.28
Average age of entrants to
full-time program: 24
TOEFL requirement: Yes
Minimum TOEFL score: 550

Oakland University

238 Elliott Hall
275 Varner Drive
Rochester, MI 48309-4493
www.oakland.edu/
business/grad
Public
Admissions: (248) 370-3287
Email: OUGradBusiness@
oakland.edu
Financial aid: (248) 370-2550
Application deadline: 07/15
In-state tuition: full time: N/A;
part time: $706/credit hour
Out-of-state tuition: full time: N/A
Room/board/expenses: N/A
College-funded aid: Yes
International student aid: Yes

Full-time enrollment: N/A
Part-time enrollment: 287
men: 65%; women:
35%; minorities: 12%;
international: 15%
Average GRE (full
time): N/A verbal; N/A
quantitative; N/A writing
TOEFL requirement: Yes
Minimum TOEFL score: 550
Most popular departments:
finance, health care
administration, human
resources management,
marketing, management
information systems

Saginaw Valley State University

7400 Bay Road
University Center, MI 48710
www.svsu.edu/mba/
Public
Admissions: (989) 964-6096
Email: gradadm@svsu.edu
Financial aid: (989) 964-4103
Application deadline: rolling
In-state tuition: full time: N/A;
part time: $564/credit hour
Out-of-state tuition: full time: N/A
Room/board/expenses: N/A
College-funded aid: Yes
International student aid: Yes
Full-time enrollment: N/A
Part-time enrollment: 61
men: 57%; women:
43%; minorities: 13%;
international: 49%
Average GRE (full
time): N/A verbal; N/A
quantitative; N/A writing
TOEFL requirement: Yes
Minimum TOEFL score: 550

University of Detroit Mercy

4001 W. McNichols Road
Detroit, MI 48221-3038
business.udmercy.edu
Private
Admissions: (800) 635-5020
Email: admissions@udmercy.edu
Financial aid: (313) 993-3350
Application deadline: rolling
Tuition: full time: $1,579/
credit hour; part time:
$1,579/credit hour
Room/board/expenses: N/A
College-funded aid: Yes
International student aid: Yes
Average student indebtedness
at graduation: $58,785
Full-time enrollment: 50
men: 62%; women:
38%; minorities: 22%;
international: 16%
Part-time enrollment: 55
men: 58%; women:
42%; minorities: 42%;
international: 9%
Acceptance rate (full time): 86%
Average GRE (full
time): N/A verbal; N/A
quantitative; N/A writing
Average GPA (full time): 3.23
Average age of entrants to
full-time program: 22
TOEFL requirement: No
Minimum TOEFL score: N/A

University of Michigan–Ann Arbor (Ross)

701 Tappan Street
Ann Arbor, MI 48109-1234
michiganross.umich.edu/
Public
Admissions: (734) 763-5796
Email: rossadmissions@
umich.edu
Financial aid: (734) 764-5139
Application deadline: 03/19
In-state tuition: full time:
$62,628; part time:
$2,056/credit hour
Out-of-state tuition:
full time: $67,628
Room/board/expenses: $23,408
College-funded aid: Yes
International student aid: Yes
Average student indebtedness
at graduation: $107,129
Full-time enrollment: 824
men: 59%; women:
41%; minorities: 23%;
international: 32%
Part-time enrollment: 402
men: 78%; women:
22%; minorities: 18%;
international: 16%
Acceptance rate (full time): 25%
Average GMAT (full time): 716
Average GRE (full
time): 160 verbal; 160
quantitative; 4.5 writing
Average GPA (full time): 3.46
Average age of entrants to
full-time program: 28
Average months of prior work
experience (full time): 66
TOEFL requirement: Yes
Minimum TOEFL score: N/A
Most popular departments:
consulting, finance, marketing,
production/operations
management, technology
Mean starting base salary for 2017
full-time graduates: $124,702
Employment location for
2017 class: Intl. 8%; N.E.
15%; M.A. 3%; S. 3%; M.W.
35%; S.W. 4%; W. 32%

University of Michigan–Dearborn

19000 Hubbard Drive
Dearborn, MI 48126-2638
umdearborn.edu/cob
Public
Admissions: (313) 593-5460
Email: umd-gradbusiness@
umich.edu
Financial aid: (313) 593-5300
Application deadline: 08/01
In-state tuition: full time: N/A;
part time: $683/credit hour
Out-of-state tuition: full time: N/A
Room/board/expenses: N/A
College-funded aid: No
International student aid: Yes
Full-time enrollment: N/A
Part-time enrollment: 124
men: 69%; women:
31%; minorities: 20%;
international: 11%
Average GRE (full
time): N/A verbal; N/A
quantitative; N/A writing
TOEFL requirement: Yes
Minimum TOEFL score: 560

Most popular departments:
finance, general management,
industrial management,
management information
systems, supply chain
management/logistics

University of Michigan–Flint

303 E. Kearsley Street
Flint, MI 48502-1950
www.umflint.edu/som/
graduate-business-programs
Public
Admissions: (810) 762-3171
Email: graduate@umflint.edu
Financial aid: (810) 762-3444
Application deadline: 08/01
In-state tuition: full time: N/A;
part time: $698/credit hour
Out-of-state tuition: full time: N/A
Room/board/expenses: N/A
College-funded aid: Yes
International student aid: Yes
Full-time enrollment: N/A
Part-time enrollment: 190
men: 63%; women:
37%; minorities: 20%;
international: 13%
Average GRE (full
time): N/A verbal; N/A
quantitative; N/A writing
TOEFL requirement: Yes
Minimum TOEFL score: N/A
Most popular departments:
accounting, finance, general
management, health care
administration, leadership

Wayne State University

5201 Cass Avenue
Prentis Building
Detroit, MI 48202
ilitchbusiness.wayne.edu/
Public
Admissions: (313) 577-4511
Email: gradbusiness@wayne.edu
Financial aid: (313) 577-2100
Application deadline: 07/01
In-state tuition: full time: N/A;
part time: $742/credit hour
Out-of-state tuition: full time: N/A
Room/board/expenses: N/A
College-funded aid: Yes
International student aid: Yes
Full-time enrollment: N/A
Part-time enrollment: 1,214
men: 55%; women:
45%; minorities: 27%;
international: 5%
Average GRE (full
time): N/A verbal; N/A
quantitative; N/A writing
TOEFL requirement: Yes
Minimum TOEFL score: 550
Most popular departments:
finance, general management,
marketing, management
information systems, supply
chain management/logistics

Western Michigan University (Haworth)

1903 W. Michigan Avenue
Kalamazoo, MI 49008-5480
wmich.edu/mba
Public
Admissions: (269) 387-5133
Email: mba-advising@wmich.edu

Financial aid: (269) 387-6000
Application deadline: 07/15
In-state tuition: full time: N/A;
part time: $596/credit hour
Out-of-state tuition: full time: N/A
Room/board/expenses: N/A
College-funded aid: Yes
International student aid: No
Full-time enrollment: N/A
Part-time enrollment: 312
men: 66%; women:
34%; minorities: 13%;
international: 18%
Average GRE (full
time): N/A verbal; N/A
quantitative; N/A writing
TOEFL requirement: Yes
Minimum TOEFL score: 500
Most popular departments:
finance, general management,
marketing, management
information systems, other

MINNESOTA

Minnesota State University–Mankato

120 Morris Hall
Mankato, MN 56001
grad.mnsu.edu
Public
Admissions: (507) 389-2321
Financial aid: (507) 389-1419
Application deadline: 06/01
In-state tuition: full time: N/A;
part time: $603/credit hour
Out-of-state tuition: full time: N/A
Room/board/expenses: N/A
College-funded aid: Yes
International student aid: Yes
Full-time enrollment: N/A
Part-time enrollment: 52
men: 65%; women:
35%; minorities: 12%;
international: 17%
Average GRE (full
time): N/A verbal; N/A
quantitative; N/A writing
TOEFL requirement: Yes
Minimum TOEFL score: 500
Most popular departments:
leadership

Minnesota State University–Moorhead[1]

1104 7th Avenue South
Moorhead, MN 56563
www.mnstate.edu/graduate/
programs
Public
Admissions: (218) 477-2134
Email: graduate@mnstate.edu
Financial aid: (218) 477-2251
Tuition: N/A
Room/board/expenses: N/A
Enrollment: N/A

St. Cloud State University (Herberger)[1]

720 Fourth Avenue S
St. Cloud, MN 56301-4498
www.stcloudstate.edu/mba
Public
Admissions: (320) 308-3212
Email: mba@stcloudstate.edu
Financial aid: N/A
Tuition: N/A
Room/board/expenses: N/A
Enrollment: N/A

University of Minnesota–Duluth (Labovitz)

1318 Kirby Drive
Duluth, MN 55812-2496
lsbe.d.umn.edu/mba
Public
Admissions: (218) 726-8839
Email: umdgrad@d.umn.edu
Financial aid: (218) 726-8000
Application deadline: 07/15
In-state tuition: full time: $941/credit hour; part time: $941/credit hour
Out-of-state tuition: full time: $941/credit hour
Room/board/expenses: N/A
College-funded aid: Yes
International student aid: Yes
Full-time enrollment: N/A
Part-time enrollment: 37
men: 78%; women: 22%; minorities: 19%; international: 3%
Average GRE (full time): N/A verbal; N/A quantitative; N/A writing
TOEFL requirement: Yes
Minimum TOEFL score: N/A

University of Minnesota–Twin Cities (Carlson)

321 19th Avenue S
Suite 4-300
Minneapolis, MN 55455
www.carlsonschool.umn.edu/degrees/master-business-administration
Public
Admissions: (612) 625-5555
Email: mba@umn.edu
Financial aid: (612) 624-1111
Application deadline: 04/01
In-state tuition: full time: $42,942; part time: $1,375/credit hour
Out-of-state tuition: full time: $53,670
Room/board/expenses: $17,000
College-funded aid: Yes
International student aid: Yes
Average student indebtedness at graduation: $64,845
Full-time enrollment: 200
men: 69%; women: 32%; minorities: 13%; international: 21%
Part-time enrollment: 919
men: 68%; women: 32%; minorities: 13%; international: 6%
Acceptance rate (full time): 37%
Average GMAT (full time): 676
Average GRE (full time): 161 verbal; 157 quantitative; 4.6 writing
Average GPA (full time): 3.35
Average age of entrants to full-time program: 29
Average months of prior work experience (full time): 59
TOEFL requirement: Yes
Minimum TOEFL score: 580
Most popular departments: finance, general management, health care administration, marketing, supply chain management/logistics
Mean starting base salary for 2017 full-time graduates: $106,129

University of St. Thomas

1000 LaSalle Avenue
SCH200
Minneapolis, MN 55403
www.stthomas.edu/business
Private
Admissions: (651) 962-8800
Email: ustmba@stthomas.edu
Financial aid: (651) 962-6550
Application deadline: 08/01
Tuition: total program: $76,904 (full time); $50,760 (part time)
Room/board/expenses: N/A
College-funded aid: Yes
International student aid: Yes
Average student indebtedness at graduation: $58,146
Full-time enrollment: 79
men: 57%; women: 43%; minorities: 16%; international: 23%
Part-time enrollment: 518
men: 58%; women: 42%; minorities: 14%; international: 3%
Acceptance rate (full time): 82%
Average GMAT (full time): 558
Average GRE (full time): N/A verbal; N/A quantitative; N/A writing
Average age of entrants to full-time program: 28
Average months of prior work experience (full time): 58
TOEFL requirement: Yes
Minimum TOEFL score: 550
Most popular departments: accounting, entrepreneurship, finance, general management, marketing

Jackson State University[1]

1400 J.R. Lynch Street
Jackson, MS 39217
www.jsums.edu/business
Public
Admissions: N/A
Financial aid: N/A
Tuition: N/A
Room/board/expenses: N/A
Enrollment: N/A

Millsaps College (Else)

1701 N. State Street
Jackson, MS 39210
millsaps.edu/mba
Private
Admissions: (601) 974-1253
Email: mbamacc@millsaps.edu
Financial aid: (601) 974-1222
Application deadline: 04/01
Tuition: full time: $982/credit hour; part time: $982/credit hour
Room/board/expenses: N/A
College-funded aid: Yes
International student aid: Yes
Full-time enrollment: 53
men: 53%; women: 47%; minorities: 23%; international: 6%

Employment location for 2017 class: Intl. 0%; N.E. 8%; M.A. 2%; S. 3%; M.W. 78%; S.W. 0%; W. 9%

Part-time enrollment: N/A
Acceptance rate (full time): 98%
Average GMAT (full time): 570
Average GRE (full time): N/A verbal; N/A quantitative; N/A writing
Average age of entrants to full-time program: 25
Average months of prior work experience (full time): 103
TOEFL requirement: Yes
Minimum TOEFL score: 550
Most popular departments: finance, general management

Mississippi College[1]

200 South Capitol Street
Clinton, MS 39058
www.mc.edu/explore/programs_mba.php
Private
Admissions: N/A
Financial aid: N/A
Tuition: N/A
Room/board/expenses: N/A
Enrollment: N/A

Mississippi State University

PO Box 5288
Mississippi State, MS 39762
www.mba.business.msstate.edu
Public
Admissions: (662) 325-1891
Email: gsb@business.msstate.edu
Financial aid: (662) 325-2450
Application deadline: 03/01
In-state tuition: total program: $11,805 (full time); part time: N/A
Out-of-state tuition: total program: $31,485 (full time)
Room/board/expenses: $19,500
College-funded aid: Yes
International student aid: Yes
Average student indebtedness at graduation: $16,124
Full-time enrollment: 23
men: 52%; women: 48%; minorities: 0%; international: 9%
Part-time enrollment: N/A
Acceptance rate (full time): 53%
Average GMAT (full time): 590
Average GRE (full time): 153 verbal; 152 quantitative; N/A writing
Average GPA (full time): 3.60
Average age of entrants to full-time program: 23
Average months of prior work experience (full time): 24
TOEFL requirement: Yes
Minimum TOEFL score: 575
Most popular departments: accounting, marketing, management information systems, other
Mean starting base salary for 2017 full-time graduates: $50,844
Employment location for 2017 class: Intl. 3%; N.E. 3%; M.A. N/A; S. 83%; M.W. N/A; S.W. 3%; W. 7%

University of Mississippi

253 Holman Hall
University, MS 38677
www.olemissbusiness.com/mba
Public
Admissions: (662) 915-5483
Email: amcgee@bus.olemiss.edu
Financial aid: (800) 891-4596
Application deadline: 07/01
In-state tuition: total program: $22,625 (full time); part time: $750/credit hour
Out-of-state tuition: total program: $53,568 (full time)
Room/board/expenses: $17,260
College-funded aid: Yes
International student aid: Yes
Average student indebtedness at graduation: $22,638
Full-time enrollment: 53
men: 66%; women: 34%; minorities: 8%; international: 4%
Part-time enrollment: N/A
Acceptance rate (full time): 32%
Average GMAT (full time): 568
Average GRE (full time): 155 verbal; 156 quantitative; 3.9 writing
Average GPA (full time): 3.38
Average age of entrants to full-time program: 24
Average months of prior work experience (full time): 21
TOEFL requirement: Yes
Minimum TOEFL score: 600
Mean starting base salary for 2017 full-time graduates: $58,647

University of Southern Mississippi

118 College Drive, #5096
Hattiesburg, MS 39406-5096
choose.usm.edu/mba.html
Public
Admissions: (601) 266-4369
Email: gc-business@usm.edu
Financial aid: (601) 266-4774
Application deadline: 04/01
In-state tuition: full time: $451/credit hour; part time: $451/credit hour
Out-of-state tuition: full time: $563/credit hour
Room/board/expenses: N/A
College-funded aid: Yes
International student aid: Yes
Full-time enrollment: 29
men: 48%; women: 52%; minorities: 3%; international: 28%
Part-time enrollment: 37
men: 54%; women: 46%; minorities: 22%; international: 0%
Acceptance rate (full time): 76%
Average GMAT (full time): 499
Average GRE (full time): 148 verbal; 151 quantitative; 3.6 writing
Average GPA (full time): 3.42
Average age of entrants to full-time program: 25
Average months of prior work experience (full time): 42
TOEFL requirement: Yes
Minimum TOEFL score: N/A
Most popular departments: general management, marketing, sports business, quantitative analysis/statistics and operations research, other

Drury University

900 North Benton Avenue
Springfield, MO 65802
www.drury.edu/mba/
Private
Admissions: (417) 873-6948
Email: grad@drury.edu
Financial aid: (417) 873-7312
Application deadline: 07/15
Tuition: full time: $695/credit hour; part time: N/A
Room/board/expenses: $13,000
College-funded aid: Yes
International student aid: Yes
Full-time enrollment: 45
men: 53%; women: 47%; minorities: 11%; international: 31%
Part-time enrollment: N/A
Acceptance rate (full time): 53%
Average GMAT (full time): 550
Average GRE (full time): N/A verbal; N/A quantitative; N/A writing
Average GPA (full time): 3.30
Average age of entrants to full-time program: 28
Average months of prior work experience (full time): 36
TOEFL requirement: Yes
Minimum TOEFL score: 500

Missouri State University

901 S. National Avenue
Glass Hall 400
Springfield, MO 65897
www.mba.missouristate.edu
Public
Admissions: (417) 836-5616
Email: COBGraduatePrograms@MissouriState.edu
Financial aid: (417) 836-5262
Application deadline: 08/25
In-state tuition: full time: $268/credit hour; part time: $268/credit hour
Out-of-state tuition: full time: $539/credit hour
Room/board/expenses: $15,018
College-funded aid: Yes
International student aid: Yes
Full-time enrollment: 204
men: 45%; women: 55%; minorities: 9%; international: 43%
Part-time enrollment: N/A
Acceptance rate (full time): 81%
Average GMAT (full time): 561
Average GRE (full time): 154 verbal; 151 quantitative; 3.7 writing
Average GPA (full time): 3.44
Average age of entrants to full-time program: 25
TOEFL requirement: Yes
Minimum TOEFL score: 550
Most popular departments: finance, general management, leadership, management information systems, quantitative analysis/statistics and operations research

Missouri University of Science & Technology

1870 Miner Circle
Rolla, MO 65409
bit.mst.edu/
Public
Admissions: (573) 341-4165
Email: admissions@mst.edu
Financial aid: (573) 341-4282
Application deadline: rolling
In-state tuition: full time: $696/credit hour; part time: $696/credit hour
Out-of-state tuition: full time: $1,268/credit hour
Room/board/expenses: $15,898
College-funded aid: Yes
International student aid: Yes
Average student indebtedness at graduation: $5,576
Full-time enrollment: 19
men: 37%; women: 63%; minorities: 5%; international: 53%
Part-time enrollment: 3
men: 33%; women: 67%; minorities: 33%; international: 0%
Acceptance rate (full time): 68%
Average GRE (full time): N/A verbal; N/A quantitative; N/A writing
Average GPA (full time): 3.66
Average age of entrants to full-time program: 28
TOEFL requirement: Yes
Minimum TOEFL score: 570
Most popular departments: general management, leadership, management information systems, quantitative analysis/statistics and operations research, technology

Rockhurst University (Helzberg)

1100 Rockhurst Road
Kansas City, MO 64110
www.rockhurst.edu/helzberg
Private
Admissions: (816) 501-4632
Email: mba@rockhurst.edu
Financial aid: (816) 501-4600
Application deadline: rolling
Tuition: full time: N/A; part time: $685/credit hour
Room/board/expenses: N/A
College-funded aid: Yes
International student aid: Yes
Full-time enrollment: N/A
Part-time enrollment: 359
men: 64%; women: 36%; minorities: 20%; international: 1%
Average GRE (full time): N/A verbal; N/A quantitative; N/A writing
TOEFL requirement: Yes
Minimum TOEFL score: 550
Most popular departments: accounting, finance, general management, health care administration, quantitative analysis/statistics and operations research

Southeast Missouri State University (Harrison)

1 University Plaza
MS 5890
Cape Girardeau, MO 63701
www.semo.edu/mba
Public
Admissions: (573) 651-2590
Email: mba@semo.edu
Financial aid: (573) 651-2039
Application deadline: 08/01
In-state tuition: full time: $270/credit hour; part time: $270/credit hour
Out-of-state tuition: full time: $504/credit hour
Room/board/expenses: $11,900
College-funded aid: Yes
International student aid: Yes
Average student indebtedness at graduation: $10,902
Full-time enrollment: 67
men: 48%; women: 52%; minorities: 3%; international: 58%
Part-time enrollment: 67
men: 54%; women: 46%; minorities: 16%; international: 9%
Acceptance rate (full time): 100%
Average GMAT (full time): 449
Average GRE (full time): 150 verbal; 146 quantitative; 3.3 writing
Average GPA (full time): 3.31
Average age of entrants to full-time program: 28
TOEFL requirement: Yes
Minimum TOEFL score: 550
Most popular departments: accounting, finance, general management, health care administration, international business

Saint Louis University (Chaifetz)

3674 Lindell Boulevard
St. Louis, MO 63108
www.slu.edu/business
Private
Admissions: (314) 977-3800
Email: gradbiz@slu.edu
Financial aid: (314) 977-2350
Application deadline: 08/01
Tuition: full time: $58,456; part time: $1,040/credit hour
Room/board/expenses: $20,734
College-funded aid: Yes
International student aid: Yes
Average student indebtedness at graduation: $57,885
Full-time enrollment: 21
men: 67%; women: 33%; minorities: 24%; international: 19%
Part-time enrollment: 149
men: 56%; women: 44%; minorities: 13%; international: 7%
Acceptance rate (full time): 59%
Average GMAT (full time): 561
Average GRE (full time): 155 verbal; 152 quantitative; N/A writing
Average GPA (full time): 3.19

Average age of entrants to full-time program: 25
Average months of prior work experience (full time): 18
TOEFL requirement: Yes
Minimum TOEFL score: N/A
Most popular departments: finance, general management, international business, marketing, supply chain management/logistics
Mean starting base salary for 2017 full-time graduates: $57,184
Employment location for 2017 class: Intl. N/A; N.E. N/A; M.A. N/A; S. N/A; M.W. 88%; S.W. N/A; W. 13%

Truman State University[1]

100 E. Normal
Kirksville, MO 63501
gradstudies.truman.edu
Public
Admissions: (660) 785-4109
Email: gradinfo@truman.edu
Financial aid: (660) 785-4130
Tuition: N/A
Room/board/expenses: N/A
Enrollment: N/A

University of Central Missouri (Harmon)

Ward Edwards 1600
Warrensburg, MO 64093
www.ucmo.edu/mba
Public
Admissions: (660) 543-8192
Email: mba@ucmo.edu
Financial aid: (660) 543-8266
Application deadline: 07/14
In-state tuition: full time: $464/credit hour; part time: $464/credit hour
Out-of-state tuition: full time: $464/credit hour
Room/board/expenses: $8,400
College-funded aid: Yes
International student aid: Yes
Full-time enrollment: 68
men: 59%; women: 41%; minorities: 24%; international: 0%
Part-time enrollment: 68
men: 59%; women: 41%; minorities: 24%; international: 0%
Acceptance rate (full time): 63%
Average GMAT (full time): 493
Average GRE (full time): 148 verbal; 149 quantitative; 3.6 writing
Average GPA (full time): 3.44
Average age of entrants to full-time program: 25
Average months of prior work experience (full time): 12
TOEFL requirement: Yes
Minimum TOEFL score: 550
Most popular departments: ethics, finance, general management, marketing, sports business

University of Missouri–Kansas City (Bloch)

5100 Rockhill Road
Kansas City, MO 64110
www.bloch.umkc.edu/graduate-program/mba
Public
Admissions: (816) 235-5254
Email: bloch@umkc.edu
Financial aid: (816) 235-1154
Application deadline: 07/10
In-state tuition: full time: $377/credit hour; part time: $377/credit hour
Out-of-state tuition: full time: $973/credit hour
Room/board/expenses: $20,118
College-funded aid: Yes
International student aid: Yes
Full-time enrollment: 52
men: 69%; women: 31%; minorities: 13%; international: 19%
Part-time enrollment: 149
men: 60%; women: 40%; minorities: 11%; international: 4%
Average GRE (full time): N/A verbal; N/A quantitative; N/A writing
TOEFL requirement: Yes
Minimum TOEFL score: 550

University of Missouri–St. Louis[1]

1 University Boulevard
St. Louis, MO 63121
mba.umsl.edu
Public
Admissions: N/A
Financial aid: N/A
Tuition: N/A
Room/board/expenses: N/A
Enrollment: N/A

University of Missouri (Trulaske)

306 Cornell Hall
Columbia, MO 65211
mba.missouri.edu
Public
Admissions: (573) 882-2750
Email: mba@missouri.edu
Financial aid: (573) 882-2750
Application deadline: 07/01
In-state tuition: full time: $360/credit hour; part time: N/A
Out-of-state tuition: full time: $986/credit hour
Room/board/expenses: $19,140
College-funded aid: Yes
International student aid: Yes
Average student indebtedness at graduation: $15,509
Full-time enrollment: 109
men: 61%; women: 39%; minorities: 7%; international: 28%
Part-time enrollment: N/A
Acceptance rate (full time): 41%
Average GMAT (full time): 654
Average GRE (full time): 155 verbal; 157 quantitative; 4.0 writing
Average GPA (full time): 3.58
Average age of entrants to full-time program: 24

Average months of prior work experience (full time): 20
TOEFL requirement: Yes
Minimum TOEFL score: N/A
Most popular departments: entrepreneurship, finance, general management, marketing, quantitative analysis/statistics and operations research
Mean starting base salary for 2017 full-time graduates: $70,065
Employment location for 2017 class: Intl. 0%; N.E. 3%; M.A. 6%; S. 11%; M.W. 58%; S.W. 17%; W. 6%

Washington University in St. Louis (Olin)

1 Brookings Drive
Campus Box 1133
St. Louis, MO 63130-4899
www.olin.wustl.edu/academicprograms/MBA/Pages/default.aspx
Private
Admissions: (314) 935-7301
Email: OlinGradAdmissions@wustl.edu
Financial aid: (314) 935-7301
Application deadline: 04/10
Tuition: full time: $57,900; part time: $1,676/credit hour
Room/board/expenses: $25,746
College-funded aid: Yes
International student aid: Yes
Average student indebtedness at graduation: $67,458
Full-time enrollment: 272
men: 68%; women: 32%; minorities: 20%; international: 39%
Part-time enrollment: 258
men: 69%; women: 31%; minorities: 19%; international: 6%
Acceptance rate (full time): 40%
Average GMAT (full time): 694
Average GRE (full time): 156 verbal; 156 quantitative; 4.0 writing
Average GPA (full time): 3.50
Average age of entrants to full-time program: 28
Average months of prior work experience (full time): 57
TOEFL requirement: Yes
Minimum TOEFL score: N/A
Most popular departments: consulting, entrepreneurship, finance, marketing, supply chain management/logistics
Mean starting base salary for 2017 full-time graduates: $106,812
Employment location for 2017 class: Intl. 7%; N.E. 11%; M.A. 7%; S. 5%; M.W. 40%; S.W. 6%; W. 25%

MONTANA

University of Montana[1]

32 Campus Drive
Missoula, MT 59812-6808
www.business.umt.edu/
Public
Admissions: N/A
Email: mba@business.umt.edu
Financial aid: N/A
Tuition: N/A

Room/board/expenses: N/A
Enrollment: N/A

NEBRASKA

Creighton University

2500 California Plaza
Omaha, NE 68178-0130
business.creighton.edu
Private
Admissions: (402) 280-2703
Email: GraduateSchool@
creighton.edu
Financial aid: (402) 280-2731
Application deadline: rolling
Tuition: full time: N/A; part
time: $850/credit hour
Room/board/expenses: N/A
College-funded aid: Yes
International student aid: Yes
Full-time enrollment: N/A
Part-time enrollment: 112
men: 67%; women:
33%; minorities: 18%;
international: 9%
Average GRE (full
time): N/A verbal; N/A
quantitative; N/A writing
TOEFL requirement: Yes
Minimum TOEFL score: 577
Most popular departments:
accounting, finance,
leadership, management
information systems

University of Nebraska–Kearney[1]

905 West 25th Street
Kearney, NE 68849
www.unk.edu
Public
Admissions: (800) 717-7881
Email: gradstudies@unk.edu
Financial aid: N/A
Tuition: N/A
Room/board/expenses: N/A
Enrollment: N/A

University of Nebraska–Lincoln

P.O. Box 880405
730 North 14th Street
Lincoln, NE 68588-0405
business.unl.edu/mba/
Public
Admissions: (402) 472-2338
Email: businessgrad@unl.edu
Financial aid: (402) 472-2030
Application deadline: 07/01
In-state tuition: full time: N/A;
part time: $388/credit hour
Out-of-state tuition: full time: N/A
Room/board/expenses: N/A
College-funded aid: Yes
International student aid: Yes
Full-time enrollment: N/A
Part-time enrollment: 41
men: 68%; women:
32%; minorities: 2%;
international: 32%
Average GRE (full
time): N/A verbal; N/A
quantitative; N/A writing
TOEFL requirement: Yes
Minimum TOEFL score: 550
Most popular departments:
finance, international
business, marketing, supply

chain management/logistics,
quantitative analysis/statistics
and operations research

University of Nebraska–Omaha

6708 Pine Street
Omaha, NE 68182-0048
mba.unomaha.edu
Public
Admissions: (402) 554-4836
Email: mba@unomaha.edu
Financial aid: (402) 554-2327
Application deadline: 07/01
In-state tuition: full time: N/A;
part time: $351/credit hour
Out-of-state tuition: full time: N/A
Room/board/expenses: N/A
College-funded aid: Yes
International student aid: Yes
Full-time enrollment: N/A
Part-time enrollment: 246
men: 58%; women: 42%;
minorities: 9%; international: 8%
Average GRE (full
time): N/A verbal; N/A
quantitative; N/A writing
TOEFL requirement: Yes
Minimum TOEFL score: 550
Most popular departments: health
care administration, human
resources management, supply
chain management/logistics,
quantitative analysis/statistics
and operations research, other

NEVADA

University of Nevada–Las Vegas

4505 Maryland Parkway
PO Box 456031
Las Vegas, NV 89154-6031
business.unlv.edu
Public
Admissions: (702) 895-3655
Email: lbsmba@unlv.edu
Financial aid: (702) 895-3682
Application deadline: 07/15
In-state tuition: full time:
$369/credit hour; part
time: $369/credit hour
Out-of-state tuition:
full time: $26,367
Room/board/expenses: N/A
College-funded aid: Yes
International student aid: Yes
Full-time enrollment: N/A
Part-time enrollment: 156
men: 63%; women:
37%; minorities: 35%;
international: 10%
Average GRE (full
time): N/A verbal; N/A
quantitative; N/A writing
TOEFL requirement: Yes
Minimum TOEFL score: 550
Most popular departments:
entrepreneurship, finance,
hotel administration,
marketing, management
information systems

University of Nevada–Reno

1664 N. Virginia Street
Reno, NV 89557
www.mba.unr.edu
Public
Admissions: (775) 682-9142
Email: raffiee@unr.edu

Financial aid: (775) 784-4666
Application deadline: 03/15
In-state tuition: full time: N/A;
part time: $364/credit hour
Out-of-state tuition: full time: N/A
Room/board/expenses: N/A
College-funded aid: Yes
International student aid: Yes
Full-time enrollment: N/A
Part-time enrollment: 208
men: 53%; women:
47%; minorities: 19%;
international: 7%
Average GRE (full
time): N/A verbal; N/A
quantitative; N/A writing
TOEFL requirement: Yes
Minimum TOEFL score: 550
Most popular departments:
entrepreneurship, finance,
general management,
marketing, management
information systems

NEW HAMPSHIRE

Dartmouth College (Tuck)

100 Tuck Hall
Hanover, NH 03755-9000
www.tuck.dartmouth.edu
Private
Admissions: (603) 646-3162
Email: tuck.admissions@
tuck.dartmouth.edu
Financial aid: (603) 646-0640
Application deadline: 04/04
Tuition: full time: $72,330;
part time: N/A
Room/board/expenses: $32,703
College-funded aid: Yes
International student aid: Yes
Full-time enrollment: 582
men: 55%; women:
45%; minorities: 20%;
international: 30%
Part-time enrollment: N/A
Acceptance rate (full time): 23%
Average GMAT (full time): 722
Average GRE (full
time): 161 verbal; 158
quantitative; 4.8 writing
Average GPA (full time): 3.52
Average age of entrants to
full-time program: 28
Average months of prior work
experience (full time): 63
TOEFL requirement: Yes
Minimum TOEFL score: N/A
Mean starting base salary for 2017
full-time graduates: $127,986
Employment location for
2017 class: Intl. 8%; N.E.
46%; M.A. 6%; S. 3%; M.W.
9%; S.W. 5%; W. 23%

University of New Hampshire (Paul)

10 Garrison Avenue
Durham, NH 03824
www.mba.unh.edu
Public
Admissions: (603) 862-1367
Email: cynthia.traver@unh.edu
Financial aid: (603) 862-3600
Application deadline: 06/01
In-state tuition: full time:
$37,033; part time:
$800/credit hour

Out-of-state tuition:
full time: $48,033
Room/board/expenses: $20,690
College-funded aid: Yes
International student aid: Yes
Average student indebtedness
at graduation: $30,866
Full-time enrollment: 34
men: 76%; women:
24%; minorities: 0%;
international: 15%
Part-time enrollment: 139
men: 73%; women: 27%;
minorities: 6%; international: 6%
Acceptance rate (full time): 86%
Average GMAT (full time): 504
Average GRE (full
time): 150 verbal; 148
quantitative; 3.8 writing
Average GPA (full time): 3.15
Average age of entrants to
full-time program: 28
Average months of prior work
experience (full time): 28
TOEFL requirement: Yes
Minimum TOEFL score: 550
Most popular departments:
entrepreneurship, finance,
international business,
marketing, management
information systems
Mean starting base salary for 2017
full-time graduates: $62,700
Employment location for 2017
class: Intl. 4%; N.E. 80%;
M.A. 4%; S. 12%; M.W.
0%; S.W. 0%; W. 0%

NEW JERSEY

Fairleigh Dickinson University (Silberman)

1000 River Road
Teaneck, NJ 07666
view2.fdu.edu/academics/
silberman-college/
Private
Admissions: (201) 692-2554
Email: grad@fdu.edu
Financial aid: (973) 443-7304
Application deadline: 08/22
Tuition: full time: $1,305/
credit hour; part time:
$1,305/credit hour
Room/board/expenses: N/A
College-funded aid: Yes
International student aid: Yes
Full-time enrollment: 248
men: 56%; women:
44%; minorities: 19%;
international: 38%
Part-time enrollment: 238
men: 56%; women:
44%; minorities: 23%;
international: 0%
Acceptance rate (full time): 72%
Average GRE (full
time): N/A verbal; N/A
quantitative; N/A writing
Average age of entrants to
full-time program: 24
TOEFL requirement: Yes
Minimum TOEFL score: 550
Most popular departments:
accounting, finance,
marketing, supply chain
management/logistics

Monmouth University

400 Cedar Avenue
West Long Branch, NJ 07764
www.monmouth.edu
Private
Admissions: (732) 571-3452
Email: gradadm@monmouth.edu
Financial aid: (732) 571-3463
Application deadline: 07/15
Tuition: full time: $1,142/
credit hour; part time:
$1,142/credit hour
Room/board/expenses: $17,524
College-funded aid: Yes
International student aid: Yes
Average student indebtedness
at graduation: $17,945
Full-time enrollment: 24
men: 58%; women:
42%; minorities: 13%;
international: 0%
Part-time enrollment: 184
men: 52%; women: 48%;
minorities: 9%; international: 7%
Acceptance rate (full time): 100%
Average GRE (full
time): N/A verbal; N/A
quantitative; N/A writing
Average GPA (full time): 3.63
Average age of entrants to
full-time program: 24
TOEFL requirement: Yes
Minimum TOEFL score: 550

Montclair State University (Feliciano)

Feliciano School of Business
1 Normal Avenue
Montclair, NJ 07043
www.montclair.edu/mba
Public
Admissions: (973) 655-5147
Email: graduate.school@
montclair.edu
Financial aid: (973) 655-4461
Application deadline: rolling
In-state tuition: full time:
$697/credit hour; part
time: $697/credit hour
Out-of-state tuition: full
time: $697/credit hour
Room/board/expenses: N/A
College-funded aid: Yes
International student aid: Yes
Full-time enrollment: N/A
Part-time enrollment: 562
men: 44%; women:
56%; minorities: 41%;
international: 16%
Average GRE (full
time): N/A verbal; N/A
quantitative; N/A writing
TOEFL requirement: Yes
Minimum TOEFL score: 550
Most popular departments:
accounting, finance,
marketing, management
information systems, other

New Jersey Institute of Technology

University Heights
Newark, NJ 07102
management.njit.edu/
Public
Admissions: (973) 596-3300
Email: admissions@njit.edu
Financial aid: (973) 596-3479

Application deadline: N/A
In-state tuition: full time: $22,690; part time: $1,073/credit hour
Out-of-state tuition: full time: $32,136
Room/board/expenses: $17,900
College-funded aid: Yes
International student aid: Yes
Average student indebtedness at graduation: $27,924
Full-time enrollment: 71
men: 62%; women: 38%; minorities: 38%; international: 46%
Part-time enrollment: 151
men: 62%; women: 38%; minorities: 57%; international: 1%
Acceptance rate (full time): 54%
Average GMAT (full time): 455
Average GRE (full time): 143 verbal; 162 quantitative; 3.1 writing
Average GPA (full time): 3.19
Average age of entrants to full-time program: 25
Average months of prior work experience (full time): 3
TOEFL requirement: Yes
Minimum TOEFL score: 550
Most popular departments: entrepreneurship, finance, management information systems, technology, other
Mean starting base salary for 2017 full-time graduates: $50,000
Employment location for 2017 class: Intl. N/A; N.E. 100%; M.A. N/A; S. N/A; M.W. N/A; S.W. N/A; W. N/A

Ramapo College of New Jersey

505 Ramapo Valley Road
Mahwah, NJ 07430
www.ramapo.edu/admissions/
Public
Admissions: (201) 684-7300
Email: admissions@ramapo.edu
Financial aid: (201) 684-7549
Application deadline: 05/01
In-state tuition: full time: N/A; part time: $946/credit hour
Out-of-state tuition: full time: N/A
Room/board/expenses: N/A
College-funded aid: Yes
International student aid: Yes
Full-time enrollment: N/A
Part-time enrollment: 63
men: 52%; women: 48%; minorities: 22%; international: 0%
Average GRE (full time): N/A verbal; N/A quantitative; N/A writing
TOEFL requirement: Yes
Minimum TOEFL score: 550

Rider University

2083 Lawrenceville Road
Lawrenceville, NJ 08648-3099
www.rider.edu/mba
Private
Admissions: (609) 895-5635
Email: gradadm@rider.edu
Financial aid: (609) 896-5360
Application deadline: rolling
Tuition: full time: N/A; part time: $1,060/credit hour
Room/board/expenses: N/A

College-funded aid: Yes
International student aid: Yes
Full-time enrollment: N/A
Part-time enrollment: 172
men: 52%; women: 48%; minorities: 34%; international: 13%
Average GRE (full time): N/A verbal; N/A quantitative; N/A writing
TOEFL requirement: Yes
Minimum TOEFL score: 550
Most popular departments: accounting, finance, international business, quantitative analysis/statistics and operations research

Rowan University (Rohrer)

201 Mullica Hill Road
Glassboro, NJ 08028
www.rowanu.com
Public
Admissions: (856) 256-5435
Email: cgceadmissions@rowan.edu
Financial aid: (856) 256-5141
Application deadline: 07/01
In-state tuition: full time: $737/credit hour; part time: $737/credit hour
Out-of-state tuition: full time: $737/credit hour
Room/board/expenses: $17,644
College-funded aid: Yes
International student aid: No
Average student indebtedness at graduation: $34,971
Full-time enrollment: 26
men: 50%; women: 50%; minorities: 31%; international: 4%
Part-time enrollment: 74
men: 57%; women: 43%; minorities: 27%; international: 0%
Average GRE (full time): N/A verbal; N/A quantitative; N/A writing
TOEFL requirement: Yes
Minimum TOEFL score: 550
Most popular departments: accounting, general management, marketing, management information systems

Rutgers, The State University of New Jersey–Camden

227 Penn Street
Camden, NJ 08102
business.camden.rutgers.edu/
Public
Admissions: (856) 225-6452
Email: Rsbcmba@camden.rutgers.edu
Financial aid: (856) 225-6039
Application deadline: 08/01
In-state tuition: full time: N/A; part time: $974/credit hour
Out-of-state tuition: full time: N/A
Room/board/expenses: N/A
College-funded aid: Yes
International student aid: Yes
Full-time enrollment: N/A
Part-time enrollment: 127
men: 59%; women: 41%; minorities: 35%; international: 8%

Average GRE (full time): N/A verbal; N/A quantitative; N/A writing
TOEFL requirement: Yes
Minimum TOEFL score: 550
Most popular departments: finance, general management, international business, marketing, production/operations management

Rutgers, The State University of New Jersey–Newark and New Brunswick

1 Washington Park
Newark, NJ 07102-3122
www.business.rutgers.edu
Public
Admissions: (973) 353-1234
Email: admit@business.rutgers.edu
Financial aid: (973) 353-5151
Application deadline: 05/01
In-state tuition: full time: $29,043; part time: $1,097/credit hour
Out-of-state tuition: full time: $48,415
Room/board/expenses: $24,000
College-funded aid: Yes
International student aid: No
Average student indebtedness at graduation: $40,550
Full-time enrollment: 118
men: 59%; women: 41%; minorities: 34%; international: 35%
Part-time enrollment: 1,040
men: 63%; women: 37%; minorities: 43%; international: 4%
Acceptance rate (full time): 37%
Average GMAT (full time): 673
Average GRE (full time): 158 verbal; 158 quantitative; N/A writing
Average GPA (full time): 3.21
Average age of entrants to full-time program: 29
Average months of prior work experience (full time): 58
TOEFL requirement: Yes
Minimum TOEFL score: 600
Most popular departments: entrepreneurship, finance, leadership, marketing, supply chain management/logistics
Mean starting base salary for 2017 full-time graduates: $97,546
Employment location for 2017 class: Intl. 0%; N.E. 68%; M.A. 6%; S. 2%; M.W. 17%; S.W. 2%; W. 4%

Seton Hall University (Stillman)

400 S. Orange Avenue
South Orange, NJ 07079
www.shu.edu/academics/business/
Private
Admissions: (973) 761-9262
Email: busgrad@shu.edu
Financial aid: (973) 761-9350
Application deadline: 05/31
Tuition: full time: N/A; part time: $1,305/credit hour
Room/board/expenses: N/A
College-funded aid: Yes

International student aid: Yes
Full-time enrollment: N/A
Part-time enrollment: 216
men: 63%; women: 38%; minorities: 25%; international: 31%
Average GRE (full time): N/A verbal; N/A quantitative; N/A writing
TOEFL requirement: Yes
Minimum TOEFL score: 607
Most popular departments: accounting, finance, general management, international business, marketing

Stevens Institute of Technology

1 Castle Point Terrace
Hoboken, NJ 07030
www.stevens.edu/admissions/graduate-admissions
Private
Admissions: (888) 783-8367
Email: graduate@stevens.edu
Financial aid: (201) 216-5555
Application deadline: 06/01
Tuition: full time: $35,716; part time: $1,554/credit hour
Room/board/expenses: $14,450
College-funded aid: Yes
International student aid: Yes
Full-time enrollment: 914
men: 65%; women: 35%; minorities: 2%; international: 94%
Part-time enrollment: 464
men: 62%; women: 38%; minorities: 28%; international: 12%
Acceptance rate (full time): 62%
Average GMAT (full time): 628
Average GRE (full time): 148 verbal; 161 quantitative; 3.2 writing
Average GPA (full time): 3.00
Average age of entrants to full-time program: 24
Average months of prior work experience (full time): 26
TOEFL requirement: Yes
Minimum TOEFL score: 537
Most popular departments: finance, general management, management information systems, quantitative analysis/statistics and operations research, other
Mean starting base salary for 2017 full-time graduates: $71,959

Stockton University

101 Vera King Farris Drive
Galloway, NJ 08205
stockton.edu/graduate/business-administration.html
Public
Admissions: (609) 626-3640
Email: gradschool@stockton.edu
Financial aid: (609) 652-4203
Application deadline: 07/01
In-state tuition: full time: N/A; part time: $608/credit hour
Out-of-state tuition: full time: N/A
Room/board/expenses: N/A
College-funded aid: Yes
Full-time enrollment: N/A
Part-time enrollment: 90
men: 41%; women: 59%; minorities: 29%; international: 1%

Average GRE (full time): N/A verbal; N/A quantitative; N/A writing
TOEFL requirement: Yes
Minimum TOEFL score: 550
Most popular departments: general management

William Paterson University (Cotsakos)[1]

1600 Valley Road
Wayne, NJ 07470
www.wpunj.edu/MBA
Public
Admissions: (973) 720-3601
Email: graduate@wpunj.edu
Financial aid: (973) 720-3945
Tuition: N/A
Room/board/expenses: N/A
Enrollment: N/A

NEW MEXICO

New Mexico State University

P.O. Box 30001
MSC 3AD
Las Cruces, NM 88003-0030
business.nmsu.edu/academics/graduate-programs/mba
Public
Admissions: (575) 646-8003
Email: mbaprog@nmsu.edu
Financial aid: (575) 646-4105
Application deadline: 07/15
In-state tuition: full time: N/A; part time: $244/credit hour
Out-of-state tuition: full time: N/A
Room/board/expenses: N/A
College-funded aid: Yes
International student aid: Yes
Full-time enrollment: N/A
Part-time enrollment: 85
men: 48%; women: 52%; minorities: N/A; international: N/A
Average GRE (full time): N/A verbal; N/A quantitative; N/A writing
TOEFL requirement: Yes
Minimum TOEFL score: 550
Most popular departments: finance, general management, management information systems, other

University of New Mexico (Anderson)

MSC05 3090
1 University of New Mexico
Albuquerque, NM 87131-0001
www.mgt.unm.edu
Public
Admissions: (505) 277-3290
Email: andersonadvising@unm.edu
Financial aid: (505) 277-8900
Application deadline: 04/01
In-state tuition: full time: $523/credit hour; part time: $523/credit hour
Out-of-state tuition: full time: $1,174/credit hour
Room/board/expenses: N/A
College-funded aid: Yes
International student aid: Yes

Full-time enrollment: 174
men: 48%; women:
52%; minorities: 48%;
international: 10%
Part-time enrollment: 126
men: 52%; women:
48%; minorities: 48%;
international: 4%
Average GRE (full
time): N/A verbal; N/A
quantitative; N/A writing
TOEFL requirement: Yes
Minimum TOEFL score: 550
Most popular departments:
finance, general management,
production/operations
management, organizational
behavior, technology

NEW YORK

Adelphi University
1 South Avenue
Garden City, NY 11530
www.adelphi.edu
Private
Admissions: (516) 877-3050
Email: admissions@adelphi.edu
Financial aid: (516) 877-3080
Application deadline: rolling
Tuition: full time: N/A; part
time: $1,210/credit hour
Room/board/expenses: N/A
College-funded aid: Yes
International student aid: Yes
Full-time enrollment: N/A
Part-time enrollment: 402
men: 53%; women:
47%; minorities: 20%;
international: 46%
Average GRE (full
time): N/A verbal; N/A
quantitative; N/A writing
TOEFL requirement: Yes
Minimum TOEFL score: N/A
Most popular departments:
accounting, finance, health
care administration, marketing

Alfred University
Saxon Drive
Alfred, NY 14802
business.alfred.edu/mba.html
Private
Admissions: (800) 541-9229
Email: gradinquiry@alfred.edu
Financial aid: (607) 871-2159
Application deadline: 08/01
Tuition: full time: $39,010;
part time: $810/credit hour
Room/board/expenses: $15,670
College-funded aid: Yes
International student aid: Yes
Full-time enrollment: 28
men: 61%; women:
39%; minorities: 29%;
international: 7%
Part-time enrollment: 20
men: 65%; women:
35%; minorities: 30%;
international: 5%
Acceptance rate (full time): 77%
Average GRE (full
time): N/A verbal; N/A
quantitative; N/A writing
Average age of entrants to
full-time program: 24
Average months of prior work
experience (full time): 16
TOEFL requirement: Yes
Minimum TOEFL score: 550

Most popular departments:
accounting, general
management, health care
administration, other

Binghamton University–SUNY
PO Box 6000
Binghamton, NY 13902-6000
www.binghamton.edu/som/
graduate-programs/index.html
Public
Admissions: (607) 777-2012
Email:
awheeler@binghamton.edu
Financial aid: (607) 777-6358
Application deadline: 03/01
In-state tuition: full time: $17,026;
part time: $613/credit hour
Out-of-state tuition:
full time: $26,716
Room/board/expenses: $19,517
College-funded aid: Yes
International student aid: Yes
Average student indebtedness
at graduation: $18,706
Full-time enrollment: 107
men: 66%; women:
34%; minorities: 19%;
international: 23%
Part-time enrollment: N/A
Acceptance rate (full time): 69%
Average GMAT (full time): 612
Average GRE (full
time): 151 verbal; 155
quantitative; 4.0 writing
Average GPA (full time): 3.53
Average age of entrants to
full-time program: 22
Average months of prior work
experience (full time): 15
TOEFL requirement: Yes
Minimum TOEFL score: 580
Most popular departments:
finance, leadership, marketing,
management information
systems, supply chain
management/logistics
Mean starting base salary for 2017
full-time graduates: $60,640
Employment location for 2017
class: Intl. N/A; N.E. 100%;
M.A. N/A; S. N/A; M.W.
N/A; S.W. N/A; W. N/A

Canisius College (Wehle)
2001 Main Street
Buffalo, NY 14208
www.canisius.edu/business/
graduate_programs.asp
Private
Admissions: (800) 950-2505
Email: gradubus@canisius.edu
Financial aid: (716) 888-2300
Application deadline: rolling
Tuition: total program:
$40,668 (full time); part
time: $819/credit hour
Room/board/expenses: $15,718
College-funded aid: Yes
International student aid: Yes
Average student indebtedness
at graduation: $27,757
Full-time enrollment: 28
men: 57%; women:
43%; minorities: 29%;
international: 7%
Part-time enrollment: 234
men: 60%; women:
40%; minorities: 8%;
international: 14%

Acceptance rate (full time): 78%
Average GMAT (full time): 488
Average GRE (full
time): 149 verbal; 144
quantitative; 3.4 writing
Average GPA (full time): 3.32
Average age of entrants to
full-time program: 24
TOEFL requirement: Yes
Minimum TOEFL score: 550
Most popular departments:
accounting, general
management, leadership,
marketing, supply chain
management/logistics
Mean starting base salary for 2017
full-time graduates: $48,417

Clarkson University
Snell Hall 322E
Box 5770
Potsdam, NY 13699-5770
www.clarkson.edu/mba
Private
Admissions: (315) 268-6613
Email: busgrad@clarkson.edu
Financial aid: (315) 268-7699
Application deadline: rolling
Tuition: total program:
$51,110 (full time); part
time: $1,138/credit hour
Room/board/expenses: $18,864
College-funded aid: Yes
International student aid: Yes
Average student indebtedness
at graduation: $40,755
Full-time enrollment: 67
men: 66%; women:
34%; minorities: 6%;
international: 16%
Part-time enrollment: 140
men: 54%; women:
46%; minorities: 18%;
international: 5%
Acceptance rate (full time): 86%
Average GMAT (full time): 601
Average GRE (full
time): 150 verbal; 152
quantitative; 3.6 writing
Average GPA (full time): 3.45
Average age of entrants to
full-time program: 24
Average months of prior work
experience (full time): 31
TOEFL requirement: Yes
Minimum TOEFL score: 550
Most popular departments:
accounting, entrepreneurship,
health care administration,
supply chain management/
logistics, other
Mean starting base salary for
2017 full-time graduates: $61,311
Employment location for 2017
class: Intl. 6%; N.E. 65%;
M.A. 12%; S. N/A; M.W.
6%; S.W. 6%; W. 6%

College at Brockport–SUNY[1]
119 Hartwell Hall
Brockport, NY 14420
www.brockport.edu/business
Public
Admissions: N/A
Financial aid: N/A
Tuition: N/A
Room/board/expenses: N/A
Enrollment: N/A

Columbia University
3022 Broadway
216 Uris Hall
New York, NY 10027
www.gsb.columbia.edu
Private
Admissions: (212) 854-1961
Email: apply@gsb.columbia.edu
Financial aid: (212) 854-4057
Application deadline: 04/11
Tuition: full time: $74,476;
part time: N/A
Room/board/expenses: $28,307
College-funded aid: Yes
International student aid: Yes
Full-time enrollment: 1,297
men: 60%; women:
40%; minorities: N/A;
international: N/A
Part-time enrollment: N/A
Acceptance rate (full time): 14%
Average GMAT (full time): 727
Average GRE (full
time): N/A verbal; N/A
quantitative; N/A writing
Average GPA (full time): 3.60
Average age of entrants to
full-time program: 28
Average months of prior work
experience (full time): 61
TOEFL requirement: Yes
Minimum TOEFL score: N/A
Most popular departments:
consulting, entrepreneurship,
finance, leadership, marketing
Mean starting base salary for 2017
full-time graduates: $128,343

Cornell University (Johnson)
Sage Hall, Cornell University
Ithaca, NY 14853-6201
www.johnson.cornell.edu
Private
Admissions: (607) 255-0600
Email: mba@johnson.cornell.edu
Financial aid: (607) 255-6116
Application deadline: 04/05
Tuition: full time: $66,894;
part time: N/A
Room/board/expenses: $25,780
College-funded aid: Yes
International student aid: Yes
Full-time enrollment: 573
men: 71%; women:
29%; minorities: 13%;
international: 33%
Part-time enrollment: N/A
Acceptance rate (full time): 30%
Average GMAT (full time): 700
Average GRE (full
time): 161 verbal; 161
quantitative; 4.5 writing
Average GPA (full time): 3.36
Average age of entrants to
full-time program: 28
Average months of prior work
experience (full time): 59
TOEFL requirement: Yes
Minimum TOEFL score: N/A
Most popular departments:
consulting, finance, leadership,
marketing, technology
Mean starting base salary for 2017
full-time graduates: $125,578
Employment location for
2017 class: Intl. 9%; N.E.
51%; M.A. 5%; S. 4%; M.W.
8%; S.W. 4%; W. 19%

CUNY Bernard M. Baruch College (Zicklin)
1 Bernard Baruch Way
New York, NY 10010
zicklin.baruch.cuny.edu
Public
Admissions: (646) 312-1300
Email: zicklingradadmissions@
baruch.cuny.edu
Financial aid: (646) 312-1370
Application deadline: N/A
In-state tuition: full time: $17,729;
part time: $685/credit hour
Out-of-state tuition:
full time: $30,709
Room/board/expenses: N/A
College-funded aid: Yes
International student aid: Yes
Full-time enrollment: 101
men: 44%; women:
56%; minorities: 22%;
international: 38%
Part-time enrollment: 460
men: 54%; women:
46%; minorities: 29%;
international: 6%
Acceptance rate (full time): 38%
Average GMAT (full time): 619
Average GRE (full
time): 154 verbal; 156
quantitative; N/A writing
Average GPA (full time): 3.31
Average age of entrants to
full-time program: 30
Average months of prior work
experience (full time): 76
TOEFL requirement: Yes
Minimum TOEFL score: N/A
Most popular departments:
accounting, finance,
general management,
marketing, production/
operations management
Mean starting base salary for 2017
full-time graduates: $80,900
Employment location for 2017
class: Intl. N/A; N.E. 100%;
M.A. N/A; S. N/A; M.W.
N/A; S.W. N/A; W. N/A

Fordham University (Gabelli)
140 W. 62nd Street
New York, NY 10023
www.fordham.edu/gabelli
Private
Admissions: (212) 636-6200
Email: admissionsgb@
fordham.edu
Financial aid: (212) 636-6700
Application deadline: 06/01
Tuition: full time: $46,575; part
time: $1,453/credit hour
Room/board/expenses: $23,380
College-funded aid: Yes
International student aid: Yes
Average student indebtedness
at graduation: $49,090
Full-time enrollment: 83
men: 57%; women:
43%; minorities: 19%;
international: 36%
Part-time enrollment: 163
men: 53%; women:
47%; minorities: 29%;
international: 6%
Acceptance rate (full time): 39%
Average GMAT (full time): 643

Average GRE (full time): 153 verbal; 154 quantitative; 4.0 writing
Average GPA (full time): 3.14
Average age of entrants to full-time program: 30
Average months of prior work experience (full time): 70
TOEFL requirement: Yes
Minimum TOEFL score: N/A
Most popular departments: finance, general management, marketing, management information systems, other
Mean starting base salary for 2017 full-time graduates: $83,328
Employment location for 2017 class: Intl. 6%; N.E. 91%; M.A. N/A; S. N/A; M.W. N/A; S.W. N/A; W. 3%

Hofstra University (Zarb)
300 Weller Hall
Hempstead, NY 11549
www.hofstra.edu/graduate
Private
Admissions: (516) 463-4723
Email: graduateadmission@hofstra.edu
Financial aid: (516) 463-8000
Application deadline: rolling
Tuition: full time: $1,322/credit hour; part time: $1,322/credit hour
Room/board/expenses: $22,254
College-funded aid: Yes
International student aid: Yes
Full-time enrollment: 90
men: 60%; women: 40%; minorities: 16%; international: 54%
Part-time enrollment: 751
men: 54%; women: 46%; minorities: 19%; international: 45%
Acceptance rate (full time): 45%
Average GMAT (full time): 568
Average GRE (full time): N/A verbal; N/A quantitative; N/A writing
Average GPA (full time): 3.42
Average age of entrants to full-time program: 25
Average months of prior work experience (full time): 50
TOEFL requirement: Yes
Minimum TOEFL score: 550
Most popular departments: accounting, finance, health care administration, marketing, quantitative analysis/statistics and operations research

Iona College (Hagan)
715 North Avenue
New Rochelle, NY 10801
www.iona.edu/academics/school-of-business.aspx
Private
Admissions: (800) 231-4662
Email: gradadmissions@iona.edu
Financial aid: (914) 633-2497
Application deadline: rolling
Tuition: full time: N/A; part time: $1,094/credit hour
Room/board/expenses: N/A
College-funded aid: Yes
International student aid: Yes

Full-time enrollment: N/A
Part-time enrollment: 242
men: 50%; women: 50%; minorities: 34%; international: 7%
Average GRE (full time): N/A verbal; N/A quantitative; N/A writing
TOEFL requirement: Yes
Minimum TOEFL score: 550
Most popular departments: accounting, finance, general management, marketing, management information systems

Ithaca College
953 Danby Road
Ithaca, NY 14850-7002
www.ithaca.edu/gradadmission
Private
Admissions: (607) 274-3124
Email: admission@ithaca.edu
Financial aid: (607) 274-3131
Application deadline: 05/15
Tuition: full time: $951/credit hour; part time: $951/credit hour
Room/board/expenses: N/A
College-funded aid: Yes
International student aid: Yes
Full-time enrollment: 36
men: 72%; women: 28%; minorities: 8%; international: 3%
Part-time enrollment: 2
men: 50%; women: 50%; minorities: 0%; international: 0%
Acceptance rate (full time): 78%
Average GRE (full time): N/A verbal; N/A quantitative; N/A writing
Average age of entrants to full-time program: 22
TOEFL requirement: Yes
Minimum TOEFL score: 550

Le Moyne College
1419 Salt Springs Road
Syracuse, NY 13214-1301
www.lemoyne.edu/madden
Private
Admissions: (315) 445-5444
Email: business@lemoyne.edu
Financial aid: (315) 445-4400
Application deadline: 07/01
Tuition: full time: $817/credit hour; part time: $817/credit hour
Room/board/expenses: N/A
College-funded aid: Yes
International student aid: Yes
Average student indebtedness at graduation: $8,330
Full-time enrollment: 55
men: 65%; women: 35%; minorities: 13%; international: 4%
Part-time enrollment: 73
men: 55%; women: 45%; minorities: 7%; international: 0%
Acceptance rate (full time): 95%
Average GMAT (full time): 475
Average GRE (full time): 151 verbal; 149 quantitative; 4.0 writing
Average GPA (full time): 3.49
Average age of entrants to full-time program: 23
Average months of prior work experience (full time): 7
TOEFL requirement: Yes
Minimum TOEFL score: 550

Mean starting base salary for 2017 full-time graduates: $54,800
Employment location for 2017 class: Intl. 0%; N.E. 83%; M.A. 8%; S. 0%; M.W. 8%; S.W. 0%; W. 0%

LIU Post
720 Northern Boulevard
Brookville, NY 11548-1300
www.liu.edu/postmba
Private
Admissions: (516) 299-2900
Email: post-enroll@liu.edu
Financial aid: (516) 299-2338
Application deadline: 08/18
Tuition: full time: $1,201/credit hour; part time: $1,201/credit hour
Room/board/expenses: $20,200
College-funded aid: Yes
International student aid: Yes
Full-time enrollment: 95
men: 61%; women: 39%; minorities: 13%; international: 33%
Part-time enrollment: 26
men: 65%; women: 35%; minorities: 35%; international: 0%
Acceptance rate (full time): 68%
Average GMAT (full time): 450
Average GRE (full time): 144 verbal; 154 quantitative; 0.0 writing
Average GPA (full time): 3.25
Average age of entrants to full-time program: 24
Average months of prior work experience (full time): 56
TOEFL requirement: Yes
Minimum TOEFL score: N/A

Manhattan College
4513 Manhattan College Parkway
Riverdale, NY 10471
manhattan.edu/
Private
Admissions: (718) 862-8200
Email: gradadmit@manhattan.edu
Financial aid: (718) 862-7178
Application deadline: rolling
Tuition: full time: $1,090/credit hour; part time: $1,090/credit hour
Room/board/expenses: N/A
College-funded aid: Yes
International student aid: Yes
Full-time enrollment: 63
men: 54%; women: 46%; minorities: N/A; international: N/A
Part-time enrollment: 24
men: 42%; women: 58%; minorities: N/A; international: N/A
Average GRE (full time): N/A verbal; N/A quantitative; N/A writing
Minimum TOEFL score: N/A
Most popular departments: accounting, finance, general management, international business, marketing

New York Institute of Technology[1]
1855 Broadway
New York, NY 10023
www.nyit.edu/degrees/management_mba
Private
Admissions: (516) 686-7520
Email: nyitgrad@nyit.edu
Financial aid: N/A
Tuition: N/A
Room/board/expenses: N/A
Enrollment: N/A

New York University (Stern)
44 W. Fourth Street
New York, NY 10012-1126
www.stern.nyu.edu
Private
Admissions: (212) 998-0600
Email: sternmba@stern.nyu.edu
Financial aid: (212) 998-0790
Application deadline: 03/15
Tuition: full time: $71,658; part time: $2,158/credit hour
Room/board/expenses: $37,384
College-funded aid: Yes
International student aid: Yes
Average student indebtedness at graduation: $120,984
Full-time enrollment: 779
men: 64%; women: 36%; minorities: 29%; international: 22%
Part-time enrollment: 1,300
men: 62%; women: 38%; minorities: 25%; international: 10%
Acceptance rate (full time): 21%
Average GMAT (full time): 714
Average GRE (full time): 162 verbal; 161 quantitative; 4.4 writing
Average GPA (full time): 3.48
Average age of entrants to full-time program: 28
Average months of prior work experience (full time): 59
TOEFL requirement: Yes
Minimum TOEFL score: N/A
Most popular departments: consulting, entrepreneurship, finance, general management, marketing
Mean starting base salary for 2017 full-time graduates: $121,146
Employment location for 2017 class: Intl. 10%; N.E. 75%; M.A. 2%; S. 1%; M.W. 1%; S.W. 1%; W. 10%

Niagara University
PO Box 1909
Niagara University, NY 14109
mba.niagara.edu
Private
Admissions: (716) 286-8051
Email: bsemski@niagara.edu
Financial aid: (716) 286-8686
Application deadline: rolling
Tuition: full time: $895/credit hour; part time: $895/credit hour
Room/board/expenses: $14,820
College-funded aid: Yes
International student aid: Yes
Full-time enrollment: 173
men: 47%; women: 53%; minorities: 15%; international: 18%

Part-time enrollment: 79
men: 51%; women: 49%; minorities: 15%; international: 19%
Average GRE (full time): N/A verbal; N/A quantitative; N/A writing
Average age of entrants to full-time program: 25
TOEFL requirement: Yes
Minimum TOEFL score: 550
Most popular departments: accounting, finance, general management, health care administration, marketing

Pace University (Lubin)
1 Pace Plaza
New York, NY 10038
www.pace.edu/lubin/sections/explore-programs/graduate-programs
Private
Admissions: (212) 346-1531
Email: graduateadmission@pace.edu
Financial aid: (914) 773-3751
Application deadline: 08/01
Tuition: full time: $1,230/credit hour; part time: $1,230/credit hour
Room/board/expenses: $23,558
College-funded aid: Yes
International student aid: Yes
Average student indebtedness at graduation: $46,461
Full-time enrollment: 192
men: 49%; women: 51%; minorities: 21%; international: 52%
Part-time enrollment: 103
men: 47%; women: 53%; minorities: 40%; international: 17%
Acceptance rate (full time): 42%
Average GMAT (full time): 543
Average GRE (full time): N/A verbal; N/A quantitative; N/A writing
Average GPA (full time): 3.59
Average age of entrants to full-time program: 24
TOEFL requirement: Yes
Minimum TOEFL score: 577
Most popular departments: accounting, finance, general management, human resources management, marketing
Mean starting base salary for 2017 full-time graduates: $62,340

Rensselaer Polytechnic Institute (Lally)
110 Eighth Street
Pittsburgh Building 5202
Troy, NY 12180-3590
lallyschool.rpi.edu
Private
Admissions: (518) 276-6565
Email: lallymba@rpi.edu
Financial aid: (518) 276-6565
Application deadline: 04/15
Tuition: full time: $53,757; part time: N/A
Room/board/expenses: $16,782
College-funded aid: Yes
International student aid: Yes

Full-time enrollment: 28
men: 39%; women:
61%; minorities: 25%;
international: 4%
Part-time enrollment: N/A
Acceptance rate (full time): 58%
Average GMAT (full time): 625
Average GRE (full
time): N/A verbal; N/A
quantitative; N/A writing
Average GPA (full time): 3.37
Average age of entrants to
full-time program: 25
Average months of prior work
experience (full time): 35
TOEFL requirement: Yes
Minimum TOEFL score: 570
Most popular departments:
entrepreneurship, finance,
manufacturing and technology
management, marketing, supply
chain management/logistics
Mean starting base salary for 2017
full-time graduates: $66,444
Employment location for 2017
class: Intl. 9%; N.E. 55%;
M.A. 18%; S. 18%; M.W.
N/A; S.W. N/A; W. N/A

Rochester Institute of Technology (Saunders)

105 Lomb Memorial Drive
Rochester, NY 14623-5608
saunders.rit.edu
Private
Admissions: (585) 475-2229
Email: gradinfo@rit.edu
Financial aid: (585) 475-2186
Application deadline: rolling
Tuition: full time: $43,840;
part time: $1,815/credit hour
Room/board/expenses: $14,690
College-funded aid: Yes
International student aid: Yes
Full-time enrollment: 146
men: 58%; women:
42%; minorities: 8%;
international: 57%
Part-time enrollment: 76
men: 57%; women:
43%; minorities: 11%;
international: 13%
Acceptance rate (full time): 45%
Average GMAT (full time): 551
Average GRE (full
time): 148 verbal; 154
quantitative; 3.4 writing
Average GPA (full time): 3.37
Average age of entrants to
full-time program: 25
Average months of prior work
experience (full time): 46
TOEFL requirement: Yes
Minimum TOEFL score: 580
Most popular departments:
finance, leadership, marketing,
management information
systems, technology
Mean starting base salary for 2017
full-time graduates: $56,747
Employment location for
2017 class: Intl. 3%; N.E.
77%; M.A. 10%; S. 3%; M.W.
N/A; S.W. 6%; W. N/A

St. Bonaventure University

3261 West State Road
St. Bonaventure, NY 14778
www.sbu.edu/admission-aid/
graduate-admissions
Private
Admissions: (716) 375-2021
Email: gradsch@sbu.edu
Financial aid: (716) 375-2528
Application deadline: 10/08
Tuition: full time: $733/credit
hour; part time: $733/credit hour
Room/board/expenses: $14,565
College-funded aid: Yes
International student aid: Yes
Average student indebtedness
at graduation: $18,802
Full-time enrollment: 79
men: 59%; women: 41%;
minorities: 9%; international: 5%
Part-time enrollment: 27
men: 52%; women: 48%;
minorities: 0%; international: 0%
Acceptance rate (full time): 100%
Average GRE (full
time): N/A verbal; N/A
quantitative; N/A writing
Average age of entrants to
full-time program: 23
TOEFL requirement: Yes
Minimum TOEFL score: 550
Most popular departments:
accounting, finance, general
management, marketing

St. John Fisher College

3690 East Avenue
Rochester, NY 14618
www.sjfc.edu/graduate-
programs/master-of-
business-administration-mba/
Private
Admissions: (585) 385-8064
Email: grad@sjfc.edu
Financial aid: (585) 385-8042
Application deadline: rolling
Tuition: full time: $1,090/
credit hour; part time:
$1,090/credit hour
Room/board/expenses: N/A
College-funded aid: Yes
International student aid: Yes
Full-time enrollment: 64
men: 50%; women: 50%;
minorities: 8%; international: 8%
Part-time enrollment: 75
men: 55%; women:
45%; minorities: 16%;
international: 0%
Acceptance rate (full time): 79%
Average GMAT (full time): 557
Average GRE (full
time): N/A verbal; N/A
quantitative; N/A writing
Average GPA (full time): 3.40
Average age of entrants to
full-time program: 22
TOEFL requirement: Yes
Minimum TOEFL score: 575
Mean starting base salary for 2017
full-time graduates: $47,046
Employment location for
2017 class: Intl. N/A; N.E.
93%; M.A. N/A; S. N/A; M.W.
N/A; S.W. 7%; W. N/A

St. John's University (Tobin)

8000 Utopia Parkway
Queens, NY 11439
www.stjohns.edu/tobin
Private
Admissions: (718) 990-3060
Email: tobingradnyc@
stjohns.edu
Financial aid: (718) 990-2000
Application deadline: 11/01
Tuition: full time: N/A/credit hour;
part time: $1,215/credit hour
Room/board/expenses: N/A
College-funded aid: Yes
International student aid: Yes
Full-time enrollment: N/A
Part-time enrollment: 319
men: 56%; women:
44%; minorities: 31%;
international: 26%
Average GRE (full
time): N/A verbal; N/A
quantitative; N/A writing
TOEFL requirement: Yes
Minimum TOEFL score: 550
Most popular departments:
accounting, finance, general
management, international
business, marketing

SUNY–Fredonia[1]

280 Central Avenue
Fredonia, NY 14063
home.fredonia.edu/
businessadministration
Private
Admissions: N/A
Financial aid: N/A
Tuition: N/A
Room/board/expenses: N/A
Enrollment: N/A

SUNY–New Paltz

1 Hawk Drive
New Paltz, NY 12561
www.newpaltz.edu/graduate
Public
Admissions: (845) 257-3947
Email: gradstudies@
newpaltz.edu
Financial aid: (845) 257-3250
Application deadline: rolling
In-state tuition: full time: $15,715;
part time: $600/credit hour
Out-of-state tuition:
full time: $25,695
Room/board/expenses: N/A
College-funded aid: Yes
International student aid: No
Full-time enrollment: 98
men: 48%; women:
52%; minorities: 29%;
international: 12%
Part-time enrollment: N/A
Acceptance rate (full time): 97%
Average GMAT (full time): 481
Average GRE (full
time): 150 verbal; 146
quantitative; 3.5 writing
Average GPA (full time): 3.39
Average age of entrants to
full-time program: 26
TOEFL requirement: Yes
Minimum TOEFL score: N/A
Most popular departments:
accounting, general
management

SUNY–Oswego

138 Rich Hall
Oswego, NY 13126
www.oswego.edu/graduate/
Public
Admissions: (315) 312-3152
Email: gradstudies@oswego.edu
Financial aid: (315) 312-2248
Application deadline: rolling
In-state tuition: full time: $15,366;
part time: $613/credit hour
Out-of-state tuition:
full time: $25,056
Room/board/expenses: $18,540
College-funded aid: Yes
International student aid: Yes
Average student indebtedness
at graduation: $23,862
Full-time enrollment: 92
men: 61%; women:
39%; minorities: 11%;
international: 9%
Part-time enrollment: 152
men: 59%; women:
41%; minorities: 22%;
international: 1%
Acceptance rate (full time): 88%
Average GMAT (full time): 500
Average GRE (full
time): N/A verbal; N/A
quantitative; N/A writing
Average GPA (full time): 3.25
Average age of entrants to
full-time program: 25
Average months of prior work
experience (full time): 82
TOEFL requirement: Yes
Minimum TOEFL score: 560
Most popular departments:
accounting, general
management, health care
administration, marketing, tax
Mean starting base salary for 2017
full-time graduates: $49,900
Employment location for 2017
class: Intl. 0%; N.E. 83%;
M.A. 17%; S. 0%; M.W.
0%; S.W. 0%; W. 0%

SUNY Polytechnic Institute[1]

100 Seymour Road
Utica, NY 13502
www.sunypoly.edu/graduate/
mbatm/
Public
Admissions: (315) 792-7347
Email: gradcenter@sunyit.edu
Financial aid: (315) 792-7210
Tuition: N/A
Room/board/expenses: N/A
Enrollment: N/A

Syracuse University (Whitman)

721 University Avenue, Suite 315
Syracuse, NY 13244-2450
whitman.syr.edu/mba/fulltime
Private
Admissions: (315) 443-9214
Email: busgrad@syr.edu
Financial aid: (315) 443-9214
Application deadline: 04/19
Tuition: full time: $46,202;
part time: N/A
Room/board/expenses: $19,516
College-funded aid: Yes
International student aid: Yes
Average student indebtedness
at graduation: $39,269

Full-time enrollment: 52
men: 58%; women:
42%; minorities: 2%;
international: 73%
Part-time enrollment: N/A
Acceptance rate (full time): 60%
Average GMAT (full time): 642
Average GRE (full time): 161
verbal; 160 quantitative;
N/A writing
Average GPA (full time): 3.43
Average age of entrants to
full-time program: 25
Average months of prior work
experience (full time): 29
TOEFL requirement: Yes
Minimum TOEFL score: 600
Most popular departments:
entrepreneurship, finance,
general management,
marketing, supply chain
management/logistics
Mean starting base salary for 2017
full-time graduates: $67,589
Employment location for
2017 class: Intl. 5%; N.E.
67%; M.A. 5%; S. 0%; M.W.
14%; S.W. 5%; W. 5%

University at Albany–SUNY

1400 Washington Avenue
Massry Center for Business
Albany, NY 12222
graduatebusiness.albany.edu
Public
Admissions: (518) 442-3980
Email: graduate@albany.edu
Financial aid: (518) 442-5757
Application deadline: 05/01
In-state tuition: total program:
$16,618 (full time); part
time: $613/credit hour
Out-of-state tuition: total
program: $24,128 (full time)
Room/board/expenses: $12,942
College-funded aid: Yes
International student aid: Yes
Full-time enrollment: 103
men: 65%; women:
35%; minorities: 34%;
international: 11%
Part-time enrollment: 189
men: 63%; women:
37%; minorities: 22%;
international: 3%
Acceptance rate (full time): 52%
Average GMAT (full time): 560
Average GRE (full
time): N/A verbal; N/A
quantitative; N/A writing
Average GPA (full time): 3.60
Average months of prior work
experience (full time): 48
TOEFL requirement: Yes
Minimum TOEFL score: 600
Most popular departments:
finance, human resources
management, marketing,
management information
systems, other
Mean starting base salary for 2017
full-time graduates: $64,000
Employment location for
2017 class: Intl. N/A; N.E.
97%; M.A. N/A; S. N/A; M.W.
3%; S.W. N/A; W. N/A

University at Buffalo–SUNY

203 Alfiero Center
Buffalo, NY 14260-4010
mgt.buffalo.edu/mba
Public
Admissions: (716) 645-3204
Email: som-apps@buffalo.edu
Financial aid: (716) 645-8232
Application deadline: 06/01
In-state tuition: full time: $19,750;
part time: $760/credit hour
Out-of-state tuition:
full time: $29,440
Room/board/expenses: $18,308
College-funded aid: Yes
International student aid: Yes
Full-time enrollment: 204
men: 61%; women:
39%; minorities: 28%;
international: 15%
Part-time enrollment: 201
men: 68%; women:
32%; minorities: 12%;
international: 3%
Acceptance rate (full time): 64%
Average GMAT (full time): 613
Average GRE (full
time): 150 verbal; 152
quantitative; N/A writing
Average GPA (full time): 3.38
Average age of entrants to
full-time program: 25
Average months of prior work
experience (full time): 29
TOEFL requirement: Yes
Minimum TOEFL score: 570
Most popular departments:
consulting, finance, health care
administration, marketing, other
Mean starting base salary for 2017
full-time graduates: $60,751
Employment location for 2017
class: Intl. 6%; N.E. 67%;
M.A. 10%; S. 8%; M.W.
3%; S.W. 0%; W. 7%

University of Rochester (Simon)

245 Gleason Hall
Rochester, NY 14627
www.simon.rochester.edu
Private
Admissions: (585) 275-3533
Email: admissions@
simon.rochester.edu
Financial aid: (585) 275-3533
Application deadline: 05/15
Tuition: full time: $47,125; part
time: $1,875/credit hour
Room/board/expenses: $17,765
College-funded aid: Yes
International student aid: Yes
Average student indebtedness
at graduation: $46,659
Full-time enrollment: 211
men: 66%; women:
34%; minorities: 29%;
international: 47%
Part-time enrollment: 159
men: 61%; women:
39%; minorities: 16%;
international: 3%
Acceptance rate (full time): 30%
Average GMAT (full time): 666
Average GRE (full
time): 156 verbal; 158
quantitative; 4.0 writing
Average GPA (full time): 3.40
Average age of entrants to
full-time program: 28

Average months of prior work
experience (full time): 61
TOEFL requirement: Yes
Minimum TOEFL score: N/A
Most popular departments:
accounting, consulting,
finance, marketing, other
Mean starting base salary for 2017
full-time graduates: $102,046
Employment location for 2017
class: Intl. 11%; N.E. 32%;
M.A. 9%; S. 13%; M.W.
17%; S.W. 0%; W. 17%

Yeshiva University (Syms)[1]

500 West 185th Street
New York, NY 10033
www.yu.edu/syms/
Private
Admissions: N/A
Financial aid: (646) 592-4166
Tuition: N/A
Room/board/expenses: N/A
Enrollment: N/A

NORTH CAROLINA

Appalachian State University (Walker)

Box 32037
Boone, NC 28608-2037
business.appstate.edu/mba
Public
Admissions: (828) 262-2130
Email: mba@appstate.edu
Financial aid: (828) 262-2190
Application deadline: 07/01
In-state tuition: total
program: $15,970 (full
time); $18,379 (part time)
Out-of-state tuition: total
program: $33,410 (full time)
Room/board/expenses: N/A
College-funded aid: Yes
International student aid: Yes
Full-time enrollment: 70
men: 60%; women: 40%;
minorities: 4%; international: 3%
Part-time enrollment: 45
men: 49%; women:
51%; minorities: 11%;
international: 4%
Acceptance rate (full time): 83%
Average GRE (full
time): N/A verbal; N/A
quantitative; N/A writing
Average GPA (full time): 3.40
Average age of entrants to
full-time program: 23
Average months of prior work
experience (full time): 48
TOEFL requirement: Yes
Minimum TOEFL score: N/A
Most popular departments:
economics, general
management, international
business, management
information systems, supply
chain management/logistics

Duke University (Fuqua)

100 Fuqua Drive
Box 90120
Durham, NC 27708-0120
www.fuqua.duke.edu/
Private
Admissions: (919) 257-9913
Email: admissions-info@
fuqua.duke.edu

Financial aid: (919) 660-7687
Application deadline: 03/20
Tuition: full time: $68,322;
part time: N/A
Room/board/expenses: $22,302
College-funded aid: Yes
International student aid: Yes
Average student indebtedness
at graduation: $114,679
Full-time enrollment: 882
men: 66%; women:
34%; minorities: 21%;
international: 37%
Part-time enrollment: N/A
Acceptance rate (full time): 22%
Average GMAT (full time): 702
Average GRE (full
time): 161 verbal; 160
quantitative; 4.5 writing
Average GPA (full time): 3.50
Average age of entrants to
full-time program: 29
Average months of prior work
experience (full time): 66
TOEFL requirement: No
Minimum TOEFL score: N/A
Most popular departments:
consulting, finance, health care
administration, marketing,
quantitative analysis/statistics
and operations research
Mean starting base salary for 2017
full-time graduates: $122,989
Employment location for 2017
class: Intl. 11%; N.E. 23%;
M.A. 6%; S. 18%; M.W.
12%; S.W. 9%; W. 21%

East Carolina University

3203 Bate Building
Greenville, NC 27858-4353
www.ecu.edu/cs-bus/grad/
Public
Admissions: (252) 328-6970
Email: gradbus@ecu.edu
Financial aid: (252) 328-6610
Application deadline: 06/01
In-state tuition: full time:
$358/credit hour; part
time: $358/credit hour
Out-of-state tuition: full
time: $1,002/credit hour
Room/board/expenses: $20,268
College-funded aid: Yes
International student aid: Yes
Average student indebtedness
at graduation: $33,163
Full-time enrollment: 181
men: 54%; women:
46%; minorities: 23%;
international: 5%
Part-time enrollment: 585
men: 54%; women:
46%; minorities: 22%;
international: 2%
Acceptance rate (full time): 96%
Average GMAT (full time): 501
Average GRE (full
time): 150 verbal; 149
quantitative; 3.0 writing
Average GPA (full time): 3.32
Average age of entrants to
full-time program: 23
TOEFL requirement: Yes
Minimum TOEFL score: 550
Most popular departments:
finance, health care
administration, marketing,
management information
systems, quantitative
analysis/statistics and
operations research

Elon University (Love)

100 Campus Drive
Elon, NC 27244-2010
elon.edu/mba
Private
Admissions: (336) 278-7600
Email: gradadm@elon.edu
Financial aid: (336) 278-7600
Application deadline: rolling
Tuition: full time: N/A; part
time: $913/credit hour
Room/board/expenses: N/A
College-funded aid: No
International student aid: No
Full-time enrollment: N/A
Part-time enrollment: 131
men: 57%; women:
43%; minorities: 21%;
international: 0%
Average GRE (full
time): N/A verbal; N/A
quantitative; N/A writing
TOEFL requirement: Yes
Minimum TOEFL score: 550
Most popular departments:
entrepreneurship, general
management, human
resources management,
leadership, marketing

Fayetteville State University

1200 Murchison Road
Newbold Station
Fayetteville, NC 28301-1033
mba.uncfsu.edu/
Public
Admissions: (910) 672-1197
Email: mbaprogram@uncfsu.edu
Financial aid: (910) 672-1325
Application deadline: 06/30
In-state tuition: full time: N/A;
part time: $233/credit hour
Out-of-state tuition: full time: N/A
Room/board/expenses: N/A
College-funded aid: Yes
International student aid: Yes
Full-time enrollment: N/A
Part-time enrollment: 322
men: 51%; women:
49%; minorities: 52%;
international: 2%
Average GRE (full
time): N/A verbal; N/A
quantitative; N/A writing
TOEFL requirement: Yes
Minimum TOEFL score: 550
Most popular departments:
entrepreneurship, finance,
general management, health
care administration, production/
operations management

Meredith College

3800 Hillsborough Street
Raleigh, NC 27607
www.meredith.edu/master-
of-business-administration
Private
Admissions: (919) 760-2281
Email: mba@meredith.edu
Financial aid: (919) 760-8565
Application deadline: 06/01
Tuition: full time: $945/credit
hour; part time: $945/credit hour
Room/board/expenses: $10,718
College-funded aid: Yes
International student aid: Yes
Average student indebtedness
at graduation: $35,925

Full-time enrollment: 64
men: 11%; women:
89%; minorities: 34%;
international: 3%
Part-time enrollment: 29
men: 28%; women:
72%; minorities: 28%;
international: 0%
Acceptance rate (full time): 81%
Average GMAT (full time): 553
Average GRE (full
time): N/A verbal; N/A
quantitative; N/A writing
Average GPA (full time): 3.14
Average age of entrants to
full-time program: 25
Average months of prior work
experience (full time): 49
TOEFL requirement: Yes
Minimum TOEFL score: 550
Most popular departments:
general management, human
resources management, other

North Carolina A&T State University

1601 E. Market Street
Greensboro, NC 27411
ncatmba.com
Public
Admissions: (336) 285-2373
Email: cdcampbe@ncat.edu
Financial aid: (336) 334-7973
Application deadline: 07/15
In-state tuition: total program:
$15,462 (full time); part
time: $583/credit hour
Out-of-state tuition: total
program: $40,272 (full time)
Room/board/expenses: $7,731
College-funded aid: Yes
International student aid: Yes
Average student indebtedness
at graduation: $35,000
Full-time enrollment: 114
men: 42%; women:
58%; minorities: 89%;
international: 9%
Part-time enrollment: N/A
Acceptance rate (full time): 72%
Average GMAT (full time): 510
Average GRE (full
time): N/A verbal; N/A
quantitative; N/A writing
Average GPA (full time): 3.52
Average age of entrants to
full-time program: 27
Average months of prior work
experience (full time): 36
TOEFL requirement: Yes
Minimum TOEFL score: 550
Most popular departments:
accounting, general
management, human resources
management, supply chain
management/logistics
Mean starting base salary for 2017
full-time graduates: $84,000

North Carolina Central University[1]

1801 Fayetteville Street
Durham, NC 27707
www.nccu.edu/academics/
business/index.cfm
Public
Admissions: (919) 530-6405
Email: mba@nccu.edu
Financial aid: N/A
Tuition: N/A
Room/board/expenses: N/A
Enrollment: N/A

North Carolina State University (Poole)

2130 Nelson Hall
Campus Box 8114
Raleigh, NC 27695-8114
www.mba.ncsu.edu
Public
Admissions: (919) 515-5584
Email: mba@ncsu.edu
Financial aid: (919) 515-2866
Application deadline: 03/01
In-state tuition: full time: $25,152; part time: $1,108/credit hour
Out-of-state tuition: full time: $41,112
Room/board/expenses: $17,813
College-funded aid: Yes
International student aid: Yes
Average student indebtedness at graduation: $36,288
Full-time enrollment: 93
men: 68%; women: 32%; minorities: 26%; international: 22%
Part-time enrollment: 281
men: 64%; women: 36%; minorities: 28%; international: 15%
Acceptance rate (full time): 41%
Average GMAT (full time): 626
Average GRE (full time): 155 verbal; 155 quantitative; 4.0 writing
Average GPA (full time): 3.40
Average age of entrants to full-time program: 29
Average months of prior work experience (full time): 61
TOEFL requirement: Yes
Minimum TOEFL score: 650
Most popular departments: entrepreneurship, marketing, supply chain management/logistics, technology, other
Mean starting base salary for 2017 full-time graduates: $80,368
Employment location for 2017 class: Intl. N/A; N.E. 7%; M.A. N/A; S. 80%; M.W. 7%; S.W. 3%; W. 3%

Queens University of Charlotte (McColl)

1900 Selwyn Avenue
Charlotte, NC 28274
mccoll.queens.edu/
Private
Admissions: (704) 337-2224
Email: mccollshool@queens.edu
Financial aid: (704) 337-2225
Application deadline: rolling
Tuition: full time: N/A; part time: $1,105/credit hour
Room/board/expenses: N/A
College-funded aid: Yes
International student aid: Yes
Full-time enrollment: N/A
Part-time enrollment: 101
men: 32%; women: 68%; minorities: 23%; international: 18%
Average GRE (full time): N/A verbal; N/A quantitative; N/A writing
TOEFL requirement: Yes
Minimum TOEFL score: 550
Most popular departments: finance, health care administration, leadership, other

University of North Carolina–Chapel Hill (Kenan-Flagler)

CB 3490, McColl Building
Chapel Hill, NC 27599-3490
www.kenan-flagler.unc.edu
Public
Admissions: (919) 962-3236
Email: mba_info@unc.edu
Financial aid: (919) 962-9096
Application deadline: N/A
In-state tuition: full time: $46,473; part time: N/A
Out-of-state tuition: full time: $61,596
Room/board/expenses: $25,672
College-funded aid: Yes
International student aid: Yes
Average student indebtedness at graduation: $96,096
Full-time enrollment: 581
men: 70%; women: 30%; minorities: 20%; international: 27%
Part-time enrollment: N/A
Acceptance rate (full time): 37%
Average GMAT (full time): 701
Average GRE (full time): 159 verbal; 157 quantitative; 4.0 writing
Average GPA (full time): 3.38
Average age of entrants to full-time program: 28
Average months of prior work experience (full time): 63
TOEFL requirement: Yes
Minimum TOEFL score: N/A
Most popular departments: consulting, entrepreneurship, finance, marketing, real estate
Mean starting base salary for 2017 full-time graduates: $111,082
Employment location for 2017 class: Intl. 2%; N.E. 20%; M.A. 16%; S. 29%; M.W. 8%; S.W. 11%; W. 14%

University of North Carolina–Charlotte (Belk)

9201 University City Boulevard
Charlotte, NC 28223
www.mba.uncc.edu
Public
Admissions: (704) 687-0815
Email: belkgradprograms@uncc.edu
Financial aid: (704) 687-7010
Application deadline: rolling
In-state tuition: full time: $13,498; part time: $9,997
Out-of-state tuition: full time: $26,932
Room/board/expenses: N/A
College-funded aid: Yes
International student aid: Yes
Full-time enrollment: N/A
Part-time enrollment: 368
men: 67%; women: 33%; minorities: 16%; international: 40%
Average GRE (full time): N/A verbal; N/A quantitative; N/A writing
TOEFL requirement: Yes
Minimum TOEFL score: 557

Most popular departments: finance, general management, international business, marketing, supply chain management/logistics

University of North Carolina–Greensboro (Bryan)

PO Box 26170
Greensboro, NC 27402-6170
mba.uncg.edu
Public
Admissions: (336) 334-5390
Email: mba@uncg.edu
Financial aid: (336) 334-5702
Application deadline: 07/01
In-state tuition: full time: $10,698; part time: $526/credit hour
Out-of-state tuition: full time: $26,988
Room/board/expenses: $12,690
College-funded aid: Yes
International student aid: Yes
Full-time enrollment: 43
men: 49%; women: 51%; minorities: 26%; international: 35%
Part-time enrollment: 111
men: 55%; women: 45%; minorities: 20%; international: 7%
Acceptance rate (full time): 77%
Average GMAT (full time): 527
Average GRE (full time): 149 verbal; 150 quantitative; 3.5 writing
Average GPA (full time): 3.40
Average age of entrants to full-time program: 24
Average months of prior work experience (full time): 33
TOEFL requirement: Yes
Minimum TOEFL score: 550
Most popular departments: finance, general management, marketing, supply chain management/logistics, quantitative analysis/statistics and operations research
Mean starting base salary for 2017 full-time graduates: $57,529
Employment location for 2017 class: Intl. N/A; N.E. N/A; M.A. 7%; S. 93%; M.W. N/A; S.W. N/A; W. N/A

University of North Carolina–Pembroke[1]

PO Box 1510
One University Drive
Pembroke, NC 28372
www.uncp.edu/grad
Public
Admissions: (910) 521-6271
Email: grad@uncp.edu
Financial aid: (910) 521-6255
Tuition: N/A
Room/board/expenses: N/A
Enrollment: N/A

University of North Carolina–Wilmington (Cameron)

601 S. College Road
Wilmington, NC 28403-5680
www.csb.uncw.edu/gradprograms
Public
Admissions: (910) 962-3903
Email: wilhelmc@uncw.edu
Financial aid: (910) 962-3177
Application deadline: 06/01
In-state tuition: total program: $18,900 (full time); $11,605 (part time)
Out-of-state tuition: total program: $18,900 (full time)
Room/board/expenses: $17,297
College-funded aid: Yes
International student aid: Yes
Full-time enrollment: 79
men: 52%; women: 48%; minorities: 14%; international: 27%
Part-time enrollment: 78
men: 64%; women: 36%; minorities: 12%; international: 0%
Acceptance rate (full time): 95%
Average GRE (full time): N/A verbal; N/A quantitative; N/A writing
Average GPA (full time): 3.26
Average age of entrants to full-time program: 25
Average months of prior work experience (full time): 20
TOEFL requirement: Yes
Minimum TOEFL score: 550
Most popular departments: consulting, finance, general management, marketing

Wake Forest University

PO Box 7659
Winston-Salem, NC 27109-7659
www.business.wfu.edu
Private
Admissions: (336) 758-5422
Email: busadmissions@wfu.edu
Financial aid: (336) 758-4424
Application deadline: rolling
Tuition: full time: N/A; part time: $38,799
Room/board/expenses: N/A
College-funded aid: Yes
International student aid: Yes
Full-time enrollment: N/A
Part-time enrollment: 311
men: 59%; women: 41%; minorities: 26%; international: 1%
Average GRE (full time): N/A verbal; N/A quantitative; N/A writing
TOEFL requirement: Yes
Minimum TOEFL score: N/A
Most popular departments: accounting, finance, general management, marketing

Western Carolina University

Forsyth Building
Cullowhee, NC 28723
businessgrad.wcu.edu
Public
Admissions: (828) 227-3174
Email: gradadmissions@email.wcu.edu
Financial aid: (828) 227-7290
Application deadline: 07/15
In-state tuition: full time: N/A; part time: N/A
Out-of-state tuition: full time: N/A
Room/board/expenses: N/A
College-funded aid: Yes
International student aid: Yes
Full-time enrollment: 45
men: 58%; women: 42%; minorities: 9%; international: 4%
Part-time enrollment: 77
men: 48%; women: 52%; minorities: 12%; international: 0%
Acceptance rate (full time): 76%
Average GMAT (full time): 424
Average GRE (full time): 150 verbal; 148 quantitative; 3.8 writing
Average GPA (full time): 3.41
Average age of entrants to full-time program: 27
TOEFL requirement: Yes
Minimum TOEFL score: 550

Winston-Salem State University[1]

RJR Center, Suite 109
Winston-Salem, NC 27110
www.wssu.edu/
Public
Admissions: (336) 750-3045
Email: graduate@wssu.edu
Financial aid: N/A
Tuition: N/A
Room/board/expenses: N/A
Enrollment: N/A

North Dakota State University

NDSU Department 2400
PO Box 6050
Fargo, ND 58108-6050
www.ndsu.edu/business/programs/graduate/mba/
Public
Admissions: (701) 231-7681
Email: paul.brown@ndsu.edu
Financial aid: N/A
Application deadline: rolling
In-state tuition: full time: $310/credit hour; part time: $310/credit hour
Out-of-state tuition: full time: $827/credit hour
Room/board/expenses: N/A
College-funded aid: Yes
International student aid: Yes
Full-time enrollment: 15
men: 60%; women: 40%; minorities: 7%; international: 80%
Part-time enrollment: 70
men: 54%; women: 46%; minorities: 7%; international: 7%
Acceptance rate (full time): 25%
Average GMAT (full time): 530

Average GRE (full time): N/A verbal; N/A quantitative; N/A writing
Average GPA (full time): 3.40
Average age of entrants to full-time program: 27
Average months of prior work experience (full time): 60
TOEFL requirement: Yes
Minimum TOEFL score: N/A
Most popular departments: general management

University of North Dakota

293 Centennial Drive
Stop 8098
Grand Forks, ND 58202-8098
business.und.edu/mba
Public
Admissions: (701) 777-3299
Email: laura.look@und.edu
Financial aid: (701) 777-4409
Application deadline: 05/15
In-state tuition: full time: $320/credit hour; part time: $320/credit hour
Out-of-state tuition: full time: $855/credit hour
Room/board/expenses: $9,300
College-funded aid: Yes
International student aid: Yes
Average student indebtedness at graduation: $25,802
Full-time enrollment: 9
men: 67%; women: 33%; minorities: 44%; international: 0%
Part-time enrollment: 18
men: 67%; women: 33%; minorities: 17%; international: 0%
Acceptance rate (full time): 89%
Average GMAT (full time): 580
Average GRE (full time): 154 verbal; 163 quantitative; 3.5 writing
Average GPA (full time): 3.61
Average age of entrants to full-time program: 25
TOEFL requirement: Yes
Minimum TOEFL score: N/A
Most popular departments: economics, entrepreneurship, general management, health care administration, marketing

OHIO

Bowling Green State University

371 Business Administration Building
Bowling Green, OH 43403-0001
www.bgsumba.com
Public
Admissions: (800) 247-8622
Email: mba@bgsu.edu
Financial aid: (419) 372-2651
Application deadline: 03/01
In-state tuition: total program: $22,644 (full time); $24,835 (part time)
Out-of-state tuition: total program: $33,944 (full time)
Room/board/expenses: N/A
College-funded aid: Yes
International student aid: Yes
Full-time enrollment: 46
men: 52%; women: 48%; minorities: 39%; international: 0%

Part-time enrollment: 90
men: 61%; women: 39%; minorities: 8%; international: 0%
Acceptance rate (full time): 45%
Average GMAT (full time): 492
Average GRE (full time): 145 verbal; 150 quantitative; 2.6 writing
Average GPA (full time): 3.80
Average age of entrants to full-time program: 25
Average months of prior work experience (full time): 18
TOEFL requirement: Yes
Minimum TOEFL score: 550
Most popular departments: accounting, finance, supply chain management/logistics

Case Western Reserve University (Weatherhead)

Peter B. Lewis Building
10900 Euclid Avenue
Cleveland, OH 44106-7235
www.weatherhead.case.edu
Private
Admissions: (216) 368-6702
Email: wsomadmissions@case.edu
Financial aid: (216) 368-8907
Application deadline: 05/31
Tuition: full time: $39,590; part time: $31,624
Room/board/expenses: $20,926
College-funded aid: Yes
International student aid: Yes
Average student indebtedness at graduation: $61,940
Full-time enrollment: 108
men: 70%; women: 30%; minorities: 19%; international: 42%
Part-time enrollment: 170
men: 63%; women: 37%; minorities: 15%; international: 6%
Acceptance rate (full time): 70%
Average GMAT (full time): 612
Average GRE (full time): 153 verbal; 153 quantitative; 4.2 writing
Average GPA (full time): 3.10
Average age of entrants to full-time program: 27
Average months of prior work experience (full time): 54
TOEFL requirement: Yes
Minimum TOEFL score: N/A
Most popular departments: accounting, finance, leadership, marketing, quantitative analysis/statistics and operations research
Mean starting base salary for 2017 full-time graduates: $81,244
Employment location for 2017 class: Intl. 5%; N.E. 2%; M.A. 5%; S. 9%; M.W. 66%; S.W. 5%; W. 9%

Cleveland State University (Ahuja)

1860 E. 18th Street, BU420
Cleveland, OH 44115
www.csuohio.edu/mba
Public
Admissions: (216) 687-5599
Email: cbacsu@csuohio.edu
Financial aid: (216) 687-5411
Application deadline: 08/17

In-state tuition: full time: $569/credit hour; part time: $569/credit hour
Out-of-state tuition: full time: $1,074/credit hour
Room/board/expenses: $15,818
College-funded aid: Yes
International student aid: Yes
Average student indebtedness at graduation: $35,562
Full-time enrollment: 205
men: 52%; women: 48%; minorities: N/A; international: N/A
Part-time enrollment: 341
men: 56%; women: 44%; minorities: N/A; international: N/A
Average GRE (full time): N/A verbal; N/A quantitative; N/A writing
TOEFL requirement: Yes
Minimum TOEFL score: 550
Most popular departments: accounting, finance, health care administration, production/operations management, supply chain management/logistics

John Carroll University (Boler)

1 John Carroll Boulevard
University Heights, OH 44118
boler.jcu.edu
Private
Admissions: (216) 397-1970
Email: gradbusiness@jcu.edu
Financial aid: (216) 397-4248
Application deadline: 07/15
Tuition: full time: N/A; part time: $870/credit hour
Room/board/expenses: N/A
College-funded aid: Yes
International student aid: Yes
Full-time enrollment: N/A
Part-time enrollment: 137
men: 67%; women: 33%; minorities: 15%; international: 7%
Average GRE (full time): N/A verbal; N/A quantitative; N/A writing
TOEFL requirement: Yes
Minimum TOEFL score: 550
Most popular departments: accounting, finance, human resources management, international business, marketing

Kent State University

PO Box 5190
Kent, OH 44242-0001
www.kent.edu/business
Public
Admissions: (330) 672-2282
Email: gradbus@kent.edu
Financial aid: (330) 672-2972
Application deadline: 03/15
In-state tuition: full time: $12,510; part time: N/A
Out-of-state tuition: full time: $21,596
Room/board/expenses: $12,750
College-funded aid: Yes
International student aid: Yes
Full-time enrollment: 57
men: 58%; women: 42%; minorities: 2%; international: 21%

Part-time enrollment: N/A
Acceptance rate (full time): 75%
Average GMAT (full time): 530
Average GRE (full time): 150 verbal; 151 quantitative; 3.7 writing
Average GPA (full time): 3.33
Average age of entrants to full-time program: 24
Average months of prior work experience (full time): 13
TOEFL requirement: Yes
Minimum TOEFL score: 550
Most popular departments: finance, general management, international business, management information systems, supply chain management/logistics
Mean starting base salary for 2017 full-time graduates: $35,866
Employment location for 2017 class: Intl. N/A; N.E. 9%; M.A. N/A; S. N/A; M.W. 64%; S.W. N/A; W. 27%

Miami University (Farmer)

800 E. High Street
Oxford, OH 45056
miamioh.edu/fsb/mba/
Public
Admissions: (513) 895-8876
Email: mba@miamioh.edu
Financial aid: (513) 529-8710
Application deadline: rolling
In-state tuition: full time: N/A; total program: $37,800 (part time)
Out-of-state tuition: full time: N/A
Room/board/expenses: N/A
College-funded aid: No
International student aid: No
Full-time enrollment: N/A
Part-time enrollment: 126
men: 72%; women: 28%; minorities: 21%; international: 3%
Average GRE (full time): N/A verbal; N/A quantitative; N/A writing
TOEFL requirement: Yes
Minimum TOEFL score: 550
Most popular departments: finance, general management, marketing

Ohio State University (Fisher)

100 Gerlach Hall
2108 Neil Avenue
Columbus, OH 43210-1144
fisher.osu.edu/graduate
Public
Admissions: (614) 292-8511
Email: mba@fisher.osu.edu
Financial aid: (614) 292-8511
Application deadline: 05/15
In-state tuition: full time: $31,139; part time: $1,574/credit hour
Out-of-state tuition: full time: $52,611
Room/board/expenses: $16,137
College-funded aid: Yes
International student aid: Yes
Average student indebtedness at graduation: $65,154
Full-time enrollment: 183
men: 69%; women: 31%; minorities: 15%; international: 31%

Part-time enrollment: 365
men: 64%; women: 36%; minorities: 18%; international: 10%
Acceptance rate (full time): 37%
Average GMAT (full time): 670
Average GRE (full time): 157 verbal; 157 quantitative; N/A writing
Average GPA (full time): 3.47
Average age of entrants to full-time program: 28
Average months of prior work experience (full time): 64
TOEFL requirement: Yes
Minimum TOEFL score: 600
Most popular departments: finance, leadership, marketing, production/operations management, supply chain management/logistics
Mean starting base salary for 2017 full-time graduates: $96,034
Employment location for 2017 class: Intl. 7%; N.E. 4%; M.A. 6%; S. 4%; M.W. 60%; S.W. 5%; W. 15%

Ohio University

1 Ohio University
College of Business Annex, 351
Athens, OH 45701
www.business.ohio.edu
Public
Admissions: (740) 593-2053
Email: mba@ohio.edu
Financial aid: (740) 593-4141
Application deadline: 03/01
In-state tuition: total program: $19,677 (full time); $40,551 (part time)
Out-of-state tuition: total program: $31,665 (full time)
Room/board/expenses: $15,700
College-funded aid: Yes
International student aid: Yes
Average student indebtedness at graduation: $31,110
Full-time enrollment: 44
men: 64%; women: 36%; minorities: 9%; international: 23%
Part-time enrollment: 102
men: 57%; women: 43%; minorities: 17%; international: 4%
Acceptance rate (full time): 36%
Average GMAT (full time): 528
Average GRE (full time): N/A verbal; N/A quantitative; N/A writing
Average GPA (full time): 3.50
Average age of entrants to full-time program: 23
Average months of prior work experience (full time): 48
TOEFL requirement: Yes
Minimum TOEFL score: 550
Most popular departments: finance, general management, health care administration, other

University of Akron

CBA 412
Akron, OH 44325-4805
mba.uakron.edu
Public
Admissions: (330) 972-7043
Email: gradcba@uakron.edu
Financial aid: (330) 972-7032
Application deadline: 07/15

In-state tuition: full time: N/A; part time: $461/credit hour
Out-of-state tuition: full time: N/A
Room/board/expenses: N/A
College-funded aid: No
International student aid: Yes
Full-time enrollment: N/A
Part-time enrollment: 310
men: 64%; women: 36%; minorities: 11%; international: 20%
Average GRE (full time): N/A verbal; N/A quantitative; N/A writing
TOEFL requirement: Yes
Minimum TOEFL score: 550
Most popular departments: accounting, general management, management information systems, tax, other

University of Cincinnati (Lindner)

606 Lindner Hall
2925 Campus Green Drive
Cincinnati, OH 45221-0020
www.business.uc.edu/mba
Public
Admissions: (513) 556-7024
Email: graduate@uc.edu
Financial aid: (513) 556-6982
Application deadline: 06/30
In-state tuition: total program: $31,437 (full time); part time: $806/credit hour
Out-of-state tuition: total program: $43,194 (full time)
Room/board/expenses: $20,000
College-funded aid: Yes
International student aid: Yes
Average student indebtedness at graduation: $26,336
Full-time enrollment: 83
men: 67%; women: 33%; minorities: 16%; international: 30%
Part-time enrollment: 130
men: 65%; women: 35%; minorities: 17%; international: 6%
Acceptance rate (full time): 52%
Average GMAT (full time): 670
Average GRE (full time): 161 verbal; 161 quantitative; 4.0 writing
Average GPA (full time): 3.45
Average age of entrants to full-time program: 26
Average months of prior work experience (full time): 31
TOEFL requirement: Yes
Minimum TOEFL score: 600
Most popular departments: entrepreneurship, health care administration, marketing, real estate, quantitative analysis/statistics and operations research
Mean starting base salary for 2017 full-time graduates: $67,129
Employment location for 2017 class: Intl. 0%; N.E. 0%; M.A. 2%; S. 11%; M.W. 78%; S.W. 9%; W. 0%

University of Dayton

300 College Park Avenue
Dayton, OH 45469-2234
business.udayton.edu/mba
Private
Admissions: (937) 229-3733
Email: mba@udayton.edu

Financial aid: (937) 229-4311
Application deadline: rolling
Tuition: full time: $980/credit hour; part time: $980/credit hour
Room/board/expenses: N/A
College-funded aid: Yes
International student aid: Yes
Full-time enrollment: 53
men: 57%; women: 43%; minorities: N/A; international: N/A
Part-time enrollment: 83
men: 60%; women: 40%; minorities: N/A; international: N/A
Acceptance rate (full time): 50%
Average GMAT (full time): 521
Average GRE (full time): 154 verbal; 152 quantitative; 4.0 writing
Average GPA (full time): 3.20
Average age of entrants to full-time program: 23
TOEFL requirement: Yes
Minimum TOEFL score: 550

University of Toledo

Stranahan Hall North
Room 3130
Toledo, OH 43606-3390
utoledo.edu/business/graduate
Public
Admissions: (419) 530-5689
Email: COBIGradPrograms@utoledo.edu
Financial aid: (419) 530-8700
Application deadline: 08/01
In-state tuition: full time: $537/credit hour; part time: N/A
Out-of-state tuition: full time: $1,003/credit hour
Room/board/expenses: N/A
College-funded aid: Yes
International student aid: Yes
Full-time enrollment: 397
men: 54%; women: 46%; minorities: 7%; international: 43%
Part-time enrollment: N/A
Acceptance rate (full time): 71%
Average GMAT (full time): 448
Average GRE (full time): N/A verbal; N/A quantitative; N/A writing
Average GPA (full time): 3.38
Average age of entrants to full-time program: 26
TOEFL requirement: Yes
Minimum TOEFL score: 550
Mean starting base salary for 2017 full-time graduates: $52,500

Wright State University (Soin)

3640 Colonel Glenn Highway
Dayton, OH 45435-0001
www.wright.edu/business
Public
Admissions: (937) 775-2953
Email: mba@wright.edu
Financial aid: (937) 775-5721
Application deadline: 08/01
In-state tuition: full time: $13,880; part time: $640/credit hour
Out-of-state tuition: full time: $23,578
Room/board/expenses: $11,376
College-funded aid: Yes
Average student indebtedness at graduation: $42,020

Full-time enrollment: 501
men: 53%; women: 47%; minorities: 21%; international: 14%
Part-time enrollment: 159
men: 59%; women: 41%; minorities: 15%; international: 5%
Acceptance rate (full time): 74%
Average GMAT (full time): 456
Average GRE (full time): 148 verbal; 150 quantitative; 3.5 writing
Average GPA (full time): 3.03
Average age of entrants to full-time program: 29
TOEFL requirement: Yes
Minimum TOEFL score: N/A
Most popular departments: economics, finance, general management, marketing, quantitative analysis/statistics and operations research

Xavier University (Williams)

3800 Victory Parkway
Cincinnati, OH 45207-1221
www.xavier.edu/MBA
Private
Admissions: (513) 745-4800
Email: mbaadmit@xavier.edu
Financial aid: (513) 745-3142
Application deadline: 08/01
Tuition: full time: $799/credit hour; part time: $799/credit hour
Room/board/expenses: $15,200
College-funded aid: Yes
International student aid: Yes
Average student indebtedness at graduation: $14,112
Full-time enrollment: 34
men: 56%; women: 44%; minorities: 12%; international: 29%
Part-time enrollment: 546
men: 68%; women: 32%; minorities: 18%; international: 3%
Acceptance rate (full time): 90%
Average GMAT (full time): 481
Average GRE (full time): 149 verbal; 148 quantitative; 3.5 writing
Average GPA (full time): 3.21
Average age of entrants to full-time program: 27
Average months of prior work experience (full time): 60
TOEFL requirement: Yes
Minimum TOEFL score: 550
Most popular departments: finance, general management, leadership, marketing, quantitative analysis/statistics and operations research
Mean starting base salary for 2017 full-time graduates: $48,500
Employment location for 2017 class: Intl. 0%; N.E. 33%; M.A. 0%; S. 0%; M.W. 67%; S.W. 0%; W. 0%

Youngstown State University (Williamson)[1]

1 University Plaza
Youngstown, OH 44555
web.ysu.edu/mba
Public
Admissions: N/A

Email: graduateschool@ysu.edu
Financial aid: N/A
Tuition: N/A
Room/board/expenses: N/A
Enrollment: N/A

OKLAHOMA

Oklahoma City University

2501 N Blackwelder
Oklahoma City, OK 73106
www.okcu.edu/mba/
Private
Admissions: (405) 208-5351
Email: gadmissions@okcu.edu
Financial aid: (405) 208-5211
Application deadline: rolling
Tuition: full time: $590/credit hour; part time: $590/credit hour
Room/board/expenses: $11,124
College-funded aid: Yes
International student aid: No
Average student indebtedness at graduation: $26,825
Full-time enrollment: 29
men: 62%; women: 38%; minorities: 17%; international: 55%
Part-time enrollment: 101
men: 55%; women: 45%; minorities: 28%; international: 0%
Acceptance rate (full time): 72%
Average GRE (full time): N/A verbal; N/A quantitative; N/A writing
Average age of entrants to full-time program: 27
TOEFL requirement: Yes
Minimum TOEFL score: N/A
Mean starting base salary for 2017 full-time graduates: $46,000

Oklahoma State University (Spears)

102 Gundersen
Stillwater, OK 74078-4022
business.okstate.edu/watson/mba/index.html
Public
Admissions: (405) 744-2951
Email: spearsmasters@okstate.edu
Financial aid: (405) 744-6604
Application deadline: 04/15
In-state tuition: full time: $223/credit hour; part time: $223/credit hour
Out-of-state tuition: full time: $849/credit hour
Room/board/expenses: $14,690
College-funded aid: Yes
International student aid: Yes
Average student indebtedness at graduation: $24,095
Full-time enrollment: 79
men: 62%; women: 38%; minorities: 8%; international: 20%
Part-time enrollment: 86
men: 67%; women: 33%; minorities: 10%; international: 3%
Acceptance rate (full time): 63%
Average GMAT (full time): 552
Average GRE (full time): 151 verbal; 155 quantitative; 3.3 writing
Average GPA (full time): 3.43

Average age of entrants to full-time program: 25
Average months of prior work experience (full time): 50
TOEFL requirement: Yes
Minimum TOEFL score: 575
Most popular departments: entrepreneurship, finance, human resources management, not-for-profit management, other
Mean starting base salary for 2017 full-time graduates: $58,142
Employment location for 2017 class: Intl. 7%; N.E. 7%; M.A. N/A; S. 14%; M.W. 14%; S.W. 50%; W. 7%

Southeastern Oklahoma State University[1]

1405 N. Fourth Avenue
PMB 4205
Durant, OK 74701-0609
www.se.edu/bus/
Public
Admissions: (580) 745-2176
Email: kluke@se.edu
Financial aid: (580) 745-2186
Tuition: N/A
Room/board/expenses: N/A
Enrollment: N/A

University of Central Oklahoma

100 N University Drive, Box 115
Edmond, OK 73034
business.uco.edu/degrees/mba/
Private
Admissions: (405) 974-5445
Email: mba@uco.edu
Financial aid: (405) 974-2727
Application deadline: rolling
Tuition: full time: $379/credit hour; part time: $379/credit hour
Room/board/expenses: $18,196
College-funded aid: Yes
International student aid: Yes
Average student indebtedness at graduation: $41,700
Full-time enrollment: 77
men: 58%; women: 42%; minorities: 18%; international: 14%
Part-time enrollment: 28
men: 46%; women: 54%; minorities: 50%; international: 11%
Average GRE (full time): N/A verbal; N/A quantitative; N/A writing
Average age of entrants to full-time program: 30
TOEFL requirement: Yes
Minimum TOEFL score: 557
Most popular departments: general management, health care administration, other

University of Oklahoma (Price)

Adams Hall
307 West Brooks
Norman, OK 73019-4004
ou.edu/mba
Public
Admissions: (405) 325-5623
Email: meganallen@ou.edu
Financial aid: (405) 325-4521

Application deadline: 05/15
In-state tuition: total program: $34,000 (full time); $27,000 (part time)
Out-of-state tuition: total program: $54,000 (full time)
Room/board/expenses: $15,000
College-funded aid: Yes
International student aid: Yes
Full-time enrollment: 80 men: 69%; women: 31%; minorities: 16%; international: 15%
Part-time enrollment: 127 men: 80%; women: 20%; minorities: 13%; international: 1%
Acceptance rate (full time): 59%
Average GMAT (full time): 639
Average GRE (full time): 158 verbal; 157 quantitative; N/A writing
Average GPA (full time): 3.60
Average age of entrants to full-time program: 24
Average months of prior work experience (full time): 16
TOEFL requirement: Yes
Minimum TOEFL score: 600
Most popular departments: entrepreneurship, finance, health care administration, management information systems, other
Mean starting base salary for 2017 full-time graduates: $73,969
Employment location for 2017 class: Intl. 5%; N.E. N/A; M.A. 5%; S. 10%; M.W. 5%; S.W. 70%; W. 5%

University of Tulsa (Collins)

800 S. Tucker Drive
Tulsa, OK 74104-9700
www.utulsa.edu/graduate/business
Private
Admissions: (918) 631-2242
Email: graduate-business@utulsa.edu
Financial aid: (918) 631-2526
Application deadline: 07/01
Tuition: full time: $900/credit hour; part time: $900/credit hour
Room/board/expenses: $19,510
College-funded aid: Yes
International student aid: Yes
Average student indebtedness at graduation: $47,484
Full-time enrollment: 36 men: 61%; women: 39%; minorities: 17%; international: 17%
Part-time enrollment: 48 men: 69%; women: 31%; minorities: 8%; international: 4%
Acceptance rate (full time): 67%
Average GMAT (full time): 590
Average GRE (full time): N/A verbal; N/A quantitative; N/A writing
Average GPA (full time): 3.50
Average age of entrants to full-time program: 24
Average months of prior work experience (full time): 33
TOEFL requirement: Yes
Minimum TOEFL score: 575
Most popular departments: accounting, finance, general management, marketing, other

Mean starting base salary for 2017 full-time graduates: $67,526
Employment location for 2017 class: Intl. 13%; N.E. N/A; M.A. N/A; S. 13%; M.W. 13%; S.W. 63%; W. N/A

OREGON

Oregon State University

443 Austin Hall
Corvallis, OR 97331
business.oregonstate.edu/mba/
Public
Admissions: (541) 737-5510
Email: mba.info@oregonstate.edu
Financial aid: (541) 737-2241
Application deadline: 08/20
In-state tuition: full time: $20,784; part time: $777/credit hour
Out-of-state tuition: full time: $35,040
Room/board/expenses: $15,678
College-funded aid: Yes
International student aid: Yes
Average student indebtedness at graduation: $40,106
Full-time enrollment: 150 men: 55%; women: 45%; minorities: 20%; international: 33%
Part-time enrollment: 44 men: 52%; women: 48%; minorities: 30%; international: 0%
Acceptance rate (full time): 36%
Average GMAT (full time): 559
Average GRE (full time): 155 verbal; 159 quantitative; 4.1 writing
Average GPA (full time): 3.40
Average age of entrants to full-time program: 29
Average months of prior work experience (full time): 80
TOEFL requirement: Yes
Minimum TOEFL score: 575
Most popular departments: entrepreneurship, finance, leadership, supply chain management/logistics, quantitative analysis/statistics and operations research
Mean starting base salary for 2017 full-time graduates: $81,416
Employment location for 2017 class: Intl. 0%; N.E. 0%; M.A. 0%; S. 0%; M.W. 0%; S.W. 0%; W. 100%

Portland State University

PO Box 751
Portland, OR 97207-0751
www.pdx.edu/sba/the-portland-mba
Public
Admissions: (503) 725-8190
Email: gradadmissions.sba@pdx.edu
Financial aid: (503) 725-5446
Application deadline: 05/01
In-state tuition: full time: $637/credit hour; part time: $637/credit hour
Out-of-state tuition: full time: $765/credit hour
Room/board/expenses: $20,000

College-funded aid: Yes
International student aid: Yes
Full-time enrollment: 28 men: 50%; women: 50%; minorities: 21%; international: 18%
Part-time enrollment: 43 men: 58%; women: 42%; minorities: 21%; international: 0%
Acceptance rate (full time): 52%
Average GMAT (full time): 572
Average GRE (full time): 156 verbal; 152 quantitative; 3.8 writing
Average GPA (full time): 3.26
Average age of entrants to full-time program: 30
Average months of prior work experience (full time): 75
TOEFL requirement: Yes
Minimum TOEFL score: 550
Most popular departments: entrepreneurship, finance, sports business, supply chain management/logistics, other
Mean starting base salary for 2017 full-time graduates: $65,296
Employment location for 2017 class: Intl. 10%; N.E. N/A; M.A. N/A; S. N/A; M.W. 20%; S.W. 10%; W. 60%

University of Oregon (Lundquist)

1208 University of Oregon
Eugene, OR 97403-1208
business.uoregon.edu/mba/
Public
Admissions: (541) 346-3306
Email: mbainfo@uoregon.edu
Financial aid: (541) 346-3221
Application deadline: N/A
In-state tuition: full time: $31,953; part time: $856/credit hour
Out-of-state tuition: full time: $42,849
Room/board/expenses: $12,921
College-funded aid: Yes
International student aid: Yes
Average student indebtedness at graduation: $63,646
Full-time enrollment: 126 men: 60%; women: 40%; minorities: 0%; international: 13%
Part-time enrollment: 4 men: 25%; women: 75%; minorities: 0%; international: 0%
Acceptance rate (full time): 51%
Average GMAT (full time): 588
Average GRE (full time): 154 verbal; 153 quantitative; 4.0 writing
Average GPA (full time): 3.39
Average age of entrants to full-time program: 27
Average months of prior work experience (full time): 49
TOEFL requirement: Yes
Minimum TOEFL score: 600
Most popular departments: accounting, entrepreneurship, finance, sports business, other
Mean starting base salary for 2017 full-time graduates: $71,477

University of Portland (Pamplin)

5000 N. Willamette Boulevard
Portland, OR 97203-5798
business.up.edu
Private
Admissions: (503) 943-7224
Email: bus-grad@up.edu
Financial aid: (503) 943-7311
Application deadline: 07/15
Tuition: full time: $1,271/credit hour; part time: $1,271/credit hour
Room/board/expenses: $11,000
College-funded aid: Yes
International student aid: Yes
Average student indebtedness at graduation: $50,145
Full-time enrollment: 36 men: 58%; women: 42%; minorities: 22%; international: 53%
Part-time enrollment: 108 men: 65%; women: 35%; minorities: 19%; international: 5%
Acceptance rate (full time): 88%
Average GMAT (full time): 551
Average GRE (full time): 149 verbal; 152 quantitative; 4.0 writing
Average GPA (full time): 3.45
Average age of entrants to full-time program: 27
Average months of prior work experience (full time): 53
TOEFL requirement: Yes
Minimum TOEFL score: 570
Most popular departments: finance, manufacturing and technology management, marketing, production/operations management, other

Willamette University (Atkinson)

900 State Street
Salem, OR 97301-3922
www.willamette.edu/mba
Private
Admissions: (503) 370-6620
Email: mba-admission@willamette.edu
Financial aid: (503) 370-6273
Application deadline: 05/01
Tuition: full time: $40,650; total program: $71,640 (part time)
Room/board/expenses: $13,078
College-funded aid: Yes
International student aid: Yes
Average student indebtedness at graduation: $63,823
Full-time enrollment: 131 men: 55%; women: 45%; minorities: 21%; international: 25%
Part-time enrollment: 119 men: 45%; women: 55%; minorities: 19%; international: 0%
Acceptance rate (full time): 60%
Average GMAT (full time): 552
Average GRE (full time): 151 verbal; 149 quantitative; 3.6 writing
Average GPA (full time): 3.13
Average age of entrants to full-time program: 26
Average months of prior work experience (full time): 18

TOEFL requirement: Yes
Minimum TOEFL score: 580
Most popular departments: accounting, entrepreneurship, finance, marketing, production/operations management
Mean starting base salary for 2017 full-time graduates: $55,306
Employment location for 2017 class: Intl. 0%; N.E. 3%; M.A. 3%; S. 0%; M.W. 0%; S.W. 3%; W. 91%

PENNSYLVANIA

Bloomsburg University of Pennsylvania

Sutliff Hall, Room 363
400 Second Street
Bloomsburg, PA 17815-1301
cob.bloomu.edu/
Public
Admissions: (570) 389-4394
Email: gradadmissions@bloomu.edu
Financial aid: (570) 389-4297
Application deadline: 06/01
In-state tuition: full time: N/A; part time: $500/credit hour
Out-of-state tuition: full time: N/A
Room/board/expenses: N/A
College-funded aid: Yes
International student aid: Yes
Full-time enrollment: N/A
Part-time enrollment: 36 men: 56%; women: 44%; minorities: N/A; international: N/A
Average GRE (full time): N/A verbal; N/A quantitative; N/A writing
TOEFL requirement: Yes
Minimum TOEFL score: 590

Carnegie Mellon University (Tepper)

5000 Forbes Avenue
Pittsburgh, PA 15213
www.tepper.cmu.edu
Private
Admissions: (412) 268-2272
Email: mba-admissions@andrew.cmu.edu
Financial aid: (412) 268-7581
Application deadline: 03/09
Tuition: full time: $64,834; part time: $1,998/credit hour
Room/board/expenses: $21,944
College-funded aid: Yes
International student aid: Yes
Full-time enrollment: 446 men: 72%; women: 28%; minorities: 26%; international: 34%
Part-time enrollment: 119 men: 77%; women: 23%; minorities: 19%; international: 10%
Acceptance rate (full time): 30%
Average GMAT (full time): 691
Average GRE (full time): 159 verbal; 162 quantitative; 4.0 writing
Average GPA (full time): 3.30
Average age of entrants to full-time program: 29
Average months of prior work experience (full time): 68
TOEFL requirement: Yes

Minimum TOEFL score: 600
Most popular departments: entrepreneurship, finance, marketing, management information systems, organizational behavior
Mean starting base salary for 2017 full-time graduates: $119,402

Clarion University of Pennsylvania

840 Wood Street
Clarion, PA 16214
www.clarion.edu/admissions/graduate
Public
Admissions: (814) 393-2337
Email: gradstudies@clarion.edu
Financial aid: (800) 672-7171
Application deadline: rolling
In-state tuition: full time: $500/credit hour; part time: $500/credit hour
Out-of-state tuition: full time: $540/credit hour
Room/board/expenses: N/A
College-funded aid: Yes
International student aid: Yes
Average student indebtedness at graduation: $31,768
Full-time enrollment: 9
men: 56%; women: 44%; minorities: 0%; international: 0%
Part-time enrollment: 104
men: 49%; women: 51%; minorities: 5%; international: 3%
Acceptance rate (full time): 100%
Average GRE (full time): N/A verbal; N/A quantitative; N/A writing
Average GPA (full time): 3.83
Average age of entrants to full-time program: 22
TOEFL requirement: Yes
Minimum TOEFL score: 550
Most popular departments: accounting, entrepreneurship, finance, general management, health care administration

Drexel University (LeBow)

3141 Chestnut Street
Philadelphia, PA 19104
www.lebow.drexel.edu/
Private
Admissions: (215) 895-6804
Email: mba@drexel.edu
Financial aid: (215) 571-4545
Application deadline: 09/01
Tuition: total program: $64,000 (full time); part time: $1,228/credit hour
Room/board/expenses: N/A
College-funded aid: Yes
International student aid: Yes
Average student indebtedness at graduation: $51,360
Full-time enrollment: 42
men: 60%; women: 40%; minorities: 19%; international: 38%
Part-time enrollment: 143
men: 52%; women: 48%; minorities: 24%; international: 3%
Acceptance rate (full time): 45%
Average GMAT (full time): 570
Average GRE (full time): 151 verbal; 151 quantitative; N/A writing
Average GPA (full time): 3.20

Average age of entrants to full-time program: 27
Average months of prior work experience (full time): 60
TOEFL requirement: Yes
Minimum TOEFL score: 577
Most popular departments: entrepreneurship, finance, general management, marketing, other
Mean starting base salary for 2017 full-time graduates: $65,625

Duquesne University (Palumbo-Donahue)

600 Forbes Avenue
704 Rockwell Hall
Pittsburgh, PA 15282
www.duq.edu/academics/schools/business/graduate
Private
Admissions: (412) 396-6276
Email: grad-bus@duq.edu
Financial aid: (412) 396-6607
Application deadline: 07/01
Tuition: total program: $50,589 (full time); part time: $1,259/credit hour
Room/board/expenses: $15,714
College-funded aid: Yes
International student aid: Yes
Average student indebtedness at graduation: $53,452
Full-time enrollment: 16
men: 63%; women: 38%; minorities: 13%; international: 13%
Part-time enrollment: 199
men: 65%; women: 35%; minorities: 7%; international: 8%
Acceptance rate (full time): 86%
Average GMAT (full time): 555
Average GRE (full time): 152 verbal; 147 quantitative; 3.8 writing
Average GPA (full time): 3.40
Average age of entrants to full-time program: 27
Average months of prior work experience (full time): 54
TOEFL requirement: Yes
Minimum TOEFL score: 577
Most popular departments: general management, other
Mean starting base salary for 2017 full-time graduates: $50,000
Employment location for 2017 class: Intl. N/A; N.E. N/A; M.A. 67%; S. N/A; M.W. N/A; S.W. 33%; W. N/A

Indiana University of Pennsylvania (Eberly)

664 Pratt Drive, Room 402
Indiana, PA 15705
www.eberly.iup.edu/mba
Public
Admissions: (724) 357-2522
Email: iup-mba@iup.edu
Financial aid: (724) 357-2218
Application deadline: rolling
In-state tuition: full time: $500/credit hour; part time: $500/credit hour
Out-of-state tuition: full time: $750/credit hour
Room/board/expenses: $15,142
College-funded aid: Yes
International student aid: Yes
Average student indebtedness at graduation: $28,160

Full-time enrollment: 150
men: 66%; women: 34%; minorities: 3%; international: 83%
Part-time enrollment: 10
men: 40%; women: 60%; minorities: 20%; international: 0%
Acceptance rate (full time): 71%
Average GMAT (full time): 463
Average GRE (full time): N/A verbal; N/A quantitative; N/A writing
Average age of entrants to full-time program: 22
TOEFL requirement: Yes
Minimum TOEFL score: 540
Most popular departments: finance, human resources management, marketing, supply chain management/logistics

King's College (McGowan)[1]

133 N. River Street
Wilkes-Barre, PA 18711
www.kings.edu/academics/colleges_and_programs/business
Private
Admissions: (570) 208-5991
Email: gradprograms@kings.edu
Financial aid: N/A
Tuition: N/A
Room/board/expenses: N/A
Enrollment: N/A

Kutztown University of Pennsylvania

PO Box 730
Kutztown, PA 19530
www.kutztown.edu/admissions/graduate-admissions.htm
Public
Admissions: (610) 683-4200
Email: graduate@kutztown.edu
Financial aid: (610) 683-4077
Application deadline: 08/01
In-state tuition: full time: $500/credit hour; part time: $500/credit hour
Out-of-state tuition: full time: $750/credit hour
Room/board/expenses: N/A
College-funded aid: Yes
International student aid: Yes
Full-time enrollment: 14
men: 64%; women: 36%; minorities: 29%; international: 7%
Part-time enrollment: 17
men: 65%; women: 35%; minorities: 6%; international: 18%
Acceptance rate (full time): 66%
Average GMAT (full time): 440
Average GRE (full time): 153 verbal; 150 quantitative; 4.0 writing
Average GPA (full time): 2.63
Average age of entrants to full-time program: 26
TOEFL requirement: Yes
Minimum TOEFL score: 550
Most popular departments: accounting, finance, human resources management, marketing, production/operations management

La Salle University

1900 W. Olney Avenue
Philadelphia, PA 19141
www.lasalle.edu/business/programs/mba
Private
Admissions: (215) 951-1057
Email: mba@lasalle.edu
Financial aid: (215) 951-1070
Application deadline: rolling
Tuition: full time: $24,280; part time: $1,000/credit hour
Room/board/expenses: N/A
College-funded aid: Yes
International student aid: Yes
Average student indebtedness at graduation: $20,201
Full-time enrollment: 63
men: 52%; women: 48%; minorities: 32%; international: 35%
Part-time enrollment: 182
men: 48%; women: 52%; minorities: 22%; international: 0%
Acceptance rate (full time): 94%
Average GMAT (full time): 456
Average GRE (full time): 143 verbal; 139 quantitative; 3.0 writing
Average GPA (full time): 3.20
Average age of entrants to full-time program: 24
Average months of prior work experience (full time): 30
TOEFL requirement: Yes
Minimum TOEFL score: 573
Most popular departments: accounting, finance, general management, marketing, other
Mean starting base salary for 2017 full-time graduates: $55,174
Employment location for 2017 class: Intl. 7%; N.E. 2%; M.A. 89%; S. 2%; M.W. N/A; S.W. N/A; W. N/A

Lehigh University

621 Taylor Street
Bethlehem, PA 18015
www.lehigh.edu/mba
Private
Admissions: (610) 758-4386
Email: mba.admissions@lehigh.edu
Financial aid: (610) 758-5285
Application deadline: 08/01
Tuition: full time: $1,075/credit hour; part time: $1,075/credit hour
Room/board/expenses: $18,170
College-funded aid: Yes
International student aid: Yes
Average student indebtedness at graduation: $0
Full-time enrollment: 14
men: 50%; women: 50%; minorities: 0%; international: 50%
Part-time enrollment: 167
men: 75%; women: 25%; minorities: 16%; international: 6%
Acceptance rate (full time): 31%
Average GRE (full time): N/A verbal; N/A quantitative; N/A writing
Average age of entrants to full-time program: 32
Average months of prior work experience (full time): 72
TOEFL requirement: Yes

Minimum TOEFL score: 600
Most popular departments: entrepreneurship, finance, marketing, supply chain management/logistics, other
Mean starting base salary for 2017 full-time graduates: $95,333

Pennsylvania State University–Erie, The Behrend College (Black)

5101 Jordan Road
Erie, PA 16563
behrend.psu.edu/
Public
Admissions: (814) 898-7255
Email: behrend.admissions@psu.edu
Financial aid: (814) 898-6162
Application deadline: 12/19
In-state tuition: full time: $874/credit hour; part time: $874/credit hour
Out-of-state tuition: full time: $1,366/credit hour
Room/board/expenses: N/A
College-funded aid: Yes
International student aid: Yes
Average student indebtedness at graduation: $48,022
Full-time enrollment: N/A
Part-time enrollment: 122
men: 70%; women: 30%; minorities: 5%; international: 0%
Average GRE (full time): N/A verbal; N/A quantitative; N/A writing
TOEFL requirement: Yes
Minimum TOEFL score: 550

Pennsylvania State University–Great Valley[1]

30 E. Swedesford Road
Malvern, PA 19355
www.sgps.psu.edu
Public
Admissions: (610) 648-3242
Email: gvadmiss@psu.edu
Financial aid: N/A
Tuition: N/A
Room/board/expenses: N/A
Enrollment: N/A

Pennsylvania State University–Harrisburg

777 W. Harrisburg Pike
Middletown, PA 17057-4898
harrisburg.psu.edu/mba
Public
Admissions: (717) 948-6250
Email: mbahbg@psu.edu
Financial aid: (717) 948-6307
Application deadline: 07/18
In-state tuition: full time: N/A; part time: $874/credit hour
Out-of-state tuition: full time: N/A
Room/board/expenses: N/A
College-funded aid: Yes
International student aid: Yes
Full-time enrollment: N/A
Part-time enrollment: 160
men: 68%; women: 33%; minorities: 8%; international: 0%

Average GRE (full
time): N/A verbal; N/A
quantitative; N/A writing
TOEFL requirement: Yes
Minimum TOEFL score: 550
Most popular departments:
accounting, finance, general
management, management
information systems, supply
chain management/logistics

Pennsylvania State University–University Park (Smeal)

220 Business Building
University Park, PA 16802-3000
www.smeal.psu.edu/mba
Public
Admissions: (814) 863-0474
Email: smealmba@psu.edu
Financial aid: (814) 865-6301
Application deadline: 04/01
In-state tuition: full time:
$26,650; part time: N/A
Out-of-state tuition:
full time: $42,094
Room/board/expenses: $21,950
College-funded aid: Yes
International student aid: Yes
Average student indebtedness
at graduation: $35,128
Full-time enrollment: 115
men: 70%; women:
30%; minorities: 16%;
international: 36%
Part-time enrollment: N/A
Acceptance rate (full time): 17%
Average GMAT (full time): 661
Average GRE (full
time): 157 verbal; 157
quantitative; 4.1 writing
Average GPA (full time): 3.47
Average age of entrants to
full-time program: 29
Average months of prior work
experience (full time): 63
TOEFL requirement: Yes
Minimum TOEFL score: 600
Most popular departments:
consulting, finance, leadership,
marketing, supply chain
management/logistics
Mean starting base salary for 2017
full-time graduates: $105,462
Employment location for 2017
class: Intl. 2%; N.E. 15%;
M.A. 9%; S. 20%; M.W.
17%; S.W. 19%; W. 19%

Robert Morris University

6001 University Boulevard
Moon Township, PA 15108-1189
admissions.rmu.edu/
onlinehome/mba-and-business
Private
Admissions: (800) 762-0097
Email: enrollmentoffice@
rmu.edu
Financial aid: (412) 397-6250
Application deadline: N/A
Tuition: full time: N/A; part
time: $925/credit hour
Room/board/expenses: N/A
College-funded aid: Yes
International student aid: Yes
Full-time enrollment: N/A

Part-time enrollment: 164
men: 63%; women: 37%;
minorities: 8%; international: 5%
Average GRE (full
time): N/A verbal; N/A
quantitative; N/A writing
TOEFL requirement: Yes
Minimum TOEFL score: 550
Most popular departments:
general management, human
resources management, tax

Shippensburg University of Pennsylvania (Grove)

1871 Old Main Drive
Shippensburg, PA 17257
www.ship.edu/mba
Public
Admissions: (717) 477-1231
Email: admiss@ship.edu
Financial aid: (717) 477-1131
Application deadline: N/A
In-state tuition: full time:
$500/credit hour; part
time: $500/credit hour
Out-of-state tuition: full
time: $750/credit hour
Room/board/expenses: $10,331
College-funded aid: Yes
International student aid: Yes
Full-time enrollment: 80
men: 74%; women:
26%; minorities: 3%;
international: 28%
Part-time enrollment: 176
men: 60%; women: 40%;
minorities: 7%; international: 0%
Acceptance rate (full time): 78%
Average GMAT (full time): 516
Average GRE (full
time): N/A verbal; N/A
quantitative; N/A writing
Average GPA (full time): 3.09
Average age of entrants to
full-time program: 30
Average months of prior work
experience (full time): 80
TOEFL requirement: Yes
Minimum TOEFL score: 500
Most popular departments:
finance, health care
administration, management
information systems, supply
chain management/logistics

St. Joseph's University (Haub)

5600 City Avenue
Philadelphia, PA 19131
www.sju.edu/haubmba
Private
Admissions: (610) 660-1690
Email: sjumba@sju.edu
Financial aid: (610) 660-1349
Application deadline: 07/15
Tuition: full time: N/A; part
time: $1,023/credit hour
Room/board/expenses: N/A
College-funded aid: Yes
International student aid: Yes
Full-time enrollment: N/A
Part-time enrollment: 421
men: 60%; women:
40%; minorities: 14%;
international: 36%
Average GRE (full
time): N/A verbal; N/A
quantitative; N/A writing

TOEFL requirement: Yes
Minimum TOEFL score: 550
Most popular departments:
finance, general management,
human resources management,
marketing, management
information systems

Temple University (Fox)

Alter Hall
1801 Liacouras Walk
Philadelphia, PA 19122-6083
sbm.temple.edu/
Public
Admissions: (215) 204-7678
Email: foxinfo@temple.edu
Financial aid: (215) 204-7678
Application deadline: 12/10
In-state tuition: full time: N/A;
part time: N/A/credit hour
Out-of-state tuition: full time: N/A;
part time: N/A/credit hour
Room/board/expenses: N/A
College-funded aid: Yes
International student aid: Yes
Full-time enrollment: N/A
Part-time enrollment: N/A
Average GRE (full
time): N/A verbal; N/A
quantitative; N/A writing
TOEFL requirement: Yes
Minimum TOEFL score: 600
Most popular departments:
entrepreneurship, finance,
international business,
marketing, quantitative
analysis/statistics and
operations research

University of Pennsylvania (Wharton)

420 Jon M. Huntsman Hall
3730 Walnut Street
Philadelphia, PA 19104
www.wharton.upenn.edu/
Private
Admissions: (215) 898-6183
Email: mbaadmiss@
wharton.upenn.edu
Financial aid: (215) 898-8728
Application deadline: 03/27
Tuition: full time: $76,580;
part time: N/A
Room/board/expenses: $32,870
College-funded aid: Yes
International student aid: Yes
Full-time enrollment: 1,737
men: 56%; women:
44%; minorities: 33%;
international: 32%
Part-time enrollment: N/A
Acceptance rate (full time): 19%
Average GMAT (full time): 730
Average GRE (full
time): N/A verbal; N/A
quantitative; N/A writing
Average GPA (full time): 3.60
Average age of entrants to
full-time program: 28
Average months of prior work
experience (full time): 60
TOEFL requirement: No
Minimum TOEFL score: N/A
Most popular departments:
entrepreneurship, finance,
general management, health
care administration, other
Mean starting base salary for 2017
full-time graduates: $135,716

Employment location for
2017 class: Intl. 11%; N.E.
43%; M.A. 7%; S. 3%; M.W.
6%; S.W. 3%; W. 26%

University of Pittsburgh (Katz)

372 Mervis Hall
Pittsburgh, PA 15260
www.business.pitt.edu/
Public
Admissions: (412) 648-1700
Email: mba@katz.pitt.edu
Financial aid: (412) 648-1700
Application deadline: 04/01
In-state tuition: total program:
$59,852 (full time); part
time: $1,277/credit hour
Out-of-state tuition: total
program: $76,416 (full time)
Room/board/expenses: $36,034
College-funded aid: Yes
International student aid: Yes
Full-time enrollment: 135
men: 65%; women:
35%; minorities: 19%;
international: 37%
Part-time enrollment: 294
men: 68%; women:
32%; minorities: 13%;
international: 1%
Acceptance rate (full time): 33%
Average GMAT (full time): 608
Average GRE (full
time): 154 verbal; 153
quantitative; 4.1 writing
Average GPA (full time): 3.41
Average age of entrants to
full-time program: 27
Average months of prior work
experience (full time): 48
TOEFL requirement: Yes
Minimum TOEFL score: N/A
Most popular departments:
finance, marketing, management
information systems,
production/operations
management, supply chain
management/logistics
Mean starting base salary for 2017
full-time graduates: $88,358
Employment location for 2017
class: Intl. 3%; N.E. 12%;
M.A. 48%; S. 3%; M.W.
18%; S.W. 9%; W. 6%

University of Scranton

800 Linden Street
Scranton, PA 18510-4632
www.scranton.edu
Private
Admissions: (570) 941-7540
Email: joseph.roback@
scranton.edu
Financial aid: (570) 941-7700
Application deadline: rolling
Tuition: full time: N/A; part
time: $965/credit hour
Room/board/expenses: N/A
College-funded aid: Yes
International student aid: Yes
Full-time enrollment: N/A
Part-time enrollment: 123
men: 61%; women:
39%; minorities: 9%;
international: 18%
Average GRE (full
time): N/A verbal; N/A
quantitative; N/A writing
TOEFL requirement: Yes
Minimum TOEFL score: 550

Most popular departments:
accounting, finance, general
management, health care
administration, production/
operations management

Villanova University

Bartley Hall
800 Lancaster Avenue
Villanova, PA 19085
mba.villanova.edu
Private
Admissions: (610) 519-4336
Email: claire.bruno@
villanova.edu
Financial aid: (610) 519-4010
Application deadline: 07/31
Tuition: full time: N/A; part
time: $1,134/credit hour
Room/board/expenses: N/A
College-funded aid: Yes
International student aid: Yes
Full-time enrollment: N/A
Part-time enrollment: 128
men: 57%; women:
43%; minorities: 13%;
international: 5%
Average GRE (full
time): N/A verbal; N/A
quantitative; N/A writing
TOEFL requirement: Yes
Minimum TOEFL score: 550
Most popular departments:
finance, general
management, international
business, marketing

West Chester University of Pennsylvania

1160 McDermott Drive
West Chester, PA 19383
www.wcupa.edu/mba
Public
Admissions: (610) 436-2943
Email: gradstudy@wcupa.edu
Financial aid: (610) 436-2627
Application deadline: rolling
In-state tuition: full time: N/A;
part time: $500/credit hour
Out-of-state tuition: full time: N/A
Room/board/expenses: N/A
College-funded aid: Yes
International student aid: Yes
Full-time enrollment: N/A
Part-time enrollment: 427
men: 61%; women:
39%; minorities: 16%;
international: 0%
Average GRE (full
time): N/A verbal; N/A
quantitative; N/A writing
TOEFL requirement: Yes
Minimum TOEFL score: 550
Most popular departments:
entrepreneurship, general
management, leadership,
production/operations
management, quantitative
analysis/statistics and
operations research

Widener University

1 University Place
Chester, PA 19013
www.widener.edu/sba
Private
Admissions: (610) 499-4330
Email:
sbagradv@mail.widener.edu
Financial aid: (610) 499-4161

Application deadline: rolling
Tuition: full time: N/A;
part time: N/A
Room/board/expenses: N/A
College-funded aid: Yes
International student aid: Yes
Full-time enrollment: 32
men: 63%; women:
38%; minorities: 22%;
international: 50%
Part-time enrollment: 35
men: 60%; women:
40%; minorities: 23%;
international: 9%
Acceptance rate (full time): 89%
Average GMAT (full time): 453
**Average GRE (full
time):** 148 verbal; 152
quantitative; 4.0 writing
Average GPA (full time): 3.16
**Average age of entrants to
full-time program:** 25
TOEFL requirement: Yes
Minimum TOEFL score: N/A

PUERTO RICO

University of
Puerto Rico–
Rio Piedras

Plaza Universitaria Building
Torre Norte, 5th Floor
San Juan, PR
business.uprrp.edu
Private
Admissions: (787) 764-0000
Email: mayra.crespo2@upr.edu
Financial aid: (787) 764-0000
Application deadline: 02/27
Tuition: full time: $142/
credit hour; part time: N/A
Room/board/expenses: $20,000
College-funded aid: Yes
International student aid: Yes
Full-time enrollment: 166
men: 55%; women:
45%; minorities: 99%;
international: 0%
Part-time enrollment: N/A
Acceptance rate (full time): 42%
Average GMAT (full time): 550
**Average GRE (full
time):** N/A verbal; N/A
quantitative; N/A writing
Average GPA (full time): 3.50
**Average age of entrants to
full-time program:** 27
**Average months of prior work
experience (full time):** 24
TOEFL requirement: No
Minimum TOEFL score: N/A
**Employment location for 2017
class:** Intl. N/A; N.E. N/A;
M.A. 20%; S. 80%; M.W.
N/A; S.W. N/A; W. N/A

RHODE ISLAND

Bryant University

1150 Douglas Pike
Smithfield, RI 02917
www.bryant.edu/
Private
Admissions: (401) 232-6707
Email: gradprog@bryant.edu
Financial aid: (401) 232-6020
Application deadline: 04/15
Tuition: full time: $1,118/
credit hour; part time: N/A
Room/board/expenses: N/A
College-funded aid: Yes
International student aid: Yes

Full-time enrollment: 41
men: 68%; women:
32%; minorities: 15%;
international: 2%
Part-time enrollment: 70
men: 60%; women:
40%; minorities: 13%;
international: 0%
Acceptance rate (full time): 63%
Average GMAT (full time): 482
**Average GRE (full
time):** N/A verbal; N/A
quantitative; N/A writing
Average GPA (full time): 3.07
**Average age of entrants to
full-time program:** 24
TOEFL requirement: Yes
Minimum TOEFL score: N/A
Most popular departments:
finance, general management,
international business, supply
chain management/logistics,
quantitative analysis/statistics
and operations research

Providence College

One Cunningham Square
Providence, RI 02918
business.providence.edu/mba/
Private
Admissions: (401) 865-2294
Email: mba@providence.edu
Financial aid: (401) 865-2286
Application deadline: 07/01
Tuition: full time: N/A;
part time: $8,004
Room/board/expenses: N/A
College-funded aid: Yes
International student aid: Yes
Full-time enrollment: N/A
Part-time enrollment: 169
men: 59%; women: 41%;
minorities: 11%; international: 1%
**Average GRE (full
time):** N/A verbal; N/A
quantitative; N/A writing
TOEFL requirement: Yes
Minimum TOEFL score: 577
Most popular departments:
accounting, finance, general
management, international
business, marketing

University of
Rhode Island[1]

7 Lippitt Road
Kingston, RI 02881
web.uri.edu/business/
Public
Admissions: (401) 874-2842
Email: gradadm@etal.uri.edu
Financial aid: N/A
Tuition: N/A
Room/board/expenses: N/A
Enrollment: N/A

SOUTH CAROLINA

The Citadel

171 Moultrie Street
Charleston, SC 29409
www.citadel.edu/csba/
Public
Admissions: (843) 953-5336
Email: cgc@citadel.edu
Financial aid: (843) 953-5187
Application deadline: 07/15
In-state tuition: full time:
$587/credit hour; part
time: $587/credit hour

Out-of-state tuition: full
time: $988/credit hour
Room/board/expenses: $24,660
College-funded aid: Yes
International student aid: Yes
**Average student indebtedness
at graduation:** $26,595
Full-time enrollment: 43
men: 60%; women:
40%; minorities: 23%;
international: 5%
Part-time enrollment: 154
men: 67%; women:
33%; minorities: 12%;
international: 1%
Average GMAT (full time): 495
Average GRE (full time): 147
verbal; 144 quantitative;
N/A writing
Average GPA (full time): 3.12
**Average age of entrants to
full-time program:** 26
TOEFL requirement: Yes
Minimum TOEFL score: 550

Clemson University

1 North Main Street
Greenville, SC 29601
www.clemson.edu/cbbs/
departments/mba
Public
Admissions: (864) 656-8173
Email: mba@clemson.edu
Financial aid: (864) 656-2280
Application deadline: 06/18
In-state tuition: full time: $18,666;
part time: $723/credit hour
Out-of-state tuition:
full time: $30,672
Room/board/expenses: $13,750
Full-time enrollment: 139
men: 63%; women:
37%; minorities: 12%;
international: 16%
Part-time enrollment: 367
men: 70%; women:
30%; minorities: 14%;
international: 2%
Acceptance rate (full time): 80%
Average GMAT (full time): 559
**Average GRE (full
time):** N/A verbal; N/A
quantitative; N/A writing
Average GPA (full time): 3.21
**Average age of entrants to
full-time program:** 26
**Average months of prior work
experience (full time):** 50
TOEFL requirement: Yes
Minimum TOEFL score: N/A
Most popular departments:
entrepreneurship, general
management, health care
administration, marketing,
quantitative analysis/statistics
and operations research
**Mean starting base salary for
2017 full-time graduates:** $71,519
**Employment location for
2017 class:** Intl. 0%; N.E.
0%; M.A. 0%; S. 94%; M.W.
3%; S.W. 3%; W. 0%

Coastal Carolina
University

PO Box 261954
Conway, SC 29528-6054
www.coastal.edu/
graduatestudies/
Public
Admissions: (843) 349-2394
Email: graduate@coastal.edu

Financial aid: (843) 349-2313
Application deadline: 06/15
In-state tuition: full time:
$576/credit hour; part
time: $576/credit hour
Out-of-state tuition: full
time: $1,041/credit hour
Room/board/expenses: $5,120
College-funded aid: Yes
International student aid: Yes
**Average student indebtedness
at graduation:** $25,156
Full-time enrollment: 58
men: 47%; women:
53%; minorities: 31%;
international: 10%
Part-time enrollment: 34
men: 53%; women:
47%; minorities: 24%;
international: 9%
Acceptance rate (full time): 99%
**Average GRE (full
time):** N/A verbal; N/A
quantitative; N/A writing
Average GPA (full time): 3.46
**Average age of entrants to
full-time program:** 24
TOEFL requirement: Yes
Minimum TOEFL score: 575

College of Charleston

66 George Street
Charleston, SC 29424
www.mbacharleston.com/
Public
Admissions: (843) 953-8112
Email: mba@cofc.edu
Financial aid: (843) 953-5540
Application deadline: 05/01
In-state tuition: total program:
$30,787 (full time); part time: N/A
Out-of-state tuition: total
program: $30,787 (full time)
Room/board/expenses: $16,202
College-funded aid: Yes
International student aid: Yes
**Average student indebtedness
at graduation:** $19,810
Full-time enrollment: 41
men: 46%; women:
54%; minorities: 5%;
international: 12%
Part-time enrollment: N/A
Acceptance rate (full time): 65%
Average GMAT (full time): 555
Average GRE (full time): 154
verbal; 151 quantitative;
N/A writing
Average GPA (full time): 3.35
**Average age of entrants to
full-time program:** 26
**Average months of prior work
experience (full time):** 81
TOEFL requirement: Yes
Minimum TOEFL score: N/A
Most popular departments:
finance, hotel administration,
marketing
**Mean starting base salary for
2017 full-time graduates:** $61,931
**Employment location for 2017
class:** Intl. N/A; N.E. 20%;
M.A. 10%; S. 67%; M.W.
3%; S.W. N/A; W. N/A

Francis Marion
University

Box 100547
Florence, SC 29501
www.fmarion.edu/business/
mba/
Public
Admissions: (843) 661-1424
Email: klawrimore@fmarion.edu
Financial aid: (843) 661-1190
Application deadline: rolling
In-state tuition: full time:
$520/credit hour; part
time: $520/credit hour
Out-of-state tuition: full
time: $1,040/credit hour
Room/board/expenses: N/A
College-funded aid: Yes
Full-time enrollment: 47
men: N/A; women:
N/A; minorities: N/A;
international: N/A
Part-time enrollment: N/A
**Average GRE (full
time):** N/A verbal; N/A
quantitative; N/A writing
TOEFL requirement: Yes
Minimum TOEFL score: N/A

South Carolina
State University

300 College Street NE
Orangeburg, SC 29117
www.scsu.edu/
schoolofgraduatestudies.aspx
Public
Admissions: (803) 536-7133
Email: graduateschool@
scsu.edu
Financial aid: (803) 536-7067
Application deadline: 06/15
In-state tuition: full time: $10,920;
part time: $607/credit hour
Out-of-state tuition:
full time: $21,500
Room/board/expenses: N/A
College-funded aid: Yes
International student aid: Yes
Full-time enrollment: 20
men: 50%; women:
50%; minorities: 100%;
international: 0%
Part-time enrollment: 11
men: 36%; women:
64%; minorities: 100%;
international: 0%
Acceptance rate (full time): 88%
**Average GRE (full
time):** N/A verbal; N/A
quantitative; N/A writing
**Average age of entrants to
full-time program:** 24
TOEFL requirement: Yes
Minimum TOEFL score: 550

University of
South Carolina
(Moore)

1014 Greene Street
Columbia, SC 29208
moore.sc.edu/
Public
Admissions: (803) 777-4346
Email: gradinfo@moore.sc.edu
Financial aid: (803) 777-8134
Application deadline: rolling
In-state tuition: total program:
$44,422 (full time); part
time: $741/credit hour

Out-of-state tuition: total program: $72,860 (full time)
Room/board/expenses: $48,855
College-funded aid: Yes
International student aid: Yes
Average student indebtedness at graduation: $68,464
Full-time enrollment: 53
men: 62%; women: 38%; minorities: 17%; international: 21%
Part-time enrollment: 435
men: 70%; women: 30%; minorities: 23%; international: 2%
Acceptance rate (full time): 74%
Average GMAT (full time): 670
Average GRE (full time): 157 verbal; 154 quantitative; 4.0 writing
Average GPA (full time): 3.50
Average age of entrants to full-time program: 29
Average months of prior work experience (full time): 61
TOEFL requirement: Yes
Minimum TOEFL score: 600
Mean starting base salary for 2017 full-time graduates: $84,206
Employment location for 2017 class: Intl. 4%; N.E. 4%; M.A. 8%; S. 68%; M.W. 12%; S.W. 0%; W. 4%

Winthrop University[1]

Thurmond Building
Rock Hill, SC 29733
www.winthrop.edu/cba
Public
Admissions: (803) 323-2204
Email: gradschool@winthrop.edu
Financial aid: N/A
Tuition: N/A
Room/board/expenses: N/A
Enrollment: N/A

SOUTH DAKOTA

Black Hills State University

1200 University Street
Spearfish, SD 57799
www.bhsu.edu/
Public
Admissions: (605) 642-6919
Email: MBA@bhsu.edu
Financial aid: (605) 718-4113
Application deadline: rolling
In-state tuition: full time: N/A; part time: N/A
Out-of-state tuition: full time: N/A
Room/board/expenses: N/A
College-funded aid: Yes
International student aid: Yes
Full-time enrollment: N/A
Part-time enrollment: 20
men: 50%; women: 50%; minorities: N/A; international: N/A
Average GRE (full time): N/A verbal; N/A quantitative; N/A writing
TOEFL requirement: Yes
Minimum TOEFL score: 500

University of South Dakota

414 E. Clark Street
Vermillion, SD 57069
www.usd.edu/mba
Public
Admissions: (605) 274-9519
Email: mba@usd.edu
Financial aid: (605) 677-5446
Application deadline: 06/01
In-state tuition: full time: $314/credit hour; part time: $444/credit hour
Out-of-state tuition: full time: $605/credit hour
Room/board/expenses: $8,800
College-funded aid: Yes
International student aid: Yes
Average student indebtedness at graduation: $28,696
Full-time enrollment: 50
men: 52%; women: 48%; minorities: 8%; international: 20%
Part-time enrollment: 210
men: 66%; women: 34%; minorities: 7%; international: 6%
Acceptance rate (full time): 97%
Average GMAT (full time): 464
Average GRE (full time): N/A verbal; N/A quantitative; N/A writing
Average GPA (full time): 3.46
Average age of entrants to full-time program: 25
Average months of prior work experience (full time): 46
TOEFL requirement: Yes
Minimum TOEFL score: 550
Most popular departments: general management, health care administration, marketing, production/operations management, other
Mean starting base salary for 2017 full-time graduates: $45,550
Employment location for 2017 class: Intl. N/A; N.E. N/A; M.A. N/A; S. N/A; M.W. 100%; S.W. N/A; W. N/A

TENNESSEE

Belmont University (Massey)

1900 Belmont Boulevard
Nashville, TN 37212
www.belmont.edu/business/graduatebusiness
Private
Admissions: (615) 460-6480
Email: masseyadmissions@belmont.edu
Financial aid: (615) 460-6403
Application deadline: 06/01
Tuition: total program: $56,650 (full time); $56,650 (part time)
Room/board/expenses: N/A
College-funded aid: Yes
International student aid: Yes
Full-time enrollment: 32
men: 53%; women: 47%; minorities: 19%; international: 9%
Part-time enrollment: 129
men: 60%; women: 40%; minorities: 18%; international: 2%
Acceptance rate (full time): 82%
Average GMAT (full time): 525
Average GRE (full time): N/A verbal; N/A quantitative; N/A writing

Average GPA (full time): 3.45
Average age of entrants to full-time program: 24
TOEFL requirement: Yes
Minimum TOEFL score: 550
Most popular departments: entrepreneurship, finance, general management, health care administration, marketing
Mean starting base salary for 2017 full-time graduates: $49,300
Employment location for 2017 class: Intl. 5%; N.E. 0%; M.A. 5%; S. 74%; M.W. 5%; S.W. 5%; W. 5%

East Tennessee State University[1]

PO Box 70699
Johnson City, TN 37614
www.etsu.edu/cbat
Public
Admissions: (423) 439-5314
Email: business@etsu.edu
Financial aid: N/A
Tuition: N/A
Room/board/expenses: N/A
Enrollment: N/A

Middle Tennessee State University[1]

PO Box 290
Murfreesboro, TN 37132
www.mtsu.edu
Public
Admissions: (615) 898-2840
Email: graduate@mtsu.edu
Financial aid: N/A
Tuition: N/A
Room/board/expenses: N/A
Enrollment: N/A

Tennessee State University[1]

330 N. 10th Avenue
Nashville, TN 37203
www.tnstate.edu/business
Public
Admissions: (615) 963-5145
Email: cobinfo@tnstate.edu
Financial aid: N/A
Tuition: N/A
Room/board/expenses: N/A
Enrollment: N/A

Tennessee Technological University

Box 5023
Cookeville, TN 38505
www.tntech.edu/mba
Public
Admissions: (931) 372-3600
Email: knicewicz@tntech.edu
Financial aid: (931) 372-3073
Application deadline: 07/01
In-state tuition: full time: $488/credit hour; part time: $488/credit hour
Out-of-state tuition: full time: $726/credit hour
Room/board/expenses: $25,600
College-funded aid: Yes
International student aid: Yes
Average student indebtedness at graduation: $12,592

Full-time enrollment: 54
men: 57%; women: 43%; minorities: 11%; international: 19%
Part-time enrollment: 191
men: 61%; women: 39%; minorities: 11%; international: 3%
Acceptance rate (full time): 100%
Average GRE (full time): N/A verbal; N/A quantitative; N/A writing
Average age of entrants to full-time program: 28
TOEFL requirement: Yes
Minimum TOEFL score: 550
Most popular departments: accounting, general management, human resources management, international business, management information systems

Union University

1050 Union University Drive
Jackson, TN 38305
www.uu.edu/academics/graduate/mba/
Private
Admissions: (731) 661-5341
Email: lpowell@uu.edu
Financial aid: (731) 661-5213
Application deadline: 08/15
Tuition: full time: $575/credit hour; part time: $575/credit hour
Room/board/expenses: N/A
College-funded aid: Yes
International student aid: Yes
Full-time enrollment: N/A
Part-time enrollment: 150
men: 56%; women: 44%; minorities: 27%; international: 1%
Average GRE (full time): N/A verbal; N/A quantitative; N/A writing
TOEFL requirement: Yes
Minimum TOEFL score: 560
Most popular departments: accounting, general management, human resources management, leadership, marketing

University of Memphis (Fogelman)

3675 Central Avenue
Memphis, TN 38152
fcbe.memphis.edu/
Public
Admissions: (901) 678-3721
Email: krishnan@memphis.edu
Financial aid: (901) 678-4825
Application deadline: 07/01
In-state tuition: full time: $609/credit hour; part time: $609/credit hour
Out-of-state tuition: full time: $1,097/credit hour
Room/board/expenses: N/A
College-funded aid: Yes
International student aid: Yes
Full-time enrollment: 37
men: 49%; women: 51%; minorities: 19%; international: 35%
Part-time enrollment: 141
men: 70%; women: 30%; minorities: 34%; international: 0%
Acceptance rate (full time): 55%

Average GMAT (full time): 508
Average GRE (full time): 153 verbal; 148 quantitative; N/A writing
Average GPA (full time): 3.44
Average age of entrants to full-time program: 25
Average months of prior work experience (full time): 52
TOEFL requirement: Yes
Minimum TOEFL score: 550
Most popular departments: accounting, finance, general management, international business, management information systems

University of Tennessee–Chattanooga

615 McCallie Avenue
Chattanooga, TN 37403
www.utc.edu/Academic/Business/
Public
Admissions: (423) 425-4666
Email: bonny-clark@utc.edu
Financial aid: (423) 425-4677
Application deadline: 06/15
In-state tuition: full time: N/A; part time: $458/credit hour
Out-of-state tuition: full time: N/A
Room/board/expenses: N/A
College-funded aid: Yes
International student aid: No
Full-time enrollment: N/A
Part-time enrollment: 150
men: 56%; women: 44%; minorities: 18%; international: 3%
Average GRE (full time): N/A verbal; N/A quantitative; N/A writing
TOEFL requirement: Yes
Minimum TOEFL score: 550
Most popular departments: accounting, finance, human resources management, marketing, other

University of Tennessee–Knoxville (Haslam)

453 Haslam Business Building
Knoxville, TN 37996-4150
mba.utk.edu
Public
Admissions: (865) 974-5033
Email: mba@utk.edu
Financial aid: (865) 974-3131
Application deadline: 02/01
In-state tuition: full time: $11,244; part time: N/A
Out-of-state tuition: full time: $29,432
Room/board/expenses: $16,000
College-funded aid: Yes
International student aid: Yes
Average student indebtedness at graduation: $33,675
Full-time enrollment: 120
men: 66%; women: 34%; minorities: 7%; international: 20%
Part-time enrollment: N/A
Acceptance rate (full time): 51%
Average GMAT (full time): 656
Average GRE (full time): 155 verbal; 155 quantitative; N/A writing

Average GPA (full time): 3.48
Average age of entrants to full-time program: 27
Average months of prior work experience (full time): 55
TOEFL requirement: Yes
Minimum TOEFL score: 600
Most popular departments: entrepreneurship, finance, marketing, supply chain management/logistics, other
Mean starting base salary for 2017 full-time graduates: $88,560
Employment location for 2017 class: Intl. N/A; N.E. 6%; M.A. N/A; S. 55%; M.W. 12%; S.W. 10%; W. 16%

University of Tennessee–Martin

103 Business Administration Building
Martin, TN 38238
www.utm.edu/departments/cbga/mba
Public
Admissions: (731) 881-7012
Email: jcunningham@utm.edu
Financial aid: (731) 881-7040
Application deadline: 07/30
In-state tuition: full time: $566/credit hour; part time: $566/credit hour
Out-of-state tuition: full time: $623/credit hour
Room/board/expenses: N/A
College-funded aid: Yes
International student aid: Yes
Full-time enrollment: 80
men: 55%; women: 45%; minorities: 15%; international: 0%
Part-time enrollment: 10
men: 30%; women: 70%; minorities: 0%; international: 0%
Acceptance rate (full time): 84%
Average GMAT (full time): 518
Average GRE (full time): 150 verbal; 146 quantitative; 3.6 writing
Average GPA (full time): 3.19
Average age of entrants to full-time program: 34
Average months of prior work experience (full time): 156
TOEFL requirement: Yes
Minimum TOEFL score: 525
Most popular departments: other

Vanderbilt University (Owen)

401 21st Avenue S
Nashville, TN 37203
business.vanderbilt.edu
Private
Admissions: (615) 322-6469
Email: mba@owen.vanderbilt.edu
Financial aid: (615) 322-3591
Application deadline: 04/30
Tuition: full time: $54,547; part time: N/A
Room/board/expenses: $20,853
College-funded aid: Yes
International student aid: Yes
Average student indebtedness at graduation: $76,759
Full-time enrollment: 347
men: 72%; women: 28%; minorities: 13%; international: 23%

Part-time enrollment: N/A
Acceptance rate (full time): 43%
Average GMAT (full time): 688
Average GRE (full time): 156 verbal; 157 quantitative; 4.0 writing
Average GPA (full time): 3.31
Average age of entrants to full-time program: 28
Average months of prior work experience (full time): 60
TOEFL requirement: Yes
Minimum TOEFL score: N/A
Most popular departments: finance, health care administration, marketing, production/operations management, organizational behavior
Mean starting base salary for 2017 full-time graduates: $113,205
Employment location for 2017 class: Intl. 3%; N.E. 15%; M.A. 3%; S. 40%; M.W. 10%; S.W. 10%; W. 20%

Abilene Christian University[1]

ACU Box 29300
Abilene, TX 79699-9300
www.acu.edu/academics/coba/index.html
Private
Admissions: (800) 460-6228
Email: info@admissions.acu.edu
Financial aid: N/A
Tuition: N/A
Room/board/expenses: N/A
Enrollment: N/A

Baylor University (Hankamer)

1 Bear Place, #98013
Waco, TX 76798-8013
www.baylor.edu/mba
Private
Admissions: (254) 710-3718
Email: mba_info@baylor.edu
Financial aid: (254) 710-2611
Application deadline: 06/15
Tuition: full time: $44,190; part time: N/A
Room/board/expenses: $19,000
College-funded aid: Yes
International student aid: Yes
Average student indebtedness at graduation: $30,700
Full-time enrollment: 96
men: 67%; women: 33%; minorities: 23%; international: 5%
Part-time enrollment: N/A
Acceptance rate (full time): 51%
Average GMAT (full time): 628
Average GRE (full time): 155 verbal; 154 quantitative; 4.1 writing
Average GPA (full time): 3.35
Average age of entrants to full-time program: 25
Average months of prior work experience (full time): 22
TOEFL requirement: Yes
Minimum TOEFL score: 600
Most popular departments: entrepreneurship, finance, health care administration, marketing, management information systems

Mean starting base salary for 2017 full-time graduates: $73,314
Employment location for 2017 class: Intl. 4%; N.E. 7%; M.A. 0%; S. 4%; M.W. 7%; S.W. 64%; W. 14%

Lamar University

4400 Martin Luther King Parkway
Beaumont, TX 77710
lamar.edu/mba
Public
Admissions: (409) 880-8888
Email: gradmissions@lamar.edu
Financial aid: (409) 880-7011
Application deadline: 07/31
In-state tuition: full time: $12,296; part time: $9,209
Out-of-state tuition: full time: $22,256
Room/board/expenses: $12,952
College-funded aid: Yes
International student aid: Yes
Average student indebtedness at graduation: $25,795
Full-time enrollment: 127
men: 50%; women: 50%; minorities: 20%; international: 24%
Part-time enrollment: N/A
Acceptance rate (full time): 80%
Average GMAT (full time): 490
Average GRE (full time): N/A verbal; N/A quantitative; N/A writing
Average GPA (full time): 3.30
Average age of entrants to full-time program: 30
TOEFL requirement: Yes
Minimum TOEFL score: 550
Most popular departments: general management, health care administration, leadership, marketing, management information systems

Midwestern State University

3410 Taft Boulevard
Wichita Falls, TX 76308
www.mwsu.edu/mba
Public
Admissions: (940) 397-4920
Email: graduateschool@mwsu.edu
Financial aid: (940) 397-4214
Application deadline: 08/01
In-state tuition: full time: $214/credit hour; part time: $214/credit hour
Out-of-state tuition: full time: $279/credit hour
Room/board/expenses: N/A
College-funded aid: Yes
International student aid: Yes
Full-time enrollment: 20
men: 60%; women: 40%; minorities: 25%; international: 25%
Part-time enrollment: 49
men: 45%; women: 55%; minorities: 16%; international: 12%
Average GRE (full time): N/A verbal; N/A quantitative; N/A writing
TOEFL requirement: Yes
Minimum TOEFL score: N/A

Prairie View A&M University

PO Box 519, MS 2300
Prairie View, TX 77446
pvamu.edu/business
Public
Admissions: (936) 261-9217
Email: mba@pvamu.edu
Financial aid: (936) 261-1000
Application deadline: 06/01
In-state tuition: full time: $242/credit hour; part time: $242/credit hour
Out-of-state tuition: full time: $695/credit hour
Room/board/expenses: $13,791
College-funded aid: Yes
International student aid: Yes
Full-time enrollment: 82
men: 41%; women: 59%; minorities: 79%; international: 16%
Part-time enrollment: 143
men: 43%; women: 57%; minorities: 89%; international: 3%
Acceptance rate (full time): 89%
Average GRE (full time): N/A verbal; N/A quantitative; N/A writing
Average age of entrants to full-time program: 28
TOEFL requirement: Yes
Minimum TOEFL score: 500
Most popular departments: accounting, finance, general management, international business, management information systems

Rice University (Jones)

PO Box 2932
Houston, TX 77252-2932
business.rice.edu
Private
Admissions: (713) 348-4918
Email: ricemba@rice.edu
Financial aid: (713) 348-4958
Application deadline: rolling
Tuition: full time: $58,794; part time: $54,044
Room/board/expenses: $24,341
College-funded aid: Yes
International student aid: Yes
Average student indebtedness at graduation: $68,531
Full-time enrollment: 228
men: 71%; women: 29%; minorities: 23%; international: 30%
Part-time enrollment: 331
men: 83%; women: 17%; minorities: 27%; international: 9%
Acceptance rate (full time): 27%
Average GMAT (full time): 711
Average GRE (full time): 160 verbal; 161 quantitative; 4.4 writing
Average GPA (full time): 3.34
Average age of entrants to full-time program: 29
Average months of prior work experience (full time): 66
TOEFL requirement: Yes
Minimum TOEFL score: N/A
Most popular departments: entrepreneurship, finance, general management, marketing, other

Mean starting base salary for 2017 full-time graduates: $113,349
Employment location for 2017 class: Intl. N/A; N.E. 4%; M.A. 3%; S. 2%; M.W. 3%; S.W. 81%; W. 6%

Sam Houston State University

PO Box 2056
Huntsville, TX 77341
www.shsu.edu/dept/graduate-admissions
Public
Admissions: (936) 294-1971
Email: graduate@shsu.edu
Financial aid: (936) 294-1724
Application deadline: 08/01
In-state tuition: full time: $300/credit hour; part time: N/A
Out-of-state tuition: full time: $715/credit hour
Room/board/expenses: $12,666
College-funded aid: Yes
International student aid: Yes
Average student indebtedness at graduation: $32,493
Full-time enrollment: 251
men: 54%; women: 46%; minorities: 33%; international: 4%
Part-time enrollment: N/A
Acceptance rate (full time): 78%
Average GMAT (full time): 552
Average GRE (full time): N/A verbal; N/A quantitative; N/A writing
Average GPA (full time): 3.50
Average age of entrants to full-time program: 30
TOEFL requirement: Yes
Minimum TOEFL score: 550
Most popular departments: economics, finance, general management

Southern Methodist University (Cox)

PO Box 750333
Dallas, TX 75275-0333
www.coxgrad.com
Private
Admissions: (214) 768-1214
Email: mbainfo@cox.smu.edu
Financial aid: (214) 768-2371
Application deadline: 05/02
Tuition: full time: $52,880; part time: $47,800
Room/board/expenses: $20,860
College-funded aid: Yes
International student aid: Yes
Full-time enrollment: 222
men: 67%; women: 33%; minorities: 17%; international: 13%
Part-time enrollment: 233
men: 70%; women: 30%; minorities: 28%; international: 6%
Acceptance rate (full time): 46%
Average GMAT (full time): 660
Average GRE (full time): 154 verbal; 153 quantitative; 4.0 writing
Average GPA (full time): 3.33
Average age of entrants to full-time program: 29
Average months of prior work experience (full time): 57
TOEFL requirement: Yes
Minimum TOEFL score: 600

Most popular departments: entrepreneurship, finance, marketing, real estate, quantitative analysis/statistics and operations research
Mean starting base salary for 2017 full-time graduates: $97,906
Employment location for 2017 class: Intl. 3%; N.E. 1%; M.A. 2%; S. 1%; M.W. 3%; S.W. 85%; W. 4%

Stephen F. Austin State University[1]
PO Box 13004
SFA Station
Nacogdoches, TX 75962-3004
www.sfasu.edu/cob/
Public
Admissions: (936) 468-2807
Email: gschool@titan.sfasu.edu
Financial aid: N/A
Tuition: N/A
Room/board/expenses: N/A
Enrollment: N/A

St. Mary's University (Greehey)
1 Camino Santa Maria
San Antonio, TX 78228-8607
www.stmarytx.edu/academics/programs/mba-values/
Private
Admissions: (210) 436-3101
Email: kthornton@stmarytx.edu
Financial aid: (210) 436-3141
Application deadline: 07/01
Tuition: full time: $900/credit hour; part time: $900/credit hour
Room/board/expenses: $20,234
College-funded aid: Yes
International student aid: Yes
Full-time enrollment: 99
men: 49%; women: 51%; minorities: 43%; international: 22%
Part-time enrollment: 41
men: 51%; women: 49%; minorities: 68%; international: 5%
Acceptance rate (full time): 94%
Average GMAT (full time): 477
Average GRE (full time): 148 verbal; 147 quantitative; 3.3 writing
Average GPA (full time): 3.26
Average age of entrants to full-time program: 29
Average months of prior work experience (full time): 12
TOEFL requirement: Yes
Minimum TOEFL score: 570
Most popular departments: general management

Texas A&M International University
5201 University Boulevard
Western Hemispheric Trade
Center, Suite 203
Laredo, TX 78041-1900
www.tamiu.edu
Public
Admissions: (956) 326-3020
Email: graduatedmissions@tamiu.edu
Financial aid: (956) 326-2225

Application deadline: 04/30
In-state tuition: full time: $77/credit hour; part time: $77/credit hour
Out-of-state tuition: full time: $492/credit hour
Room/board/expenses: $10,976
College-funded aid: Yes
International student aid: Yes
Average student indebtedness at graduation: $32,651
Full-time enrollment: 57
men: 63%; women: 37%; minorities: 60%; international: 37%
Part-time enrollment: 113
men: 44%; women: 56%; minorities: 90%; international: 7%
Acceptance rate (full time): 91%
Average GMAT (full time): 373
Average GRE (full time): 145 verbal; 149 quantitative; 3.0 writing
Average GPA (full time): 2.99
Average age of entrants to full-time program: 28
Average months of prior work experience (full time): 77
TOEFL requirement: Yes
Minimum TOEFL score: 550
Most popular departments: accounting, finance, general management, international business, management information systems

Texas A&M University–College Station (Mays)
4117 TAMU
390 Wehner Building
College Station, TX 77843-4117
mays.tamu.edu/mbaprograms
Public
Admissions: (979) 845-4714
Email: mbaprograms@mays.tamu.edu
Financial aid: (979) 845-3236
Application deadline: 04/11
In-state tuition: full time: $36,079; part time: $67,950
Out-of-state tuition: full time: $52,471
Room/board/expenses: $23,992
College-funded aid: Yes
International student aid: Yes
Full-time enrollment: 122
men: 75%; women: 25%; minorities: 29%; international: 20%
Part-time enrollment: 89
men: 74%; women: 26%; minorities: 33%; international: 2%
Acceptance rate (full time): 34%
Average GMAT (full time): 638
Average GRE (full time): 156 verbal; 155 quantitative; 3.9 writing
Average GPA (full time): 3.27
Average age of entrants to full-time program: 29
Average months of prior work experience (full time): 66
TOEFL requirement: Yes
Minimum TOEFL score: N/A

Most popular departments: entrepreneurship, finance, marketing, supply chain management/logistics, quantitative analysis/statistics and operations research
Mean starting base salary for 2017 full-time graduates: $105,910
Employment location for 2017 class: Intl. 4%; N.E. 9%; M.A. 2%; S. 33%; M.W. 11%; S.W. 38%; W. 2%

Texas A&M University–Commerce
PO Box 3011
Commerce, TX 75429-3011
www.tamu-commerce.edu/graduateprograms
Public
Admissions: (903) 886-5163
Email: graduate.school@tamuc.edu
Financial aid: (903) 886-5091
Application deadline: 07/28
In-state tuition: full time: $202/credit hour; part time: $202/credit hour
Out-of-state tuition: full time: $617/credit hour
Room/board/expenses: N/A
College-funded aid: Yes
International student aid: Yes
Full-time enrollment: N/A
Part-time enrollment: 1,522
men: 48%; women: 52%; minorities: 43%; international: 14%
Average GRE (full time): N/A verbal; N/A quantitative; N/A writing
TOEFL requirement: Yes
Minimum TOEFL score: 550
Most popular departments: accounting, finance, health care administration, international business, marketing

Texas A&M University–Corpus Christi[1]
6300 Ocean Drive
Corpus Christi, TX 78412-5807
www.cob.tamucc.edu/prstudents/graduate.html
Public
Admissions: (361) 825-2177
Email: gradweb@tamucc.edu
Financial aid: (361) 825-2338
Tuition: N/A
Room/board/expenses: N/A
Enrollment: N/A

Texas Christian University (Neeley)
PO Box 298540
Fort Worth, TX 76129
www.mba.tcu.edu
Private
Admissions: (817) 257-7531
Email: mbainfo@tcu.edu
Financial aid: (817) 257-7531
Application deadline: 11/01
Tuition: full time: $56,385; part time: $35,190
Room/board/expenses: $22,700
College-funded aid: Yes
International student aid: Yes

Average student indebtedness at graduation: $35,468
Full-time enrollment: 91
men: 74%; women: 26%; minorities: 12%; international: 27%
Part-time enrollment: 147
men: 72%; women: 28%; minorities: 12%; international: 1%
Acceptance rate (full time): 54%
Average GMAT (full time): 640
Average GRE (full time): 154 verbal; 156 quantitative; 4.4 writing
Average GPA (full time): 3.34
Average age of entrants to full-time program: 29
Average months of prior work experience (full time): 60
TOEFL requirement: Yes
Minimum TOEFL score: 600
Most popular departments: consulting, finance, health care administration, marketing, supply chain management/logistics
Mean starting base salary for 2017 full-time graduates: $93,093
Employment location for 2017 class: Intl. 3%; N.E. 0%; M.A. 3%; S. 6%; M.W. 3%; S.W. 71%; W. 13%

Texas Southern University (Jones)
3100 Cleburne Avenue
Houston, TX 77004
www.tsu.edu/academics/colleges_schools/Jesse_H_Jones_School_of_Business/
Public
Admissions: (713) 313-7309
Email: haidern@tsu.edu
Financial aid: (713) 313-7480
Application deadline: 07/15
In-state tuition: full time: $7,660; part time: $5,353
Out-of-state tuition: full time: $14,330
Room/board/expenses: N/A
College-funded aid: Yes
International student aid: Yes
Full-time enrollment: 173
men: 46%; women: 54%; minorities: 71%; international: 29%
Part-time enrollment: N/A
Acceptance rate (full time): 60%
Average GMAT (full time): 340
Average GRE (full time): N/A verbal; N/A quantitative; N/A writing
Average GPA (full time): 3.09
Average age of entrants to full-time program: 27
Average months of prior work experience (full time): 56
TOEFL requirement: Yes
Minimum TOEFL score: 550
Most popular departments: accounting, general management, health care administration, management information systems, other

Texas State University (McCoy)
601 University Drive
San Marcos, TX 78666-4616
www.txstate.edu
Public
Admissions: (512) 245-3591
Email: gradcollege@txstate.edu
Financial aid: (512) 245-2315
Application deadline: 06/01
In-state tuition: total program: $23,894 (full time); $23,894 (part time)
Out-of-state tuition: total program: $41,030 (full time)
Room/board/expenses: N/A
College-funded aid: Yes
International student aid: Yes
Average student indebtedness at graduation: $14,611
Full-time enrollment: 23
men: 61%; women: 39%; minorities: 43%; international: 4%
Part-time enrollment: 226
men: 58%; women: 42%; minorities: 27%; international: 4%
Acceptance rate (full time): 43%
Average GMAT (full time): 554
Average GRE (full time): 151 verbal; 154 quantitative; N/A writing
Average GPA (full time): 3.37
Average age of entrants to full-time program: 25
Average months of prior work experience (full time): 43
TOEFL requirement: Yes
Minimum TOEFL score: N/A
Most popular departments: general management, health care administration, human resources management, international business, manufacturing and technology management
Mean starting base salary for 2017 full-time graduates: $55,000

Texas Tech University (Rawls)[1]
PO Box 42101
Lubbock, TX 79409-2101
texastechmba.com
Public
Admissions: (806) 742-3184
Email: rawls.mba@ttu.edu
Financial aid: (806) 742-0454
Tuition: N/A
Room/board/expenses: N/A
Enrollment: N/A

Texas Wesleyan University[1]
1201 Wesleyan Street
Fort Worth, TX 76105
txwes.edu/
Private
Admissions: (817) 531-4422
Email: graduate@txwes.edu
Financial aid: (817) 531-4420
Tuition: N/A
Room/board/expenses: N/A
Enrollment: N/A

University of Dallas

1845 East Northgate Drive
Irving, TX 75062
www.udallas.edu/cob/
Private
Admissions: (972) 721-5004
Email: admiss@udallas.edu
Financial aid: N/A
Application deadline: rolling
Tuition: full time: N/A; part time: $1,250/credit hour
Room/board/expenses: N/A
College-funded aid: Yes
International student aid: Yes
Full-time enrollment: N/A
Part-time enrollment: 731
men: N/A; women: N/A; minorities: N/A; international: N/A
Average GRE (full time): N/A verbal; N/A quantitative; N/A writing
TOEFL requirement: Yes
Minimum TOEFL score: 550
Most popular departments: accounting, finance, general management, management information systems, technology

University of Houston (Bauer)

334 Melcher Hall, Suite 330
Houston, TX 77204-6021
www.bauer.uh.edu/graduate
Public
Admissions: (713) 743-0700
Email: mba@uh.edu
Financial aid: (713) 743-2062
Application deadline: 06/01
In-state tuition: full time: $24,592; part time: $15,148
Out-of-state tuition: full time: $40,042
Room/board/expenses: $17,884
College-funded aid: Yes
International student aid: Yes
Full-time enrollment: 85
men: 69%; women: 31%; minorities: 27%; international: 32%
Part-time enrollment: 327
men: 70%; women: 30%; minorities: 35%; international: 19%
Acceptance rate (full time): 55%
Average GMAT (full time): 612
Average GRE (full time): 156 verbal; 158 quantitative; 3.6 writing
Average GPA (full time): 3.23
Average age of entrants to full-time program: 30
Average months of prior work experience (full time): 70
TOEFL requirement: Yes
Minimum TOEFL score: 603
Mean starting base salary for 2017 full-time graduates: $74,224
Employment location for 2017 class: Intl. 5%; N.E. 0%; M.A. 0%; S. 5%; M.W. 5%; S.W. 86%; W. 0%

University of Houston–Clear Lake

2700 Bay Area Boulevard
Houston, TX 77058
www.uhcl.edu/admissions
Public
Admissions: (281) 283-2500
Email: admissions@uhcl.edu

Financial aid: (281) 283-2480
Application deadline: 08/01
In-state tuition: full time: N/A; part time: $451/credit hour
Out-of-state tuition: full time: N/A
Room/board/expenses: N/A
College-funded aid: Yes
International student aid: Yes
Full-time enrollment: N/A
Part-time enrollment: 314
men: 45%; women: 55%; minorities: 48%; international: 5%
Average GRE (full time): N/A verbal; N/A quantitative; N/A writing
TOEFL requirement: Yes
Minimum TOEFL score: 550
Most popular departments: finance, human resources management, international business, manufacturing and technology management, other

University of Houston–Downtown

320 North Main Street
Houston, TX 77002
www.uhd.edu/admissions/Pages/admissions-index.aspx
Public
Admissions: (713) 221-8093
Email: gradadmissions@uhd.edu
Financial aid: (713) 221-8041
Application deadline: 08/15
In-state tuition: full time: N/A; part time: $435/credit hour
Out-of-state tuition: full time: N/A
Room/board/expenses: N/A
College-funded aid: Yes
International student aid: Yes
Full-time enrollment: N/A
Part-time enrollment: 1,069
men: 43%; women: 57%; minorities: 77%; international: 3%
Average GRE (full time): N/A verbal; N/A quantitative; N/A writing
TOEFL requirement: Yes
Minimum TOEFL score: 550
Most popular departments: finance, general management, human resources management, leadership, supply chain management/logistics

University of Houston–Victoria[1]

University West, Room 214
3007 N. Ben Wilson
Victoria, TX 77901
www.uhv.edu/business
Public
Admissions: (361) 570-4110
Email: admissions@uhv.edu
Financial aid: (361) 570-4131
Tuition: N/A
Room/board/expenses: N/A
Enrollment: N/A

University of North Texas

1155 Union Circle, #311160
Denton, TX 76203-5017
www.cob.unt.edu
Public
Admissions: (940) 369-8977
Email: mbacob@unt.edu
Financial aid: (940) 565-2302

Application deadline: 06/15
In-state tuition: full time: $303/credit hour; part time: $303/credit hour
Out-of-state tuition: full time: $719/credit hour
Room/board/expenses: $31,435
College-funded aid: Yes
International student aid: Yes
Full-time enrollment: 14
men: 29%; women: 71%; minorities: 21%; international: 0%
Part-time enrollment: 312
men: 60%; women: 40%; minorities: 27%; international: 13%
Acceptance rate (full time): 74%
Average GMAT (full time): 473
Average GRE (full time): N/A verbal; N/A quantitative; N/A writing
Average GPA (full time): 3.64
Average age of entrants to full-time program: 24
TOEFL requirement: Yes
Minimum TOEFL score: 550
Most popular departments: accounting, finance, general management, marketing, organizational behavior

University of St. Thomas–Houston

3800 Montrose Boulevard
Houston, TX 77006
www.stthom.edu/bschool
Private
Admissions: (713) 525-2100
Email: cameron@stthom.edu
Financial aid: (713) 525-2170
Application deadline: 07/15
Tuition: full time: N/A; part time: $1,163/credit hour
Room/board/expenses: N/A
College-funded aid: Yes
International student aid: Yes
Full-time enrollment: N/A
Part-time enrollment: 213
men: 48%; women: 52%; minorities: 49%; international: 26%
Average GRE (full time): N/A verbal; N/A quantitative; N/A writing
TOEFL requirement: Yes
Minimum TOEFL score: N/A
Most popular departments: accounting, finance, general management, international business, marketing

University of Texas–Arlington

UTA Box 19377
Arlington, TX 76019-0376
wweb.uta.edu/business/gradbiz
Public
Admissions: (817) 272-3004
Email: gradbiz@uta.edu
Financial aid: (817) 272-3561
Application deadline: 06/15
In-state tuition: full time: N/A; part time: $7,760
Out-of-state tuition: full time: N/A
Room/board/expenses: N/A
College-funded aid: Yes
International student aid: Yes
Full-time enrollment: N/A

Part-time enrollment: 442
men: 57%; women: 43%; minorities: 26%; international: 41%
Average GRE (full time): N/A verbal; N/A quantitative; N/A writing
TOEFL requirement: Yes
Minimum TOEFL score: 550
Most popular departments: accounting, finance, general management, human resources management, management information systems

University of Texas–Austin (McCombs)

MBA Program
2110 Speedway, Stop B6004
Austin, TX 78712-1750
www.mccombs.utexas.edu/MBA/Full-Time
Public
Admissions: (512) 471-7698
Email: TexasMBA@mccombs.utexas.edu
Financial aid: (512) 471-7698
Application deadline: 04/03
In-state tuition: full time: $35,324; total program: $111,310 (part time)
Out-of-state tuition: full time: $51,804
Room/board/expenses: $19,060
College-funded aid: Yes
International student aid: Yes
Average student indebtedness at graduation: $82,812
Full-time enrollment: 527
men: 62%; women: 38%; minorities: 23%; international: 26%
Part-time enrollment: 453
men: 73%; women: 27%; minorities: 33%; international: 9%
Acceptance rate (full time): 28%
Average GMAT (full time): 703
Average GRE (full time): 158 verbal; 158 quantitative; 4.3 writing
Average GPA (full time): 3.48
Average age of entrants to full-time program: 29
Average months of prior work experience (full time): 70
TOEFL requirement: Yes
Minimum TOEFL score: 620
Most popular departments: consulting, entrepreneurship, finance, marketing, management information systems
Mean starting base salary for 2017 full-time graduates: $116,403
Employment location for 2017 class: Intl. 3%; N.E. 8%; M.A. 0%; S. 7%; M.W. 3%; S.W. 57%; W. 20%

University of Texas–Dallas

800 W. Campbell Road, SM 40
Richardson, TX 75080-3021
jindal.utdallas.edu/mba
Public
Admissions: (972) 883-6191
Email: mba@utdallas.edu
Financial aid: (972) 883-2941
Application deadline: 05/01
In-state tuition: full time: $16,499; part time: $15,097

Out-of-state tuition: full time: $32,166
Room/board/expenses: $16,000
College-funded aid: Yes
International student aid: Yes
Average student indebtedness at graduation: $7,345
Full-time enrollment: 100
men: 74%; women: 26%; minorities: 18%; international: 35%
Part-time enrollment: 759
men: 66%; women: 34%; minorities: 27%; international: 41%
Acceptance rate (full time): 24%
Average GMAT (full time): 678
Average GRE (full time): 157 verbal; 155 quantitative; 4.0 writing
Average GPA (full time): 3.50
Average age of entrants to full-time program: 28
Average months of prior work experience (full time): 60
TOEFL requirement: Yes
Minimum TOEFL score: 550
Most popular departments: accounting, finance, management information systems, production/operations management, supply chain management/logistics
Mean starting base salary for 2017 full-time graduates: $87,522
Employment location for 2017 class: Intl. 0%; N.E. 4%; M.A. 0%; S. 14%; M.W. 0%; S.W. 71%; W. 11%

University of Texas–El Paso

500 W. University Avenue
El Paso, TX 79968
mba.utep.edu
Public
Admissions: (915) 747-7726
Email: mba@utep.edu
Financial aid: (915) 747-5204
Application deadline: 11/15
In-state tuition: full time: $432/credit hour; part time: $432/credit hour
Out-of-state tuition: full time: $917/credit hour
Room/board/expenses: $24,358
College-funded aid: Yes
International student aid: Yes
Average student indebtedness at graduation: $29,153
Full-time enrollment: 39
men: 54%; women: 46%; minorities: 69%; international: 13%
Part-time enrollment: 129
men: 53%; women: 47%; minorities: 72%; international: 16%
Acceptance rate (full time): 84%
Average GMAT (full time): 524
Average GRE (full time): N/A verbal; N/A quantitative; N/A writing
Average GPA (full time): 3.35
Average age of entrants to full-time program: 26
Average months of prior work experience (full time): 59
TOEFL requirement: Yes
Minimum TOEFL score: 600

Most popular departments:
finance, general management, human resources management, international business, marketing
Mean starting base salary for 2017 full-time graduates: $74,000
Employment location for 2017 class: Intl. N/A; N.E. N/A; M.A. N/A; S. N/A; M.W. N/A; S.W. 100%; W. N/A

University of Texas of the Permian Basin[1]

4901 E. University
Odessa, TX 79762
www.utpb.edu/
Public
Admissions: (432) 552-2605
Email: Admissions@utpb.edu
Financial aid: (432) 552-2620
Tuition: N/A
Room/board/expenses: N/A
Enrollment: N/A

University of Texas–Rio Grande Valley

1201 W University Drive
Edinburg, TX 78539
www.utrgv.edu/graduate/for-future-students/how-to-apply/index.htm
Public
Admissions: (956) 665-3661
Financial aid: (888) 882-4026
Application deadline: 04/15
In-state tuition: full time: $6,719; part time: $416/credit hour
Out-of-state tuition:
full time: $14,189
Room/board/expenses: $11,238
College-funded aid: Yes
International student aid: Yes
Full-time enrollment: 45
men: 67%; women: 33%; minorities: 49%; international: 44%
Part-time enrollment: 159
men: 51%; women: 49%; minorities: 76%; international: 4%
Acceptance rate (full time): 82%
Average GRE (full time): N/A verbal; N/A quantitative; N/A writing
Average age of entrants to full-time program: 30
TOEFL requirement: Yes
Minimum TOEFL score: 550
Most popular departments:
accounting, finance, general management, marketing, management information systems

University of Texas–San Antonio

1 UTSA Circle
San Antonio, TX 78249
www.graduateschool.utsa.edu
Public
Admissions: (210) 458-4331
Email: GraduateAdmissions@utsa.edu
Financial aid: (210) 458-8000
Application deadline: 06/15
In-state tuition: full time: $405/credit hour; part time: $405/credit hour

Out-of-state tuition: full time: $1,319/credit hour
Room/board/expenses: $15,595
College-funded aid: Yes
International student aid: Yes
Full-time enrollment: 73
men: 51%; women: 49%; minorities: 48%; international: 14%
Part-time enrollment: 174
men: 63%; women: 37%; minorities: 43%; international: 2%
Acceptance rate (full time): 59%
Average GMAT (full time): 527
Average GRE (full time): 154 verbal; 153 quantitative; 3.0 writing
Average GPA (full time): 3.30
Average age of entrants to full-time program: 25
Average months of prior work experience (full time): 31
TOEFL requirement: Yes
Minimum TOEFL score: 550
Mean starting base salary for 2017 full-time graduates: $59,000
Employment location for 2017 class: Intl. N/A; N.E. N/A; M.A. N/A; S. N/A; M.W. N/A; S.W. 100%; W. N/A

University of Texas–Tyler[1]

3900 University Boulevard
Tyler, TX 75799
www.uttyler.edu/cbt/
Public
Admissions: (903) 566-7360
Email: cbtinfo@uttyler.edu
Financial aid: N/A
Tuition: N/A
Room/board/expenses: N/A
Enrollment: N/A

West Texas A&M University

WTAMU Box 60768
Canyon, TX 79016
www.wtamu.edu/academics/online-mba.aspx
Public
Admissions: (806) 651-2501
Email: lmills@wtamu.edu
Financial aid: (806) 651-2059
Application deadline: rolling
In-state tuition: total program: $14,800 (full time); $15,300 (part time)
Out-of-state tuition: total program: $16,800 (full time)
Room/board/expenses: $15,000
College-funded aid: Yes
International student aid: Yes
Average student indebtedness at graduation: $19,000
Full-time enrollment: 370
men: 59%; women: 41%; minorities: 50%; international: 16%
Part-time enrollment: 930
men: 55%; women: 45%; minorities: 56%; international: 1%
Acceptance rate (full time): 74%
Average GMAT (full time): 540
Average GRE (full time): N/A verbal; N/A quantitative; N/A writing
Average GPA (full time): 3.48

Average age of entrants to full-time program: 26
Average months of prior work experience (full time): 18
TOEFL requirement: Yes
Minimum TOEFL score: 525
Most popular departments:
accounting, finance, health care administration, marketing, management information systems
Mean starting base salary for 2017 full-time graduates: $76,000
Employment location for 2017 class: Intl. 13%; N.E. 0%; M.A. 0%; S. 0%; M.W. 6%; S.W. 75%; W. 6%

UTAH

Brigham Young University (Marriott)

W-437 TNRB
Provo, UT 84602
mba.byu.edu
Private
Admissions: (801) 422-3500
Email: mba@byu.edu
Financial aid: (801) 422-5195
Application deadline: 05/01
Tuition: full time: $12,680; part time: N/A
Room/board/expenses: $20,792
College-funded aid: Yes
International student aid: Yes
Average student indebtedness at graduation: $39,953
Full-time enrollment: 302
men: 78%; women: 22%; minorities: 9%; international: 19%
Part-time enrollment: N/A
Acceptance rate (full time): 47%
Average GMAT (full time): 680
Average GRE (full time): N/A verbal; N/A quantitative; N/A writing
Average GPA (full time): 3.49
Average age of entrants to full-time program: 30
Average months of prior work experience (full time): 50
TOEFL requirement: Yes
Minimum TOEFL score: 590
Most popular departments:
entrepreneurship, finance, human resources management, marketing, supply chain management/logistics
Mean starting base salary for 2017 full-time graduates: $102,534
Employment location for 2017 class: Intl. 2%; N.E. 5%; M.A. 2%; S. 7%; M.W. 20%; S.W. 23%; W. 41%

Southern Utah University

351 W. University Boulevard
Cedar City, UT 84720
www.suu.edu/business
Public
Admissions: (435) 586-7740
Email: businessgrad@suu.edu
Financial aid: (435) 586-7734
Application deadline: 07/01
In-state tuition: total program: $14,002 (full time); $15,106 (part time)
Out-of-state tuition: total program: $38,710 (full time)

Room/board/expenses: N/A
College-funded aid: Yes
International student aid: Yes
Full-time enrollment: 19
men: 79%; women: 21%; minorities: N/A; international: N/A
Part-time enrollment: 18
men: 56%; women: 44%; minorities: N/A; international: N/A
Average GRE (full time): N/A verbal; N/A quantitative; N/A writing
TOEFL requirement: Yes
Minimum TOEFL score: 525

University of Utah (Eccles)

1655 E. Campus Center Drive
Room 1113
Salt Lake City, UT 84112-9301
eccles.utah.edu/programs/mba/
Public
Admissions: (801) 585-6291
Email: stephanie.geisler@eccles.utah.edu
Financial aid: (801) 585-6291
Application deadline: 05/01
In-state tuition: total program: $59,000 (full time); $58,800 (part time)
Out-of-state tuition: total program: $60,000 (full time)
Room/board/expenses: $17,500
College-funded aid: Yes
International student aid: Yes
Full-time enrollment: 133
men: 73%; women: 27%; minorities: 5%; international: 15%
Part-time enrollment: 288
men: 76%; women: 24%; minorities: 8%; international: 1%
Acceptance rate (full time): 44%
Average GMAT (full time): 637
Average GRE (full time): 161 verbal; 159 quantitative; 4.6 writing
Average GPA (full time): 3.49
Average age of entrants to full-time program: 28
Average months of prior work experience (full time): 48
TOEFL requirement: Yes
Minimum TOEFL score: 600
Most popular departments:
entrepreneurship, general management, marketing, quantitative analysis/statistics and operations research, technology
Mean starting base salary for 2017 full-time graduates: $88,143
Employment location for 2017 class: Intl. 0%; N.E. 4%; M.A. 0%; S. 2%; M.W. 8%; S.W. 8%; W. 79%

Utah State University (Huntsman)[1]

3500 Old Main Hill
Logan, UT 84322-3500
www.huntsman.usu.edu/mba/
Public
Admissions: (435) 797-3624
Email: HuntsmanMBA@usu.edu
Financial aid: N/A
Tuition: N/A

Room/board/expenses: N/A
Enrollment: N/A

Utah Valley University[1]

800 W. University Parkway
Orem, UT 84058
www.uvu.edu/woodbury
Public
Admissions: (801) 863-8367
Financial aid: N/A
Tuition: N/A
Room/board/expenses: N/A
Enrollment: N/A

Weber State University (Goddard)

2750 N. University Park
Boulevard, MC102
Layton, UT 84041-9099
weber.edu/mba
Public
Admissions: (801) 395-3528
Email: mba@weber.edu
Financial aid: (801) 626-7569
Application deadline: 05/01
In-state tuition: full time: N/A; part time: $685/credit hour
Out-of-state tuition: full time: N/A
Room/board/expenses: N/A
College-funded aid: Yes
International student aid: Yes
Full-time enrollment: N/A
Part-time enrollment: 236
men: 72%; women: 28%; minorities: N/A; international: N/A
Average GRE (full time): N/A verbal; N/A quantitative; N/A writing
TOEFL requirement: Yes
Minimum TOEFL score: 550

VERMONT

University of Vermont

55 Colchester Avenue
Burlington, VT 05405
www.uvm.edu/si-mba
Public
Admissions: (802) 656-2699
Email: si-mba@uvm.edu
Financial aid: (802) 656-5700
Application deadline: 07/15
In-state tuition: total program: $29,580 (full time); part time: N/A
Out-of-state tuition: total program: $51,564 (full time)
Room/board/expenses: $16,338
College-funded aid: Yes
International student aid: Yes
Average student indebtedness at graduation: $41,730
Full-time enrollment: 30
men: 47%; women: 53%; minorities: 3%; international: 7%
Part-time enrollment: N/A
Acceptance rate (full time): 82%
Average GMAT (full time): 504
Average GRE (full time): 159 verbal; 154 quantitative; 4.2 writing
Average GPA (full time): 3.30
Average age of entrants to full-time program: 31
Average months of prior work experience (full time): 97
TOEFL requirement: Yes
Minimum TOEFL score: 550

Most popular departments: entrepreneurship, other
Mean starting base salary for 2017 full-time graduates: $64,700
Employment location for 2017 class: Intl. N/A; N.E. 90%; M.A. N/A; S. N/A; M.W. N/A; S.W. N/A; W. 10%

VIRGINIA

College of William and Mary (Mason)

PO Box 8795
Williamsburg, VA 23187-8795
mason.wm.edu
Public
Admissions: (757) 221-2944
Email: admissions@ mason.wm.edu
Financial aid: (757) 221-2944
Application deadline: 07/15
In-state tuition: full time: $32,106; part time: $825/credit hour
Out-of-state tuition: full time: $43,278
Room/board/expenses: $18,500
College-funded aid: Yes
International student aid: Yes
Average student indebtedness at graduation: $64,927
Full-time enrollment: 204
men: 66%; women: 34%; minorities: 13%; international: 41%
Part-time enrollment: 196
men: 61%; women: 39%; minorities: 24%; international: 2%
Acceptance rate (full time): 60%
Average GMAT (full time): 617
Average GRE (full time): 152 verbal; 149 quantitative; 3.5 writing
Average GPA (full time): 3.33
Average age of entrants to full-time program: 31
Average months of prior work experience (full time): 51
TOEFL requirement: Yes
Minimum TOEFL score: N/A
Most popular departments: consulting, entrepreneurship, finance, general management, marketing
Mean starting base salary for 2017 full-time graduates: $84,966
Employment location for 2017 class: Intl. 0%; N.E. 9%; M.A. 59%; S. 4%; M.W. 9%; S.W. 9%; W. 9%

George Mason University

4400 University Drive
Fairfax, VA 22030
business.gmu.edu
Public
Admissions: (703) 993-2136
Email: mba@gmu.edu
Financial aid: (703) 993-2353
Application deadline: 04/01
In-state tuition: full time: N/A; part time: $950/credit hour
Out-of-state tuition: full time: N/A
Room/board/expenses: N/A
College-funded aid: Yes
International student aid: Yes
Full-time enrollment: N/A

Part-time enrollment: 252
men: 56%; women: 44%; minorities: 34%; international: 8%
Average GRE (full time): N/A verbal; N/A quantitative; N/A writing
TOEFL requirement: Yes
Minimum TOEFL score: N/A

James Madison University

Showker Hall
Harrisonburg, VA 22807
www.jmu.edu/cob/mba
Public
Admissions: (540) 568-3058
Email: mccoynta@jmu.edu
Financial aid: (540) 568-3139
Application deadline: 07/01
In-state tuition: full time: N/A; part time: $500/credit hour
Out-of-state tuition: full time: N/A
Room/board/expenses: N/A
College-funded aid: Yes
International student aid: Yes
Full-time enrollment: N/A
Part-time enrollment: 42
men: 62%; women: 38%; minorities: 12%; international: 7%
Average GRE (full time): N/A verbal; N/A quantitative; N/A writing
TOEFL requirement: Yes
Minimum TOEFL score: 570
Most popular departments: entrepreneurship, general management, leadership, marketing, organizational behavior

Longwood University[1]

201 High Street
Farmville, VA 23909
www.longwood.edu/business/
Public
Admissions: (877) 267-7883
Email: graduate@longwood.edu
Financial aid: N/A
Tuition: N/A
Room/board/expenses: N/A
Enrollment: N/A

Old Dominion University

1026 Constant Hall
Norfolk, VA 23529
odu.edu/mba
Public
Admissions: (757) 683-3585
Email: mbainfo@odu.edu
Financial aid: (757) 683-3683
Application deadline: 06/01
In-state tuition: full time: $496/credit hour; part time: $496/credit hour
Out-of-state tuition: full time: $1,249/credit hour
Room/board/expenses: $19,393
College-funded aid: Yes
International student aid: Yes
Full-time enrollment: 15
men: 47%; women: 53%; minorities: 27%; international: 40%
Part-time enrollment: 85
men: 55%; women: 45%; minorities: 14%; international: 6%

Average GRE (full time): N/A verbal; N/A quantitative; N/A writing
TOEFL requirement: Yes
Minimum TOEFL score: 550
Most popular departments: entrepreneurship, health care administration, public administration, supply chain management/logistics, other

Radford University

PO Box 6956
Radford, VA 24142
www.radford.edu
Public
Admissions: (540) 831-5724
Email: gradcollege@radford.edu
Financial aid: (540) 831-5408
Application deadline: 08/01
In-state tuition: full time: $347/credit hour; part time: $347/credit hour
Out-of-state tuition: full time: $702/credit hour
Room/board/expenses: $14,609
College-funded aid: Yes
International student aid: Yes
Full-time enrollment: 9
men: 44%; women: 56%; minorities: 0%; international: 33%
Part-time enrollment: 32
men: 66%; women: 34%; minorities: 3%; international: 9%
Acceptance rate (full time): 71%
Average GMAT (full time): 500
Average GRE (full time): N/A verbal; N/A quantitative; N/A writing
Average GPA (full time): 3.59
Average age of entrants to full-time program: 28
Average months of prior work experience (full time): 96
TOEFL requirement: Yes
Minimum TOEFL score: 550
Most popular departments: general management

Shenandoah University (Byrd)

Halpin Harrison, Room 103
Winchester, VA 22601
www.su.edu/
Private
Admissions: (540) 665-4581
Email: admit@su.edu
Financial aid: (540) 665-4538
Application deadline: 05/15
Tuition: full time: $16,120; part time: $860/credit hour
Room/board/expenses: $14,280
College-funded aid: Yes
International student aid: Yes
Average student indebtedness at graduation: $35,960
Full-time enrollment: 53
men: 66%; women: 34%; minorities: 17%; international: 49%
Part-time enrollment: 46
men: 37%; women: 63%; minorities: 33%; international: 4%
Acceptance rate (full time): 98%
Average GRE (full time): N/A verbal; N/A quantitative; N/A writing
Average GPA (full time): 3.18

Average age of entrants to full-time program: 27
TOEFL requirement: Yes
Minimum TOEFL score: 550
Most popular departments: general management
Mean starting base salary for 2017 full-time graduates: $31,875

University of Richmond (Robins)

1 Gateway Road
Richmond, VA 23173
robins.richmond.edu/mba/
Private
Admissions: (804) 289-8553
Email: mba@richmond.edu
Financial aid: (804) 289-8438
Application deadline: 05/15
Tuition: full time: N/A; part time: $1,440/credit hour
Room/board/expenses: N/A
College-funded aid: Yes
International student aid: Yes
Full-time enrollment: N/A
Part-time enrollment: 79
men: 63%; women: 37%; minorities: 22%; international: 4%
Average GRE (full time): N/A verbal; N/A quantitative; N/A writing
TOEFL requirement: Yes
Minimum TOEFL score: 600

University of Virginia (Darden)

PO Box 6550
Charlottesville, VA 22906-6550
www.darden.virginia.edu
Public
Admissions: (434) 924-1817
Email: darden@virginia.edu
Financial aid: (434) 924-7739
Application deadline: 05/01
In-state tuition: full time: $63,482; part time: N/A
Out-of-state tuition: full time: $65,800
Room/board/expenses: $27,168
College-funded aid: Yes
International student aid: Yes
Average student indebtedness at graduation: $104,686
Full-time enrollment: 671
men: 62%; women: 38%; minorities: N/A; international: N/A
Part-time enrollment: N/A
Acceptance rate (full time): 24%
Average GMAT (full time): 713
Average GRE (full time): 162 verbal; 161 quantitative; 5.0 writing
Average GPA (full time): 3.50
Average age of entrants to full-time program: 27
Average months of prior work experience (full time): 58
TOEFL requirement: No
Minimum TOEFL score: N/A
Most popular departments: consulting, entrepreneurship, finance, general management, marketing
Mean starting base salary for 2017 full-time graduates: $124,684

Employment location for 2017 class: Intl. 10%; N.E. 25%; M.A. 14%; S. 13%; M.W. 6%; S.W. 12%; W. 20%

Virginia Commonwealth University

301 W. Main Street
Richmond, VA 23284-4000
business.vcu.edu
Public
Admissions: (804) 828-4622
Email: gsib@vcu.edu
Financial aid: (804) 828-6669
Application deadline: 07/01
In-state tuition: full time: $14,437; part time: $632/credit hour
Out-of-state tuition: full time: $26,458
Room/board/expenses: N/A
College-funded aid: Yes
International student aid: Yes
Full-time enrollment: N/A
Part-time enrollment: 175
men: 58%; women: 42%; minorities: N/A; international: N/A
Average GRE (full time): N/A verbal; N/A quantitative; N/A writing
TOEFL requirement: Yes
Minimum TOEFL score: 600
Most popular departments: entrepreneurship, finance, general management, international business, quantitative analysis/statistics and operations research

Virginia Tech (Pamplin)

1044 Pamplin Hall (0209)
Blacksburg, VA 24061
www.mba.vt.edu
Public
Admissions: (703) 538-8410
Email: mba@vt.edu
Financial aid: (540) 231-5179
Application deadline: 08/01
In-state tuition: full time: N/A; part time: $796/credit hour
Out-of-state tuition: full time: N/A
Room/board/expenses: N/A
College-funded aid: Yes
International student aid: Yes
Full-time enrollment: N/A
Part-time enrollment: 182
men: 61%; women: 39%; minorities: 40%; international: 1%
Average GRE (full time): N/A verbal; N/A quantitative; N/A writing
TOEFL requirement: Yes
Minimum TOEFL score: 550
Most popular departments: finance, general management, international business, management information systems, technology

WASHINGTON

Eastern Washington University[1]

668 N. Riverpoint Boulevard
Suite A
Spokane, WA 99202-1677
www.ewu.edu/mba
Public
Admissions: (509) 828-1248
Email: mbaprogram@ewu.edu
Financial aid: N/A
Tuition: N/A
Room/board/expenses: N/A
Enrollment: N/A

Gonzaga University

502 E. Boone Avenue
Spokane, WA 99258-0009
www.gonzaga.edu/mba
Private
Admissions: (509) 313-4622
Email: chatman@gonzaga.edu
Financial aid: (509) 313-6581
Application deadline: 05/30
Tuition: full time: $975/credit
hour; part time: $975/credit hour
Room/board/expenses: $12,227
College-funded aid: Yes
International student aid: Yes
Full-time enrollment: 94
men: 53%; women:
47%; minorities: 19%;
international: 5%
Part-time enrollment: 154
men: 53%; women:
47%; minorities: 19%;
international: 5%
Acceptance rate (full time): 74%
Average GMAT (full time): 537
**Average GRE (full
time):** 156 verbal; 156
quantitative; N/A writing
Average GPA (full time): 3.47
**Average age of entrants to
full-time program:** 24
TOEFL requirement: Yes
Minimum TOEFL score: 570
Most popular departments:
accounting, entrepreneurship,
finance, marketing, tax

Pacific Lutheran University

Morken Center for Learning
and Technology, Room 176
Tacoma, WA 98447
www.plu.edu/mba
Private
Admissions: (253) 535-7252
Email: plumba@plu.edu
Financial aid: (253) 535-8491
Application deadline: rolling
Tuition: full time: $1,205/
credit hour; part time:
$1,205/credit hour
Room/board/expenses: $14,078
College-funded aid: Yes
International student aid: Yes
**Average student indebtedness
at graduation:** $38,175
Full-time enrollment: 52
men: 46%; women:
54%; minorities: 31%;
international: 6%
Part-time enrollment: 7
men: 43%; women:
57%; minorities: 29%;
international: 0%
Acceptance rate (full time): 94%

Average GMAT (full time): 515
**Average GRE (full
time):** 149 verbal; 147
quantitative; 3.5 writing
Average GPA (full time): 3.43
**Average age of entrants to
full-time program:** 27
**Average months of prior work
experience (full time):** 90
TOEFL requirement: Yes
Minimum TOEFL score: 570
Most popular departments:
entrepreneurship, general
management, health care
administration, supply
chain management/
logistics, technology

Seattle Pacific University[1]

3307 Third Avenue W, Suite 201
Seattle, WA 98119-1950
www.spu.edu/sbe
Private
Admissions: (206) 281-2753
Email: drj@spu.edu
Financial aid: (206) 281-2469
Tuition: N/A
Room/board/expenses: N/A
Enrollment: N/A

Seattle University (Albers)

901 12th Avenue
PO Box 222000
Seattle, WA 98122-1090
www.seattleu.edu/business/
graduate/
Private
Admissions: (206) 296-5904
Email: janshan@seattleu.edu
Financial aid: (206) 220-8020
Application deadline: 08/01
Tuition: full time: N/A; part
time: $850/credit hour
Room/board/expenses: N/A
College-funded aid: Yes
International student aid: Yes
Full-time enrollment: N/A
Part-time enrollment: 345
men: 57%; women:
43%; minorities: 28%;
international: 11%
**Average GRE (full
time):** N/A verbal; N/A
quantitative; N/A writing
TOEFL requirement: Yes
Minimum TOEFL score: 580
Most popular departments:
accounting, finance, marketing,
management information
systems, quantitative
analysis/statistics and
operations research

University of Washington–Bothell[1]

18115 Campus Way NW
Box 358533
Bothell, WA 98011
www.uwb.edu/mba
Public
Admissions: (425) 352-5394
Email: uwbmba@uw.edu
Financial aid: N/A
Tuition: N/A
Room/board/expenses: N/A
Enrollment: N/A

University of Washington (Foster)

PO Box 353223
Seattle, WA 98195-3223
mba.washington.edu
Public
Admissions: (206) 543-4661
Email: mba@uw.edu
Financial aid: (206) 543-4661
Application deadline: 03/15
In-state tuition: full time:
$33,339; part time: $25,290
Out-of-state tuition:
full time: $48,606
Room/board/expenses: $29,768
College-funded aid: Yes
International student aid: Yes
**Average student indebtedness
at graduation:** $45,045
Full-time enrollment: 221
men: 60%; women:
40%; minorities: 15%;
international: 34%
Part-time enrollment: 382
men: 62%; women:
38%; minorities: 25%;
international: 6%
Acceptance rate (full time): 22%
Average GMAT (full time): 693
**Average GRE (full
time):** 160 verbal; 158
quantitative; 4.5 writing
Average GPA (full time): 3.39
**Average age of entrants to
full-time program:** 28
**Average months of prior work
experience (full time):** 68
TOEFL requirement: Yes
Minimum TOEFL score: 600
Most popular departments:
consulting, entrepreneurship,
finance, manufacturing
and technology
management, marketing
**Mean starting base salary for 2017
full-time graduates:** $119,904
**Employment location for
2017 class:** Intl. 2%; N.E.
0%; M.A. 0%; S. 0%; M.W.
0%; S.W. 2%; W. 96%

University of Washington–Tacoma (Milgard)

1900 Commerce Street
Box 358420
Tacoma, WA 98402
www.tacoma.uw.edu/milgard/
mba/overview
Public
Admissions: (253) 692-5630
Email: uwtmba@uw.edu
Financial aid: (253) 692-4374
Application deadline: 06/01
In-state tuition: full time: N/A;
part time: $1,537/credit hour
Out-of-state tuition: full time: N/A
Room/board/expenses: N/A
College-funded aid: Yes
International student aid: Yes
Full-time enrollment: N/A
Part-time enrollment: 50
men: 56%; women:
44%; minorities: 34%;
international: 0%
**Average GRE (full
time):** N/A verbal; N/A
quantitative; N/A writing
TOEFL requirement: Yes
Minimum TOEFL score: 580

Washington State University[1]

PO Box 644744
Pullman, WA 99164-4744
business.wsu.edu/
graduate-programs/
Public
Admissions: (509) 335-7617
Email: mba@wsu.edu
Financial aid: (509) 335-9711
Tuition: N/A
Room/board/expenses: N/A
Enrollment: N/A

Western Washington University[1]

516 High Street, MS 9072
Bellingham, WA 98225-9072
www.cbe.wwu.edu/mba/
Public
Admissions: (360) 650-3898
Email: mba@wwu.edu
Financial aid: N/A
Tuition: N/A
Room/board/expenses: N/A
Enrollment: N/A

WEST VIRGINIA

Marshall University (Lewis)

1 John Marshall Drive
Huntington, WV 25755-2020
www.marshall.edu/lcob/
Public
Admissions: (800) 642-9842
Email: johnson73@marshall.edu
Financial aid: (800) 438-5390
Application deadline: 08/01
In-state tuition: full time:
$484/credit hour; part
time: $484/credit hour
Out-of-state tuition: full
time: $1,141/credit hour
Room/board/expenses: N/A
College-funded aid: Yes
International student aid: Yes
Full-time enrollment: 149
men: 62%; women:
38%; minorities: N/A;
international: N/A
Part-time enrollment: 64
men: 53%; women:
47%; minorities: N/A;
international: N/A
Acceptance rate (full time): 87%
**Average GRE (full
time):** N/A verbal; N/A
quantitative; N/A writing
Average GPA (full time): 3.21
TOEFL requirement: Yes
Minimum TOEFL score: N/A
Most popular departments:
finance, general management,
health care administration,
human resources
management, marketing

West Virginia University[1]

PO Box 6027
Morgantown, WV 26506
www.be.wvu.edu
Public
Admissions: (304) 293-7811
Email: mba@wvu.edu
Financial aid: (304) 293-5242

Tuition: N/A
Room/board/expenses: N/A
Enrollment: N/A

WISCONSIN

Marquette University

PO Box 1881
Milwaukee, WI 53201-1881
www.marquette.edu/gsm
Private
Admissions: (414) 288-7145
Email: mba@Marquette.edu
Financial aid: (414) 288-7137
Application deadline: rolling
Tuition: full time: $1,100/
credit hour; part time:
$1,100/credit hour
Room/board/expenses: $16,662
College-funded aid: Yes
International student aid: Yes
Full-time enrollment: 92
men: 40%; women:
60%; minorities: 10%;
international: 38%
Part-time enrollment: 195
men: 71%; women: 29%;
minorities: 9%; international: 5%
Acceptance rate (full time): 76%
Average GMAT (full time): 581
**Average GRE (full
time):** 153 verbal; 154
quantitative; 4.1 writing
Average GPA (full time): 3.48
**Average age of entrants to
full-time program:** 24
TOEFL requirement: Yes
Minimum TOEFL score: N/A
Most popular departments:
accounting, finance, human
resources management,
international business

University of Wisconsin–Eau Claire[1]

Schneider Hall 215
Eau Claire, WI 54702-4004
www.uwec.edu/academics/
college-business/
Public
Admissions: (715) 836-5415
Email: uwecmba@uwec.edu
Financial aid: (715) 836-5606
Tuition: N/A
Room/board/expenses: N/A
Enrollment: N/A

University of Wisconsin–La Crosse[1]

1725 State Street
La Crosse, WI 54601
www.uwlax.edu
Public
Admissions: (608) 785-8939
Email: admissions@uwlax.edu
Financial aid: (608) 785-8604
Tuition: N/A
Room/board/expenses: N/A
Enrollment: N/A

University of Wisconsin–Madison

975 University Avenue
Madison, WI 53706-1323
wsb.wisc.edu
Public
Admissions: (608) 262-4000
Email: mba@wsb.wisc.edu
Financial aid: (608) 262-3060

Application deadline: 04/11
In-state tuition: full time:
$18,712; part time: $20,043
Out-of-state tuition:
full time: $36,576
Room/board/expenses: $21,084
College-funded aid: Yes
International student aid: Yes
**Average student indebtedness
at graduation:** $20,226
Full-time enrollment: 203
men: 65%; women:
35%; minorities: 17%;
international: 20%
Part-time enrollment: 157
men: 69%; women:
31%; minorities: 11%;
international: 3%
Acceptance rate (full time): 30%
Average GMAT (full time): 678
**Average GRE (full
time):** 158 verbal; 157
quantitative; 4.5 writing
Average GPA (full time): 3.35
**Average age of entrants to
full-time program:** 28
**Average months of prior work
experience (full time):** 60
TOEFL requirement: Yes
Minimum TOEFL score: N/A
Most popular departments:
finance, general
management, marketing,
production/operations
management, real estate
**Mean starting base salary for 2017
full-time graduates:** $97,237
**Employment location for
2017 class:** Intl. 4%; N.E.
9%; M.A. 0%; S. 4%; M.W.
58%; S.W. 8%; W. 17%

University of Wisconsin– Milwaukee (Lubar)

PO Box 742
Milwaukee, WI 53201-9863
lubar.uwm.edu
Public
Admissions: (414) 229-5403
Email: mba-ms@uwm.edu
Financial aid: (414) 229-4541
Application deadline: rolling
In-state tuition: full time:
N/A; part time: $14,532
Out-of-state tuition: full time: N/A
Room/board/expenses: N/A
College-funded aid: Yes

International student aid: Yes
Full-time enrollment: N/A
Part-time enrollment: 433
men: 61%; women:
39%; minorities: 16%;
international: 10%
**Average GRE (full
time):** N/A verbal; N/A
quantitative; N/A writing
TOEFL requirement: Yes
Minimum TOEFL score: 550
Most popular departments:
accounting, finance, general
management, management
information systems

University of Wisconsin–Oshkosh

800 Algoma Boulevard
Oshkosh, WI 54901
www.uwosh.edu/cob
Public
Admissions: (800) 633-1430
Email: mba@uwosh.edu
Financial aid: (920) 424-3377
Application deadline: rolling
In-state tuition: full time: $758/
credit hour; part time: N/A
Out-of-state tuition: full
time: $1,266/credit hour
Room/board/expenses: N/A
College-funded aid: Yes
International student aid: Yes
Full-time enrollment: 12
men: 75%; women:
25%; minorities: 17%;
international: 0%
Part-time enrollment: 397
men: 64%; women:
36%; minorities: 10%;
international: 0%
Acceptance rate (full time): 100%
Average GMAT (full time): 470
**Average GRE (full
time):** 154 verbal; 144
quantitative; 2.5 writing
Average GPA (full time): 3.11
**Average age of entrants to
full-time program:** 32
**Average months of prior work
experience (full time):** 105
TOEFL requirement: Yes
Minimum TOEFL score: 550
Most popular departments: health
care administration, other

University of Wisconsin–Parkside

900 Wood Road
PO Box 2000
Kenosha, WI 53141-2000
uwp.edu/learn/programs/
mbamasters.cfm
Public
Admissions: (262) 595-2243
Email: admissions@uwp.edu
Financial aid: (262) 595-2574
Application deadline: 08/15
In-state tuition: full time:
$498/credit hour; part
time: $498/credit hour
Out-of-state tuition: full
time: $1,020/credit hour
Room/board/expenses: $9,000
College-funded aid: Yes
International student aid: Yes
Full-time enrollment: 17
men: 47%; women:
53%; minorities: 18%;
international: 47%
Part-time enrollment: 55
men: 56%; women:
44%; minorities: 16%;
international: 11%
Acceptance rate (full time): 92%
Average GMAT (full time): 395
**Average GRE (full
time):** N/A verbal; N/A
quantitative; N/A writing
Average GPA (full time): 3.35
**Average age of entrants to
full-time program:** 28
**Average months of prior work
experience (full time):** 36
TOEFL requirement: Yes
Minimum TOEFL score: 550
Most popular departments:
finance, general
management, international
business, marketing,
organizational behavior

University of Wisconsin–River Falls

410 S. Third Street
River Falls, WI 54022-5001
www.uwrf.edu/mba
Public
Admissions: (715) 425-3335
Email: mbacbe@uwrf.edu
Financial aid: (715) 425-4111
Application deadline: rolling

In-state tuition: full time:
$692/credit hour; part
time: $692/credit hour
Out-of-state tuition: full
time: $692/credit hour
Room/board/expenses: N/A
College-funded aid: Yes
International student aid: Yes
Full-time enrollment: 26
men: 73%; women:
27%; minorities: N/A;
international: N/A
Part-time enrollment: 65
men: 57%; women:
43%; minorities: N/A;
international: N/A
Acceptance rate (full time): 100%
Average GMAT (full time): 277
**Average GRE (full
time):** N/A verbal; N/A
quantitative; N/A writing
**Average age of entrants to
full-time program:** 24
TOEFL requirement: Yes
Minimum TOEFL score: 550

University of Wisconsin– Whitewater

800 W. Main Street
Whitewater, WI 53190
www.uww.edu/cobe
Public
Admissions: (262) 472-1945
Email: gradbus@uww.edu
Financial aid: (262) 472-1130
Application deadline: 07/15
In-state tuition: full time: $9,492;
part time: $527/credit hour
Out-of-state tuition:
full time: $19,018
Room/board/expenses: $6,950
College-funded aid: Yes
International student aid: Yes
**Average student indebtedness
at graduation:** $8,000
Full-time enrollment: 62
men: 60%; women:
40%; minorities: 11%;
international: 6%
Part-time enrollment: 454
men: 58%; women:
42%; minorities: 11%;
international: 6%
Acceptance rate (full time): 68%
Average GMAT (full time): 506
**Average GRE (full
time):** N/A verbal; N/A
quantitative; N/A writing

Average GPA (full time): 3.30
**Average age of entrants to
full-time program:** 27
**Average months of prior work
experience (full time):** 50
TOEFL requirement: Yes
Minimum TOEFL score: 550
Most popular departments:
finance, general management,
marketing, supply chain
management/logistics, other
**Mean starting base salary for 2017
full-time graduates:** $57,000

WYOMING

University of Wyoming

1000 E. University Avenue
Department 3275
Laramie, WY 82071-3275
www.uwyo.edu/mba/
Public
Admissions: (307) 766-5160
Email: admissions@uwyo.edu
Financial aid: (307) 766-3506
Application deadline: 06/30
In-state tuition: full time: $683/
credit hour; part time: N/A
Out-of-state tuition: full
time: $1,143/credit hour
Room/board/expenses: $5,800
College-funded aid: Yes
International student aid: Yes
Full-time enrollment: 38
men: 71%; women: 29%;
minorities: 5%; international: 3%
Part-time enrollment: N/A
Acceptance rate (full time): 65%
Average GMAT (full time): 610
**Average GRE (full
time):** 156 verbal; 155
quantitative; 4.0 writing
Average GPA (full time): 3.00
**Average age of entrants to
full-time program:** 25
**Average months of prior work
experience (full time):** 10
TOEFL requirement: Yes
Minimum TOEFL score: N/A
Most popular departments:
finance, international
business, other

Online Business Programs

NCLUDED IN THIS directory are **319 regionally accredited U.S. institutions** that offer business degree programs that can be completed primarily through distance education. Among them, **281 schools award online MBAs and 165 award master of business degrees that are not MBAs**; for institutions reporting both, you will find information for each degree type. Data were submitted to U.S. News in a statistical survey conducted in the summer and autumn of 2017. Only schools that provided their data have profiles in this directory.

KEY TO THE TERMINOLOGY

N/A. Not available from the school or not applicable.

Email. The address of the admissions office. If instead of an email address a website is given in this field, the website will automatically present an email screen programmed to reach the admissions office.

Application deadline. For fall 2018 enrollment. "Rolling" means there is no application deadline; the school acts on applications as they are received.

Program can be completed entirely online. "Yes" means there are no requirements to come to campus. "No" indicates some limited face-to-face attendance mandates for events like orientations, group sessions and exams. "Depends" means there may be variation among programs.

Total program cost. For the 2017-2018 academic year, the tuition required to earn the full degree from start to finish. Tuition is for the program with largest enrollment.

Tuition per credit. The cost per credit hour for the 2017-2018 academic year. Tuition is for the program with largest enrollment.

Acceptance rate. Percentage of applicants who were offered admittance during the 2016-2017 academic year.

Test scores required. For the 2016-2017 academic year.

Average Graduate Management Admission Test (GMAT) score. Calculated for students who entered in the 2016-2017 academic year.

Average Graduate Record Examinations (GRE) score. Verbal, quantitative and writing scores calculated for students who entered in the 2016-2017 academic year.

Average age of entrants. Calculated for new entrants in the 2016-2017 academic year.

Students with prior work experience. Calculated for students who entered in the 2016-2017 academic year. Refers to post-baccalaureate work experience only.

Enrollment. The count of students enrolled at least once during the 2016-2017 academic year.

Average class size. Calculation of students per course in October 2016. Includes students attending class on campus in the case of blended courses delivered both online and in person.

Most popular concentrations. Based on highest student demand.

Completion. Includes three distinct elements: the three-year graduation rate among new entrants from the 2013-2014 academic year; the number of credits students need to earn a degree; the estimated time needed for completing the program with the largest enrollment starting in the 2017-2018 academic year.

College-funded aid available. "Yes" means the school provided its own financial aid to students during the 2016-2017 academic year.

Graduates with debt. Calculated for 2016-2017 graduates who incurred business program debt.

ALABAMA

Auburn University (Harbert)
Public

ONLINE MBA PROGRAM(S)
harbert.auburn.edu/
Admissions: (334) 844-4060
Email: mbadmis@auburn.edu
Financial aid: (334) 844-4634
Application deadline: rolling
Program can be completed entirely online: No
Total program cost: $34,425 full-time in-state, $34,425 part-time in-state, $34,425 full-time out-of-state, $34,425 part-time out-of-state
Tuition per credit: $875 full-time in-state, $875 part-time in-state, $875 full-time out-of-state, $875 part-time out-of-state
Acceptance rate: 78%
Test scores required: GMAT or GRE
Average GMAT: 577
Average GRE: 154 verbal, 154 quantitative, 3.9 writing
Average age of entrants: 32
Students with prior work experience: 96%
Enrollment: 353, 73% men, 27% women, 14% minority, 1% international
Average class size: 28
Most popular MBA concentrations: finance, marketing, management information systems, supply chain management/logistics, quantitative analysis/statistics and operations research
Completion: Three year graduation rate: 77%; credits needed to graduate: 39; target time to graduate: 2.5 years
College funded aid available: Domestic: No; International: No
Graduates with debt: 27%; average amount of debt $10,281

ONLINE BUSINESS PROGRAM(S)
harbert.auburn.edu/
Admissions: (334) 844-4060
Email: mbadmis@auburn.edu
Financial aid: (334) 844-4634
Application deadline: rolling
Program can be completed entirely online: No
Total program cost: $26,550 full-time in-state, $26,550 part-time in-state, $26,550 full-time out-of-state, $26,550 part-time out-of-state
Tuition per credit: $875 full-time in-state, $875 part-time in-state, $875 full-time out-of-state, $875 part-time out-of-state
Acceptance rate: 67%
Test scores required: GMAT or GRE
Average GMAT: 566
Average GRE: 151 verbal, 150 quantitative, 3.6 writing
Average age of entrants: 31
Students with prior work experience: 94%
Enrollment: 150, 64% men, 36% women, 13% minority, 1% international
Average class size: 24

Most popular business concentrations: accounting, finance, management information systems, quantitative analysis/statistics and operations research
Completion: Three year graduation rate: 93%; credits needed to graduate: 30; target time to graduate: 2 years
College funded aid available: Domestic: No; International: No
Graduates with debt: 38%; average amount of debt $14,323

Auburn University–Montgomery
Public

ONLINE MBA PROGRAM(S)
www.aum.edu/admissions
Admissions: (334) 244-3615
Email: admissions@aum.edu
Financial aid: (334) 244-3571
Application deadline: rolling
Program can be completed entirely online: Depends
Total program cost: $11,550 full-time in-state, $11,550 part-time in-state, $12,210 full-time out-of-state, $12,210 part-time out-of-state
Tuition per credit: $385 full-time in-state, $385 part-time in-state, $407 full-time out-of-state, $407 part-time out-of-state
Test scores required: GMAT
Completion: Credits needed to graduate: 30; target time to graduate: 2 years

Jacksonville State University
Public

ONLINE MBA PROGRAM(S)
www.jsu.edu/graduate/index.html
Admissions: (256) 782-5329
Email: graduate@jsu.edu
Financial aid: (256) 782-5006
Application deadline: rolling
Program can be completed entirely online: Yes
Total program cost: $11,460 full-time in-state, $11,460 part-time in-state, $11,460 full-time out-of-state, $11,460 part-time out-of-state
Tuition per credit: $382 full-time in-state, $382 part-time in-state, $382 full-time out-of-state, $382 part-time out-of-state
Acceptance rate: 50%
Test scores required: GMAT
Average GMAT: 466
Average age of entrants: 27
Students with prior work experience: 52%
Enrollment: 79, 46% men, 54% women, 28% minority
Completion: Three year graduation rate: 45%; credits needed to graduate: 30; target time to graduate: 2 years

Samford University (Brock)
Private

ONLINE MBA PROGRAM(S)
www.samford.edu/business
Admissions: (205) 726-2040
Email: eagambre@samford.edu
Financial aid: (205) 726-2905
Application deadline: rolling
Program can be completed entirely online: Yes
Total program cost: $39,000 full-time in-state, $39,000 part-time in-state, $39,000 full-time out-of-state, $39,000 part-time out-of-state
Tuition per credit: $813 full-time in-state, $813 part-time in-state, $813 full-time out-of-state, $813 part-time out-of-state
Acceptance rate: 55%
Test scores required: GMAT or GRE
Average GMAT: 566
Average GRE: 157 verbal, 151 quantitative, 4.0 writing
Average age of entrants: 28
Enrollment: 123, 57% men, 43% women, 11% minority, 5% international
Average class size: 20
Most popular MBA concentrations: entrepreneurship, finance, marketing
Completion: Three year graduation rate: 69%; credits needed to graduate: 36; target time to graduate: 2 years
College funded aid available: Domestic: Yes
Graduates with debt: 16%; average amount of debt $31,846

Troy University
Public

ONLINE MBA PROGRAM(S)
admission.troy.edu
Admissions: (800) 414-5756
Email: admit@troy.edu
Financial aid: (334) 670-3182
Application deadline: rolling
Program can be completed entirely online: Yes
Total program cost: $17,784 full-time in-state, $8,892 part-time in-state, $35,568 full-time out-of-state, $17,784 part-time out-of-state
Tuition per credit: $494 full-time in-state, $494 part-time in-state, $988 full-time out-of-state, $988 part-time out-of-state
Acceptance rate: 60%
Test scores required: GMAT or GRE
Average GMAT: 460
Average GRE: 143 verbal, 145 quantitative
Average age of entrants: 30
Enrollment: 124, 44% men, 56% women, 39% minority
Average class size: 22
Most popular MBA concentrations: general management
Completion: Target time to graduate: 2 years
College funded aid available: Domestic: Yes; International: Yes

ONLINE BUSINESS PROGRAM(S)
admission.troy.edu
Admissions: (800) 414-5756
Email: admit@troy.edu
Financial aid: (334) 670-3182
Application deadline: rolling
Program can be completed entirely online: Yes
Total program cost: $17,784 full-time in-state, $8,892 part-time in-state, $35,668 full-time out-of-state, $17,784 part-time out-of-state
Tuition per credit: $494 full-time in-state, $494 part-time in-state, $988 full-time out-of-state, $988 part-time out-of-state
Acceptance rate: 98%
Test scores required: GMAT or GRE
Average GMAT: 240
Average GRE: 143 verbal, 142 quantitative
Average age of entrants: 35
Enrollment: 807, 38% men, 62% women, 38% minority
Average class size: 25
Most popular business concentrations: e-commerce, general management, human resources management, leadership, other
Completion: Three year graduation rate: 33%; target time to graduate: 2 years
College funded aid available: Domestic: Yes; International: Yes

University of Alabama (Manderson)
Public

ONLINE BUSINESS PROGRAM(S)
www.graduate.ua.edu
Admissions: (205) 348-7221
Email: graduate.school@ua.edu
Financial aid: (205) 348-6756
Application deadline: rolling
Program can be completed entirely online: Yes
Total program cost: N/A
Tuition per credit: $372 full-time in-state, $372 part-time in-state, $372 full-time out-of-state, $372 part-time out-of-state
Acceptance rate: 82%
Test scores required: GMAT or GRE
Average GMAT: 605
Average GRE: 150 verbal, 154 quantitative, 4.0 writing
Average age of entrants: 36
Students with prior work experience: 100%
Enrollment: 174, 57% men, 43% women, N/A minority, N/A international
Average class size: 25
Most popular business concentrations: general management, marketing, production/operations management
Completion: Three year graduation rate: 94%; credits needed to graduate: 30; target time to graduate: 2 years

College funded aid available: Domestic: Yes; International: Yes
Graduates with debt: 10%; average amount of debt $13,000

University of Alabama–Birmingham
Public

ONLINE MBA PROGRAM(S)
www.uab.edu/graduate/
Admissions: (205) 934-8227
Email: gradschool@uab.edu
Financial aid: (205) 934-8223
Application deadline: rolling
Program can be completed entirely online: Yes
Total program cost: $39,168 part-time in-state, $39,168 full-time out-of-state, $39,168 part-time out-of-state
Tuition per credit: $1,088 full-time in-state, $1,088 part-time in-state, $1,088 full-time out-of-state, $1,088 part-time out-of-state
Acceptance rate: 75%
Average GMAT: 507
Average GRE: 150 verbal, 145 quantitative, 3.0 writing
Average age of entrants: 31
Enrollment: 27, 52% men, 48% women, 30% minority, 7% international
Average class size: 29
Most popular MBA concentrations: finance, health care administration, marketing, management information systems
Completion: Credits needed to graduate: 36
College funded aid available: Domestic: Yes; International: Yes

ONLINE BUSINESS PROGRAM(S)
www.uab.edu/graduate/
Admissions: (205) 934-8227
Email: gradschool@uab.edu
Financial aid: (205) 934-8223
Application deadline: rolling
Program can be completed entirely online: Yes
Total program cost: $32,640 part-time in-state, $32,640 part-time out-of-state
Tuition per credit: $1,088 full-time in-state, $1,088 part-time in-state, $1,088 full-time out-of-state, $1,088 part-time out-of-state
Acceptance rate: 92%
Test scores required: GMAT or GRE
Average GMAT: 510
Average age of entrants: 33
Students with prior work experience: 80%
Enrollment: 100, 39% men, 61% women, 24% minority
Average class size: 19
Most popular business concentrations: accounting
Completion: Credits needed to graduate: 30; target time to graduate: 2 years
College funded aid available: Domestic: Yes; International: Yes
Graduates with debt: 74%; average amount of debt $35,045

University of North Alabama
Public

ONLINE MBA PROGRAM(S)
www.una.edu/mba/index.html
Admissions: (256) 765-4103
Email: ztcrowell@una.edu
Financial aid: (256) 765-4279
Application deadline: rolling
Program can be completed entirely online: Yes
Total program cost: $14,450 full-time in-state, $14,450 part-time in-state, $14,450 full-time out-of-state, $14,450 part-time out-of-state
Tuition per credit: $425 full-time in-state, $425 part-time in-state, $425 full-time out-of-state, $425 part-time out-of-state
Acceptance rate: 88%
Average GMAT: 470
Average GRE: 147 verbal, 146 quantitative
Average age of entrants: 34
Students with prior work experience: 24%
Enrollment: 819, 55% men, 45% women, 35% minority, 7% international
Average class size: 35
Most popular MBA concentrations: finance, general management, health care administration, human resources management, management information systems
Completion: Three year graduation rate: 68%; credits needed to graduate: 34; target time to graduate: 2 years
College funded aid available: Domestic: Yes; International: Yes
Graduates with debt: 26%; average amount of debt $32,770

ALASKA

University of Alaska–Fairbanks
Public

ONLINE MBA PROGRAM(S)
www.uaf.edu/admissions
Admissions: (800) 478-1823
Email: admissions@uaf.edu
Financial aid: (888) 474-7256
Application deadline: rolling
Program can be completed entirely online: Yes
Total program cost: $18,300 full-time in-state, $18,300 part-time in-state, $18,300 full-time out-of-state, $18,300 part-time out-of-state
Tuition per credit: $555 full-time in-state, $555 part-time in-state, $555 full-time out-of-state, $555 part-time out-of-state
Average class size: 27
Most popular MBA concentrations: general management
Completion: Credits needed to graduate: 30; target time to graduate: 2 years

College funded aid available: Domestic: Yes; International: Yes
Graduates with debt: 29%; average amount of debt $21,534

ARIZONA

Arizona State University (Carey)

Public

ONLINE MBA PROGRAM(S)

wpcarey.asu.edu/mba
Admissions: (480) 965-3332
Email: wpcareymasters@asu.edu
Financial aid: (480) 965-6890
Application deadline: Domestic: 06/05; International: 02/06
Program can be completed entirely online: Yes
Total program cost: $59,584
full-time in-state, $59,584
full-time out-of-state
Tuition per credit: $1,216
full-time in-state, $1,216
part-time in-state, $1,216
full-time out-of-state, $1,216
part-time out-of-state
Acceptance rate: 57%
Test scores required: GMAT or GRE
Average GMAT: 591
Average GRE: 156 verbal, 154 quantitative, 4.1 writing
Average age of entrants: 31
Students with prior work experience: 99%
Enrollment: 402, 74% men, 26% women, 30% minority, 2% international
Average class size: 50
Most popular MBA concentrations: finance, international business, marketing, supply chain management/logistics, other
Completion: Three year graduation rate: 97%; credits needed to graduate: 49; target time to graduate: 2 years
College funded aid available: Domestic: Yes; International: Yes
Graduates with debt: 53%; average amount of debt $47,567

ONLINE BUSINESS PROGRAM(S)

wpcarey.asu.edu/masters-programs
Admissions: (480) 965-3332
Email: wpcareymasters@asu.edu
Financial aid: (480) 965-6890
Application deadline: N/A
Program can be completed entirely online: Yes
Total program cost: $30,540
full-time in-state, $30,540
full-time out-of-state
Tuition per credit: $1,018
full-time in-state, $1,020
part-time in-state, $1,018
full-time out-of-state, $1,020
part-time out-of-state
Acceptance rate: 72%
Test scores required: GMAT or GRE
Average GMAT: 634
Average GRE: 155 verbal, 155 quantitative, 4.0 writing
Average age of entrants: 34

Students with prior work experience: 95%
Enrollment: 206, 74% men, 26% women, 35% minority, 3% international
Average class size: 35
Most popular business concentrations: management information systems, other
Completion: Three year graduation rate: 94%; credits needed to graduate: 30; target time to graduate: 1.5 years
College funded aid available: Domestic: Yes; International: Yes
Graduates with debt: 59%; average amount of debt $45,634

Northcentral University

Private

ONLINE MBA PROGRAM(S)

www.ncu.edu
Admissions: (866) 776-0331
Email: information@ncu.edu
Financial aid: (888) 327-2877
Application deadline: rolling
Program can be completed entirely online: Yes
Total program cost: $28,230
full-time in-state, $28,230
part-time in-state, $28,230
full-time out-of-state, $28,230
part-time out-of-state
Tuition per credit: $901 full-time in-state, $901 part-time in-state, $901 full-time out-of-state, $901 part-time out-of-state
Test scores required: No
Average class size: 1
Most popular MBA concentrations: entrepreneurship, finance, general management, health care administration, human resources management
Completion: Target time to graduate: 2 years

ONLINE BUSINESS PROGRAM(S)

www.ncu.edu
Admissions: (866) 776-0331
Email: information@ncu.edu
Financial aid: (888) 327-2877
Application deadline: N/A
Program can be completed entirely online: Yes
Total program cost: $25,770
full-time in-state, $25,770
part-time in-state, $25,770
full-time out-of-state, $25,770
part-time out-of-state
Tuition per credit: $824
full-time in-state, $824
part-time in-state, $824
full-time out-of-state, $824
part-time out-of-state
Test scores required: No
Average class size: 1
Most popular business concentrations: accounting, leadership
Completion: Target time to graduate: 2 years

Northern Arizona University

Public

ONLINE BUSINESS PROGRAM(S)

nau.edu/gradcol/admissions/
Admissions: (928) 523-4348
Email: graduate@nau.edu
Financial aid: (928) 523-4951
Application deadline: rolling
Program can be completed entirely online: Yes
Total program cost: $14,760
full-time in-state, $19,800
part-time in-state, $14,760
full-time out-of-state, $19,800
part-time out-of-state
Tuition per credit: $410
full-time in-state, $550
part-time in-state, $410
full-time out-of-state, $550
part-time out-of-state
Acceptance rate: 99%
Test scores required: No
Average GRE: 147 verbal, 144 quantitative, 3.0 writing
Average age of entrants: 39
Enrollment: 306, 40% men, 60% women, 33% minority
Average class size: 11
Most popular business concentrations: health care administration, leadership, public administration
Completion: Three year graduation rate: 71%; credits needed to graduate: 36; target time to graduate: 2 years
College funded aid available: Domestic: Yes; International: Yes
Graduates with debt: 50%; average amount of debt $42,798

University of Arizona (Eller)

Public

ONLINE MBA PROGRAM(S)

ellermba.arizona.edu/
Admissions: (520) 621-4008
Email: jderanek@eller.arizona.edu
Financial aid: (520) 621-5065
Application deadline: rolling
Program can be completed entirely online: Yes
Total program cost: $27,000
full-time in-state, $18,000
part-time in-state, $27,000
full-time out-of-state, $18,000
part-time out-of-state
Tuition per credit: $1,000
full-time in-state, $1,000
part-time in-state, $1,000
full-time out-of-state, $1,000
part-time out-of-state
Acceptance rate: 85%
Test scores required: GMAT
Average GMAT: 591
Average age of entrants: 32
Students with prior work experience: 97%
Enrollment: 273, 73% men, 27% women, 28% minority, 2% international
Average class size: 60
Most popular MBA concentrations: entrepreneurship, finance, general management, marketing, management information systems

Completion: Three year graduation rate: 92%; credits needed to graduate: 45; target time to graduate: 2.5 years
College funded aid available: Domestic: Yes; International: Yes
Graduates with debt: 54%; average amount of debt $45,106

ARKANSAS

Arkansas State University–Jonesboro

Public

ONLINE MBA PROGRAM(S)

www.astate.edu/college/graduate-school
Admissions: (870) 972-3035
Email: broe@astate.edu
Financial aid: (870) 972-2310
Application deadline: rolling
Program can be completed entirely online: Yes
Total program cost: $20,130
full-time in-state, $20,130
part-time in-state, $20,130
full-time out-of-state, $20,130
part-time out-of-state
Tuition per credit: $610 full-time in-state, $610 part-time in-state, $610 full-time out-of-state, $610 part-time out-of-state
Acceptance rate: 83%
Test scores required: GMAT or GRE
Average GMAT: 608
Average GRE: 157 verbal, 156 quantitative, 5.0 writing
Average age of entrants: 34
Students with prior work experience: 88%
Enrollment: 190, 57% men, 43% women, 21% minority
Average class size: 28
Most popular MBA concentrations: finance, health care administration, international business, management information systems, supply chain management/logistics
Completion: Three year graduation rate: 93%; credits needed to graduate: 33; target time to graduate: 2.5 years
College funded aid available: Domestic: Yes; International: Yes
Graduates with debt: 54%; average amount of debt $16,760

Southern Arkansas University

Public

ONLINE MBA PROGRAM(S)

www.saumag.edu/graduate
Admissions: (870) 235-4150
Email: kkbloss@saumag.edu
Financial aid: (870) 235-4025
Application deadline: rolling
Program can be completed entirely online: Yes
Total program cost: N/A
Tuition per credit: $285
full-time in-state, $285
part-time in-state, $425
full-time out-of-state, $425
part-time out-of-state

Test scores required: GMAT or GRE
Average class size: 17
Most popular MBA concentrations: entrepreneurship, general management, supply chain management/logistics, other
Completion: Credits needed to graduate: 30; target time to graduate: 2 years
College funded aid available: Domestic: Yes; International: Yes

University of Central Arkansas

Public

ONLINE MBA PROGRAM(S)

www.uca.edu/graduateschool
Admissions: (501) 450-3124
Financial aid: (501) 450-3140
Application deadline: rolling
Program can be completed entirely online: Yes
Total program cost: N/A
Tuition per credit: $325
full-time in-state, $325
part-time in-state, $325
full-time out-of-state, $325
part-time out-of-state
Acceptance rate: 59%
Test scores required: GMAT or GRE
Enrollment: 138, 53% men, 47% women, 22% minority, 19% international
Average class size: 25
Most popular MBA concentrations: finance, health care administration, management information systems
College funded aid available: Domestic: Yes
Graduates with debt: 39%; average amount of debt $18,437

CALIFORNIA

Alliant International University

Private

ONLINE MBA PROGRAM(S)

www.alliant.edu/asm/asm-admissions/
Admissions: (866) 825-5426
Email: admissions@alliant.edu
Financial aid: (858) 635-4700
Application deadline: rolling
Program can be completed entirely online: Yes
Total program cost: $16,200
full-time in-state, $8,100
part-time in-state, $16,200
full-time out-of-state, $8,100
part-time out-of-state
Tuition per credit: $675 full-time in-state, $675 part-time in-state, $675 full-time out-of-state, $675 part-time out-of-state
Test scores required: No
Enrollment: 22, 45% men, 55% women, N/A minority, N/A international
Average class size: 12
Completion: Credits needed to graduate: 36; target time to graduate: 2 years
College funded aid available: Domestic: Yes; International: Yes

Azusa Pacific University

Private

ONLINE BUSINESS PROGRAM(S)

www.apu.edu
Admissions: (626) 815-4570
Email: lwitte@apu.edu
Financial aid: (626) 815-4570
Application deadline: rolling
Program can be completed entirely online: Yes
Total program cost: N/A
Tuition per credit:
Acceptance rate: 94%
Test scores required: No
Enrollment: 160, 42% men, 58% women, 41% minority, 12% international

Brandman University

Private

ONLINE MBA PROGRAM(S)

www.brandman.edu/admissions
Admissions: (800) 746-0082
Email: adminfo@brandman.edu
Financial aid: (800) 746-0082
Application deadline: rolling
Program can be completed entirely online: Yes
Total program cost: $30,720 full-time in-state, $30,720 part-time in-state, $30,720 full-time out-of-state, $30,720 part-time out-of-state
Tuition per credit: $640 full-time in-state, $640 part-time in-state, $640 full-time out-of-state, $640 part-time out-of-state
Acceptance rate: 99%
Test scores required: No
Average age of entrants: 35
Enrollment: 186, 48% men, 52% women, 40% minority
Average class size: 20
Most popular MBA concentrations: general management, health care administration, human resources management, leadership, marketing
Completion: Three year graduation rate: 64%; credits needed to graduate: 48; target time to graduate: 2 years
College funded aid available: Domestic: Yes; International: Yes
Graduates with debt: 62%; average amount of debt $61,126

ONLINE BUSINESS PROGRAM(S)

www.brandman.edu/admissions
Admissions: (800) 746-0082
Email: adminfo@brandman.edu
Financial aid: (800) 746-0082
Application deadline: rolling
Program can be completed entirely online: Yes
Total program cost: $23,040 full-time in-state, $23,040 part-time in-state, $23,040 full-time out-of-state, $23,040 part-time out-of-state
Tuition per credit: $640 full-time in-state, $640 part-time in-state, $640 full-time out-of-state, $640 part-time out-of-state
Acceptance rate: 100%
Test scores required: No

Average age of entrants: 35
Enrollment: 244, 46% men, 54% women, 28% minority
Average class size: 20
Most popular business concentrations: human resources management, leadership, public administration
Completion: Three year graduation rate: 74%; credits needed to graduate: 36; target time to graduate: 1.5 years
College funded aid available: Domestic: Yes; International: Yes
Graduates with debt: 42%; average amount of debt $45,680

California Baptist University

Private

ONLINE MBA PROGRAM(S)

www.cbuonline.edu
Admissions: (951) 343-9000
Email: cbuonline@calbaptist.edu
Financial aid: (951) 343-4236
Application deadline: rolling
Program can be completed entirely online: Yes
Total program cost: $23,832 full-time in-state, $23,832 part-time in-state, $23,832 full-time out-of-state, $23,832 part-time out-of-state
Tuition per credit: $662 full-time in-state, $662 part-time in-state, $662 full-time out-of-state, $662 part-time out-of-state
Acceptance rate: 92%
Test scores required: No
Average age of entrants: 33
Students with prior work experience: 100%
Enrollment: 91, 49% men, 51% women, 60% minority
Average class size: 17
Most popular MBA concentrations: accounting, general management
Completion: Three year graduation rate: 71%; credits needed to graduate: 36; target time to graduate: 1.5 years
College funded aid available: Domestic: Yes; International: Yes
Graduates with debt: 83%; average amount of debt $31,522

ONLINE BUSINESS PROGRAM(S)

www.cbuonline.edu
Admissions: (951) 343-9000
Email: cbuonline@calbaptist.edu
Financial aid: (951) 343-4236
Application deadline: rolling
Program can be completed entirely online: Yes
Total program cost: $19,860 full-time in-state, $19,860 part-time in-state, $19,860 full-time out-of-state, $19,860 part-time out-of-state
Tuition per credit: $662 full-time in-state, $662 part-time in-state, $662 full-time out-of-state, $662 part-time out-of-state
Acceptance rate: 88%
Test scores required: No

Average age of entrants: 32
Students with prior work experience: 100%
Enrollment: 38, 37% men, 63% women, 55% minority
Average class size: 16
Most popular business concentrations: accounting
Completion: Credits needed to graduate: 30; target time to graduate: 1 year
College funded aid available: Domestic: Yes; International: Yes
Graduates with debt: 86%; average amount of debt $22,782

California State University–Dominguez Hills

Public

ONLINE MBA PROGRAM(S)

mbaonline.csudh.edu
Admissions: (310) 243-3646
Email: mbaonline@csudh.edu
Financial aid: (310) 243-3691
Application deadline: rolling
Program can be completed entirely online: Yes
Total program cost: $13,800 full-time in-state, $13,800 part-time in-state, $13,800 full-time out-of-state, $13,800 part-time out-of-state
Tuition per credit: $460 full-time in-state, $460 part-time in-state, $460 full-time out-of-state, $460 part-time out-of-state
Acceptance rate: 60%
Test scores required: GMAT or GRE
Average GMAT: 485
Students with prior work experience: 100%
Enrollment: 47, 49% men, 51% women, 62% minority
Average class size: 18
Most popular MBA concentrations: finance, general management, human resources management, international business, marketing
Completion: Three year graduation rate: 67%; credits needed to graduate: 30; target time to graduate: 1.5 years
College funded aid available: Domestic: No; International: No

California State University–Fullerton (Mihaylo)

Public

ONLINE BUSINESS PROGRAM(S)

business.fullerton.edu/msit
Admissions: (657) 278-2574
Email: msit@fullerton.edu
Financial aid: (657) 278-3128
Application deadline: Domestic: 05/31
Program can be completed entirely online: No
Total program cost: $8,970 full-time in-state, $10,410 part-time in-state, $20,850 full-time out-of-state, $22,920 part-time out-of-state

Tuition per credit: $299 full-time in-state, $347 part-time in-state, $695 full-time out-of-state, $743 part-time out-of-state
Acceptance rate: 66%
Test scores required: GMAT or GRE
Average GMAT: 559
Average GRE: 152 verbal, 153 quantitative, 4.2 writing
Average age of entrants: 31
Students with prior work experience: 92%
Enrollment: 50, 80% men, 20% women, 42% minority, 2% international
Average class size: 28
Most popular business concentrations: e-commerce, manufacturing and technology management, management information systems, technology, other
Completion: Three year graduation rate: 84%; credits needed to graduate: 30; target time to graduate: 1.5 years
College funded aid available: Domestic: Yes; International: No
Graduates with debt: 48%; average amount of debt $16,567

California State University–Sacramento

Public

ONLINE BUSINESS PROGRAM(S)

www.csus.edu/cba/graduate/
Admissions: (916) 278-2895
Email: cbagrad@csus.edu
Financial aid: (916) 278-2676
Application deadline: Domestic: 04/01
Program can be completed entirely online: Yes
Total program cost: $22,200 full-time in-state, $22,200 part-time in-state, $22,200 full-time out-of-state, $22,200 part-time out-of-state
Tuition per credit: $740 full-time in-state, $740 part-time in-state, $740 full-time out-of-state, $740 part-time out-of-state
Acceptance rate: 77%
Test scores required: gre
Average GMAT: 543
Average age of entrants: 34
Students with prior work experience: 54%
Enrollment: 50, 58% men, 42% women, 40% minority
Average class size: 20
Most popular business concentrations: accounting
Completion: Three year graduation rate: 93%; credits needed to graduate: 30; target time to graduate: 1.5 years
College funded aid available: International: No

California State University–San Bernardino

Public

ONLINE MBA PROGRAM(S)

jhbc.csusb.edu/mba
Admissions: (909) 537-5703
Email: mbaonline@csusb.edu

Financial aid: (909) 537-7651
Application deadline: rolling
Program can be completed entirely online: Yes
Total program cost: $36,000 full-time in-state, $36,000 part-time in-state, $36,000 full-time out-of-state, $36,000 part-time out-of-state
Tuition per credit: $750 full-time in-state, $750 part-time in-state, $750 full-time out-of-state, $750 part-time out-of-state
Acceptance rate: 90%
Test scores required: No
Average age of entrants: 37
Students with prior work experience: 100%
Enrollment: 135, 52% men, 48% women, 63% minority, 2% international
Average class size: 24
Most popular MBA concentrations: general management
Completion: Three year graduation rate: 67%; credits needed to graduate: 48; target time to graduate: 1.5 years
College funded aid available: Domestic: No; International: No
Graduates with debt: 55%; average amount of debt $36,797

California State University–Stanislaus

Public

ONLINE MBA PROGRAM(S)

www.csustan.edu/omba
Admissions: (209) 667-3683
Email: kkidd@csustan.edu
Financial aid: (209) 667-3337
Application deadline: Domestic: 06/30; International: 06/30
Program can be completed entirely online: Yes
Total program cost: N/A
Tuition per credit: $800 full-time in-state, $800 part-time in-state, $800 full-time out-of-state, $800 part-time out-of-state
Acceptance rate: 71%
Test scores required: GMAT or GRE
Average age of entrants: 28
Students with prior work experience: 88%
Enrollment: 24, 46% men, 54% women, N/A minority, N/A international
Completion: Credits needed to graduate: 30; target time to graduate: 2 years
College funded aid available: Domestic: No; International: No

National University

Private

ONLINE MBA PROGRAM(S)

www.nu.edu/onlineeducation.html
Admissions: (855) 355-6288
Email: onlineadmissions@nu.edu
Financial aid: (858) 642-8513
Application deadline: rolling
Program can be completed entirely online: Yes

Total program cost: $14,976
full-time in-state, $7,488
part-time in-state, $14,976
full-time out-of-state, $7,488
part-time out-of-state
Tuition per credit: $416 full-time
in-state, $416 part-time in-state,
$416 full-time out-of-state,
$416 part-time out-of-state
Acceptance rate: 100%
Test scores required: No
Average age of entrants: 33
Enrollment: 728, 53% men,
47% women, 48% minority,
19% international
Average class size: 18
Most popular MBA
concentrations: general
management
Completion: Three year
graduation rate: 60%; credits
needed to graduate: 63; target
time to graduate: 2 years
College funded aid
available: Domestic: Yes;
International: Yes
Graduates with debt: 33%;
average amount of debt $21,928

ONLINE BUSINESS PROGRAM(S)

www.nu.edu/
onlineeducation.html
Admissions: (855) 355-6288
Email: onlineadmissions@nu.edu
Financial aid: (858) 642-8513
Application deadline: rolling
Program can be completed
entirely online: Yes
Total program cost: $14,976
full-time in-state, $7,488
part-time in-state, $14,976
full-time out-of-state, $7,488
part-time out-of-state
Tuition per credit: $416 full-time
in-state, $416 part-time in-state,
$416 full-time out-of-state,
$416 part-time out-of-state
Acceptance rate: 100%
Test scores required: No
Average age of entrants: 36
Enrollment: 666, 48%
men, 52% women, 57%
minority, 3% international
Average class size: 16
Most popular business
concentrations: accounting,
general management,
human resources
management, international
business, leadership
Completion: Three year
graduation rate: 52%; credits
needed to graduate: 54; target
time to graduate: 2 years
College funded aid
available: Domestic: Yes;
International: Yes
Graduates with debt: 44%;
average amount of debt $20,449

Pepperdine University (Graziadio)

Private

ONLINE MBA PROGRAM(S)

mbaonline.pepperdine.edu/
lp-ap/?access_code=pep-
mba-seo2&utm_campaign=
pep-mba-seo2
Admissions: (310) 568-5535
Email: GSBM.Admission@
pepperdine.edu

Financial aid: (310) 568-5530
Application deadline: rolling
Program can be completed
entirely online: No
Total program cost: $89,180
full-time in-state, $89,180
part-time in-state, $89,180
full-time out-of-state, $89,180
part-time out-of-state
Tuition per credit: $1,715
full-time in-state, $1,715
part-time in-state, $1,715
full-time out-of-state, $1,715
part-time out-of-state
Acceptance rate: 72%
Test scores required:
GMAT or GRE
Average GMAT: 586
Average GRE: 152 verbal, 147
quantitative, 4.0 writing
Average age of entrants: 33
Students with prior work
experience: 99%
Enrollment: 361, 53% men,
47% women, 31% minority,
5% international
Average class size: 23
Most popular MBA
concentrations: finance, general
management, leadership,
marketing, management
information systems
Completion: Three year
graduation rate: 73%; credits
needed to graduate: 52; target
time to graduate: 2 years
College funded aid
available: Domestic: Yes;
International: Yes
Graduates with debt:
60%; average amount
of debt $54,000

Point Loma Nazarene University

Private

ONLINE MBA PROGRAM(S)

www.pointloma.edu/grad
Admissions: (866) 692-4723
Email: gradinfo@pointloma.edu
Financial aid: (619) 563-2849
Application deadline: rolling
Program can be completed
entirely online: Yes
Total program cost: $34,650
full-time in-state, $34,650
part-time in-state, $34,650
full-time out-of-state, $34,650
part-time out-of-state
Tuition per credit: $825
full-time in-state, $825
part-time in-state, $825
full-time out-of-state, $825
part-time out-of-state
Acceptance rate: 100%
Test scores required:
GMAT or GRE
Average age of entrants: 34
Enrollment: 11, 82% men,
18% women, 64% minority
Average class size: 10
Completion: Credits needed
to graduate: 42; target time
to graduate: 2 years
College funded aid
available: Domestic: Yes;
International: Yes

St. Mary's College of California

Private

ONLINE MBA PROGRAM(S)

www.saintmarysmba.com
Admissions: (925) 631-4888
Email: smcmba@stmarys-ca.edu
Financial aid: (925) 631-4836
Application deadline: Domestic:
04/15; International: 04/15
Program can be completed
entirely online: No
Total program cost: $67,000
full-time in-state, $67,000
part-time in-state, $67,000
full-time out-of-state, $67,000
part-time out-of-state
Tuition per credit: $1,396
full-time in-state, $1,396
part-time in-state, $1,396
full-time out-of-state, $1,396
part-time out-of-state
Acceptance rate: 88%
Test scores required: No
Average age of entrants: 38
Students with prior work
experience: 100%
Enrollment: 83, 48% men,
52% women, 49% minority,
2% international
Average class size: 14
Most popular MBA concentrations:
entrepreneurship, finance,
international business,
marketing, quantitative
analysis/statistics and
operations research
Completion: Credits needed
to graduate: 48; target time
to graduate: 1.5 years
College funded aid
available: Domestic: Yes;
International: Yes
Graduates with debt: 65%

ONLINE BUSINESS PROGRAM(S)

www.saintmarysmba.com
Admissions: (925) 631-4888
Email: smcmba@stmarys-ca.edu
Financial aid: (925) 631-4686
Application deadline: Domestic:
03/18; International: 03/18
Program can be completed
entirely online: No
Total program cost: $35,000
full-time in-state, $35,000
part-time in-state, $35,000
full-time out-of-state, $35,000
part-time out-of-state
Tuition per credit: $875 full-time
in-state, $875 part-time in-state,
$875 full-time out-of-state,
$875 part-time out-of-state
Acceptance rate: 92%
Test scores required:
GMAT or GRE
Average GMAT: 583
Average GRE: 155 verbal,
158 quantitative
Average age of entrants: 33
Students with prior work
experience: 100%
Enrollment: 90, 57% men,
43% women, 57% minority,
11% international
Average class size: 19
Completion: Three year
graduation rate: 89%; credits
needed to graduate: 45; target
time to graduate: 1.5 years
College funded aid
available: Domestic: Yes;
International: Yes

University of La Verne

Private

ONLINE MBA PROGRAM(S)

laverne.edu/online/
prospective-students/
Admissions: (909) 448-4086
Email: laverneonline@
laverne.edu
Financial aid: (909) 448-4180
Application deadline: rolling
Program can be completed
entirely online: Yes
Total program cost: N/A
Tuition per credit: $830
full-time in-state, $830
part-time in-state, $830
full-time out-of-state, $830
part-time out-of-state
Acceptance rate: 51%
Test scores required: No
Average age of entrants: 36
Enrollment: 187, 42% men,
58% women, 52% minority
Average class size: 19
Most popular MBA
concentrations: finance, general
management, leadership,
marketing, supply chain
management/logistics
Completion: Three year
graduation rate: 58%; credits
needed to graduate: 33; target
time to graduate: 2.5 years
College funded aid
available: Domestic: Yes;
International: Yes
Graduates with debt:
74%; average amount
of debt $60,952

University of San Diego

Private

ONLINE BUSINESS PROGRAM(S)

www.sandiego.edu/msscm
Admissions: (619) 260-4860
Email: msscminfo@sandiego.edu
Financial aid: (619) 260-4720
Application deadline: rolling
Program can be completed
entirely online: No
Total program cost: $51,120
part-time in-state, $51,120
part-time out-of-state
Tuition per credit: $1,420
full-time in-state, $1,420
part-time in-state, $1,420
full-time out-of-state, $1,420
part-time out-of-state
Acceptance rate: 79%
Test scores required: No
Average age of entrants: 34
Students with prior work
experience: 100%
Enrollment: 68, 43% men,
57% women, 46% minority
Average class size: 15
Most popular business
concentrations: supply chain
management/logistics
Completion: Three year
graduation rate: 83%; credits
needed to graduate: 36; target
time to graduate: 2 years
College funded aid available:
Domestic: Yes
Graduates with debt: 27%;
average amount of debt $39,178

University of Southern California (Marshall)

Private

ONLINE MBA PROGRAM(S)

onlinemba.marshall.usc.edu/
admissions
Admissions: (213) 821-6947
Email: onlinemba@
marshall.usc.edu
Financial aid: (213) 740-4444
Application deadline: rolling
Program can be completed
entirely online: No
Total program cost: $95,618
full-time in-state, $95,618
part-time in-state, $95,618
full-time out-of-state, $95,618
part-time out-of-state
Tuition per credit: $1,847
full-time in-state, $1,847
part-time in-state, $1,847
full-time out-of-state, $1,847
part-time out-of-state
Acceptance rate: 56%
Test scores required:
GMAT or GRE
Average GMAT: 624
Average GRE: 153 verbal, 150
quantitative, 4.0 writing
Average age of entrants: 34
Students with prior work
experience: 100%
Enrollment: 88, 66% men,
34% women, 50% minority
Average class size: 23
Completion: Credits needed
to graduate: 51; target time
to graduate: 1.5 years
College funded aid available:
Domestic: No; International: No
Graduates with debt: 61%;
average amount of debt $66,780

ONLINE BUSINESS PROGRAM(S)

www.marshall.usc.edu/
Admissions: (213) 740-9507
Email: learning@
marshall.usc.edu
Financial aid: (213) 740-4444
Application deadline: rolling
Program can be completed
entirely online: Yes
Total program cost: $50,139
full-time in-state, $50,139
full-time out-of-state
Tuition per credit: $1,847
full-time in-state, $1,847
part-time in-state, $1,847
full-time out-of-state, $1,847
part-time out-of-state
Acceptance rate: 70%
Test scores required: No
Average age of entrants: 33
Students with prior work
experience: 66%
Enrollment: 132, 60%
men, 40% women, 53%
minority, 6% international
Average class size: 31
Most popular business
concentrations: accounting,
production/operations
management, supply chain
management/logistics,
quantitative analysis/statistics
and operations research, tax
Completion: Three year
graduation rate: 83%; credits
needed to graduate: 27; target
time to graduate: 2 years

College funded aid available: Yes; International: Yes
Graduates with debt: 61%; average amount of debt $51,303

COLORADO

Colorado Christian University

Private

ONLINE MBA PROGRAM(S)

www.ccu.edu/ccu/grad/
Admissions: (720) 872-5602
Email: bgrimm@ccu.edu
Financial aid: (303) 963-3233
Application deadline: rolling
Program can be completed entirely online: Yes
Total program cost: $21,645 full-time in-state, $21,645 part-time in-state, $21,645 full-time out-of-state, $21,645 part-time out-of-state
Tuition per credit: $555 full-time in-state, $555 part-time in-state, $555 full-time out-of-state, $555 part-time out-of-state
Test scores required: No
Enrollment: 139, 44% men, 56% women, 34% minority
Average class size: 15
Most popular MBA concentrations: accounting, health care administration, leadership, other
Completion: Credits needed to graduate: 39; target time to graduate: 1.5 years
College funded aid available: Domestic: Yes; International: Yes

Colorado State University

Public

ONLINE MBA PROGRAM(S)

biz.colostate.edu/academics/
graduate-programs/mba/
online-mba/how-to-apply
Admissions: (970) 491-1129
Email: gradadmissions@business.colostate.edu
Financial aid: (970) 491-6321
Application deadline: rolling
Program can be completed entirely online: Yes
Total program cost: N/A
Tuition per credit: $946 full-time in-state, $946 part-time in-state, $946 full-time out-of-state, $946 part-time out-of-state
Acceptance rate: 86%
Test scores required: No
Average GMAT: 524
Average GRE: 154 verbal, 154 quantitative, 4.0 writing
Average age of entrants: 35
Students with prior work experience: 89%
Enrollment: 838, 67% men, 33% women, 21% minority, 1% international
Average class size: 35

Most popular MBA concentrations: finance, general management, leadership, marketing, supply chain management/logistics
Completion: Three year graduation rate: 64%; credits needed to graduate: 42; target time to graduate: 2.5 years
College funded aid available: Domestic: No; International: No
Graduates with debt: 35%; average amount of debt $40,238

ONLINE BUSINESS PROGRAM(S)

biz.colostate.edu/cismaster/
pages.apply.aspx
Admissions: (970) 491-1129
Email: gradadmissions@business.colostate.edu
Financial aid: (970) 491-6321
Application deadline: rolling
Program can be completed entirely online: Yes
Total program cost: N/A
Tuition per credit: $817 full-time in-state, $817 part-time in-state, $817 full-time out-of-state, $817 part-time out-of-state
Acceptance rate: 86%
Test scores required: GMAT or GRE
Average GMAT: 590
Average GRE: 155 verbal, 151 quantitative, 4.0 writing
Average age of entrants: 36
Students with prior work experience: 98%
Enrollment: 171, 68% men, 32% women, 26% minority, 1% international
Average class size: 26
Most popular business concentrations: management information systems, quantitative analysis/statistics and operations research, technology
Completion: Three year graduation rate: 41%; credits needed to graduate: 33; target time to graduate: 2.5 years
College funded aid available: Domestic: No; International: No
Graduates with debt: 38%; average amount of debt $23,106

Colorado State University–Global Campus

Public

ONLINE BUSINESS PROGRAM(S)

csuglobal.edu/graduate/
admissions/admissions-process
Admissions: (800) 920-6723
Email: Admissions@CSUGlobal.edu
Financial aid: (800) 462-7845
Application deadline: rolling
Program can be completed entirely online: Yes
Total program cost: $18,000 full-time in-state, $18,000 part-time in-state, $18,000 full-time out-of-state, $18,000 part-time out-of-state
Tuition per credit: $500 full-time in-state, $500 part-time in-state, $500 full-time out-of-state, $500 part-time out-of-state
Acceptance rate: 99%

Test scores required: No
Average age of entrants: 34
Enrollment: 4,687, 39% men, 61% women, 28% minority
Average class size: 9
Most popular business concentrations: finance, general management, human resources management, leadership, organizational behavior
Completion: Three year graduation rate: 49%; credits needed to graduate: 36; target time to graduate: 2.5 years
College funded aid available: Domestic: Yes; International: Yes
Graduates with debt: 63%; average amount of debt $36,521

Colorado Technical University

Proprietary

ONLINE MBA PROGRAM(S)

www.coloradotech.edu/
admissions
Admissions: (855) 230-0555
Email: enroll@coloradotech.edu
Financial aid: (847) 851-7167
Application deadline: rolling
Program can be completed entirely online: Yes
Total program cost: $28,080 full-time in-state, $28,080 part-time in-state, $28,080 full-time out-of-state, $28,080 part-time out-of-state
Tuition per credit: $585 full-time in-state, $585 part-time in-state, $585 full-time out-of-state, $585 part-time out-of-state
Acceptance rate: 100%
Test scores required: No
Average age of entrants: 38
Enrollment: 2,300, 37% men, 63% women, 53% minority
Average class size: 22
Most popular MBA concentrations: entrepreneurship, general management, health care administration, human resources management, other
Completion: Three year graduation rate: 65%; credits needed to graduate: 48; target time to graduate: 1.5 years
College funded aid available: Domestic: Yes; International: Yes
Graduates with debt: 82%; average amount of debt $27,021

ONLINE BUSINESS PROGRAM(S)

www.coloradotech.edu/
admissions
Admissions: (855) 230-0555
Email: enroll@coloradotech.edu
Financial aid: (847) 851-7167
Application deadline: rolling
Program can be completed entirely online: Yes
Total program cost: $28,080 full-time in-state, $28,080 part-time in-state, $28,080 full-time out-of-state, $28,080 part-time out-of-state
Tuition per credit: $585 full-time in-state, $585 part-time in-state, $585 full-time out-of-state, $585 part-time out-of-state

Acceptance rate: 100%
Test scores required: No
Average age of entrants: 40
Enrollment: 1,408, 39% men, 61% women, 55% minority
Average class size: 20
Most popular business concentrations: accounting, general management, health care administration, organizational behavior, other
Completion: Three year graduation rate: 54%; credits needed to graduate: 48; target time to graduate: 1.5 years
College funded aid available: Domestic: Yes; International: Yes
Graduates with debt: 82%; average amount of debt $26,450

Regis University

Private

ONLINE MBA PROGRAM(S)

www.regis.edu/cps/admissions/
applying-to-college-for-
professional%20studies/
graduate-admissions.aspx
Admissions: (800) 388-2366
Email: regisadm@regis.edu
Financial aid: (303) 458-4126
Application deadline: rolling
Program can be completed entirely online: Yes
Total program cost: N/A
Tuition per credit: $950 full-time in-state, $950 part-time in-state, $950 full-time out-of-state, $950 part-time out-of-state
Acceptance rate: 91%
Test scores required: No
Average age of entrants: 33
Enrollment: 932, 49% men, 51% women, 31% minority, 5% international
Average class size: 13
Most popular MBA concentrations: accounting, general management, leadership, marketing
Completion: Three year graduation rate: 58%; credits needed to graduate: 36; target time to graduate: 2 years
Graduates with debt: 51%; average amount of debt $55,187

ONLINE BUSINESS PROGRAM(S)

www.regis.edu/cps/admissions/
applying-to-college-for-
professional%20studies/
graduate-admissions.aspx
Admissions: (800) 388-2366
Email: regisadm@regis.edu
Financial aid: (303) 458-4126
Application deadline: rolling
Program can be completed entirely online: Yes
Total program cost: N/A
Tuition per credit: $850 full-time in-state, $850 part-time in-state, $850 full-time out-of-state, $850 part-time out-of-state
Acceptance rate: 94%
Test scores required: No
Average age of entrants: 35
Enrollment: 656, 31% men, 69% women, 29% minority, 1% international
Average class size: 18

Most popular business concentrations: accounting, human resources management, leadership, not-for-profit management
Completion: Three year graduation rate: 55%; credits needed to graduate: 30; target time to graduate: 2 years
College funded aid available: Domestic: Yes; International: Yes
Graduates with debt: 64%; average amount of debt $51,373

University of Colorado–Colorado Springs

Public

ONLINE MBA PROGRAM(S)

www.uccs.edu/business/
academics/masters-degree.html
Admissions: (719) 255-3122
Email: cobgrad@uccs.edu
Financial aid: (719) 255-3460
Application deadline: rolling
Program can be completed entirely online: Yes
Total program cost: N/A
Tuition per credit: $726 full-time in-state, $790 part-time in-state, $834 full-time out-of-state, $834 part-time out-of-state
Acceptance rate: 78%
Average GMAT: 593
Average GRE: 154 verbal, 154 quantitative, 4.0 writing
Average age of entrants: 35
Enrollment: 108, 49% men, 51% women, 19% minority, 4% international
Average class size: 18
Most popular MBA concentrations: finance, general management, health care administration, international business, other
Completion: Credits needed to graduate: 36; target time to graduate: 3 years
College funded aid available: Domestic: No; International: No

University of Denver (Daniels)

Private

ONLINE BUSINESS PROGRAM(S)

daniels.du.edu/
graduate-students/admissions/
Admissions: (303) 732-6186
Email: daniels@du.edu
Financial aid: (303) 871-4098
Application deadline: Domestic: 05/01; International: 03/15
Program can be completed entirely online: No
Total program cost: $63,360 full-time in-state, $63,360 part-time in-state, $63,360 full-time out-of-state, $63,360 part-time out-of-state
Tuition per credit: $1,320 full-time in-state, $1,320 part-time in-state, $1,320 full-time out-of-state, $1,320 part-time out-of-state
Acceptance rate: 100%
Test scores required: No
Average GMAT: N/A

Average age of entrants: 39
Students with prior work experience: 100%
Enrollment: 58, 78% men, 22% women, 16% minority
Average class size: 9
Most popular business concentrations: real estate, other
Completion: Three year graduation rate: 59%; credits needed to graduate: 48; target time to graduate: 1.5 years
College funded aid available: Domestic: Yes; International: Yes
Graduates with debt: 45%

CONNECTICUT

Albertus Magnus College
Private

ONLINE MBA PROGRAM(S)
www.albertus.edu/
business-administration/ms/
Admissions: (203) 773-8505
Email: admissions-pgs@
albertus.edu
Financial aid: (203) 773-8508
Application deadline: rolling
Program can be completed entirely online: Yes
Total program cost: N/A
Tuition per credit: $902
full-time in-state, $902
part-time in-state, $902
full-time out-of-state, $902
part-time out-of-state
Test scores required: No
Enrollment: 201, 37% men, 63% women, 55% minority, 3% international
Average class size: 7
Most popular MBA concentrations: accounting, general management
Completion: Credits needed to graduate: 48; target time to graduate: 2 years
Graduates with debt: 70%; average amount of debt $30,706

ONLINE BUSINESS PROGRAM(S)
www.albertus.edu/
graduate-degrees/
Admissions: (203) 773-8505
Email: admissions-pgs@
albertus.edu
Financial aid: (203) 773-8508
Application deadline: rolling
Program can be completed entirely online: Yes
Total program cost: N/A
Tuition per credit: $902
full-time in-state, $902
part-time in-state, $902
full-time out-of-state, $902
part-time out-of-state
Test scores required: No
Enrollment: 147, 31% men, 69% women, 50% minority
Average class size: 7
Most popular business concentrations:
accounting, leadership, organizational behavior
Completion: Credits needed to graduate: 30; target time to graduate: 2 years
College funded aid available:
Domestic: No; International: No
Graduates with debt: 20%; average amount of debt $17,746

Post University
Proprietary

ONLINE MBA PROGRAM(S)
post.edu/admissions/
online-students/graduate
Admissions: (203) 596-6164
Email: adpadmissions@post.edu
Financial aid: (203) 591-5641
Application deadline: rolling
Program can be completed entirely online: Yes
Total program cost: $26,280
full-time in-state, $26,280
part-time in-state, $26,280
full-time out-of-state, $26,280
part-time out-of-state
Tuition per credit: $730 full-time in-state, $730 part-time in-state, $730 full-time out-of-state, $730 part-time out-of-state
Acceptance rate: 50%
Test scores required: No
Average age of entrants: 35
Students with prior work experience: 100%
Enrollment: 412, 57% men, 43% women, 21% minority, 1% international
Average class size: 12
Most popular MBA concentrations: consulting, entrepreneurship, finance, leadership, other
Completion: Three year graduation rate: 34%; credits needed to graduate: 36; target time to graduate: 2 years
College funded aid available: Domestic: Yes; International: Yes
Graduates with debt: 15%; average amount of debt $18,072

ONLINE BUSINESS PROGRAM(S)
post.edu/admissions
Admissions: (203) 596-6164
Email: adpadmissions@post.edu
Financial aid: (800) 345-2562
Application deadline: rolling
Program can be completed entirely online: Yes
Total program cost: $18,750
full-time in-state, $18,750
part-time in-state, $18,750
full-time out-of-state, $18,750
part-time out-of-state
Tuition per credit: $625
full-time in-state, $625
part-time in-state, $625
full-time out-of-state, $625
part-time out-of-state
Acceptance rate: 83%
Test scores required: No
Average age of entrants: 38
Students with prior work experience: 100%
Enrollment: 60, 42% men, 58% women, 30% minority
Average class size: 5
Most popular business concentrations: accounting
Completion: Credits needed to graduate: 30; target time to graduate: 2 years
College funded aid available: Domestic: Yes; International: Yes
Graduates with debt: 80%; average amount of debt $22,618

Quinnipiac University
Private

ONLINE MBA PROGRAM(S)
www.qu.edu/schools/business/
programs/mba.html
Admissions: (203) 582-7259
Email: jonathan.feldman@
quinnipiac.edu
Financial aid: (203) 582-3638
Application deadline: rolling
Program can be completed entirely online: Yes
Total program cost: $42,550
full-time in-state, $42,550
part-time in-state, $42,550
full-time out-of-state, $42,550
part-time out-of-state
Tuition per credit: $925
full-time in-state, $925
part-time in-state, $925
full-time out-of-state, $925
part-time out-of-state
Acceptance rate: 63%
Test scores required:
GMAT or GRE
Average GMAT: 535
Average GRE: 158 verbal, 153 quantitative, 3.8 writing
Average age of entrants: 33
Students with prior work experience: 82%
Enrollment: 323, 52% men, 48% women, 15% minority
Average class size: 32
Most popular MBA concentrations: finance, general management, health care administration, marketing, supply chain management/logistics
Completion: Three year graduation rate: 63%; credits needed to graduate: 46; target time to graduate: 4 years
College funded aid available: Domestic: No; International: No
Graduates with debt: 53%; average amount of debt $41,248

ONLINE BUSINESS PROGRAM(S)
quonline.quinnipiac.edu/
Admissions: (203) 582-7529
Email: jonathan.feldman@
quinnipiac.edu
Financial aid: (203) 582-8384
Application deadline: rolling
Program can be completed entirely online: Yes
Total program cost: $30,525
full-time in-state, $30,525
part-time in-state, $30,525
full-time out-of-state, $30,525
part-time out-of-state
Tuition per credit: $925
full-time in-state, $925
part-time in-state, $925
full-time out-of-state, $925
part-time out-of-state
Acceptance rate: 88%
Test scores required: No
Average age of entrants: 38
Students with prior work experience: 98%
Enrollment: 455, 39% men, 61% women, N/A minority, N/A international
Average class size: 27
Most popular business concentrations: general management, health care administration, human resources management, leadership, quantitative

analysis/statistics and operations research
Completion: Three year graduation rate: 78%; credits needed to graduate: 33; target time to graduate: 2 years
College funded aid available:
Domestic: No; International: No
Graduates with debt: 58%; average amount of debt $34,777

University of Bridgeport
Private

ONLINE MBA PROGRAM(S)
www.bridgeport.edu
Admissions: (203) 576-4552
Email: mba@bridgeport.edu
Financial aid: (203) 576-4566
Application deadline: rolling
Program can be completed entirely online: Yes
Total program cost: N/A
Tuition per credit: $805
full-time in-state, $805
part-time in-state, $805
full-time out-of-state, $805
part-time out-of-state
Acceptance rate: 60%
Test scores required: No
Average age of entrants: 33
Enrollment: 145, 39% men, 61% women, 53% minority, 10% international
Average class size: 10
Most popular MBA concentrations: accounting, finance, general management, international business, marketing
Completion: Credits needed to graduate: 30; target time to graduate: 2 years
College funded aid available: Domestic: Yes; International: Yes

University of Connecticut
Public

ONLINE BUSINESS PROGRAM(S)
www.msaccounting.
business.uconn.edu
Admissions: (860) 486-8180
Email: ricki.livingston@
business.uconn.edu
Financial aid: (860) 486-2819
Application deadline: rolling
Program can be completed entirely online: No
Total program cost: $24,750
full-time in-state, $24,750
part-time in-state, $24,750
full-time out-of-state, $24,750
part-time out-of-state
Tuition per credit: $825
full-time in-state, $825
part-time in-state, $825
full-time out-of-state, $825
part-time out-of-state
Acceptance rate: 90%
Test scores required: gre
Average GMAT: 608
Average age of entrants: 28
Students with prior work experience: 71%
Enrollment: 238, 59% men, 41% women, 10% minority, 6% international
Average class size: 30

Most popular business concentrations: accounting
Completion: Three year graduation rate: 88%; credits needed to graduate: 30; target time to graduate: 1 year
College funded aid available:
Domestic: No; International: No
Graduates with debt: 38%; average amount of debt $18,980

University of Hartford (Barney)
Private

ONLINE MBA PROGRAM(S)
www.hartford.edu/barney/mba/
admission/default.aspx
Admissions: (860) 768-5003
Email: mbainfo@hartford.edu
Financial aid: (860) 768-4282
Application deadline: rolling
Program can be completed entirely online: Yes
Total program cost: $35,445
full-time in-state, $35,445
part-time in-state, $35,445
full-time out-of-state, $35,445
part-time out-of-state
Tuition per credit: $695
full-time in-state, $695
part-time in-state, $695
full-time out-of-state, $695
part-time out-of-state
Acceptance rate: 67%
Average GMAT: 561
Average age of entrants: 30
Enrollment: 349, 50% men, 50% women, 22% minority, 6% international
Average class size: 25
Completion: Credits needed to graduate: 51; target time to graduate: 2 years

ONLINE BUSINESS PROGRAM(S)
www.hartford.edu/barney/
graduate/admission/default.aspx
Admissions: (860) 768-4198
Email: bmbainfo@hartford.edu
Financial aid: (860) 768-4784
Application deadline: N/A
Program can be completed entirely online: Yes
Total program cost: N/A
Tuition per credit: $695
full-time in-state, $695
part-time in-state, $695
full-time out-of-state, $695
part-time out-of-state
Acceptance rate: 68%
Average GMAT: 520
Average GRE: 135 verbal, 157 quantitative, 2.5 writing
Average age of entrants: 29
Students with prior work experience: 63%
Enrollment: 98, 54% men, 46% women, 26% minority, 2% international
Average class size: 25

DELAWARE

University of Delaware (Lerner)
Public

ONLINE MBA PROGRAM(S)
business.online.udel.edu/mba
Admissions: (302) 831-4626
Email: onlinemba@udel.edu

Financial aid: (302) 831-8189
Application deadline: rolling
Program can be completed entirely online: Yes
Total program cost: $35,750
full-time in-state, $35,750
part-time in-state, $35,750
full-time out-of-state, $35,750
part-time out-of-state
Tuition per credit: $812 full-time in-state, $812 part-time in-state, $812 full-time out-of-state, $812 part-time out-of-state
Acceptance rate: 63%
Test scores required: GMAT or GRE
Average GMAT: 580
Average GRE: 154 verbal, 155 quantitative, 4.5 writing
Average age of entrants: 34
Students with prior work experience: 98%
Enrollment: 240, 40% men, 60% women, 22% minority, 5% international
Average class size: 20
Most popular MBA concentrations: finance, health care administration, international business, leadership, other
Completion: Three year graduation rate: 80%; credits needed to graduate: 44; target time to graduate: 1.5 years
College funded aid available: Domestic: Yes; International: Yes
Graduates with debt: 89%; average amount of debt $29,029

Wilmington University
Private

ONLINE MBA PROGRAM(S)
www.wilmu.edu/business/mba_index.aspx
Admissions: N/A
Financial aid: N/A
Application deadline: rolling
Program can be completed entirely online: Yes
Total program cost: N/A
Tuition per credit: $466
full-time in-state, $466
part-time in-state, $466
full-time out-of-state, $466
part-time out-of-state
Acceptance rate: 100%
Average age of entrants: 33
Enrollment: 724, 43% men, 57% women, 36% minority, 1% international
Average class size: 17
Most popular MBA concentrations: general management, health care administration, marketing, management information systems, other
Completion: Credits needed to graduate: 36

ONLINE BUSINESS PROGRAM(S)
www.wilmu.edu/onlinelearning/
Admissions: N/A
Financial aid: N/A
Application deadline: rolling
Program can be completed entirely online: Yes
Total program cost: N/A

Tuition per credit: $466
full-time in-state, $466
part-time in-state, $466
full-time out-of-state, $466
part-time out-of-state
Acceptance rate: 100%
Average age of entrants: 37
Enrollment: 379, 25% men, 75% women, 42% minority
Average class size: 17
College funded aid available: Domestic: Yes

DISTRICT OF COLUMBIA

American University (Kogod)
Private

ONLINE MBA PROGRAM(S)
onlinebusiness.american.edu
Admissions: (202) 885-2831
Email: admissions@onlinebusiness.american.edu
Financial aid: (202) 885-6500
Application deadline: rolling
Program can be completed entirely online: No
Total program cost: $78,816
full-time in-state, $78,816
part-time in-state, $78,816
full-time out-of-state, $78,816
part-time out-of-state
Tuition per credit: $1,642
full-time in-state, $1,642
part-time in-state, $1,642
full-time out-of-state, $1,642
part-time out-of-state
Acceptance rate: 83%
Test scores required: No
Average GMAT: 520
Average GRE: 148 verbal, 149 quantitative, 3.0 writing
Average age of entrants: 31
Students with prior work experience: 98%
Enrollment: 365, 51% men, 49% women, 58% minority
Average class size: 13
Most popular MBA concentrations: consulting, finance, marketing, quantitative analysis/statistics and operations research, other
Completion: Credits needed to graduate: 48; target time to graduate: 2 years
College funded aid available: Domestic: Yes; International: Yes

ONLINE BUSINESS PROGRAM(S)
onlinebusiness.american.edu
Admissions: (202) 885-2831
Email: admissions@onlinebusiness.american.edu
Financial aid: (202) 885-6500
Application deadline: rolling
Program can be completed entirely online: No
Total program cost: $54,186
full-time in-state, $54,186
part-time in-state, $54,186
full-time out-of-state, $54,186
part-time out-of-state
Tuition per credit: $1,642
full-time in-state, $1,642
part-time in-state, $1,642
full-time out-of-state, $1,642
part-time out-of-state
Acceptance rate: 79%
Test scores required: No
Average GMAT: 700

Average GRE: 156 verbal, 154 quantitative, 4.0 writing
Average age of entrants: 32
Students with prior work experience: 93%
Enrollment: 132, 55% men, 45% women, 49% minority, 1% international
Average class size: 14
Most popular business concentrations: consulting, finance, marketing, management information systems, quantitative analysis/statistics and operations research
Completion: Credits needed to graduate: 33; target time to graduate: 1.5 years
College funded aid available: Domestic: Yes; International: Yes
Graduates with debt: 77%; average amount of debt $49,073

George Washington University
Private

ONLINE MBA PROGRAM(S)
business.gwu.edu/programs/online-programs/
Admissions: (202) 994-1212
Email: business@gwu.edu
Financial aid: (202) 994-7850
Application deadline: Domestic: 07/13; International: 07/13
Program can be completed entirely online: Yes
Total program cost: $97,958
full-time in-state, $97,958
part-time in-state, $97,958
full-time out-of-state, $97,958
part-time out-of-state
Tuition per credit: $1,765
full-time in-state, $1,765
part-time in-state, $1,765
full-time out-of-state, $1,765
part-time out-of-state
Acceptance rate: 63%
Test scores required: GMAT or GRE
Average GMAT: 599
Average GRE: 154 verbal, 151 quantitative, 4.0 writing
Average age of entrants: 38
Students with prior work experience: 100%
Enrollment: 403, 50% men, 50% women, 45% minority, 3% international
Average class size: 42
Most popular MBA concentrations: consulting, entrepreneurship, finance, health care administration, international business
Completion: Three year graduation rate: 68%; credits needed to graduate: 55; target time to graduate: 3 years
College funded aid available: Domestic: Yes; International: No
Graduates with debt: 54%; average amount of debt $65,479

ONLINE BUSINESS PROGRAM(S)
business.gwu.edu/programs/online-programs/
Admissions: (202) 994-1212
Email: business@gwu.edu
Financial aid: (202) 994-7850
Application deadline: rolling
Program can be completed entirely online: No

Total program cost: $59,580
full-time in-state, $59,580
part-time in-state, $59,580
full-time out-of-state, $59,580
part-time out-of-state
Tuition per credit: $1,655
full-time in-state, $1,655
part-time in-state, $1,655
full-time out-of-state, $1,655
part-time out-of-state
Acceptance rate: 74%
Test scores required: No
Average GMAT: 590
Average GRE: 157 verbal, 157 quantitative, 4.0 writing
Average age of entrants: 40
Students with prior work experience: 100%
Enrollment: 56, 54% men, 46% women, 48% minority, 5% international
Average class size: 28
Most popular business concentrations: other
Completion: Three year graduation rate: 64%; credits needed to graduate: 36; target time to graduate: 2.5 years
College funded aid available: Domestic: Yes; International: No
Graduates with debt: 35%; average amount of debt $30,099

Georgetown University (McDonough)
Private

ONLINE BUSINESS PROGRAM(S)
msbonline.georgetown.edu/admissions
Admissions: (866) 531-4825
Email: msfadmissions@georgetown.edu
Financial aid: (202) 687-4547
Application deadline: Domestic: 06/01; International: 06/01
Program can be completed entirely online: No
Total program cost: $73,312
full-time in-state, $73,312
part-time in-state, $73,312
full-time out-of-state, $73,312
part-time out-of-state
Tuition per credit: $2,291
full-time in-state, $2,291
part-time in-state, $2,291
full-time out-of-state, $2,291
part-time out-of-state
Acceptance rate: 31%
Test scores required: GMAT or GRE
Average GMAT: 661
Average GRE: 155 verbal, 149 quantitative
Average age of entrants: 30
Students with prior work experience: 93%
Enrollment: 86, 79% men, 21% women, 30% minority
Average class size: 40
Most popular business concentrations: finance
Completion: Three year graduation rate: 82%; credits needed to graduate: 32; target time to graduate: 2 years
College funded aid available: Domestic: Yes; International: Yes
Graduates with debt: 58%; average amount of debt $75,290

FLORIDA

Embry-Riddle Aeronautical University–Worldwide
Private

ONLINE MBA PROGRAM(S)
worldwide.erau.edu/admissions/
Admissions: (800) 522-6787
Email: wwadmissions@erau.edu
Financial aid: (866) 567-7202
Application deadline: rolling
Program can be completed entirely online: Yes
Total program cost: N/A
Tuition per credit: $640
full-time in-state, $640
part-time in-state, $640
full-time out-of-state, $640
part-time out-of-state
Acceptance rate: 95%
Test scores required: No
Average GMAT: 514
Average GRE: 145 verbal, 142 quantitative, 3.5 writing
Average age of entrants: 34
Enrollment: 974, 80% men, 20% women, 26% minority, 8% international
Average class size: 9
Most popular MBA concentrations: finance, international business, leadership, marketing, technology
Completion: Three year graduation rate: 35%; credits needed to graduate: 33; target time to graduate: 2 years
College funded aid available: Domestic: Yes; International: Yes
Graduates with debt: 19%; average amount of debt $13,688

ONLINE BUSINESS PROGRAM(S)
worldwide.erau.edu/admissions
Admissions: (800) 522-6787
Email: wwadmissions@erau.edu
Financial aid: (866) 567-7202
Application deadline: rolling
Program can be completed entirely online: Yes
Total program cost: $7,680
full-time in-state, $7,680
part-time in-state, $7,680
full-time out-of-state, $7,680
part-time out-of-state
Tuition per credit: $640
full-time in-state, $640
part-time in-state, $640
full-time out-of-state, $640
part-time out-of-state
Acceptance rate: 95%
Test scores required: No
Average GMAT: 460
Average GRE: 156 verbal, 154 quantitative, 3.3 writing
Average age of entrants: 36
Enrollment: 2,570, 73% men, 27% women, 32% minority, 1% international
Average class size: 10
Most popular business concentrations: general management, leadership, manufacturing and technology management, supply chain management/logistics, other
Completion: Three year graduation rate: 31%; credits needed to graduate: 30; target time to graduate: 2 years

College funded aid
available: Domestic: Yes;
International: Yes
Graduates with debt: 18%;
average amount of debt $12,465

Florida A&M University

Public

ONLINE MBA PROGRAM(S)

elearning.famu.edu/
pos-sbl.php#pos
Admissions: (850) 599-3796
Email: famuonline@famu.edu
Financial aid: (850) 599-3730
Application deadline: rolling
Program can be completed
entirely online: Yes
Total program cost: N/A
Tuition per credit: $792 full-time
in-state, $792 part-time in-state,
$792 full-time out-of-state,
$792 part-time out-of-state
Test scores required: No
Enrollment: 15, 13% men, 87%
women, 100% minority
Most popular MBA
concentrations: general
management
Completion: Credits
needed to graduate: 43

Florida Atlantic University

Public

ONLINE MBA PROGRAM(S)

business.fau.edu
Admissions: (561) 297-2470
Email: omba@fau.edu
Financial aid: (561) 297-3530
Application deadline: rolling
Program can be completed
entirely online: Yes
Total program cost: $32,000
full-time in-state, $32,000
part-time in-state, $32,000
full-time out-of-state, $32,000
part-time out-of-state
Tuition per credit: $800
full-time in-state, $800
part-time in-state, $800
full-time out-of-state, $800
part-time out-of-state
Acceptance rate: 68%
Test scores required: No
Average GMAT: 526
Average GRE: 150 verbal, 148
quantitative, 3.5 writing
Average age of entrants: 33
Students with prior work
experience: 100%
Enrollment: 224, 50% men,
50% women, N/A minority,
N/A international
Average class size: 32
Most popular MBA
concentrations: general
management, health care
administration, hotel
administration, international
business, sports business
Completion: Credits needed
to graduate: 40; target time
to graduate: 2 years
College funded aid
available: Domestic: Yes;
International: Yes
Graduates with debt: 62%;
average amount of debt $37,032

ONLINE BUSINESS PROGRAM(S)

business.fau.edu
Admissions: (561) 297-0525
Email: jknox6@fau.edu
Financial aid: (561) 297-3530
Application deadline: rolling
Program can be completed
entirely online: Yes
Total program cost: $19,200
full-time in-state, $12,800
part-time in-state, $19,200
full-time out-of-state, $12,800
part-time out-of-state
Tuition per credit: $1,067
full-time in-state, $1,067
part-time in-state, $1,067
full-time out-of-state, $1,067
part-time out-of-state
Acceptance rate: 68%
Test scores required: No
Average GMAT: 527
Average age of entrants: 34
Students with prior work
experience: 78%
Enrollment: 584, 42% men,
58% women, N/A minority,
N/A international
Average class size: 32
Most popular business
concentrations: accounting,
health care administration, tax
Completion: Three year
graduation rate: 56%; credits
needed to graduate: 30; target
time to graduate: 2 years
College funded aid available:
Domestic: Yes; International: No
Graduates with debt:
60%; average amount
of debt $40,000

Florida Institute of Technology

Private

ONLINE MBA PROGRAM(S)

www.fit.edu
Admissions: (321) 674-7118
Email: gradadm-olocp@fit.edu
Financial aid: (321) 674-8070
Application deadline: rolling
Program can be completed
entirely online: Yes
Total program cost: N/A
Tuition per credit: $896
full-time in-state, $896
part-time in-state, $896
full-time out-of-state, $896
part-time out-of-state
Acceptance rate: 42%
Test scores required: No
Average GMAT: 531
Average age of entrants: 34
Enrollment: 968, 51%
men, 49% women, 42%
minority, 1% international
Average class size: 18
Most popular MBA
concentrations: general
management, health care
administration, production/
operations management,
supply chain management/
logistics, other
Completion: Three year
graduation rate: 50%; credits
needed to graduate: 36; target
time to graduate: 2 years
College funded aid available:
Domestic: No; International: No
Graduates with debt: 63%;
average amount of debt $40,675

ONLINE BUSINESS PROGRAM(S)

www.fit.edu
Admissions: (321) 674-7118
Email: gradadm-olocp@fit.edu
Financial aid: (321) 674-8070
Application deadline: rolling
Program can be completed
entirely online: Yes
Total program cost: N/A
Tuition per credit: $777 full-time
in-state, $777 part-time in-state,
$777 full-time out-of-state,
$777 part-time out-of-state
Acceptance rate: 47%
Test scores required: No
Average age of entrants: 33
Enrollment: 650, 66%
men, 34% women, 38%
minority, 2% international
Average class size: 18
Most popular business
concentrations: health care
administration, production/
operations management,
supply chain management/
logistics, technology, other
Completion: Three year
graduation rate: 48%; credits
needed to graduate: 33; target
time to graduate: 2 years
College funded aid available:
Domestic: No; International: No
Graduates with debt: 31%;
average amount of debt $34,352

Florida International University

Public

ONLINE MBA PROGRAM(S)

business.fiu.edu
Admissions: (305) 348-3125
Email: chapman@fiu.edu
Financial aid: (305) 348-4234
Application deadline: rolling
Program can be completed
entirely online: Depends
Total program cost: $42,000
full-time in-state, $42,000
part-time in-state, $42,000
full-time out-of-state, $42,000
part-time out-of-state
Tuition per credit: $1,000
full-time in-state, $1,000
part-time in-state, $1,000
full-time out-of-state, $1,000
part-time out-of-state
Acceptance rate: 62%
Test scores required: No
Average GMAT: 533
Average GRE: 146 verbal, 145
quantitative, 3.0 writing
Average age of entrants: 32
Students with prior work
experience: 100%
Enrollment: 650, 52%
men, 48% women, 75%
minority, 2% international
Average class size: 13
Most popular MBA
concentrations: finance, general
management, health care
administration, international
business, marketing
Completion: Three year
graduation rate: 81%; credits
needed to graduate: 42; target
time to graduate: 1.5 years
College funded aid available:
Domestic: Yes
Graduates with debt: 80%;
average amount of debt $34,828

ONLINE BUSINESS PROGRAM(S)

business.fiu.edu
Admissions: (305) 348-3125
Email: chapman@fiu.edu
Financial aid: (305) 348-4234
Application deadline: rolling
Program can be completed
entirely online: Yes
Total program cost: $35,000
full-time in-state, $35,000
part-time in-state, $35,000
full-time out-of-state, $35,000
part-time out-of-state
Tuition per credit: $921 full-time
in-state, $921 part-time in-state,
$921 full-time out-of-state,
$921 part-time out-of-state
Acceptance rate: 40%
Test scores required: No
Average GMAT: 570
Average GRE: 149 verbal, 145
quantitative, 3.0 writing
Average age of entrants: 34
Students with prior work
experience: 71%
Enrollment: 134, 40%
men, 60% women, 66%
minority, 3% international
Average class size: 13
Most popular business
concentrations: human
resources management,
international business,
real estate
Completion: Three year
graduation rate: 85%; credits
needed to graduate: 36; target
time to graduate: 1.5 years
College funded aid available:
Domestic: No; International: No
Graduates with debt: 89%;
average amount of debt $36,215

Florida Southern College

Private

ONLINE MBA PROGRAM(S)

www.flsouthern.edu/sage/
graduate/master-of-business-
administration.aspx
Admissions: (863) 680-4205
Email: fscadm@flsouthern.edu
Financial aid: (863) 680-4140
Application deadline: rolling
Program can be completed
entirely online: No
Total program cost: $34,100
full-time in-state, $34,100
part-time in-state, $34,100
full-time out-of-state, $34,100
part-time out-of-state
Tuition per credit: $775 full-time
in-state, $775 part-time in-state,
$775 full-time out-of-state,
$775 part-time out-of-state
Test scores required:
GMAT or GRE
Enrollment: 8, 62% men,
38% women, N/A minority
Most popular MBA
concentrations: accounting,
general management, health
care administration, supply
chain management/logistics
Completion: Credits
needed to graduate: 44
College funded aid
available: Domestic: Yes;
International: Yes

Florida State University

Public

ONLINE MBA PROGRAM(S)

admissions.fsu.edu/gradapp
Admissions: (850) 644-6455
Email: graduateadmissions@
admin.fsu.edu
Financial aid: (850) 644-0539
Application deadline: rolling
Program can be completed
entirely online: Yes
Total program cost: $30,427
full-time in-state, $30,427
part-time in-state, $31,599
full-time out-of-state, $31,599
part-time out-of-state
Tuition per credit: $750 full-time
in-state, $750 part-time in-state,
$750 full-time out-of-state,
$750 part-time out-of-state
Acceptance rate: 57%
Test scores required:
GMAT or GRE
Average GMAT: 565
Average GRE: 155 verbal,
153 quantitative
Average age of entrants: 35
Students with prior work
experience: 100%
Enrollment: 213, 72%
men, 28% women, 22%
minority, 1% international
Average class size: 19
Most popular MBA
concentrations: general
management, real estate
Completion: Three year
graduation rate: 66%; credits
needed to graduate: 39; target
time to graduate: 2 years
College funded aid
available: Domestic: Yes;
International: Yes
Graduates with debt: 33%;
average amount of debt $27,566

ONLINE BUSINESS PROGRAM(S)

admissions.fsu.edu/gradapp
Admissions: (850) 644-6455
Email: graduateadmissions@
admin.fsu.edu
Financial aid: (850) 644-0539
Application deadline:
Domestic: 03/01
Program can be completed
entirely online: Yes
Total program cost: $25,745
full-time in-state, $25,745
part-time in-state, $26,737
full-time out-of-state, $26,737
part-time out-of-state
Tuition per credit: $750 full-time
in-state, $750 part-time in-state,
$750 full-time out-of-state,
$750 part-time out-of-state
Acceptance rate: 84%
Test scores required:
GMAT or GRE
Average GMAT: 549
Average GRE: 152 verbal,
149 quantitative
Average age of entrants: 37
Students with prior work
experience: 100%
Enrollment: 126, 59% men,
41% women, 25% minority,
2% international
Average class size: 16
Most popular business
concentrations:
insurance, management
information systems

Completion: Three year graduation rate: 81%; credits needed to graduate: 33; target time to graduate: 2 years
College funded aid available: Domestic: Yes; International: Yes
Graduates with debt: 25%; average amount of debt $33,372

Keiser University

Private

ONLINE MBA PROGRAM(S)

www.keiseruniversity.edu/
Admissions: (954) 318-1620
Financial aid: (954) 318-1620
Application deadline: N/A
Program can be completed entirely online: Yes
Total program cost: N/A
Tuition per credit: $946 full-time in-state, $946 part-time in-state, $946 full-time out-of-state, $946 part-time out-of-state
Enrollment: 406, 37% men, 63% women, 72% minority, 7% international
Average class size: 12
Most popular MBA concentrations: accounting, general management, health care administration, international business, marketing
Completion: Three year graduation rate: 75%; target time to graduate: 3 years

ONLINE BUSINESS PROGRAM(S)

www.keiseruniversity.edu/
Admissions: (954) 318-1620
Email: ryounkins@keiseruniversity.edu
Financial aid: (954) 318-1620
Application deadline: N/A
Program can be completed entirely online: Yes
Total program cost: N/A
Tuition per credit: $946 full-time in-state, $946 part-time in-state, $946 full-time out-of-state, $946 part-time out-of-state
Enrollment: 88, 39% men, 61% women, 76% minority
Average class size: 12
Most popular business concentrations: accounting, general management
Completion: Three year graduation rate: 81%; target time to graduate: 3 years

Lynn University

Private

ONLINE MBA PROGRAM(S)

onlinemba.lynn.edu/admissions/
Admissions: (561) 237-7834
Email: spruitt@lynn.edu
Financial aid: (561) 237-7973
Application deadline: rolling
Program can be completed entirely online: Yes
Total program cost: $26,640 full-time in-state, $26,640 part-time in-state, $26,640 full-time out-of-state, $26,640 part-time out-of-state

Tuition per credit: $740 full-time in-state, $740 part-time in-state, $740 full-time out-of-state, $740 part-time out-of-state
Acceptance rate: 85%
Test scores required: No
Average age of entrants: 29
Enrollment: 604, 49% men, 51% women, 23% minority, 26% international
Average class size: 19
Most popular MBA concentrations: entrepreneurship, finance, human resources management, international business, marketing
Completion: Three year graduation rate: 83%; credits needed to graduate: 37; target time to graduate: 1 year
College funded aid available: Domestic: Yes; International: Yes
Graduates with debt: 48%; average amount of debt $35,018

Nova Southeastern University

Private

ONLINE MBA PROGRAM(S)

www.huizenga.nova.edu
Admissions: (954) 262-5163
Email: zeida@nova.edu
Financial aid: (954) 262-7456
Application deadline: rolling
Program can be completed entirely online: Yes
Total program cost: $37,785 full-time in-state, $37,785 part-time in-state, $37,785 full-time out-of-state, $37,785 part-time out-of-state
Tuition per credit: $895 full-time in-state, $895 part-time in-state, $895 full-time out-of-state, $895 part-time out-of-state
Acceptance rate: 91%
Test scores required: GMAT or GRE
Enrollment: 1,493, 36% men, 64% women, 70% minority, 5% international
Most popular MBA concentrations: entrepreneurship, finance, general management, human resources management, marketing
Completion: Credits needed to graduate: 39; target time to graduate: 2.5 years
College funded aid available: Domestic: Yes; International: Yes

ONLINE BUSINESS PROGRAM(S)

www.huizenga.nova.edu
Admissions: (954) 262-5163
Email: zeida@nova.edu
Financial aid: (954) 262-7456
Application deadline: rolling
Program can be completed entirely online: Depends
Total program cost: $34,905 full-time in-state, $34,905 part-time in-state, $34,905 full-time out-of-state, $34,905 part-time out-of-state
Tuition per credit: $895 full-time in-state, $895 part-time in-state, $895 full-time out-of-state, $895 part-time out-of-state

Acceptance rate: 90%
Test scores required: GMAT or GRE
Enrollment: 289, 38% men, 62% women, 61% minority, 2% international
Average class size: 20
Completion: Credits needed to graduate: 40; target time to graduate: 2.5 years
College funded aid available: Domestic: Yes

Southeastern University

Private

ONLINE MBA PROGRAM(S)

seu.edu
Admissions: (863) 667-5999
Email: admission@seu.edu
Financial aid: (863) 667-8760
Application deadline: rolling
Program can be completed entirely online: Yes
Total program cost: N/A
Tuition per credit: $525 full-time in-state, $525 part-time in-state, $525 full-time out-of-state, $525 part-time out-of-state
Test scores required: No
Most popular MBA concentrations: leadership
Completion: Credits needed to graduate: 39

Stetson University

Private

ONLINE MBA PROGRAM(S)

www.stetson.edu/graduate
Admissions: (386) 822-7100
Email: gradadmissions@stetson.edu
Financial aid: (386) 822-7120
Application deadline: rolling
Program can be completed entirely online: Yes
Total program cost: $24,150 full-time in-state, $24,150 part-time in-state, $24,150 full-time out-of-state, $24,150 part-time out-of-state
Tuition per credit: $1,000 full-time in-state, $1,000 part-time in-state, $1,000 full-time out-of-state, $1,000 part-time out-of-state
Acceptance rate: 100%
Test scores required: No
Average age of entrants: 36
Enrollment: 25, 48% men, 52% women, 36% minority
Average class size: 6
Most popular MBA concentrations: general management
Completion: Three year graduation rate: 53%; credits needed to graduate: 30; target time to graduate: 2.5 years
College funded aid available: Domestic: No; International: No
Graduates with debt: 33%; average amount of debt $26,594

ONLINE BUSINESS PROGRAM(S)

www.stetson.edu/graduate
Admissions: (386) 822-7100
Email: gradadmissions@stetson.edu
Financial aid: (386) 822-7120
Application deadline: rolling
Program can be completed entirely online: Yes
Total program cost: $25,820 full-time in-state, $25,820 part-time in-state, $25,820 full-time out-of-state, $25,820 part-time out-of-state
Tuition per credit: $784 full-time in-state, $784 part-time in-state, $784 full-time out-of-state, $784 part-time out-of-state
Acceptance rate: 62%
Test scores required: GMAT or GRE
Average GMAT: 530
Average age of entrants: 29
Enrollment: 23, 39% men, 61% women, 26% minority
Average class size: 18
Most popular business concentrations: accounting
Completion: Three year graduation rate: 78%; credits needed to graduate: 30; target time to graduate: 1 year
Graduates with debt: 43%; average amount of debt $24,458

University of Florida (Hough)

Public

ONLINE MBA PROGRAM(S)

www.floridamba.ufl.edu
Admissions: (352) 392-7992
Email: FloridaMBA@warrington.ufl.edu
Financial aid: (352) 273-4960
Application deadline: rolling
Program can be completed entirely online: No
Total program cost: $58,000 part-time in-state, $58,000 part-time out-of-state
Tuition per credit: $531 full-time in-state, $1,208 part-time in-state, $1,255 full-time out-of-state, $1,208 part-time out-of-state
Acceptance rate: 46%
Test scores required: GMAT or GRE
Average GMAT: 588
Average GRE: 152 verbal, 151 quantitative
Average age of entrants: 30
Students with prior work experience: 100%
Enrollment: 456, 65% men, 35% women, 27% minority, 7% international
Average class size: 47
Most popular MBA concentrations: entrepreneurship, finance, general management, international business, marketing
Completion: Three year graduation rate: 93%; credits needed to graduate: 48; target time to graduate: 2 years
College funded aid available: Domestic: No; International: No
Graduates with debt: 57%; average amount of debt $48,044

University of Miami

Private

ONLINE MBA PROGRAM(S)

miami.edu/online
Admissions: (800) 411-2290
Email: onlineinfo@miami.edu
Financial aid: (305) 284-3115
Application deadline: rolling
Program can be completed entirely online: Yes
Total program cost: $82,320 full-time in-state, $82,320 part-time in-state, $82,320 full-time out-of-state, $82,320 part-time out-of-state
Tuition per credit: $1,960 full-time in-state, $1,960 part-time in-state, $1,960 full-time out-of-state, $1,960 part-time out-of-state
Acceptance rate: 55%
Test scores required: GMAT
Average GMAT: 588
Average age of entrants: 33
Students with prior work experience: 100%
Enrollment: 45, 56% men, 44% women, 33% minority
Average class size: 12
Completion: Credits needed to graduate: 42; target time to graduate: 2 years
College funded aid available: Domestic: Yes; International: Yes
Graduates with debt: 50%; average amount of debt $48,000

ONLINE BUSINESS PROGRAM(S)

miami.edu/online
Admissions: (800) 411-2290
Email: onlineinfo@miami.edu
Financial aid: (305) 284-3115
Application deadline: rolling
Program can be completed entirely online: Yes
Total program cost: $62,720 full-time in-state, $62,720 part-time in-state, $62,720 full-time out-of-state, $62,720 part-time out-of-state
Tuition per credit: $1,960 full-time in-state, $1,960 part-time in-state, $1,960 full-time out-of-state, $1,960 part-time out-of-state
Acceptance rate: 61%
Test scores required: GMAT or GRE
Average GMAT: 330
Average age of entrants: 33
Students with prior work experience: 100%
Enrollment: 130, 50% men, 50% women, 24% minority
Average class size: 15
Completion: Credits needed to graduate: 32; target time to graduate: 1.5 years
College funded aid available: Domestic: Yes; International: Yes
Graduates with debt: 25%; average amount of debt $29,000

University of South Florida

Public

ONLINE MBA PROGRAM(S)
www.usf.edu/business/
graduate/mba-online/
Admissions: (813) 974-3335
Email: aartis@usf.edu
Financial aid: (813) 974-4700
Application deadline: rolling
**Program can be completed
entirely online:** Depends
Total program cost: $28,800
full-time in-state, $28,800
part-time in-state, $28,800
full-time out-of-state, $28,800
part-time out-of-state
Tuition per credit: $900
full-time in-state, $900
part-time in-state, $900
full-time out-of-state, $900
part-time out-of-state
Acceptance rate: 56%
Test scores required:
GMAT or GRE
Average GMAT: N/A
Average age of entrants: 30
**Students with prior work
experience:** 100%
Enrollment: 3, 33% men, 67%
women, 67% minority
**Most popular MBA
concentrations:** other
Completion: Credits needed
to graduate: 32; target time
to graduate: 2 years
College funded aid available:
Domestic: No; International: No

University of South Florida– St. Petersburg (Tiedemann)

Public

ONLINE MBA PROGRAM(S)
www.usfsp.edu/mba
Admissions: (727) 873-4622
Email: mba@usfsp.edu
Financial aid: (727) 873-4128
Application deadline: rolling
**Program can be completed
entirely online:** Yes
Total program cost: $16,617
full-time in-state, $16,617
part-time in-state, $32,664
full-time out-of-state, $32,664
part-time out-of-state
Tuition per credit: $462
full-time in-state, $462
part-time in-state, $907
full-time out-of-state, $907
part-time out-of-state
Acceptance rate: 48%
Test scores required:
GMAT or GRE
Average GMAT: 540
Average GRE: 152 verbal, 151
quantitative, 4.0 writing
Average age of entrants: 33
**Students with prior work
experience:** 80%
Enrollment: 296, 53%
men, 47% women, 24%
minority, 2% international
Average class size: 25
**Most popular MBA
concentrations:** finance, general
management, international
business, management
information systems, other

Completion: Three year
graduation rate: 77%; credits
needed to graduate: 36; target
time to graduate: 2 years
**College funded aid
available:** Domestic: Yes;
International: Yes
Graduates with debt:
41%; average amount
of debt $30,988

Warner University

Private

ONLINE MBA PROGRAM(S)
www.warner.edu
Admissions: (863) 638-7212
Email: admissions@warner.edu
Financial aid: (863) 638-7202
Application deadline: N/A
**Program can be completed
entirely online:** Depends
Total program cost: $20,016
full-time in-state, $20,016
part-time in-state, $20,016
full-time out-of-state, $20,016
part-time out-of-state
Tuition per credit: $556
full-time in-state, $556
part-time in-state, $556
full-time out-of-state, $556
part-time out-of-state
Average class size: 11
**Most popular MBA
concentrations:** accounting,
human resources management,
international business
Completion: Three year
graduation rate: 76%; credits
needed to graduate: 36; target
time to graduate: 2 years
**College funded aid
available:** Domestic: Yes;
International: Yes
Graduates with debt: 68%;
average amount of debt $39,789

ONLINE BUSINESS PROGRAM(S)
www.warner.edu
Admissions: (863) 638-7212
Email: admissions@warner.edu
Financial aid: (863) 638-7202
Application deadline: N/A
**Program can be completed
entirely online:** Depends
Total program cost: $20,016
full-time in-state, $20,016
part-time in-state, $20,016
full-time out-of-state, $20,016
part-time out-of-state
Tuition per credit: $556
full-time in-state, $556
part-time in-state, $556
full-time out-of-state, $556
part-time out-of-state
Average class size: 13
**Most popular business
concentrations:** general
management
Completion: Three year
graduation rate: 64%; credits
needed to graduate: 36; target
time to graduate: 2 years
College funded aid available:
Domestic: No; International: No
Graduates with debt: 100%;
average amount of debt $44,672

GEORGIA

Brenau University

Private

ONLINE MBA PROGRAM(S)
www.brenau.edu/apply-now/
graduate-admissions/
Admissions: (770) 534-6162
Email: ngoss@brenau.edu
Financial aid: (770) 534-6152
Application deadline: rolling
**Program can be completed
entirely online:** Yes
Total program cost: $30,825
full-time in-state, $30,825
part-time in-state, $30,825
full-time out-of-state, $30,825
part-time out-of-state
Tuition per credit: $685
full-time in-state, $685
part-time in-state, $685
full-time out-of-state, $685
part-time out-of-state
Acceptance rate: 56%
Test scores required: No
Average age of entrants: 34
**Students with prior work
experience:** 100%
Enrollment: 486, 24% men,
76% women, 63% minority
Average class size: 13
**Most popular MBA
concentrations:** accounting,
general management,
health care administration,
human resources
management, production/
operations management
Completion: Three year
graduation rate: 60%; credits
needed to graduate: 45; target
time to graduate: 1.5 years
College funded aid available:
Domestic: No; International: No
Graduates with debt: 84%;
average amount of debt $48,307

Columbus State University (Turner)

Public

ONLINE MBA PROGRAM(S)
admissions.columbusstate.edu/
grad/
Admissions: (706) 507-8079
Email: boadu_sonya@
columbusstate.edu
Financial aid: (706) 507-8898
Application deadline: Domestic:
06/30; International: 06/01
**Program can be completed
entirely online:** No
Total program cost: $22,170
part-time in-state, $22,170
part-time out-of-state
Tuition per credit: $739 full-time
in-state, $739 part-time in-state,
$739 full-time out-of-state,
$739 part-time out-of-state
Acceptance rate: 84%
Test scores required:
GMAT or GRE
Average GMAT: 478
Average GRE: 151 verbal, 148
quantitative, 3.8 writing
Average age of entrants: 33
**Students with prior work
experience:** 100%
Enrollment: 23, 39% men,
61% women, 61% minority
Average class size: 5

**Most popular MBA
concentrations:** general
management
Completion: Three year
graduation rate: 92%; credits
needed to graduate: 30; target
time to graduate: 2 years
**College funded aid
available:** Domestic: Yes;
International: Yes
Graduates with debt:
33%; average amount
of debt $20,496

Georgia College & State University (Bunting)

Public

ONLINE MBA PROGRAM(S)
webmba.gcsu.edu
Admissions: (478) 445-5115
Email: mba@gcsu.edu
Financial aid: (478) 445-5149
Application deadline: rolling
**Program can be completed
entirely online:** No
Total program cost: $22,170
full-time in-state, $22,170
part-time in-state, $22,170
full-time out-of-state, $22,170
part-time out-of-state
Tuition per credit: $739 full-time
in-state, $739 part-time in-state,
$739 full-time out-of-state,
$739 part-time out-of-state
Acceptance rate: 91%
Test scores required:
GMAT or GRE
Average GMAT: 526
Average GRE: 151 verbal, 150
quantitative, 3.8 writing
Average age of entrants: 36
**Students with prior work
experience:** 100%
Enrollment: 59, 63% men,
37% women, 34% minority
Average class size: 15
Completion: Three year
graduation rate: 88%; credits
needed to graduate: 30; target
time to graduate: 1.5 years
College funded aid available:
Domestic: Yes; International: No
Graduates with debt: 36%;
average amount of debt $27,469

ONLINE BUSINESS PROGRAM(S)
mlscm.gcsu.edu
Admissions: (478) 445-5115
Email: mlscm@gcsu.edu
Financial aid: (478) 445-5149
Application deadline: rolling
**Program can be completed
entirely online:** No
Total program cost: $14,010
full-time in-state, $14,010
part-time in-state, $14,010
full-time out-of-state, $14,010
part-time out-of-state
Tuition per credit: $467 full-time
in-state, $467 part-time in-state,
$467 full-time out-of-state,
$467 part-time out-of-state
Acceptance rate: 89%
Test scores required:
GMAT or GRE
Average GMAT: 587
Average GRE: 159 verbal, 153
quantitative, 3.9 writing
Average age of entrants: 37
**Students with prior work
experience:** 98%

Enrollment: 102, 64% men,
36% women, 26% minority
Average class size: 24
Completion: Credits needed
to graduate: 30; target time
to graduate: 1.5 years
College funded aid available:
Domestic: Yes; International: No
Graduates with debt: 43%;
average amount of debt $26,187

Georgia Southern University

Public

ONLINE MBA PROGRAM(S)
cogs.georgiasouthern.edu/
admission/
Admissions: (912) 478-5384
Email: gradadmissions@
georgiasouthern.edu
Financial aid: (912) 478-5413
Application deadline: rolling
**Program can be completed
entirely online:** No
Total program cost: $13,302
full-time in-state, $13,302
part-time in-state, $13,302
full-time out-of-state, $13,302
part-time out-of-state
Tuition per credit: $739 full-time
in-state, $739 part-time in-state,
$739 full-time out-of-state,
$739 part-time out-of-state
Acceptance rate: 92%
Test scores required:
GMAT or GRE
Average GMAT: 535
Average GRE: 151 verbal, 152
quantitative, 3.0 writing
Average age of entrants: 34
Enrollment: 140, 65%
men, 35% women, 33%
minority, 4% international
Average class size: 31
**Most popular MBA
concentrations:** general
management
Completion: Credits needed
to graduate: 30; target time
to graduate: 2 years
College funded aid available:
Domestic: No; International: No
Graduates with debt: 61%;
average amount of debt $30,248

ONLINE BUSINESS PROGRAM(S)
cogs.georgiasouthern.edu/
admission/
Admissions: (912) 478-5384
Email: gradadmissions@
georgiasouthern.edu
Financial aid: (912) 478-5413
Application deadline: rolling
**Program can be completed
entirely online:** Yes
Total program cost: $7,380
full-time in-state, $7,380
part-time in-state, $7,380
full-time out-of-state, $7,380
part-time out-of-state
Tuition per credit: $410 full-time
in-state, $410 part-time in-state,
$410 full-time out-of-state,
$410 part-time out-of-state
Acceptance rate: 73%
Test scores required:
GMAT or GRE
Average GMAT: 501
Average GRE: 156 verbal, 151
quantitative, 4.0 writing
Average age of entrants: 30

Enrollment: 96, 39% men, 61% women, 29% minority, 3% international
Average class size: 20
Most popular business concentrations: accounting, economics
Completion: Three year graduation rate: 67%; credits needed to graduate: 30; target time to graduate: 2 years
College funded aid available: Domestic: No; International: No
Graduates with debt: 59%; average amount of debt $25,926

Kennesaw State University (Coles)
Public

ONLINE MBA PROGRAM(S)

graduate.kennesaw.edu/admissions/
Admissions: (470) 578-4377
Email: ksugrad@kennesaw.edu
Financial aid: (470) 578-2044
Application deadline: rolling
Program can be completed entirely online: Depends
Total program cost: $22,170 part-time in-state, $22,170 part-time out-of-state
Tuition per credit: $739 full-time in-state, $739 part-time in-state, $739 full-time out-of-state, $739 part-time out-of-state
Acceptance rate: 67%
Test scores required: GMAT or GRE
Average GMAT: 573
Average age of entrants: 35
Students with prior work experience: 100%
Enrollment: 213, 47% men, 53% women, 42% minority
Average class size: 33
Completion: Three year graduation rate: 91%; credits needed to graduate: 30; target time to graduate: 1.5 years
College funded aid available: Domestic: Yes; International: Yes
Graduates with debt: 50%; average amount of debt $9,862

Mercer University–Atlanta (Stetson)
Private

ONLINE MBA PROGRAM(S)

business.mercer.edu
Admissions: (678) 547-6159
Email: whiteside_l@mercer.edu
Financial aid: (678) 547-6467
Application deadline: rolling
Program can be completed entirely online: Yes
Total program cost: $26,640 full-time in-state, $26,640 part-time in-state, $26,640 full-time out-of-state, $26,640 part-time out-of-state
Tuition per credit: $740 full-time in-state, $740 part-time in-state, $740 full-time out-of-state, $740 part-time out-of-state
Acceptance rate: 57%
Test scores required: GMAT or GRE
Average GMAT: 528

Average GRE: 152 verbal, 153 quantitative
Average age of entrants: 28
Students with prior work experience: 91%
Enrollment: 78, 53% men, 47% women, N/A minority, N/A international
Average class size: 19
Most popular MBA concentrations: economics, entrepreneurship, finance, health care administration, marketing
Completion: Credits needed to graduate: 36; target time to graduate: 2 years
College funded aid available: Domestic: Yes; International: No
Graduates with debt: 70%; average amount of debt $20,000

University of Georgia (Terry)
Public

ONLINE BUSINESS PROGRAM(S)

www.terry.uga.edu/mit
Admissions: (706) 542-3589
Email: cpiercy@uga.edu
Financial aid: (706) 542-6147
Application deadline: rolling
Program can be completed entirely online: Yes
Total program cost: $26,400 full-time in-state, $26,400 part-time in-state, $26,400 full-time out-of-state, $26,400 part-time out-of-state
Tuition per credit: $825 full-time in-state, $825 part-time in-state, $825 full-time out-of-state, $825 part-time out-of-state
Acceptance rate: 80%
Test scores required: GMAT or GRE
Average GMAT: 525
Average GRE: 151 verbal, 152 quantitative
Average age of entrants: 35
Students with prior work experience: 100%
Enrollment: 26, 65% men, 35% women, 50% minority
Average class size: 17
Most popular business concentrations: e-commerce, management information systems, technology
Completion: Credits needed to graduate: 32; target time to graduate: 2 years
College funded aid available: Domestic: No; International: No
Graduates with debt: 52%; average amount of debt $39,276

University of West Georgia
Public

ONLINE MBA PROGRAM(S)

www.westga.edu/academics/business/webmba-regular-admissions.php
Admissions: (678) 839-5355
Email: hudombon@westga.edu
Financial aid: (678) 839-6421
Application deadline: Domestic: 07/30; International: 06/01

Program can be completed entirely online: Depends
Total program cost: N/A
Tuition per credit: $739 full-time in-state, $739 part-time in-state, $739 full-time out-of-state, $739 part-time out-of-state
Acceptance rate: 90%
Test scores required: GMAT or GRE
Average GMAT: 437
Average GRE: 147 verbal, 146 quantitative, 3.3 writing
Average age of entrants: 35
Enrollment: 115, 46% men, 54% women, 38% minority, 4% international
Average class size: 14
Most popular MBA concentrations: accounting, economics, finance, marketing, management information systems
Completion: Three year graduation rate: 91%; credits needed to graduate: 30; target time to graduate: 1.5 years
Graduates with debt: 63%; average amount of debt $25,755

Valdosta State University (Langdale)
Public

ONLINE MBA PROGRAM(S)

www.valdosta.edu/academics/graduate-school/
Admissions: (229) 333-5694
Email: rlwaters@valdosta.edu
Financial aid: (229) 333-5935
Application deadline: N/A
Program can be completed entirely online: Yes
Total program cost: $22,170 full-time in-state, $22,170 part-time in-state, $22,170 full-time out-of-state, $22,170 part-time out-of-state
Tuition per credit: $739 full-time in-state, $739 part-time in-state, $739 full-time out-of-state, $739 part-time out-of-state
Acceptance rate: 100%
Test scores required: GMAT or GRE
Average GMAT: 522
Average GRE: 145 verbal, 143 quantitative, 3.5 writing
Average age of entrants: 35
Enrollment: 15, 53% men, 47% women, 40% minority
Average class size: 28
Most popular MBA concentrations: general management, health care administration
Completion: Credits needed to graduate: 30; target time to graduate: 1.5 years
College funded aid available: Domestic: Yes; International: Yes
Graduates with debt: 57%; average amount of debt $34,934

IDAHO

Boise State University
Public

ONLINE MBA PROGRAM(S)

degree.boisestate.edu/admissions.aspx
Admissions: (855) 290-3840
Email: OnlineMBA@boisestate.edu
Financial aid: (208) 426-1664
Application deadline: rolling
Program can be completed entirely online: Yes
Total program cost: $36,750 full-time in-state, $36,750 part-time in-state, $36,750 full-time out-of-state, $36,750 part-time out-of-state
Tuition per credit: $750 full-time in-state, $750 part-time in-state, $750 full-time out-of-state, $750 part-time out-of-state
Acceptance rate: 76%
Test scores required: GMAT or GRE
Average GMAT: 590
Average GRE: 148 verbal, 151 quantitative
Average age of entrants: 34
Students with prior work experience: 98%
Enrollment: 209, 76% men, 24% women, 15% minority
Average class size: 28
Completion: Three year graduation rate: 83%; credits needed to graduate: 49; target time to graduate: 2 years
College funded aid available: Domestic: Yes; International: Yes
Graduates with debt: 25%; average amount of debt $39,576

ONLINE BUSINESS PROGRAM(S)

online.boisestate.edu/masters-degrees/accountancy/admissions/
Admissions: (208) 426-5921
Email: online@boisestate.edu
Financial aid: (208) 426-1664
Application deadline: rolling
Program can be completed entirely online: Yes
Total program cost: $13,500 full-time in-state, $13,500 part-time in-state, $13,500 full-time out-of-state, $13,500 part-time out-of-state
Tuition per credit: $450 full-time in-state, $450 part-time in-state, $450 full-time out-of-state, $450 part-time out-of-state
Completion: Credits needed to graduate: 30; target time to graduate: 2 years

ILLINOIS

American InterContinental University
Proprietary

ONLINE MBA PROGRAM(S)

www.aiuniv.edu/admissions
Admissions: (877) 701-3800
Email: enroll@aiuonline.edu
Financial aid: (877) 221-5800
Application deadline: rolling

Program can be completed entirely online: Yes
Total program cost: $27,936 full-time in-state, $27,936 part-time in-state, $27,936 full-time out-of-state, $27,936 part-time out-of-state
Tuition per credit: $582 full-time in-state, $582 part-time in-state, $582 full-time out-of-state, $582 part-time out-of-state
Acceptance rate: 100%
Test scores required: No
Average age of entrants: 38
Enrollment: 2,043, 30% men, 70% women, 62% minority
Average class size: 13
Most popular MBA concentrations: general management, health care administration, human resources management, production/operations management, other
Completion: Three year graduation rate: 54%; credits needed to graduate: 48; target time to graduate: less than 1 year
College funded aid available: Domestic: Yes; International: Yes
Graduates with debt: 85%; average amount of debt $30,577

Concordia University Chicago
Private

ONLINE MBA PROGRAM(S)

gradschool.cuchicago.edu/academics/mba/admissions/
Admissions: (708) 209-4093
Email: grad.admission@cuchicago.edu
Financial aid: (708) 209-3347
Application deadline: rolling
Program can be completed entirely online: Yes
Total program cost: $25,560 full-time in-state, $25,560 part-time in-state, $25,560 full-time out-of-state, $25,560 part-time out-of-state
Tuition per credit: $710 full-time in-state, $710 part-time in-state, $710 full-time out-of-state, $710 part-time out-of-state
Acceptance rate: 98%
Test scores required: No
Average age of entrants: 33
Enrollment: 218, 37% men, 63% women, 47% minority
Average class size: 12
Most popular MBA concentrations: finance, general management, health care administration, leadership, sports business
Completion: Three year graduation rate: 24%; credits needed to graduate: 36; target time to graduate: 2 years
College funded aid available: Domestic: Yes; International: Yes
Graduates with debt: 42%; average amount of debt $35,867

DeVry University (Keller)

Proprietary

ONLINE MBA PROGRAM(S)

www.keller.edu/online-learning/online-mba-and-online-graduate-programs
Admissions: (800) 839-9009
Financial aid: N/A
Application deadline: rolling
Program can be completed entirely online: Yes
Total program cost: $36,768 full-time in-state, $36,768 part-time in-state, $36,768 full-time out-of-state, $36,768 part-time out-of-state
Tuition per credit: $766 full-time in-state, $766 part-time in-state, $766 full-time out-of-state, $766 part-time out-of-state
Acceptance rate: 90%
Test scores required: No
Average age of entrants: 35
Enrollment: 2,283, 41% men, 59% women, 42% minority, 3% international
Average class size: 19
Most popular MBA concentrations: accounting, finance, general management, human resources management, other
Completion: Three year graduation rate: 33%; credits needed to graduate: 48; target time to graduate: 2 years
College funded aid available: Domestic: Yes; International: No
Graduates with debt: 72%; average amount of debt $40,545

ONLINE BUSINESS PROGRAM(S)

www.keller.edu/online-learning/online-masters-degree-programs.html
Admissions: (800) 839-9009
Financial aid: N/A
Application deadline: rolling
Program can be completed entirely online: Yes
Total program cost: $34,470 full-time in-state, $34,470 part-time in-state, $34,470 full-time out-of-state, $34,470 part-time out-of-state
Tuition per credit: $766 full-time in-state, $766 part-time in-state, $766 full-time out-of-state, $766 part-time out-of-state
Acceptance rate: 89%
Test scores required: No
Average age of entrants: 36
Enrollment: 2,519, 40% men, 60% women, 45% minority, 3% international
Average class size: 18
Most popular business concentrations: accounting, finance, human resources management, management information systems, other
Completion: Three year graduation rate: 37%; credits needed to graduate: 45; target time to graduate: 2 years
College funded aid available: Domestic: Yes; International: No
Graduates with debt: 74%; average amount of debt $36,780

Eastern Illinois University

Public

ONLINE MBA PROGRAM(S)

www.eiu.edu/graduate/aboutadmissions.php
Admissions: (217) 581-2220
Email: Graduate@eiu.edu
Financial aid: (217) 581-7812
Application deadline: rolling
Program can be completed entirely online: Yes
Total program cost: $19,800 part-time in-state, $19,800 part-time out-of-state
Tuition per credit: $600 full-time in-state, $600 part-time in-state, $600 full-time out-of-state, $600 part-time out-of-state
Acceptance rate: 100%
Test scores required: No
Average GMAT: 460
Average age of entrants: 31
Students with prior work experience: 100%
Enrollment: 24, 46% men, 54% women, N/A minority, N/A international
Average class size: 14
Most popular MBA concentrations: accounting, general management, other
Completion: Credits needed to graduate: 33; target time to graduate: 2 years
College funded aid available: Domestic: Yes; International: No

Governors State University

Public

ONLINE MBA PROGRAM(S)

www.govst.edu/admissions/
Admissions: (708) 534-4490
Email: admissions@govst.edu
Financial aid: N/A
Application deadline: rolling
Program can be completed entirely online: Yes
Total program cost: $8,472 full-time in-state, $4,236 part-time in-state, $16,944 full-time out-of-state, $8,472 part-time out-of-state
Tuition per credit: $353 full-time in-state, $353 part-time in-state, $706 full-time out-of-state, $706 part-time out-of-state
Acceptance rate: 47%
Average age of entrants: 37
Enrollment: 12, 25% men, 75% women, 58% minority
Average class size: 19
Completion: Credits needed to graduate: 48
College funded aid available: Domestic: Yes

Greenville University

Private

ONLINE MBA PROGRAM(S)

www.greenville.edu/admissions/adult_grad/
Admissions: (618) 664-7130
Email: admissions@greenville.edu
Financial aid: (618) 664-7109
Application deadline: rolling
Program can be completed entirely online: Yes
Total program cost: N/A
Tuition per credit: $434 full-time in-state, $434 part-time in-state, $434 full-time out-of-state, $434 part-time out-of-state
Test scores required: No
Enrollment: 59, 53% men, 47% women, 20% minority, 7% international
Completion: Credits needed to graduate: 39; target time to graduate: 2 years
College funded aid available: Domestic: Yes

ONLINE BUSINESS PROGRAM(S)

www.greenville.edu/admissions/adult_grad/
Admissions: (618) 664-7100
Email: admissions@greenville.edu
Financial aid: (618) 664-7109
Application deadline: rolling
Program can be completed entirely online: Yes
Total program cost: $14,322 full-time in-state, $14,322 part-time in-state, $14,322 full-time out-of-state, $14,322 part-time out-of-state
Tuition per credit: $434 full-time in-state, $434 part-time in-state, $434 full-time out-of-state, $434 part-time out-of-state
Test scores required: No
Enrollment: 20, 55% men, 45% women, 10% minority
Most popular business concentrations: general management
Completion: Credits needed to graduate: 33; target time to graduate: 2 years
College funded aid available: Domestic: Yes

Judson University

Private

ONLINE MBA PROGRAM(S)

www.judsonu.edu/admissions/
Admissions: (847) 628-2510
Email: admissions@judsonu.edu
Financial aid: (847) 628-2531
Application deadline: rolling
Program can be completed entirely online: Yes
Total program cost: $25,350 full-time in-state, $25,350 part-time in-state, $25,350 full-time out-of-state, $25,350 part-time out-of-state
Tuition per credit: $665 full-time in-state, $665 part-time in-state, $665 full-time out-of-state, $665 part-time out-of-state
Acceptance rate: 64%
Test scores required: No
Average age of entrants: 36
Enrollment: 9, 67% men, 33% women, N/A minority, N/A international
Average class size: 8
Completion: Credits needed to graduate: 37; target time to graduate: 2 years

McKendree University

Private

ONLINE MBA PROGRAM(S)

www.mckendree.edu/admission/info/graduate/home/index.php
Admissions: (618) 537-6576
Email: graduate@mckendree.edu
Financial aid: (618) 537-6530
Application deadline: rolling
Program can be completed entirely online: Yes
Total program cost: $17,820 full-time in-state, $17,820 part-time in-state, $17,820 full-time out-of-state, $17,820 part-time out-of-state
Tuition per credit: $495 full-time in-state, $495 part-time in-state, $495 full-time out-of-state, $495 part-time out-of-state
Acceptance rate: 60%
Test scores required: No
Average age of entrants: 33
Enrollment: 151, 38% men, 62% women, 18% minority, 1% international
Average class size: 15
Most popular MBA concentrations: general management, human resources management
Completion: Three year graduation rate: 89%; credits needed to graduate: 36; target time to graduate: 2 years
Graduates with debt: 54%; average amount of debt $14,998

North Park University

Private

ONLINE MBA PROGRAM(S)

www.northpark.edu/academics/online-education/
Admissions: (773) 244-5518
Email: jdonor@northpark.edu
Financial aid: (773) 244-5506
Application deadline: rolling
Program can be completed entirely online: Yes
Total program cost: $41,410 full-time in-state, $41,410 part-time in-state, $41,410 full-time out-of-state, $41,410 part-time out-of-state
Tuition per credit: $1,150 full-time in-state, $1,150 part-time in-state, $1,150 full-time out-of-state, $1,150 part-time out-of-state
Acceptance rate: 93%
Test scores required: No
Average age of entrants: 32
Students with prior work experience: 98%
Enrollment: 95, 31% men, 69% women, 34% minority
Average class size: 12
Most popular MBA concentrations: accounting, human resources management, not-for-profit management, organizational behavior, other
College funded aid available: Domestic: Yes
Graduates with debt: 50%; average amount of debt $12,000

Completion: Three year graduation rate: 62%; credits needed to graduate: 36; target time to graduate: 2 years
College funded aid available: Domestic: Yes; International: Yes
Graduates with debt: 30%; average amount of debt $20,000

ONLINE BUSINESS PROGRAM(S)

www.northpark.edu/academics/colleges-and-schools/school-of-business-and-nonprofit-management/
Admissions: (773) 244-5518
Email: lscrementi@northpark.edu
Financial aid: (773) 244-5506
Application deadline: rolling
Program can be completed entirely online: Yes
Total program cost: $41,410 full-time in-state, $41,410 part-time in-state, $41,410 full-time out-of-state, $41,410 part-time out-of-state
Tuition per credit: $1,150 full-time in-state, $1,150 part-time in-state, $1,150 full-time out-of-state, $1,150 part-time out-of-state
Acceptance rate: 96%
Test scores required: No
Average age of entrants: 32
Students with prior work experience: 98%
Enrollment: 60, 30% men, 70% women, 35% minority
Average class size: 12
Most popular business concentrations: human resources management, not-for-profit management, organizational behavior, other
Completion: Three year graduation rate: 71%; credits needed to graduate: 36; target time to graduate: 2 years
College funded aid available: Domestic: Yes; International: Yes
Graduates with debt: 25%; average amount of debt $20,000

Olivet Nazarene University

Private

ONLINE MBA PROGRAM(S)

graduate.olivet.edu
Admissions: (877) 965-4838
Email: gradadmissions@olivet.edu
Financial aid: N/A
Application deadline: rolling
Program can be completed entirely online: Yes
Total program cost: N/A
Tuition per credit: $675 full-time in-state, $675 part-time in-state, $675 full-time out-of-state, $675 part-time out-of-state
Test scores required: No
Enrollment: 121, N/A minority, N/A international
Most popular MBA concentrations: health care administration, leadership, not-for-profit management, other
Completion: Target time to graduate: 2 years

ONLINE BUSINESS PROGRAM(S)
graduate.olivet.edu
Admissions: (877) 965-4838
Email: gradadmissions@olivet.edu
Financial aid: N/A
Application deadline: rolling
Program can be completed entirely online: Yes
Total program cost: N/A
Tuition per credit: $675 full-time in-state, $675 part-time in-state, $675 full-time out-of-state, $675 part-time out-of-state
Test scores required: No
Enrollment: 43, N/A minority, N/A international
Completion: Credits needed to graduate: 36; target time to graduate: 2 years
College funded aid available: Domestic: Yes; International: Yes
Graduates with debt: 65%; average amount of debt $26,975

Southern Illinois University–Carbondale
Public

ONLINE MBA PROGRAM(S)
onlinegrad.business.siu.edu
Admissions: (618) 453-3030
Email: GradPrograms@business.siu.edu
Financial aid: (618) 453-4334
Application deadline: Domestic: 06/01; International: 04/15
Program can be completed entirely online: Yes
Total program cost: $35,868 full-time in-state, $35,868 part-time in-state, $35,868 full-time out-of-state, $35,868 part-time out-of-state
Tuition per credit: $854 full-time in-state, $854 part-time in-state, $854 full-time out-of-state, $854 part-time out-of-state
Acceptance rate: 80%
Test scores required: GMAT or GRE
Average age of entrants: 36
Students with prior work experience: 100%
Enrollment: 122, 62% men, 38% women, 18% minority
Average class size: 20
Most popular MBA concentrations: general management, other
Completion: Three year graduation rate: 86%; credits needed to graduate: 42; target time to graduate: 2 years
College funded aid available: Domestic: No; International: No
Graduates with debt: 44%; average amount of debt $46,196

University of Illinois–Springfield
Public

ONLINE BUSINESS PROGRAM(S)
www.uis.edu/admissions
Admissions: (888) 977-4847
Email: admissions@uis.edu
Financial aid: (217) 206-6724
Application deadline: rolling

Program can be completed entirely online: Yes
Total program cost: N/A
Tuition per credit: $403 full-time in-state, $403 part-time in-state, $403 full-time out-of-state, $403 part-time out-of-state
Acceptance rate: 85%
Test scores required: GMAT or GRE
Average age of entrants: 35
Students with prior work experience: 93%
Enrollment: 170, 69% men, 31% women, 38% minority, 12% international
Average class size: 20
Most popular business concentrations: management information systems
Completion: Three year graduation rate: 45%; credits needed to graduate: 36; target time to graduate: 2.5 years
College funded aid available: Domestic: Yes; International: Yes
Graduates with debt: 25%; average amount of debt $32,205

University of St. Francis
Private

ONLINE MBA PROGRAM(S)
www.stfrancis.edu/admissions/graduate
Admissions: (800) 735-7500
Email: admissions@stfrancis.edu
Financial aid: (866) 890-8331
Application deadline: rolling
Program can be completed entirely online: Yes
Total program cost: N/A
Tuition per credit: $798 full-time in-state, $798 part-time in-state, $798 full-time out-of-state, $798 part-time out-of-state
Acceptance rate: 43%
Test scores required: No
Average age of entrants: 33
Enrollment: 150, 43% men, 57% women, 29% minority, 1% international
Average class size: 13
Most popular MBA concentrations: finance, general management, health care administration, human resources management, supply chain management/logistics
Completion: Three year graduation rate: 62%; credits needed to graduate: 36; target time to graduate: 2 years
College funded aid available: Domestic: Yes; International: No
Graduates with debt: 50%; average amount of debt $29,187

ONLINE BUSINESS PROGRAM(S)
www.stfrancis.edu/admissions/graduate
Admissions: (800) 735-7500
Email: admissions@stfrancis.edu
Financial aid: (866) 890-8331
Application deadline: rolling
Program can be completed entirely online: Yes
Total program cost: N/A

Tuition per credit: $748 full-time in-state, $748 part-time in-state, $748 full-time out-of-state, $748 part-time out-of-state
Acceptance rate: 41%
Test scores required: No
Average GMAT: N/A
Average age of entrants: 40
Enrollment: 84, 33% men, 67% women, 31% minority, 4% international
Average class size: 14
Most popular business concentrations: general management, health care administration, human resources management, supply chain management/logistics
Completion: Three year graduation rate: 62%; credits needed to graduate: 36; target time to graduate: 2 years
College funded aid available: Domestic: Yes; International: No
Graduates with debt: 65%; average amount of debt $33,523

Western Illinois University
Public

ONLINE MBA PROGRAM(S)
www.wiu.edu/cbt/mba
Admissions: (309) 298-2442
Email: grad-office@wiu.edu
Financial aid: (309) 298-2446
Application deadline: rolling
Program can be completed entirely online: Yes
Total program cost: N/A
Tuition per credit: $324 full-time in-state, $324 part-time in-state, $324 full-time out-of-state, $324 part-time out-of-state
Test scores required: GMAT or GRE
Average class size: 16
Most popular MBA concentrations: accounting, finance, general management, international business, supply chain management/logistics
Completion: Credits needed to graduate: 33; target time to graduate: 2 years
College funded aid available: Domestic: Yes; International: Yes

Anderson University
Private

ONLINE MBA PROGRAM(S)
www.anderson.edu/admissions
Admissions: (765) 641-3043
Email: agsenrollment@anderson.edu
Financial aid: N/A
Application deadline: rolling
Program can be completed entirely online: Yes
Total program cost: $20,350 full-time in-state, $20,350 part-time in-state, $20,350 full-time out-of-state, $20,350 part-time out-of-state

Tuition per credit: $550 full-time in-state, $550 part-time in-state, $550 full-time out-of-state, $550 part-time out-of-state
Most popular MBA concentrations: entrepreneurship, finance, international business, leadership, other
Completion: Credits needed to graduate: 37; target time to graduate: 2 years

Ball State University (Miller)
Public

ONLINE MBA PROGRAM(S)
bsu.edu/mba
Admissions: (765) 285-1931
Email: mba@bsu.edu
Financial aid: (765) 285-5600
Application deadline: rolling
Program can be completed entirely online: Yes
Total program cost: $12,060 full-time in-state, $12,060 part-time in-state, $18,090 full-time out-of-state, $18,090 part-time out-of-state
Tuition per credit: $402 full-time in-state, $402 part-time in-state, $603 full-time out-of-state, $603 part-time out-of-state
Acceptance rate: 92%
Test scores required: GMAT or GRE
Average GMAT: 564
Average GRE: 154 verbal, 155 quantitative, 4.0 writing
Average age of entrants: 29
Students with prior work experience: 92%
Enrollment: 293, 65% men, 35% women, 9% minority, 1% international
Average class size: 29
Most popular MBA concentrations: entrepreneurship, finance, health care administration, supply chain management/logistics, other
Completion: Three year graduation rate: 61%; credits needed to graduate: 30; target time to graduate: 3 years
College funded aid available: Domestic: Yes; International: Yes
Graduates with debt: 44%; average amount of debt $29,863

Indiana Institute of Technology
Private

ONLINE MBA PROGRAM(S)
www.indianatech.edu/prospectivestudents/online/pages/default.aspx
Admissions: (800) 288-1766
Email: cps@indianatech.edu
Financial aid: (260) 422-5561
Application deadline: rolling
Program can be completed entirely online: Yes
Total program cost: N/A

Tuition per credit: $495 full-time in-state, $495 part-time in-state, $495 full-time out-of-state, $495 part-time out-of-state
Acceptance rate: 99%
Test scores required: No
Average age of entrants: 35
Enrollment: 389, 44% men, 56% women, 29% minority, 5% international
Average class size: 13
Most popular MBA concentrations: accounting, general management, health care administration, human resources management, marketing

ONLINE BUSINESS PROGRAM(S)
www.indianatech.edu/admission-aid/
Admissions: (800) 288-1766
Email: cps@indianatech.edu
Financial aid: (260) 422-5561
Application deadline: rolling
Program can be completed entirely online: Yes
Total program cost: N/A
Tuition per credit: $396 full-time in-state, $396 part-time in-state, $396 full-time out-of-state, $396 part-time out-of-state
Acceptance rate: 99%
Test scores required: No
Average age of entrants: 37
Enrollment: 162, 35% men, 65% women, 45% minority, 3% international
Average class size: 13
Most popular business concentrations: general management, leadership
Completion: Target time to graduate: 2 years

Indiana University–Bloomington (Kelley)
Public

ONLINE MBA PROGRAM(S)
kelley.iu.edu/onlinemba/admissions/page36806.html
Admissions: (877) 785-4713
Email: kdirect@indiana.edu
Financial aid: (812) 856-7026
Application deadline: rolling
Program can be completed entirely online: No
Total program cost: $67,830 full-time in-state, $67,830 part-time in-state, $67,830 full-time out-of-state, $67,830 part-time out-of-state
Tuition per credit: $1,330 full-time in-state, $1,330 part-time in-state, $1,330 full-time out-of-state, $1,330 part-time out-of-state
Acceptance rate: 75%
Test scores required: GMAT or GRE
Average GMAT: 639
Average GRE: 156 verbal, 158 quantitative, 4.0 writing
Average age of entrants: 31
Students with prior work experience: 100%
Enrollment: 703, 74% men, 26% women, 14% minority, 12% international
Average class size: 31

Most popular MBA **concentrations:** finance, general management, marketing, supply chain management/logistics, quantitative analysis/statistics and operations research **Completion:** Three year graduation rate: 86%; credits needed to graduate: 51; target time to graduate: 3 years **College funded aid available:** Domestic: Yes; International: Yes **Graduates with debt:** 43%; average amount of debt $56,046

ONLINE BUSINESS PROGRAM(S)
kelley.iu.edu/onlinemba/
Admissions: (877) 785-4713
Email: ajherman@indiana.edu
Financial aid: (812) 856-7026
Application deadline: rolling
Program can be completed entirely online: Depends
Total program cost: $39,900 full-time in-state, $39,900 part-time in-state, $39,900 full-time out-of-state, $39,900 part-time out-of-state
Tuition per credit: $1,330 full-time in-state, $1,330 part-time in-state, $1,330 full-time out-of-state, $1,330 part-time out-of-state
Acceptance rate: 69%
Test scores required: GMAT or GRE
Average GMAT: 614
Average GRE: 154 verbal, 156 quantitative, 4.0 writing
Average age of entrants: 34
Students with prior work experience: 100%
Enrollment: 216, 80% men, 20% women, 17% minority, 12% international
Average class size: 31
Most popular business concentrations: finance, general management, marketing, supply chain management/logistics, quantitative analysis/statistics and operations research
Completion: Three year graduation rate: 70%; credits needed to graduate: 30; target time to graduate: 2 years
College funded aid available: Domestic: Yes; International: Yes
Graduates with debt: 42%; average amount of debt $55,118

University of Southern Indiana
Public

ONLINE MBA PROGRAM(S)
www.usi.edu/graduatestudies/
Admissions: (812) 465-7015
Email: Graduate.Studies@usi.edu
Financial aid: (812) 464-1767
Application deadline: rolling
Program can be completed entirely online: Yes
Total program cost: $12,900 full-time in-state, $12,900 part-time in-state, $12,900 full-time out-of-state, $12,900 part-time out-of-state

Tuition per credit: $430 full-time in-state, $430 part-time in-state, $430 full-time out-of-state, $430 part-time out-of-state
Acceptance rate: 86%
Test scores required: GMAT or GRE
Average GMAT: 495
Average GRE: 147 verbal, 148 quantitative, 3.0 writing
Average age of entrants: 34
Students with prior work experience: 6%
Enrollment: 293, 51% men, 49% women, 18% minority, 1% International
Average class size: 39
Most popular MBA concentrations: accounting, health care administration, human resources management, industrial management, other
Completion: Credits needed to graduate: 30; target time to graduate: 1.5 years
College funded aid available: Domestic: Yes; International: Yes

IOWA

Briar Cliff University
Private

ONLINE BUSINESS PROGRAM(S)
www.briarcliff.edu
Admissions: (712) 279-1628
Email: admissioins@briarcliff.edu
Financial aid: (712) 279-5239
Application deadline: rolling
Program can be completed entirely online: Yes
Total program cost: $405 full-time in-state, $405 part-time in-state, $405 full-time out-of-state, $405 part-time out-of-state
Tuition per credit: $405 full-time in-state, $405 part-time in-state, $405 full-time out-of-state, $405 part-time out-of-state
Acceptance rate: 77%
Test scores required: No
Average age of entrants: 28
Students with prior work experience: 44%
Enrollment: 65, 46% men, 54% women, N/A minority, N/A international
Average class size: 10
Most popular business concentrations: health care administration, human resources management, leadership, sports business, technology
Completion: Three year graduation rate: 100%; credits needed to graduate: 33; target time to graduate: 1.5 years
College funded aid available: Domestic: Yes
Graduates with debt: 95%

Maharishi University of Management
Private

ONLINE MBA PROGRAM(S)
www.mum.edu/admissions/welcome.html
Admissions: (641) 472-1110
Email: bmylett@mum.edu
Financial aid: (641) 472-1156
Application deadline: rolling
Program can be completed entirely online: Yes
Total program cost: N/A
Tuition per credit: $450 full-time in-state, $450 part-time in-state, $450 full-time out-of-state, $450 part-time out-of-state
Test scores required: No
Average GMAT: N/A
Average class size: 28
Completion: Credits needed to graduate: 60; target time to graduate: 3 years

ONLINE BUSINESS PROGRAM(S)
www.mum.edu/admissions/welcome.html
Admissions: (641) 472-1110
Email: bmylett@mum.edu
Financial aid: (641) 472-1156
Application deadline: N/A
Program can be completed entirely online: Yes
Total program cost: $27,000 full-time in-state, $27,000 part-time in-state, $27,000 full-time out-of-state, $27,000 part-time out-of-state
Tuition per credit: $450 full-time in-state, $450 part-time in-state, $450 full-time out-of-state, $450 part-time out-of-state
Average class size: 20
Completion: Credits needed to graduate: 58; target time to graduate: 3 years

Upper Iowa University
Private

ONLINE MBA PROGRAM(S)
uiu.edu/future/index.html
Admissions: (563) 425-5253
Email: wissmillerr@uiu.edu
Financial aid: (563) 425-5170
Application deadline: rolling
Program can be completed entirely online: Yes
Total program cost: $19,260 full-time in-state, $19,260 part-time in-state, $19,260 full-time out-of-state, $19,260 part-time out-of-state
Tuition per credit: $535 full-time in-state, $535 part-time in-state, $535 full-time out-of-state, $535 part-time out-of-state
Acceptance rate: 56%
Test scores required: No
Average age of entrants: 35
Enrollment: 471, 38% men, 62% women, 22% minority, 1% international
Average class size: 12

Most popular MBA **concentrations:** accounting, finance, general management, human resources management, other **Completion:** Three year graduation rate: 60%; credits needed to graduate: 36; target time to graduate: 2 years **College funded aid available:** Domestic: Yes; International: No **Graduates with debt:** 86%; average amount of debt $59,922

KANSAS

Baker University
Private

ONLINE MBA PROGRAM(S)
www.bakeru.edu/spgs/mba/
Admissions: (913) 491-4432
Email: ruth.miller@bakeru.edu
Financial aid: (785) 594-4595
Application deadline: rolling
Program can be completed entirely online: Yes
Total program cost: $26,620 full-time in-state, $26,620 part-time in-state, $26,620 full-time out-of-state, $26,620 part-time out-of-state
Tuition per credit: $670 full-time in-state, $670 part-time in-state, $670 full-time out-of-state, $670 part-time out-of-state
Test scores required: No
Enrollment: 222, 50% men, 50% women, N/A minority, N/A international
Average class size: 13
Most popular MBA concentrations: finance, health care administration, human resources management
Completion: Credits needed to graduate: 39; target time to graduate: 2 years
College funded aid available: Domestic: Yes; International: No
Graduates with debt: 72%; average amount of debt $44,731

ONLINE BUSINESS PROGRAM(S)
www.bakeru.edu
Admissions: (913) 491-4432
Email: ruth.miller@bakeru.edu
Financial aid: (785) 594-4595
Application deadline: rolling
Program can be completed entirely online: Yes
Total program cost: $22,135 full-time in-state, $22,135 part-time in-state, $22,135 full-time out-of-state, $22,135 part-time out-of-state
Tuition per credit: $555 full-time in-state, $555 part-time in-state, $555 full-time out-of-state, $555 part-time out-of-state
Test scores required: No
Enrollment: 84, 27% men, 73% women, N/A minority, N/A international
Average class size: 13
Most popular business concentrations: finance, health care administration, human resources management, marketing

Completion: Credits needed to graduate: 39; target time to graduate: 2 years
College funded aid available: Domestic: Yes; International: No
Graduates with debt: 60%; average amount of debt $44,693

Emporia State University
Public

ONLINE MBA PROGRAM(S)
www.emporia.edu/grad/admissions
Admissions: (620) 341-5456
Email: jwilling@emporia.edu
Financial aid: (620) 341-5457
Application deadline: rolling
Program can be completed entirely online: Yes
Total program cost: $12,357 full-time in-state, $12,357 part-time in-state, $16,920 full-time out-of-state, $16,920 part-time out-of-state
Tuition per credit: $343 full-time in-state, $343 part-time in-state, $470 full-time out-of-state, $470 part-time out-of-state
Acceptance rate: 93%
Test scores required: GMAT or GRE
Average age of entrants: 28
Students with prior work experience: 0%
Enrollment: 40, 40% men, 60% women, 5% minority
Average class size: 20
Most popular MBA concentrations: accounting
Completion: Credits needed to graduate: 36; target time to graduate: 2 years
College funded aid available: Domestic: Yes; International: Yes
Graduates with debt: 10%; average amount of debt $32,673

ONLINE BUSINESS PROGRAM(S)
www.emporia.edu/grad/admissions
Admissions: (620) 341-5456
Email: jwilling@emporia.edu
Financial aid: (620) 341-5457
Application deadline: rolling
Program can be completed entirely online: Yes
Total program cost: $12,357 full-time in-state, $12,357 part-time in-state, $16,920 full-time out-of-state, $16,920 part-time out-of-state
Tuition per credit: $343 full-time in-state, $343 part-time in-state, $470 full-time out-of-state, $470 part-time out-of-state
Acceptance rate: 100%
Test scores required: GMAT or GRE
Average age of entrants: 34
Enrollment: 47, 38% men, 62% women, 11% minority, 2% international
Average class size: 20
Most popular business concentrations: accounting
Completion: Credits needed to graduate: 30; target time to graduate: 2 years

College funded aid
available: Domestic: Yes;
International: Yes
Graduates with debt: 10%;
average amount of debt $32,673

Fort Hays State University

Public

ONLINE MBA PROGRAM(S)

www.fhsu.edu/mba
Admissions: (785) 628-5696
Email: gradcoordinator@
fhsu.edu
Financial aid: (785) 628-4408
Application deadline: rolling
**Program can be completed
entirely online:** Yes
Total program cost: $12,527
full-time in-state, $12,527
part-time in-state, $12,527
full-time out-of-state, $12,527
part-time out-of-state
Tuition per credit: $400
full-time in-state, $400
part-time in-state, $400
full-time out-of-state, $400
part-time out-of-state
Acceptance rate: 55%
Test scores required:
GMAT or GRE
Average GMAT: 452
Average GRE: 146 verbal, 146
quantitative, 4.0 writing
Average age of entrants: 28
**Students with prior work
experience:** 92%
Enrollment: 120, 43% men,
57% women, 18% minority,
5% international
Average class size: 23
**Most popular MBA
concentrations:** finance,
general management,
health care administration,
human resources
management, marketing
Completion: Three year
graduation rate: 57%; credits
needed to graduate: 34; target
time to graduate: 2 years
**College funded aid
available:** Domestic: Yes;
International: Yes
Graduates with debt: 52%;
average amount of debt $27,835

Friends University

Private

ONLINE MBA PROGRAM(S)

www.friends.edu/admissions
Admissions: (316) 295-5872
Email: learn@friends.edu
Financial aid: (316) 295-5120
Application deadline: rolling
**Program can be completed
entirely online:** Yes
Total program cost: $20,430
full-time in-state, $20,430
part-time in-state, $20,430
full-time out-of-state, $20,430
part-time out-of-state
Tuition per credit: $681 full-time
in-state, $681 part-time in-state,
$681 full-time out-of-state,
$681 part-time out-of-state
Acceptance rate: 78%
Test scores required: No
Average age of entrants: 34
Enrollment: 153, 42% men,
58% women, 34% minority

Average class size: 12
**Most popular MBA
concentrations:** accounting,
health care administration,
supply chain management/
logistics, other
Completion: Credits needed
to graduate: 30; target time
to graduate: 2 years
College funded aid available:
Domestic: No; International: No
Graduates with debt: 72%;
average amount of debt $28,493

ONLINE BUSINESS PROGRAM(S)

www.friends.edu/admissions/
Admissions: (316) 295-5872
Email: learn@friends.edu
Financial aid: (316) 295-5120
Application deadline: rolling
**Program can be completed
entirely online:** Yes
Total program cost: $20,430
full-time in-state, $20,430
part-time in-state, $20,430
full-time out-of-state, $20,430
part-time out-of-state
Tuition per credit: $681 full-time
in-state, $681 part-time in-state,
$681 full-time out-of-state,
$681 part-time out-of-state
Acceptance rate: 80%
Test scores required: No
Average age of entrants: 36
Enrollment: 55, 38% men,
62% women, 36% minority
Average class size: 10
**Most popular business
concentrations:** health care
administration, management
information systems
Completion: Credits needed
to graduate: 33; target time
to graduate: 2 years
College funded aid available:
Domestic: No; International: No
Graduates with debt: 64%;
average amount of debt $32,840

Kansas State University

Public

ONLINE MBA PROGRAM(S)

www.k-state.edu/onlinemba
Admissions: (785) 532-6191
Email: grad@ksu.edu
Financial aid: (785) 532-6420
Application deadline: rolling
**Program can be completed
entirely online:** No
Total program cost: $32,500
full-time in-state, $32,500
part-time in-state, $32,500
full-time out-of-state, $32,500
part-time out-of-state
Tuition per credit: $833
full-time in-state, $833
part-time in-state, $833
full-time out-of-state, $833
part-time out-of-state
Acceptance rate: 97%
Test scores required: GMAT
Average GMAT: 633
Average GRE: 150 verbal, 153
quantitative, 3.0 writing
Average age of entrants: 35
**Students with prior work
experience:** 100%
Enrollment: 81, 64% men,
36% women, 16% minority
Average class size: 16

**Most popular MBA
concentrations:** general
management
Completion: Credits needed
to graduate: 33; target time
to graduate: 2.5 years
**College funded aid
available:** Domestic: Yes;
International: Yes
Graduates with debt: 47%;
average amount of debt $50,072

Southwestern College

Private

ONLINE MBA PROGRAM(S)

ps.sckans.edu/
admissions-center
Admissions: (888) 684-5335
Email: enrollment@sckans.edu
Financial aid: (620) 229-6387
Application deadline: rolling
**Program can be completed
entirely online:** Yes
Total program cost: N/A
Tuition per credit: $662
full-time in-state, $662
part-time in-state, $662
full-time out-of-state, $662
part-time out-of-state
Acceptance rate: 68%
Test scores required: No
Average age of entrants: 31
Enrollment: 49, 71% men,
29% women, 27% minority,
2% international
Average class size: 6
**Most popular MBA
concentrations:** finance,
general management
Completion: Three year
graduation rate: 53%; credits
needed to graduate: 33; target
time to graduate: 2 years
College funded aid available:
Domestic: Yes; International: No
Graduates with debt:
33%; average amount
of debt $30,856

ONLINE BUSINESS PROGRAM(S)

ps.sckans.edu/
admissions-center
Admissions: (888) 684-5335
Email: enrollment@sckans.edu
Financial aid: (620) 229-6387
Application deadline: rolling
**Program can be completed
entirely online:** Yes
Total program cost: N/A
Tuition per credit: $599
full-time in-state, $599
part-time in-state, $599
full-time out-of-state, $599
part-time out-of-state
Acceptance rate: 82%
Test scores required: No
Average age of entrants: 37
Enrollment: 105, 71% men,
29% women, 29% minority
Average class size: 8
**Most popular business
concentrations:** general
management, leadership, other
Completion: Three year
graduation rate: 52%; credits
needed to graduate: 33; target
time to graduate: 2 years
College funded aid available:
Domestic: Yes; International: No
Graduates with debt: 50%;
average amount of debt $32,947

Tabor College

Private

ONLINE MBA PROGRAM(S)

tabor.edu/online/
admissions-enrollment/
Admissions: (316) 729-6333
Email: learn@tabor.edu
Financial aid: (316) 729-6333
Application deadline: rolling
**Program can be completed
entirely online:** Yes
Total program cost: $20,476
full-time in-state, $20,476
part-time in-state, $20,476
full-time out-of-state, $20,476
part-time out-of-state
Tuition per credit: $521 full-time
in-state, $521 part-time in-state,
$521 full-time out-of-state,
$521 part-time out-of-state
Acceptance rate: 81%
Test scores required: No
Enrollment: 28, 68% men,
32% women, N/A minority,
N/A international
**Most popular MBA
concentrations:** leadership, other
Completion: Credits needed
to graduate: 36; target time
to graduate: 2 years
**College funded aid
available:** Domestic: Yes;
International: Yes

University of Kansas

Public

ONLINE MBA PROGRAM(S)

onlinemba.ku.edu/admissions
Admissions: (855) 639-7799
Email: onlineinfo@ku.edu
Financial aid: (785) 864-4700
Application deadline: rolling
**Program can be completed
entirely online:** Yes
Total program cost: $35,700
full-time in-state, $35,700
part-time in-state, $35,700
full-time out-of-state, $35,700
part-time out-of-state
Tuition per credit: $850
full-time in-state, $850
part-time in-state, $850
full-time out-of-state, $850
part-time out-of-state
Acceptance rate: 73%
Test scores required:
GMAT or GRE
Average GMAT: 556
Average GRE: 154 verbal, 156
quantitative, 4.2 writing
Average age of entrants: 33
**Students with prior work
experience:** 93%
Enrollment: 234, 68%
men, 32% women, 16%
minority, 1% international
Average class size: 37
**Most popular MBA
concentrations:** finance,
general management,
leadership, marketing
Completion: Credits needed
to graduate: 42; target time
to graduate: 2.5 years
College funded aid available:
Domestic: No; International: No

University of St. Mary

Private

ONLINE MBA PROGRAM(S)

www.stmary.edu/
admissions.aspx
Admissions: (913) 758-6308
Email: John.Shultz@stmary.edu
Financial aid: (913) 758-6172
Application deadline: rolling
**Program can be completed
entirely online:** Yes
Total program cost: $22,140
full-time in-state, $22,140
part-time in-state, $22,140
full-time out-of-state, $22,140
part-time out-of-state
Tuition per credit: $615 full-time
in-state, $615 part-time in-state,
$615 full-time out-of-state,
$615 part-time out-of-state
Acceptance rate: 97%
Test scores required: No
Average age of entrants: 33
Enrollment: 317, 42%
men, 58% women, 37%
minority, 1% international
Average class size: 14
**Most popular MBA
concentrations:** finance,
general management,
health care administration,
human resources
management, marketing
Completion: Three year
graduation rate: 65%; credits
needed to graduate: 36; target
time to graduate: 2 years
College funded aid available:
Domestic: No; International: No
Graduates with debt: 69%;
average amount of debt $34,480

Wichita State University (Barton)

Public

ONLINE MBA PROGRAM(S)

www.wichita.edu/gradschool
Admissions: (316) 978-3095
Email: wsugradschool@
wichita.edu
Financial aid: (316) 978-3430
Application deadline: rolling
**Program can be completed
entirely online:** Yes
Total program cost: $7,128
full-time in-state, $3,564
part-time in-state, $7,128
full-time out-of-state, $3,564
part-time out-of-state
Tuition per credit: $294
full-time in-state, $294
part-time in-state, $294
full-time out-of-state, $294
part-time out-of-state
Acceptance rate: 72%
Test scores required:
GMAT or GRE
Average GRE: 151 verbal, 149
quantitative, 3.4 writing
Average age of entrants: 28
Enrollment: 223, 66%
men, 34% women, 20%
minority, 9% international
Average class size: 16
**Most popular MBA
concentrations:** general
management, marketing
Completion: Credits needed
to graduate: 36; target time
to graduate: 2 years

College funded aid available: Domestic: Yes; International: Yes
Graduates with debt: 57%; average amount of debt $15,528

KENTUCKY

Campbellsville University

Private

ONLINE MBA PROGRAM(S)

www.campbellsville.edu/mba
Admissions: (270) 789-5221
Email: mkbamwine@campbellsville.edu
Financial aid: (270) 789-5013
Application deadline: rolling
Program can be completed entirely online: Yes
Total program cost: $18,900 full-time in-state, $18,900 part-time in-state, $18,900 full-time out-of-state, $18,900 part-time out-of-state
Tuition per credit: $525 full-time in-state, $525 part-time in-state, $525 full-time out-of-state, $525 part-time out-of-state
Acceptance rate: 49%
Test scores required: GMAT or GRE
Average GMAT: 420
Average GRE: 150 verbal, 145 quantitative, 3.1 writing
Average age of entrants: 31
Students with prior work experience: 0%
Enrollment: 83, 48% men, 52% women, 18% minority, 1% international
Average class size: 25
Most popular MBA concentrations: health care administration, human resources management, international business, marketing, technology
Completion: Three year graduation rate: 58%; credits needed to graduate: 36; target time to graduate: 2 years
College funded aid available: Domestic: No; International: No
Graduates with debt: 46%; average amount of debt $15,928

ONLINE BUSINESS PROGRAM(S)

www.campbellsville.edu/mml
Admissions: (270) 789-5221
Email: mkbamwine@campbellsville.edu
Financial aid: (270) 789-5013
Application deadline: rolling
Program can be completed entirely online: Yes
Total program cost: $15,750 full-time in-state, $15,750 part-time in-state, $15,750 full-time out-of-state, $15,750 part-time out-of-state
Tuition per credit: $525 full-time in-state, $525 part-time in-state, $525 full-time out-of-state, $525 part-time out-of-state
Acceptance rate: 71%
Test scores required: GMAT or GRE
Average GMAT: 350
Average GRE: 147 verbal, 145 quantitative, 3.0 writing

Average age of entrants: 40
Enrollment: 37, 51% men, 49% women, 22% minority
Average class size: 18
Most popular business concentrations: general management, leadership
Completion: Three year graduation rate: 61%; credits needed to graduate: 30; target time to graduate: 2 years
College funded aid available: Domestic: No; International: No
Graduates with debt: 75%; average amount of debt $19,044

University of the Cumberlands

Private

ONLINE MBA PROGRAM(S)

www.ucumberlands.edu/
Admissions: (606) 539-4390
Email: mba@ucumberlands.edu
Financial aid: (606) 539-4220
Application deadline: rolling
Program can be completed entirely online: Yes
Total program cost: $9,450 full-time in-state, $9,450 part-time in-state, $9,450 full-time out-of-state, $9,450 part-time out-of-state
Tuition per credit: $315 full-time in-state, $315 part-time in-state, $315 full-time out-of-state, $315 part-time out-of-state
Acceptance rate: 77%
Test scores required: No
Average age of entrants: 33
Students with prior work experience: 92%
Enrollment: 227, 7% minority
Average class size: 28
Most popular MBA concentrations: accounting
Completion: Three year graduation rate: 88%; credits needed to graduate: 30; target time to graduate: 1.5 years
College funded aid available: Domestic: No; International: No

Western Kentucky University (Ford)

Public

ONLINE MBA PROGRAM(S)

www.wku.edu/mba/
Admissions: (270) 745-5458
Email: gfcb@wku.edu
Financial aid: (270) 745-2755
Application deadline: rolling
Program can be completed entirely online: Depends
Total program cost: $21,210 full-time in-state, $21,210 part-time in-state, $21,210 full-time out-of-state, $21,210 part-time out-of-state
Tuition per credit: $707 full-time in-state, $707 part-time in-state, $707 full-time out-of-state, $707 part-time out-of-state
Acceptance rate: 96%
Test scores required: GMAT
Average GMAT: 523
Average age of entrants: 29
Students with prior work experience: 89%

Enrollment: 92, 54% men, 46% women, 7% minority
Average class size: 18
Most popular MBA concentrations: accounting, finance, marketing, organizational behavior, other
Completion: Three year graduation rate: 79%; credits needed to graduate: 33; target time to graduate: 2 years
Graduates with debt: 62%; average amount of debt $25,312

LOUISIANA

Louisiana State University– Baton Rouge (Ourso)

Public

ONLINE MBA PROGRAM(S)

lsuonline.lsu.edu/programs/1138/master-business-administration
Admissions: (225) 578-8867
Email: lwhitm3@lsu.edu
Financial aid: (225) 578-3103
Application deadline: rolling
Program can be completed entirely online: Yes
Total program cost: $42,462 full-time in-state, $42,462 part-time in-state, $42,462 full-time out-of-state, $42,462 part-time out-of-state
Tuition per credit: $1,011 full-time in-state, $1,011 part-time in-state, $1,011 full-time out-of-state, $1,011 part-time out-of-state
Acceptance rate: 55%
Test scores required: No
Average GMAT: 540
Average GRE: 145 verbal, 150 quantitative, 4.0 writing
Average age of entrants: 32
Students with prior work experience: 73%
Enrollment: 137, 75% men, 25% women, 23% minority
Average class size: 20
Completion: Three year graduation rate: 94%; credits needed to graduate: 42; target time to graduate: 2.5 years
College funded aid available: Domestic: No; International: No
Graduates with debt: 49%; average amount of debt $49,709

Louisiana State University–Shreveport

Public

ONLINE MBA PROGRAM(S)

www.lsus.edu/academics/graduate-studies/graduate-programs/online-master-of-business-administration
Admissions: (318) 797-5268
Email: tami.knotts@lsus.edu
Financial aid: (318) 797-5346
Application deadline: N/A
Total program cost: $12,474 full-time in-state, $12,474 part-time in-state, $12,474 full-time out-of-state, $12,474 part-time out-of-state

Tuition per credit: $350 full-time in-state, $350 part-time in-state, $350 full-time out-of-state, $350 part-time out-of-state
Acceptance rate: 90%
Enrollment: 1,175, 51% men, 49% women, 31% minority, 3% international
Most popular MBA concentrations: accounting, finance, general management, marketing, other
Completion: Credits needed to graduate: 30

ONLINE BUSINESS PROGRAM(S)

www.lsus.edu/academics/graduate-studies/graduate-programs/online-master-of-business-administration
Admissions: (318) 795-2400
Email: mary.harvison@lsus.edu
Financial aid: (318) 797-5346
Application deadline: N/A
Total program cost: $12,474 full-time in-state, $12,474 part-time in-state, $12,474 full-time out-of-state, $12,474 part-time out-of-state
Tuition per credit: $350 full-time in-state, $350 part-time in-state, $350 full-time out-of-state, $350 part-time out-of-state
Acceptance rate: 96%
Enrollment: 438, 26% men, 74% women, 36% minority, 1% international
Most popular business concentrations: health care administration, not-for-profit management

Louisiana Tech University

Public

ONLINE MBA PROGRAM(S)

www.latech.edu/graduate_school
Admissions: (318) 257-2924
Email: gschool@latech.edu
Financial aid: (318) 257-2641
Application deadline: rolling
Program can be completed entirely online: Yes
Total program cost: $8,010 full-time in-state, $7,740 part-time in-state, $15,895 full-time out-of-state, $7,740 part-time out-of-state
Tuition per credit: $456 full-time in-state, $445 part-time in-state, $719 full-time out-of-state, $445 part-time out-of-state
Acceptance rate: 55%
Test scores required: GMAT or GRE
Average GMAT: 476
Average GRE: 147 verbal, 148 quantitative, 3.1 writing
Average age of entrants: 27
Enrollment: 39, 54% men, 46% women, 23% minority, 3% international
Average class size: 30
Most popular MBA concentrations: entrepreneurship, finance
Completion: Credits needed to graduate: 30; target time to graduate: 1 year

College funded aid available: Domestic: Yes; International: Yes
Graduates with debt: 38%; average amount of debt $16,731

McNeese State University (Burton)

Public

ONLINE MBA PROGRAM(S)

www.becomeacowboy.com
Admissions: (337) 475-5504
Email: admissions@mcneese.edu
Financial aid: (337) 475-5068
Application deadline: Domestic: 05/01
Program can be completed entirely online: Yes
Total program cost: N/A
Tuition per credit: $891 full-time in-state, $891 part-time in-state, $1,330 full-time out-of-state, $1,330 part-time out-of-state
Test scores required: GMAT or GRE
Enrollment: 12, 75% men, 25% women, N/A minority
Average class size: 10
Completion: Credits needed to graduate: 30
College funded aid available: Domestic: No; International: No

ONLINE BUSINESS PROGRAM(S)

www.becomeacowboy.com
Admissions: (337) 475-5065
Email: admissions@mcneese.edu
Financial aid: (337) 475-5065
Application deadline: Domestic: 05/01
Program can be completed entirely online: Yes
Total program cost: N/A
Tuition per credit: $891 full-time in-state, $891 part-time in-state, $1,330 full-time out-of-state, $1,330 part-time out-of-state
Test scores required: No
Enrollment: 2, 50% men, 50% women
Completion: Target time to graduate: 1.5 years
College funded aid available: Domestic: No; International: No

University of Louisiana–Monroe

Public

ONLINE MBA PROGRAM(S)

www.ulm.edu/gradschool/
Admissions: (318) 342-1041
Email: gradadmissions@ulm.edu
Financial aid: (318) 342-5329
Application deadline: rolling
Program can be completed entirely online: Yes
Total program cost: $17,500 full-time in-state, $17,500 part-time in-state, $17,500 full-time out-of-state, $17,500 part-time out-of-state
Tuition per credit: $583 full-time in-state, $583 part-time in-state, $583 full-time out-of-state, $583 part-time out-of-state
Acceptance rate: 70%

Test scores required:
GMAT or GRE
Average GMAT: 514
Average GRE: 148 verbal, 148 quantitative, 3.3 writing
Average age of entrants: 26
Students with prior work experience: 100%
Enrollment: 67, 64% men, 36% women, 19% minority, 1% international
Average class size: 17
Most popular MBA concentrations: general management
Completion: Three year graduation rate: 24%; credits needed to graduate: 30; target time to graduate: 2 years
College funded aid available: Domestic: Yes; International: Yes
Graduates with debt: 50%; average amount of debt $25,071

MAINE

Husson University
Private

ONLINE MBA PROGRAM(S)

www.husson.edu/
mba-admissions
Admissions: (207) 992-4994
Email: graduateschool@
husson.edu
Financial aid: (207) 973-1090
Application deadline: rolling
Program can be completed entirely online: Yes
Total program cost: $16,704
full-time in-state, $16,704
part-time in-state, $16,704
full-time out-of-state, $16,704
part-time out-of-state
Tuition per credit: $464
full-time in-state, $464
part-time in-state, $464
full-time out-of-state, $464
part-time out-of-state
Acceptance rate: 79%
Test scores required: No
Average age of entrants: 33
Enrollment: 82, 32% men, 68% women, 7% minority
Average class size: 20
Most popular MBA concentrations: general management, health care administration, organizational behavior, other
Completion: Credits needed to graduate: 36; target time to graduate: 1.5 years
College funded aid available: Domestic: Yes; International: Yes

Maine Maritime Academy
Public

ONLINE BUSINESS PROGRAM(S)

mainemaritime.edu/academics/
graduate-programs/
Admissions: (207) 326-2212
Email: online@mma.edu
Financial aid: (207) 326-2339
Application deadline: rolling
Program can be completed entirely online: Yes

Total program cost: $28,800
full-time in-state, $28,800
part-time in-state, $28,800
full-time out-of-state, $28,800
part-time out-of-state
Tuition per credit: $900
full-time in-state, $900
part-time in-state, $900
full-time out-of-state, $900
part-time out-of-state
Acceptance rate: 82%
Test scores required:
GMAT or GRE
Average GRE: 150 verbal, 142 quantitative, 5.0 writing
Average age of entrants: 31
Students with prior work experience: 100%
Enrollment: 19, N/A minority, N/A international
Average class size: 10
Most popular business concentrations: supply chain management/logistics
Completion: Credits needed to graduate: 36; target time to graduate: 2 years
College funded aid available: Domestic: Yes; International: Yes
Graduates with debt: 40%; average amount of debt $10,000

University of Maine
Public

ONLINE MBA PROGRAM(S)

umaine.edu/business/
degrees-and-programs/mba/
Admissions: (207) 581-1968
Email: mba@maine.edu
Financial aid: (207) 581-1324
Application deadline: rolling
Program can be completed entirely online: Yes
Total program cost: $12,870
full-time in-state, $12,870
part-time in-state, $16,080
full-time out-of-state, $16,080
part-time out-of-state
Tuition per credit: $429
full-time in-state, $429
part-time in-state, $536
full-time out-of-state, $536
part-time out-of-state
Acceptance rate: 72%
Test scores required:
GMAT or GRE
Average GMAT: 568
Average GRE: 154 verbal, 152 quantitative, 4.0 writing
Average age of entrants: 31
Enrollment: 38, 55% men, 45% women, 5% minority, 5% international
Average class size: 25
Completion: Credits needed to graduate: 30; target time to graduate: 2.5 years
College funded aid available: Domestic: Yes; International: Yes

Frostburg State University
Public

ONLINE MBA PROGRAM(S)

www.frostburg.edu/academics/
majorminors/graduate/
ms-business-administration.php
Admissions: (301) 687-4595
Email: vmmazer@frostburg.edu
Financial aid: (301) 687-4301
Application deadline: rolling
Total program cost: $14,868
full-time in-state, $14,868
part-time in-state, $19,116
full-time out-of-state, $19,116
part-time out-of-state
Tuition per credit: $413 full-time in-state, $413 part-time in-state, $531 full-time out-of-state, $531 part-time out-of-state
Acceptance rate: 76%
Average GMAT: 510
Average GRE: 153 verbal, 158 quantitative, 4.5 writing
Average age of entrants: 31
Enrollment: 258, 51% men, 49% women, 22% minority, 2% international
Average class size: 21
Completion: Three year graduation rate: 38%; target time to graduate: 3 years
Graduates with debt: 32%; average amount of debt $27,000

ONLINE BUSINESS PROGRAM(S)

www.frostburg.edu/academics/
majorminors/graduate/
ms-business-administration.php
Admissions: (301) 687-4595
Email: vmmazer@frostburg.edu
Financial aid: (301) 687-4301
Application deadline: N/A
Total program cost: $14,868
full-time in-state, $14,868
part-time in-state, $19,116
full-time out-of-state, $19,116
part-time out-of-state
Tuition per credit: $413 full-time in-state, $413 part-time in-state, $531 full-time out-of-state, $531 part-time out-of-state
Acceptance rate: 76%
Average GMAT: 510
Average GRE: 153 verbal, 158 quantitative, 4.5 writing
Average age of entrants: 34
Enrollment: 258, 51% men, 49% women, 22% minority, 2% international
Average class size: 21
Completion: Three year graduation rate: 38%; target time to graduate: 3 years
Graduates with debt: 32%; average amount of debt $27,000

Morgan State University (Graves)
Public

ONLINE MBA PROGRAM(S)

www.morgan.edu/online
Admissions: (443) 885-4720
Email: online@morgan.edu
Financial aid: (443) 885-3170
Application deadline: Domestic: 05/01; International: 04/01

Program can be completed entirely online: Yes
Total program cost: $30,000
full-time in-state, $30,000
full-time out-of-state
Tuition per credit: $3,300
full-time in-state, $3,300
part-time in-state, $3,300
full-time out-of-state, $3,300
part-time out-of-state
Acceptance rate: 100%
Test scores required:
GMAT or GRE
Average GRE: 147 verbal, 143 quantitative
Average age of entrants: 31
Enrollment: 5, 40% men, 60% women, 100% minority
Average class size: 13
Completion: Credits needed to graduate: 33; target time to graduate: 2 years
College funded aid available: Domestic: Yes; International: No
Graduates with debt: 100%; average amount of debt $7,500

ONLINE BUSINESS PROGRAM(S)

www.morgan.edu/
online_education/
online_admissions.html
Admissions: (443) 885-3396
Email: joseph.wells@morgan.edu
Financial aid: (443) 885-3172
Application deadline: Domestic: 03/15; International: 03/15
Program can be completed entirely online: Yes
Total program cost: $30,000
full-time in-state, $30,000
full-time out-of-state
Tuition per credit: $412 full-time in-state, $412 part-time in-state, $810 full-time out-of-state, $810 part-time out-of-state
Acceptance rate: 88%
Test scores required: No
Average age of entrants: 37
Enrollment: 7, 29% men, 71% women, 100% minority
Average class size: 18
Completion: Credits needed to graduate: 30; target time to graduate: 2 years
College funded aid available: Domestic: No; International: No

Salisbury University
Public

ONLINE MBA PROGRAM(S)

www.salisbury.edu/gsr/
gradstudies/default.html
Admissions: (410) 677-0047
Email: mba@salisbury.edu
Financial aid: (410) 543-6165
Application deadline: rolling
Program can be completed entirely online: Yes
Total program cost: $22,500
full-time in-state, $22,500
full-time out-of-state
Tuition per credit: $750 full-time in-state, $750 part-time in-state, $750 full-time out-of-state, $750 part-time out-of-state
Test scores required:
GMAT or GRE
Enrollment: 20, 60% men, 40% women, 15% minority
Average class size: 20
Completion: Credits needed to graduate: 30; target time to graduate: 1 year

College funded aid available: Domestic: Yes; International: Yes

University of Baltimore
Public

ONLINE MBA PROGRAM(S)

www.ubalt.edu/admission/
graduate/index.cfm
Admissions: (410) 837-6565
Email: admission@ubalt.edu
Financial aid: (410) 837-4772
Application deadline: rolling
Program can be completed entirely online: Yes
Total program cost: $39,552
full-time in-state, $39,552
part-time in-state, $39,552
full-time out-of-state, $39,552
part-time out-of-state
Tuition per credit: $824
full-time in-state, $824
part-time in-state, $824
full-time out-of-state, $824
part-time out-of-state
Acceptance rate: 89%
Test scores required:
GMAT or GRE
Average GMAT: 518
Average GRE: 148 verbal, 145 quantitative, 4.0 writing
Average age of entrants: 31
Students with prior work experience: 88%
Enrollment: 512, 48% men, 52% women, 36% minority, 6% international
Average class size: 26
Most popular MBA concentrations: general management, other
Completion: Three year graduation rate: 57%; credits needed to graduate: 36; target time to graduate: 1.5 years
College funded aid available: Domestic: Yes; International: Yes
Graduates with debt: 51%; average amount of debt $47,847

University of Maryland– College Park (Smith)
Public

ONLINE MBA PROGRAM(S)

onlinemba.umd.edu/
Admissions: (877) 807-8741
Email: admissions@
onlineprograms.umd.edu
Financial aid: (301) 314-9565
Application deadline: rolling
Program can be completed entirely online: No
Total program cost: $83,970
full-time in-state, $83,970
part-time in-state, $83,970
full-time out-of-state, $83,970
part-time out-of-state
Tuition per credit: $1,555
full-time in-state, $1,555
part-time in-state, $1,555
full-time out-of-state, $1,555
part-time out-of-state
Acceptance rate: 74%
Test scores required:
GMAT or GRE

Average GMAT: 614
Average GRE: 158 verbal, 155 quantitative
Average age of entrants: 32
Students with prior work experience: 100%
Enrollment: 369, 66% men, 34% women, N/A minority, N/A international
Average class size: 18
Most popular MBA concentrations: finance, general management, marketing, management information systems, supply chain management/logistics
Completion: Three year graduation rate: 100%; credits needed to graduate: 54; target time to graduate: 2 years
College funded aid available: Domestic: Yes; International: Yes

MASSACHUSETTS

Babson College (Olin)

Private

ONLINE MBA PROGRAM(S)

babson.edu/admission/graduate/working-professionals-programs/Pages/blended-learning-program.aspx
Admissions: (781) 239-4317
Email: gradadmissions@babson.edu
Financial aid: N/A
Application deadline: Domestic: 09/01
Program can be completed entirely online: No
Total program cost: $87,025 full-time in-state, $87,025 part-time in-state, $87,025 full-time out-of-state, $87,025 part-time out-of-state
Tuition per credit: $1,853 full-time in-state, $1,853 part-time in-state, $1,853 full-time out-of-state, $1,853 part-time out-of-state
Acceptance rate: 90%
Test scores required: No
Average age of entrants: 33
Students with prior work experience: 100%
Enrollment: 449, 61% men, 39% women, 28% minority, 6% international
Average class size: 35
Most popular MBA concentrations: entrepreneurship, marketing
Completion: Three year graduation rate: 93%; credits needed to graduate: 46; target time to graduate: 2 years
College funded aid available: Domestic: Yes
Graduates with debt: 51%; average amount of debt $64,495

Bay Path University

Private

ONLINE MBA PROGRAM(S)

graduate.baypath.edu/
Admissions: (413) 565-1332
Email: graduate@baypath.edu
Financial aid: (413) 565-1256
Application deadline: N/A
Total program cost: N/A

Tuition per credit: $815 full-time in-state, $815 part-time in-state, $815 full-time out-of-state, $815 part-time out-of-state

ONLINE BUSINESS PROGRAM(S)

graduate.baypath.edu/
Admissions: (413) 565-1332
Email: graduate@baypath.edu
Financial aid: (413) 565-1256
Application deadline: N/A
Total program cost: N/A
Tuition per credit: $815 full-time in-state, $815 part-time in-state, $815 full-time out-of-state, $815 part-time out-of-state

Bentley University

Private

ONLINE BUSINESS PROGRAM(S)

admissions.bentley.edu/graduate
Admissions: (781) 891-2108
Email: applygrad@bentley.edu
Financial aid: (781) 891-3441
Application deadline: rolling
Program can be completed entirely online: Depends
Total program cost: $44,450 full-time in-state, $44,450 part-time in-state, $44,450 full-time out-of-state, $44,450 part-time out-of-state
Tuition per credit: $1,481 full-time in-state, $1,481 part-time in-state, $1,481 full-time out-of-state, $1,481 part-time out-of-state
Acceptance rate: 84%
Test scores required: GMAT or GRE
Average GMAT: 594
Average age of entrants: 28
Students with prior work experience: 62%
Enrollment: 237, 42% men, 58% women, 12% minority, 19% international
Average class size: 25
Most popular business concentrations: finance, leadership, tax, technology
Completion: Three year graduation rate: 82%; credits needed to graduate: 30; target time to graduate: 2 years
College funded aid available: Domestic: Yes; International: Yes
Graduates with debt: 35%; average amount of debt $29,834

Boston University

Private

ONLINE BUSINESS PROGRAM(S)

www.bu.edu/met/admissions/apply-now/graduate-degree-program/
Admissions: (617) 358-8162
Email: adsadmissions@bu.edu
Financial aid: (617) 358-3993
Application deadline: rolling
Program can be completed entirely online: Yes
Total program cost: $34,400 part-time in-state, $34,400 part-time out-of-state
Tuition per credit: $860 full-time in-state, $860 part-time in-state, $860 full-time out-of-state, $860 part-time out-of-state

Acceptance rate: 89%
Test scores required: No
Average GMAT: 625
Average GRE: 150 verbal, 155 quantitative, 3.7 writing
Average age of entrants: 34
Students with prior work experience: 97%
Enrollment: 758, 49% men, 51% women, 29% minority, 11% international
Average class size: 34
Most popular business concentrations: finance, international business, marketing, quantitative analysis/statistics and operations research, other
Completion: Three year graduation rate: 63%; credits needed to graduate: 40; target time to graduate: 3 years
College funded aid available: Domestic: Yes; International: Yes
Graduates with debt: 43%; average amount of debt $41,177

Fitchburg State University

Public

ONLINE MBA PROGRAM(S)

www.fitchburgstate.edu/admissions
Admissions: (978) 665-3144
Email: admissions@fitchburgstate.edu
Financial aid: (978) 665-3156
Application deadline: rolling
Program can be completed entirely online: Yes
Total program cost: $11,310 full-time in-state, $11,310 part-time in-state, $11,310 full-time out-of-state, $11,310 part-time out-of-state
Tuition per credit: $177 full-time in-state, $177 part-time in-state, $177 full-time out-of-state, $177 part-time out-of-state
Acceptance rate: 100%
Test scores required: No
Average age of entrants: 34
Enrollment: 173, 45% men, 55% women, 33% minority
Average class size: 23
Most popular MBA concentrations: general management, human resources management
Completion: Three year graduation rate: 88%; credits needed to graduate: 30; target time to graduate: 4 years
College funded aid available: Domestic: Yes; International: Yes

Lasell College

Private

ONLINE MBA PROGRAM(S)

www.lasell.edu/admissions/graduate-admission.html
Admissions: (617) 243-2400
Email: gradinfo@lasell.edu
Financial aid: (617) 243-2227
Application deadline: rolling
Program can be completed entirely online: Yes

Total program cost: $21,600 full-time in-state, $21,600 part-time in-state, $21,600 full-time out-of-state, $21,600 part-time out-of-state
Tuition per credit: $600 full-time in-state, $600 part-time in-state, $600 full-time out-of-state, $600 part-time out-of-state
Acceptance rate: 95%
Test scores required: No
Average age of entrants: 31
Students with prior work experience: 100%
Enrollment: 25, 20% men, 80% women, 28% minority
Average class size: 5
Most popular MBA concentrations: general management
Completion: Credits needed to graduate: 36; target time to graduate: 1.5 years
College funded aid available: Domestic: No; International: No
Graduates with debt: 29%; average amount of debt $26,585

ONLINE BUSINESS PROGRAM(S)

www.lasell.edu/admissions/graduate-admission.html
Admissions: (617) 243-2400
Email: gradinfo@lasell.edu
Financial aid: (617) 243-2227
Application deadline: rolling
Program can be completed entirely online: Yes
Total program cost: $21,600 full-time in-state, $21,600 part-time in-state, $21,600 full-time out-of-state, $21,600 part-time out-of-state
Tuition per credit: $600 full-time in-state, $600 part-time in-state, $600 full-time out-of-state, $600 part-time out-of-state
Acceptance rate: 90%
Test scores required: No
Average age of entrants: 30
Enrollment: 168, 27% men, 73% women, 20% minority, 20% international
Average class size: 13
Most popular business concentrations: general management, hotel administration, human resources management, marketing, other
Completion: Three year graduation rate: 64%; credits needed to graduate: 36; target time to graduate: 1.5 years
College funded aid available: Domestic: No; International: No
Graduates with debt: 66%; average amount of debt $33,503

New England College of Business and Finance

Proprietary

ONLINE MBA PROGRAM(S)

www.necb.edu/admissions/about-admissions/
Admissions: (617) 603-6937
Email: kirsten.thompson@necb.edu
Financial aid: (205) 795-9605

Application deadline: rolling
Program can be completed entirely online: Yes
Total program cost: $36,420 full-time in-state, $36,420 part-time in-state, $36,420 full-time out-of-state, $36,420 part-time out-of-state
Tuition per credit: $1,012 full-time in-state, $1,012 part-time in-state, $1,012 full-time out-of-state, $1,012 part-time out-of-state
Acceptance rate: 92%
Test scores required: No
Average age of entrants: 33
Students with prior work experience: 86%
Enrollment: 166, 31% men, 69% women, 30% minority
Average class size: 15
Most popular MBA concentrations: finance, health care administration, human resources management, other
Completion: Three year graduation rate: 68%; credits needed to graduate: 36; target time to graduate: 1.5 years
College funded aid available: Domestic: Yes; International: Yes
Graduates with debt: 58%; average amount of debt $32,000

ONLINE BUSINESS PROGRAM(S)

www.necb.edu/admissions/about-admissions/
Admissions: (617) 603-6937
Email: kirsten.thompson@necb.edu
Financial aid: (205) 795-9605
Application deadline: rolling
Program can be completed entirely online: Yes
Total program cost: $30,350 full-time in-state, $30,350 part-time in-state, $30,350 full-time out-of-state, $30,350 part-time out-of-state
Tuition per credit: $1,012 full-time in-state, $1,012 part-time in-state, $1,012 full-time out-of-state, $1,012 part-time out-of-state
Acceptance rate: 85%
Test scores required: No
Average age of entrants: 37
Students with prior work experience: 95%
Enrollment: 170, 25% men, 75% women, 30% minority, 4% international
Average class size: 9
Most popular business concentrations: accounting, other
Completion: Three year graduation rate: 85%; credits needed to graduate: 30; target time to graduate: 1.5 years
College funded aid available: Domestic: Yes; International: Yes
Graduates with debt: 62%; average amount of debt $33,500

Northeastern University

Private

ONLINE MBA PROGRAM(S)

onlinebusiness.
northeastern.edu/
Admissions: N/A
Email: onlinegradbusiness@
neu.edu
Financial aid: (617) 373-5899
Application deadline: rolling
**Program can be completed
entirely online:** Yes
Total program cost: $78,000
full-time in-state, $78,000
part-time in-state, $78,000
full-time out-of-state, $78,000
part-time out-of-state
Tuition per credit: $1,560
full-time in-state, $1,560
part-time in-state, $1,560
full-time out-of-state, $1,560
part-time out-of-state
Acceptance rate: 88%
Test scores required: No
Average age of entrants: 34
**Students with prior work
experience:** 100%
Enrollment: 709, 59% men,
41% women, 27% minority,
5% international
Average class size: 17
Most popular MBA concentrations:
entrepreneurship, finance,
international business,
marketing, supply chain
management/logistics
Completion: Three year
graduation rate: 50%; credits
needed to graduate: 50; target
time to graduate: 2 years
**College funded aid
available:** Domestic: Yes;
International: Yes

ONLINE BUSINESS PROGRAM(S)

onlinebusiness.
northeastern.edu/
Admissions: N/A
Email:
onlinegradbusiness@neu.edu
Financial aid: (617) 373-5899
Application deadline: rolling
**Program can be completed
entirely online:** Yes
Total program cost: $46,800
full-time in-state, $46,800
part-time in-state, $46,800
full-time out-of-state, $46,800
part-time out-of-state
Tuition per credit: $1,560
full-time in-state, $1,560
part-time in-state, $1,560
full-time out-of-state, $1,560
part-time out-of-state
Acceptance rate: 90%
Test scores required: No
Average age of entrants: 35
**Students with prior work
experience:** 100%
Enrollment: 174, 60% men,
40% women, 25% minority,
6% international
Average class size: 12
**Most popular business
concentrations:**
finance, tax, other
Completion: Three year
graduation rate: 42%; credits
needed to graduate: 30; target
time to graduate: 1.5 years

Suffolk University (Sawyer)

Private

ONLINE MBA PROGRAM(S)

www.suffolk.edu/admission/
graduate.php
Admissions: (617) 573-8302
Email: grad.admission@
suffolk.edu
Financial aid: (617) 573-8470
Application deadline: rolling
**Program can be completed
entirely online:** Yes
Total program cost: $21,360
full-time in-state, $21,360
full-time out-of-state
Tuition per credit: $1,424
full-time in-state, $1,424
part-time in-state, $1,424
full-time out-of-state, $1,424
part-time out-of-state
Acceptance rate: 85%
Average GMAT: 310
Average GRE: 149 verbal, 144
quantitative, 4.0 writing
Average age of entrants: 27
**Students with prior work
experience:** 100%
Enrollment: 38, 47% men,
53% women, 18% minority
Average class size: 13
Completion: Three year
graduation rate: 29%; credits
needed to graduate: 34; target
time to graduate: 1.5 years
**College funded aid
available:** Domestic: Yes;
International: Yes

University of Massachusetts–Amherst (Isenberg)

Public

ONLINE MBA PROGRAM(S)

www.isenberg.umass.edu
Admissions: (413) 545-5608
Email:
mba@isenberg.umass.edu
Financial aid: (413) 545-0801
Application deadline: rolling
**Program can be completed
entirely online:** Yes
Total program cost: $35,100
full-time in-state, $35,100
part-time in-state, $35,100
full-time out-of-state, $35,100
part-time out-of-state
Tuition per credit: $900
full-time in-state, $900
part-time in-state, $900
full-time out-of-state, $900
part-time out-of-state
Acceptance rate: 85%
Test scores required:
GMAT or GRE
Average GMAT: 579
Average GRE: 157 verbal, 156
quantitative, 4.0 writing
Average age of entrants: 37
**Students with prior work
experience:** 99%
Enrollment: 1,344, 69%
men, 31% women, 24%
minority, 5% international
Average class size: 48

**Most popular MBA
concentrations:** finance, health
care administration, marketing,
management information
systems, production/
operations management
Completion: Three year
graduation rate: 54%; credits
needed to graduate: 39; target
time to graduate: 4 years
College funded aid available:
Domestic: No; International: No
Graduates with debt: 19%;
average amount of debt $36,126

ONLINE BUSINESS PROGRAM(S)

www.isenberg.umass.edu
Admissions: (413) 545-5608
Email: msa@isenberg.umass.edu
Financial aid: (413) 545-0801
Application deadline: rolling
**Program can be completed
entirely online:** Yes
Total program cost: $24,000
full-time in-state, $24,000
part-time in-state, $24,000
full-time out-of-state, $24,000
part-time out-of-state
Tuition per credit: $800
full-time in-state, $800
part-time in-state, $800
full-time out-of-state, $800
part-time out-of-state
Acceptance rate: 80%
Test scores required:
GMAT or GRE
Average GMAT: 550
Average age of entrants: 25
Enrollment: 169, 52%
men, 48% women, 20%
minority, 9% international
Average class size: 29
**Most popular business
concentrations:** accounting
Completion: Credits needed
to graduate: 30; target
time to graduate: 1 year
College funded aid available:
Domestic: No; International: No
Graduates with debt: 49%;
average amount of debt $21,348

University of Massachusetts–Boston

Public

ONLINE BUSINESS PROGRAM(S)

www.umb.edu/admissions/grad
Admissions: (617) 287-6400
Email: bos.gadm@umb.edu
Financial aid: (617) 287-6300
Application deadline: Domestic:
06/01; International: 06/01
**Program can be completed
entirely online:** No
Total program cost: $20,700
part-time in-state, $20,700
full-time out-of-state, $20,700
part-time out-of-state
Tuition per credit: $575 full-time
in-state, $575 part-time in-state,
$575 full-time out-of-state,
$575 part-time out-of-state
Acceptance rate: 88%
Test scores required: No
Average age of entrants: 33
Enrollment: 80, 15% men,
85% women, 22% minority
Average class size: 11

**Most popular business
concentrations:** health care
administration, leadership,
organizational behavior, public
administration, public policy
Completion: Three year
graduation rate: 45%; credits
needed to graduate: 36; target
time to graduate: 2 years
College funded aid available:
Domestic: Yes; International: No
Graduates with debt:
47%; average amount
of debt $33,053

University of Massachusetts–Dartmouth (Charlton)

Public

ONLINE MBA PROGRAM(S)

www.umassd.edu/extension/
programs/
Admissions: (508) 999-8604
Email: graduate@umassd.edu
Financial aid: (508) 999-8643
Application deadline: rolling
**Program can be completed
entirely online:** Yes
Total program cost: N/A
Tuition per credit: $553
full-time in-state, $553
part-time in-state, $553
full-time out-of-state, $553
part-time out-of-state
Acceptance rate: 81%
Test scores required: GMAT
Average GMAT: 509
Average GRE: 154 verbal, 148
quantitative, 4.0 writing
Average age of entrants: 36
Enrollment: 68, 53% men,
47% women, 22% minority,
1% international
Average class size: 26
**Most popular MBA
concentrations:** general
management
Completion: Credits needed
to graduate: 30; target time
to graduate: 2 years
College funded aid available:
International: No

ONLINE BUSINESS PROGRAM(S)

www.umassd.edu/extension/
programs/msinhealth
caremanagementmshm
Admissions: (508) 999-8604
Email: graduate@umassd.edu
Financial aid: (508) 999-8643
Application deadline: rolling
**Program can be completed
entirely online:** Yes
Total program cost: N/A
Tuition per credit: $553
full-time in-state, $553
part-time in-state, $553
full-time out-of-state, $553
part-time out-of-state
Acceptance rate: 86%
Test scores required: gre
Average age of entrants: 36
Enrollment: 7, 29% men, 71%
women, 57% minority
Average class size: 28
Completion: Credits needed
to graduate: 30; target time
to graduate: 2 years
College funded aid available:
International: No

University of Massachusetts–Lowell

Public

ONLINE MBA PROGRAM(S)

continuinged.uml.edu/
online/mba/
Admissions: (800) 656-4723
Email: mba@uml.edu
Financial aid: (978) 934-4220
Application deadline: rolling
**Program can be completed
entirely online:** Yes
Total program cost: $19,200
full-time in-state, $19,200
part-time in-state, $19,200
full-time out-of-state, $19,200
part-time out-of-state
Tuition per credit: $640
full-time in-state, $640
part-time in-state, $640
full-time out-of-state, $640
part-time out-of-state
Acceptance rate: 92%
Test scores required:
GMAT or GRE
Average GMAT: 539
Average age of entrants: 38
**Students with prior work
experience:** 99%
Enrollment: 564, 66% men,
34% women, 14% minority,
56% international
Average class size: 25
**Most popular MBA
concentrations:** finance,
international business,
leadership, marketing,
management information
systems
Completion: Three year
graduation rate: 55%; credits
needed to graduate: 30; target
time to graduate: 3 years
College funded aid available:
Domestic: No; International: No
Graduates with debt: 20%;
average amount of debt $38,433

ONLINE BUSINESS PROGRAM(S)

continuinged.uml.edu/
online/mba/
Admissions: (800) 656-4723
Email: mba@uml.edu
Financial aid: (978) 934-4220
Application deadline: rolling
**Program can be completed
entirely online:** Yes
Total program cost: $19,200
full-time in-state, $19,200
part-time in-state, $19,200
full-time out-of-state, $19,200
part-time out-of-state
Tuition per credit: $640
full-time in-state, $640
part-time in-state, $640
full-time out-of-state, $640
part-time out-of-state
Acceptance rate: 90%
Test scores required:
GMAT or GRE
Average GMAT: 553
Average age of entrants: 31
**Students with prior work
experience:** 96%
Enrollment: 87, 54% men,
46% women, 28% minority,
1% international
Average class size: 22
**Most popular business
concentrations:**
accounting, finance

Completion: Credits needed to graduate: 30; target time to graduate: 3 years
College funded aid available: Domestic: No; International: No
Graduates with debt: 38%; average amount of debt $25,603

Western New England University

Private

ONLINE MBA PROGRAM(S)

www1.wne.edu/admissions/graduate/index.cfm
Admissions: (800) 325-1122
Email: study@wne.edu
Financial aid: (413) 796-2080
Application deadline: rolling
Program can be completed entirely online: Yes
Total program cost: $29,644
part-time in-state, $29,644
part-time out-of-state
Tuition per credit: $824
full-time in-state, $824
part-time in-state, $824
full-time out-of-state, $824
part-time out-of-state
Acceptance rate: 66%
Test scores required: GMAT or GRE
Average GMAT: 480
Average age of entrants: 30
Students with prior work experience: 77%
Enrollment: 85, 59% men, 41% women, 13% minority, 5% international
Most popular MBA concentrations: general management
Completion: Credits needed to graduate: 36; target time to graduate: 2 years
College funded aid available: Domestic: No; International: No

ONLINE BUSINESS PROGRAM(S)

www1.wne.edu/admissions/graduate/index.cfm
Admissions: (800) 325-1122
Email: study@wne.edu
Financial aid: (413) 796-2080
Application deadline: rolling
Program can be completed entirely online: Yes
Total program cost: $24,720
full-time in-state, $24,720
part-time in-state, $24,720
full-time out-of-state, $24,720
part-time out-of-state
Tuition per credit: $824
full-time in-state, $824
part-time in-state, $824
full-time out-of-state, $824
part-time out-of-state
Acceptance rate: 91%
Test scores required: GMAT or GRE
Average GMAT: 473
Average age of entrants: 29
Students with prior work experience: 74%
Enrollment: 49, 53% men, 47% women, 4% minority
Most popular business concentrations: accounting, leadership

Completion: Credits needed to graduate: 30; target time to graduate: 2 years
College funded aid available: Domestic: No; International: No

Worcester Polytechnic Institute

Private

ONLINE MBA PROGRAM(S)

business.wpi.edu
Admissions: (508) 831-4665
Email: business@wpi.edu
Financial aid: (508) 831-5469
Application deadline: rolling
Program can be completed entirely online: No
Total program cost: $69,936
full-time in-state, $69,936
part-time in-state, $69,936
full-time out-of-state, $69,936
part-time out-of-state
Tuition per credit: $1,457
full-time in-state, $1,457
part-time in-state, $1,457
full-time out-of-state, $1,457
part-time out-of-state
Acceptance rate: 92%
Test scores required: GMAT or GRE
Average GMAT: 555
Average age of entrants: 35
Students with prior work experience: 100%
Enrollment: 169, 66% men, 34% women, 16% minority, 12% international
Average class size: 20
Most popular MBA concentrations: manufacturing and technology management, production/operations management, organizational behavior, supply chain management/logistics, technology
Completion: Three year graduation rate: 95%; credits needed to graduate: 48; target time to graduate: 2.5 years
College funded aid available: Domestic: Yes; International: Yes
Graduates with debt: 50%; average amount of debt $10,000

MICHIGAN

Andrews University

Private

ONLINE MBA PROGRAM(S)

www.andrews.edu/grad/admission/
Admissions: (269) 471-6321
Email: graduate@andrews.edu
Financial aid: (269) 471-6040
Application deadline: rolling
Program can be completed entirely online: No
Total program cost: $17,721
full-time in-state, $17,721
part-time in-state, $17,721
full-time out-of-state, $17,721
part-time out-of-state
Tuition per credit: $537 full-time in-state, $537 part-time in-state, $537 full-time out-of-state, $537 part-time out-of-state
Acceptance rate: 86%

Test scores required: GMAT
Average GMAT: 337
Average GRE: 149 verbal, 153 quantitative, 3.5 writing
Average age of entrants: 28
Students with prior work experience: 52%
Enrollment: 35, 49% men, 51% women, 77% minority, 9% international
Average class size: 7
Most popular MBA concentrations: general management
Completion: Credits needed to graduate: 33; target time to graduate: 2 years
College funded aid available: Domestic: No; International: No

Central Michigan University

Public

ONLINE MBA PROGRAM(S)

global.cmich.edu/onlinemba/default.aspx?dc=mba
Admissions: (877) 268-4636
Email: cmuglobal@cmich.edu
Financial aid: (800) 664-2681
Application deadline: rolling
Program can be completed entirely online: Yes
Total program cost: N/A
Tuition per credit: $600
full-time in-state, $600
part-time in-state, $600
full-time out-of-state, $600
part-time out-of-state
Acceptance rate: 34%
Test scores required: GMAT
Average GMAT: 499
Average age of entrants: 31
Enrollment: 241, 59% men, 41% women, 19% minority, 1% international
Average class size: 22
Most popular MBA concentrations: general management, human resources management, marketing, management information systems, supply chain management/logistics
Completion: Three year graduation rate: 72%; credits needed to graduate: 36; target time to graduate: 2.5 years
College funded aid available: Domestic: Yes; International: Yes
Graduates with debt: 15%; average amount of debt $13,548

Cornerstone University

Private

ONLINE MBA PROGRAM(S)

www.cornerstone.edu/pgs-business-degrees
Admissions: (800) 947-2382
Email: pgs.information@cornerstone.edu
Financial aid: (616) 222-1424
Application deadline: rolling
Program can be completed entirely online: Yes

Total program cost: $19,000
full-time in-state, $19,000
part-time in-state, $19,000
full-time out-of-state, $19,000
part-time out-of-state
Tuition per credit: $500
full-time in-state, $500
part-time in-state, $500
full-time out-of-state, $500
part-time out-of-state
Acceptance rate: 51%
Test scores required: No
Average age of entrants: 35
Enrollment: 72, 47% men, 53% women, 25% minority
Average class size: 10
Most popular MBA concentrations: finance, health care administration, international business, other
Completion: Three year graduation rate: 62%; credits needed to graduate: 38; target time to graduate: 2 years
College funded aid available: Domestic: No; International: No

ONLINE BUSINESS PROGRAM(S)

www.cornerstone.edu/pgs-business-degrees
Admissions: (800) 947-2382
Email: pgs.information@cornerstone.edu
Financial aid: (616) 222-1424
Application deadline: rolling
Program can be completed entirely online: Yes
Total program cost: $16,560
full-time in-state, $16,560
part-time in-state, $16,560
full-time out-of-state, $16,560
part-time out-of-state
Tuition per credit: $460
full-time in-state, $460
part-time in-state, $460
full-time out-of-state, $460
part-time out-of-state
Acceptance rate: 50%
Test scores required: No
Average age of entrants: 35
Enrollment: 17, 29% men, 71% women, 59% minority
Average class size: 8
Most popular business concentrations: leadership
Completion: Credits needed to graduate: 36; target time to graduate: 1.5 years
College funded aid available: Domestic: No; International: No

Eastern Michigan University

Public

ONLINE BUSINESS PROGRAM(S)

cob.emich.edu
Admissions: (734) 487-4444
Email: cob_graduate@emich.edu
Financial aid: (734) 487-0455
Application deadline: rolling
Program can be completed entirely online: Yes
Total program cost: $26,028
full-time in-state, $26,028
part-time in-state, $26,028
full-time out-of-state, $26,028
part-time out-of-state
Tuition per credit: $723 full-time in-state, $723 part-time in-state, $723 full-time out-of-state, $723 part-time out-of-state
Acceptance rate: 61%
Test scores required: No

Average age of entrants: 32
Students with prior work experience: 100%
Enrollment: 68, 19% men, 81% women, 25% minority
Average class size: 13
Most popular business concentrations: marketing
Completion: Three year graduation rate: 69%; credits needed to graduate: 36; target time to graduate: 2 years
College funded aid available: Domestic: Yes; International: No
Graduates with debt: 48%; average amount of debt $18,238

Ferris State University

Public

ONLINE MBA PROGRAM(S)

www.ferris.edu/mba-online/
Admissions: (231) 591-3932
Email: tetsworc@ferris.edu
Financial aid: (231) 591-2115
Application deadline: rolling
Program can be completed entirely online: Yes
Total program cost: $27,072
full-time in-state, $27,072
part-time in-state, $27,072
full-time out-of-state, $27,072
part-time out-of-state
Tuition per credit: $564
full-time in-state, $564
part-time in-state, $564
full-time out-of-state, $564
part-time out-of-state
Acceptance rate: 34%
Test scores required: GMAT or GRE
Average GMAT: 530
Average GRE: 150 verbal, 153 quantitative, 4.0 writing
Average age of entrants: 29
Students with prior work experience: 45%
Enrollment: 116, 48% men, 52% women, 13% minority
Average class size: 17
Most popular MBA concentrations: general management, other
Completion: Three year graduation rate: 70%; credits needed to graduate: 48; target time to graduate: 2 years
College funded aid available: Domestic: Yes; International: Yes
Graduates with debt: 55%; average amount of debt $32,390

ONLINE BUSINESS PROGRAM(S)

ferris.edu/admissions/homepage.htm
Admissions: (231) 591-3932
Email: CharlotteTetsworth@ferris.edu
Financial aid: (231) 591-2115
Application deadline: rolling
Program can be completed entirely online: No
Total program cost: $18,612
full-time in-state, $18,612
part-time in-state, $27,918
full-time out-of-state, $27,918
part-time out-of-state
Tuition per credit: $564
full-time in-state, $564
part-time in-state, $846
full-time out-of-state, $846
part-time out-of-state

Acceptance rate: 32%
Test scores required:
GMAT or GRE
Average GMAT: N/A
Average GRE: 143 verbal, 148 quantitative, 3.0 writing
Average age of entrants: 25
Students with prior work experience: 67%
Enrollment: 72, 62% men, 38% women, 4% minority, 69% international
Average class size: 14
Most popular business concentrations: other
Completion: Three year graduation rate: 96%; credits needed to graduate: 33; target time to graduate: 1.5 years
College funded aid available: Domestic: Yes; International: Yes
Graduates with debt: 13%; average amount of debt $29,470

Kettering University
Private

ONLINE MBA PROGRAM(S)
online.kettering.edu
Admissions: (810) 762-9575
Email: cwallace@kettering.edu
Financial aid: (810) 762-7859
Application deadline: rolling
Program can be completed entirely online: Yes
Total program cost: $42,720
full-time in-state, $42,720 part-time in-state, $42,720 full-time out-of-state, $42,720 part-time out-of-state
Tuition per credit: $890
full-time in-state, $890 part-time in-state, $890 full-time out-of-state, $890 part-time out-of-state
Test scores required: No
Most popular MBA concentrations: general management, leadership, production/operations management, supply chain management/logistics, technology
Completion: Credits needed to graduate: 48; target time to graduate: 2 years
College funded aid available: Domestic: No; International: No

ONLINE BUSINESS PROGRAM(S)
online.kettering.edu
Admissions: (810) 762-9575
Email: cwallace@kettering.edu
Financial aid: (810) 762-7859
Application deadline: rolling
Program can be completed entirely online: Yes
Total program cost: $34,800
full-time in-state, $34,800 part-time in-state, $34,800 full-time out-of-state, $34,800 part-time out-of-state
Tuition per credit: $870 full-time in-state, $870 part-time in-state, $870 full-time out-of-state, $870 part-time out-of-state
Test scores required: No
Average class size: 12
Most popular business concentrations: production/operations management, supply chain management/logistics

Completion: Credits needed to graduate: 40; target time to graduate: 2.5 years
College funded aid available: Domestic: Yes; International: Yes

Lawrence Technological University
Private

ONLINE MBA PROGRAM(S)
www.ltu.edu/futurestudents/
Admissions: (800) 225-5588
Email: admissions@ltu.edu
Financial aid: (248) 204-2126
Application deadline: rolling
Program can be completed entirely online: Yes
Total program cost: N/A
Tuition per credit: $960
full-time in-state, $960 part-time in-state, $960 full-time out-of-state, $960 part-time out-of-state
Acceptance rate: 60%
Test scores required: No
Average age of entrants: 32
Enrollment: 166, 61% men, 39% women, 22% minority, 11% international
Average class size: 19
Most popular MBA concentrations: finance, marketing, management information systems, other
Completion: Three year graduation rate: 40%; credits needed to graduate: 36; target time to graduate: 3 years
College funded aid available: Domestic: Yes; International: Yes
Graduates with debt: 28%; average amount of debt $66,490

Madonna University
Private

ONLINE MBA PROGRAM(S)
www.madonna.edu/grad
Admissions: (734) 432-5667
Email: grad@madonna.edu
Financial aid: (734) 432-5662
Application deadline: rolling
Program can be completed entirely online: Yes
Total program cost: N/A
Tuition per credit: $790 full-time in-state, $790 part-time in-state, $790 full-time out-of-state, $790 part-time out-of-state
Acceptance rate: 100%
Test scores required: No
Average age of entrants: 24
Enrollment: 30, 40% men, 60% women, N/A minority, 100% international
Average class size: 20
Completion: Three year graduation rate: 65%; credits needed to graduate: 45; target time to graduate: 1.5 years
College funded aid available: Domestic: No; International: No

Michigan State University (Broad)
Public

ONLINE BUSINESS PROGRAM(S)
michiganstateuniversityonline.com/programs/masters-degree/ms-management-strategy-leadership/
Admissions: (517) 355-1878
Email: MS-MGT@broad.msu.edu
Financial aid: (517) 432-1155
Application deadline: rolling
Program can be completed entirely online: Yes
Total program cost: $32,700
full-time in-state, $32,700 part-time in-state, $32,700 full-time out-of-state, $32,700 part-time out-of-state
Tuition per credit: $1,090
full-time in-state, $1,090 part-time in-state, $1,090 full-time out-of-state, $1,090 part-time out-of-state
Acceptance rate: 94%
Test scores required: No
Average age of entrants: 39
Students with prior work experience: 85%
Enrollment: 534, 66% men, 34% women, 8% minority
Average class size: 36
Most popular business concentrations: other
Completion: Three year graduation rate: 89%; credits needed to graduate: 30; target time to graduate: 1.5 years
College funded aid available: Domestic: No; International: No
Graduates with debt: 46%; average amount of debt $47,014

Northwood University
Private

ONLINE MBA PROGRAM(S)
www.northwood.edu/academics/graduate/admissions-requirements.aspx
Admissions: (989) 837-4895
Email: Rca@northwood.edu
Financial aid: (800) 622-9000
Application deadline: rolling
Program can be completed entirely online: Yes
Total program cost: $37,080
full-time in-state, $37,080 part-time in-state, $37,080 full-time out-of-state, $37,080 part-time out-of-state
Tuition per credit: $1,030
full-time in-state, $1,030 part-time in-state, $1,030 full-time out-of-state, $1,030 part-time out-of-state
Acceptance rate: 72%
Test scores required: No
Average age of entrants: 34
Enrollment: 150, 51% men, 49% women, 21% minority, 3% international
Average class size: 15
Most popular MBA concentrations: general management
Completion: Credits needed to graduate: 36; target time to graduate: 2 years

College funded aid available: Domestic: Yes; International: Yes
Graduates with debt: 94%; average amount of debt $44,562

ONLINE BUSINESS PROGRAM(S)
www.northwood.edu/graduate/admission-requirements.aspx
Admissions: (989) 837-4895
Email: rca@nothwood.edu
Financial aid: (800) 622-9000
Application deadline: rolling
Program can be completed entirely online: Yes
Total program cost: $23,610
full-time in-state, $23,610 part-time in-state, $23,610 full-time out-of-state, $23,610 part-time out-of-state
Tuition per credit: $787 full-time in-state, $787 part-time in-state, $787 full-time out-of-state, $787 part-time out-of-state
Acceptance rate: 100%
Test scores required: No
Average age of entrants: 38
Students with prior work experience: 100%
Enrollment: 92, 40% men, 60% women, 26% minority
Average class size: 15
Most popular business concentrations: leadership, organizational behavior
Completion: Three year graduation rate: 52%; credits needed to graduate: 30; target time to graduate: 2 years
College funded aid available: Domestic: No; International: No
Graduates with debt: 76%; average amount of debt $42,753

University of Michigan–Dearborn
Public

ONLINE MBA PROGRAM(S)
umdearborn.edu/cob/graduate-programs
Admissions: (313) 593-5460
Email: umd-gradbusiness@umich.edu
Financial aid: (313) 593-5300
Application deadline: rolling
Program can be completed entirely online: Yes
Total program cost: N/A
Tuition per credit: $883
full-time in-state, $883 part-time in-state, $1,376 full-time out-of-state, $1,376 part-time out-of-state
Acceptance rate: 44%
Test scores required: GMAT or GRE
Average GMAT: 589
Average GRE: 157 verbal, 153 quantitative, 4.0 writing
Average age of entrants: 29
Students with prior work experience: 100%
Enrollment: 117, 62% men, 38% women, 21% minority, 4% international
Average class size: 27
Most popular MBA concentrations: finance, international business, marketing, management information systems, supply chain management/logistics

Completion: Three year graduation rate: 33%; credits needed to graduate: 48; target time to graduate: 2.5 years
College funded aid available: Domestic: Yes; International: Yes
Graduates with debt: 22%; average amount of debt $45,551

ONLINE BUSINESS PROGRAM(S)
umdearborn.edu/cob/grad-programs/
Admissions: (313) 593-5460
Email: umd-gradbusiness@umich.edu
Financial aid: (313) 593-5300
Application deadline: rolling
Program can be completed entirely online: Yes
Total program cost: N/A
Tuition per credit: $883
full-time in-state, $883 part-time in-state, $1,376 full-time out-of-state, $1,376 part-time out-of-state
Acceptance rate: 39%
Test scores required: GMAT or GRE
Average GMAT: 600
Average age of entrants: 29
Students with prior work experience: 100%
Enrollment: 36, 78% men, 22% women, 33% minority, 6% international
Average class size: 27
Most popular business concentrations: finance
Completion: Three year graduation rate: 27%; credits needed to graduate: 30; target time to graduate: 1.5 years
College funded aid available: Domestic: Yes; International: Yes
Graduates with debt: 42%; average amount of debt $51,969

Concordia University–St. Paul
Private

ONLINE MBA PROGRAM(S)
www.csp.edu/admission/graduate/
Admissions: (651) 641-8230
Email: graduateadmission@csp.edu
Financial aid: (651) 603-6300
Application deadline: rolling
Program can be completed entirely online: Yes
Total program cost: $27,500
full-time in-state, $27,500 part-time in-state, $27,500 full-time out-of-state, $27,500 part-time out-of-state
Tuition per credit: $625
full-time in-state, $625 part-time in-state, $625 full-time out-of-state, $625 part-time out-of-state
Acceptance rate: 69%
Test scores required: No
Average age of entrants: 35
Enrollment: 423, 48% men, 52% women, 26% minority, 14% international
Average class size: 13

Most popular MBA concentrations: general management, health care administration, other
Completion: Three year graduation rate: 87%; credits needed to graduate: 44; target time to graduate: 3 years
College funded aid available: Domestic: No; International: Yes
Graduates with debt: 78%; average amount of debt $37,080

ONLINE BUSINESS PROGRAM(S)
www.csp.edu/admission/graduate/
Admissions: (651) 641-8230
Email: graduateadmission@csp.edu
Financial aid: (651) 603-6300
Application deadline: rolling
Program can be completed entirely online: Yes
Total program cost: $15,300 full-time in-state, $15,300 part-time in-state, $15,300 full-time out-of-state, $15,300 part-time out-of-state
Tuition per credit: $475 full-time in-state, $475 part-time in-state, $475 full-time out-of-state, $475 part-time out-of-state
Acceptance rate: 79%
Test scores required: No
Average age of entrants: 34
Enrollment: 182, 24% men, 76% women, 19% minority
Average class size: 11
Most popular business concentrations: human resources management, leadership
Completion: Three year graduation rate: 64%; credits needed to graduate: 36; target time to graduate: 2 years
College funded aid available: Domestic: No; International: Yes
Graduates with debt: 78%; average amount of debt $28,123

Minnesota State University–Moorhead
Public

ONLINE MBA PROGRAM(S)
www.mnstate.edu/graduate/admission.aspx
Admissions: (218) 477-2134
Email: graduate@mnstate.edu
Financial aid: (218) 477-2251
Application deadline: rolling
Program can be completed entirely online: Yes
Total program cost: $14,393 full-time in-state, $14,393 part-time in-state, $28,786 full-time out-of-state, $28,786 part-time out-of-state
Tuition per credit: $389 full-time in-state, $389 part-time in-state, $778 full-time out-of-state, $778 part-time out-of-state
Acceptance rate: 100%
Test scores required: GMAT
Average age of entrants: 33
Enrollment: 34, 56% men, 44% women, N/A minority, N/A international
Average class size: 13

Most popular MBA concentrations: general management, health care administration
Completion: Credits needed to graduate: 37; target time to graduate: 2 years
College funded aid available: Domestic: Yes

MISSISSIPPI
Belhaven University
Private

ONLINE MBA PROGRAM(S)
online.belhaven.edu
Admissions: (601) 965-7043
Email: onlineadmission@belhaven.edu
Financial aid: (601) 968-5920
Application deadline: rolling
Program can be completed entirely online: Yes
Total program cost: $20,340 full-time in-state, $20,340 part-time in-state, $20,340 full-time out-of-state, $20,340 part-time out-of-state
Tuition per credit: $540 full-time in-state, $540 part-time in-state, $540 full-time out-of-state, $540 part-time out-of-state
Acceptance rate: 50%
Test scores required: No
Average age of entrants: 30
Enrollment: 326, 23% men, 77% women, 73% minority
Average class size: 12
Most popular MBA concentrations: health care administration, human resources management, leadership, sports business
Completion: Three year graduation rate: 43%; credits needed to graduate: 39; target time to graduate: 2 years
College funded aid available: Domestic: No; International: No
Graduates with debt: 52%; average amount of debt $58,174

ONLINE BUSINESS PROGRAM(S)
online.belhaven.edu
Admissions: (601) 965-7043
Email: onlineadmission@belhaven.edu
Financial aid: (601) 968-5920
Application deadline: rolling
Program can be completed entirely online: Yes
Total program cost: $18,900 full-time in-state, $18,900 part-time in-state, $18,900 full-time out-of-state, $18,900 part-time out-of-state
Tuition per credit: $540 full-time in-state, $540 part-time in-state, $540 full-time out-of-state, $540 part-time out-of-state
Acceptance rate: 71%
Test scores required: No
Average age of entrants: 33
Enrollment: 743, 25% men, 75% women, 29% minority
Average class size: 12
Most popular business concentrations: health care administration, human

resources management, leadership, public administration, sports business
Completion: Three year graduation rate: 48%; credits needed to graduate: 36; target time to graduate: 2 years
College funded aid available: Domestic: No; International: No
Graduates with debt: 64%; average amount of debt $59,663

Jackson State University
Public

ONLINE MBA PROGRAM(S)
www.jsums.edu/graduateschool/
Admissions: (601) 979-4327
Email: kenneth.russ@jsums.edu
Financial aid: (601) 979-2227
Application deadline: Domestic: 03/15
Program can be completed entirely online: Yes
Total program cost: N/A
Tuition per credit: $462 full-time in-state, $462 part-time in-state, $462 full-time out-of-state, $462 part-time out-of-state
Test scores required: GMAT or GRE
Average class size: 20
Completion: Credits needed to graduate: 30; target time to graduate: 1 year
College funded aid available: Domestic: No; International: No
Graduates with debt: 88%; average amount of debt $28,138

Mississippi College
Private

ONLINE MBA PROGRAM(S)
www.mc.edu/admissions/
Admissions: (601) 925-3800
Email: admissions@mc.edu
Financial aid: (601) 925-3212
Application deadline: N/A
Program can be completed entirely online: Yes
Total program cost: $17,640 full-time in-state, $17,640 part-time in-state, $17,640 full-time out-of-state, $17,640 part-time out-of-state
Tuition per credit: $588 full-time in-state, $588 part-time in-state, $588 full-time out-of-state, $588 part-time out-of-state
Test scores required: GMAT
Most popular MBA concentrations: accounting, finance, general management, management information systems
Completion: Credits needed to graduate: 30; target time to graduate: 1.5 years

Mississippi State University
Public

ONLINE MBA PROGRAM(S)
distance.msstate.edu/mba
Admissions: (662) 325-7281
Email: csmith@business.msstate.edu
Financial aid: (662) 325-2450
Application deadline: rolling
Program can be completed entirely online: Yes
Total program cost: $13,680 full-time in-state, $13,680 part-time in-state, $13,680 full-time out-of-state, $13,680 part-time out-of-state
Tuition per credit: $456 full-time in-state, $456 part-time in-state, $456 full-time out-of-state, $456 part-time out-of-state
Acceptance rate: 63%
Test scores required: GMAT or GRE
Average GMAT: 596
Average GRE: 155 verbal, 154 quantitative, 3.9 writing
Average age of entrants: 29
Students with prior work experience: 88%
Enrollment: 245, 80% men, 20% women, 10% minority, 2% international
Average class size: 25
Most popular MBA concentrations: general management, industrial management, marketing, management information systems, quantitative analysis/statistics and operations research
Completion: Three year graduation rate: 62%; credits needed to graduate: 30; target time to graduate: 2 years
College funded aid available: Domestic: Yes; International: Yes
Graduates with debt: 26%; average amount of debt $29,428

ONLINE BUSINESS PROGRAM(S)
distance.msstate.edu/msis
Admissions: (662) 325-7281
Email: csmith@business.msstate.edu
Financial aid: (662) 325-2450
Application deadline: rolling
Program can be completed entirely online: Yes
Total program cost: $13,680 full-time in-state, $13,680 part-time in-state, $13,680 full-time out-of-state, $13,680 part-time out-of-state
Tuition per credit: $456 full-time in-state, $456 part-time in-state, $456 full-time out-of-state, $456 part-time out-of-state
Acceptance rate: 44%
Test scores required: GMAT or GRE
Average GMAT: 553
Average GRE: 150 verbal, 155 quantitative, 4.0 writing
Average age of entrants: 32
Enrollment: 18, 89% men, 11% women, 22% minority, 6% international

Average class size: 13
Most popular business concentrations: accounting, finance, general management, marketing, management information systems
Completion: Credits needed to graduate: 30; target time to graduate: 2 years
College funded aid available: Domestic: Yes; International: Yes
Graduates with debt: 25%; average amount of debt $30,423

University of Mississippi
Public

ONLINE MBA PROGRAM(S)
www.olemissbusiness.com/mba/pmba/index.html
Admissions: (662) 915-5483
Email: ajones@bus.olemiss.edu
Financial aid: (800) 891-4596
Application deadline: rolling
Program can be completed entirely online: Yes
Total program cost: $29,700 full-time in-state, $29,700 part-time in-state, $29,700 full-time out-of-state, $29,700 part-time out-of-state
Tuition per credit: $750 full-time in-state, $750 part-time in-state, $750 full-time out-of-state, $750 part-time out-of-state
Acceptance rate: 45%
Test scores required: GMAT or GRE
Average GMAT: 583
Average GRE: 153 verbal, 154 quantitative, 3.7 writing
Average age of entrants: 30
Students with prior work experience: 100%
Enrollment: 131, 80% men, 20% women, 5% minority, 1% international
Average class size: 43
Completion: Three year graduation rate: 49%; credits needed to graduate: 36; target time to graduate: 2 years
College funded aid available: Domestic: No; International: No
Graduates with debt: 22%; average amount of debt $23,566

University of Southern Mississippi
Public

ONLINE MBA PROGRAM(S)
usm.edu/graduate-school
Admissions: (601) 266-4369
Email: graduateschool@usm.edu
Financial aid: (601) 266-4774
Application deadline: Domestic: 06/01; International: 05/01
Program can be completed entirely online: Depends
Total program cost: $12,162 full-time in-state, $14,883 part-time in-state, $14,162 full-time out-of-state, $18,579 part-time out-of-state
Tuition per credit: $369 full-time in-state, $451 part-time in-state, $429 full-time out-of-state, $563 part-time out-of-state
Acceptance rate: 96%

Test scores required: GMAT or GRE
Average GRE: 148 verbal, 147 quantitative, 4.0 writing
Average age of entrants: 34
Students with prior work experience: 100%
Enrollment: 52, 42% men, 58% women, 15% minority
Average class size: 27
Most popular MBA concentrations: sports business, quantitative analysis/statistics and operations research, other
Completion: Credits needed to graduate: 33; target time to graduate: 2 years
College funded aid available: Domestic: No; International: No

MISSOURI

Columbia College
Private

ONLINE MBA PROGRAM(S)
www.ccis.edu/onlinemba/
Admissions: (573) 875-7352
Email: onlinegrad@ccis.edu
Financial aid: (573) 875-7860
Application deadline: rolling
Program can be completed entirely online: Yes
Total program cost: N/A
Tuition per credit: $415 full-time in-state, $415 part-time in-state, $415 full-time out-of-state, $415 part-time out-of-state
Acceptance rate: 93%
Test scores required: No
Average age of entrants: 36
Students with prior work experience: 91%
Enrollment: 806, 41% men, 59% women, 26% minority, 5% international
Average class size: 11
Most popular MBA concentrations: accounting, general management, human resources management
Completion: Three year graduation rate: 58%; credits needed to graduate: 36; target time to graduate: 2.5 years
College funded aid available: Domestic: No; International: No
Graduates with debt: 60%; average amount of debt $47,560

Fontbonne University
Private

ONLINE MBA PROGRAM(S)
www.fontbonne.edu/admission/eveningonline/
Admissions: (314) 863-2220
Email: jhavis@fontbonne.edu
Financial aid: (314) 889-4686
Application deadline: rolling
Program can be completed entirely online: Yes
Total program cost: $26,856 full-time in-state, $26,856 part-time in-state, $26,856 full-time out-of-state, $26,856 part-time out-of-state
Tuition per credit: $728 full-time in-state, $728 part-time in-state, $728 full-time out-of-state, $728 part-time out-of-state
Test scores required: No

Most popular MBA concentrations: supply chain management/logistics
Completion: Credits needed to graduate: 36
College funded aid available: Domestic: No; International: No

ONLINE BUSINESS PROGRAM(S)
www.fontbonne.edu/admissions/evening_online/
Admissions: (314) 863-2220
Financial aid: (314) 889-4686
Application deadline: rolling
Program can be completed entirely online: Yes
Total program cost: $22,380 full-time in-state, $22,380 part-time in-state, $22,380 full-time out-of-state, $22,380 part-time out-of-state
Tuition per credit: $728 full-time in-state, $728 part-time in-state, $728 full-time out-of-state, $728 part-time out-of-state
Test scores required: No
College funded aid available: Domestic: No; International: No

Lindenwood University
Private

ONLINE MBA PROGRAM(S)
www.lindenwood.edu/admissions/
Admissions: (636) 949-4933
Email: eveningadmissions@lindenwood.edu
Financial aid: (636) 949-4925
Application deadline: rolling
Program can be completed entirely online: Yes
Total program cost: $19,500 full-time in-state, $19,500 part-time in-state, $19,500 full-time out-of-state, $19,500 part-time out-of-state
Tuition per credit: $500 full-time in-state, $500 part-time in-state, $500 full-time out-of-state, $500 part-time out-of-state
Acceptance rate: 67%
Test scores required: No
Average GMAT: 520
Average age of entrants: 30
Students with prior work experience: 67%
Enrollment: 160, 44% men, 56% women, 21% minority, 3% international
Average class size: 15
Most popular MBA concentrations: accounting, general management, leadership, not-for-profit management
Completion: Three year graduation rate: 43%; credits needed to graduate: 39; target time to graduate: 1.5 years
College funded aid available: Domestic: Yes; International: Yes
Graduates with debt: 46%; average amount of debt $13,530

ONLINE BUSINESS PROGRAM(S)
www.lindenwood.edu/admissions/
Admissions: (636) 949-4933
Email: eveningadmissions@lindenwood.edu

Financial aid: (636) 949-4925
Application deadline: rolling
Program can be completed entirely online: Yes
Total program cost: $18,500 full-time in-state, $18,500 part-time in-state, $18,500 full-time out-of-state, $18,500 part-time out-of-state
Tuition per credit: $500 full-time in-state, $500 part-time in-state, $500 full-time out-of-state, $500 part-time out-of-state
Acceptance rate: 46%
Test scores required: No
Average age of entrants: 35
Students with prior work experience: 78%
Enrollment: 18, 28% men, 72% women, 61% minority
Average class size: 18
Most popular business concentrations: accounting, leadership, not-for-profit management
Completion: Three year graduation rate: 50%; credits needed to graduate: 37; target time to graduate: 1.5 years
College funded aid available: Domestic: Yes; International: Yes
Graduates with debt: 76%; average amount of debt $11,718

Maryville University of St. Louis
Private

ONLINE MBA PROGRAM(S)
www.maryville.edu/adults
Admissions: (314) 529-9571
Email: gradprograms@maryville.edu
Financial aid: (314) 529-9360
Application deadline: rolling
Program can be completed entirely online: Yes
Total program cost: N/A
Tuition per credit: $714 full-time in-state, $714 part-time in-state, $714 full-time out-of-state, $714 part-time out-of-state
Acceptance rate: 94%
Test scores required: No
Average age of entrants: 34
Enrollment: 209, 46% men, 54% women, 27% minority
Average class size: 15
Most popular MBA concentrations: general management, health care administration, human resources management
Completion: Credits needed to graduate: 36; target time to graduate: 2 years
College funded aid available: Domestic: Yes; International: Yes
Graduates with debt: 76%; average amount of debt $18,785

ONLINE BUSINESS PROGRAM(S)
online.maryville.edu/
Admissions: (314) 529-9571
Email: gradprograms@maryville.edu
Financial aid: (314) 529-9360
Application deadline: rolling
Program can be completed entirely online: Yes
Total program cost: N/A

Tuition per credit: $816 full-time in-state, $800 part-time in-state, $816 full-time out-of-state, $816 part-time out-of-state
Acceptance rate: 97%
Test scores required: No
Average age of entrants: 36
Enrollment: 187, 65% men, 35% women, 37% minority
Average class size: 15
Completion: Credits needed to graduate: 36; target time to graduate: 2 years
College funded aid available: Domestic: Yes; International: Yes

Missouri State University
Public

ONLINE MBA PROGRAM(S)
www.mba.missouristate.edu
Admissions: (417) 836-5616
Email: COBGraduatePrograms@MissouriState.edu
Financial aid: (417) 836-5262
Application deadline: rolling
Program can be completed entirely online: Yes
Total program cost: $9,405 full-time in-state, $9,405 part-time in-state, $9,405 full-time out-of-state, $9,405 part-time out-of-state
Tuition per credit: $285 full-time in-state, $285 part-time in-state, $285 full-time out-of-state, $285 part-time out-of-state
Acceptance rate: 85%
Test scores required: GMAT or GRE
Average GMAT: 552
Average GRE: 154 verbal, 153 quantitative, 4.0 writing
Average age of entrants: 31
Enrollment: 143, 64% men, 36% women, 14% minority, 1% international
Average class size: 24
Most popular MBA concentrations: finance, management information systems, other
Completion: Credits needed to graduate: 33; target time to graduate: 1.5 years
College funded aid available: Domestic: Yes; International: Yes

ONLINE BUSINESS PROGRAM(S)
cybersecurity.missouristate.edu/admissionrequirements.htm
Admissions: (417) 836-5616
Email: COBGraduatePrograms@MissouriState.edu
Financial aid: (417) 836-5262
Application deadline: rolling
Program can be completed entirely online: Yes
Total program cost: $8,550 full-time in-state, $8,550 part-time in-state, $8,550 full-time out-of-state, $8,550 part-time out-of-state
Tuition per credit: $285 full-time in-state, $285 part-time in-state, $285 full-time out-of-state, $285 part-time out-of-state
Acceptance rate: 77%

Test scores required: GMAT or GRE
Average age of entrants: 33
Enrollment: 29, 83% men, 17% women, 21% minority, 3% international
Average class size: 19
Completion: Credits needed to graduate: 30; target time to graduate: 1.5 years
College funded aid available: Domestic: Yes; International: Yes

Missouri University of Science & Technology
Public

ONLINE MBA PROGRAM(S)
futurestudents.mst.edu/
Admissions: (573) 341-4075
Email: lks@mst.edu
Financial aid: (573) 341-4282
Application deadline: rolling
Program can be completed entirely online: Yes
Total program cost: $43,200 full-time in-state, $43,200 part-time in-state, $43,200 full-time out-of-state, $43,200 part-time out-of-state
Tuition per credit: $1,200 full-time in-state, $1,200 part-time in-state, $1,200 full-time out-of-state, $1,200 part-time out-of-state
Acceptance rate: 91%
Test scores required: GMAT or GRE
Average GMAT: 620
Average GRE: 145 verbal, 154 quantitative, 3.0 writing
Average age of entrants: 30
Students with prior work experience: 90%
Enrollment: 83, 57% men, 43% women, 16% minority, 24% international
Average class size: 17
Most popular MBA concentrations: entrepreneurship, general management, leadership, marketing, management information systems
Completion: Three year graduation rate: 100%; credits needed to graduate: 36; target time to graduate: 3 years
College funded aid available: Domestic: Yes; International: Yes
Graduates with debt: 35%; average amount of debt $3,527

ONLINE BUSINESS PROGRAM(S)
futurestudents.mst.edu/
Admissions: (573) 341-4075
Email: lynns@mst.edu
Financial aid: (573) 341-4282
Application deadline: rolling
Program can be completed entirely online: Yes
Total program cost: $36,000 full-time in-state, $36,000 part-time in-state, $36,000 full-time out-of-state, $36,000 part-time out-of-state
Tuition per credit: $1,200 full-time in-state, $1,200 part-time in-state, $1,200 full-time out-of-state, $1,200 part-time out-of-state
Acceptance rate: 64%

Test scores required: GMAT or GRE
Average GMAT: 543
Average GRE: 145 verbal, 156 quantitative, 3.0 writing
Average age of entrants: 24
Students with prior work experience: 90%
Enrollment: 67, 46% men, 54% women, 3% minority, 88% international
Average class size: 17
Most popular business concentrations: leadership, management information systems, supply chain management/logistics, technology, other
Completion: Three year graduation rate: 88%; credits needed to graduate: 30; target time to graduate: 3 years
College funded aid available: Domestic: Yes; International: Yes
Graduates with debt: 24%; average amount of debt $3,555

Northwest Missouri State University

Public

ONLINE MBA PROGRAM(S)

www.nwmissouri.edu/online/admission.htm
Admissions: (660) 562-1562
Email: admissions@nwmissouri.edu
Financial aid: (660) 562-1363
Application deadline: rolling
Program can be completed entirely online: Yes
Total program cost: $13,530
full-time in-state, $13,530
part-time in-state, $13,530
full-time out-of-state, $13,530
part-time out-of-state
Tuition per credit: $400
full-time in-state, $400
part-time in-state, $400
full-time out-of-state, $400
part-time out-of-state
Test scores required: GMAT or GRE
Enrollment: 158, 39% men, 61% women, 11% minority, 1% international
Most popular MBA concentrations: general management, human resources management, marketing
Completion: Credits needed to graduate: 33
College funded aid available: Domestic: Yes; International: Yes

Park University

Private

ONLINE MBA PROGRAM(S)

www.park.edu/admissions/graduate/index.html
Admissions: (816) 559-5625
Email: gradschool@park.edu
Financial aid: (816) 584-6714
Application deadline: rolling
Program can be completed entirely online: Yes

Total program cost: $20,592
full-time in-state, $20,592
part-time in-state, $20,592
full-time out-of-state, $20,592
part-time out-of-state
Tuition per credit: $624
full-time in-state, $624
part-time in-state, $624
full-time out-of-state, $624
part-time out-of-state
Acceptance rate: 93%
Test scores required: No
Average age of entrants: 36
Enrollment: 721, 50% men, 50% women, 47% minority, 1% international
Average class size: 19
Most popular MBA concentrations: finance, general management, human resources management, management information systems, other
Completion: Credits needed to graduate: 33; target time to graduate: 2 years
College funded aid available: Domestic: Yes; International: Yes
Graduates with debt: 43%; average amount of debt $18,670

ONLINE BUSINESS PROGRAM(S)

www.park.edu/admissions/graduate/index.html
Admissions: (816) 559-5625
Email: gradschool@park.edu
Financial aid: (816) 584-6714
Application deadline: rolling
Program can be completed entirely online: Yes
Total program cost: $19,764
full-time in-state, $19,764
part-time in-state, $19,764
full-time out-of-state, $19,764
part-time out-of-state
Tuition per credit: $549
full-time in-state, $549
part-time in-state, $549
full-time out-of-state, $549
part-time out-of-state
Acceptance rate: 100%
Test scores required: No
Average age of entrants: 34
Enrollment: 281, 37% men, 63% women, 39% minority, 8% international
Average class size: 14
Most popular business concentrations: accounting, finance, human resources management, international business, management information systems
Completion: Credits needed to graduate: 36; target time to graduate: 2 years
College funded aid available: Domestic: Yes; International: Yes

Southeast Missouri State University (Harrison)

Public

ONLINE MBA PROGRAM(S)

www.semo.edu/admissions
Admissions: (573) 651-2590
Email: admissions@semo.edu
Financial aid: (573) 651-2253
Application deadline: rolling
Program can be completed entirely online: Yes

Total program cost: N/A
Tuition per credit: $334
full-time in-state, $334
part-time in-state, $334
full-time out-of-state, $334
part-time out-of-state
Acceptance rate: 100%
Test scores required: GMAT or GRE
Average GMAT: 555
Average GRE: 154 verbal, 157 quantitative
Average age of entrants: 33
Enrollment: 74, 80% men, 20% women, 18% minority, 1% international
Average class size: 22
Most popular MBA concentrations: general management, health care administration, sports business
Completion: Three year graduation rate: 62%; credits needed to graduate: 33; target time to graduate: 2.5 years
College funded aid available: Domestic: Yes; International: Yes
Graduates with debt: 37%

ONLINE BUSINESS PROGRAM(S)

www.semo.edu/admissions
Admissions: (573) 651-2590
Email: admissions@semo.edu
Financial aid: (573) 651-2253
Application deadline: rolling
Program can be completed entirely online: Yes
Total program cost: N/A
Tuition per credit: $334
full-time in-state, $334
part-time in-state, $334
full-time out-of-state, $334
part-time out-of-state
Acceptance rate: 83%
Test scores required: GMAT or GRE
Average GMAT: 490
Average GRE: 147 verbal, 155 quantitative
Average age of entrants: 38
Enrollment: 37, 41% men, 59% women, 11% minority, 5% international
Average class size: 25
Most popular business concentrations: general management, health care administration
Completion: Credits needed to graduate: 30; target time to graduate: 2.5 years
College funded aid available: Domestic: Yes; International: Yes
Graduates with debt: 29%

University of Central Missouri (Harmon)

Public

ONLINE MBA PROGRAM(S)

www.ucmo.edu/mba/admission.cfm
Admissions: (660) 543-8192
Email: mba@ucmo.edu
Financial aid: (660) 543-8266
Application deadline: rolling
Program can be completed entirely online: Yes

Total program cost: $11,228
full-time in-state, $11,228
part-time in-state, $11,228
full-time out-of-state, $11,228
part-time out-of-state
Tuition per credit: $340
full-time in-state, $340
part-time in-state, $340
full-time out-of-state, $340
part-time out-of-state
Acceptance rate: 64%
Test scores required: GMAT or GRE
Average GMAT: 490
Average GRE: 147 verbal, 148 quantitative, 3.5 writing
Average age of entrants: 29
Students with prior work experience: 76%
Enrollment: 17, 59% men, 41% women, 24% minority
Average class size: 15
Most popular MBA concentrations: general management, international business, marketing, sports business
Completion: Credits needed to graduate: 33; target time to graduate: 1 year
College funded aid available: Domestic: Yes; International: Yes

Webster University

Private

ONLINE MBA PROGRAM(S)

www.webster.edu/admissions/graduate/
Admissions: (314) 246-7646
Email: mcwill@webster.edu
Financial aid: (314) 246-7080
Application deadline: rolling
Program can be completed entirely online: Yes
Total program cost: N/A
Tuition per credit: $780 full-time in-state, $780 part-time in-state, $780 full-time out-of-state, $780 part-time out-of-state
Acceptance rate: 92%
Test scores required: No
Average age of entrants: 33
Enrollment: 603, 52% men, 48% women, 50% minority, 1% international
Average class size: 17
Most popular MBA concentrations: finance, general management, human resources management, leadership, supply chain management/logistics
Completion: Three year graduation rate: 41%; credits needed to graduate: 36; target time to graduate: 2.5 years
College funded aid available: Domestic: No; International: No
Graduates with debt: 50%; average amount of debt $53,107

ONLINE BUSINESS PROGRAM(S)

www.webster.edu/admissions/graduate/
Admissions: (314) 246-7646
Email: mcwill@webster.edu
Financial aid: (314) 246-7080
Application deadline: rolling
Program can be completed entirely online: Yes
Total program cost: N/A

Tuition per credit: $780 full-time in-state, $780 part-time in-state, $780 full-time out-of-state, $780 part-time out-of-state
Acceptance rate: 96%
Test scores required: No
Average age of entrants: 36
Enrollment: 1,226, 53% men, 47% women, 59% minority
Average class size: 17
Most popular business concentrations: general management, human resources management, leadership, management information systems, supply chain management/logistics
Completion: Three year graduation rate: 51%; credits needed to graduate: 37; target time to graduate: 2.5 years
College funded aid available: Domestic: No; International: No
Graduates with debt: 39%; average amount of debt $57,548

William Woods University

Private

ONLINE MBA PROGRAM(S)

www.williamwoods.edu/admissions/online/index.html
Admissions: (800) 995-3159
Email: onlineadmissions@williamwoods.edu
Financial aid: (573) 592-1793
Application deadline: rolling
Program can be completed entirely online: Yes
Total program cost: N/A
Tuition per credit: $350
full-time in-state, $350
part-time in-state, $350
full-time out-of-state, $350
part-time out-of-state
Acceptance rate: 100%
Test scores required: No
Average age of entrants: 31
Enrollment: 104, 39% men, 61% women, 20% minority, 1% international
Average class size: 11
Most popular MBA concentrations: entrepreneurship
Completion: Credits needed to graduate: 30; target time to graduate: 2 years
College funded aid available: Domestic: Yes; International: Yes

ONLINE BUSINESS PROGRAM(S)

www.williamwoods.edu/admissions/index.html
Admissions: (800) 995-3159
Email: onlineadmissions@williamwoods.edu
Financial aid: (573) 592-1793
Application deadline: rolling
Program can be completed entirely online: Yes
Total program cost: N/A
Tuition per credit: $350
full-time in-state, $350
part-time in-state, $350
full-time out-of-state, $350
part-time out-of-state
Acceptance rate: 100%
Test scores required: No
Average age of entrants: 38
Enrollment: 12, 25% men, 75% women, 17% minority
Average class size: 5

Most popular business concentrations: health care administration
Completion: Credits needed to graduate: 30; target time to graduate: 2.5 years
College funded aid available: Domestic: No; International: No

NEBRASKA

Bellevue University
Private

ONLINE BUSINESS PROGRAM(S)
bellevue.edu/admissions-tuition/admission-requirements/master-admissions
Admissions: (402) 557-7282
Email: dubay@bellevue.edu
Financial aid: (402) 557-7095
Application deadline: rolling
Program can be completed entirely online: Yes
Total program cost: $20,340
full-time in-state, $20,340
part-time in-state, $20,340
full-time out-of-state, $20,340
part-time out-of-state
Tuition per credit: $565
full-time in-state, $565
part-time in-state, $565
full-time out-of-state, $565
part-time out-of-state
Acceptance rate: 81%
Test scores required: No
Average age of entrants: 36
Enrollment: 886, 39% men, 61% women, 47% minority
Average class size: 12
Most popular business concentrations: finance, health care administration, human resources management, marketing, other
Completion: Credits needed to graduate: 36; target time to graduate: 2.5 years
College funded aid available: Domestic: Yes; International: Yes
Graduates with debt: 66%; average amount of debt $34,000

Creighton University
Private

ONLINE MBA PROGRAM(S)
gradschool.creighton.edu/future-students
Admissions: (402) 280-2703
Email: gradschool@creighton.edu
Financial aid: (402) 280-2351
Application deadline: rolling
Program can be completed entirely online: Yes
Total program cost: $36,300
full-time in-state, $36,300
part-time in-state, $36,300
full-time out-of-state, $36,300
part-time out-of-state
Tuition per credit: $1,100
full-time in-state, $1,100
part-time in-state, $1,100
full-time out-of-state, $1,100
part-time out-of-state
Acceptance rate: 56%
Test scores required: GMAT or GRE
Average GMAT: 517
Average GRE: 149 verbal, 151 quantitative

Average age of entrants: 32
Students with prior work experience: 97%
Enrollment: 71, 65% men, 35% women, 24% minority
Average class size: 14
Most popular MBA concentrations: economics, finance, leadership, marketing, management information systems
Completion: Credits needed to graduate: 33; target time to graduate: 2.5 years
College funded aid available: Domestic: Yes; International: Yes
Graduates with debt: 32%; average amount of debt $16,861

ONLINE BUSINESS PROGRAM(S)
gradschool.creighton.edu/future-students
Admissions: (402) 280-2703
Email: gradschool@creighton.edu
Financial aid: (402) 280-2351
Application deadline: rolling
Program can be completed entirely online: Yes
Total program cost: $36,000
full-time in-state, $36,000
part-time in-state, $36,000
full-time out-of-state, $36,000
part-time out-of-state
Tuition per credit: $1,200
full-time in-state, $1,200
part-time in-state, $1,200
full-time out-of-state, $1,200
part-time out-of-state
Acceptance rate: 70%
Test scores required: GMAT or GRE
Average GMAT: 504
Average GRE: 155 verbal, 154 quantitative
Average age of entrants: 32
Students with prior work experience: 86%
Enrollment: 121, 85% men, 15% women, 21% minority
Average class size: 14
Most popular business concentrations: finance, other
Completion: Three year graduation rate: 69%; credits needed to graduate: 30; target time to graduate: 2.5 years
College funded aid available: Domestic: Yes; International: Yes
Graduates with debt: 32%; average amount of debt $46,908

University of Nebraska–Lincoln
Public

ONLINE MBA PROGRAM(S)
business.unl/mba/
Admissions: (402) 472-2338
Email: businessgrad@unl.edu
Financial aid: (402) 472-3484
Application deadline: Domestic: 07/01; International: 04/01
Program can be completed entirely online: Yes
Total program cost: $30,240
full-time in-state, $30,240
part-time in-state, $30,240
full-time out-of-state, $30,240
part-time out-of-state

Tuition per credit: $630
full-time in-state, $630
part-time in-state, $630
full-time out-of-state, $630
part-time out-of-state
Acceptance rate: 86%
Test scores required: GMAT or GRE
Average GMAT: 603
Average GRE: 153 verbal, 155 quantitative, 4.0 writing
Average age of entrants: 32
Students with prior work experience: 91%
Enrollment: 389, 79% men, 21% women, 10% minority, 6% international
Average class size: 36
Most popular MBA concentrations: finance, international business, marketing, supply chain management/logistics, quantitative analysis/statistics and operations research
Completion: Three year graduation rate: 44%; credits needed to graduate: 48; target time to graduate: 3.5 years
College funded aid available: Domestic: No; International: No
Graduates with debt: 33%; average amount of debt $31,503

NEVADA

University of Nevada–Reno
Public

ONLINE MBA PROGRAM(S)
www.unr.edu/grad/admissions
Admissions: (775) 784-4652
Email: courtnees@unr.edu
Financial aid: (775) 784-4666
Application deadline: rolling
Program can be completed entirely online: Yes
Total program cost: $30,000
full-time in-state, $30,000
part-time in-state, $30,000
full-time out-of-state, $30,000
part-time out-of-state
Tuition per credit: $833
full-time in-state, $833
part-time in-state, $833
full-time out-of-state, $833
part-time out-of-state
Acceptance rate: 100%
Test scores required: GMAT or GRE
Average GMAT: 428
Average GRE: 164 verbal, 149 quantitative, 3.0 writing
Average age of entrants: 37
Students with prior work experience: 100%
Enrollment: 66, 61% men, 39% women, 24% minority
Average class size: 29
Completion: Three year graduation rate: 96%; credits needed to graduate: 36; target time to graduate: 2 years
Graduates with debt: 31%; average amount of debt $19,005

ONLINE BUSINESS PROGRAM(S)
www.unr.edu/emba
Admissions: (775) 784-4652
Email: courtnees@unr.edu
Financial aid: (775) 784-4666
Application deadline: N/A
Total program cost: N/A

Tuition per credit: $833
full-time in-state, $833
part-time in-state, $833
full-time out-of-state, $833
part-time out-of-state

NEW HAMPSHIRE

Franklin Pierce University
Private

ONLINE MBA PROGRAM(S)
www.franklinpierce.edu/admissions/index.htm
Admissions: (800) 325-1090
Email: cgps@franklinpierce.edu
Financial aid: (877) 372-7347
Application deadline: rolling
Program can be completed entirely online: Yes
Total program cost: $25,935
full-time in-state, $25,935
part-time in-state, $25,935
full-time out-of-state, $25,935
part-time out-of-state
Tuition per credit: $665
full-time in-state, $665
part-time in-state, $665
full-time out-of-state, $665
part-time out-of-state
Acceptance rate: 100%
Test scores required: No
Average age of entrants: 31
Students with prior work experience: 69%
Enrollment: 224, 46% men, 54% women, 13% minority, 4% international
Average class size: 15
Most popular MBA concentrations: health care administration, human resources management, leadership, sports business, other
Completion: Three year graduation rate: 51%; credits needed to graduate: 39; target time to graduate: 2 years
College funded aid available: Domestic: Yes; International: Yes
Graduates with debt: 73%; average amount of debt $27,835

Granite State College
Public

ONLINE BUSINESS PROGRAM(S)
www.granite.edu/become-a-student/apply-now/graduate-apply-now/
Admissions: (888) 228-3000
Email: gsc.admissions@granite.edu
Financial aid: (888) 228-1392
Application deadline: rolling
Program can be completed entirely online: Yes
Total program cost: $15,750
full-time in-state, $15,750
part-time in-state, $16,800
full-time out-of-state, $16,800
part-time out-of-state
Tuition per credit: $525
full-time in-state, $525
part-time in-state, $560
full-time out-of-state, $560
part-time out-of-state
Acceptance rate: 98%
Test scores required: No
Average age of entrants: 38

Students with prior work experience: 92%
Enrollment: 156, 36% men, 64% women, 6% minority
Average class size: 6
Most popular business concentrations: general management, human resources management, leadership, not-for-profit management, production/operations management
Completion: Three year graduation rate: 64%; credits needed to graduate: 30; target time to graduate: 1.5 years
College funded aid available: Domestic: Yes
Graduates with debt: 43%; average amount of debt $21,028

New England College
Private

ONLINE MBA PROGRAM(S)
www.nec.edu/sgps/prospective
Admissions: (603) 428-2252
Email: graduateadmission@nec.edu
Financial aid: (603) 428-2226
Application deadline: rolling
Program can be completed entirely online: Yes
Total program cost: $23,800
full-time in-state, $23,800
part-time in-state, $23,800
full-time out-of-state, $23,800
part-time out-of-state
Tuition per credit: $595
full-time in-state, $595
part-time in-state, $595
full-time out-of-state, $595
part-time out-of-state
Acceptance rate: 99%
Test scores required: No
Average age of entrants: 37
Students with prior work experience: 98%
Enrollment: 170, 42% men, 58% women, 6% minority, 2% international
Average class size: 13
Most popular MBA concentrations: health care administration, leadership, not-for-profit management, sports business, other
Completion: Three year graduation rate: 82%; credits needed to graduate: 40; target time to graduate: 1.5 years
College funded aid available: Domestic: No; International: No
Graduates with debt: 38%; average amount of debt $24,261

ONLINE BUSINESS PROGRAM(S)
www.nec.edu/sgps/prospective
Admissions: (603) 428-2252
Email: graduateadmission@nec.edu
Financial aid: (603) 428-2226
Application deadline: rolling
Program can be completed entirely online: Yes
Total program cost: $27,200
full-time in-state, $27,200
part-time in-state, $27,200
full-time out-of-state, $27,200
part-time out-of-state

Tuition per credit: $680 full-time in-state, $680 part-time in-state, $680 full-time out-of-state, $680 part-time out-of-state
Acceptance rate: 100%
Test scores required: No
Average age of entrants: 35
Students with prior work experience: 86%
Enrollment: 251, 35% men, 65% women, 6% minority, 1% international
Average class size: 14
Most popular business concentrations: accounting, health care administration, not-for-profit management, production/operations management, real estate
Completion: Three year graduation rate: 66%; credits needed to graduate: 40; target time to graduate: 1.5 years
College funded aid available: Domestic: No; International: No
Graduates with debt: 73%; average amount of debt $25,579

University of New Hampshire (Paul)

Public

ONLINE MBA PROGRAM(S)

paulcollege.unh.edu/graduate
Admissions: (603) 862-1367
Email: mba.info@unh.edu
Financial aid: (603) 862-3671
Application deadline: N/A
Program can be completed entirely online: Yes
Total program cost: $38,400 full-time in-state, $38,400 part-time in-state, $42,240 full-time out-of-state, $42,240 part-time out-of-state
Tuition per credit: $800 full-time in-state, $800 part-time in-state, $880 full-time out-of-state, $880 part-time out-of-state
Acceptance rate: 94%
Test scores required: GMAT
Average GMAT: 542
Average age of entrants: 33
Students with prior work experience: 100%
Enrollment: 80, 66% men, 34% women, 10% minority, 5% international
Average class size: 24
Most popular MBA concentrations: finance, international business, marketing, management information systems, other
Completion: Three year graduation rate: 42%; credits needed to graduate: 48; target time to graduate: 3 years
College funded aid available: Domestic: No; International: No
Graduates with debt: 50%; average amount of debt $27,029

NEW JERSEY

Montclair State University

Public

ONLINE MBA PROGRAM(S)

www.montclair.edu/graduate
Admissions: (973) 655-4497
Email: gradschool@montclair.edu
Financial aid: (973) 655-4461
Application deadline: rolling
Program can be completed entirely online: Yes
Total program cost: $10,383 part-time in-state, $10,383 part-time out-of-state
Tuition per credit: $692 full-time in-state, $692 part-time in-state, $692 full-time out-of-state, $692 part-time out-of-state
Acceptance rate: 65%
Average age of entrants: 29
Enrollment: 161, 33% men, 67% women, 45% minority, 1% international
Average class size: 25
Completion: Credits needed to graduate: 36; target time to graduate: 2 years
College funded aid available: Domestic: Yes; International: No

New Jersey Institute of Technology

Public

ONLINE MBA PROGRAM(S)

www.njit.edu/admissions
Admissions: (973) 596-3306
Email: stephen.eck@njit.edu
Financial aid: (973) 596-3476
Application deadline: rolling
Program can be completed entirely online: Depends
Total program cost: $51,504 full-time in-state, $59,904 full-time out-of-state
Tuition per credit: $1,073 full-time in-state, $1,073 part-time in-state, $1,248 full-time out-of-state, $1,248 part-time out-of-state
Acceptance rate: 70%
Test scores required: No
Average GMAT: 567
Average GRE: 155 verbal, 153 quantitative, 3.9 writing
Average age of entrants: 31
Students with prior work experience: 95%
Enrollment: 102, 60% men, 40% women, 52% minority
Average class size: 23
Most popular MBA concentrations: finance, general management, marketing, management information systems, technology
Completion: Three year graduation rate: 43%; credits needed to graduate: 48; target time to graduate: 3.5 years
College funded aid available: Domestic: No; International: No
Graduates with debt: 73%; average amount of debt $55,921

ONLINE BUSINESS PROGRAM(S)

www.njit.edu/admissions
Admissions: (973) 596-3306
Email: eck@njit.edu
Financial aid: (973) 596-3476
Application deadline: rolling
Program can be completed entirely online: Depends
Total program cost: $32,190 full-time in-state, $37,440 full-time out-of-state
Tuition per credit: $1,073 full-time in-state, $1,073 part-time in-state, $1,248 full-time out-of-state, $1,248 part-time out-of-state
Acceptance rate: 63%
Test scores required: No
Average GRE: 149 verbal, 155 quantitative, 3.8 writing
Average age of entrants: 33
Students with prior work experience: 86%
Enrollment: 13, 77% men, 23% women, 46% minority
Average class size: 26
Most popular business concentrations: general management, management information systems, organizational behavior, technology, other
Completion: Credits needed to graduate: 30; target time to graduate: 2 years
College funded aid available: Domestic: No; International: No

Rider University

Private

ONLINE MBA PROGRAM(S)

www.rider.edu/admissions/graduate/apply
Admissions: (609) 896-5036
Email: admissions@rider.edu
Financial aid: (609) 896-5380
Application deadline: rolling
Program can be completed entirely online: Yes
Total program cost: N/A
Tuition per credit: $1,060 full-time in-state, $1,060 part-time in-state, $1,060 full-time out-of-state, $1,060 part-time out-of-state
Acceptance rate: 93%
Average age of entrants: 38
Enrollment: 6, 67% men, 33% women, 50% minority
Average class size: 17
Completion: Credits needed to graduate: 33; target time to graduate: 1 year
College funded aid available: Domestic: Yes; International: No

ONLINE BUSINESS PROGRAM(S)

www.rider.edu/admissions/graduate/apply
Admissions: (609) 896-5036
Email: admissions@rider.edu
Financial aid: (609) 896-5178
Application deadline: rolling
Program can be completed entirely online: Yes
Total program cost: N/A
Tuition per credit: $1,060 full-time in-state, $1,060 part-time in-state, $1,060 full-time out-of-state, $1,060 part-time out-of-state
Acceptance rate: 65%

Average age of entrants: 31
Enrollment: 31, 58% men, 42% women, 45% minority
Average class size: 11
Most popular business concentrations: accounting, other
Completion: Three year graduation rate: 89%; credits needed to graduate: 30; target time to graduate: 1.5 years
College funded aid available: Domestic: Yes; International: No
Graduates with debt: 88%; average amount of debt $24,987

Rowan University (Rohrer)

Public

ONLINE MBA PROGRAM(S)

rowanu.com/graduate/admissions
Admissions: (856) 256-4747
Email: global@rowan.edu
Financial aid: (856) 256-5141
Application deadline: rolling
Program can be completed entirely online: Yes
Total program cost: N/A
Tuition per credit: $891 full-time in-state, $891 part-time in-state, $891 full-time out-of-state, $891 part-time out-of-state
Acceptance rate: 52%
Test scores required: GMAT or GRE
Average GMAT: 510
Average age of entrants: 32
Students with prior work experience: 0%
Enrollment: 52, 56% men, 44% women, 17% minority, 2% international
Average class size: 22
Most popular MBA concentrations: general management
Completion: Credits needed to graduate: 36; target time to graduate: 2 years
College funded aid available: Domestic: Yes; International: Yes
Graduates with debt: 50%; average amount of debt $17,194

Rutgers University–Camden

Public

ONLINE MBA PROGRAM(S)

online.rutgers.edu/master-business-admin/
Admissions: (856) 225-6452
Email: Rsbcmba@camden.rutgers.edu
Financial aid: (856) 225-6039
Application deadline: rolling
Program can be completed entirely online: Yes
Total program cost: $52,752 full-time in-state, $52,752 part-time in-state, $52,752 full-time out-of-state, $52,752 part-time out-of-state
Tuition per credit: $1,256 full-time in-state, $1,256 part-time in-state, $1,256 full-time out-of-state, $1,256 part-time out-of-state
Acceptance rate: 66%

Test scores required: GMAT or GRE
Average GMAT: 575
Average GRE: 152 verbal, 153 quantitative
Average age of entrants: 33
Students with prior work experience: 100%
Enrollment: 208, 53% men, 47% women, 47% minority
Average class size: 29
Most popular MBA concentrations: finance, general management, international business, marketing
Completion: Credits needed to graduate: 42; target time to graduate: 3 years
College funded aid available: Domestic: No; International: No
Graduates with debt: 25%; average amount of debt $38,876

Rutgers University–New Brunswick and Newark

Public

ONLINE BUSINESS PROGRAM(S)

business.rutgers.edu/admissions
Admissions: (973) 353-1234
Email: rkwan@business.rutgers.edu
Financial aid: (973) 353-1234
Application deadline: rolling
Program can be completed entirely online: Yes
Total program cost: $36,000 full-time in-state, $36,000 part-time in-state, $36,000 full-time out-of-state, $36,000 part-time out-of-state
Tuition per credit: $1,200 full-time in-state, $1,200 part-time in-state, $1,200 full-time out-of-state, $1,200 part-time out-of-state
Acceptance rate: 75%
Test scores required: No
Average age of entrants: 34
Students with prior work experience: 98%
Enrollment: 295, 51% men, 49% women, 34% minority, 2% international
Average class size: 16
Most popular business concentrations: accounting, supply chain management/logistics
Completion: Three year graduation rate: 51%; credits needed to graduate: 30; target time to graduate: 3 years
College funded aid available: Domestic: Yes; International: No
Graduates with debt: 63%; average amount of debt $42,615

Stevens Institute of Technology

Private

ONLINE MBA PROGRAM(S)

www.stevens.edu/admissions/graduate-admissions
Admissions: (888) 783-8367
Email: graduate@stevens.edu
Financial aid: (201) 216-8142
Application deadline: rolling

Program can be completed entirely online: Yes
Total program cost: $68,988
full-time in-state, $68,988
part-time in-state, $68,988
full-time out-of-state, $68,988
part-time out-of-state
Tuition per credit: $1,554
full-time in-state, $1,554
part-time in-state, $1,554
full-time out-of-state, $1,554
part-time out-of-state
Acceptance rate: 74%
Test scores required:
GMAT or GRE
Average GMAT: 578
Average age of entrants: 38
Students with prior work experience: 100%
Enrollment: 88, 52% men, 48% women, 31% minority
Average class size: 16
Most popular MBA concentrations: general management, management information systems, quantitative analysis/statistics and operations research, other
Completion: Credits needed to graduate: 48; target time to graduate: 4 years
College funded aid available: Domestic: Yes; International: Yes
Graduates with debt: 1%; average amount of debt $24,325

ONLINE BUSINESS PROGRAM(S)

www.stevens.edu/admissions/graduate-admissions
Admissions: (888) 783-8367
Email: graduate@stevens.edu
Financial aid: (201) 216-8142
Application deadline: rolling
Program can be completed entirely online: Yes
Total program cost: $51,741
full-time in-state, $51,741
part-time in-state, $51,741
full-time out-of-state, $51,741
part-time out-of-state
Tuition per credit: $1,554
full-time in-state, $1,554
part-time in-state, $1,554
full-time out-of-state, $1,554
part-time out-of-state
Acceptance rate: 66%
Test scores required:
GMAT or GRE
Average GMAT: 655
Average GRE: 157 verbal, 158 quantitative, 4.0 writing
Average age of entrants: 32
Students with prior work experience: 89%
Enrollment: 184, 68% men, 32% women, 27% minority
Average class size: 14
Most popular business concentrations: general management, management information systems, quantitative analysis/statistics and operations research, other
Completion: Three year graduation rate: 37%; credits needed to graduate: 36; target time to graduate: 2 years
College funded aid available: Domestic: Yes; International: Yes
Graduates with debt: 19%; average amount of debt $39,350

NEW MEXICO

New Mexico State University

Public

ONLINE MBA PROGRAM(S)

gradadmissions.nmsu.edu
Admissions: (575) 646-5746
Email: gradinfo@nmsu.edu
Financial aid: (575) 646-4105
Application deadline: Domestic: 07/15; International: 04/15
Program can be completed entirely online: No
Total program cost: $8,780
full-time in-state, $8,780
part-time in-state, $30,618
full-time out-of-state, $30,618
part-time out-of-state
Tuition per credit: $244
full-time in-state, $244
part-time in-state, $851
full-time out-of-state, $851
part-time out-of-state
Acceptance rate: 100%
Average age of entrants: 36
Enrollment: 63, 44% men, 56% women, N/A minority, N/A international
Average class size: 22
Most popular MBA concentrations: finance, other
Completion: Credits needed to graduate: 36; target time to graduate: 2 years
College funded aid available: Domestic: Yes; International: Yes

NEW YORK

Clarkson University

Private

ONLINE MBA PROGRAM(S)

www.clarkson.edu/graduate-admissions/
Admissions: (315) 268-6613
Email: busgrad@clarkson.edu
Financial aid: (315) 268-3904
Application deadline: rolling
Program can be completed entirely online: No
Total program cost: $54,624
full-time in-state, $54,624
part-time in-state, $54,624
full-time out-of-state, $54,624
part-time out-of-state
Tuition per credit: $1,138
full-time in-state, $1,138
part-time in-state, $1,138
full-time out-of-state, $1,138
part-time out-of-state
Acceptance rate: 45%
Test scores required:
GMAT or GRE
Average GMAT: 520
Average GRE: 154 verbal, 156 quantitative, 4.0 writing
Average age of entrants: 30
Students with prior work experience: 66%
Enrollment: 230, 56% men, 44% women, 17% minority, 6% international
Average class size: 10
Most popular MBA concentrations: general management, health care administration, supply chain management/logistics

Completion: Three year graduation rate: 79%; credits needed to graduate: 48; target time to graduate: 2 years
College funded aid available: Domestic: Yes; International: Yes
Graduates with debt: 37%; average amount of debt $42,831

ONLINE BUSINESS PROGRAM(S)

www.clarkson.edu/graduate-admissions
Admissions: (315) 268-6613
Email: busgrad@clarkson.edu
Financial aid: (315) 268-3904
Application deadline: rolling
Program can be completed entirely online: No
Total program cost: $40,968
full-time in-state, $40,968
part-time in-state, $40,968
full-time out-of-state, $40,968
part-time out-of-state
Tuition per credit: $1,138
full-time in-state, $1,138
part-time in-state, $1,138
full-time out-of-state, $1,138
part-time out-of-state
Acceptance rate: 52%
Test scores required:
GMAT or GRE
Average age of entrants: 38
Enrollment: 23, 30% men, 70% women, 26% minority, 4% international
Average class size: 12
Completion: Credits needed to graduate: 36; target time to graduate: 1.5 years
College funded aid available: Domestic: Yes; International: Yes
Graduates with debt: 36%

D'Youville College

Private

ONLINE MBA PROGRAM(S)

www.dyc.edu
Admissions: N/A
Financial aid: (716) 829-7500
Application deadline: rolling
Program can be completed entirely online: Yes
Total program cost: $27,000
full-time in-state, $27,000
part-time in-state, $27,000
full-time out-of-state, $27,000
part-time out-of-state
Tuition per credit: $750 full-time in-state, $750 part-time in-state, $750 full-time out-of-state, $750 part-time out-of-state
Average age of entrants: 0
Most popular MBA concentrations: general management
Completion: Credits needed to graduate: 36

Hofstra University (Zarb)

Private

ONLINE MBA PROGRAM(S)

www.hofstra.edu/graduate
Admissions: (800) 463-7672
Email: graduateadmission@hofstra.edu
Financial aid: (516) 463-8000
Application deadline: rolling
Program can be completed entirely online: Depends

Total program cost: $76,600
full-time in-state, $76,600
full-time out-of-state
Tuition per credit: $1,596
full-time in-state, $1,596
part-time in-state, $1,596
full-time out-of-state, $1,596
part-time out-of-state
Acceptance rate: 75%
Average age of entrants: 34
Students with prior work experience: 76%
Enrollment: 47, 57% men, 43% women, 36% minority
Average class size: 22
Most popular MBA concentrations: finance, general management, health care administration, management information systems
Completion: Three year graduation rate: 91%; credits needed to graduate: 45; target time to graduate: 2 years
College funded aid available: Domestic: Yes; International: Yes
Graduates with debt: 33%

Keuka College

Private

ONLINE BUSINESS PROGRAM(S)

www.keuka.edu/admissions/cps
Admissions: (315) 279-5117
Email: adlearn@keuka.edu
Financial aid: (315) 279-5646
Application deadline: rolling
Program can be completed entirely online: Yes
Total program cost: N/A
Tuition per credit:
Acceptance rate: 100%
Test scores required: No
Average age of entrants: 38
Enrollment: 21, 29% men, 71% women, N/A minority
Average class size: 11
Completion: Credits needed to graduate: 40; target time to graduate: 1.5 years
College funded aid available: Domestic: Yes; International: Yes

Marist College

Private

ONLINE MBA PROGRAM(S)

www.marist.edu/admission/graduate/
Admissions: (845) 575-3800
Email: graduate@marist.edu
Financial aid: (845) 575-3000
Application deadline: rolling
Program can be completed entirely online: Yes
Total program cost: $28,800
full-time in-state, $28,800
part-time in-state, $28,800
full-time out-of-state, $28,800
part-time out-of-state
Tuition per credit: $800
full-time in-state, $800
part-time in-state, $800
full-time out-of-state, $800
part-time out-of-state
Acceptance rate: 42%
Test scores required:
GMAT or GRE
Average GMAT: 531
Average GRE: 151 verbal, 148 quantitative, 4.0 writing

Average age of entrants: 31
Students with prior work experience: 93%
Enrollment: 228, 57% men, 43% women, 17% minority
Average class size: 22
Most popular MBA concentrations: finance, general management, health care administration, leadership
Completion: Three year graduation rate: 47%; credits needed to graduate: 36; target time to graduate: 2 years
College funded aid available: Domestic: Yes; International: Yes
Graduates with debt: 36%; average amount of debt $32,510

ONLINE BUSINESS PROGRAM(S)

www.marist.edu/admission/graduate/
Admissions: (845) 575-3800
Email: graduate@marist.edu
Financial aid: (845) 575-3230
Application deadline: rolling
Program can be completed entirely online: Yes
Total program cost: $33,600
full-time in-state, $33,600
part-time in-state, $33,600
full-time out-of-state, $33,600
part-time out-of-state
Tuition per credit: $800
full-time in-state, $800
part-time in-state, $800
full-time out-of-state, $800
part-time out-of-state
Acceptance rate: 42%
Test scores required: GMAT
Average GRE: 155 verbal, 148 quantitative, 3.9 writing
Average age of entrants: 32
Students with prior work experience: 94%
Enrollment: 299, 49% men, 51% women, 31% minority
Average class size: 22
Most popular business concentrations: health care administration, leadership, not-for-profit management, public administration
Completion: Three year graduation rate: 68%; credits needed to graduate: 42; target time to graduate: 2 years
College funded aid available: Domestic: Yes; International: Yes
Graduates with debt: 36%; average amount of debt $31,802

Mercy College

Private

ONLINE MBA PROGRAM(S)

www.mercy.edu/admissions/
Admissions: (877) 637-2946
Email: admissions@mercy.edu
Financial aid: (877) 637-2946
Application deadline: rolling
Program can be completed entirely online: Yes
Total program cost: N/A
Tuition per credit: $876 full-time in-state, $876 part-time in-state, $876 full-time out-of-state, $876 part-time out-of-state
Acceptance rate: 27%
Test scores required: No
Average age of entrants: 28

Enrollment: 39, 36% men, 64% women, 59% minority, 3% international
Average class size: 18
Most popular MBA concentrations: finance, general management, international business, marketing, quantitative analysis/statistics and operations research
Completion: Credits needed to graduate: 57; target time to graduate: 1 year

ONLINE BUSINESS PROGRAM(S)
www.mercy.edu/admissions/
Admissions: (877) 637-2946
Email: admissions@mercy.edu
Financial aid: (877) 637-2946
Application deadline: rolling
Program can be completed entirely online: Yes
Total program cost: N/A
Tuition per credit: $876 full-time in-state, $876 part-time in-state, $876 full-time out-of-state, $876 part-time out-of-state
Test scores required: No
Enrollment: 62, 27% men, 73% women, 68% minority
Average class size: 18
Most popular business concentrations: accounting, human resources management, leadership
Completion: Credits needed to graduate: 57; target time to graduate: 2 years
College funded aid available: Domestic: Yes

Monroe College
Proprietary

ONLINE MBA PROGRAM(S)
www.monroecollege.edu/
Online-Learning/
Admissions: (718) 933-6700
Financial aid: (718) 933-6700
Application deadline: rolling
Program can be completed entirely online: Depends
Total program cost: $29,376 full-time in-state, $29,376 part-time in-state, $29,376 full-time out-of-state, $29,376 part-time out-of-state
Tuition per credit: $816 full-time in-state, $816 part-time in-state, $816 full-time out-of-state, $816 part-time out-of-state
Acceptance rate: 57%
Test scores required: No
Average GMAT: N/A
Average age of entrants: 32
Students with prior work experience: 87%
Enrollment: 152, 21% men, 79% women, 74% minority, 15% international
Average class size: 19
Most popular MBA concentrations: entrepreneurship, finance, general management, health care administration, marketing
Completion: Three year graduation rate: 65%; credits needed to graduate: 37; target time to graduate: 3 years
College funded aid available: Domestic: Yes; International: Yes
Graduates with debt: 83%; average amount of debt $25,765

Rochester Institute of Technology
Private

ONLINE MBA PROGRAM(S)
www.rit.edu/emba/
admissions-requirements
Admissions: (585) 475-2729
Email: awilliams@saunders.rit.edu
Financial aid: (585) 475-2186
Application deadline: rolling
Program can be completed entirely online: No
Total program cost: $70,000 full-time in-state, $70,000 full-time out-of-state
Tuition per credit: $1,489 full-time in-state, $1,489 part-time in-state, $1,489 full-time out-of-state, $1,489 part-time out-of-state
Acceptance rate: 74%
Test scores required: No
Average age of entrants: 39
Students with prior work experience: 100%
Enrollment: 39, 51% men, 49% women, 23% minority
Average class size: 21
Completion: Credits needed to graduate: 47; target time to graduate: 1.5 years
College funded aid available: Domestic: Yes; International: Yes
Graduates with debt: 67%; average amount of debt $52,961

ONLINE BUSINESS PROGRAM(S)
admissions.rit.edu
Admissions: (585) 475-2729
Email: sgriffin@saunders.rit.edu
Financial aid: (585) 475-2186
Application deadline: rolling
Program can be completed entirely online: Yes
Total program cost: N/A
Tuition per credit: $1,035 full-time in-state, $1,035 part-time in-state, $1,035 full-time out-of-state, $1,035 part-time out-of-state
Acceptance rate: 86%
Test scores required: No
Average age of entrants: 30
Students with prior work experience: 86%
Enrollment: 56, 29% men, 71% women, 11% minority, 30% international
Most popular business concentrations: human resources management, leadership
Completion: Credits needed to graduate: 33

SUNY Polytechnic Institute
Public

ONLINE MBA PROGRAM(S)
sunypoly.edu/admissions/
graduate.html
Admissions: (315) 792-7347
Email: graduate@sunypoly.edu
Financial aid: (315) 792-7210
Application deadline: Domestic: 07/01; International: 07/01
Program can be completed entirely online: Yes

Total program cost: $29,400 full-time in-state, $29,424 part-time in-state, $48,780 full-time out-of-state, $48,768 part-time out-of-state
Tuition per credit: $613 full-time in-state, $613 part-time in-state, $1,016 full-time out-of-state, $1,016 part-time out-of-state
Acceptance rate: 95%
Test scores required: GMAT or GRE
Average GMAT: 479
Average age of entrants: 30
Enrollment: 112, 55% men, 45% women, 20% minority
Average class size: 22
Most popular MBA concentrations: e-commerce, finance, health care administration, human resources management, marketing
Completion: Three year graduation rate: 89%; credits needed to graduate: 48; target time to graduate: 1.5 years
College funded aid available: Domestic: Yes; International: Yes

ONLINE BUSINESS PROGRAM(S)
sunypoly.edu/
office-graduate-studies.html
Admissions: (315) 792-7347
Email: graduate@sunypoly.edu
Financial aid: (315) 792-7210
Application deadline: Domestic: 07/01; International: 07/01
Program can be completed entirely online: Yes
Total program cost: N/A
Tuition per credit: $453 full-time in-state, $453 part-time in-state, $925 full-time out-of-state, $925 part-time out-of-state
Acceptance rate: 97%
Test scores required: GMAT or GRE
Average GMAT: 485
Average age of entrants: 34
Enrollment: 61, 54% men, 46% women, 34% minority
Average class size: 19
Most popular business concentrations: accounting
Completion: Three year graduation rate: 44%; credits needed to graduate: 33; target time to graduate: 1.5 years
College funded aid available: Domestic: Yes; International: Yes

SUNY–Oswego
Public

ONLINE MBA PROGRAM(S)
www.oswego.edu/mba
Admissions: (315) 312-3152
Email: mba@oswego.edu
Financial aid: (315) 312-2248
Application deadline: rolling
Program can be completed entirely online: Yes
Total program cost: $22,050 full-time in-state, $22,050 part-time in-state, $36,585 full-time out-of-state, $36,585 part-time out-of-state

Tuition per credit: $613 full-time in-state, $613 part-time in-state, $1,016 full-time out-of-state, $1,016 part-time out-of-state
Acceptance rate: 78%
Test scores required: GMAT
Average GMAT: 544
Average GRE: 154 verbal, 152 quantitative, 4.0 writing
Average age of entrants: 34
Students with prior work experience: 98%
Enrollment: 198, 60% men, 40% women, 21% minority
Average class size: 22
Most popular MBA concentrations: accounting, finance, general management, health care administration, marketing
Completion: Three year graduation rate: 71%; credits needed to graduate: 36; target time to graduate: 2 years
College funded aid available: Domestic: Yes; International: Yes
Graduates with debt: 46%; average amount of debt $24,017

St. Bonaventure University
Private

ONLINE MBA PROGRAM(S)
www.sbu.edu/admission-aid/
graduate-admissions
Admissions: (716) 375-2021
Email: gradsch@sbu.edu
Financial aid: (716) 375-2528
Application deadline: N/A
Program can be completed entirely online: Yes
Total program cost: $30,786 full-time in-state, $30,786 part-time in-state, $30,786 full-time out-of-state, $30,786 part-time out-of-state
Tuition per credit: $733 full-time in-state, $733 part-time in-state, $733 full-time out-of-state, $733 part-time out-of-state
Acceptance rate: 88%
Test scores required: GMAT or GRE
Average age of entrants: 30
Students with prior work experience: 96%
Enrollment: 56, 50% men, 50% women, 21% minority, 4% international
Average class size: 15
Most popular MBA concentrations: accounting, finance, general management, marketing
Completion: Credits needed to graduate: 42; target time to graduate: 2 years
College funded aid available: Domestic: No; International: No

St. John's University (Tobin)
Private

ONLINE BUSINESS PROGRAM(S)
www.stjohns.edu/
admission-aid/
graduate-admission
Admissions: (718) 277-5113
Email: steigera@stjohns.edu

Financial aid: (718) 990-2000
Application deadline: N/A
Program can be completed entirely online: Yes
Total program cost: N/A
Tuition per credit: $1,215 full-time in-state, $1,215 part-time in-state, $1,215 full-time out-of-state, $1,215 part-time out-of-state
Acceptance rate: 92%
Test scores required: GMAT or GRE
Average GMAT: 550
Average age of entrants: 32
Students with prior work experience: 47%
Enrollment: 40, 60% men, 40% women, 20% minority, 2% international
Average class size: 18
Most popular business concentrations: accounting, tax
Completion: Three year graduation rate: 56%; credits needed to graduate: 32; target time to graduate: 2 years
College funded aid available: Domestic: Yes; International: Yes
Graduates with debt: 38%; average amount of debt $49,092

St. Joseph's College New York
Private

ONLINE MBA PROGRAM(S)
www.sjcny.edu/online/
admissions/graduate
Admissions: (631) 687-4514
Financial aid: (631) 687-2611
Application deadline: rolling
Program can be completed entirely online: Yes
Total program cost: $12,854 full-time in-state, $12,854 part-time in-state, $12,854 full-time out-of-state, $12,854 part-time out-of-state
Tuition per credit: $520 full-time in-state, $520 part-time in-state, $520 full-time out-of-state, $520 part-time out-of-state
Acceptance rate: 100%
Average age of entrants: 33
Enrollment: 63, 27% men, 73% women, 33% minority
Average class size: 17
Most popular MBA concentrations: health care administration, other
Completion: Credits needed to graduate: 36; target time to graduate: 2 years
College funded aid available: Domestic: No; International: No
Graduates with debt: 75%; average amount of debt $35,733

ONLINE BUSINESS PROGRAM(S)
www.sjcny.edu/online/
admissions/graduate
Admissions: (631) 687-4514
Email: cseifert@sjcny.edu
Financial aid: (631) 687-2611
Application deadline: rolling
Program can be completed entirely online: Yes

Total program cost: $12,854 full-time in-state, $6,427 part-time in-state, $12,854 full-time out-of-state, $6,427 part-time out-of-state
Tuition per credit: $520 full-time in-state, $520 part-time in-state, $520 full-time out-of-state, $520 part-time out-of-state
Acceptance rate: 100%
Average age of entrants: 35
Enrollment: 28, 25% men, 75% women, 50% minority
Average class size: 17
Most popular business concentrations: general management, health care administration, human resources management, other
Completion: Credits needed to graduate: 36; target time to graduate: 2 years
College funded aid available: Domestic: No; International: No

Stony Brook University–SUNY

Public

ONLINE BUSINESS PROGRAM(S)

www.stonybrook.edu/spd/
Admissions: (631) 632-7050
Email: SPD@stonybrook.edu
Financial aid: (631) 632-6840
Application deadline: Domestic: 06/15; International: 06/01
Program can be completed entirely online: Yes
Total program cost: N/A
Tuition per credit: $453 full-time in-state, $453 part-time in-state, $925 full-time out-of-state, $925 part-time out-of-state
Acceptance rate: 96%
Test scores required: No
Average age of entrants: 30
Students with prior work experience: 100%
Enrollment: 162, 18% men, 82% women, 36% minority
Average class size: 19
Most popular business concentrations: human resources management
Completion: Three year graduation rate: 59%; credits needed to graduate: 30; target time to graduate: 2.5 years
College funded aid available: International: No
Graduates with debt: 44%; average amount of debt $26,826

Syracuse University (Whitman)

Private

ONLINE MBA PROGRAM(S)

onlinebusiness.syr.edu/admissions/overview/
Admissions: (315) 443-9214
Email: admissions@onlinebusiness.syr.edu
Financial aid: (315) 443-1513
Application deadline: rolling
Program can be completed entirely online: Depends

Total program cost: $81,000 full-time in-state, $81,000 part-time in-state, $81,000 full-time out-of-state, $81,000 part-time out-of-state
Tuition per credit: $1,500 full-time in-state, $1,500 part-time in-state, $1,500 full-time out-of-state, $1,500 part-time out-of-state
Acceptance rate: 77%
Average GMAT: 580
Average GRE: 158 verbal, 155 quantitative, 4.0 writing
Average age of entrants: 35
Students with prior work experience: 100%
Enrollment: 1,102, 69% men, 31% women, 37% minority, 1% international
Average class size: 16
Most popular MBA concentrations: entrepreneurship, finance, general management, marketing, supply chain management/logistics
Completion: Three year graduation rate: 68%; credits needed to graduate: 54; target time to graduate: 2 years
College funded aid available: Domestic: No; International: No
Graduates with debt: 59%; average amount of debt $74,200

ONLINE BUSINESS PROGRAM(S)

onlinebusiness.syr.edu/admissions/overview/
Admissions: (315) 443-9214
Email: admissions@onlinebusiness.syr.edu
Financial aid: (315) 443-1513
Application deadline: rolling
Program can be completed entirely online: Yes
Total program cost: $51,000 full-time in-state, $51,000 part-time in-state, $51,000 full-time out-of-state, $51,000 part-time out-of-state
Tuition per credit: $1,500 full-time in-state, $1,500 part-time in-state, $1,500 full-time out-of-state, $1,500 part-time out-of-state
Acceptance rate: 75%
Average GMAT: 633
Average GRE: 154 verbal, 156 quantitative, 4.0 writing
Average age of entrants: 37
Students with prior work experience: 100%
Enrollment: 124, 51% men, 49% women, 38% minority, 3% international
Average class size: 16
Completion: Credits needed to graduate: 30; target time to graduate: 1 year
College funded aid available: Domestic: No; International: No
Graduates with debt: 86%; average amount of debt $40,317

Utica College

Private

ONLINE MBA PROGRAM(S)

www.onlineuticacollege.com/
Admissions: (315) 792-3010
Email: admiss@utica.edu
Financial aid: (315) 792-3215
Application deadline: rolling

Program can be completed entirely online: Yes
Total program cost: N/A
Tuition per credit: $650 full-time in-state, $650 part-time in-state, $650 full-time out-of-state, $650 part-time out-of-state
Acceptance rate: 88%
Test scores required: No
Average age of entrants: 31
Enrollment: 251, 47% men, 53% women, 24% minority, 1% international
Average class size: 14
Most popular MBA concentrations: accounting, entrepreneurship, health care administration, insurance
Completion: Three year graduation rate: 68%; credits needed to graduate: 60; target time to graduate: 2 years
College funded aid available: Domestic: No; International: No
Graduates with debt: 52%; average amount of debt $12,058

NORTH CAROLINA

East Carolina University

Public

ONLINE MBA PROGRAM(S)

www.ecu.edu/cs-bus/grad/
Admissions: (252) 328-6970
Email: gradbus@ecu.edu
Financial aid: (252) 328-6610
Application deadline: rolling
Program can be completed entirely online: Yes
Total program cost: $11,807 full-time in-state, $11,807 part-time in-state, $33,078 full-time out-of-state, $33,078 part-time out-of-state
Tuition per credit: $358 full-time in-state, $358 part-time in-state, $1,002 full-time out-of-state, $1,002 part-time out-of-state
Acceptance rate: 77%
Test scores required: GMAT or GRE
Average GMAT: 507
Average GRE: 152 verbal, 151 quantitative, 4.0 writing
Average age of entrants: 31
Enrollment: 840, 53% men, 47% women, 21% minority, 2% international
Average class size: 27
Most popular MBA concentrations: finance, health care administration, marketing, management information systems, supply chain management/logistics
Completion: Three year graduation rate: 49%; credits needed to graduate: 54; target time to graduate: 2.5 years
College funded aid available: Domestic: Yes; International: Yes
Graduates with debt: 49%; average amount of debt $31,363

Fayetteville State University

Public

ONLINE MBA PROGRAM(S)

mba.uncfsu.edu/
Admissions: (910) 672-2910
Email: mbaprogram@uncfsu.edu
Financial aid: (910) 672-1325
Application deadline: rolling
Program can be completed entirely online: Yes
Total program cost: $6,591 full-time in-state, $6,591 part-time in-state, $16,478 full-time out-of-state, $16,478 part-time out-of-state
Tuition per credit: $183 full-time in-state, $183 part-time in-state, $458 full-time out-of-state, $458 part-time out-of-state
Acceptance rate: 72%
Average GMAT: 482
Average GRE: 147 verbal, 149 quantitative, 3.2 writing
Average age of entrants: 36
Students with prior work experience: 94%
Enrollment: 248, 52% men, 48% women, 48% minority, 2% international
Average class size: 35
Most popular MBA concentrations: finance, general management, health care administration, marketing, production/operations management
Completion: Three year graduation rate: 40%; credits needed to graduate: 36; target time to graduate: 2 years
College funded aid available: Domestic: Yes; International: Yes

North Carolina State University (Poole)

Public

ONLINE MBA PROGRAM(S)

mba.ncsu.edu/admissions/
Admissions: (919) 513-5584
Email: jennifer_arthur@ncsu.edu
Financial aid: (919) 515-2866
Application deadline: rolling
Program can be completed entirely online: No
Total program cost: $44,955 full-time in-state, $44,955 part-time in-state, $74,555 full-time out-of-state, $74,555 part-time out-of-state
Tuition per credit: $1,123 full-time in-state, $1,123 part-time in-state, $1,863 full-time out-of-state, $1,863 part-time out-of-state
Acceptance rate: 58%
Average GMAT: 601
Average GRE: 155 verbal, 158 quantitative, 4.0 writing
Average age of entrants: 34
Students with prior work experience: 100%
Enrollment: 311, 66% men, 34% women, 21% minority, 2% international
Average class size: 36
Most popular MBA concentrations: entrepreneurship, finance, marketing, supply chain management/logistics, other

Completion: Three year graduation rate: 93%; credits needed to graduate: 40; target time to graduate: 3 years
College funded aid available: Domestic: No; International: No
Graduates with debt: 47%; average amount of debt $42,327

Queens University of Charlotte (McColl)

Private

ONLINE MBA PROGRAM(S)

online.queens.edu/master-of-business-administration-online-overview
Admissions: (704) 337-2465
Email: info@online.queens.edu
Financial aid: (704) 337-2512
Application deadline: rolling
Program can be completed entirely online: No
Total program cost: $39,780 full-time in-state, $39,780 part-time in-state, $39,780 full-time out-of-state, $39,780 part-time out-of-state
Tuition per credit: $1,105 full-time in-state, $1,105 part-time in-state, $1,105 full-time out-of-state, $1,105 part-time out-of-state
Acceptance rate: 85%
Test scores required: No
Average GRE: 153 verbal, 150 quantitative, 4.0 writing
Average age of entrants: 35
Students with prior work experience: 100%
Enrollment: 95, 37% men, 63% women, 36% minority, 1% international
Average class size: 17
Completion: Credits needed to graduate: 36; target time to graduate: 2 years
College funded aid available: Domestic: No; International: No
Graduates with debt: 45%; average amount of debt $46,298

University of North Carolina–Chapel Hill (Kenan-Flagler)

Public

ONLINE MBA PROGRAM(S)

onlinemba.unc.edu/admissions/admissions-overview/
Admissions: (919) 962-8919
Email: OnlineMBA@unc.edu
Financial aid: (919) 962-0135
Application deadline: rolling
Program can be completed entirely online: Depends
Total program cost: $114,048 full-time in-state, $114,048 part-time in-state, $114,048 full-time out-of-state, $114,048 part-time out-of-state
Tuition per credit: $1,728 full-time in-state, $1,728 part-time in-state, $1,728 full-time out-of-state, $1,728 part-time out-of-state
Acceptance rate: 55%
Average GMAT: 652
Average GRE: 160 verbal, 160 quantitative, 5.0 writing

Average age of entrants: 33
Students with prior work experience: 100%
Enrollment: 1,862, 75% men, 25% women, 21% minority, 5% international
Average class size: 13
Most popular MBA concentrations: consulting, finance, general management, leadership, marketing
Completion: Three year graduation rate: 92%; credits needed to graduate: 66; target time to graduate: 2 years
College funded aid available: Domestic: Yes; International: Yes
Graduates with debt: 35%; average amount of debt $72,225

University of North Carolina–Pembroke

Public

ONLINE MBA PROGRAM(S)

www.uncp.edu/grad
Admissions: (910) 521-6271
Email: grad@uncp.edu
Financial aid: (910) 521-6255
Application deadline: rolling
Program can be completed entirely online: Yes
Total program cost: N/A
Tuition per credit: $208 full-time in-state, $208 part-time in-state, $736 full-time out-of-state, $736 part-time out-of-state
Acceptance rate: 100%
Average age of entrants: 32
Enrollment: 70, 36% men, 64% women, 49% minority
Most popular MBA concentrations: accounting, finance, general management, international business, marketing
Completion: Credits needed to graduate: 36
College funded aid available: Domestic: Yes; International: Yes
Graduates with debt: 66%; average amount of debt $31,800

Western Carolina University

Public

ONLINE BUSINESS PROGRAM(S)

www.wcu.edu/academics/edoutreach/distance-online-programs/index.asp
Admissions: (828) 227-7397
Email: distance@wcu.edu
Financial aid: (828) 227-7290
Application deadline: rolling
Program can be completed entirely online: Yes
Total program cost: N/A
Tuition per credit: $291 full-time in-state, $291 part-time in-state, $845 full-time out-of-state, $845 part-time out-of-state
Acceptance rate: 96%
Test scores required: GMAT or GRE
Average GMAT: 350
Average GRE: 146 verbal, 147 quantitative, 3.6 writing

Average age of entrants: 35
Enrollment: 189, 56% men, 44% women, 38% minority, 3% international
Average class size: 20
Completion: Three year graduation rate: 56%; credits needed to graduate: 36; target time to graduate: 2 years
College funded aid available: Domestic: Yes; International: Yes
Graduates with debt: 29%; average amount of debt $32,218

NORTH DAKOTA

Minot State University

Public

ONLINE BUSINESS PROGRAM(S)

www.minotstateu.edu/graduate/future_students/admission_requirements.shtml
Admissions: (701) 858-3413
Email: penny.brandt@minotstateu.edu
Financial aid: (701) 858-3875
Application deadline: Domestic: 07/30; International: 05/30
Program can be completed entirely online: Yes
Total program cost: $8,940 full-time in-state, $8,940 part-time in-state, $8,940 full-time out-of-state, $8,940 part-time out-of-state
Tuition per credit: $298 full-time in-state, $298 part-time in-state, $298 full-time out-of-state, $298 part-time out-of-state
Acceptance rate: 96%
Test scores required: GMAT or GRE
Average GRE: 149 verbal, 159 quantitative, 4.0 writing
Enrollment: 111, 71% men, 29% women, 46% minority
Average class size: 16
Most popular business concentrations: general management, management information systems
Completion: Three year graduation rate: 75%; credits needed to graduate: 30; target time to graduate: 2 years
College funded aid available: Domestic: Yes; International: Yes

University of North Dakota

Public

ONLINE MBA PROGRAM(S)

business.und.edu/academics/mba/index.cfm
Admissions: (701) 777-5892
Email: kate.menzies@und.edu
Financial aid: (701) 777-4409
Application deadline: rolling
Program can be completed entirely online: Yes
Total program cost: $19,152 full-time in-state, $19,152 part-time in-state, $19,152 full-time out-of-state, $19,152 part-time out-of-state

Tuition per credit: $383 full-time in-state, $383 part-time in-state, $383 full-time out-of-state, $383 part-time out-of-state
Acceptance rate: 79%
Test scores required: GMAT or GRE
Average GMAT: 581
Average GRE: 156 verbal, 153 quantitative, 4.0 writing
Average age of entrants: 32
Enrollment: 98, 79% men, 21% women, 5% minority, 7% international
Average class size: 20
Most popular MBA concentrations: entrepreneurship, general management, health care administration, marketing, public administration
Completion: Three year graduation rate: 64%; credits needed to graduate: 43; target time to graduate: 2.5 years
College funded aid available: Domestic: No; International: No
Graduates with debt: 36%; average amount of debt $19,123

ONLINE BUSINESS PROGRAM(S)

business.und.edu/academics/msae/index.cfm
Admissions: (701) 777-5892
Email: kate.menzies@und.edu
Financial aid: (701) 777-4409
Application deadline: rolling
Program can be completed entirely online: Yes
Total program cost: $14,112 full-time in-state, $14,112 part-time in-state, $14,112 full-time out-of-state, $14,112 part-time out-of-state
Tuition per credit: $383 full-time in-state, $383 part-time in-state, $383 full-time out-of-state, $383 part-time out-of-state
Acceptance rate: 58%
Test scores required: GMAT or GRE
Average GMAT: 645
Average GRE: 159 verbal, 158 quantitative, 4.0 writing
Average age of entrants: 41
Enrollment: 51, 86% men, 14% women, 8% minority, 10% international
Average class size: 18
Most popular business concentrations: economics
Completion: Three year graduation rate: 45%; credits needed to graduate: 30; target time to graduate: 2 years
College funded aid available: Domestic: No; International: No
Graduates with debt: 42%; average amount of debt $19,752

OHIO

Ashland University

Private

ONLINE MBA PROGRAM(S)

www.ashland.edu/graduate-admissions/mba-programs
Admissions: (419) 289-5214
Email: mba@ashland.edu
Financial aid: (419) 289-5002
Application deadline: rolling

Program can be completed entirely online: Yes
Total program cost: $24,450 full-time in-state, $24,450 part-time in-state, $24,450 full-time out-of-state, $24,450 part-time out-of-state
Tuition per credit: $815 full-time in-state, $815 part-time in-state, $815 full-time out-of-state, $815 part-time out-of-state
Acceptance rate: 87%
Test scores required: No
Average age of entrants: 27
Students with prior work experience: 100%
Enrollment: 270, 51% men, 49% women, 23% minority, 3% international
Average class size: 30
Most popular MBA concentrations: finance, human resources management, production/operations management, supply chain management/logistics, other
Completion: Three year graduation rate: 100%; credits needed to graduate: 30; target time to graduate: 2 years
College funded aid available: Domestic: Yes; International: No
Graduates with debt: 44%; average amount of debt $32,686

Baldwin Wallace University

Private

ONLINE MBA PROGRAM(S)

www.bw.edu/graduate-admission/
Admissions: (440) 826-2064
Email: bpeterso@bw.edu
Financial aid: (440) 826-2081
Application deadline: rolling
Program can be completed entirely online: No
Total program cost: N/A
Tuition per credit: $948 full-time in-state, $948 part-time in-state, $948 full-time out-of-state, $948 part-time out-of-state
Acceptance rate: 65%
Test scores required: GMAT
Average GMAT: N/A
Average age of entrants: 34
Students with prior work experience: 100%
Enrollment: 52, 56% men, 44% women, 12% minority
Average class size: 17
Most popular MBA concentrations: general management
Completion: Three year graduation rate: 79%; credits needed to graduate: 38; target time to graduate: 2 years
College funded aid available: Domestic: Yes; International: Yes
Graduates with debt: 43%; average amount of debt $38,068

Cedarville University

Private

ONLINE MBA PROGRAM(S)

www.cedarville.edu/admissions/graduate.aspx
Admissions: (888) 233-2784
Email: gradadmissions@cedarville.edu
Financial aid: (937) 766-7866
Application deadline: rolling
Program can be completed entirely online: Yes
Total program cost: $21,456 full-time in-state, $21,456 part-time in-state, $21,456 full-time out-of-state, $21,456 part-time out-of-state
Tuition per credit: $596 full-time in-state, $596 part-time in-state, $596 full-time out-of-state, $596 part-time out-of-state
Acceptance rate: 79%
Test scores required: No
Average age of entrants: 27
Students with prior work experience: 65%
Enrollment: 32, 78% men, 22% women, 6% minority, 3% international
Average class size: 8
Most popular MBA concentrations: general management, production/operations management, other
Completion: Three year graduation rate: 58%; credits needed to graduate: 36; target time to graduate: 2 years
College funded aid available: Domestic: No; International: No
Graduates with debt: 35%; average amount of debt $15,625

Cleveland State University (Ahuja)

Public

ONLINE MBA PROGRAM(S)

www.csuohio.edu/graduate-admissions
Admissions: (216) 687-9370
Email: d.easler@csuohio.edu
Financial aid: (216) 687-5411
Application deadline: rolling
Program can be completed entirely online: Yes
Total program cost: $35,000 full-time in-state, $35,000 part-time in-state, $35,000 full-time out-of-state, $35,000 part-time out-of-state
Tuition per credit: $1,029 full-time in-state, $1,029 part-time in-state, $1,029 full-time out-of-state, $1,029 part-time out-of-state
Acceptance rate: 79%
Test scores required: GMAT or GRE
Average GMAT: 625
Average GRE: 155 verbal, 155 quantitative, 2.8 writing
Average age of entrants: 28
Enrollment: 26, 62% men, 38% women, 23% minority, 4% international
Average class size: 17
Most popular MBA concentrations: general management

Completion: Three year graduation rate: 68%; credits needed to graduate: 34; target time to graduate: 1 year
College funded aid available: Domestic: Yes; International: Yes
Graduates with debt: 38%; average amount of debt $12,928

Kent State University

Public

ONLINE MBA PROGRAM(S)

www.kent.edu/business/online.mba
Admissions: (330) 672-2282
Email: gradbus@kent.edu
Financial aid: (330) 672-6000
Application deadline: rolling
Program can be completed entirely online: Yes
Total program cost: $29,880
full-time in-state, $29,880
part-time in-state, $29,880
full-time out-of-state, $29,880
part-time out-of-state
Tuition per credit: $830
full-time in-state, $830
part-time in-state, $830
full-time out-of-state, $830
part-time out-of-state
Test scores required: GMAT or GRE
Most popular MBA concentrations: international business, supply chain management/logistics, other
Completion: Credits needed to graduate: 36; target time to graduate: 2 years

Ohio Dominican University

Private

ONLINE MBA PROGRAM(S)

ohiodominican.edu
Admissions: (614) 251-4721
Email: naughtoj@ohiodominican.edu
Financial aid: (614) 251-4954
Application deadline: rolling
Program can be completed entirely online: Yes
Total program cost: $21,600
full-time in-state, $21,600
part-time in-state, $21,600
full-time out-of-state, $21,600
part-time out-of-state
Tuition per credit: $600
full-time in-state, $600
part-time in-state, $600
full-time out-of-state, $600
part-time out-of-state
Acceptance rate: 93%
Test scores required: No
Average age of entrants: 34
Enrollment: 230, 51% men, 49% women, 30% minority, 2% international
Average class size: 13
Completion: Three year graduation rate: 73%; credits needed to graduate: 36; target time to graduate: 2 years
College funded aid available: Domestic: No; International: No
Graduates with debt: 55%

Ohio University

Public

ONLINE MBA PROGRAM(S)

onlinemba.ohio.edu
Admissions: (800) 622-3124
Email: mba@ohio.edu
Financial aid: (740) 593-9853
Application deadline: rolling
Program can be completed entirely online: Yes
Total program cost: $35,140
part-time in-state, $35,805
part-time out-of-state
Tuition per credit: $1,004
part-time in-state, $1,023
part-time out-of-state
Acceptance rate: 81%
Test scores required: No
Average age of entrants: 32
Students with prior work experience: 100%
Enrollment: 815, 60% men, 40% women, 21% minority, 1% international
Average class size: 54
Most popular MBA concentrations: finance, general management, health care administration, other
Completion: Three year graduation rate: 77%; credits needed to graduate: 35; target time to graduate: 2 years
College funded aid available: Domestic: No; International: No
Graduates with debt: 47%; average amount of debt $15,100

ONLINE BUSINESS PROGRAM(S)

onlinemba.ohio.edu
Admissions: (800) 622-3124
Email: mba@ohio.edu
Financial aid: (740) 593-9853
Application deadline: rolling
Program can be completed entirely online: Yes
Total program cost: $35,140
part-time in-state, $35,805
part-time out-of-state
Tuition per credit: $1,004
full-time in-state, $1,004
part-time in-state, $1,023
full-time out-of-state, $1,023
part-time out-of-state
Acceptance rate: 81%
Test scores required: No
Average age of entrants: 32
Students with prior work experience: 100%
Enrollment: 815, 60% men, 40% women, 21% minority, 1% international
Average class size: 54
Most popular business concentrations: finance, general management, health care administration, other
Completion: Three year graduation rate: 77%; credits needed to graduate: 35; target time to graduate: 2 years
College funded aid available: Domestic: No; International: No
Graduates with debt: 47%; average amount of debt $15,100

University of Cincinnati

Public

ONLINE MBA PROGRAM(S)

aponline.uc.edu/programs/master-of-business-administration.aspx#admissions
Admissions: (513) 556-7024
Email: jason.dickman@uc.edu
Financial aid: (513) 556-3076
Application deadline: rolling
Program can be completed entirely online: Yes
Total program cost: $28,920
full-time in-state, $30,628
part-time in-state, $40,677
full-time out-of-state, $31,198
part-time out-of-state
Tuition per credit: $964
full-time in-state, $806
part-time in-state, $1,356
full-time out-of-state, $821
part-time out-of-state
Acceptance rate: 76%
Test scores required: GMAT or GRE
Average GMAT: 616
Average GRE: 159 verbal, 158 quantitative, 4.0 writing
Average age of entrants: 34
Students with prior work experience: 97%
Enrollment: 218, 56% men, 44% women, 20% minority, 2% international
Average class size: 45
Most popular MBA concentrations: health care administration, marketing, other
Completion: Three year graduation rate: 42%; credits needed to graduate: 38; target time to graduate: 1.5 years
College funded aid available: Domestic: Yes; International: Yes
Graduates with debt: 48%; average amount of debt $42,987

ONLINE BUSINESS PROGRAM(S)

aponline.uc.edu/programs/ms-in-taxation.aspx
Admissions: (513) 556-7024
Email: jason.dickman@uc.edu
Financial aid: (513) 556-3076
Application deadline: rolling
Program can be completed entirely online: Yes
Total program cost: $28,920
full-time in-state, $24,180
part-time in-state, $36,177
full-time out-of-state, $24,630
part-time out-of-state
Tuition per credit: $964
full-time in-state, $806
part-time in-state, $1,206
full-time out-of-state, $821
part-time out-of-state
Acceptance rate: 88%
Test scores required: GMAT or GRE
Average GMAT: 420
Average age of entrants: 36
Students with prior work experience: 85%
Enrollment: 44, 52% men, 48% women, 16% minority
Average class size: 22
Most popular business concentrations: tax, other

Completion: Three year graduation rate: 65%; credits needed to graduate: 30; target time to graduate: 2 years
College funded aid available: Domestic: Yes; International: Yes
Graduates with debt: 40%

University of Dayton

Private

ONLINE MBA PROGRAM(S)

onlinemba.udayton.edu/admission/
Admissions: (937) 229-1850
Email: gradadmission@udayton.edu
Financial aid: N/A
Application deadline: rolling
Program can be completed entirely online: No
Total program cost: $37,500
full-time in-state, $37,500
part-time in-state, $37,500
full-time out-of-state, $37,500
part-time out-of-state
Tuition per credit: $1,250
full-time in-state, $1,250
part-time in-state, $1,250
full-time out-of-state, $1,250
part-time out-of-state
Acceptance rate: 81%
Average age of entrants: 35
Enrollment: 20, 85% men, 15% women, N/A minority, N/A international
Completion: Credits needed to graduate: 30; target time to graduate: 2.5 years

University of Findlay

Private

ONLINE MBA PROGRAM(S)

www.findlay.edu
Admissions: (800) 472-9502
Email: admissions@findlay.edu
Financial aid: (419) 434-5678
Application deadline: rolling
Program can be completed entirely online: Yes
Total program cost: $21,780
full-time in-state, $21,780
part-time in-state, $21,780
full-time out-of-state, $21,780
part-time out-of-state
Tuition per credit: $660
full-time in-state, $660
part-time in-state, $660
full-time out-of-state, $660
part-time out-of-state
Acceptance rate: 88%
Test scores required: No
Average age of entrants: 23
Enrollment: 373, 53% men, 47% women, 2% minority, 36% international
Average class size: 20
Most popular MBA concentrations: accounting, general management, health care administration
Completion: Credits needed to graduate: 33; target time to graduate: 1.5 years
College funded aid available: Domestic: Yes; International: Yes

Walsh University

Private

ONLINE MBA PROGRAM(S)

www.walsh.edu/graduate-programs
Admissions: (330) 490-7181
Email: adice@walsh.edu
Financial aid: (330) 490-7146
Application deadline: rolling
Program can be completed entirely online: Yes
Total program cost: $12,330
full-time in-state, $8,220
part-time in-state, $12,330
full-time out-of-state, $8,220
part-time out-of-state
Tuition per credit: $685
full-time in-state, $685
part-time in-state, $685
full-time out-of-state, $685
part-time out-of-state
Acceptance rate: 78%
Test scores required: GMAT
Average GMAT: 483
Enrollment: 200, 42% men, 58% women, 9% minority, 3% international
Average class size: 15
Most popular MBA concentrations: entrepreneurship, general management, health care administration, marketing
Completion: Credits needed to graduate: 36; target time to graduate: 2 years
College funded aid available: Domestic: Yes; International: No
Graduates with debt: 59%; average amount of debt $42,752

Wright State University (Soin)

Public

ONLINE MBA PROGRAM(S)

www.wright.edu/onlinemba
Admissions: (937) 775-2437
Email: mba@wright.edu
Financial aid: (937) 775-5721
Application deadline: rolling
Program can be completed entirely online: No
Total program cost: $29,760
full-time in-state, $29,760
part-time in-state, $50,732
full-time out-of-state, $50,732
part-time out-of-state
Tuition per credit: $640
full-time in-state, $640
part-time in-state, $1,091
full-time out-of-state, $1,091
part-time out-of-state
Acceptance rate: 84%
Test scores required: No
Average GMAT: 456
Average GRE: 147 verbal, 151 quantitative, 3.0 writing
Average age of entrants: 30
Enrollment: 667, 55% men, 45% women, 16% minority, 16% international
Average class size: 28
Most popular MBA concentrations: economics, finance, general management, marketing, quantitative analysis/statistics and operations research
Completion: Credits needed to graduate: 46; target time to graduate: 2 years

College funded aid available:
Domestic: Yes
Graduates with debt: 38%;
average amount of debt $40,375

ONLINE BUSINESS PROGRAM(S)
www.wright.edu/graduate-school/admissions/apply-now
Admissions: (937) 775-2895
Email: Donald.Hopkins@wright.edu
Financial aid: (937) 775-5721
Application deadline: rolling
Program can be completed entirely online: No
Total program cost: $29,335
full-time in-state, $40,425
full-time out-of-state
Tuition per credit: $889 full-time in-state, $915 part-time in-state, $1,225 full-time out-of-state, $1,225 part-time out-of-state
Acceptance rate: 72%
Test scores required: No
Average GMAT: 892
Average GRE: 146 verbal, 150 quantitative, 3.2 writing
Students with prior work experience: 12%
Enrollment: 33, 67% men, 33% women, N/A minority, N/A international
Average class size: 18
Most popular business concentrations: management information systems, supply chain management/logistics
Completion: Three year graduation rate: 97%; credits needed to graduate: 33; target time to graduate: 1 year
College funded aid available:
Domestic: Yes

OKLAHOMA

Cameron University
Public

ONLINE MBA PROGRAM(S)
www.cameron.edu/business/graduate
Admissions: (580) 581-2289
Email: admissions@cameron.edu
Financial aid: (580) 581-2293
Application deadline: rolling
Program can be completed entirely online: Yes
Total program cost: $10,230
full-time in-state, $10,230
part-time in-state, $13,530
full-time out-of-state, $13,530
part-time out-of-state
Tuition per credit: $310 full-time in-state, $310 part-time in-state, $410 full-time out-of-state, $410 part-time out-of-state
Acceptance rate: 66%
Test scores required:
GMAT or GRE
Average GMAT: 480
Average age of entrants: 32
Students with prior work experience: 93%
Enrollment: 128, 52% men, 48% women, 18% minority, 27% international
Average class size: 14
Completion: Three year graduation rate: 18%; credits needed to graduate: 33; target time to graduate: 2 years

College funded aid available: Domestic: Yes;
International: Yes
Graduates with debt: 23%;
average amount of debt $17,407

Oklahoma City University
Private

ONLINE BUSINESS PROGRAM(S)
www.okcu.edu/admissions/graduate/
Admissions: (405) 208-5094
Email: maharrington@okcu.edu
Financial aid: (405) 208-5154
Application deadline: rolling
Program can be completed entirely online: Depends
Total program cost: $17,700
full-time in-state, $17,700
part-time in-state, $17,700
full-time out-of-state, $17,700
part-time out-of-state
Tuition per credit: $590
full-time in-state, $590
part-time in-state, $590
full-time out-of-state, $590
part-time out-of-state
Acceptance rate: 91%
Test scores required: No
Average GMAT: 355
Average age of entrants: 35
Students with prior work experience: 100%
Enrollment: 199, 68% men, 32% women, 24% minority
Average class size: 22
Most popular business concentrations: economics, finance, general management, leadership, public policy
Completion: Credits needed to graduate: 30; target time to graduate: 2 years
College funded aid available: Domestic: Yes
Graduates with debt: 23%;
average amount of debt $26,931

Oklahoma State University (Spears)
Public

ONLINE MBA PROGRAM(S)
business.okstate.edu/watson/mba/index.html
Admissions: (405) 744-2951
Email: spearsmasters@okstate.edu
Financial aid: (405) 744-6604
Application deadline: Domestic: 07/01; International: 03/01
Program can be completed entirely online: Yes
Total program cost: $9,378
full-time in-state, $9,378
part-time in-state, $12,946
full-time out-of-state, $12,946
part-time out-of-state
Tuition per credit: $223
full-time in-state, $223
part-time in-state, $308
full-time out-of-state, $308
part-time out-of-state
Acceptance rate: 82%
Test scores required:
GMAT or GRE
Average GMAT: 563
Average GRE: 152 verbal, 152 quantitative, 3.8 writing
Average age of entrants: 29

Students with prior work experience: 97%
Enrollment: 285, 78% men, 22% women, 19% minority, 1% international
Average class size: 21
Most popular MBA concentrations: entrepreneurship, human resources management, management information systems, not-for-profit management, other
Completion: Three year graduation rate: 56%; credits needed to graduate: 42; target time to graduate: 2.5 years
College funded aid available: Domestic: No; International: No
Graduates with debt: 8%;
average amount of debt $31,994

ONLINE BUSINESS PROGRAM(S)
business.okstate.edu/watson/
Admissions: (405) 744-2951
Email: spearsmasters@okstate.edu
Financial aid: (405) 744-6604
Application deadline: Domestic: 07/01; International: 03/01
Program can be completed entirely online: Yes
Total program cost: $7,368
full-time in-state, $7,368
part-time in-state, $10,172
full-time out-of-state, $10,172
part-time out-of-state
Tuition per credit: $223
full-time in-state, $223
part-time in-state, $308
full-time out-of-state, $308
part-time out-of-state
Acceptance rate: 94%
Test scores required:
GMAT or GRE
Average GMAT: 502
Average GRE: 153 verbal, 154 quantitative, 4.0 writing
Average age of entrants: 32
Students with prior work experience: 89%
Enrollment: 85, 79% men, 21% women, 24% minority, 6% international
Average class size: 21
Most popular business concentrations: entrepreneurship, management information systems, not-for-profit management
Completion: Three year graduation rate: 39%; credits needed to graduate: 33; target time to graduate: 3 years
College funded aid available: Domestic: No; International: No
Graduates with debt: 15%;
average amount of debt $10,221

University of Oklahoma
Public

ONLINE BUSINESS PROGRAM(S)
www.ou.edu/content/admissions/apply/graduate.html
Admissions: (405) 325-6765
Email: gradadm@ou.edu
Financial aid: (405) 325-4521
Application deadline: N/A
Total program cost: N/A
Tuition per credit: $213 full-time in-state, $213 part-time in-state, $824 full-time out-of-state, $824 part-time out-of-state

University of Tulsa (Collins)
Private

ONLINE BUSINESS PROGRAM(S)
business.utulsa.edu/
Admissions: (918) 631-2242
Email: graduate-business@utulsa.edu
Financial aid: (918) 631-2527
Application deadline: rolling
Program can be completed entirely online: Depends
Total program cost: $30,600
full-time in-state, $30,600
part-time in-state, $30,600
full-time out-of-state, $30,600
part-time out-of-state
Tuition per credit: $900
full-time in-state, $900
part-time in-state, $900
full-time out-of-state, $900
part-time out-of-state
Acceptance rate: 92%
Test scores required:
GMAT or GRE
Average GMAT: 567
Average age of entrants: 33
Students with prior work experience: 100%
Enrollment: 115, 82% men, 18% women, 12% minority, 5% international
Average class size: 18
Completion: Credits needed to graduate: 34; target time to graduate: 2 years
College funded aid available: Domestic: No; International: No

OREGON

Northwest Christian University
Private

ONLINE MBA PROGRAM(S)
www.nwcu.edu/graduate/
Admissions: (541) 684-7201
Email: admissions@nwcu.edu
Financial aid: (541) 684-7291
Application deadline: N/A
Program can be completed entirely online: Yes
Total program cost: $23,400
full-time in-state, $23,400
part-time in-state, $23,400
full-time out-of-state, $23,400
part-time out-of-state
Tuition per credit: $650
full-time in-state, $650
part-time in-state, $650
full-time out-of-state, $650
part-time out-of-state
Enrollment: 116, 53% men, 47% women, 26% minority
Most popular MBA concentrations: accounting, other
Completion: Credits needed to graduate: 36; target time to graduate: 1 year

Portland State University
Public

ONLINE MBA PROGRAM(S)
thehealthcaremba.org/
Admissions: (503) 725-8001
Email: gradadmissions.sba@pdx.edu
Financial aid: N/A
Application deadline: Domestic: 06/01; International: 06/01
Program can be completed entirely online: No
Total program cost: $41,904
full-time in-state, $41,904
part-time out-of-state
Tuition per credit: $582
full-time in-state, $582
part-time in-state, $582
full-time out-of-state, $582
part-time out-of-state
Acceptance rate: 75%
Average GMAT: 675
Average GRE: 162 verbal, 154 quantitative, 4.3 writing
Average age of entrants: 39
Students with prior work experience: 100%
Enrollment: 119, 51% men, 49% women, N/A minority, N/A international
Average class size: 46
Most popular MBA concentrations: health care administration
Completion: Three year graduation rate: 81%; credits needed to graduate: 72; target time to graduate: 3 years

ONLINE BUSINESS PROGRAM(S)
www.pdx.edu/sba/graduate-business-programs-admissions
Admissions: (503) 725-8001
Email: gradadmissions.sba@pdx.edu
Financial aid: (503) 725-5442
Application deadline: rolling
Program can be completed entirely online: No
Total program cost: $36,868
full-time in-state, $36,868
part-time in-state, $39,936
full-time out-of-state, $39,936
part-time out-of-state
Tuition per credit: $709 full-time in-state, $709 part-time in-state, $768 full-time out-of-state, $768 part-time out-of-state
Acceptance rate: 67%
Test scores required: No
Average GMAT: 547
Average GRE: 153 verbal, 150 quantitative, 4.0 writing
Average age of entrants: 36
Students with prior work experience: 91%
Enrollment: 34, 59% men, 41% women, 18% minority, 12% international
Average class size: 36
Most popular business concentrations: supply chain management/logistics
Completion: Three year graduation rate: 74%; credits needed to graduate: 52; target time to graduate: 2 years
College funded aid available: Domestic: Yes; International: Yes

PENNSYLVANIA

California University of Pennsylvania
Public

ONLINE MBA PROGRAM(S)
www.calu.edu/academics/
graduate-programs/
business-administration/
admissions/index.htm
Admissions: (724) 938-5900
Email: chawdry@calu.edu
Financial aid: (724) 938-4415
Application deadline: rolling
Program can be completed
entirely online: Yes
Total program cost: $18,000
full-time in-state, $18,000
part-time in-state, $27,000
full-time out-of-state, $27,000
part-time out-of-state
Tuition per credit: $500
full-time in-state, $500
part-time in-state, $750
full-time out-of-state, $750
part-time out-of-state
Acceptance rate: 65%
Test scores required: No
Average age of entrants: 35
Enrollment: 110, 50% men,
50% women, 13% minority,
1% international
Average class size: 31
Most popular MBA concentrations:
entrepreneurship, health
care administration
Completion: Credits needed
to graduate: 36; target
time to graduate: 1 year
College funded aid available:
Domestic: Yes
Graduates with debt: 45%;
average amount of debt $41,000

ONLINE BUSINESS PROGRAM(S)
www.calu.edu/academics/
online-programs/index.htm
Admissions: (724) 938-4000
Email: calugo@calu.edu
Financial aid: N/A
Application deadline: rolling
Program can be completed
entirely online: Yes
Total program cost: $18,000
full-time in-state, $18,000
part-time in-state, $27,000
full-time out-of-state, $27,000
part-time out-of-state
Tuition per credit: $500
full-time in-state, $500
part-time in-state, $750
full-time out-of-state, $750
part-time out-of-state
Acceptance rate: 71%
Test scores required: No
Average age of entrants: 29
Enrollment: 118, 64% men,
36% women, 13% minority
Average class size: 31
Most popular business
concentrations:
entrepreneurship, general
management, health care
administration, international
business, leadership
Completion: Credits needed
to graduate: 36; target
time to graduate: 1 year
College funded aid
available: Domestic: Yes;
International: Yes
Graduates with debt: 60%;
average amount of debt $41,000

Carnegie Mellon University (Tepper)
Private

ONLINE MBA PROGRAM(S)
tepper.cmu.edu/
prospective-students/masters/
mba/program-options
Admissions: (412) 268-2273
Email: mba-admissions@
andrew.cmu.edu
Financial aid: (412) 268-7581
Application deadline: Domestic:
04/20; International: 04/20
Program can be completed
entirely online: No
Total program cost: $128,000
part-time in-state, $128,000
part-time out-of-state
Tuition per credit: $1,998
full-time in-state, $1,998
part-time in-state, $1,998
full-time out-of-state, $1,998
part-time out-of-state
Acceptance rate: 54%
Test scores required:
GMAT or GRE
Average GMAT: 651
Average GRE: 155 verbal, 163
quantitative, 4.0 writing
Average age of entrants: 29
Students with prior work
experience: 97%
Enrollment: 146, 29% men,
71% women, 38% minority,
14% international
Average class size: 24
Most popular MBA concentrations:
entrepreneurship, finance,
marketing, production/
operations management,
technology
Completion: Three year
graduation rate: 100%; credits
needed to graduate: 64; target
time to graduate: 2.5 years
College funded aid available:
Domestic: No; International: No
Graduates with debt:
44%; average amount
of debt $90,445

Chatham University
Private

ONLINE MBA PROGRAM(S)
www.chatham.edu/admission/
Admissions: (412) 365-1290
Email: admission@chatham.edu
Financial aid: (412) 365-2781
Application deadline: Domestic:
07/01; International: 07/01
Program can be completed
entirely online: Yes
Total program cost: N/A
Tuition per credit: $903
full-time in-state, $903
part-time in-state, $903
full-time out-of-state, $903
part-time out-of-state
Acceptance rate: 100%
Test scores required: No
Average age of entrants: 31
Students with prior work
experience: 100%
Enrollment: 18, 22% men,
78% women, 11% minority,
17% international
Average class size: 15
Most popular MBA
concentrations: health
care administration

Completion: Credits needed
to graduate: 36; target time
to graduate: 2 years
College funded aid available:
Domestic: Yes

Clarion University of Pennsylvania
Public

ONLINE MBA PROGRAM(S)
www.clarion.edu/admissions
Admissions: (814) 393-2306
Email: gradstudies@clarion.edu
Financial aid: (814) 393-2315
Application deadline: rolling
Program can be completed
entirely online: Yes
Total program cost: $15,000
full-time in-state, $15,000
part-time in-state, $16,200
full-time out-of-state, $16,200
part-time out-of-state
Tuition per credit: $500
full-time in-state, $500
part-time in-state, $540
full-time out-of-state, $540
part-time out-of-state
Acceptance rate: 92%
Test scores required:
GMAT or GRE
Average GMAT: 520
Average age of entrants: 29
Students with prior work
experience: 82%
Enrollment: 140, 50% men,
50% women, 14% minority,
4% international
Average class size: 29
Most popular MBA concentrations:
entrepreneurship, finance,
health care administration,
international business, not-
for-profit management
Completion: Three year
graduation rate: 49%; credits
needed to graduate: 30; target
time to graduate: 2.5 years
College funded aid
available: Domestic: Yes;
International: Yes
Graduates with debt: 56%;
average amount of debt $31,768

ONLINE BUSINESS PROGRAM(S)
www.clarion.edu/admissions
Admissions: (814) 393-2306
Email: gradstudies@clarion.edu
Financial aid: (814) 393-2315
Application deadline: rolling
Program can be completed
entirely online: Yes
Total program cost: $15,000
full-time in-state, $15,000
part-time in-state, $16,200
full-time out-of-state, $16,200
part-time out-of-state
Tuition per credit: $500
full-time in-state, $500
part-time in-state, $540
full-time out-of-state, $540
part-time out-of-state
Acceptance rate: 100%
Test scores required: No
Average GMAT: 475
Average age of entrants: 32
Students with prior work
experience: 63%
Enrollment: 19, 32% men,
68% women, 16% minority,
5% international
Average class size: 17

Most popular business
concentrations: accounting
Completion: Credits needed
to graduate: 30; target time
to graduate: 1.5 years
College funded aid
available: Domestic: Yes;
International: Yes
Graduates with debt: 50%;
average amount of debt $10,141

DeSales University
Private

ONLINE MBA PROGRAM(S)
www.desales.edu/home/
admissions-financial-aid
Admissions: (610) 282-1100
Email:
gradadmissions@desales.edu
Financial aid: (610) 282-1100
Application deadline: rolling
Program can be completed
entirely online: Yes
Total program cost: N/A
Tuition per credit: $840
full-time in-state, $840
part-time in-state, $840
full-time out-of-state, $840
part-time out-of-state
Acceptance rate: 87%
Test scores required: No
Average age of entrants: 34
Students with prior work
experience: 100%
Enrollment: 625, 48%
men, 52% women, 24%
minority, 1% international
Average class size: 14
Most popular MBA
concentrations: accounting,
general management,
health care administration,
marketing, supply chain
management/logistics
Completion: Three year
graduation rate: 60%; credits
needed to graduate: 36; target
time to graduate: 2.5 years
College funded aid
available: Domestic: Yes;
International: Yes
Graduates with debt: 15%;
average amount of debt $9,200

Delaware Valley University
Private

ONLINE MBA PROGRAM(S)
www.delval.edu/admission/
graduate-admission
Admissions: (215) 489-4469
Email:
pamela.heffner@delval.edu
Financial aid: (215) 489-2975
Application deadline: rolling
Program can be completed
entirely online: Yes
Total program cost: $1,604
full-time in-state, $802
part-time in-state, $1,604
full-time out-of-state, $802
part-time out-of-state
Tuition per credit: $802
full-time in-state, $802
part-time in-state, $802
full-time out-of-state, $802
part-time out-of-state
Acceptance rate: 98%
Test scores required: No
Average age of entrants: 33

Students with prior work
experience: 97%
Enrollment: 115, 55% men,
45% women, 16% minority,
1% international
Average class size: 12
Most popular MBA
concentrations: general
management, supply chain
management/logistics, other
Completion: Three year
graduation rate: 72%; credits
needed to graduate: 30; target
time to graduate: 3.5 years
College funded aid available:
Domestic: No; International: No

Drexel University (LeBow)
Private

ONLINE MBA PROGRAM(S)
www.lebow.drexel.edu/
academics/graduate/resources/
admissions
Admissions: (215) 895-0285
Email: mba@drexel.edu
Financial aid: (215) 571-4545
Application deadline: rolling
Program can be completed
entirely online: Yes
Total program cost: $64,005
part-time in-state, $64,005
part-time out-of-state
Tuition per credit: $1,306
full-time in-state, $1,306
part-time in-state, $1,306
full-time out-of-state, $1,306
part-time out-of-state
Acceptance rate: 92%
Test scores required:
GMAT or GRE
Average GMAT: 567
Average age of entrants: 34
Students with prior work
experience: 100%
Enrollment: 190, 56%
men, 44% women, 34%
minority, 5% international
Average class size: 25
Most popular MBA concentrations:
entrepreneurship,
finance, marketing
Completion: Three year
graduation rate: 89%; credits
needed to graduate: 49; target
time to graduate: 2.5 years
College funded aid
available: Domestic: Yes;
International: Yes
Graduates with debt: 69%;
average amount of debt $57,629

Duquesne University (Palumbo-Donahue)
Private

ONLINE BUSINESS PROGRAM(S)
www.duq.edu/academics/
schools/business/graduate
Admissions: (412) 396-6276
Email: grad-bus@duq.edu
Financial aid: (412) 396-6607
Application deadline: rolling
Program can be completed
entirely online: Yes
Total program cost: $28,020
full-time in-state, $28,020
part-time in-state, $28,020
full-time out-of-state, $28,020
part-time out-of-state

Tuition per credit: $934
full-time in-state, $934
part-time in-state, $934
full-time out-of-state, $934
part-time out-of-state
Acceptance rate: 91%
Test scores required:
GMAT or GRE
Average GMAT: 513
Average GRE: 151 verbal, 145
quantitative, 4.0 writing
Average age of entrants: 32
**Students with prior work
experience:** 76%
Enrollment: 37, 54% men,
46% women, 16% minority,
3% international
Average class size: 13
Completion: Credits needed
to graduate: 30; target time
to graduate: 2 years
College funded aid available:
Domestic: No; International: No

La Salle University

Private

ONLINE MBA PROGRAM(S)

www.lasalle.edu/grad/
Admissions: (215) 951-1100
Email: grad@lasalle.edu
Financial aid: (215) 951-1974
Application deadline: rolling
**Program can be completed
entirely online:** Yes
Total program cost: $34,983
full-time in-state, $34,983
part-time in-state, $34,983
full-time out-of-state, $34,983
part-time out-of-state
Tuition per credit: $897 full-time
in-state, $897 part-time in-state,
$897 full-time out-of-state,
$897 part-time out-of-state
**Most popular MBA
concentrations:** accounting,
finance, general management,
marketing, management
information systems
Completion: Credits needed
to graduate: 36; target time
to graduate: 2.5 years

Lehigh University

Private

ONLINE MBA PROGRAM(S)

www.lehigh.edu/mba
Admissions: (610) 758-3418
Email:
mba.admissions@lehigh.edu
Financial aid: (610) 758-5285
Application deadline: rolling
**Program can be completed
entirely online:** No
Total program cost: $39,075
full-time in-state, $39,075
part-time in-state, $39,075
full-time out-of-state, $39,075
part-time out-of-state
Tuition per credit: $1,075
full-time in-state, $1,075
part-time in-state, $1,075
full-time out-of-state, $1,075
part-time out-of-state
Acceptance rate: 77%
Test scores required:
GMAT or GRE
Average GMAT: 636
Average GRE: 156 verbal, 158
quantitative, 4.0 writing
Average age of entrants: 34

**Students with prior work
experience:** 100%
Enrollment: 200, 74%
men, 26% women, 16%
minority, 4% international
Average class size: 23
**Most popular MBA
concentrations:** finance,
international business,
marketing, supply chain
management/logistics
Completion: Three year
graduation rate: 75%; credits
needed to graduate: 36; target
time to graduate: 3 years
**College funded aid
available:** Domestic: Yes;
International: Yes
Graduates with debt: 5%;
average amount of debt $13,525

Pennsylvania State University– World Campus

Public

ONLINE MBA PROGRAM(S)

www.worldcampus.psu.edu/
admissions
Admissions: (800) 252-3592
Email: wdadmissions@
outreach.psu.edu
Financial aid: (800) 252-3592
Application deadline: rolling
**Program can be completed
entirely online:** No
Total program cost: $56,880
full-time in-state, $56,880
part-time in-state, $56,880
full-time out-of-state, $56,880
part-time out-of-state
Tuition per credit: $1,185
full-time in-state, $1,185
part-time in-state, $1,185
full-time out-of-state, $1,185
part-time out-of-state
Acceptance rate: 83%
Test scores required:
GMAT or GRE
Average GMAT: 542
Average GRE: 154 verbal, 150
quantitative, 4.0 writing
Average age of entrants: 33
**Students with prior work
experience:** 100%
Enrollment: 259, 66%
men, 34% women, 19%
minority, 3% international
Average class size: 27
**Most popular MBA
concentrations:** accounting,
entrepreneurship, finance,
human resources management,
quantitative analysis/statistics
and operations research
Completion: Three year
graduation rate: 87%; credits
needed to graduate: 48; target
time to graduate: 2 years
**College funded aid
available:** Domestic: Yes;
International: Yes
Graduates with debt: 35%;
average amount of debt $47,083

ONLINE BUSINESS PROGRAM(S)

www.worldcampus.psu.edu/
admissions
Admissions: (800) 252-3592
Email: wdadmissions@
outreach.psu.edu
Financial aid: (800) 252-3592
Application deadline: rolling

**Program can be completed
entirely online:** Depends
Total program cost: $31,650
full-time in-state, $31,650
part-time in-state, $31,650
full-time out-of-state, $31,650
part-time out-of-state
Tuition per credit: $1,055
full-time in-state, $1,055
part-time in-state, $1,055
full-time out-of-state, $1,055
part-time out-of-state
Acceptance rate: 78%
Test scores required:
GMAT or GRE
Average GMAT: 549
Average GRE: 154 verbal, 154
quantitative, 4.0 writing
Average age of entrants: 33
**Students with prior work
experience:** 89%
Enrollment: 637, 69% men,
31% women, 21% minority,
14% international
Average class size: 20
**Most popular business
concentrations:** accounting,
finance, general management,
manufacturing and technology
management, supply chain
management/logistics
Completion: Three year
graduation rate: 81%; credits
needed to graduate: 30; target
time to graduate: 2 years
**College funded aid
available:** Domestic: Yes;
International: Yes
Graduates with debt: 27%;
average amount of debt $35,246

Point Park University

Private

ONLINE MBA PROGRAM(S)

online.pointpark.edu/
admissions/
Admissions: (412) 392-3808
Email: enroll@pointpark.edu
Financial aid: (412) 392-3930
Application deadline: rolling
**Program can be completed
entirely online:** Yes
Total program cost: N/A
Tuition per credit: $595
full-time in-state, $595
part-time in-state, $595
full-time out-of-state, $595
part-time out-of-state
Acceptance rate: 88%
Test scores required: No
Enrollment: 78, 38% men,
62% women, 23% minority
Average class size: 20
Completion: Credits needed
to graduate: 36; target time
to graduate: 1.5 years
College funded aid available:
Domestic: No; International: No

ONLINE BUSINESS PROGRAM(S)

online.pointpark.edu
Admissions: (412) 392-3808
Email: enroll@pointpark.edu
Financial aid: (412) 392-3930
Application deadline: rolling
**Program can be completed
entirely online:** Yes
Total program cost: N/A
Tuition per credit: $595
full-time in-state, $595
part-time in-state, $595
full-time out-of-state, $595
part-time out-of-state
Acceptance rate: 84%

Test scores required: No
Enrollment: 56, 21% men,
79% women, 25% minority
Average class size: 15

Robert Morris University

Private

ONLINE MBA PROGRAM(S)

www.rmu.edu/online
Admissions: (412) 397-6300
Email:
onlineadmissions@rmu.edu
Financial aid: (412) 397-6250
Application deadline: rolling
**Program can be completed
entirely online:** Yes
Total program cost: N/A
Tuition per credit: $925
full-time in-state, $925
part-time in-state, $925
full-time out-of-state, $925
part-time out-of-state
Acceptance rate: 100%
Test scores required: GMAT
Average GMAT: 570
Average age of entrants: 30
**Students with prior work
experience:** 71%
Enrollment: 87, 66% men,
34% women, 1% minority
Average class size: 9
**Most popular MBA
concentrations:** finance
Completion: Three year
graduation rate: 82%; credits
needed to graduate: 36
Graduates with debt: 28%;
average amount of debt $34,662

ONLINE BUSINESS PROGRAM(S)

www.rmu.edu/online
Admissions: (412) 397-6300
Email:
onlineadmissions@rmu.edu
Financial aid: (412) 397-6250
Application deadline: rolling
**Program can be completed
entirely online:** Yes
Total program cost: N/A
Tuition per credit: $905
full-time in-state, $905
part-time in-state, $905
full-time out-of-state, $905
part-time out-of-state
Acceptance rate: 100%
Average GMAT: 570
Average age of entrants: 29
**Students with prior work
experience:** 100%
Enrollment: 21, 24% men,
76% women, 10% minority
Average class size: 14
**Most popular business
concentrations:** human
resources management
Completion: Credits
needed to graduate: 30
Graduates with debt:
50%; average amount
of debt $30,034

Saint Vincent College

Private

ONLINE BUSINESS PROGRAM(S)

www.stvincent.edu/
admission-aid/
graduate-students
Admissions: N/A
Financial aid: N/A
Application deadline: rolling

**Program can be completed
entirely online:** Depends
Total program cost: $23,832
full-time in-state, $23,832
part-time in-state, $23,832
full-time out-of-state, $23,832
part-time out-of-state
Tuition per credit: $662
full-time in-state, $662
part-time in-state, $662
full-time out-of-state, $662
part-time out-of-state
Acceptance rate: 79%
Test scores required: No
Average GMAT: 550
Average age of entrants: 35
**Students with prior work
experience:** 82%
Enrollment: 34, 59% men,
41% women, 15% minority,
15% international
Average class size: 11
**Most popular business
concentrations:** general
management, leadership,
production/operations
management, organizational
behavior, quantitative
analysis/statistics and
operations research
Completion: Credits needed
to graduate: 6; target time
to graduate: 2 years
**College funded aid
available:** Domestic: Yes;
International: Yes
Graduates with debt: 10%

Shippensburg University of Pennsylvania (Grove)

Public

ONLINE MBA PROGRAM(S)

www.ship.edu/graduate
Admissions: (717) 477-1213
Email: gradschool@ship.edu
Financial aid: (717) 477-1131
Application deadline: rolling
**Program can be completed
entirely online:** Depends
Total program cost: $18,180
full-time in-state, $18,180
part-time in-state, $18,840
full-time out-of-state, $18,840
part-time out-of-state
Tuition per credit: $500
full-time in-state, $500
part-time in-state, $510
full-time out-of-state, $510
part-time out-of-state
Acceptance rate: 88%
Test scores required: No
Average GMAT: 533
Average age of entrants: 31
**Students with prior work
experience:** 96%
Enrollment: 172, 63% men,
37% women, 3% minority
Average class size: 18
**Most popular MBA
concentrations:** finance, health
care administration, supply
chain management/logistics,
quantitative analysis/statistics
and operations research
Completion: Three year
graduation rate: 59%; credits
needed to graduate: 30; target
time to graduate: 2 years
College funded aid available:
Domestic: Yes; International: No
Graduates with debt: 63%

St. Francis University
Private

ONLINE MBA PROGRAM(S)
www.francis.edu/admissions/
Admissions: (814) 472-3026
Email: nbauman@francis.edu
Financial aid: (814) 472-3945
Application deadline: rolling
Program can be completed entirely online: Yes
Total program cost: $31,500 full-time in-state, $31,500 part-time in-state, $31,500 full-time out-of-state, $31,500 part-time out-of-state
Tuition per credit: $875 full-time in-state, $875 part-time in-state, $875 full-time out-of-state, $875 part-time out-of-state
Test scores required: GMAT
Enrollment: 23, 57% men, 43% women, N/A minority
Most popular MBA concentrations: accounting, finance, health care administration, human resources management, marketing
Completion: Credits needed to graduate: 45
College funded aid available: Domestic: Yes

ONLINE BUSINESS PROGRAM(S)
www.francis.edu/admissions/
Admissions: N/A
Financial aid: (814) 472-3010
Application deadline: rolling
Total program cost: $26,250 full-time in-state, $26,250 part-time in-state, $26,250 full-time out-of-state, $26,250 part-time out-of-state
Tuition per credit: $875 full-time in-state, $875 part-time in-state, $875 full-time out-of-state, $875 part-time out-of-state
Most popular business concentrations: human resources management
College funded aid available: Domestic: Yes; International: Yes

St. Joseph's University (Haub)
Private

ONLINE MBA PROGRAM(S)
www.sju.edu/majors-programs/graduate-business
Admissions: (610) 660-1690
Email: sjumba@sju.edu
Financial aid: (610) 660-1349
Application deadline: rolling
Program can be completed entirely online: Depends
Total program cost: N/A
Tuition per credit: $1,023 full-time in-state, $1,023 part-time in-state, $1,023 full-time out-of-state, $1,023 part-time out-of-state
Acceptance rate: 82%
Test scores required: GMAT or GRE
Average GMAT: 479
Average GRE: 152 verbal, 150 quantitative, 4.0 writing
Average age of entrants: 31
Enrollment: 374, 57% men, 43% women, 20% minority

Average class size: 18
Most popular MBA concentrations: finance, general management, health care administration, marketing, management information systems
Completion: Three year graduation rate: 48%; credits needed to graduate: 33; target time to graduate: 2 years
College funded aid available: Domestic: Yes; International: Yes
Graduates with debt: 40%; average amount of debt $46,600

ONLINE BUSINESS PROGRAM(S)
www.sju.edu/majors-programs/graduate-business
Admissions: (610) 660-1690
Email: sjums@sju.edu
Financial aid: (610) 660-1349
Application deadline: rolling
Program can be completed entirely online: Yes
Total program cost: N/A
Tuition per credit: $1,023 full-time in-state, $1,023 part-time in-state, $1,023 full-time out-of-state, $1,023 part-time out-of-state
Acceptance rate: 76%
Test scores required: GMAT or GRE
Average GMAT: 527
Average GRE: 157 verbal, 152 quantitative, 4.0 writing
Average age of entrants: 34
Enrollment: 311, 59% men, 41% women, 30% minority
Average class size: 19
Most popular business concentrations: finance, human resources management, marketing, management information systems
Completion: Three year graduation rate: 77%; credits needed to graduate: 30; target time to graduate: 2 years
College funded aid available: Domestic: Yes; International: Yes
Graduates with debt: 48%; average amount of debt $33,211

Temple University (Fox)
Public

ONLINE BUSINESS PROGRAM(S)
www.fox.temple.edu/onlinemba/index.html
Admissions: (215) 204-5890
Email: foxinfo@temple.edu
Financial aid: (215) 204-5890
Application deadline: rolling
Program can be completed entirely online: Yes
Total program cost: $33,420 full-time in-state, $33,420 part-time in-state, $33,420 full-time out-of-state, $33,420 part-time out-of-state
Tuition per credit: $1,114 full-time in-state, $1,114 part-time in-state, $1,114 full-time out-of-state, $1,114 part-time out-of-state
Acceptance rate: 58%
Test scores required: GMAT or GRE

Average GMAT: 555
Average GRE: 150 verbal, 154 quantitative, 5.0 writing
Average age of entrants: 33
Students with prior work experience: 100%
Enrollment: 112, 30% men, 70% women, 27% minority
Average class size: 20
Most popular business concentrations: human resources management, marketing, management information systems
Completion: Credits needed to graduate: 30; target time to graduate: 2 years
College funded aid available: Domestic: Yes; International: Yes

University of Scranton
Private

ONLINE MBA PROGRAM(S)
elearning.scranton.edu/
Admissions: (866) 373-9547
Email: onlineprograms@scranton.edu
Financial aid: (570) 941-7700
Application deadline: rolling
Program can be completed entirely online: Yes
Total program cost: $34,740 full-time in-state, $34,740 part-time in-state, $34,740 full-time out-of-state, $34,740 part-time out-of-state
Tuition per credit: $965 full-time in-state, $965 part-time in-state, $965 full-time out-of-state, $965 part-time out-of-state
Acceptance rate: 95%
Test scores required: No
Average age of entrants: 33
Students with prior work experience: 100%
Enrollment: 453, 55% men, 45% women, 24% minority
Average class size: 13
Most popular MBA concentrations: accounting, general management, health care administration, international business, production/operations management
Completion: Three year graduation rate: 50%; credits needed to graduate: 48; target time to graduate: 2 years
College funded aid available: Domestic: No; International: No
Graduates with debt: 52%; average amount of debt $20,634

ONLINE BUSINESS PROGRAM(S)
elearning.scranton.edu/macc
Admissions: (866) 373-9547
Email: onlineprograms@scranton.edu
Financial aid: (570) 941-7700
Application deadline: rolling
Program can be completed entirely online: Yes
Total program cost: $26,850 full-time in-state, $26,850 part-time in-state, $26,850 full-time out-of-state, $26,850 part-time out-of-state

Tuition per credit: $895 full-time in-state, $895 part-time in-state, $895 full-time out-of-state, $895 part-time out-of-state
Acceptance rate: 100%
Test scores required: No
Average age of entrants: 32
Enrollment: 145, 48% men, 52% women, N/A minority, N/A international
Average class size: 14
Most popular business concentrations: accounting
Completion: Credits needed to graduate: 30; target time to graduate: 2 years
Graduates with debt: 14%; average amount of debt $21,517

Villanova University
Private

ONLINE MBA PROGRAM(S)
www.villanova.edu/business/graduate
Admissions: (610) 519-4336
Email: claire.bruno@villanova.edu
Financial aid: (610) 519-4010
Application deadline: rolling
Program can be completed entirely online: No
Total program cost: $64,800 full-time in-state, $64,800 part-time in-state, $64,800 full-time out-of-state, $64,800 part-time out-of-state
Tuition per credit: $1,350 full-time in-state, $1,350 part-time in-state, $1,350 full-time out-of-state, $1,350 part-time out-of-state
Acceptance rate: 75%
Test scores required: GMAT or GRE
Average GMAT: 560
Average GRE: 153 verbal, 152 quantitative, 4.0 writing
Average age of entrants: 32
Students with prior work experience: 100%
Enrollment: 243, 59% men, 41% women, 17% minority, 1% international
Average class size: 21
Most popular MBA concentrations: accounting, economics, finance, general management, marketing
Completion: Credits needed to graduate: 48; target time to graduate: 2 years
College funded aid available: Domestic: Yes; International: Yes
Graduates with debt: 69%; average amount of debt $35,837

ONLINE BUSINESS PROGRAM(S)
www.villanova.edu/business/graduate
Admissions: (610) 519-4336
Email: claire.bruno@villanova.edu
Financial aid: (610) 519-4010
Application deadline: rolling
Program can be completed entirely online: Yes
Total program cost: $43,200 full-time in-state, $43,200 part-time in-state, $43,200 full-time out-of-state, $43,200 part-time out-of-state

Tuition per credit: $1,200 full-time in-state, $1,200 part-time in-state, $1,200 full-time out-of-state, $1,200 part-time out-of-state
Acceptance rate: 82%
Test scores required: No
Average GMAT: 657
Average GRE: 156 verbal, 160 quantitative, 4.0 writing
Average age of entrants: 39
Students with prior work experience: 99%
Enrollment: 311, 59% men, 41% women, 9% minority, 1% international
Average class size: 21
Most popular business concentrations: accounting, finance, general management, production/operations management, technology
Completion: Three year graduation rate: 100%; credits needed to graduate: 36; target time to graduate: 2 years
College funded aid available: Domestic: Yes; International: Yes
Graduates with debt: 51%; average amount of debt $29,466

Waynesburg University
Private

ONLINE MBA PROGRAM(S)
www.waynesburg.edu/graduate/graduate-majors/master-of-business-administration
Admissions: (724) 743-4420
Email: dmariner@waynesburg.edu
Financial aid: (724) 852-3208
Application deadline: rolling
Program can be completed entirely online: Yes
Total program cost: $23,760 full-time in-state, $23,760 part-time in-state, $23,760 full-time out-of-state, $23,760 part-time out-of-state
Tuition per credit: $660 full-time in-state, $660 part-time in-state, $660 full-time out-of-state, $660 part-time out-of-state
Acceptance rate: 60%
Average age of entrants: 33
Enrollment: 220, 62% men, 38% women, 9% minority
Average class size: 21
Most popular MBA concentrations: finance, leadership, other
Completion: Credits needed to graduate: 36; target time to graduate: 1 year
College funded aid available: Domestic: No; International: No
Graduates with debt: 35%; average amount of debt $22,500

West Chester University of Pennsylvania
Public

ONLINE MBA PROGRAM(S)
www.wcupa.edu/grad
Admissions: (610) 436-2943
Email: gradstudy@wcupa.edu
Financial aid: (610) 436-2627
Application deadline: rolling
Program can be completed entirely online: Yes
Total program cost: $15,000
full-time in-state, $15,000
part-time in-state, $15,300
full-time out-of-state, $15,300
part-time out-of-state
Tuition per credit: $500
full-time in-state, $500
part-time in-state, $510
full-time out-of-state, $510
part-time out-of-state
Acceptance rate: 91%
Test scores required: GMAT or GRE
Average GMAT: 522
Average GRE: 151 verbal, 151 quantitative, 4.0 writing
Average age of entrants: 33
Students with prior work experience: 98%
Enrollment: 399, 60% men, 40% women, 17% minority
Average class size: 24
Most popular MBA concentrations: entrepreneurship, general management, leadership, production/operations management, quantitative analysis/statistics and operations research
Completion: Three year graduation rate: 83%; credits needed to graduate: 30; target time to graduate: 1.5 years
College funded aid available: Domestic: Yes; International: Yes
Graduates with debt: 33%; average amount of debt $22,351

Widener University
Private

ONLINE MBA PROGRAM(S)
onlineprograms.widener.edu/mba/online-mba-program
Admissions: N/A
Financial aid: N/A
Application deadline: rolling
Program can be completed entirely online: Yes
Total program cost: N/A
Tuition per credit: $1,004
full-time in-state, $1,004
part-time in-state, $1,004
full-time out-of-state, $1,004
part-time out-of-state
Acceptance rate: 87%
Enrollment: 53, 55% men, 45% women, 30% minority

RHODE ISLAND
Johnson & Wales University
Private

ONLINE MBA PROGRAM(S)
online.jwu.edu/
Admissions: (401) 598-4400
Email: onlineadmissions@jwu.edu

Financial aid: (401) 598-2499
Application deadline: rolling
Program can be completed entirely online: Yes
Total program cost: N/A
Tuition per credit: $482
full-time in-state, $482
part-time in-state, $482
full-time out-of-state, $482
part-time out-of-state
Acceptance rate: 66%
Test scores required: No
Average age of entrants: 36
Enrollment: 453, 35% men, 65% women, 36% minority
Average class size: 19
Most popular MBA concentrations: finance, general management, hotel administration, human resources management, not-for-profit management
Completion: Three year graduation rate: 63%; credits needed to graduate: 54; target time to graduate: 2 years
College funded aid available: Domestic: No; International: No
Graduates with debt: 84%

ONLINE BUSINESS PROGRAM(S)
online.jwu.edu/admissions/graduate
Admissions: (401) 598-4400
Email: onlineadmissions@jwu.edu
Financial aid: (401) 598-2499
Application deadline: rolling
Program can be completed entirely online: Yes
Total program cost: N/A
Tuition per credit: $482
full-time in-state, $482
part-time in-state, $482
full-time out-of-state, $482
part-time out-of-state
Acceptance rate: 65%
Test scores required: No
Average age of entrants: 33
Enrollment: 111, 26% men, 74% women, 32% minority
Average class size: 19
Most popular business concentrations: finance, hotel administration, human resources management, not-for-profit management, sports business
Completion: Credits needed to graduate: 45; target time to graduate: 1.5 years
College funded aid available: Domestic: No; International: No
Graduates with debt: 90%

SOUTH CAROLINA
Charleston Southern University
Private

ONLINE MBA PROGRAM(S)
www.csuniv.edu/mba
Admissions: (843) 863-7050
Email: jsbrown@csuniv.edu
Financial aid: (843) 863-7050
Application deadline: rolling
Program can be completed entirely online: Depends

Total program cost: $20,625
full-time in-state, $20,625
part-time in-state, $20,625
full-time out-of-state, $20,625
part-time out-of-state
Tuition per credit: $625
full-time in-state, $625
part-time in-state, $625
full-time out-of-state, $625
part-time out-of-state
Acceptance rate: 76%
Test scores required: No
Average age of entrants: 34
Enrollment: 50, N/A minority, N/A international
Most popular MBA concentrations: accounting, finance, general management, human resources management, leadership
Completion: Credits needed to graduate: 33
College funded aid available: International: No

ONLINE BUSINESS PROGRAM(S)
www.csuniv.edu/mba
Admissions: (843) 863-7050
Email: jsbrown@csuniv.edu
Financial aid: (843) 863-7050
Application deadline: rolling
Program can be completed entirely online: Yes
Total program cost: $20,625
full-time in-state, $20,625
part-time in-state, $20,625
full-time out-of-state, $20,625
part-time out-of-state
Tuition per credit: $625
full-time in-state, $625
part-time in-state, $625
full-time out-of-state, $625
part-time out-of-state
Acceptance rate: 83%
Test scores required: No
Average age of entrants: 34
Enrollment: 19, N/A minority, N/A international
Most popular business concentrations: accounting, finance, general management, human resources management, leadership
Completion: Credits needed to graduate: 33
College funded aid available: International: No

The Citadel
Public

ONLINE MBA PROGRAM(S)
www.citadel.edu/root/mba
Admissions: (843) 953-5089
Email: cgc@citadel.edu
Financial aid: (843) 953-5187
Application deadline: rolling
Program can be completed entirely online: Yes
Total program cost: N/A
Tuition per credit: $695
full-time in-state, $695
part-time in-state, $695
full-time out-of-state, $695
part-time out-of-state
Test scores required: GMAT or GRE
Completion: Credits needed to graduate: 54

Coastal Carolina University (Wall)
Public

ONLINE MBA PROGRAM(S)
www.coastal.edu/business/gradprograms
Admissions: (843) 349-2761
Email: gradbus@coastal.edu
Financial aid: (843) 349-2313
Application deadline: N/A
Total program cost: N/A
Tuition per credit: $576 full-time in-state, $576 part-time in-state, $1,041 full-time out-of-state, $1,041 part-time out-of-state

North Greenville University
Private

ONLINE MBA PROGRAM(S)
gradschool.ngu.edu
Admissions: (864) 663-7507
Email: justin.pitts@ngu.edu
Financial aid: (864) 663-7507
Application deadline: rolling
Program can be completed entirely online: Yes
Total program cost: $450
full-time in-state, $18,900
part-time in-state, $18,900
full-time out-of-state, $18,900
part-time out-of-state
Tuition per credit: $450
full-time in-state, $450
part-time in-state, $450
full-time out-of-state, $450
part-time out-of-state
Test scores required: No
Average class size: 15
Completion: Credits needed to graduate: 36; target time to graduate: 1.5 years

ONLINE BUSINESS PROGRAM(S)
www.ngu.edu/graduate-admissions-page.php
Admissions: (864) 663-7507
Email: justin.pitts@ngu.edu
Financial aid: (864) 977-7058
Application deadline: rolling
Program can be completed entirely online: Yes
Total program cost: $16,680
full-time in-state, $16,680
part-time in-state, $16,680
full-time out-of-state, $16,680
part-time out-of-state
Tuition per credit: $450
full-time in-state, $450
part-time in-state, $450
full-time out-of-state, $450
part-time out-of-state
Acceptance rate: 97%
Average age of entrants: 29
Students with prior work experience: 100%
Enrollment: 139, 41% men, 59% women, N/A minority, N/A international
Average class size: 15
Most popular business concentrations: human resources management
Completion: Credits needed to graduate: 36; target time to graduate: 1.5 years
College funded aid available: Domestic: Yes; International: Yes

SOUTH DAKOTA
Dakota State University
Public

ONLINE MBA PROGRAM(S)
dsu.edu/graduate-students/mba
Admissions: (605) 256-5799
Email: gradoffice@dsu.edu
Financial aid: (605) 256-5152
Application deadline: rolling
Program can be completed entirely online: Yes
Total program cost: N/A
Tuition per credit: $444
full-time in-state, $444
part-time in-state, $444
full-time out-of-state, $444
part-time out-of-state
Acceptance rate: 100%
Test scores required: GMAT or GRE
Average age of entrants: 33
Enrollment: N/A minority, 2% international
Average class size: 10
Most popular MBA concentrations: general management, management information systems
Completion: Credits needed to graduate: 36; target time to graduate: 2 years
College funded aid available: Domestic: Yes; International: No
Graduates with debt: 42%; average amount of debt $22,792

Dakota Wesleyan University
Private

ONLINE MBA PROGRAM(S)
www.dwu.edu/admissions
Admissions: (605) 995-2650
Email: admissions@dwu.edu
Financial aid: (605) 995-2656
Application deadline: rolling
Program can be completed entirely online: Yes
Total program cost: $14,400
full-time in-state, $7,200
part-time in-state, $14,400
full-time out-of-state, $7,200
part-time out-of-state
Tuition per credit: $400
full-time in-state, $400
part-time in-state, $400
full-time out-of-state, $400
part-time out-of-state
Acceptance rate: 68%
Test scores required: No
Average GMAT: N/A
Average age of entrants: 32
Students with prior work experience: 81%
Enrollment: 43, 56% men, 44% women, 16% minority
Average class size: 13
Most popular MBA concentrations: leadership
Completion: Three year graduation rate: 85%; credits needed to graduate: 36; target time to graduate: 1.5 years
College funded aid available: Domestic: No; International: No
Graduates with debt: 40%; average amount of debt $21,317

University of Sioux Falls

Private

ONLINE MBA PROGRAM(S)

usiouxfalls.edu/mba
Admissions: (605) 331-6708
Email: mba@usiouxfalls.edu
Financial aid: (605) 331-6621
Application deadline: rolling
Program can be completed entirely online: Yes
Total program cost: $13,680
full-time in-state, $13,680
part-time in-state, $13,680
full-time out-of-state, $13,680
part-time out-of-state
Tuition per credit: $380
full-time in-state, $380
part-time in-state, $380
full-time out-of-state, $380
part-time out-of-state
Acceptance rate: 100%
Test scores required: No
Average age of entrants: 33
Students with prior work experience: 100%
Enrollment: 21, 67% men, 33% women, N/A minority, N/A international
Average class size: 15
Most popular MBA concentrations: general management, health care administration
Completion: Credits needed to graduate: 36; target time to graduate: 2 years
College funded aid available: Domestic: Yes; International: No

University of South Dakota

Public

ONLINE MBA PROGRAM(S)

www.usd.edu/graduate-school/apply-now
Admissions: (605) 658-6136
Email: Brittany.E.Wagner@usd.edu
Financial aid: (605) 658-6250
Application deadline: rolling
Program can be completed entirely online: No
Total program cost: $14,660
full-time in-state, $14,660
part-time in-state, $14,660
full-time out-of-state, $14,660
part-time out-of-state
Tuition per credit: $444
full-time in-state, $444
part-time in-state, $444
full-time out-of-state, $444
part-time out-of-state
Acceptance rate: 95%
Test scores required: GMAT
Average GMAT: 520
Average age of entrants: 32
Students with prior work experience: 87%
Enrollment: 267, 70% men, 30% women, 7% minority, 7% international
Average class size: 28
Most popular MBA concentrations: general management, health care administration, marketing, supply chain management/logistics, other

Completion: Three year graduation rate: 38%; credits needed to graduate: 33; target time to graduate: 2 years
College funded aid available: Domestic: No; International: No
Graduates with debt: 35%; average amount of debt $27,993

ONLINE BUSINESS PROGRAM(S)

www.usd.edu/academics/graduate-studies
Admissions: (605) 658-6138
Email: grad@usd.edu
Financial aid: (605) 677-5446
Application deadline: rolling
Program can be completed entirely online: Yes
Total program cost: $13,327
full-time in-state, $13,327
part-time in-state, $13,327
full-time out-of-state, $13,327
part-time out-of-state
Tuition per credit: $444
full-time in-state, $444
part-time in-state, $444
full-time out-of-state, $444
part-time out-of-state
Acceptance rate: 69%
Test scores required: gre
Average GMAT: 544
Average age of entrants: 35
Students with prior work experience: 53%
Enrollment: 103, 52% men, 48% women, 13% minority, 11% international
Average class size: 29
Most popular business concentrations: accounting
Completion: Three year graduation rate: 36%; credits needed to graduate: 30; target time to graduate: 2 years
College funded aid available: Domestic: No; International: No
Graduates with debt: 35%; average amount of debt $29,275

TENNESSEE

Austin Peay State University

Public

ONLINE BUSINESS PROGRAM(S)

www.apsu.edu/grad-studies/management.php
Admissions: (931) 221-7662
Email: gradadmissions@apsu.edu
Financial aid: (931) 221-7907
Application deadline: rolling
Program can be completed entirely online: Yes
Total program cost: N/A
Tuition per credit: $427 full-time in-state, $427 part-time in-state, $641 full-time out-of-state, $641 part-time out-of-state
Acceptance rate: 55%
Average GMAT: 451
Average age of entrants: 32
Students with prior work experience: 0%
Enrollment: 71, 48% men, 52% women, 15% minority
Average class size: 13
Most popular business concentrations: general management

Completion: Three year graduation rate: 65%; credits needed to graduate: 30; target time to graduate: 1 year
College funded aid available: Domestic: Yes

Bethel University

Private

ONLINE MBA PROGRAM(S)

bethelsuccess.net/programs/graduate/
Admissions: (844) 415-2151
Email: bevilla@bethelu.edu
Financial aid: (731) 352-8423
Application deadline: rolling
Program can be completed entirely online: Yes
Total program cost: $21,420
full-time in-state, $21,420
part-time in-state, $21,420
full-time out-of-state, $21,420
part-time out-of-state
Tuition per credit: $595
full-time in-state, $595
part-time in-state, $595
full-time out-of-state, $595
part-time out-of-state
Acceptance rate: 80%
Test scores required: No
Average age of entrants: 37
Students with prior work experience: 0%
Enrollment: 877, 31% men, 69% women, 58% minority
Average class size: 20
Most popular MBA concentrations: general management, health care administration, human resources management, other
Completion: Three year graduation rate: 73%; credits needed to graduate: 30; target time to graduate: 2 years
College funded aid available: Domestic: No
Graduates with debt: 81%; average amount of debt $30,672

Bryan College

Private

ONLINE MBA PROGRAM(S)

www.bryan.edu/adult-education
Admissions: (877) 256-7008
Email: ags@bryan.edu
Financial aid: (423) 775-7460
Application deadline: rolling
Program can be completed entirely online: Yes
Total program cost: $19,620
full-time in-state, $19,620
part-time in-state, $19,620
full-time out-of-state, $19,620
part-time out-of-state
Tuition per credit: $545
full-time in-state, $545
part-time in-state, $545
full-time out-of-state, $545
part-time out-of-state
Test scores required: No
Enrollment: 92, N/A minority, N/A international
Most popular MBA concentrations: general management, human resources management, marketing, other

King University

Private

ONLINE MBA PROGRAM(S)

online.king.edu
Admissions: (800) 391-8252
Email: admissions@king.edu
Financial aid: (423) 652-4725
Application deadline: rolling
Program can be completed entirely online: Yes
Total program cost: $21,780
full-time in-state, $21,780
part-time in-state, $21,780
full-time out-of-state, $21,780
part-time out-of-state
Tuition per credit: $605
full-time in-state, $605
part-time in-state, $605
full-time out-of-state, $605
part-time out-of-state
Acceptance rate: 52%
Test scores required: No
Average age of entrants: 34
Students with prior work experience: 100%
Enrollment: 159, 31% men, 69% women, 21% minority, 1% international
Average class size: 12
Most popular MBA concentrations: accounting, finance, human resources management, leadership, marketing
Completion: Three year graduation rate: 78%; credits needed to graduate: 36; target time to graduate: 1.5 years
College funded aid available: Domestic: No; International: No
Graduates with debt: 82%; average amount of debt $33,035

Tennessee Technological University

Public

ONLINE MBA PROGRAM(S)

www.tntech.edu/cob/mba/requirements/
Admissions: (931) 372-3600
Email: knicewicz@tntech.edu
Financial aid: (931) 372-3073
Application deadline: rolling
Program can be completed entirely online: Yes
Total program cost: $14,640
full-time in-state, $14,640
part-time in-state, $36,420
full-time out-of-state, $36,420
part-time out-of-state
Tuition per credit: $488
full-time in-state, $488
part-time in-state, $726
full-time out-of-state, $726
part-time out-of-state
Acceptance rate: 54%
Test scores required: GMAT or GRE
Average GMAT: 508
Average GRE: 152 verbal, 151 quantitative, 4.0 writing
Average age of entrants: 29

Enrollment: 282, 65% men, 35% women, 11% minority, 6% international
Average class size: 25
Most popular MBA concentrations: finance, general management, human resources management, international business, management information systems
Completion: Three year graduation rate: 83%; credits needed to graduate: 30; target time to graduate: 1.5 years
College funded aid available: Domestic: Yes; International: No
Graduates with debt: 25%; average amount of debt $8,178

University of Memphis (Fogelman)

Public

ONLINE MBA PROGRAM(S)

www.memphis.edu/
Admissions: (901) 678-4212
Email: jdhaliwl@memphis.edu
Financial aid: (901) 678-4685
Application deadline: rolling
Program can be completed entirely online: Yes
Total program cost: $19,668
full-time in-state, $19,668
part-time in-state, $27,753
full-time out-of-state, $27,753
part-time out-of-state
Tuition per credit: $596
full-time in-state, $596
part-time in-state, $841
full-time out-of-state, $841
part-time out-of-state
Acceptance rate: 95%
Test scores required: GMAT or GRE
Average GMAT: 553
Average GRE: 154 verbal, 150 quantitative, 4.0 writing
Average age of entrants: 32
Students with prior work experience: 80%
Enrollment: 110, 67% men, 33% women, 28% minority
Average class size: 41
Most popular MBA concentrations: accounting, finance, general management, marketing, management information systems
Completion: Three year graduation rate: 62%; credits needed to graduate: 33; target time to graduate: 2 years
College funded aid available: Domestic: Yes; International: Yes

University of Tennessee–Chattanooga

Public

ONLINE MBA PROGRAM(S)

www.utc.edu/onlinemba
Admissions: (423) 425-1730
Email: christine-estoye@utc.edu
Financial aid: (423) 425-4677
Application deadline: rolling
Program can be completed entirely online: Yes

Total program cost: $28,944 full-time in-state, $28,944 part-time in-state, $28,944 full-time out-of-state, $28,944 part-time out-of-state
Tuition per credit: $804 full-time in-state, $804 part-time in-state, $804 full-time out-of-state, $804 part-time out-of-state
Acceptance rate: 80%
Test scores required: GMAT or GRE
Average GMAT: 523
Average GRE: 152 verbal, 149 quantitative, 3.7 writing
Average age of entrants: 34
Students with prior work experience: 100%
Enrollment: 193, 49% men, 51% women, 19% minority, 1% international
Average class size: 27
Most popular MBA concentrations: other
Completion: Credits needed to graduate: 36; target time to graduate: 2 years
College funded aid available: Domestic: Yes; International: Yes
Graduates with debt: 56%; average amount of debt $34,678

University of Tennessee–Martin

Public

ONLINE MBA PROGRAM(S)

www.utm.edu/gradstudies/index.php
Admissions: (731) 881-7012
Email: graduatestudies@utm.edu
Financial aid: (731) 881-7031
Application deadline: Domestic: 07/31
Program can be completed entirely online: Yes
Total program cost: N/A
Tuition per credit: $516 full-time in-state, $516 part-time in-state, $567 full-time out-of-state, $567 part-time out-of-state
Acceptance rate: 92%
Test scores required: GMAT or GRE
Average GMAT: 486
Average GRE: 157 verbal, 149 quantitative, 4.0 writing
Average age of entrants: 35
Students with prior work experience: 100%
Enrollment: 89, 62% men, 38% women, 13% minority, 1% international
Average class size: 18
Most popular MBA concentrations: general management
Completion: Three year graduation rate: 62%; credits needed to graduate: 38; target time to graduate: 2 years
College funded aid available: Domestic: Yes; International: No
Graduates with debt: 25%; average amount of debt $27,548

TEXAS

Abilene Christian University

Private

ONLINE MBA PROGRAM(S)

www.acu.edu/content/dam/acu_2016/documents/acudallas_admissions.pdf
Admissions: (855) 219-7300
Email: gradonline@acu.edu
Financial aid: (800) 460-6228
Application deadline: rolling
Program can be completed entirely online: Yes
Total program cost: $25,200 full-time in-state, $25,200 part-time in-state, $25,200 full-time out-of-state, $25,200 part-time out-of-state
Tuition per credit: $700 full-time in-state, $700 part-time in-state, $700 full-time out-of-state, $700 part-time out-of-state
Acceptance rate: 96%
Test scores required: No
Average age of entrants: 35
Students with prior work experience: 100%
Enrollment: 123, 58% men, 42% women, 37% minority, 1% international
Average class size: 11
Most popular MBA concentrations: general management, health care administration, supply chain management/logistics
Completion: Target time to graduate: 2 years

ONLINE BUSINESS PROGRAM(S)

www.acu.edu/content/dam/acu_2016/documents/acudallas_admissions.pdf
Admissions: (855) 219-7300
Email: gradonline@acu.edu
Financial aid: (800) 460-6228
Application deadline: rolling
Program can be completed entirely online: Yes
Total program cost: N/A
Tuition per credit: $700 full-time in-state, $700 part-time in-state, $700 full-time out-of-state, $700 part-time out-of-state
Acceptance rate: 87%
Test scores required: No
Average age of entrants: 31
Students with prior work experience: 100%
Enrollment: 35, 57% men, 43% women, 49% minority, 3% international
Average class size: 11
Most popular business concentrations: supply chain management/logistics
Completion: Target time to graduate: 2 years

Angelo State University

Public

ONLINE MBA PROGRAM(S)

www.angelo.edu/dept/graduate-studies/
Admissions: (325) 942-2169
Email: graduate.studies@angelo.edu
Financial aid: (325) 942-2246
Application deadline: rolling
Program can be completed entirely online: Yes
Total program cost: $6,402 full-time in-state, $6,402 part-time in-state, $18,810 full-time out-of-state, $18,810 part-time out-of-state
Tuition per credit: $214 full-time in-state, $214 part-time in-state, $629 full-time out-of-state, $629 part-time out-of-state
Acceptance rate: 95%
Test scores required: GMAT or GRE
Average GMAT: 373
Average GRE: 155 verbal, 154 quantitative
Average age of entrants: 30
Enrollment: 136, 61% men, 39% women, 28% minority, 4% international
Average class size: 41
Most popular MBA concentrations: general management
Completion: Credits needed to graduate: 30; target time to graduate: 1 year
College funded aid available: Domestic: No; International: No
Graduates with debt: 48%; average amount of debt $18,270

Baylor University (Hankamer)

Private

ONLINE MBA PROGRAM(S)

www.baylor.edu/business/onlinemba
Admissions: (254) 710-4162
Email: mary_reinhardt@baylor.edu
Financial aid: (254) 710-2611
Application deadline: rolling
Program can be completed entirely online: Yes
Total program cost: $49,296 full-time in-state, $24,648 part-time in-state, $49,296 full-time out-of-state, $24,648 part-time out-of-state
Tuition per credit: $1,027 full-time in-state, $1,027 part-time in-state, $1,027 full-time out-of-state, $1,027 part-time out-of-state
Acceptance rate: 69%
Test scores required: No
Average GMAT: 570
Average GRE: 149 verbal, 147 quantitative
Average age of entrants: 35
Enrollment: 148, 74% men, 26% women, 34% minority, 1% international
Average class size: 50
Most popular MBA concentrations: general management

Completion: Three year graduation rate: 77%; credits needed to graduate: 48; target time to graduate: 2 years
College funded aid available: Domestic: Yes; International: Yes
Graduates with debt: 72%; average amount of debt $47,968

ONLINE BUSINESS PROGRAM(S)

www.baylor.edu/business/onlinemba
Admissions: (254) 710-4163
Email: laurie_Wilson@baylor.edu
Financial aid: (254) 710-8650
Application deadline: rolling
Program can be completed entirely online: Yes
Total program cost: $49,296 full-time in-state, $24,648 part-time in-state, $49,296 full-time out-of-state, $24,648 part-time out-of-state
Tuition per credit: $1,027 full-time in-state, $1,027 part-time in-state, $1,027 full-time out-of-state, $1,027 part-time out-of-state
Acceptance rate: 69%
Test scores required: No
Average GMAT: 570
Average GRE: 149 verbal, 147 quantitative
Average age of entrants: 35
Enrollment: 148, 74% men, 26% women, 34% minority, 1% international
Average class size: 50
Completion: Three year graduation rate: 77%; credits needed to graduate: 48; target time to graduate: 2 years
College funded aid available: Domestic: Yes; International: Yes
Graduates with debt: 72%; average amount of debt $47,968

Dallas Baptist University

Private

ONLINE MBA PROGRAM(S)

www.dbu.edu/graduate
Admissions: (214) 333-5242
Email: graduate@dbu.edu
Financial aid: (214) 333-5363
Application deadline: rolling
Program can be completed entirely online: Yes
Total program cost: $32,616 full-time in-state, $32,616 part-time in-state, $32,616 full-time out-of-state, $32,616 part-time out-of-state
Tuition per credit: $906 full-time in-state, $906 part-time in-state, $906 full-time out-of-state, $906 part-time out-of-state
Acceptance rate: 48%
Test scores required: GMAT
Enrollment: 580, 44% men, 56% women, 30% minority, 35% international
Average class size: 13
Most popular MBA concentrations: finance, general management, health care administration, marketing, management information systems

Completion: Three year graduation rate: 77%; credits needed to graduate: 48; target time to graduate: 2 years
College funded aid available: Domestic: Yes; International: Yes
College funded aid available: Domestic: Yes; International: Yes

ONLINE BUSINESS PROGRAM(S)

dbu.edu/graduate
Admissions: (214) 333-5242
Email: graduate@dbu.edu
Financial aid: (214) 333-5363
Application deadline: rolling
Program can be completed entirely online: Yes
Total program cost: $32,616 full-time in-state, $32,616 part-time in-state, $32,616 full-time out-of-state, $32,616 part-time out-of-state
Tuition per credit: $906 full-time in-state, $906 part-time in-state, $906 full-time out-of-state, $906 part-time out-of-state
Acceptance rate: 52%
Test scores required: gre
Enrollment: 77, 21% men, 79% women, 52% minority, 14% international
Average class size: 13
Most popular business concentrations: general management, health care administration, human resources management
Completion: Credits needed to graduate: 36; target time to graduate: 2.5 years
College funded aid available: Domestic: Yes; International: Yes

Hardin-Simmons University

Private

ONLINE MBA PROGRAM(S)

hsutx.edu/academics/kelley/graduate/mba
Admissions: N/A
Financial aid: N/A
Application deadline: rolling
Program can be completed entirely online: Yes
Total program cost: $13,500 full-time in-state, $13,500 full-time out-of-state
Tuition per credit: $750 full-time in-state, $750 part-time in-state, $750 full-time out-of-state, $750 part-time out-of-state
Test scores required: GMAT or GRE
Most popular MBA concentrations: finance, general management, marketing, sports business
Completion: Target time to graduate: 2 years

Houston Baptist University

Private

ONLINE BUSINESS PROGRAM(S)

hbu.edu/the-graduate-school
Admissions: (281) 649-3269
Email: gradadmissions@hbu.edu
Financial aid: (281) 649-3747
Application deadline: N/A
Program can be completed entirely online: Yes
Total program cost: N/A

Tuition per credit: $550 full-time in-state, $550 part-time in-state, $550 full-time out-of-state, $550 part-time out-of-state
Average class size: 0
Most popular business concentrations: human resources management
Completion: Credits needed to graduate: 33; target time to graduate: 2 years

Lamar University
Public

ONLINE MBA PROGRAM(S)
www.lamar.edu
Admissions: (409) 880-8888
Email: gradmissions@lamar.edu
Financial aid: (409) 880-7011
Application deadline: rolling
Program can be completed entirely online: Yes
Total program cost: $19,584 full-time in-state, $19,584 part-time in-state, $19,584 full-time out-of-state, $19,584 part-time out-of-state
Tuition per credit: $408 full-time in-state, $408 part-time in-state, $408 full-time out-of-state, $408 part-time out-of-state
Acceptance rate: 87%
Test scores required: GMAT
Average GMAT: 473
Average age of entrants: 37
Enrollment: 107, 49% men, 51% women, 41% minority
Average class size: 28
Most popular MBA concentrations: health care administration, leadership, management information systems
Completion: Credits needed to graduate: 36; target time to graduate: 1.5 years
Graduates with debt: 100%; average amount of debt $26,259

Sam Houston State University
Public

ONLINE MBA PROGRAM(S)
www.shsu.edu/~coba/programs/graduate.html
Admissions: (936) 294-1971
Email: graduate@shsu.edu
Financial aid: (936) 294-1774
Application deadline: Domestic: 08/01; International: 06/25
Program can be completed entirely online: Yes
Total program cost: $10,800 full-time in-state, $10,800 part-time in-state, $10,800 full-time out-of-state, $10,800 part-time out-of-state
Tuition per credit: $300 full-time in-state, $300 part-time in-state, $300 full-time out-of-state, $300 part-time out-of-state
Acceptance rate: 82%
Test scores required: GMAT
Average GMAT: 530
Average GRE: 152 verbal, 153 quantitative
Average age of entrants: 33

Enrollment: 291, 57% men, 43% women, 35% minority, 3% international
Average class size: 20
Most popular MBA concentrations: economics, finance, general management
Completion: Three year graduation rate: 42%; credits needed to graduate: 36; target time to graduate: 2 years
College funded aid available: Domestic: Yes; International: Yes
Graduates with debt: 53%; average amount of debt $29,360

ONLINE BUSINESS PROGRAM(S)
www.shsu.edu/~coba/programs/graduate.html
Admissions: (936) 294-1971
Email: graduate@shsu.edu
Financial aid: (936) 294-1774
Application deadline: Domestic: 08/01; International: 06/25
Program can be completed entirely online: Yes
Total program cost: $10,800 full-time in-state, $10,800 part-time in-state, $10,800 full-time out-of-state, $10,800 part-time out-of-state
Tuition per credit: $300 full-time in-state, $300 part-time in-state, $300 full-time out-of-state, $300 part-time out-of-state
Acceptance rate: 86%
Test scores required: gre
Average age of entrants: 43
Students with prior work experience: 0%
Enrollment: 16, 56% men, 44% women, 44% minority
Average class size: 20
Most popular business concentrations: production/operations management
Completion: Credits needed to graduate: 36; target time to graduate: 2 years
College funded aid available: Domestic: Yes; International: Yes

Schreiner University
Private

ONLINE MBA PROGRAM(S)
www.schreiner.edu/admission/
Admissions: (830) 792-7223
Email: admissions@schreiner.edu
Financial aid: (830) 792-7223
Application deadline: N/A
Total program cost: N/A
Tuition per credit: $647 full-time in-state, $647 part-time in-state, $647 full-time out-of-state, $647 part-time out-of-state
Acceptance rate: 100%
Average age of entrants: 33
Students with prior work experience: 47%
Enrollment: 34, 38% men, 62% women, N/A minority, N/A international
Average class size: 12
Completion: Target time to graduate: 1 year

Tarleton State University
Public

ONLINE MBA PROGRAM(S)
www.tarleton.edu/coba
Admissions: (254) 968-9055
Email: coba@tarleton.edu
Financial aid: (254) 968-9070
Application deadline: Domestic: 08/21; International: 06/15
Program can be completed entirely online: Yes
Total program cost: N/A
Tuition per credit: $210 full-time in-state, $210 part-time in-state, $623 full-time out-of-state, $623 part-time out-of-state
Acceptance rate: 56%
Test scores required: GMAT or GRE
Enrollment: 112, 51% men, 49% women, 16% minority
Completion: Credits needed to graduate: 30
Graduates with debt: 100%; average amount of debt $45,953

ONLINE BUSINESS PROGRAM(S)
www.tarleton.edu/coba
Admissions: (254) 968-9055
Email: coba@tarleton.edu
Financial aid: (254) 968-9070
Application deadline: Domestic: 08/21; International: 06/15
Program can be completed entirely online: Yes
Total program cost: N/A
Tuition per credit: $210 full-time in-state, $210 part-time in-state, $623 full-time out-of-state, $623 part-time out-of-state
Acceptance rate: 68%
Test scores required: GMAT or GRE
Enrollment: 114, 33% men, 67% women, 33% minority
Most popular business concentrations: human resources management, management information systems
Completion: Credits needed to graduate: 30
Graduates with debt: 63%; average amount of debt $37,518

Texas A&M University–Central Texas
Public

ONLINE MBA PROGRAM(S)
www.tamuct.edu/graduate-studies/index.html
Admissions: (254) 519-5447
Email: graduatestudies@tamuct.edu
Financial aid: (254) 501-5854
Application deadline: Domestic: 10/13; International: 10/13
Program can be completed entirely online: Yes
Total program cost: $7,560 full-time in-state, $7,560 part-time in-state, $23,400 full-time out-of-state, $23,400 part-time out-of-state
Tuition per credit: $210 full-time in-state, $210 part-time in-state, $650 full-time out-of-state, $650 part-time out-of-state

Acceptance rate: 97%
Test scores required: No
Average GRE: 142 verbal, 141 quantitative
Average age of entrants: 36
Students with prior work experience: 0%
Enrollment: 210, 54% men, 46% women, 57% minority, 4% international
Average class size: 7
Most popular MBA concentrations: finance, general management, human resources management, marketing, management information systems
Completion: Three year graduation rate: 100%; credits needed to graduate: 36; target time to graduate: 2 years
College funded aid available: Domestic: Yes; International: Yes
Graduates with debt: 65%; average amount of debt $36,874

ONLINE BUSINESS PROGRAM(S)
www.tamuct.edu/graduate-studies/index.html
Admissions: (254) 519-5447
Email: graduatestudies@tamuct.edu
Financial aid: (254) 501-5854
Application deadline: Domestic: 10/13; International: 10/13
Program can be completed entirely online: Yes
Total program cost: $7,560 full-time in-state, $7,560 part-time in-state, $23,400 full-time out-of-state, $23,400 part-time out-of-state
Tuition per credit: $210 full-time in-state, $210 part-time in-state, $650 full-time out-of-state, $650 part-time out-of-state
Acceptance rate: 100%
Test scores required: No
Average GMAT: N/A
Average age of entrants: 38
Enrollment: 51, 55% men, 45% women, 59% minority, 6% international
Average class size: 17
Most popular business concentrations: human resources management, leadership, marketing, management information systems, organizational behavior
Completion: Three year graduation rate: 100%; credits needed to graduate: 36; target time to graduate: 2 years
College funded aid available: Domestic: Yes; International: Yes
Graduates with debt: 65%; average amount of debt $36,874

Texas A&M International University
Public

ONLINE MBA PROGRAM(S)
www.tamiu.edu/prospect/graduate.shtml
Admissions: (956) 326-3020
Email: GraduateSchool@tamiu.edu

Financial aid: (956) 326-2225
Application deadline: rolling
Program can be completed entirely online: Yes
Total program cost: $2,310 full-time in-state, $2,310 part-time in-state, $14,760 full-time out-of-state, $14,760 part-time out-of-state
Tuition per credit: $77 full-time in-state, $77 part-time in-state, $492 full-time out-of-state, $492 part-time out-of-state
Acceptance rate: 100%
Average GMAT: 430
Average GRE: 145 verbal, 143 quantitative, 2.6 writing
Average age of entrants: 27
Students with prior work experience: 88%
Enrollment: 99, 66% men, 34% women, 54% minority, 41% international
Average class size: 20
Most popular MBA concentrations: general management, international business, other
Completion: Three year graduation rate: 83%; credits needed to graduate: 30; target time to graduate: 2 years
College funded aid available: Domestic: Yes; International: No
Graduates with debt: 21%; average amount of debt $21,406

Texas A&M University–Commerce
Public

ONLINE MBA PROGRAM(S)
www.tamu-commerce.edu/graduateprograms
Admissions: (903) 886-5163
Email: graduate.school@tamuc.edu
Financial aid: (903) 886-5096
Application deadline: Domestic: 07/28; International: 05/26
Program can be completed entirely online: Yes
Total program cost: $6,060 full-time in-state, $6,060 part-time in-state, $18,510 full-time out-of-state, $18,510 part-time out-of-state
Tuition per credit: $202 full-time in-state, $202 part-time in-state, $617 full-time out-of-state, $617 part-time out-of-state
Acceptance rate: 61%
Test scores required: No
Average GMAT: 416
Average GRE: 146 verbal, 145 quantitative, 3.0 writing
Average age of entrants: 32
Enrollment: 1,252, 54% men, 46% women, 45% minority, 5% international
Average class size: 26
Most popular MBA concentrations: accounting, finance, general management, marketing, quantitative analysis/statistics and operations research
Completion: Three year graduation rate: 51%; credits needed to graduate: 30; target time to graduate: 2 years

College funded aid available: Domestic: Yes; International: Yes
Graduates with debt: 47%; average amount of debt $33,426

ONLINE BUSINESS PROGRAM(S)
www.tamu-commerce.edu/graduateprograms
Admissions: (903) 886-5163
Email: graduate.school@tamuc.edu
Financial aid: (903) 886-5091
Application deadline: Domestic: 07/28; International: 05/26
Program can be completed entirely online: Yes
Total program cost: $6,060 full-time in-state, $6,060 part-time in-state, $18,510 full-time out-of-state, $18,510 part-time out-of-state
Tuition per credit: $202 full-time in-state, $202 part-time in-state, $617 full-time out-of-state, $617 part-time out-of-state
Acceptance rate: 60%
Test scores required: No
Average GMAT: 435
Average GRE: 144 verbal, 146 quantitative, 3.0 writing
Average age of entrants: 32
Enrollment: 1,416, 46% men, 54% women, 41% minority, 14% international
Average class size: 27
Most popular business concentrations: accounting, finance, general management, marketing, quantitative analysis/statistics and operations research
Completion: Three year graduation rate: 60%; credits needed to graduate: 30; target time to graduate: 2 years
College funded aid available: Domestic: Yes; International: Yes
Graduates with debt: 45%; average amount of debt $35,063

Texas A&M University–Kingsville
Public

ONLINE MBA PROGRAM(S)
www.tamuk.edu/cba
Admissions: (361) 593-2501
Email: Jesus.Carmona@tamuk.edu
Financial aid: (361) 593-2175
Application deadline: Domestic: 07/15; International: 06/01
Program can be completed entirely online: Yes
Total program cost: $5,791 full-time in-state, $5,381 part-time in-state, $18,241 full-time out-of-state, $17,831 part-time out-of-state
Tuition per credit: $250 full-time in-state, $250 part-time in-state, $595 full-time out-of-state, $595 part-time out-of-state
Acceptance rate: 87%
Test scores required: GMAT or GRE
Average GMAT: 425

Average GRE: 145 verbal, 146 quantitative
Average age of entrants: 28
Students with prior work experience: 35%
Enrollment: 90, 53% men, 47% women, 67% minority, 4% international
Average class size: 30
Completion: Three year graduation rate: 71%; credits needed to graduate: 30; target time to graduate: 1 year
College funded aid available: Domestic: Yes; International: Yes
Graduates with debt: 53%; average amount of debt $31,270

Texas Southern University (Jones)
Public

ONLINE MBA PROGRAM(S)
www.tsu.edu/emba
Admissions: (713) 313-7776
Email: srinis@tsu.edu
Financial aid: (713) 313-7480
Application deadline: rolling
Program can be completed entirely online: Yes
Total program cost: N/A
Tuition per credit: $1,000 full-time in-state, $1,000 part-time in-state, $1,000 full-time out-of-state, $1,000 part-time out-of-state
Acceptance rate: 75%
Test scores required: No
Average age of entrants: 38
Students with prior work experience: 100%
Enrollment: 55, 56% men, 44% women, 98% minority
Average class size: 14
Most popular MBA concentrations: general management
Completion: Credits needed to graduate: 36; target time to graduate: 2 years
College funded aid available: Domestic: No; International: No

Texas Wesleyan University
Private

ONLINE MBA PROGRAM(S)
txwes.edu/admissions/graduate/
Admissions: (817) 531-4930
Email: graduate@txwes.edu
Financial aid: (817) 531-4420
Application deadline: rolling
Program can be completed entirely online: Yes
Total program cost: N/A
Tuition per credit: $836 full-time in-state, $836 part-time in-state, $836 full-time out-of-state, $836 part-time out-of-state
Test scores required: GMAT
Most popular MBA concentrations: accounting, health care administration, supply chain management/logistics, other

University of Dallas
Private

ONLINE MBA PROGRAM(S)
udallas.edu/cob/academics/mba/index.php
Admissions: (972) 721-5004
Email: admiss@udallas.edu
Financial aid: (972) 721-5266
Application deadline: N/A
Total program cost: $37,500 full-time in-state, $37,500 part-time in-state, $37,500 full-time out-of-state, $37,500 part-time out-of-state
Tuition per credit:
Average GMAT: 494
Average GRE: 153 verbal, 146 quantitative, 3.1 writing

ONLINE BUSINESS PROGRAM(S)
www.udallas.edu/cob
Admissions: (972) 721-5004
Email: admiss@udallas.edu
Financial aid: (972) 721-5266
Application deadline: rolling
Program can be completed entirely online: Yes
Total program cost: $7,500 full-time in-state, $3,750 part-time in-state, $7,500 full-time out-of-state, $3,750 part-time out-of-state
Tuition per credit: $1,250 full-time in-state, $1,250 part-time in-state, $1,250 full-time out-of-state, $1,250 part-time out-of-state
Test scores required: No
Enrollment: 302, 64% men, 36% women, N/A minority, N/A international
Most popular business concentrations: accounting, finance, other
Completion: Credits needed to graduate: 30
College funded aid available: Domestic: Yes; International: Yes

University of Houston–Clear Lake
Public

ONLINE MBA PROGRAM(S)
www.uhcl.edu/admissions
Admissions: (281) 283-2500
Email: admissions@uhcl.edu
Financial aid: (281) 283-2480
Application deadline: rolling
Program can be completed entirely online: Yes
Total program cost: $17,592 full-time in-state, $17,592 part-time in-state, $34,728 full-time out-of-state, $34,728 part-time out-of-state
Tuition per credit: $451 full-time in-state, $451 part-time in-state, $950 full-time out-of-state, $950 part-time out-of-state
Acceptance rate: 41%
Test scores required: GMAT
Average GMAT: 504
Enrollment: 69, 51% men, 49% women, 38% minority, 9% international
Average class size: 22

Most popular MBA concentrations: finance, human resources management, international business, manufacturing and technology management, other
Completion: Three year graduation rate: 42%; credits needed to graduate: 36; target time to graduate: 2 years
College funded aid available: Domestic: Yes; International: Yes
Graduates with debt: 31%; average amount of debt $39,225

ONLINE BUSINESS PROGRAM(S)
www.uhcl.edu/admissions
Admissions: (281) 283-2500
Email: admissions@uhcl.edu
Financial aid: (281) 283-2480
Application deadline: rolling
Program can be completed entirely online: Yes
Total program cost: $17,592 full-time in-state, $17,592 part-time in-state, $34,728 full-time out-of-state, $34,728 part-time out-of-state
Tuition per credit: $451 full-time in-state, $451 part-time in-state, $950 full-time out-of-state, $950 part-time out-of-state
Acceptance rate: 38%
Test scores required: No
Average GMAT: 478
Enrollment: 46, 28% men, 72% women, 46% minority, 2% international
Average class size: 15
Most popular business concentrations: finance, human resources management
Completion: Three year graduation rate: 48%; credits needed to graduate: 36; target time to graduate: 2 years
College funded aid available: Domestic: Yes; International: Yes
Graduates with debt: 65%; average amount of debt $35,417

University of North Texas
Public

ONLINE MBA PROGRAM(S)
www.cob.unt.edu/programs/masters/onlinecourses.php
Admissions: (940) 369-8977
Email: MBACoB@unt.edu
Financial aid: (940) 565-2302
Application deadline: rolling
Program can be completed entirely online: Depends
Total program cost: $16,331 full-time in-state, $18,012 part-time in-state, $31,271 full-time out-of-state, $32,952 part-time out-of-state
Tuition per credit: $303 full-time in-state, $303 part-time in-state, $719 full-time out-of-state, $719 part-time out-of-state
Acceptance rate: 61%
Test scores required: GMAT or GRE
Average GMAT: 530
Average GRE: 150 verbal, 148 quantitative, 3.2 writing
Average age of entrants: 30

Students with prior work experience: 92%
Enrollment: 205, 60% men, 40% women, 24% minority
Average class size: 23
Most popular MBA concentrations: finance, general management, human resources management, marketing
Completion: Three year graduation rate: 69%; credits needed to graduate: 36; target time to graduate: 2 years
College funded aid available: Domestic: Yes
Graduates with debt: 36%; average amount of debt $42,862

University of Texas of the Permian Basin
Public

ONLINE MBA PROGRAM(S)
www.utpb.edu/admissions/index.html
Admissions: (432) 552-2605
Email: admissions@utpb.edu
Financial aid: (432) 552-2620
Application deadline: rolling
Program can be completed entirely online: Yes
Total program cost: $9,059 full-time in-state, $9,059 part-time in-state, $10,739 full-time out-of-state, $10,739 part-time out-of-state
Tuition per credit: $189 full-time in-state, $189 part-time in-state, $224 full-time out-of-state, $224 part-time out-of-state
Acceptance rate: 53%
Test scores required: GMAT
Average GMAT: 503
Average age of entrants: 30
Enrollment: 63, 60% men, 40% women, 44% minority, 2% international
Average class size: 25
Most popular MBA concentrations: finance, general management
Completion: Three year graduation rate: 6%; credits needed to graduate: 48; target time to graduate: 4 years
College funded aid available: Domestic: No; International: No
Graduates with debt: 34%; average amount of debt $3,679

University of Texas–Dallas
Public

ONLINE MBA PROGRAM(S)
jindal.utdallas.edu/
Admissions: (972) 883-6282
Email: mba@utdallas.edu
Financial aid: (972) 883-4037
Application deadline: rolling
Program can be completed entirely online: Yes
Total program cost: $46,816 full-time in-state, $49,178 part-time in-state, $83,084 full-time out-of-state, $83,428 part-time out-of-state
Tuition per credit: $717 full-time in-state, $764 part-time in-state, $1,402 full-time out-of-state, $1,410 part-time out-of-state
Acceptance rate: 34%

Test scores required:
GMAT or GRE
Average GMAT: 617
Average GRE: 154 verbal, 156 quantitative, 3.7 writing
Average age of entrants: 29
Students with prior work experience: 100%
Enrollment: 310, 67% men, 33% women, 38% minority, 5% international
Average class size: 34
Most popular MBA concentrations: accounting, finance, marketing, management information systems, supply chain management/logistics
Completion: Three year graduation rate: 57%; credits needed to graduate: 53; target time to graduate: 4 years
College funded aid available: Domestic: Yes; International: Yes
Graduates with debt: 39%; average amount of debt $13,415

ONLINE BUSINESS PROGRAM(S)

jindal.utdallas.edu/
Admissions: (972) 883-6282
Email: mba@utdallas.edu
Financial aid: (972) 883-4037
Application deadline: rolling
Program can be completed entirely online: Yes
Total program cost: $31,592 full-time in-state, $33,264 part-time in-state, $56,264 full-time out-of-state, $56,538 part-time out-of-state
Tuition per credit: $717 full-time in-state, $764 part-time in-state, $1,402 full-time out-of-state, $1,410 part-time out-of-state
Acceptance rate: 44%
Test scores required: GMAT or GRE
Average GMAT: 599
Average GRE: 154 verbal, 156 quantitative, 3.6 writing
Average age of entrants: 29
Students with prior work experience: 93%
Enrollment: 506, 52% men, 48% women, 31% minority, 39% international
Average class size: 34
Most popular business concentrations: accounting, finance, marketing, management information systems, supply chain management/logistics
Completion: Three year graduation rate: 64%; credits needed to graduate: 36; target time to graduate: 3 years
College funded aid available: Domestic: Yes; International: Yes
Graduates with debt: 17%; average amount of debt $4,375

University of Texas–Rio Grande Valley
Public

ONLINE MBA PROGRAM(S)

www.utrgv.edu/accelerated/programs/master-of-business-administration/index.htm
Admissions: N/A
Financial aid: N/A
Application deadline: N/A
Total program cost: N/A

Tuition per credit: $472 full-time in-state, $472 part-time in-state, $831 full-time out-of-state, $831 part-time out-of-state
Test scores required: GMAT or GRE
Enrollment: 206, 60% men, 40% women, 74% minority, 4% international
Completion: Target time to graduate: 1 year

University of Texas–Tyler
Public

ONLINE MBA PROGRAM(S)

www.uttyler.edu/graduate
Admissions: (903) 566-7457
Email: ogs@uttyler.edu
Financial aid: (903) 566-7181
Application deadline: rolling
Program can be completed entirely online: Yes
Total program cost: $13,400 full-time in-state, $16,800 part-time in-state, $28,340 full-time out-of-state, $31,740 part-time out-of-state
Tuition per credit: $372 full-time in-state, $762 part-time in-state, $787 full-time out-of-state, $1,177 part-time out-of-state
Acceptance rate: 84%
Test scores required: GMAT or GRE
Average GMAT: 463
Average GRE: 147 verbal, 147 quantitative
Average age of entrants: 33
Students with prior work experience: 22%
Enrollment: 1,504, 40% men, 60% women, 45% minority, 2% international
Average class size: 62
Most popular MBA concentrations: general management, health care administration, marketing, other
Completion: Credits needed to graduate: 36; target time to graduate: 2 years
College funded aid available: Domestic: No; International: No
Graduates with debt: 56%; average amount of debt $70,356

University of the Incarnate Word
Private

ONLINE MBA PROGRAM(S)

online.uiw.edu/
Admissions: (210) 832-5631
Email: jweber@uiwtx.edu
Financial aid: (210) 829-3912
Application deadline: rolling
Program can be completed entirely online: Yes
Total program cost: $27,490 full-time in-state, $27,490 part-time in-state, $27,490 full-time out-of-state, $27,490 part-time out-of-state
Tuition per credit: $915 full-time in-state, $915 part-time in-state, $915 full-time out-of-state, $915 part-time out-of-state
Acceptance rate: 96%
Test scores required: No
Average GMAT: 530

Average GRE: 147 verbal, 146 quantitative, 3.0 writing
Average age of entrants: 33
Students with prior work experience: 100%
Enrollment: 319, 60% men, 40% women, 67% minority
Average class size: 21
Most popular MBA concentrations: general management, human resources management, real estate, quantitative analysis/statistics and operations research
Completion: Three year graduation rate: 62%; credits needed to graduate: 30; target time to graduate: less than 1 year
College funded aid available: Domestic: Yes; International: No
Graduates with debt: 58%; average amount of debt $39,614

ONLINE BUSINESS PROGRAM(S)

sps.uiw.edu/admissions/graduate
Admissions: (210) 757-0202
Email: jweber@uiwtx.edu
Financial aid: (210) 829-3912
Application deadline: rolling
Program can be completed entirely online: Yes
Total program cost: $27,490 full-time in-state, $27,490 part-time in-state, $27,490 full-time out-of-state, $27,490 part-time out-of-state
Tuition per credit: $915 full-time in-state, $915 part-time in-state, $915 full-time out-of-state, $915 part-time out-of-state
Acceptance rate: 98%
Test scores required: No
Average GMAT: 415
Average GRE: 149 verbal, 144 quantitative, 3.3 writing
Average age of entrants: 35
Students with prior work experience: 100%
Enrollment: 717, 54% men, 46% women, 57% minority
Average class size: 22
Most popular business concentrations: arts administration, health care administration, leadership, organizational behavior, other
Completion: Three year graduation rate: 72%; credits needed to graduate: 30; target time to graduate: less than 1 year
College funded aid available: Domestic: Yes; International: No
Graduates with debt: 57%; average amount of debt $24,712

West Texas A&M University
Public

ONLINE MBA PROGRAM(S)

www.wtamu.edu/graduateschool
Admissions: (806) 651-2731
Email: graduateschool@wtamu.edu
Financial aid: (806) 651-2059
Application deadline: rolling
Program can be completed entirely online: Yes

Total program cost: $13,935 full-time in-state, $15,300 part-time in-state, $14,400 full-time out-of-state, $16,035 part-time out-of-state
Tuition per credit: $335 full-time in-state, $380 part-time in-state, $365 full-time out-of-state, $410 part-time out-of-state
Acceptance rate: 63%
Test scores required: No
Average GMAT: 550
Average GRE: 154 verbal, 159 quantitative, 4.0 writing
Average age of entrants: 30
Students with prior work experience: 94%
Enrollment: 1,005, 55% men, 45% women, 46% minority, 5% international
Average class size: 38
Most popular MBA concentrations: general management, health care administration, marketing, management information systems, organizational behavior
Completion: Three year graduation rate: 87%; credits needed to graduate: 31; target time to graduate: 1.5 years
College funded aid available: Domestic: Yes; International: Yes
Graduates with debt: 34%; average amount of debt $9,200

ONLINE BUSINESS PROGRAM(S)

www.wtamu.edu/graduateschool
Admissions: (806) 651-2731
Email: graduateschool@wtamu.edu
Financial aid: (806) 651-2059
Application deadline: rolling
Program can be completed entirely online: Yes
Total program cost: $15,410 full-time in-state, $17,000 part-time in-state, $16,725 full-time out-of-state, $17,885 part-time out-of-state
Tuition per credit: $335 full-time in-state, $380 part-time in-state, $365 full-time out-of-state, $410 part-time out-of-state
Acceptance rate: 64%
Test scores required: No
Average GMAT: 550
Average GRE: 158 verbal, 156 quantitative, 4.5 writing
Average age of entrants: 28
Students with prior work experience: 92%
Enrollment: 200, 58% men, 42% women, 40% minority, 2% international
Average class size: 31
Most popular business concentrations: economics, finance, management information systems
Completion: Three year graduation rate: 84%; credits needed to graduate: 36; target time to graduate: 1.5 years
College funded aid available: Domestic: Yes; International: Yes
Graduates with debt: 33%; average amount of debt $9,100

Southern Utah University
Public

ONLINE MBA PROGRAM(S)

www.suu.edu/business/mba/
Admissions: (435) 586-7740
Email: businessgrad@suu.edu
Financial aid: (435) 586-7734
Application deadline: rolling
Program can be completed entirely online: Yes
Total program cost: $14,004 full-time in-state, $15,505 part-time in-state, $14,004 full-time out-of-state, $15,505 part-time out-of-state
Tuition per credit: $6,623 full-time in-state, $2,870 part-time in-state, $6,623 full-time out-of-state, $2,870 part-time out-of-state
Acceptance rate: 83%
Test scores required: GMAT or GRE
Average GMAT: 500
Average GRE: 152 verbal, 150 quantitative
Enrollment: 66, 67% men, 33% women, 35% minority
Average class size: 13
Completion: Three year graduation rate: 95%; credits needed to graduate: 30; target time to graduate: 1 year
College funded aid available: Domestic: Yes; International: Yes
Graduates with debt: 36%; average amount of debt $13,409

ONLINE BUSINESS PROGRAM(S)

www.suu.edu/business/macc/
Admissions: (435) 586-7740
Email: businessgrad@suu.edu
Financial aid: (435) 586-7741
Application deadline: rolling
Program can be completed entirely online: Yes
Total program cost: $13,246 full-time in-state, $14,350 part-time in-state, $13,246 full-time out-of-state, $14,350 part-time out-of-state
Tuition per credit: $441 full-time in-state, $478 part-time in-state, $441 full-time out-of-state, $478 part-time out-of-state
Acceptance rate: 98%
Test scores required: GMAT or GRE
Average GMAT: 513
Average GRE: 148 verbal, 143 quantitative
Average age of entrants: 29
Enrollment: 90, 40% men, 60% women, 32% minority
Average class size: 17
Most popular business concentrations: accounting, tax, other
Completion: Three year graduation rate: 98%; credits needed to graduate: 30; target time to graduate: 1 year
College funded aid available: Domestic: Yes; International: Yes
Graduates with debt: 23%; average amount of debt $10,669

University of Utah (Eccles)

Public

ONLINE MBA PROGRAM(S)

eccles.utah.edu/programs/mba/
mba-online/admissions/
Admissions: (801) 587-8870
Email: mbaonline@utah.edu
Financial aid: (801) 581-6211
Application deadline: rolling
**Program can be completed
entirely online:** Yes
Total program cost: $58,800
full-time in-state, $58,800
part-time in-state, $58,800
full-time out-of-state, $58,800
part-time out-of-state
Tuition per credit: $1,225
full-time in-state, $1,225
part-time in-state, $1,225
full-time out-of-state, $1,225
part-time out-of-state
Acceptance rate: 71%
Test scores required:
GMAT or GRE
Average GMAT: 562
Average GRE: 154 verbal,
154 quantitative
Average age of entrants: 32
**Students with prior work
experience:** 100%
Enrollment: 119, 71% men,
29% women, 8% minority
Average class size: 35
**Most popular MBA
concentrations:** accounting,
finance, leadership,
management information
systems, quantitative
analysis/statistics and
operations research
Completion: Credits needed
to graduate: 48; target time
to graduate: 2 years
College funded aid available:
Domestic: Yes
Graduates with debt: 50%;
average amount of debt $37,600

Westminster College

Private

ONLINE MBA PROGRAM(S)

www.westminstercollege.edu/
graduate/programs/
project-based-mba
Admissions: (801) 832-2200
Email: admissions@
westminstercollege.edu
Financial aid: (801) 832-2500
Application deadline: rolling
**Program can be completed
entirely online:** Depends
Total program cost: $54,600
full-time in-state, $54,600
part-time in-state, $54,600
full-time out-of-state, $54,600
part-time out-of-state
Tuition per credit: $1,400
full-time in-state, $1,400
part-time in-state, $1,400
full-time out-of-state, $1,400
part-time out-of-state
Test scores required: No
Enrollment: 52, 54% men,
46% women, 13% minority
Average class size: 6
Most popular MBA concentrations:
entrepreneurship, finance,
international business,
leadership, production/
operations management

Completion: Three year
graduation rate: 75%; credits
needed to graduate: 39; target
time to graduate: 1.5 years
**College funded aid
available:** Domestic: Yes;
International: Yes

VIRGINIA

George Mason University

Public

ONLINE BUSINESS PROGRAM(S)

business.gmu.edu/msa/
Admissions: (703) 993-2136
Email: msa@gmu.edu
Financial aid: (703) 993-2353
Application deadline: Domestic:
04/01; International: 02/15
**Program can be completed
entirely online:** No
Total program cost: N/A
Tuition per credit: $973 full-time
in-state, $973 part-time in-state,
$1,787 full-time out-of-state,
$1,787 part-time out-of-state
Acceptance rate: 89%
Average age of entrants: 34
**Students with prior work
experience:** 94%
Enrollment: 31, 23% men,
77% women, 48% minority
Average class size: 21
**Most popular business
concentrations:** accounting
Completion: Credits needed
to graduate: 30; target time
to graduate: 2 years
College funded aid available:
Domestic: Yes

James Madison University

Public

ONLINE MBA PROGRAM(S)

www.jmu.edu/cob/graduate/
mba/infosec/admissions.shtml
Admissions: (540) 568-3058
Email: mccoynta@jmu.edu
Financial aid: (540) 568-3139
Application deadline: rolling
**Program can be completed
entirely online:** No
Total program cost: $37,800
full-time in-state, $37,800
part-time in-state, $37,800
full-time out-of-state, $37,800
part-time out-of-state
Tuition per credit: $900
full-time in-state, $900
part-time in-state, $900
full-time out-of-state, $900
part-time out-of-state
Acceptance rate: 92%
Test scores required:
GMAT or GRE
Average GMAT: 518
Average age of entrants: 35
**Students with prior work
experience:** 100%
Enrollment: 45, 73% men,
27% women, 31% minority
Average class size: 15
**Most popular MBA
concentrations:** accounting,
general management, marketing,
management information
systems, technology

Completion: Three year
graduation rate: 95%; credits
needed to graduate: 42; target
time to graduate: 2.5 years
College funded aid available:
Domestic: No; International: No
Graduates with debt: 43%;
average amount of debt $20,344

Liberty University

Private

ONLINE MBA PROGRAM(S)

www.luonline.com/
index.cfm?pid=21793
Admissions: (434) 582-9595
Email:
luoadmissions@liberty.edu
Financial aid: (434) 582-2270
Application deadline: rolling
**Program can be completed
entirely online:** Yes
Total program cost: N/A
Tuition per credit: $565 full-time
in-state, $615 part-time in-state,
$565 full-time out-of-state,
$615 part-time out-of-state
Acceptance rate: 31%
Test scores required: No
Average GMAT: 410
Average GRE: 146 verbal, 144
quantitative, 4.0 writing
Average age of entrants: 35
Enrollment: 4,078, 50% men,
50% women, 27% minority
Average class size: 19
**Most popular MBA
concentrations:** general
management, health care
administration, human
resources management,
leadership
Completion: Three year
graduation rate: 41%; credits
needed to graduate: 45; target
time to graduate: 2.5 years
**College funded aid
available:** Domestic: Yes;
International: Yes
Graduates with debt: 56%;
average amount of debt $39,027

ONLINE BUSINESS PROGRAM(S)

www.luonline.com/
index.cfm?pid=21793
Admissions: (434) 582-9595
Email:
luoadmissions@liberty.edu
Financial aid: (434) 582-2270
Application deadline: rolling
**Program can be completed
entirely online:** Yes
Total program cost: N/A
Tuition per credit: $565 full-time
in-state, $615 part-time in-state,
$565 full-time out-of-state,
$615 part-time out-of-state
Acceptance rate: 74%
Test scores required: No
Average GMAT: 519
Average GRE: 146 verbal, 142
quantitative, 3.0 writing
Average age of entrants: 35
Enrollment: 4,534, 50% men,
50% women, 31% minority
Average class size: 19
**Most popular business
concentrations:**
accounting, health care
administration, leadership,
marketing, management
information systems

Longwood University

Public

ONLINE MBA PROGRAM(S)

www.longwood.edu/
business/mba
Admissions: (434) 395-2043
Email: MBA@longwood.edu
Financial aid: (434) 395-2077
Application deadline: rolling
**Program can be completed
entirely online:** No
Total program cost: $20,988
full-time in-state, $20,988
part-time in-state, $42,588
full-time out-of-state, $42,588
part-time out-of-state
Tuition per credit: $373 full-time
in-state, $373 part-time in-state,
$973 full-time out-of-state,
$973 part-time out-of-state
Acceptance rate: 88%
Test scores required:
GMAT or GRE
Average GMAT: 454
Average age of entrants: 31
**Students with prior work
experience:** 81%
Enrollment: 27, 59% men,
41% women, 22% minority
Average class size: 13
**Most popular MBA
concentrations:** general
management, real estate
Completion: Credits needed
to graduate: 36; target time
to graduate: 2 years
**College funded aid
available:** Domestic: Yes;
International: Yes

Lynchburg College

Private

ONLINE MBA PROGRAM(S)

www.lynchburg.edu/graduate/
master-of-business-
administration/admission-
information/
Admissions: N/A
Financial aid: (434) 544-8228
Application deadline: rolling
**Program can be completed
entirely online:** Depends
Total program cost: $11,610
full-time in-state, $3,870
part-time in-state, $11,610
full-time out-of-state, $3,870
part-time out-of-state
Tuition per credit: $645
full-time in-state, $645
part-time in-state, $645
full-time out-of-state, $645
part-time out-of-state
Acceptance rate: 65%
Test scores required:
GMAT or GRE
Average GMAT: 502
Average GRE: 156 verbal,
153 quantitative
Average age of entrants: 30
**Students with prior work
experience:** 80%

Enrollment: 33, 67% men,
33% women, 9% minority,
9% international
Completion: Credits needed
to graduate: 36; target time
to graduate: 2 years
**College funded aid
available:** Domestic: Yes;
International: Yes
Graduates with debt: 18%;
average amount of debt $12,270

Marymount University

Private

ONLINE MBA PROGRAM(S)

www.marymount.edu/
admissions/graduate
Admissions: (703) 284-5901
Email: grad.admissions@
marymount.edu
Financial aid: (703) 284-1530
Application deadline: rolling
Total program cost: N/A
Tuition per credit: $975 full-time
in-state, $975 part-time in-state,
$975 full-time out-of-state,
$975 part-time out-of-state
Acceptance rate: 93%
Test scores required:
GMAT or GRE
Average GMAT: 378
Average GRE: 146 verbal, 144
quantitative, 3.3 writing
Average age of entrants: 30
Enrollment: 132, 39% men,
61% women, 38% minority,
12% international
Average class size: 15
Completion: Target time
to graduate: 2 years

ONLINE BUSINESS PROGRAM(S)

www.marymount.edu/
admissions/graduate
Admissions: (703) 284-5901
Email: grad.admissions@
marymount.edu
Financial aid: (703) 284-1530
Application deadline: rolling
**Program can be completed
entirely online:** Yes
Total program cost: N/A
Tuition per credit: $990
full-time in-state, $990
part-time in-state, $990
full-time out-of-state, $990
part-time out-of-state
Acceptance rate: 98%
Test scores required: No
Average GRE: 156 verbal, 154
quantitative, 4.0 writing
Average age of entrants: 35
**Students with prior work
experience:** 80%
Enrollment: 93, 59% men,
41% women, 52% minority,
12% international
Average class size: 16
**Most popular business
concentrations:** e-commerce,
leadership, management
information systems,
technology, other
Completion: Three year
graduation rate: 85%; credits
needed to graduate: 36; target
time to graduate: 2 years
**College funded aid
available:** Domestic: Yes;
International: Yes
Graduates with debt: 44%

Old Dominion University

Public

ONLINE MBA PROGRAM(S)

www.odu.edu/business/
departments/mba/investigate/
admission
Admissions: (757) 683-3585
Email: mbainfo@odu.edu
Financial aid: (757) 683-3683
Application deadline: rolling
**Program can be completed
entirely online:** Yes
Total program cost: $19,840
full-time in-state, $19,840
part-time in-state, $21,520
full-time out-of-state, $21,520
part-time out-of-state
Tuition per credit: $496
full-time in-state, $496
part-time in-state, $539
full-time out-of-state, $538
part-time out-of-state
Acceptance rate: 63%
Test scores required:
GMAT or GRE
Average GMAT: 549
Average GRE: 158 verbal, 155
quantitative, 4.0 writing
Average age of entrants: 31
**Students with prior work
experience:** 97%
Enrollment: 61, 56% men,
44% women, 20% minority
Average class size: 17
**Most popular MBA
concentrations:** health
care administration, public
administration, supply chain
management/logistics,
transportation, other
Completion: Credits needed
to graduate: 40; target time
to graduate: 2 years
**College funded aid
available:** Domestic: Yes;
International: Yes
Graduates with debt: 67%;
average amount of debt $18,904

Regent University

Private

ONLINE MBA PROGRAM(S)

www.regent.edu/sbl/
admissions-information/
Admissions: (757) 352-4400
Email:
SBLAdmissions@regent.edu
Financial aid: (757) 352-4125
Application deadline: rolling
**Program can be completed
entirely online:** Yes
Total program cost: $27,300
full-time in-state, $27,300
part-time in-state, $27,300
full-time out-of-state, $27,300
part-time out-of-state
Tuition per credit: $650
full-time in-state, $650
part-time in-state, $650
full-time out-of-state, $650
part-time out-of-state
Acceptance rate: 32%
Test scores required: No
Average age of entrants: 35
Enrollment: 512, 44%
men, 56% women, 54%
minority, 5% international
Average class size: 18

Most popular MBA concentrations:
entrepreneurship, finance,
general management, health
care administration, human
resources management
Completion: Three year
graduation rate: 50%; credits
needed to graduate: 42; target
time to graduate: 1.5 years
**College funded aid
available:** Domestic: Yes;
International: Yes
Graduates with debt: 55%;
average amount of debt $38,944

ONLINE BUSINESS PROGRAM(S)

www.regent.edu/sbl/
admissions-information/
Admissions: (757) 352-4400
Email: SBLAdmissions@
regent.edu
Financial aid: (757) 352-4125
Application deadline: rolling
**Program can be completed
entirely online:** Yes
Total program cost: $21,450
full-time in-state, $21,450
part-time in-state, $21,450
full-time out-of-state, $21,450
part-time out-of-state
Tuition per credit: $650
full-time in-state, $650
part-time in-state, $650
full-time out-of-state, $650
part-time out-of-state
Acceptance rate: 38%
Test scores required: No
Average GRE: 147 verbal, 140
quantitative, 3.3 writing
Average age of entrants: 40
Enrollment: 323, 40%
men, 60% women, 51%
minority, 5% international
Average class size: 25
**Most popular business
concentrations:** consulting,
human resources management,
leadership, not-for-profit
management, other
Completion: Three year
graduation rate: 56%; credits
needed to graduate: 33; target
time to graduate: 1.5 years
**College funded aid
available:** Domestic: Yes;
International: Yes
Graduates with debt: 56%;
average amount of debt $37,370

City University of Seattle

Private

ONLINE MBA PROGRAM(S)

www.cityu.edu/admissions-
financialaid/index.aspx
Admissions: (888) 422-4898
Email: info@cityu.edu
Financial aid: (206) 239-4535
Application deadline: rolling
**Program can be completed
entirely online:** Yes
Total program cost: $33,024
full-time in-state, $33,024
part-time in-state, $33,024
full-time out-of-state, $33,024
part-time out-of-state
Tuition per credit: $688
full-time in-state, $688
part-time in-state, $688
full-time out-of-state, $688
part-time out-of-state

Acceptance rate: 75%
Test scores required: No
Average age of entrants: 29
**Students with prior work
experience:** 9%
Enrollment: 1,169, 51%
men, 49% women, N/A
minority, N/A international
Average class size: 10
**Most popular MBA
concentrations:** finance, general
management, international
business, marketing, technology
Completion: Credits needed
to graduate: 48; target time
to graduate: 2.5 years
College funded aid available:
Domestic: Yes; International: No
Graduates with debt: 13%;
average amount of debt $12,467

ONLINE BUSINESS PROGRAM(S)

www.cityu.edu/admissions-
financialaid/index.aspx
Admissions: (888) 422-4898
Email: info@cityu.edu
Financial aid: (206) 239-4535
Application deadline: rolling
**Program can be completed
entirely online:** Yes
Total program cost: $30,960
full-time in-state, $30,960
part-time in-state, $30,960
full-time out-of-state, $30,960
part-time out-of-state
Tuition per credit: $688
full-time in-state, $688
part-time in-state, $688
full-time out-of-state, $688
part-time out-of-state
Acceptance rate: 71%
Test scores required: No
Average age of entrants: 35
**Students with prior work
experience:** 6%
Enrollment: 163, 57% men,
43% women, N/A minority,
N/A international
Average class size: 10
**Most popular business
concentrations:** international
business, management
information systems,
production/operations
management, supply
chain management/
logistics, technology
Completion: Credits needed
to graduate: 45; target time
to graduate: 2.5 years
College funded aid available:
Domestic: Yes; International: No
Graduates with debt: 12%;
average amount of debt $12,467

Northwest University

Private

ONLINE MBA PROGRAM(S)

online.northwestu.edu
Admissions: (866) 327-0264
Email: online@northwestu.edu
Financial aid: (425) 889-5336
Application deadline: rolling
**Program can be completed
entirely online:** Yes
Total program cost: $29,406
full-time in-state, $29,406
part-time in-state, $29,406
full-time out-of-state, $29,406
part-time out-of-state

Tuition per credit: $754 full-time
in-state, $754 full-time in-state,
$754 full-time out-of-state,
$754 part-time out-of-state
Acceptance rate: 79%
Test scores required: No
Average age of entrants: 31
**Students with prior work
experience:** 100%
Enrollment: 26, 46% men,
54% women, 31% minority,
4% international
Average class size: 7
Completion: Credits needed
to graduate: 39; target time
to graduate: 2 years
College funded aid available:
Domestic: No; International: No
Graduates with debt: 78%;
average amount of debt $37,829

Washington State University

Public

ONLINE MBA PROGRAM(S)

omba.wsu.edu
Admissions: (877) 960-2029
Email:
admissions@wsumba.com
Financial aid: (509) 335-9711
Application deadline: rolling
**Program can be completed
entirely online:** Yes
Total program cost: $34,000
full-time in-state, $34,000
part-time in-state, $34,000
full-time out-of-state, $34,000
part-time out-of-state
Tuition per credit: $775 full-time
in-state, $775 part-time in-state,
$775 full-time out-of-state,
$775 part-time out-of-state
Acceptance rate: 66%
Test scores required: GMAT
Average GMAT: 568
Average GRE: 155 verbal, 155
quantitative, 3.8 writing
Average age of entrants: 36
**Students with prior work
experience:** 98%
Enrollment: 852, 67%
men, 33% women, 24%
minority, 4% international
Average class size: 24
**Most popular MBA
concentrations:** finance, hotel
administration, international
business, marketing
Completion: Three year
graduation rate: 66%; credits
needed to graduate: 32; target
time to graduate: 2 years
**College funded aid
available:** Domestic: Yes;
International: Yes
Graduates with debt: 29%;
average amount of debt $31,145

University of Charleston

Private

ONLINE BUSINESS PROGRAM(S)

www.ucwv.edu/academics/
online-programs/
Admissions: N/A
Financial aid: N/A
Application deadline: N/A
Total program cost: N/A

Tuition per credit: $425
full-time in-state, $425
part-time in-state, $425
full-time out-of-state, $425
part-time out-of-state

West Virginia University

Public

ONLINE MBA PROGRAM(S)

be.wvu.edu/online-mba/
index.htm
Admissions: (304) 293-5505
Email: eavitullo@mail.wvu.edu
Financial aid: (304) 293-5242
Application deadline: Domestic:
07/01; International: 07/01
**Program can be completed
entirely online:** No
Total program cost: $47,904
full-time in-state, $47,904
part-time in-state, $47,904
full-time out-of-state, $47,904
part-time out-of-state
Tuition per credit: $998
full-time in-state, $998
part-time in-state, $998
full-time out-of-state, $998
part-time out-of-state
Acceptance rate: 93%
Test scores required:
GMAT or GRE
Average GMAT: 512
Average GRE: 149 verbal, 145
quantitative, 4.1 writing
Average age of entrants: 31
**Students with prior work
experience:** 84%
Enrollment: 86, 67% men,
33% women, N/A minority,
N/A international
Average class size: 27
Completion: Three year
graduation rate: 87%; credits
needed to graduate: 48; target
time to graduate: 2 years
College funded aid available:
Domestic: Yes; International: No
Graduates with debt: 50%;
average amount of debt $24,192

ONLINE BUSINESS PROGRAM(S)

www.be.wvu.edu/
graduate/index.htm
Admissions: (304) 293-2333
Email: mba@wvu.edu
Financial aid: (304) 293-5242
Application deadline: Domestic:
07/01; International: 09/01
**Program can be completed
entirely online:** No
Total program cost: $23,952
full-time in-state, $23,952
part-time in-state, $23,952
full-time out-of-state, $23,952
part-time out-of-state
Tuition per credit: $998
full-time in-state, $998
part-time in-state, $998
full-time out-of-state, $998
part-time out-of-state
Acceptance rate: 78%
Test scores required:
GMAT or GRE
Average GMAT: 498
Average GRE: 156 verbal, 157
quantitative, 4.1 writing
Average age of entrants: 31
**Students with prior work
experience:** 98%
Enrollment: 47, 66% men,
34% women, 21% minority
Average class size: 24

Completion: Credits needed to graduate: 30; target time to graduate: 1 year
College funded aid available: Domestic: Yes; International: No
Graduates with debt: 36%; average amount of debt $44,194

WISCONSIN

Cardinal Stritch University

Private

ONLINE MBA PROGRAM(S)

www.stritch.edu/admissions/request-information
Admissions: (414) 410-4042
Email: admissions@stritch.edu
Financial aid: (414) 410-4048
Application deadline: N/A
Program can be completed entirely online: Yes
Total program cost: $23,400 full-time in-state, $23,400 part-time in-state, $23,400 full-time out-of-state, $23,400 part-time out-of-state
Tuition per credit: $650 full-time in-state, $650 part-time in-state, $650 full-time out-of-state, $650 part-time out-of-state
Test scores required: No
Completion: Credits needed to graduate: 36

Concordia University Wisconsin

Private

ONLINE MBA PROGRAM(S)

online.cuw.edu
Admissions: (877) 366-3063
Email: onlineadmissions@cuw.edu
Financial aid: (262) 243-4392
Application deadline: rolling
Program can be completed entirely online: Yes
Total program cost: $27,261 full-time in-state, $27,261 part-time in-state, $27,261 full-time out-of-state, $27,261 part-time out-of-state
Tuition per credit: $699 full-time in-state, $699 part-time in-state, $699 full-time out-of-state, $699 part-time out-of-state
Acceptance rate: 51%
Test scores required: No
Average age of entrants: 31
Students with prior work experience: 98%
Enrollment: 175, 37% men, 63% women, N/A minority, N/A international
Average class size: 7

Most popular MBA concentrations: accounting, finance, general management, health care administration, human resources management
Completion: Credits needed to graduate: 39; target time to graduate: 2 years
College funded aid available: Domestic: Yes; International: No
Graduates with debt: 36%

ONLINE BUSINESS PROGRAM(S)

online.cuw.edu
Admissions: (877) 366-3063
Email: onlineadmissions@cuw.edu
Financial aid: (262) 243-4392
Application deadline: rolling
Program can be completed entirely online: Yes
Total program cost: $22,368 full-time in-state, $22,368 part-time in-state, $22,368 full-time out-of-state, $22,368 part-time out-of-state
Tuition per credit: $699 full-time in-state, $699 part-time in-state, $699 full-time out-of-state, $699 part-time out-of-state
Acceptance rate: 67%
Test scores required: No
Average age of entrants: 36
Students with prior work experience: 100%
Enrollment: 44, 23% men, 77% women, N/A minority, N/A international
Average class size: 5
Most popular business concentrations: leadership
Completion: Credits needed to graduate: 32; target time to graduate: 1.5 years
College funded aid available: Domestic: Yes; International: No
Graduates with debt: 40%

Edgewood College

Private

ONLINE MBA PROGRAM(S)

www.edgewood.edu/admissions/graduate-students
Admissions: (608) 663-3297
Email: tkantor@edgewood.edu
Financial aid: (608) 663-4300
Application deadline: rolling
Program can be completed entirely online: Depends
Total program cost: N/A
Tuition per credit: $930 full-time in-state, $930 part-time in-state, $930 full-time out-of-state, $930 part-time out-of-state
Test scores required: GMAT or GRE
Average class size: 14
Most popular MBA concentrations: finance, general management, health care administration, marketing

Completion: Credits needed to graduate: 37; target time to graduate: 2 years

ONLINE BUSINESS PROGRAM(S)

www.edgewood.edu/academics/programs/details/business/graduate
Admissions: (608) 663-3297
Email: jalsteen@edgewood.edu
Financial aid: (608) 663-4300
Application deadline: rolling
Program can be completed entirely online: Yes
Total program cost: N/A
Tuition per credit: $930 full-time in-state, $930 part-time in-state, $930 full-time out-of-state, $930 part-time out-of-state
Test scores required: GMAT or GRE
Average class size: 14
Most popular business concentrations: accounting, organizational behavior
Completion: Credits needed to graduate: 30; target time to graduate: 2 years

Herzing University

Private

ONLINE MBA PROGRAM(S)

www.herzing.edu
Admissions: (866) 508-6748
Email: admissions@herzing.edu
Financial aid: (866) 508-0748
Application deadline: rolling
Program can be completed entirely online: Yes
Total program cost: $26,130 full-time in-state, $26,130 part-time in-state, $26,130 full-time out-of-state, $26,130 part-time out-of-state
Tuition per credit: $670 full-time in-state, $670 part-time in-state, $670 full-time out-of-state, $670 part-time out-of-state
Acceptance rate: 89%
Test scores required: No
Average age of entrants: 37
Enrollment: 214, 27% men, 73% women, 46% minority
Average class size: 14
Most popular MBA concentrations: general management, health care administration, human resources management, technology, other
Completion: Three year graduation rate: 59%; credits needed to graduate: 39; target time to graduate: 1.5 years
College funded aid available: Domestic: Yes; International: Yes
Graduates with debt: 84%; average amount of debt $42,633

University of Wisconsin MBA Consortium

Public

ONLINE MBA PROGRAM(S)

www.wisconsinonlinemba.org/
Admissions: (715) 836-6019
Email: mba@uwec.edu
Financial aid: (715) 836-5606
Application deadline: rolling
Program can be completed entirely online: Yes
Total program cost: $20,250 full-time in-state, $20,250 part-time in-state, $20,250 full-time out-of-state, $20,250 part-time out-of-state
Tuition per credit: $675 full-time in-state, $675 part-time in-state, $675 full-time out-of-state, $675 part-time out-of-state
Acceptance rate: 82%
Test scores required: GMAT or GRE
Average GMAT: 590
Average GRE: 154 verbal, 153 quantitative, 3.7 writing
Average age of entrants: 31
Students with prior work experience: 98%
Enrollment: 316, 58% men, 42% women, 10% minority, 2% international
Average class size: 25
Most popular MBA concentrations: finance, general management, health care administration, marketing, management information systems
Completion: Three year graduation rate: 88%; credits needed to graduate: 30; target time to graduate: 3 years
College funded aid available: Domestic: No; International: No
Graduates with debt: 44%; average amount of debt $31,715

University of Wisconsin–Platteville

Public

ONLINE BUSINESS PROGRAM(S)

www.uwplatt.edu/distance-education
Admissions: (608) 342-1468
Email: disted@uwplatt.edu
Financial aid: (608) 342-1836
Application deadline: rolling
Program can be completed entirely online: Yes
Total program cost: $19,500 full-time in-state, $19,500 part-time in-state, $19,500 full-time out-of-state, $19,500 part-time out-of-state
Tuition per credit: $650 full-time in-state, $650 part-time in-state, $650 full-time out-of-state, $650 part-time out-of-state

Acceptance rate: 98%
Test scores required: No
Average age of entrants: 37
Enrollment: 850, 54% men, 46% women, N/A minority, N/A international
Average class size: 13
Most popular business concentrations: general management, leadership, manufacturing and technology management, organizational behavior, supply chain management/logistics
Completion: Three year graduation rate: 29%; credits needed to graduate: 30; target time to graduate: 3 years
College funded aid available: Domestic: No; International: No

University of Wisconsin–Whitewater

Public

ONLINE MBA PROGRAM(S)

www.uww.edu/cobe/onlinemba
Admissions: (262) 473-1945
Email: gradbus@uww.edu
Financial aid: (262) 472-1130
Application deadline: rolling
Program can be completed entirely online: Yes
Total program cost: $22,968 full-time in-state, $22,968 part-time in-state, $22,968 full-time out-of-state, $22,968 part-time out-of-state
Tuition per credit: $638 full-time in-state, $638 part-time in-state, $638 full-time out-of-state, $638 part-time out-of-state
Acceptance rate: 71%
Test scores required: GMAT or GRE
Average GMAT: 504
Average GRE: 154 verbal, 148 quantitative, 4.8 writing
Average age of entrants: 30
Students with prior work experience: 97%
Enrollment: 329, 60% men, 40% women, 11% minority, 5% international
Average class size: 37
Most popular MBA concentrations: finance, general management, marketing, supply chain management/logistics, other
Completion: Three year graduation rate: 79%; credits needed to graduate: 36; target time to graduate: 1.5 years
College funded aid available: Domestic: Yes; International: Yes
Graduates with debt: 32%; average amount of debt $12,138

INDEX OF

On-Campus MBA Programs

Online Business Programs

More @ usnews.com/bschool

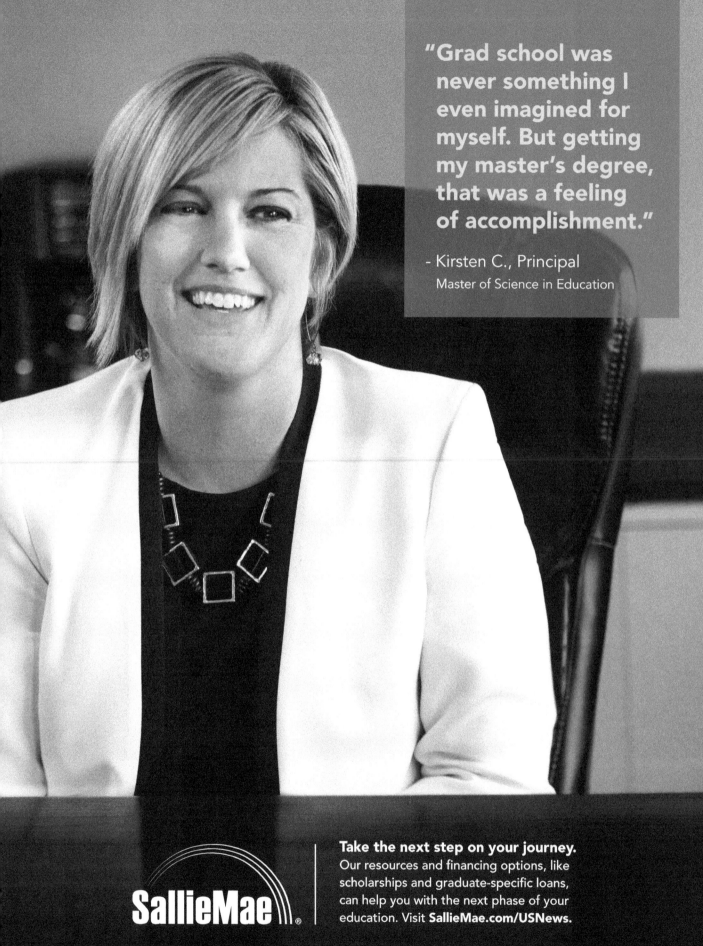

"Grad school was never something I even imagined for myself. But getting my master's degree, that was a feeling of accomplishment."

- Kirsten C., Principal
Master of Science in Education

Take the next step on your journey.
Our resources and financing options, like scholarships and graduate-specific loans, can help you with the next phase of your education. Visit **SallieMae.com/USNews.**

SallieMae®

CPSIA information can be obtained
at www.ICGtesting.com
Printed in the USA
BVHW021335240419
546415BV00009B/437/P

9 781931 469890